Perspectives on the Past

Perspectives on the Past

Theoretical Biases
in Mediterranean
Hunter-Gatherer Research

Edited by Geoffrey A. Clark

UNIVERSITY OF PENNSYLVANIA PRESS   Philadelphia

U.S. Library of Congress Cataloging-in-Publication Data
Perspectives on the past : theoretical biases in Mediterranean hunter-gatherer
   research / edited by Geoffrey A. Clark.
        p.   cm.
   Includes bibliographical references and index.
   ISBN 0-8122-8190-X
   1. Paleolithic period—Mediterranean Region.   2. Mesolithic period—
Mediterranean Region.   3. Hunting and gathering societies—Mediterranean
Region.   4. Archaeology—Research—Mediterranean Region.   5. Mediterranean
Region—Antiquities.   I. Clark, Geoffrey A.
GN772.25.A1P47   1991
909'.09822—dc20   91-16444
                                                                        CIP

This volume is dedicated to the Anthropology Program of the National Science Foundation, without whose assistance I would never have had the opportunity to complete my graduate education, let alone embark on a career as a research scientist. I hope the NSF will consider its money to have been well spent.

Contents

Figures and Tables

TABLES

Preface

This is a book about what archaeologists of a certain kind think they do, rather than about what other archaeologists (or philosophers of science) think they *should* be doing. Except in the broad sense of a shared area of interest, it is not a book of "facts" or "discoveries." It originated in a symposium on "Paradigmatic Biases in Levantine Hunter-Gatherer Research" held at the Phoenix meetings of the Society for American Archaeology in April 1988, and consists of first-person accounts by workers active in field research on various aspects of Pleistocene and early Holocene hunter-gatherer adaptations in the Mediterranean Basin. These individuals play a large role in creating what we think we know about prehistoric hunter-gatherers in this important area of Old World research and, for that reason, perhaps deserve a hearing. Since a number of distinct, but overlapping research traditions are represented here, each with it own sets of biases, construals of the research endeavor vary from one writer to the next. Some modal tendencies in this variation emerge, however, and are identified in the Introduction and the Epilogue. Construals of archaeology range from a straightforward extension of history, projected back into the preliterate past, to the anthropological paradigm that governs most American work. I hope that readers will find these diverse accounts to be as interesting for their different constructions of the past as they are for their similarities, for it should be evident that, while they must postulate its existence, archaeologists do not "discover" a past that is "out there" to be perceived and apprehended by any informed observer. Rather, they create a past out of their preconceptions and biases about what the world of archaeological data is really like. This book aims to give a reader some insight into that process—to show him or her what the world of archaeology is really like, as seen through the eyes of some of its practitioners. Archaeology as a process of construction and testing thus differs from the popular misconception that it is a process of discovery. The same might be said of any discipline that is, or aspires to be, a science.

Although they differ among themselves in terms of orientation, most *Perspectives* contributors are both realists and positivists in the sense that they believe that an archaeological reality exists that is fundamentally independent of our perceptions of it, and that we can hope to grasp the nature of that reality through application of one form or another of "the scientific method"—the formulation of expectations about the nature of pattern in data, and the subsequent empirical checking of the validity or accuracy of those patterns. This construal of science necessarily involves the advancement and potential refutation of generalizations and hypotheses, and thus entails some kind of a deductive component to the process of evaluation of the credibility of ideas, since prediction (or retrodiction) is an essential function of all scientific theories, however incomplete they might be.

Archaeological theories are, of course, very incomplete, and are usually so poorly developed conceptually that they cannot be refuted or falsified in any direct way. Since the criterion of falsifiability is sometimes invoked to separate "scientific" theories from "non- or pseudoscientific" ones, and has occasionally been used in assaults on the scientific character of evolutionary biology (from which I believe we receive our mandate), it has been proposed that such theories should not be required to satisfy the same criteria as those of physical science. This is a moot point in the present context, since no *Perspectives* contributors (in fact, no archaeologists with whose work I am familiar) would try to claim that our theories are the equivalents of those in physical science. Nevertheless, there is a wistful quality to some of the papers, including my own, that it would be eminently desirable if we could somehow distance ourselves from our strict empiricist tendencies and reject the view that observations are necessarily more reliable sources of knowledge than theories (see Brush 1989 for a discussion of these issues in physics). Linking observations with theories in a convincing manner is perhaps the major challenge of the archaeology of the 1990s.

Preparation of the manuscript prior to submission has been a long and arduous process, and I would like to thank Patricia Smith, Acquisitions Editor, University of Pennsylvania Press, for her continuing support. Marsha Schweitzer and Marian Glick, Department of Anthropology, Arizona State University, were responsible, respectively, for manuscript preparation and for the compilation of the master bibliography. Unflappable Marsha deserves a special accolade for her highly efficient, patient preparation of the final copy, a task that she somehow managed to accomplish in a timely fashion despite many other competing demands on her energies. Nancy Coinman (University of Tulsa) came up with the title, *Perspectives on the Past,* much shorter and more manageable than the one originally contemplated. Lynette Heller (Arizona State University) compiled the index. Finally, I wish to acknowledge the support of the College of Liberal Arts & Sciences, Arizona State University, and its erstwhile Dean, Samuel Kirkpatrick (now President of the University of Texas, San Antonio), for a partial subvention to underwrite some of the costs of publication. The present Dean, Gary Krahenbuhl, and his associate, Regents Professor of Physics, Marybeth Stearns, also enthusiastically supported the project, as did Department of Anthropology Chair Charles L. Redman. I am grateful to all these individuals and organizations, and to any others inadvertently omitted, for providing me with the moral support and financial assistance necessary to complete this work. I hope it will find favor in their eyes.

Geoffrey A. Clark
Arizona State University

Perspectives on the Past

Chapter 1
Introduction

Geoffrey A. Clark

Prehistoric archaeology is, once again, breaking apart as an integrated discipline. In recent years, there has been a proliferation of "alternative" archaeologies, characterized by alternative theories and methodologies that share little in the way of common goals, objectives and ideals (cf., e.g., Hodder 1985, Binford 1987a, Spaulding 1988). Sometimes lumped under the rubric of "post-processual" archaeology, these diverse approaches are a reaction to mounting dissatisfaction with the "scientific" or "processual" archaeologies of Britain and the United States that have been dominant in those countries since the mid-1970s (see, e.g., Watson et al. 1984). The positivist infrastructure of processual archaeology—its legacy from western science—is currently being assailed by "post-processualists," "neo-structuralists," "structural marxists," and "symbolic" and "contextual archaeologists" of various persuasions. While several philosophically and historically distinct perspectives are represented in these assaults, its critics seem to be agreed that processual archaeology has been a failure, that the scientific method and the quest for law-like generalizations have produced few significant advances in our understanding of the past, and that we should look instead to symbolic anthropology for rules and principles that would help us make sense of an archaeological record. Archaeology is redefined as an historical discipline or a humanity, in which meaning and sense are ever-changing, contextual, and dependent upon the symbolic order. Interpretation is sometimes considered a direct, intuitive process and is substituted for verification or refutation. The past is marketed as a consumer product, with contemporary sociopolitical objectives in mind. In short, we are once again in an era of polemic and controversy, somewhat reminiscent of the early 1970s, in which the existing conventions that underlie knowledge claims are being ferociously debated and radical alternatives are being proposed.

It is not, however, the intent of this book to formulate a reasoned response to the claims of the radical critique. Most *Perspectives* contributors appear to subscribe to what I would consider to be positivist biases. There is the widely shared view that, while there may be substance to some of the criticisms leveled at the *results* of processual archaeology, the radical critique has alienated many potential adherents by utterly rejecting any notion of a disinterested evaluation of the credibility of its knowledge claims. Although they differ among themselves in other matters paradigmatic, *Perspectives* contributors appear to support the notion of an empirically verifiable reality that exists apart from our perceptions of it—a major point of departure with some of the more extreme post-processualist views. There is also the recognition that perceptions of that reality might be faulty or incomplete, and are certainly paradigm dependent, but that does not obviate its existence. It is, therefore, one thing to argue that because science is paradigm dependent, the results of scientific inquiry must always be subjective. It is quite another to assert, as Hodder (1984) has done, that we should reject explanation and verification altogether and essentially become humanists, interpreting, or better, creating a past of our choosing out of our view of our own culture and/or our culturally conditioned perceptions of the ethnographically recorded cultures of others (Binford 1987a).

Origins of the Book Project

The idea for the book originated in a series of international archaeological conferences that I had attended over the last five or six years. These were thematic, "big issue" meetings (e.g., the role of archaeozoology in prehistoric research designs, the biocultural origins of modern humans, systematics in Levantine prehistory, the "neanderthals" and their place in human evolution, etc.). They all shared a concern with one or another aspect of Upper Pleistocene/early Holocene hunter-gatherer adaptations and human evolution in the circum-Mediterranean region. What struck me most about these meetings were the enormous differences in the paradigmatic biases that different workers brought to the resolution of problems more or less held in common (or thought to be held in common). At times, these differences were so great that there was literally no common basis for discussion (I could give some amusing—or appalling—examples, depending on one's point of view). People were, and continue to be, "talking past" one another. There also seemed to be little appreciation that such epistemological issues existed and/or that they had significant effects on the research enterprise, with some workers evidently subscribing to the strict empiricist notion that "the facts speak for themselves." Obviously, I do not think that is the case at all, but it should be noted that strict empiricism is alive and well in the late 1980s, especially in what might be called the "indigenous" Old World research traditions that have produced so much circum-Mediterranean archaeology. The "indigenous" research traditions are poorly represented in this volume, for reasons that are explored below.

Perspectives is about the effects of paradigmatic biases and regional research traditions on our capacity to understand and make sense of the human past. As Binford and Sabloff (1982) recently expressed it, a paradigm is a "worldview"—a statement about the way the world, or some portion of it, is perceived to be. A theory is juxtaposed with a paradigm and is an argument invoked or constructed to explain *why* the world is as it appears to be. Paradigms can exist at several (at least three) conceptual levels but the most common usage, after Thomas Kuhn (1962), refers to paradigm at the level of the metaphysic. Kuhn thought that metaphysical paradigms were closed logical systems and that all lower level sociological and construct (or methodological) paradigms were derived from them—a view for which he was often criticized (e.g., Masterman 1970). The metaphysical paradigms of Old World prehistorians are the intended objects of scrutiny here, although, since paradigm boundaries are never wholly impermeable either "horizontally" (that is, between metaphysical paradigms) or "vertically" (between the metaphysic and its constituent paradigms), there is considerable discussion of lower order (especially sociological) paradigms (Figure 1.1). The contributors are all scholars *active in field research*—they are the people who are creating, for better or worse, the archaeological record of hunter-gatherers in the circum-Mediterranean region. The opinion is sometimes expressed that those who actually do field research are neither interested in, nor, in most cases, qualified to write papers about theoretical topics. In fact, one reviewer of the book prospectus allowed that there is a nearly unbridgeable gap between the "field" and the "theoretical" archaeologist—admittedly a widely held sentiment, but not one that I share. It was also pointed out that many archaeologists tend to compartmentalize the practical and theoretical aspects of their work, and that few successfully integrate the two (see Thomas 1983 for a similar view). I acknowledge the latter to be true, regard it as a problem, chalk it up to the relative immaturity of the field, and do not know how to rectify it. It constitutes one of the motivations for the book—an effort to make assumptions and biases explicit (or at least more explicit than is usually the case in most published work, which tends to be relatively "problem specific").

Obviously, the book project had to be constrained by various, rather

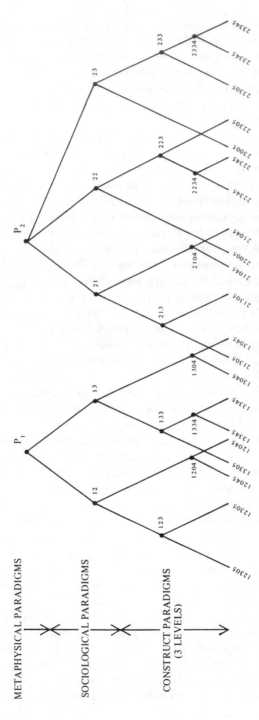

FIGURE 1.1. A schematic representation of Masterman's (1970) metaphysical, sociological, and construct paradigms. Metaphysical paradigm P_1 has two and P_2 three sociological paradigms. Each of these in turn contains a variable number of overlapping construct paradigms, themselves characterized by three levels. Paradigm boundaries below the level of the metaphysic are typically ill-defined (from Clark 1987a).

stringent, parameters. I decided to restrict it to the circum-Mediterranean region and to the Upper Pleistocene/early Holocene time frame (which includes only hunter-gatherer adaptations, although the transition to domestication economies is accomplished at the end of this period). Any data papers have been *absolutely precluded*. What I wanted people to try to do was to "make their biases explicit," to try to articulate the basic, fundamental premises under which *they* conduct the research enterprise. Predictably, I suppose, I was not wholly successful in achieving what one reviewer described as my *True Confessions* approach. I was interested in eliciting first-person accounts from scholars active in a particular kind of circum-Mediterranean field research. What I sometimes got instead were personal reactions to what contributors perceived to be the ruling theoretical and methodological biases operative in their particular research domains, which is not the same thing. However, it is by no means a "bad" thing, since, by confronting the preconceptions of the dominant paradigm, contributors were also forced to confront their own. Whatever virtues and defects the essays might prove to have, I hope that readers will agree that they are honest accounts with a minimum of posturing and moralizing.

Biases About Biases

In light of my own prejudices about archaeology as a scientific discipline (rather than as a humanistic enterprise or as a vehicle for promoting a sociopolitical agenda) it should be noted that the contributors all share at least that much by way of orientation (i.e., that archaeology is a scientific discipline). However, there are enormous differences among them in respect of (1) assumptions about the nature of culture and past human behavior, (2) differences in the systematics employed to address these problems, (3) different perceptions of the resolution attainable in the archaeological and paleontological records, (4) different views of the diagenetic processes that have transformed those records, and (5) different perceptions about how pervasive change is, and what causes it to occur. These biases in turn determine which biological and cultural variables are regarded as significant to monitor, and how much difference "makes a difference" (that is, how much difference is significant in phylogenetic or behavioral terms). In short, there are a number of discernible paradigms for Old World prehistory at the level of the metaphysic, and they tend to be differentiated among themselves, and to part company with their Americanist counterparts, along the lines of national or regional research traditions.

It should be noted that no position is taken here on general philosophy of science issues regarding what form a metaphysical paradigm should take, or what the research models derived from it should look like, or what roles induction, abduction, deduction, and covering laws should play in such a model (see, e.g., Fritz and Plog 1970; Morgan 1973, 1974; Salmon 1975, 1976, 1982; Watson et al. 1971, 1974). It is my opinion (and, evidently, that of most contributors) that rigid adherence to strictly defined models developed in philosophy of science contexts is neither necessary, realistic, nor particularly productive in terms of the conduct of archaeological research (see also Watson et al. 1974). Our capacity to contribute original, non-trivial insights to an elucidation of the general processes of human social behavior (which I take to be our singular, shared objective) is in no sense diminished by a failure to subscribe to a particular philosophy of science paradigm. This position comes from the realization that what had been widely represented as relatively cut-and-dried philosophy of science issues (e.g., primacy of a deductive-nomological approach, a confirmatory systematics, etc.) are in fact hotly contested issues within the boundaries of that very discipline (Clark 1982).

Structure of the Book

The book is organized into four major sections, comprising a category of general essays, and those relating to four geographical regions ordered from West to East. Within regions, papers are arranged in a rough chronological order from "early" to "late." There is an Epilogue, in which I try to identify some of the biases that appear to be more or less held in common by contributors. These have to do with general notions of evolution, adaptation, and ecology and, more specifically, with the interdependence of cultural and biological evolutionary models, site formation processes, the biases of archaeological "lumpers" and "splitters," and how these taxonomic considerations affect the range of variability thought to exist in archaeological assemblages and in collections of human skeletal material.

Part I—Paradigmatic Biases in Hunter-Gatherer Research

Part I comprises general papers by Mueller-Wille and Dickson, Straus, Clark and Sackett. Catherine Mueller-Wille and Bruce Dickson write about the southwestern European Upper Paleolithic in terms of what they call "the basic model"—essentially the changes wrought by the *Man the Hunter* (Lee and De Vore 1968a) volume on archaeologists' conceptions of hunter-gatherer adaptations—now experiencing critical reappraisal. They regard the basic model as nearly universal (i.e., widely adopted by both European and American prehistorians) and contend that a paradigm that allows for greater social complexity and subsistence-intensive adaptations is tending to replace it among many American (although not among Continental) Upper Paleolithic workers. The essay reviews the basic model in terms of its assumptions and limitations, discusses the emergent paradigm, summarizes and critiques some key examples of contemporary American and European research, and illustrates some of the problems with middle range theory raised by the new approaches. Assumptions and methodological implications of contemporary models of southwestern European hunter-gatherer adaptations are explored, and European and American perspectives are compared.

In some contrast, the essays by Lawrence Straus and myself are more "personal." Both present "histories" of events and personalities regarded as significant in our formal educations, followed by discussions of how those events have helped to shape our perspectives and how our biases are played out in the formulation of research designs. Basic similarities in overall orientation are attributed to similar educational backgrounds, although Straus can claim the distinction of a family history populated by previous generations of prehistorians (the only contributor to be able to do so) Straus advocates a multistage research protocol that progresses from intrasite to intersite to regional comparisons, in order to identify and contrast adaptive strategies of late Pleistocene hunter-gatherers in Spain, France and, most recently, Portugal. Both Straus and I de-emphasize traditional European typological systematics, and are inclined to reject altogether claims for the "cultural" or "ethnic" reality of the standard Upper Paleolithic European analytical units. I argue that a cultural materialist paradigm is appropriate for hunter-gatherer studies and defend eclecticism as inevitable, given the fragmentation of archaeology and the absence of general archaeological theory. A loose kind of functionalism is advocated by both workers, but one that does not entail the notion of a smoothly integrated, internally regulated system proposed by anthropological theorists. Sites are perceived as places in the landscape that were used in different, albeit modal, ways over millennia by groups of people who are beyond the resolution of "ethnicity." Differences and similarities in artifact assemblages explained under the "indigenous" paradigm by recourse to temporally sequent ethnic or cultural differences are, we feel, most likely related to differences and similarities in recurrent suites of human activities at particular places and moments in time.

Jim Sackett's essay is a provocative critique of what he refers to as the *phylogenetic paradigm*—the Straus/Clark construal of the systematics underlying French Upper Paleolithic archaeology. In an effort to address what he thinks are misconceptions of the phylogenetic paradigm, Sackett identifies four stages or eras which encompass French prehistoric archaeology after its "heroic" (pre-1860s) age. These are the Formative era (early 1860s–ca. 1900), the Traditional era (ca. 1900–1950), the Bordesian era (ca. 1950–early 1980s) and the Modern or Contemporary era (post–1980). The Traditional era is singled out for special emphasis, and the work of its dominant figures—Breuil and Peyrony—is viewed as fundamental to understanding developments after World War II. The basic tenets of the phylogenetic paradigm are seen to originate in the 1900–1950 interval, and a construal of these tenets is presented and contrasted with the Straus/Clark characterization of them. An effort is made to explore the logic of inquiry underlying the development of archaeological systematics that accounts for the rather special nature of French taxonomic schemata and for the difficulties Americans encounter in trying to understand them.

Part II—Paradigms for the Franco-Iberian Paleolithic and Mesolithic

Papers by Barton, Harrold, Chase, Davidson, González Morales, Dibble and Debénath exemplify work in the western part of the Mediterranean. Mike Barton's essay is concerned with the interpretation of Middle Paleolithic chipped stone artifacts, in particular the retouched pieces that figure so prominently in the "indigenous" systematics of Continental prehistorians. He suggests that current interpretive frameworks are usually based on implicit, but misleading, analogies with the metal-using technologies of the modern industrial world, and that this paradigm has widespread implications for the significance accorded variability in lithic assemblages. An alternative paradigm is proposed that focuses on the range of factors that affect the form of lithics prior to loss or discard. Whether retouched pieces can be considered "tools" in the sense of planned, intentionally modified artifacts is called into question.

Frank Harrold's contribution focuses on the current debate about the nature of the Middle/Upper Paleolithic transition, which he likens to the parable of the blind men and the elephant (each was touching a different part of the elephant, and each was certain that he alone perceived the true nature of the beast). The indigenous and American paradigms are contrasted in respect of implicit assumptions about questions that can legitimately be asked of an ancient archaeological record, and what kinds of evidence, analytical units, and methodologies are suitable for answering them. It is suggested that paradigm conflict can sometimes serve to sharpen perceptions of "the true nature of the beast"—the biological and behavioral changes that accompanied the appearance of modern humans.

The essay by Phil Chase also focuses on the Middle/Upper Paleolithic transition, but is concerned with archaeozoology rather than the chipped stone artifacts that occupy the attention of many scholars. Chase suggests that, while archaeozoologists can often detect the presence or absence of major kinds of behavioral phenomena (perhaps more accurately than lithic studies), there are serious difficulties with the economic models that are invoked to explain them. Because of alleged differences in adaptation, a clear implication of Middle/Upper Paleolithic "replacement" scenarios is that significant economic changes should coincide with changes in the archaeology. So far, however, these have eluded detection.

Iain Davidson's paper critiques two aspects of Upper Paleolithic research in Spain. The proper role of the typological systematics that underlie the traditional "indigenous" paradigm is assessed, and the indigenous paradigm is contrasted with the technological approaches now finding favor with some Anglo-American workers. Attempts to break free of the confines of the indigenous paradigm are viewed as only partly successful because, Davidson argues, its basic analytical units are so ingrained into every aspect of research designs that to ignore them altogether would be to produce a piece of work that would be unintelligible to most of one's colleagues. Davidson suggests that more adequate technological systematics might help to redress the historic imbalance in favor of typology. The second theme addresses the reasons why scholars might wish to break with the tenets of the indigenous paradigm. Dissatisfaction with its capacity to deal in meaningful ways with culture process questions is seen as paramount, and Davidson urges us to concentrate instead on developing approaches that will allow for a better grasp of the short term behaviors that create an archaeological record. Like some other contributors, he detects a fundamental shift in archaeologists' perceptions of the nature of archaeological sites, and advocates development of a systematics that will allow us to cope more effectively with the complex patterning of the palimpsests with which we must routinely come to terms.

Manolo R. González Morales presents a critique of the functionalism of Straus and Clark, arguing that Godelier's (1974, 1977) marxist-materialist perspective is better able to accommodate, and ultimately explain, the full range of processes involved in the transition from the late Upper Paleolithic to the Neolithic in Cantabrian Spain. Since it is a major point of contrast between the two periods, the disappearance of paleolithic art is singled out as a topic for special emphasis. González Morales contends that ecological-functionalist perspectives cannot deal very effectively with the ideological sphere and that art cannot be divorced from its broader social milieu. The implication is that the ideological context of art might have varied independently of the socio-economic and ecological contexts that are targeted by most Anglo-American workers. Whatever its context might have been, the disappearance of art at the end of the Upper Paleolithic is real enough, a significant "fact" that demands a more satisfactory explanation than that offered by functionalist perspectives.

The essay by Harold Dibble and André Debénath is the only one co-authored by a "native informant" (Debénath) and a representative of the American intellectual tradition (Dibble). Dibble and Debénath are collaborating on work at the French Middle and Upper Paleolithic site of Combe Capelle. They suggest that, while differences in paradigmatic biases can be overlooked, ignored, or compartmentalized when they exist as abstractions in the literature, they must be confronted directly when researchers from different intellectual traditions begin to work together in a cooperative venture. The chapter contrasts the natural science paradigm, which is the dominant one in French prehistory, with the paradigm of processual archaeology endorsed by most post-1970 American workers. The focus is on Middle Paleolithic issues and problems—the research area emphasized by both authors. Amicable collaboration is possible, they suggest, because the two traditions share many common, complementary methodologies, which in turn produce data useful to each of them (albeit for different ends).

Part III—Paradigms for the Paleomesolithic of Italy and Cyprus

The central part of the Mediterranean Basin is represented by contributions from Stiner, Kuhn, Bietti and Simmons. Mary Stiner's essay focuses on the effects of taphonomy on perceptions of site contextual integrity, and how recognition of more complex site formation processes has affected what archaeologists believe they can learn from paleolithic cave sites. She perceives a fundamental conflict between paradigms that seek to reconstruct past events (the traditionalist view) and those that seek to understand the evolution of behavioral systems. Adherents of the latter perspective are increasingly turning their attention to questions of hominid behavioral adaptations that see adaptation within the context of larger animal communities (the community ecology approach). Stiner argues that the community ecology paradigm represents a viable alternative to the traditionalist view because it capitalizes on the "contaminated" archaeofaunas that, without exception, make up the paleolithic archaeological record. The community ecology approach focuses on the resource procurement relationships of hominids and other sympatric predatory species that together account for the paleolithic faunal inventory. The mix of carnivore and hominid components in Italian Middle and Upper Paleolithic cave and rockshelter sites opens up many opportunities for the study of human adaptations. Properly applied to a large enough data base, the approach should allow for the recognition of some of the boundaries of the hominid food niche through interspecies comparisons of schedules and sequences of cave use, prey choice, and access to and treatment of carcasses relative to particular places and "slices" of time.

Steve Kuhn's chapter nicely complements that of Stiner, since it also deals with Italian paleolithic archaeology. He emphasizes technology, however, and contrasts traditional European typological systematics (which arise in his opinion, from an essentially historical view of prehistory) with those demanded of the evolutionary paradigm favored by most Anglo-American workers. In the context of an evolutionary approach to prehistory, technology is viewed as a strategically organized set of behaviors that relate to the design of implements and to the provisioning of individuals, corporate units, and places with modified and unmodified raw materials in response to anticipated needs. Kuhn suggests that, in order to study the technological strategies of prehistoric humans, it is necessary first to take assemblages and artifacts "apart" analytically in order to understand the sequence of behaviors which led to the presence of individual items in their observed forms and frequencies in an archaeological record.

Amilcare Bietti's contribution is a general discussion of what he considers to be the "pseudonormal science" paradigm of Italian paleolithic archaeology. He suggests that, properly speaking, Italian paleolithic archaeology remains in the "protoparadigm" stage in the sense that, while there is some agreement among workers about the nature of ancient archaeological deposits and what it is reasonable to expect to learn from them, there is neither awareness nor explicit discussion of these paradigmatic issues and many interregional differences in underlying assumptions. The "pseudonormal science" activities of Italian researchers are described and attributed to what Bietti calls the "chronotypological protoparadigm." With its origins in the French natural science tradition, and more particularly in the typological systematics of Georges Laplace, the chronotypological protoparadigm aims to establish (sometimes in the face of contradictory radiometric evidence) chronological sequences using morphological and stylistic attributes of certain classes of retouched stone tools. The effects of these biases are viewed as all-pervasive, encompassing excavation procedures, data collection, and analysis. Explanation is strictly ad hoc and, in Bietti's view, simplistic. Bietti is critical of many aspects of current Italian archaeological practice and, although he identifies areas where change is evident, sees little hope for a Kuhn-like "scientific revolution" in the absence of a genuine paradigm characterized by a common sense of problem, canons of evidence (i.e., standards relating to data acquisition and analysis), and a commonly shared scientific language.

In some contrast to the more general essays of Stiner, Kuhn and Bietti, Alan Simmons' chapter deals with the history of a single site, the Akrotiri-Aetokremnos rockshelter, on the southern tip of the Akrotiri Peninsula on the south coast of Cyprus. Tests had revealed an apparent association of aceramic cultural remains with hundreds of thousands of bones of pygmy hippopotamus, a species thought to have gone extinct long before the appearance of humans on the island. Initial radiocarbon dates of ca. 9500 B.C. indicated that the site might be the earliest evidence for a human presence on Cyprus. These two "facts" (the hippo/artifact association and the dates), which Simmons regards as reasonably well-documented according to the canons of evidence of the American research tradition, were nevertheless greeted with marked skepticism by the French and French-influenced Cypriot archaeological establishments that dominate Cypriot research. The essay summarizes the case for a pre-neolithic human presence on Cyprus, and discusses the reactions to this "anomaly" and their implications for the preservation of the establishment paradigm. It is the history of a "paradigm crisis" in miniature that called into question fundamental establishment views about the nature and timing of the colonization process and the relationship between humans and the extinction of island faunas.

Part IV—Paradigms for Levantine Epipaleolithic Research

Part IV comprises five essays concerned mainly with the paradigms that govern epipaleolithic systematics in Israel and Jordan. Steve Rosen's essay is the exception; it is an insightful discussion of the effects of modern political history on the archaeology of the Holy Land. He argues that biases inherent in the archaeologies of the world powers that have shaped the course of Levantine political history have affected systematics from the highest, most abstract levels (e.g., conceptions of culture) down to the sociological and methodological levels. The early frameworks were British or French, and to a considerable extent transferred concepts, terminology, and methods directly from European research traditions. Although the post-World War II era saw the emergence of indigenous national archaeologies (and, in Israel, the development of a cadre of professional prehistorians), the intraregional antagonisms of the area affect the location of research, preclude or obstruct communication, and result in different paradigms that reflect in part the lingering influence of the League of Nations mandate. In aggregate these factors negatively effect the capacity to generate and test hypotheses about regional variability, interregional networks, and regional archaeological systematics in general. There are, in effect, two or three partly distinct, partly overlapping research traditions which are, in each case, amalgams of different colonial archaeological heritages modified locally according to post-World War II political developments.

The epipaleolithic of the Levant is presently an area of accelerated research activity, largely because of post-1970 Israeli work headed by Ofer Bar-Yosef and his students and more recent, although no less spectacular, research in Syria and Jordan. The Natufian, in particular, has become the object of intense scrutiny, and the papers by Olszewski, Donaldson and Henry all deal with one or another aspect of it. Deborah Olszewski's essay questions the evidence for precocious social complexity in prehistoric hunter-gatherer contexts previously regarded as egalitarian. She focuses on recent models for social complexity in the sedentary but pre-agricultural Natufian, and is able to show that many concepts and terms underlying epipaleolithic systematics (e.g., base camps, storage facilities, "ranking" in mortuary data) are either conceptually ambiguous and/or lack adequate operational definitions. She asks how we measure social complexity in the Natufian context. Her answer is that Levantine archaeologists have been too uncritical in developing archaeological monitors of complexity. After clarifying some of these conceptual and definitional issues, she assesses the case for Natufian social complexity and comes to the conclusion that the Natufian indeed represents a significant organizational transformation, but not necessarily the non-egalitarian, ranked, chiefdom-like entity that it is sometimes represented as being.

The chapter by Marcie Donaldson also concerns Levantine epipaleolithic systematics. Donaldson identifies a fundamental paradox in the logic of epipaleolithic studies: although the Levantine epipaleolithic is generally acknowledged to be a period of significant economic and social transformation, our understanding of it is grounded almost exclusively in lithic analyses. What one might imagine to be crucial data related to the very economic and social changes that supposedly define this period of transition are in fact relegated to secondary importance, if they are used at all. She suggests that this bias, attributed to the dominance of European-derived normative, typological systematics, can account for some of the schizophrenic aspects of epipaleolithic research. While typological approaches have their uses, those uses are seen as limited to the formulation of normative classificatory schemata, the meaning of which is neither clear nor agreed upon by consensus. She argues that technological and metrical analyses, raw material studies, and regionally oriented paleoenvironmental and paleoeconomic research can be used independently of typological systematics to generate hypotheses about Levantine epipaleolithic adaptations and to confirm or refute hypotheses developed by the traditional approaches.

Don Henry's contribution complements those of Olszewski and Donaldson, but approaches the Natufian from a very different perspective. Henry suggests that, traditionally, sedentary foraging societies in both ethnographic and archaeological contexts have been characterized as stable adaptive systems that emerge in extraordinarily "rich" environmental settings, and in which foraging and sedentism are seen as complementary strategies. The Natufian is the Levantine archetype for what could be called the "complementarity model." An alternative perspective is offered in which "foraging" and "sedentism" are viewed as mutually contradictory from the point of view of a society's long-term survival. The systemic evolution of the Natufian is traced over a 2,000-year period, and the stability of a Natufian-like precursor to domestication economies is called into question. Environmental change and its effects on resource distributions, resource stress, sedentism and its consequences for population growth are important variables in an argument that attempts to show why complex foraging was destined to fail over the long run, and why it was a terminal Pleistocene-early Holocene phenomenon in the Levant.

The essay by Ofer Bar-Yosef is similar to those of Straus and Clark in its return to a more personal statement of how his intellectual and cultural "roots" in post-war Israel have acted in concert to shape his views. Bar-Yosef sees the present as an extension of the 1970s, an era in which the range of prehistoric research, and the number of researchers, increased enormously over previous decades, causing a collapse of the informal, face-to-face interaction among prehistorians typical of earlier periods. This phenomenon is attributed to the worldwide, post-war democratization of science in general, only manifest in archaeology after a delay of some two decades. In the Israel of the 1960s, when he received his formal training, prehistory was dominated by the European research traditions, especially those of France and England. A prehistorian with a wide range of interests spanning all Levantine preceramic periods, Bar-Yosef makes a distinction between the paradigms that govern Lower and Middle Paleolithic research, on the one hand, and those that affect "later" prehistory (the Upper Paleolithic, but especially the Epipaleolithic, Neolithic), on the other. Inferences about the earlier periods are necessarily going to be restricted to various kinds of pattern searches that, ideally, would also take into account a variety of natural site formation processes. Because most uniformitarian assumptions about culture and behavior cannot be sustained (i.e., the hominids involved were not like ourselves) and because the range of data preserved is typically very restricted, inferences will be limited to aspects of technology and subsistence. Inferences about later prehistory (i.e., that created by modern humans) are shaped by history and by our capacity to identify identity-conscious social groups in the residues of the past. While Bar-Yosef admits this approach is somewhat problematic when dealing with the Upper Paleolithic, the Epipaleolithic and Neolithic sequences in southwest Asia are thought to represent the continuous social histories of groups that can be defined and traced archaeologically. Although the assumptions that underlie them are similar, separate paradigms for the Epipaleolithic and the Neolithic are outlined and illustrated with Levantine data.

The last paper, by Suzanne and Paul Fish, differs from the rest in that Old and New World paradigms for the transition from foraging to domestication in arid regions are compared. Both authors can claim long involvement with these issues both in the American Southwest and in the Levant. In each area, they contend, regional paradigms have emerged that identify processes leading from one classificatory endpoint to the other on a scale of transitional development. And, although many of the same criteria are employed in both areas to judge the positions of assemblages, sites, and archaeological cultures along this scale, there is a tendency for these constructs to become reified in such fixed combinations in sequences that rearrangement becomes extremely difficult or is precluded altogether. The transition from mobile foragers to sedentary agriculturalists is contrasted in terms of notions of process in the two regions, which are similar in some environmental and archaeological respects but very different in evolutionary trajectories and in biases brought to bear on this important question. Problems of confirmation and refutation of alternative positions are discussed. It is concluded that a weakness of regional paradigms is a failure to acknowledge variability among different elements at different scales. Paradigm territorial boundaries that circumscribe cultural diversity for the sake of comprehension can become deterrents to new insights as well as aids of understanding.

Concluding Remarks

Because of long national and regional research traditions, much of our image of the earlier phases of Old World prehistory derives from research in the Mediterranean Basin and in the countries that border it (especially France, Spain, Italy, and the Levant). Statements about how the "producers" of this knowledge go about their work should, therefore, be of interest to anyone who has more than a passing acquaintance with contemporary prehistoric archaeology. The essays in the book are directed at a professional, rather than a popular audience, however, since most non-professionals conceive of archaeology as little more than a discovery process in which the "meaning" of "facts" is erroneously thought to be straightforward and relatively self-evident. A recent Sigma Xi survey showed that only about ten percent of the American public think of science as a method of inquiry, as opposed to any other definition they might give it (the most common one was "an accumulation of facts"). If anything, the survey showed that public understanding of science had declined over the past decade. The point, though, is that the inferential basis for knowledge claims is never made explicit in the public sector, and there is no tradition within anthropology of extensive discussion of these metaphysical issues. Yet, so long as people have sought to reconcile their views of the natural and social worlds, and the place of humans in them, they have struggled to create world views that are both satisfying on a personal level and "cognitively adequate" (Kitchener 1988:3). If it does nothing else, it is my hope that *Perspectives* will make the point that paradigmatic biases structure the research process from start to finish, and to a much greater extent than most people realize. Since there are legitimate differences of opinion about how to conduct the research enterprise, the book addresses the broader scientific and philosophical issue of the part science plays in the creation of "world views" of the human past. It should, therefore, be of some interest to prehistoric archaeologists of all persuasions (i.e., not just hunter-gatherer specialists, nor Mediterranean archaeologists, nor Old World prehistorians). Finally, the book is "timely." It constitutes both a sampler and a defense of a major "kind" of modern archaeology that views the field as a scientific enterprise that is part of the positivist legacy of western science. In this role, I would like to believe that it is a moderate response to the radical critique, and to the profusion of "alternative" archaeologies that I mentioned at the beginning of this introduction.

When I first raised the issue of the *Perspectives* volume, and so long as it remained an abstraction, I received a lot of encouragement from archaeologists of all persuasions and on both sides of the Atlantic. However, the pages of the book are mainly filled with the writings of younger scholars or those in the middle phases of their careers. There are relatively few contributors who would universally be regarded as "big names" (probably the most prominent are Sackett and Bar-Yosef). In compiling a list of potential contributors, I asked more than a dozen senior scholars who figure prominently in circum-Mediterranean hunter-gatherer research. Although some of them vacillated for a while, in the end I didn't get many "takers" and I wondered why.

It occurred to me that senior scholars are perhaps *least likely* to want to contribute to a book of this kind. The reason is fairly obvious. Archaeology is a field that is very poorly developed conceptually and epistemologically, and which has an exceptionally strong empiricist tradition. Prominent figures usually have relatively well-established, published positions within the research structure of their particular areas and problem domains and are, in consequence, usually unwilling to stick their necks out and try to make their operating assumptions explicit. After all, why should they? They have nothing to gain from it, and the discipline neither requires nor expects them to do it. The paradigmatic biases that govern the archaeological research enterprise are often rather unimpressive—a mishmash of an individual's formal education, combined with the compromises they have learned they must make if they are to cope successfully with actual data sets in "real world" situations. It is to the credit of those contributors with reputations that they are willing to expose their often-less-than-noble biases and assumptions to the discipline at large. There is not a little irony in this since these nebulous entities structure the research enterprise from start to finish and affect it at every level. I count it a strength of the book that most contributors are younger scholars who are currently, or have recently been, involved in hunter-gatherer field research. These younger workers also tend to be much more aware of the epistemological issues and questions that underlie all archaeological research than are the older scholars. A dose of epistemology is much more usually part of their formal academic preparation than it was for previous generations.

Finally, and paradoxically, there are few representatives of what I would call the "indigenous" Old World research traditions. In fact, the clearest explication of the logic of inquiry underlying French systematics is written by an American—James Sackett (see also Sackett 1981). As was the case with senior scholars, I solicited essays from thirteen prominent French, German, Spanish, British, Italian, Israeli, and Jordanian prehistorians (and one British scholar working in Greece, one Canadian working in North Africa). Only André Debénath (France), Amilcare Bietti (Italy), Manuel González Morales (Spain), and Ofer Bar-Yosef (Israel) responded. In my opinion, the reasons for the poor turnout amongst European prehistorians go deeper than the overcommitment that afflicts us all. To put it bluntly, there is no conception of epistemology in the archaeological research traditions of the Continent, nor much awareness that such a thing even exists. A concern with epistemological issues is essentially confined to the archaeological liter-ature of the United States and, to a lesser extent, England. Why this is so is not at all clear to me, and is especially puzzling in light of its Con-tinental origins. However, it should be noted that these concerns are limited to a relatively small (but growing) number of Anglo-American workers and, quite regardless of research tradition, it is obviously per-fectly possible to practice archaeology successfully throughout one's career without ever confronting the inferential basis for knowledge claims. That this is so is a telling commentary on the state of the field, and one that sets it apart from a mature discipline like physics, in which paradigms at every level are relatively well defined and understood (if not agreed upon) by most practicing professionals (see, e.g., Dunnell 1982, Clark 1987a, Kitchener 1988). Nor have the relative merits of paradigms been debated for decades in the literature, as they have in some "big science" fields. By now, it is something of a platitude to point out that our "world view" underwent a radical change with the advent of processual archaeology in the mid/late 1960s. We should not forget, however, that the defeat of the old culture historical paradigm is still very recent and, on a global scale, only very partial. While processual-ism is under attack from various quarters in England and the United States, in most of the Old World the construction of regional culture histories remains the primary objective of archaeological research.

While engaged in editing the book manuscript, I came to wonder if an irreducible "bedrock minimum" metaphysical paradigm might exist that could be claimed to underlie all of the perspectives represented here. It was clear that different "world views" existed about the nature of the past and of man's place in it, yet Americanist perspectives were so at variance with "indigenous" European views that the irreducible paradigm could never be that of anthropology—even a passing ac-quaintance with European natural science and historical traditions ruled that out entirely. I eventually came to the conclusion that, if such a thing exists, the "paradigm with a capital P" must consist of an eclectic mix of terms and concepts borrowed piecemeal from biological and cultural evolution, with the proportional contributions of each of them varying from one tradition to the next, and, within traditions, over time. Why evolution? Evolution is *the* central organizing principle for the scientific study of the natural world and is of fundamental impor-tance to a number of the social sciences, including anthropology, and to "hybrid disciplines" like prehistoric archaeology and paleoanthropol-ogy. While in my opinion just what constitutes evolution varies quite a bit from one research tradition to another (Brace 1988, Clark 1989a, b), the concept of evolution itself has an undeniable centrality with no real rivals, and is in fact no more controversial or disputed in science than gravity and electricity are in conventional physics (a point utterly lost on "creation science" advocates). Like gravitation and electricity, evolution is both a "fact" and a "theory." By this, I mean that sufficient observations and hypotheses testing them combine to form a robust theory with considerable explanatory power. A "fact," in turn, can be defined as a conventional understanding based on confirmable observation. Facts are evaluated through the formulation of hypotheses which attempt to frame questions of interest as testable propositions. Theories—arguments invoked to tell us why the world is as it seems— are logical constructs based on facts and hypotheses that both organize and explain phenomena of interest. Scientific theories are constantly subject to evaluation, modification, and (however difficult this might be in anthropology) refutation as new evidence and new hypotheses emerge. Because they have predictive and explanatory capabilities, theories function to guide investigation. So it is with evolution. There is, of course, absolutely nothing new or controversial here. These are concepts and relationships that most would acknowledge underlie all of western science; evolution is, of course, a product of western science. It is difficult for me to imagine "anti-evolutionary" prehistorians, while I can easily count among my friends and colleagues prehistorians who are "anti"- or "non-anthropological." Some of these issues are explored at greater length in the Epilogue.

Part I: Paradigmatic Biases in the Earlier Phases of Circum-Mediterranean Archaeological Research

Chapter 2
An Examination of Some Models of Late Pleistocene Society in Southwestern Europe

Catherine S. Mueller-Wille and
D. Bruce Dickson

Introduction

A generation ago the *Man the Hunter* volume (Lee and DeVore 1968a) inspired a transformation in the way archaeologists thought about the hunting and gathering subsistence adaptation. In the two decades following the book's publication, a view of hunting and gathering life which we term here the "basic model" was in general use among prehistorians seeking to interpret the material remains left by prehistoric foraging peoples. That model is now experiencing critical reappraisal, and a paradigm of a more socially complex and subsistence-intensive adaptation is replacing the basic model among many students of the European Upper Paleolithic. This chapter is concerned with the paradigmatic reformulation that is taking place in southwestern European Paleolithic studies. It consists of four parts: (1) a review of the basic model of hunting and gathering sociocultural systems and a discussion of its major limitations, (2) a brief summary of the revised view of the complexity of prehistoric foraging sociocultural systems, (3) a summary and critique of some key examples of contemporary research in southwestern European prehistory guided by this revised view, and (4) a discussion of some of the problems of testing and verification raised by those new approaches.

The Basic Model of Hunting and Gathering Sociocultural Systems[1]

By the end of the nineteenth century, most archaeologists had concluded that the paleolithic peoples of southwestern Europe were food collectors or hunter-gatherers. Although it has been common ever since for scholars to examine historically or ethnographically known hunting and gathering groups as analogues of paleolithic peoples, the *Man the Hunter* volume stimulated a more systematic comparative use of ethnography. The historical and ethnographic corpus available for comparison is quite large. It contains accounts of food collecting societies located chiefly in the subarctic and arctic (or circumpolar) zones of Eurasia and North America, the deserts and steppes of North and South America, the Congo rain forests, arid southern Africa, various heavily forested regions of southern Asia, India and the Philippines, and the Australian continent. Nonetheless, most analogues for modeling paleolithic societies were drawn from a very limited number of these societies. Based on data drawn from some, but far from all, of the societies in this corpus, a general picture of hunting and gathering life was composed by anthropologists and prehistorians. This set of generalizations is referred to by Dickson (1990) as the "basic model" of the food collecting adaptation. The basic model which achieved widest acceptance in paleolithic research held that hunting-and-gathering societies are characterized by: (1) a simple technology, (2) subsistence systems capable of producing relatively low levels of food energy, (3) a diet in which plants contribute a greater percentage of the calories than animals, (4) little emphasis on accumulation of wealth, food or other kinds of surplus, (5) a low density of population per square kilometer, (6) dependence upon wild food resources which tend to be spatially dispersed and to fluctuate (often either seasonally or over the long run) in their availability, (7) a population size determined by the amount of wild foodstuffs collectable during the season of minimum availability, (8) a band level of social organization, (9) reliance upon kinship as the most important principle of social organization, (10) economic distribution and exchange based on reciprocity, (11) bands as corporate groups holding land resources in common but granting unrestricted access to these resources to all members of the band, (12) an absence of full time specialization beyond that based on the sexual division of labor, (13) an absence of ascribed statuses and roles beyond those of age and sex, and (14) feuding but no true warfare.

Limitations of the Basic Model

Until recently, prehistorians have relied almost exclusively on variants of the foregoing basic model of the hunting and gathering adaptation in their reconstructions of Upper Paleolithic socio-cultural systems in southwestern Europe and elsewhere. Certainly extrapolation from this model to the presumed behavior of our ancient ancestors is superior to the purely rationalist approach of the "If I were a cave man, I would . . ." variety. However, there are a number of theoretical and practical limitations to the uncritical use of the basic model in the interpretation of paleolithic culture.

Perhaps the most important limitation of the model is that only a portion of the hunting and gathering societies known to science have been utilized in its formulation. Therefore, it accommodates only a fraction of the variation reported among known food collectors and tends to depend overmuch on such intensively-studied peoples as the !Kung (Lewin 1988a). The relevance of this limited selection of foraging adaptations to Upper Paleolithic Europe is problematical.

Further, Upper Paleolithic hunting and gathering peoples inhabited many environments that have no equivalent in the historic or modern world. For example, western and central Europe seem to have supported a forest-tundra and cold loess steppe or grassland environment during late glacial times. This environment has been compared to the arctic and subarctic environments of Canada and Alaska by scholars seeking to use modern Inuit culture as a source of ethnographic analogy with the European Upper Paleolithic. Butzer (1971:463) suggests that, due to its position on the globe, western Europe received solar radiation at a decidedly more favorable angle than does the modern circumpolar zone. Further, the region would not have experienced the long periods of annual darkness characteristic of land located within the Arctic Circle. As a result, the late Pleistocene tundra and grasslands of the region would have been far more productive than similar cold adapted plant assemblages in the modern world. The astounding size of the animal biomass in Late Glacial Europe apparently was due to the wealth of plant life at that time. Further, according to Butzer (1971) the diversity of animal life known from that region has no equal in the modern arctic and subarctic regions of the Earth.

Upper Paleolithic peoples in Europe hunted numerous animal species now altogether extinct, regionally extinct, or far less abundantly available to historic and modern hunting peoples. Both the paleontological and archaeological records suggest that the numbers of large mammals in the northern hemisphere during the late Pleistocene has no modern equivalent. In contrast, most modern hunter-gatherers live in environments with comparatively low animal biomass. The small size of their social groups in part reflects this paucity. Extrapolations from peoples like the !Kung San of the Kalahari desert to the Upper Paleolithic of Europe are thus particularly questionable.

Upper Paleolithic hunting and gathering peoples inhabited environments of prime subsistence potential, while modern hunter-gatherers generally occupy only marginal ones. By the late Pleistocene, hunting and gathering peoples occupied a large portion of the earth's surface from the tropics to the subarctic in both the Old and the New Worlds. After the close of that epoch, food-collecting subsistence systems began to be replaced in prime environments by those based on agriculture and herding. By historic times, modern hunting and gathering peoples persisted only in circumpolar, desert, steppe, or heavily forested environments which were decidedly marginal or inhospitable from the standpoint of agriculture or pastoral nomadism.

Upper Paleolithic peoples must have subsisted entirely upon the hunting and gathering of wild foodstuffs; very few ethnographically known hunter-gatherers do so. Examples of hunting and gathering peoples living entirely independent of surrounding food producing economies are comparatively rare in the ethnographic literature. The majority of the hunter-gatherers known to science have (or had) established symbiotic ties, trading arrangements, or patron/client relations with agricultural peoples by the time their cultures were studied. In other instances, the food collectors had been conquered or exploited by settled peoples. In addition, European expansion beginning in the sixteenth century subjected many of them to missionizing, colonization, warfare, and dependency on market exchange. Leacock (1982:160) points out that, as a consequence, "in most instances, people with a gatherer-hunter heritage have not lived solely as gatherer-hunters for a long time." They are far from perfect analogues for the paleolithic subsistence systems which were presumably based entirely on food collection.

The assumption that modern hunting and gathering peoples retain the institutions and behavior patterns of the paleolithic period is unwarranted. Food-collecting sociocultural systems have surely developed and changed over the millennia just as have more complex social formations. Most modern hunting and gathering peoples are descendants of peoples who felt the full brunt of European expansion and colonial acquisition. These people were dispossessed of their lands and subjected to the sustained impact of the market and mission. As a result, many experienced substantial cultural impoverishment. Of course, this process did not begin in the sixteenth century. Formerly universal in their distribution, societies based on hunting and gathering have been gradually giving way to those based on agriculture and pastoral nomadism for the last 8,000 years. Many modern food collectors may in fact be the descendants of pottery-using agricultural peoples who abandoned food production when they were driven from their former territories into marginal lands by stronger groups. For example, the Cheyenne, quintessential equestrian hunters of the North American Great Plains, originally practiced the characteristic mixed horticultural and hunting-gathering subsistence of other native American peoples in the woodlands of the Great Lakes region. In fact, they still were sowing catch crops of maize in various river valleys on the northwestern High Plains as recently as 1865 (Grinnell 1962:250–253). Schrire has suggested that the !Kung themselves were formerly agriculturalists (Schrire 1980).

Finally, stringent application of the uniformitarian principle "that people in the past behaved much as they do in the present, with similar social structure, economic strategies, and cognitive abilities" (Bailey 1983a:3) may distort our perception of the archaeological record of the Upper Paleolithic period. The assumption is a useful operational tool, but if it leads us to conclude in advance that past foraging adaptations must be mirrored in the present, it may preclude recognition of real differences between past and present behavior. For example, Foley (cited in Lewin 1988a:1147) notes that, although anatomically modern in most senses, Late Pleistocene *Homo sapiens sapiens* were generally larger and more robust than modern peoples, and their populations exhibited more pronounced dimorphism. Foley hypothesizes that Late Pleistocene subsistence centered to a great degree on large mammal hunting and that this hunting was done by men. Large mammal hunting would selectively favor large males possessed of physical strength and stamina while the activities associated with the female role would not. Reduced sexual dimorphism in post-Pleistocene hunter-gatherer populations may thus indicate that selective pressures no longer favored large males. Foley concludes from this that the subsistence strategies practiced by historic hunter-gatherers may be a post-Pleistocene development that reflects the increased importance of plant gathering. Thus the ethnographically known hunter-gatherer adaptation, characterized by sexual division of labor, food sharing, and central place foraging, may be relatively recent behavior. Whether or not Foley's interpretation finds adequate support in the data, it provides an important warning against the unreflective application of uniformitarian principles to the Pleistocene archaeological record.

The Complexity of Prehistoric Foraging Systems

Recognition of the foregoing has led contemporary scholars to conclude that there are no exact historic or modern analogues for Upper Paleolithic society and, therefore, to question the relevance of the basic model—drawn as it is from the ethnography of historic and modern foraging peoples—for the interpretation of Upper Paleolithic life. In recent research there is a noticeable effort to build models free of what

Wobst (1978) called "the tyranny of the ethnographic record." Consequently, the picture of late Upper Paleolithic European subsistence and settlement systems emerging from this research departs from the basic model in a number of fundamental ways. Perhaps the most significant departure is the suggestion that the foraging societies of the southwestern European Upper Paleolithic may have been socially and culturally more complex than most ethnographically known hunter-gatherers.

In the extensive anthropological literature dealing with social and cultural complexity, a variety of indicators or measures have been used. Lists of such indicators generally include the presence of ascribed status differentiation; legitimate, full-time authority; increased sedentism; burials with differential treatment; sophisticated art styles; intensification in food procurement and production; political and military competition; territoriality; and high population densities and population aggregates. Until quite recently, the notion that social and cultural complexity could only be associated with food-producing rather than food-collecting economies was an article of faith among prehistorians. However, a number of recent studies now point to evidence that such features have in fact been found at various times and places among prehistoric hunting and gathering peoples (e.g., cf. Bailey 1983a, Price and Brown 1985).

Bailey (1983a:1–6) notes that there is growing evidence that some of the higher organizational structures of modern hunter-gatherers, such as integration of local bands into larger units through social and kinship ties and possibly initial status differentiation, may be found in the European Upper Paleolithic. Many of the newer models of Upper Paleolithic subsistence and settlement assume that some degree of social complexity developed within that period. Before proceeding to a discussion of some of these models, a short discussion of some of the relevant issues of social complexity and intensification is thus in order here.

Price and Brown (1985) have attempted to provide order to the discussion of the emergence of complexity by separately discussing its conditions, consequences, and causes. They note that three conditions are generally found associated with increasing cultural complexity and resource intensification: social circumscription, the presence of an abundant resource base, and a trend toward population increase. They focus on the consequences of intensification among hunters and gatherers which are most visible archaeologically: changes in productivity, settlement, and decision making. They suggest that with increasing sociocultural complexity one would expect an increase in the number of implements and localities in use; subsistence equipment (such as tools and sites) would become more diverse in form, more specialized, and more abundant. New tools and facilities would exhibit specificity for certain resource procurement tasks, and procurement activities would be more diversified and more specialized in numbers of new species and habitats exploited (Price and Brown 1985:11). Additions to the diet would generally come from lower levels on the food chain, or be more costly in terms of procurement and/or processing, such as shellfish, fish, nuts, and dangerous animal prey. Changes in settlement should include a reduction in mobility, more pronounced territorial behavior, settlements of larger size and/or longer duration, and increased differentiation of sites both internally and in their kind and location. Status differentiation and inequality are proposed as the means by which decision making authority is designated. Exchange systems may operate to maintain alliances, and to furnish higher status individuals with the trappings of their positions.

Price and Brown review various arguments on the causes of increased intensification and complexity. Re-adaptation to changed environments coupled with demographic stress is a commonly cited causal agent, such as in Binford's (1968) discussion of subsistence and settlement change at the end of the Pleistocene. Population increase has been proposed as a prime mover (Cohen 1977). While many of the assumptions underlying population increase models have been challenged, it is nevertheless commonly cited as a casual agent (e.g., Clark 1987b). Redding (1988) formulates a general model in which population stress leads to changes in subsistence organization. Migration, diversification, and storage are posited as successive tactical moves to ameliorate stress, followed by a strategic shift to domestication if the carrying capacity of a region continues to be approached. In contrast, some structuralist approaches see demographic pressure as the *result* of a series of causes, the most important of which are changes in the relations of production (Bender 1978). Since population pressure, the necessity of adapting to environmental change, and response to changes in social organization are the most commonly invoked causes of the emergence of cultural complexity, it is perhaps fair to suggest that a great many contemporary prehistorians consciously or unconsciously accept Flannery's (1972) dictum that change in human society is always a reaction to stress. Nonetheless, there is presently no firm consensus on the source of the "stress" that is most important in generating increased complexity. Many contemporary scholars are uncomfortable with unicausal explanations and see a number of internal and external causes working together as instrumental.

Some Contemporary Models of Southwestern European Upper Paleolithic Subsistence and Settlement

We turn now to a discussion of a number of contemporary models of late Upper Paleolithic subsistence and settlement systems in southwestern Europe which posit a slightly more complex society than that presented in the "basic model." Most of our models for interpreting the material remains of prehistoric peoples have been based on the recognition that hunters and gatherers move over extensive areas in the course of their annual rounds, and use a number of different camp sites and kinds of sites. These movements are generally assumed to be seasonal, and there is growing evidence that this assumption is, in some cases at least, correct. As a consequence of these assumptions, contemporary environmentalist studies tend to share two major goals: to recognize the boundaries of ancient exploitation territories and delineate regions which were culturally and behaviorally meaningful to the paleolithic people themselves, and to determine the place of individual sites within that exploitation territory. This has led to the recognition of the importance of regional studies within a broad spatial and geographic framework. If we can begin to recognize such exploitation territories, and regions which were culturally/behaviorally meaningful in the Upper Paleolithic, a major step in understanding the past will have been made.

Models developed toward this end in the last decade or so may be roughly divided into two groups: (1) those that focus on the physical environment and demographic change as primary conditioners of human adaptation systems, and (2) those in which the "social environment" is emphasized as having a significant effect on man's adaptation to his physical environment. This is not to say that either group focuses on one aspect of human society and ignores the other, merely that either the physical *or* social environment is primarily stressed. Among the scholars emphasizing changes in the physical environment and demographic variables as primary explanations of culture change in southwestern Europe are Lawrence Straus, Geoffrey Clark, Geoffrey Bailey, and Paul Bahn. Those emphasizing the importance of the social environment in cultural patterning include Anne Sieveking, Michael Jochim, Clive Gamble, Marcia Madden, and Margaret Conkey. We will briefly discuss some models used by these researchers in their work, as examples of the way in which our basic paradigms affect our interpretation of the data. Clearly, there are many discussions of models in the literature not mentioned here. We do not offer a comprehensive view of all pertinent literature, but have chosen these particular authors as they offer specific examples of points we wish to discuss.

Physical Environmental Models

Lawrence Straus and Geoffrey Clark

A number of archaeologists working within a basic environmentalist/adaptational framework have focused on Cantabrian Spain. Faunal and lithic assemblage variability and site placement, and possible correspondences of these with environmental change, have been major research themes in this area. Freeman (1973), looking at faunal assemblages as evidence of human adaptation rather than as climatic markers, notes a significant change between pre-Magdalenian and Magdalenian faunas, with the latter period characterized by intensification in red deer and shellfish procurement, along with diversification to dangerous and solitary species. Straus (1977) and Clark (1987b) have re-examined these changes, and suggest that they are related to a sharp increase in population density around 20 kyr BP (see also Clark and Yi 1983, Clark and Straus 1986).

Straus (1975, 1976) also examines Solutrean lithic assemblage variability, correlating it with two distinct geographic sub-regions in Vasco-Cantabria. He identifies two basic types of assemblages, one characterized by high percentages of endscrapers, sidescrapers, denticulated and notched pieces, and Solutrean foliate points; the other by high percentages of burins, truncated pieces, and backed bladelets. The former assemblages are found in the Asturias and Santander regions, while the latter are concentrated in the Basque country to the east. Straus interprets these differences as strictly functional, since sites in Asturias/Santander have generally yielded faunal assemblages distinct from those found in the Basque country. Large numbers of red deer, horse, and large bovids (*Bos* and/or *Bison*), consistent with a mosaic environment of woods and grasslands, are found in the former area. In contrast, Solutrean sites in the more steeply mountainous Basque country generally produce few of the above species, but contain numerous alpine caprids such as chamois and ibex, as well as fur-bearing carnivores such as fox and various mustelids.

Straus suggests that the apparent correlation between the two different types of artifact assemblages, geographical regions, and faunal collections probably indicates that, at least by the Late Solutrean, two contrastive adaptive poses had developed in northern Spain. That is, the two distinct artifact assemblages resulted from differences in the hunting and processing requirements of animals pursued in the two regions. The basic paradigm underlying this argument is that of variability explained as different adaptational responses to different environments. If Straus is correct in asserting that the makeup of the two tool assemblages directly reflects the different array of animals exploited, the frequency and geographic distribution of these assemblages should have changed over time in response to the changes in climate and biogeography that occurred during the late and terminal Pleistocene in the region.

In collaboration with Clark, Straus sets out to test this notion using the site of La Riera cave and the surrounding region (Clark and Straus 1983). They begin their analysis with the assumption that climatic change and demographic pressure caused such adaptational shifts.

Since the end of the Middle Paleolithic . . . until the initial appearance of domestication . . . , hunter-gatherer populations in Cantabria have responded to often severe macro-climatic changes, and to regional demographic pressure by systematic adjustment in modes of subsistence linked to changes in settlement pattern (Clark and Straus 1983:131).

In fact, Clark and Straus find evidence that both types of lithic assemblages occur through time at La Riera, cross-cutting a number of the traditional culture-stratigraphic units, as do the different faunas. No clear correlation is recognized among the culture-stratigraphic units identified at La Riera, episodes of environmental/climatic change, or changes in the lithic and faunal assemblages. In other words, the authors find very little or no correlation between fluctuations in the late Pleistocene climate of Cantabrian Spain and changes in human adaptation as measured by shifts in the tool kit.

On the other hand, they find that pronounced changes in lithic raw material procurement patterns generally corresponded to breaks between the culture-stratigraphic units, and that the extent to which flint-knapping was practiced *in situ* in the cave varied from occupation layer to layer. Clark and Straus (1983:140) interpret these changes in raw material procurement and processing as evidence that the overall subsistence-settlement pattern, in which they were possibly "embedded" (Binford 1979), changed at the same time. Finally, although change in the La Riera faunas did not correlate with climate change, it did appear to be directional. The percentage of red deer in the deposits increased markedly after 20,000 B.P.; new resources such as marine fish, shellfish, and wild boar appeared, and limpet shells declined in size in the later deposits in the cave (Clark and Straus 1986). Outside La Riera, the site survey data revealed that the numbers of Upper Paleolithic sites increased per unit time, which Clark and Straus interpret as evidence of population growth. Lacking a correlation between environmental and adaptive change, they conclude that population growth and a resulting pressure on the existing resource base was the primary cause of the changes in subsistence and settlement pattern. In other words, faced with growing populations stressing the resource base at a given level of technology and tactics, hunters intensified their exploitation of existing red deer populations and began tapping the hitherto neglected marine and shoreline resources.

Clark and Straus's use of lithic analysis to model Upper Paleolithic subsistence and settlement is a refreshing contrast to the long-established archaeological practice of simply applying cultural labels to lists of tool types. Their work is a direct rejection of "ethnic identity" as the sole explanation of lithic variability in the Upper Paleolithic period. However, it should be noted that, in defining their two assemblage types, Straus (1977) and Clark and Straus (1983) retain the standard Upper Paleolithic stone tool type definitions that formed the basis for the ethnic identity model. Consequently, their types may be mixtures of stylistic, functional, and other formal criteria. It seems unlikely, therefore, that the variation between the distribution of two assemblages of such tool types could be the result of exclusively functional differences between them. Additionally, the notion that two adaptational poses characterized by the same lithic artifact assemblages would cyclically recur over a 15,000-year period is difficult for us to accept. Nevertheless, their interpretation of the two assemblages remains quite functionally specific.

Insofar as the form of the defining retouched tool groups is distinctive, a functional interpretation is implied with backed bladelet rich assemblages perhaps representing a broad spectrum of activities related to hunting contexts in which the microliths functioned as disposable weapon points and edges, the notch/denticulated dominated assemblages related to processing activities in general, including the processing of vegetal matter for which we have no direct archaeological evidence (Clark and Straus 1983:147).

While the recurrent patterns of lithic variability identified by these authors are interesting and important, their functional explanation in its current form appears inadequate, and additional definition and the testing of alternate hypotheses is in order.

Geoffrey Bailey

An objection to the "causality" in the above interpretation of Cantabrian culture change is voiced by Bailey (1983b), who asserts that Clark and Straus have not defined the independent variable of environmental change with sufficient precision (Editor's note: Clark and Straus disagree [1986]). He notes that what we call the environment is, after all, composed of many factors, not all of which are closely covariant or subject to change at the same rate. Bailey suggests that, for Cantabria, the lowered snow line and drop in sea level that characterized the later paleolithic period would have had a substantially more significant impact on human adaptation than Clark and Straus are willing to admit. He hypothesizes that the increase in red deer exploitation noted through time at La Riera may actually signal environmental change, on the grounds that deteriorating climatic conditions may have favored the more adaptable red deer over certain other game species, and that the lowered sea level and widened coastal plain may have resulted in an expansion in red deer carrying capacity. Thus at this point we cannot be certain whether the absence of a clear correlation between environmental change and assemblage change in Clark and Straus's Cantabrian data indicates that these two variables were not related, or is due to the fact that the two variables were not operationally defined with sufficient precision.

Bailey, Clark, and Straus are nevertheless looking at essentially the same phenomena, but have chosen to emphasize different factors as causal explanations. Whether change came about because of actual population increase, or because deteriorating climatic conditions necessitated adaptational shifts, proposed imbalances between populations and their resources are the underlying causal factor invoked by all three authors.

Paul Bahn

Bahn (1983), in a regional study of late Pleistocene economies in the French Pyrenees, attempts to trace economic development through changes in faunal assemblages and site location, also emphasizing environmental and demographic factors as primary causes of change. As in Cantabria, Bahn finds a shift in faunal assemblages with the Magdalenian, which includes both a greater diversity of species represented and a very heavy dependence on one or two herbivore species (reindeer, largely replaced by red deer toward the close of the Pleistocene).

Like Bailey et al. (1983) for Epirus and Conkey (1980) for Cantabria, Bahn finds a hierarchy of sites in the Pyrenean region, with Isturitz and Mas d'Azil representing probable major aggregation sites, then a large category of smaller habitation sites (base camps) and a number of task-specific work camps or transitory encampments. Bahn supports this hierarchical division with evidence on the locations of each type of site, topographic features, and available resources. In terms of causal factors, Bahn suggests that while environmental change sometimes replaced one species with another, as in the rise and fall of reindeer frequencies, overall it seems to have had little influence on exploitation methods in the Pyrenees. Population pressure, he suggests, was a constant spur to the increasing intensification of one species and exploitation of minor resources, while topography played a major role in the spatial distribution of sites from the Mousterian through the Magdalenian. The major difference from Cantabrian patterns is that Bahn finds more site specialization than is evident in Cantabria.

In summary, the physical environmental models discussed here look to changes in the external environment as causes for apparent culture change. Factors such as climatic change, topography, and availability of resources are examined. Population pressure is cited by all four authors discussed here as an underlying cause of culture change. However, Bailey also makes a case for the difficulty of conclusively excluding environmental change and cites problems with identifying population stress in the archaeological record, let alone determining whether it is cause or effect. The notion of increasing complexity within the course of the Upper Paleolithic is based on archaeological evidence of intensification in the exploitation of staple economic species, together with greater diversification of resources that are difficult to procure or process, greater site size and density, and increases in the number and types of implements and localities in use. Whether social correlates such as specialization of labor, well-defined territories, status differentiation, and increased reliance on exchange systems and more complex social networks are also to be found remains largely untested. These issues are discussed in the following section.

Social Environmental Models

An alternative, or complementary, paradigm for the explanation of patterning and variability in the Upper Paleolithic is that of an increasingly complex social environment. Bailey (1983b:187) sees three principal sources of "inspiration" for emphasis on the social dimensions of hunter-gatherer behavior:

1. simulation studies of mating networks and their spatial and social implications (Wobst 1974, 1976)
2. Marxist-inspired theories of social evolution, with emphasis on the social relations of production. This paradigm provides a point of contact between theory and archaeological studies of prehistoric subsistence (Bender 1978, 1981; Ingold 1980, 1987)
3. growing interest in the potential for interpreting symbolic com-

munication embodied in the more obviously stylistic features of paleolithic material culture (portable and parietal art, supposed items of adornment, burial associations) and their implications for changes in social organization (Wobst 1977, Harrold 1980, Conkey 1978, 1980, 1985; Gamble 1982; Jochim 1983; Dickson 1990).

Whatever the philosophical background, a unifying concept in social organizational models is the "regional social unit": the group of people who consistently would have had social contact, be it marriage exchange, trade alliance, shared religious beliefs and practices, and so forth. In two seminal papers, Wobst (1974, 1976) proposed the "mating network" as the fundamental unit of regional analysis. He emphasized the tendency of peripheral groups to move toward the center of the group's territory, at the cost of increased investment in social rituals, to help reinforce long-distance exchanges, symbolize group affiliation, and create role differentiation and the emergence of authority figures who can mediate disputes. A number of "social environmentalists" have elaborated on Wobst's ideas in examining the role of social organization in human adaptation.

Marcia Madden

Madden emphasizes that ancient foraging sociocultural systems, no less than recent ones, were not isolated, self-contained, and discrete social entities; rather, they were networks "of rather loosely defined groups and communities linked by a variety of social relationships, often extending over vast regions and even entire continents (1983: 191)." Allowing for hyperbole, she suggests that these networks were created and maintained through social rather than purely economic linkages; that is, through kinship ties, marriage, and other such relations.

She develops two key concepts: the "social interaction field" and the "social network system." The social interaction field refers to any form of exchange, regardless of the medium of exchange and the nature of the risks and obligations involved. Hunter-gatherers typically are part of a number of differently organized social interaction fields: trading fields exchanging goods, marriage fields exchanging partners, political fields exchanging information or alliance support, and so on. The sum total of these overlapping sets of social interaction Madden calls the social network system, and emphasizes that such systems are not to be confused with political entities like tribes or bands, with which they may or may not overlap. This emphasis makes the social network system a particularly appropriate concept for archaeology, in that the archaeological record may contain evidence of variations in the degree of interaction in the past, but is seldom sufficiently complete to allow the type of social formations involved in that interaction to be specified with confidence.

Madden then proposes three general types of models of social network system among hunters and gatherers, assuming that a minimum number of individuals is necessary to ensure the viability of a population through time, that groups must maintain a network of exchange relationships to allow for this minimal social interaction, and that participants in these exchange relations will be rational; that is, they will seek to minimize costs and risks. The three models predict different configurations of network relationships based on the interaction of population density, resource competition, and distance between local groups. They result from the calculation of the costs and risks of maintaining social interactions over very long distance as against those of imposing social boundaries between groups. The models are:

Type 1: undifferentiated network system

Type 2: differentiated network system due to distance

Type 3: differentiated network system due to imposed social boundaries.

The Type 1 model, the undifferentiated network system, is predicted for cases of low population density. Within such systems, the boundaries circumscribing social interaction fields, to the extent that they exist at all, would be "vague and fluctuating" and the degree of intergroup interaction would be most intense between immediate neighbors. The patchy nature of interaction within such systems would support "an uneven (but nonetheless) continuous flow of interactions across the entire system." (Madden 1983:193)

The Type 2 model, the differentiated network system due to distance, assumes that distance between groups is so large that exchange between them is infrequent and "expensive" to maintain. This network has great potential for division into two or more discrete systems as local groups turn inward or weak links with distant groups cease to be maintained. The dissolution of a social interaction network depends on whether or not groups within it calculate that the costs of maintaining it outweigh the costs of ceasing to participate. Of course, only groups that are sufficiently large to ensure their own demographic viability can willingly sever their connections with the larger network.

The Type 3 model, the differentiated network system due to imposed social boundaries, is characteristic of regions in which the distance between groups decreases so much that exploitation territories overlap and competition for resources ensues, rendering maintenance of an undifferentiated network system undesirable, even impossible. Under these conditions, the model predicts that division(s) within the social network system will be developed and imposed by the groups in order to preserve their exclusive right to exploitation of territory and/ or resources. Under these conditions, more formalized and structured linkages would result, and there may be increased frequency of exchange relationships between bounded groups.

It is a basic assumption of our discipline that the extent and intensity of interaction between groups of people tends to be reflected in the degree of similarity between their styles and symbols. Madden uses this assumption in testing her model. She predicts that minimal social bounding encountered in social network systems of Type 1 should produce the least stylistic differentiation, those of Type 3 the most differentiation *between* network systems and the most stylistic similarity *within* a system. Development of increasing interaction (that is, movement from the conditions of Type 1 through 2 to 3) should be reflected archaeologically in a pattern of increasing stylistic and symbolic homogeneity within a network. Madden tests the predictive value of her models using stylistic variation in lithic artifacts from the Norwegian Mesolithic. Unfortunately, insufficient stylistic variation in this period makes conclusions difficult—probably a general defect for all prehistoric hunter-gatherers. Nonetheless, her model seems to have great potential for paleolithic studies when combined with other approaches. For example, when her approach is used in conjunction with Sackett's (1977) notion of "isochrestic style," far stronger conclusions about her Mesolithic data could possibly be made. Her Type 2 model, in particular, nicely predicts the increased social boundaries coincident with increasing population density in Norway during this period. Her Type 1 model may also provide insight into the apparent lack of "stylistic" variability in the Mousterian which has heretofore proved so puzzling. If one assumes a population in Europe during the Middle Paleolithic so sparse that it has no modern counterpart in a comparable environment, the vast regions with apparently no stylistic variability may be more understandable.

The study of style in Upper Paleolithic art has been advanced in the last decade by research emphasizing how it might have aided hunting and gathering populations in adapting to their environment. Among researchers working on understanding the symbolic communication possibly encoded in paleolithic art are Sieveking (1976), Gamble (1982), Jochim (1983), Conkey (1980, 1985, 1987), and Mithen (1988, 1989).

Anne Sieveking

Sieveking (1976) develops a subsistence-settlement model for analyzing Magdalenian IV art in an attempt to discern the territorial and social divisions that might have emerged in southwestern France as a consequence of seasonally shifting settlement. Based on the similarity of Magdalenian IV mobiliary art between the Vezère region and the French central Pyrenees, Sieveking hypothesizes either that (1) these two regions represent the north and south migratory limits of identical groups of people, or (2) the groups from each region were in periodic close contact. She rejects the first explanation on the basis that the two regions are close environmental analogues of one another, and suggests that seasonally migratory herd animals like reindeer would probably have summered in the Dordogne and the Central Pyrenees, but would have left both regions with the onset of winter.

Sieveking suggests that during the Magdalenian IV, more-or-less independent and self-contained subsistence and settlement systems must have developed in the western Pyrenees and the Adour Valley on the one hand, and the central Pyrenees-Garonne Valley-Vezère region, on the other. Because of their relative isolation from one another, the independent systems eventually would have developed discernibly different regional variants of Magdalenian artistic traditions. In fact, at least during phase IV, the Magdalenian mobiliary art remains remarkably homogeneous. Instead of artistic parochialism, she finds styles and motifs in mobiliary art shared widely throughout southwestern France. Sieveking concludes from this:

that the geographical area of interrelated people is much larger than one might have expected and that there must have been a lot of cross traffic as well as riverine communication in southwest France during the later stages of the Magdalenian (Sieveking 1976:593).

Sieveking assumes that the Magdalenian subsistence-settlement system in southwestern Europe was based on intensive reindeer hunting as the primary subsistence activity. Since the location and availability of this resource varies over the year, she thinks that Magdalenian subsistence poses and settlement pattern changed systematically in response to this variation, that changes were closely scheduled against the seasons, and that this pattern was followed across large distances. As a consequence, contacts between independent hunting bands occurred over a vast area in southwestern Europe. The perceived relative homogeneity of the art of the final phases of the Upper Paleolithic is taken to be a result of wide-ranging seasonal contact between reindeer-hunting bands.

Clive Gamble

Like Sieveking, Gamble (1982) regards reindeer hunting as a primary subsistence activity in the southwestern European Upper Paleolithic. However, he views it as a precarious form of subsistence specialization in which small, dispersed groups are forced to cope with changing and uncertain patterns of reindeer migrations, seasonal availability, and population density. Further, Gamble does not view parietal and mobiliary art of the Upper Paleolithic as a passive reflector of the extent or intensity of socioeconomic relations. Instead, he suggests that the art of the period was a key mechanism of communication among hunting peoples. By facilitating and broadening social interaction, the artistic traditions of the period were what made the reindeer hunting adaptation possible in Europe in the first place. He suggests that the stimulus for the appearance of art during the Upper Paleolithic was certain "changes in the amount and kind of information needed by paleolithic societies (Gamble 1986:92)." By "information" he does not mean the conscious metaphysics or aesthetics of the Upper Paleolithic artistic tradition, but information of a distinctly practical sort: viz., knowledge of the movement of animal herds or the availability of food over a wide area. Gamble suggests that the art made transmission of such information possible because of a shared system of understanding and ideology, coupled with other social institutions. Connections among scattered groups of reindeer hunters could also have been maintained through widely ramifying ties of kinship, marriage partner exchange, and long distance trade. In addition to providing a mode of information sharing, connections of this kind might have served as a kind of insurance, enabling groups who were temporarily unsuccessful in the food quest to obtain aid or access to the territory of more fortunate groups within the system.

Gamble (1982) illustrates his thesis with the widely distributed Venus figurines. These artifacts have been recovered from the Pyrenees to European Russia, and are attributed to a portion of the Upper Paleolithic that Gamble asserts (probably erroneously) can be narrowed to between 25,000 and 23,000 B.P. Although the figurines can be sorted into at least three stylistic classes, they nonetheless are remarkably similar in style. In Gamble's view, artistic homogeneity of this kind over such a vast area indicates that these figurines are the material remains of a system of shared understanding and intercommunication that was equally widespread. In a related manner, Conkey (1978, 1980) interprets the decorative motifs she isolates on Spanish Magdalenian carved bone implements as a kind of artistic "grammar" developed to facilitate intercommunication among Vasco-Cantabrian hunting groups.

Michael Jochim

Jochim (1983) approaches paleolithic art with a similar view. He too is struck by the general homogeneity of Magdalenian art, but notes that it was not uniform during all phases of the tradition. Cave art in particular varies through time in respect to stylistic uniformity from region to region, while portable art waxes and wanes in general popularity and the extent of its geographic distribution. Oblivious to the possibility of sampling error, Jochim (1983:216) hypothesizes that these artistic trends are ultimately related to changes in strategy and emphasis in the Magdalenian subsistence economy.

According to Jochim, reindeer hunting and salmon fishing have profoundly different implications for human population size, settlement technology, and social organization and interaction. Citing ethnographic sources, he suggests that the degree of dependence of hunter-gatherers upon reindeer appears to be inversely related to human population density. That is, the greater the importance of reindeer, the lower the human population density. Ethnographic evidence suggests that the converse is true of salmon exploitation; the magnitude of human population density and the degree of dependence on salmon are directly related. Jochim further states that salmon and reindeer share many similar characteristics: both are subject to long term cyclical fluctuation in population size, both can be taken either by individuals or groups, both produce storable foodstuffs, and both occur in restricted localities.

Salmon, however, use the same river for spawning year after year, and are therefore far more predictable than reindeer, which commonly shift their migration routes depending on local conditions. To Jochim, this means that groups which increase their reliance upon salmon fishing will, over time, tend to develop an increasingly sedentary settlement pattern during a part of their seasonal cycle, cluster around the most suitable fishing locations, and develop a territorial exclusiveness which isolates them from neighboring groups. In contrast, the essential lack of predictability of the reindeer means that groups which seek to intensify exploitation of that species will, over time, tend to maintain a mobile and flexible settlement pattern, develop mechanisms for assembling large task groups on a seasonal basis, develop regional means of sharing information about reindeer herd movements, and develop webs of social affiliation and marriage ties with surrounding groups.

Jochim suggests that socioeconomic systems centering on salmon exploitation become closed, exclusive, and characterized by relatively limited ties to surrounding systems. While we wonder whether any such groups actually existed, Jochim thinks that such societies would tend to resolve intragroup conflict by, for example, mediation at centralized ceremonial sites. The closed nature of such societies would be reflected in distinct and highly regionalized artistic traditions. In contrast, socioeconomic systems emphasizing reindeer hunting, which require mobility, wide-ranging communication, periodic aggregation, social flexibility, and interconnectivity are likely to develop open networks enabling discrete social units to interface with neighboring societies. The existence of such interacting networks should be reflected artistically in continuous, rather than discrete, distributions of motifs and art objects. Compared to the parochialism of the art of closed systems, the art of reindeer hunters should be broadly distributed and homogeneous over contiguous regions.

Jochim used this bipolar scheme to interpret Leroi-Gourhan's (1965, 1968) four-period developmental sequence of Upper Paleolithic art. Leroi-Gourhan's Style I Primitive period, dating to between ca. 32,000 to 25,000 years ago, is characterized chiefly by the appearance, explosive growth, and widespread distribution of mobile art objects such as Venus figurines. The homogeneity, ubiquity, and portability of Style I art suggest to Jochim that it is the material reflection of the open communication networks whose widely ramifying ties, he hypothesizes, will develop in hunting economies centered on the reindeer. Cave art does not appear on a significant scale until Leroi-Gourhan's Style II period between ca. 25,000 and 19,000 B.P. Jochim (1983:217) notes that the beginning of this period correlates with the onset (under the traditional scheme) of the final glacial maximum. He hypothesizes that settlement during this period was chiefly limited to southwestern Europe, and concludes that this area began to experience population pressure as peoples from surrounding regions retreated there in the face of climatic deterioration further north. He suggests that the cave art sites that appear at this time might represent loci for group ceremonial activity directed in part at developing intragroup solidarity and mediation.

In the Style III period from ca. 19,000 to 15,000 B.P., cave art becomes increasingly abundant and elaborate, and begins for the first time to exhibit a distinctly regional character in the Dordogne, the Lot Valley, the Pyrenees, and Cantabria. During the same period, he suggests, portable art becomes relatively rare (Leroi-Gourhan 1965, Jochim 1983:217, but cf. Conkey 1985, Straus 1987c). Jochim interprets these developments as reflective of changes in subsistence emphasis in the late Solutrean and early Magdalenian traditions. But he admits that this decline in portable art is puzzling:

it may be related to the general decrease in mobility and the declining need for maintaining widespread affiliation. This together with the regionalization of the cave art styles, might reflect the formation of more closed communication networks during the Solutrean (Jochim 1983:217).

The economic trends in the Style IV period from ca. 15,000 to 10,000 B.P. are more complex, according to Jochim (1983:218). The beginning of the period witnesses a great increase in the number of painted caves and a corresponding breakdown in regional stylistic diversity. This is followed somewhat later in the period by a decline in parietal art, a "tremendous proliferation of portable art," and the appearance of burials that become both more abundant and more homogeneous throughout Europe (Jochim 1983:219).

Jochim, like Sieveking, Gamble, and Conkey, emphasizes the social utility of Upper Paleolithic art and religion. Its emergence and characteristics are responses to the environmental conditions of the late Upper Pleistocene epoch and prevailing social conditions during the European Upper Paleolithic. It should prove possible to test Jochim's thesis against existing archaeological and paleoenvironmental data. However, in order to reject his thesis, it will be necessary to show either that there is no correlation between the sequence of climatic change in Europe and the alternations between uniformity and regional distinctiveness in the art of the period, or that his reconstruction of the subsistence, or trajectory of subsistence change, during the Upper Paleolithic is in error.

The demonstration of a temporal correlation between artistic change and climate change during the Upper Paleolithic is not an easy task. Jochim uses stylistic time periods for Upper Paleolithic art developed by Leroi-Gourhan (1965). However, these stylistic periods constitute a relative sequence based on a stylistic seriation of motifs, and the "softness" of the dates makes correlations between them and the chronometrically dated trajectory of paleoenvironmental change problematical. Jochim tacitly acknowledges this problem when, with no stated justification, he assigns new dates to Leroi-Gourhan's periods that depart from the original ranges, sometimes by as much as a millennium or more.

Mellars (1985) asserts that Jochim's reconstruction of the subsistence system of the later Upper Paleolithic is also in error. He disputes Jochim's claim that salmon harvesting was an important subsistence activity during the Upper Paleolithic by marshaling evidence indicating that salmon bones have not simply been overlooked in the excavation of sites of the period (see also Clark and Straus 1983, Straus and Clark 1986). A small number of salmon bones, along with the bones of the other fish species, have been reported from late Upper Paleolithic period sites, but Mellars notes that when they do occur, salmon represents a smaller percentage of the total fish bones than do species such as the smaller river trout and pike. In contrast, fish bones are an important part of the faunal assemblages from terminal Magdalenian and Azilian sites, a fact which suggests to Mellars that the dearth of salmon remains from earlier periods is not an artifact of poor preservation or recovery techniques, but evidence that salmon was not a primary part of the diet during the Magdalenian, and that fishing became an important element only in postglacial times.

Mellars (1985:279) also thinks that Jochim (and by implication, Gamble) has been misled by ethnographic accounts of historic reindeer-hunting peoples in Siberia and in the North American Arctic. In those regions reindeer migrate over vast distances and can use a number of alternative routes between their summer and winter grazing areas, and reindeer-hunting is indeed a precarious undertaking that scatters hunting groups and places a high premium on shared information. However, Mellars contends that these conditions did not pertain to southwestern Europe during the Late Pleistocene. The geography of that region would have necessitated only a short migration between the coastal wintering areas and the summer pastures of the Masif Central, Cantabria, and the Pyrenees. Further, these migratory poles are connected by a set of narrow, east-west trending river valleys. Since it is precisely within the lower foothill zones cut by these river valleys that the greatest concentration of Upper Paleolithic sites are found, Mellars concludes that peoples of this period had located in these places in order to be strategically placed for the interception of the annual migration of the reindeer herds. Such placement meant that the reindeer herds "were probably never very far removed from the main centers of Upper Paleolithic settlement over the full range of their annual cycle" (Mellars 1985:279). Finally, Mellars notes that even in seasons in which reindeer were relatively scarce, the high animal biomass of full glacial southwestern Europe probably meant that a host of alternative game species would be available (Guthrie 1989). (Editor's Note: this is certainly *not* true in France.)

The Sieveking, Gamble, and Jochim models all suffer from insufficiently supported basic assumptions concerning subsistence. As Freeman (1973) noted well before these models were posited:

Baseless speculation such as the one sometimes advanced that Magdalenian occupations throughout western Europe flourished on a predictable subsistence base of reindeer herds and salmon runs are to be deplored. Intuitively appealing as such a suggestion may be to those unfamiliar with the details of the regional sequences in question, it does not accord with the facts in many regions, and is probably not entirely true even for the Dordogne.

While Jochim developed his model to explain the flowering of art in southwestern France and Cantabria, reindeer are particularly rare in Cantabrian sites, although this area is notably rich in both parietal and mobiliary art. There is no evidence of reliance on salmon.

Margaret Conkey

Conkey (1978, 1980, 1985) also interprets Upper Paleolithic art in the context of social organization, but attempts a closer focus. She (1980) looks at relative variability in design elements on engraved bone and antler as a way of testing the hypothesized use of Altamira (Santander) as a major aggregation site. While difficulties with the resolution of the data from the thick and mixed levels from Altamira prevent strong conclusions, her methodology holds great promise. Her discussion of variability in ethnographic aggregation/dispersion patterns provides a timely warning to those who write too glibly of such patterning. Further methodological considerations are brought up in her reexamination of the role paleolithic art played in ritual communication and social elaboration (Conkey 1985).

Conkey is more exact in methodology and more careful about assumptions than preceding students of paleolithic art. She notes that, while the emergence of complex adaptations among hunter-gatherers by the close of the Pleistocene is widely assumed, few of the indications of this complexity are as yet substantiated in any way (1985:300) (something that might be said of the entire Price and Brown-edited volume). She suggests that, before we can formulate useful models, we must define the full range of temporal and regional diversity of paleolithic visual imagery. Previous attempts at general explanations have masked the full range of variability. Following an explicit discussion of model and methodology, Conkey (1985) examines classes of imagery involving formalized systems of production, particularly engraved bone and antler, with some discussion of human figurines and "body ornaments." She identifies recognizable sets of motifs or design elements that characterize regional assemblages of engraved bone and antler, and notes marked regional variability in densities and distribution of engraved bone in Magdalenian assemblages from Cantabria, the Pyrenées, the Périgord, and southwestern Germany. At this point, we have only tantalizing glimpses of what the data may offer. For example, Conkey notes that 80 percent of engraved pieces in the Périgord come from only four late sites. What implications that might have for models of aggregation, social boundaries, or cultural hierarchies remain to be examined when more detailed studies of systems of imagery are available.

In her 1987 review of research in the field, Conkey again calls for studies detailing the diversity of the materials, contexts, and styles of paleolithic visual imagery. She substitutes the term "visual imagery" for "paleolithic art," as the latter assumes both an aesthetic interpretation and that all the various images are somehow functionally the same. Her stress on the need for research emphasizing both diversity and context are more than timely. She tends to apologize: "Although this appears to be an empirical and descriptive goal (if interpreted narrowly), it is so only in part" (1987:417). There is no need to be apologetic about the call for better definition of data, as some empiricists might argue that useful models can only be built and tested on a solid data base. Better knowledge of the temporal and regional diversity in media and context, as well as regional lithic, faunal, and environmental sequences, will allow the formulation of testable models and hypotheses "about organizational dynamics and change within the Upper Paleolithic that may contribute to understanding of where, when, and what kinds of complexity or elaboration may have occurred" (Conkey 1985:303), rather than the painting of an "intuitively appealing" picture of either subsistence or social organization.

In summary, like the external environmental models, contemporary views of Upper Paleolithic social organization depart from the basic model. Rather than viewing Upper Paleolithic hunters and gatherers in southwestern Europe as members of the tiny, isolated "band" formations of the basic model, these scholars envision them as integrated into vast regional networks, emphasizing marriage ties, information exchange, and social and religious interaction. In such networks, the existence of full time specialists beyond those social categories defined by sex and age appears a real possibility. By facilitating the sharing of both information and risk, these regional networks are seen as contributing directly to the adaptive success of the peoples of southwestern Europe (see also Soffer 1985 for eastern Europe).

In these models, it is assumed that human sociocultural systems in southwestern Europe became more complex during the Upper Paleolithic. However, reaching consensus on the nature of this complexity or the evidence needed to demonstrate it will prove more difficult. General models can only be tested by the specific definition of conditions and consequences of intensification and complexity, combined with detailed studies of patterned variability in lithic, faunal, environmental, and visual imagery assemblages, treated together on a regional basis. A call for a return to understanding the record in detail is not to be dismissed as lowly empiricism. As our models become more sophisticated and more detailed, more is demanded of the data. We turn to a brief consideration of these questions in the final section of this chapter.

Middle Range Theory

The first sections of this chapter were concerned with a discussion of general models of hunter-gatherer adaptation and their application to the specific circumstances of the southwestern European Upper Paleolithic. We now take a look at what Lewis Binford has called "middle range theory" (1977a:6): the development of operational concepts by which the researcher moves from the material data of the archaeological record to an interpretation of the pattern of past human behavior that created it.

The construction of both general models of hunting and gathering behavior and of middle range considerations of how such behaviors will be materially represented has generally been carried on in an eclectic fashion using concepts drawn from ethnology, ethology, demography, ecology, and other disciplines. While these concepts have sometimes proven to be of interpretive value, there are inherent difficulties in attempting to interpret the prehistorians' data by applying models devised by other sciences with other data sets. Among these are the difficulties with ethnographic analogy and uniformitarianism alluded to above. As Binford notes:

theories and explanations for observed phenomena developed in other fields can certainly be used as a basis for inference in archaeology. Yet we frequently find ourselves in a situation where the inferences so obtained are perhaps neither useful nor germane to the solution of our problems as archaeologists. . . . What I am suggesting . . . is that archaeologists cannot wait for other fields to develop the necessary principles which will permit them to make reliable inferences about the past (1983b:17).

Borrowed concepts are not tailored to fit our data, and, all too often when the fit is bad, it is assumed that the data must be faulty, because the concept has been tested in its own context. This low opinion of our data is not without cause; archaeological data are not what many fields would consider adequate. But the shortcomings of the material record have led to appeals for "a special use of theoretical procedures" (Bailey 1983a:2), in which theoretical models are used not so much to explain patterns of past behavior as to aid in recreating those patterns by "filling in gaps" with what "should be" there. By adopting this procedure, archaeologists use the model to tell them what patterns "should" appear, rather than explaining and interpreting directly observed or independently verifiable patterns visible in the record. This "filling in" is untestable, circular in its reasoning, and probably misleading. When we predict what "should" be under water or in the unsurveyed uplands, or what has presumably been disturbed or lost, we are in danger of assuming the validity of our conclusions before we have data to test them. For the Upper Paleolithic, assumptions of seasonal migration, cultural complexity, or demographic pressure are in some danger of being accepted as conclusions without sufficiently rigorous testing.

The strength of archaeological data lies in the long span of time they represent and in the record of human biocultural evolutionary change they contain. These features make archaeological data unique. At some time in the past, hominids shifted from a predominantly biological to predominantly cultural mode of adaptation, and the archaeological record is one of the few sources of information about that change (Wolpoff 1980). Consequently, knowledge of the human evolutionary career is archaeology's preeminent contribution to human understanding. We must of course continue to cooperate with comparative ethnology and other fields of research to formulate general principles, but also remain aware that our data are unique, and that our own contribution to general as well as to middle range theory is mandated.

Finally, we must expect that the archaeological record contains patterns of material remains that cannot be interpreted in terms of behavior known from the ethnographic or historical record. But how can we possibly reconstruct prehistoric social and cultural formations that have no parallels in the present? We suggest: by continuing to develop methods of examining patterning and variability—among artifacts, among assemblages, among site types, faunal remains, topographic situations. We have barely begun to identify regional variability in the patterning of the material record through time and across space. Until that is done, testing of our theories and assumptions is only partial and preliminary. We cannot "do science" without theories and sets of testable hypotheses, but a continual interplay is involved. Sufficient hard data from which to build suitable hypotheses are also needed. As prehistorians we should feel committed neither to producing what Wobst termed "ethnography with a shovel," nor to bringing the human past into conformity with the theoretical predictions of demography, ethology, ecology, or any other field. Rather, paleolithic archaeologists must continue to concentrate on identifying and understanding patterned variability in prehistory on its own terms. Not only will this provide an immediate benefit to the discipline, but it will ultimately contribute to the general theoretical understanding of the development of human behavior. The proliferation of new models of Upper Paleolithic subsistence and settlement in southwestern Europe is an indication of the overall vitality of contemporary research in this historically important period and area. While applauding this vitality, we would like to call attention to a few areas we think are neglected by current researchers.

We are concerned with the lack of a theoretical framework in which faunal, lithic, environmental, and other data can be analyzed in combination as parts of an integrated system. While progress in middle range theory building is being made for many of these types of data, there is a tendency for individual studies to concentrate on one or perhaps two of them, and for other lines of evidence to be slighted or ignored. Data sets frequently are not well integrated in regional studies, or even in many site reports. In particular, interpretation of lithic data in explicating past behavior has been noticeably less advanced than that of environmental or faunal studies, in part because we have had no other disciplines to interact with and borrow from in this sphere, in part because the causes of artifact variability are not understood, and in part because the middle range theory that would allow the transformation of artifact variability into patterns of behavior remains relatively rudimentary. However, the number of chapters in this book specifically addressing assemblage and typological variability suggests a renewed interest in lithics, happily directed precisely to many of the problems and questions discussed above.

Suggestions for Lithic Analysis

Bailey (1983c:8) has noted that "stone artifact analysis has tended to gain a certain notoriety in the wider archaeological community as a rather sterile end in itself, rather than a means to a further end." However, lithics are the most abundant remains, sometimes the *only* remains, of human activity at a site. Paleolithic stone tool analysis has also suffered from the normative paradigm of separate "cultures," traditionally held by some European scholars to account for most observed variability. While we are largely past the point of purely descriptive lithic analyses using standard type lists and culture designations, simply substituting function for culture to account for variability is equally perilous.

Topics in lithic studies that hold promise for European paleolithic research include production methods, use and recycling, assemblage intra- and intersite variability, and style. Most such studies will depend on the availability of good interpretive models and typologies. We cannot continue to use the established retouched tool typologies to try to correlate "assemblages" with environment, topography, site type, or whatever. These typologies were useful in their time for establishing a culture/historic framework but we no longer use them for that: from an American perspective, dating the Upper Paleolithic is accomplished by absolute dating methods and stratigraphic studies. Chronology is still a major problem for the Middle Paleolithic, but the established typologies (*la méthode Bordes*) were of little use in that regard anyway.

Now that most archaeological research has shifted to other questions, new typologies must be developed to answer those questions. As has often been noted, the extant typologies are mixtures of morphological, functional, stylistic, and what might be called "lateral recycling" attributes (Dibble 1987a–c). Since it cannot partition sources of variation, such a mixture renders any analysis based on it impossible to interpret. Specific attributes must be chosen to answer specific questions.

In addition, the normative "culture" analytic terms should only be used as a *lingua franca* and even then with great caution. There is more potential for confusion than understanding when processual archaeologists interact with archaeologists who to a greater or lesser degree subscribe to the normative cultural paradigm. We suggest that these terms be avoided where possible in explanatory discussions—but the fact is we have rejected the culture explanation, and have not provided another. There may well be some reality to such terms as "Aurignacian III" or "Magdalenian IV" but to determine what the nature of that reality might be, we will need to reexamine whole assemblages from the point of view of the new explanatory paradigms.

Strictly "technical" lithic studies are also needed to provide solid data for inference on behavior. Debitage analyses can illuminate tool production methods, and may identify specific activity areas (Fish 1979). Studies of formal tool classes will aid in the interpretation of typological variability, a concern central to prehistoric research. In our judgment, the lithic analysis of three contemporary scholars, Dibble (1987a–c), Marks (1983a), and Sackett (1977, 1982, 1985, 1986) offer particular promise in this regard.

Dibble's (1987) examination of Middle Paleolithic scrapers has elucidated the role re-use and re-modification play in the scraper "types," and shows that studies of reduction processes will be of great use in clarifying differences and similarities among different assemblages. The major implication, of course, is that the classic Bordesian scraper "types" probably represent nothing more than successive general stages in re-use and resharpening of different kinds of blanks. As he notes, "Whether these differences are due to cultural or other factors such as differences in raw material, or technology that led to the production of differently shaped flake blanks, is a question that should be addressed" (Dibble 1987a:116). Until we can make better judgments about the causes underlying lithic variability, stone tools will remain relatively useless in evaluating the kinds of models discussed here. If we can separately identify functional and stylistic variability, lithics could play as integral a part in the identification and definition of sociocultural regions in the paleolithic as visual imagery promises to do.

Marks (1983a) has re-examined the Middle to Upper Paleolithic transition in the Levant by studying reduction sequences and core technologies using almost 200 reconstructed cores from the open site of Boker Tachtit, in the central Negev desert of Israel. From this analysis he concluded that two separate paths led from the Mousterian to the Upper Paleolithic, passing through an early Upper Paleolithic stage characterized by the use of a hard hammer and single platform core reduction strategy. One path led to the blade-rich Ahmarian; the other to the flake-dominated Levantine Aurignacian. Such detailed analyses of reduction sequences will help clarify the profusion of assemblages types and "cultures" in the Levant, a necessary prerequisite to the formulation of processual models. Strict definition of regional variability among artifact assemblages, and the examination of the causes underlying such variability, are basic to the testing of models of hunter-gatherer systematics in the paleolithic.

Another perennial problem in late Pleistocene lithic studies is the question of whether the variability among stone tool assemblages is partly attributable to "stylistic" differences. While not providing an answer, Sackett's notion of "isochrestic" style (Sackett 1977, 1982, 1985, 1986) appears to be one of the more promising approaches. As Sackett frames it:

The approach is based on the consideration that style is fundamentally a question not of whether formal variation happens to be decorative or functional, but rather of the choices made by the artisan (1985:278).

Thus, Sackett rejects a "style vs. function" dichotomy: style exists wherever artisans make specific and consistent choices which, insofar as they are learned, become diagnostic of the group to which the artisans belong. "Alternative models of profiling a scraper bevel or of spalling a burin edge can be equally as stylistic as alternative design elements on the body of a pot" (1985:278). For those archaeologists for whom the term style is a gloss for words like "decorative" or "nonfunctional," Sackett's definition of style appears to be an unacceptable enlargement of the word's meaning (e.g., Clark 1989c, Binford 1989b). However, given the absence of design element equivalents on most Pleistocene stone tools, the "isochrestic" notion of style is a concept with which many of us can feel comfortable, although allowance must be made for constraints on the toolmaker imposed by the nature of the raw material and level of technology. As an example of new approaches on a regional scale, we briefly examine how Sackett's notion of isochrestic style could be usefully applied in testing Madden's models of social networks systems.

Madden (1983), using Norwegian Mesolithic data to attempt to test her models of social networks, concluded that such a test was not practical because of inadequate data. She notes:

> With respect to the variation that is known to exist [between southeastern and southwestern Norway], it appears that the greatest variability occurs in technological and functional attributes rather than stylistic ones. Thus variation exists in the frequencies of specific tool types, particularly axes and burins, or in certain technological features such as use of raw materials and specific manufacturing techniques (1983:199).

She also reports similar geographical differences in production of microliths and "microburins," and in the manufacturing (flake vs. core) and finishing techniques of axes. While functional variation cannot be decisively ruled out, isochrestic style could very well be represented in the choice of manufacturing and finishing technique, and possibly raw material choice as well. If the isochrestic view of style is applied to the same data, Madden's conclusions would appear to be considerably strengthened.

A final method we will discuss is that of use-wear analysis. While initially thought to be promising, such studies have often encountered technical difficulties that severely limit either interpretation or "generalizability" of results. Straus et al. (1988) did a use-wear analysis on 43 pieces from a Magdalenian assemblage at the Abri Dufaure in the French Pyrenees. They report that hide and bone/antler processing took place, but there is no evidence of wood or plant working. Since a sample was selected from only the less-patinated pieces that retained clear use-wear, attempts to infer what activities did or did not take place appear to be limited by sample selectivity. Of perhaps more interest is the very detailed way in which lithic sources were identified: all were located within a two-hour walk of the site. Debitage analysis indicates that this local flint was brought in with little or no prior modification. Faunal studies show that Dufaure was occupied mainly during the winter and spring. Combining this site-specific research with Bahn's (1984) regional study of the Upper Paleolithic of the Pyrenees, a valuable picture of the occupations at Dufaure should emerge, including its position in the proposed site hierarchy, distances traveled for resources, subsistence modes, and position in an annual migration cycle. All of this information would have important consequences for the models of paleolithic society discussed in the third part of this chapter. We will include a few suggestions here, but a detailed research design directed toward an evaluation of a regional subsistence/settlement model would include many more lines of evidence.

Assumptions about seasonal migration, site hierarchy, and group aggregations could be independently examined using lithic and visual imagery assemblage variability. For example, detailed stylistic analyses of both lithic and engraved bone/antler assemblages on a regional basis could be employed to evaluate the idea of a hierarchical system of sites, and the relative position of individual sites in that hierarchy. Major sites where groups aggregated would be expected to have a greater diversity of lithic and visual imagery styles, to be larger, and to contain extralocal objects (both lithic raw materials and "exotic" items) brought from longer distances. Short-term logistical camps would be expected to be smaller, to contain a narrower range of stylistic choices in tools and imagery, and to demonstrate a more restricted range in raw material procurement and possibly food debris. An intermediate range of sites between these two "types" might be identified on the basis of relative site size, stylistic and functional diversity, and topographical location. The relative importance of manufacturing vs. maintenance activities at various sites could be approached by the amount and kind of debitage.

Our closing point is simply that the proliferation of new perspectives demands more detailed description and analysis of all classes of data, within a regional frame of reference, if the models are to be reliably tested. Archaeologists must make use of all available lines of regional evidence to test adequately the credibility of the new paradigms of social complexity and settlement organization in the European Upper Paleolithic.

Note

1. For an extended discussion of the "basic model" and its limitations, see Dickson (1990:159–196).

Chapter 3
Paradigm Found? A Research Agenda for Study of the Upper and Post-Paleolithic in Southwest Europe

Lawrence Guy Straus

By Way of Introduction: A Personal Archaeological History

My beliefs about and practical approach to prehistoric archaeology are the products of my personal and educational backgrounds and of a long, varied history of archaeological fieldwork begun at an early age. My maternal great grandfather, Louis Magnant, a schoolteacher in the Charente (southwest France), was an early prehistorian who discovered the Lower and Middle Paleolithic site of Balzac. His son (my grandfather), Professor Guy Magnant of Bordeaux, was a very active amateur prehistorian in the years before, during, and immediately after World War I. He amassed a sizeable collection through surface survey and quarry observation (notably in Charente, Indre-et-Loire, and in the war zones of northern France) and through excavations at such notable Mousterian and Upper Paleolithic sites as Le Petit Puymoyen and Le Placard in Charente (Straus 1985a). Although he died long before my birth, I was familiar with his collections (left in his office in Bordeaux virtually untouched since his death) from my early childhood and was brought up on stories of his investigations and friendships with such greats of early French prehistory as Victor Commont, Denis Peyrony and Henri Breuil. (In fact, it turned out that my mother was a classmate of François Bordes at the University of Bordeaux before different natural science interests led them to pursue their respective doctorates at the Sorbonne.) Thus the paleolithic prehistory of southwest Europe can be said to run in my veins.

But a childhood spent in an historic New England town (Portsmouth, New Hampshire) was the direct source of my deep interest in the past as an avid reader of history books. I grew up surrounded by the decaying vestiges of a once glorious colonial past, which included an early period bloodstained with Indian wars. History, specifically the debates concerning New Hampshire's decisive role in ratifying the U.S. Constitution, was the subject of my first publications (Straus 1968) and European-Indian relations were also of interest to me in my early years (Straus n.d.a). By age fourteen I was conducting my own archaeological investigations at the newly established Strawberry Banke Historic Restoration Project, of which I was a charter member. Entrance into the Phillips Exeter Academy in 1963 brought me into contact with Dr. Eugene Finch, adviser to the Archaeology Club and past President (and influential member) of the New Hampshire Archaeological Society. Dr. Finch (an English teacher, historian, and naturalist) and the weekend "digs" of these two groups instilled in me an appreciation of practical field methods and of the ephemeral nature of the material record left behind by aboriginal hunter-gatherers. In contrast, a summer (1966) of excavating a Chalcolithic ossuary and a Roman pottery factory, both in France, taught me something of the problems of uncovering and documenting high-density, structural sites. Work the following summer with a University of Colorado crew at Mesa Verde (where Ezra Zubrow was one of Dave Breternitz's foremen), provided a change of venue, and an appreciation of the broad similarities in terms of archaeological remains and problems with early food-production systems in southern Europe.

In 1967 I entered the College of the University of Chicago because of the reputation of its Anthropology Department. At the recommendation of then graduate students John Fritz and Fred Plog, I met the late Paul S. Martin at the Field Museum and was admitted as an N.S.F. Undergraduate Research Participation Grantee to his well-known Vernon, Arizona, field school. Two books were required reading before joining the expedition in Gallup, New Mexico: *New Perspectives in Archaeology*, edited by Lewis and Sally Binford, and *The Structure of Scientific Revolutions* by Thomas Kuhn (who was an invited visiting lecturer at Vernon that memorable summer of 1968). Paris, Prague—and Vernon! Paul Martin's staff included Zubrow, Fred and Steve Plog (the latter in his pre-archaeological days), Mark Leone, and Craig Morris. Having experienced somewhat more traditional Southwestern archaeology at Mesa Verde, I was unimpressed with the excavation we did on the Carter Ranch, but I learned many a valuable lesson on Chris White's "systematic, stratified, unaligned sample" survey of a large part of that famous piece of east-central Arizona real estate (compass-skewing, iron-rich volcanics, no maps, bad air photos, and all!). Paul

Martin was a unique source of traditional knowledge on Southwest ruins (many of which he had dug himself) and on ceramic typology (much of which he had personally defined in his decades of research in the region); his "conversion" to the "New Archaeology" made quite an impression on me (even if his *mea culpa* published several years later in *American Antiquity* [Martin 1971] struck me as a bit sad).

We URP grantees not only had to dig, survey, do artifact processing, and attend lectures, but also carry out original research projects under the guidance of the staff. I chose to try to demonstrate the existence of nascent social stratifcation among the prehistoric pueblos through an analysis of burials (Straus n.d.b). The possibility of revealing aspects of the social organization of extinct human groups à la *New Perspectives* (and in the shadow of the Carter Ranch and Broken-K sites themselves!) was heady stuff for a college freshman—as was our odyssey to the Pecos Conference in El Paso. Revolution (of all sorts) was in the air. Even so, I was troubled by what I saw as attempts to "find" proof of "deduced" hypotheses in the archaeological data at all costs. And I wondered about the general validity of laws of human behavior—sometimes no more than disguised common sense.

In my sophomore year at Chicago, I took an intensive individual reading course on French paleolithic archaeology with F. Clark Howell. That course, emphasizing the now-classic writings of François Bordes and Denise de Sonneville-Bordes, became my empirical underpinning for the work to come, beginning with a summer spent excavating with Bordes at Pech de l'Azé II. Digging with Bordes brought my grandfather's collections and Clark Howell's lessons to life, and I began to experience the electricity of the then-new Bordes-Binford debate over the significance of differences among the assemblages of Mousterian tools (tools like those in the drawers in Bordeaux and Chicago and in the dirt at Pech de l'Azé). A rented bicycle and public transportation permitted me to see many of the major paleolithic sites and museums of the Dordogne and of the Ariège. Among others, I was to meet Bordes's then-senior students, Jean-Philippe Rigaud and Henri Laville—now long-time friends and colleagues. And I was converted to a belief in the fundamental importance of stratified cave/rockshelter sites in order to study long-term change through time (whether from a normative or processual perspective) (see Straus 1979b, 1990a).

Back in Chicago I was swept up both by the politico-social events of the times and, with the return of Leslie Freeman from the Cueva Morín excavations, by the New Archaeology. The interassemblage variability debate was the burning archaeological issue, transcending the Middle Paleolithic to herald an era of *explanation* in archaeology, replacing normative "pigeon-holing." I "hung out" with the likes of Chuck Redman, Geof Clark, Tom Cook, Greg Possehl, Jane Buikstra and Don Johanson—the young Turks of archaeology and human paleontology at Chicago, who held regular, (usually) serious discussion sessions in Hyde Park apartments. Besides classes with Freeman, I began taking the series of courses with Karl Butzer which would develop into the second edition of his *Environment and Archaeology* (subtitled "An Ecological Approach to Prehistory"). Those courses taught me how to evaluate critically and use constructively natural science data and to begin to grapple with the complexities of man-land relations in the past. But my anthropological education at Chicago included heavy doses of the classics of social anthropology (Durkheim, Radcliffe-Brown, Malinowski, Evans-Pritchard, Linton, Fred Eggan [in person] et al.) and lessons in the intricacies of researching "man-man" relations (such as dealing with Indian Census data with Brenda Beck). Under Freeman, I got "hands-on" typological experience by classifying the large Garrod collection from Tabūn at Chicago. In fact, I waded through the conflicting theories of archaeological typology (and the then-new approach known as "numerical taxonomy") in an Honors A.B. paper (which was also accepted as an A.M. thesis at Chicago). After reading Semenov's *Prehistoric Technology*, Phil Walker and I dabbled in lithic microwear studies, then (1971) beginning to be thought to be a very promising technique for determining artifact function (Straus and Walker 1978).

I further diversified my base of archaeological field experiences in 1970 and 1971 by working in Illinois: first as a field school supervisor for S.I.U. at a colonial fort excavation and at a Mississippian site near Kinkaid, and then as a supervisor for Stuart Struever at the Koster site. The latter experience exposed me to the benefits and difficulties of conducting large scale, multi/interdisciplinary archaeological research; but it did not convert me to lower Illinois Valley archaeology, since my heart was still in Europe and the vexing issues raised by the Bordeses, the Binfords, and Freeman.

As a C.I.C. Traveling Scholar, I interrupted the beginning of my graduate studies at Chicago with a very productive semester at the University of Michigan, which focused on cultural ecology (notably with Kent Flannery, Dick Ford, Henry Wright, Roy Rappoport, and Ed Wilmsen) and environmental reconstruction (particularly with Margaret Davis). Playing "devil's advocate" with Wilmsen, who was developing his ecological models of hunter-gatherer settlement-subsistence behavior, and engaging in spirited discussions with fellow students (the likes of Mike Jochim, Barbara Luedtke, Polly Wiessner, Greg Johnson, Bob Wenke, Bob Schacht, et al.) made that cold, damp semester a most memorable one, as did the opportunity of acting as interpreter for H.

and M.-A. deLumley as they displayed and explained the significance of the Arago skull in Ann Arbor. I also was fortunate to meet and develop a healthy respect for James Griffin. The Ann Arbor experience was also intellectually valuable, as I prepared to go to Spain at the invitation of Geof Clark—supposedly to bring Southwest methods of systematic survey to the paleolithic of the Old World.

As it turned out, the North Burgos Archaeological Project of 1972 quickly discovered that random sample survey techniques on the northern Meseta would not produce paleolithic sites, due to millennia of tilted upland surface erosion (something Butzer had warned me about back in Chicago). The lessons of reality forced us to target caves, rockshelters, and river terrace exposures. Although some evidence of paleolithic habitation was discovered, the resulting largely negative evidence said something significant about the nature of Upper Paleolithic settlement in northern Iberia: that the coastal zone was richer in resources and environmentally more habitable during the Last Glacial (as it is today) than even the entrenched valleys of the bleak Meseta (Clark and Straus 1979) (Figure 3.1).

The Solutrean Problem

Freeman had proposed to me that the Solutrean of Cantabrian Spain would make a good dissertation subject, basically because it had been only very partially (and normatively) studied up to that time (1972). So I briefly surveyed the state of the Solutrean collections in Spanish museums and then undertook to develop a dissertation proposal consonant with the goals of "Processual Archaeology." I was influenced particularly by the views of Sally Binford (1972) concerning the Upper Paleolithic. In addition I approached the problem of the Cantabrian Solutrean with a perspective influenced by the Cambridge school of economic prehistory (e.g., J. G. D. Clark 1971, Vita-Finzi and Higgs 1970). The Solutrean collections were not just ensembles of artistic objects to be ordered into theoretical phases, as many predecessors had done (e.g., Jordá 1955, Corchón 1971); they were part of the residues of the activities of prehistoric hunter-gatherers in different places on the Würm Upper Pleniglacial landscapes—activities involving subsistence procurement and processing, artifact manufacture and maintenance, feature construction, etc., by different kinds of work groups, at different seasons and in different habitats.

The Solutrean research was undertaken under the premise that interassemblage variability could be due to change through time, functional differences among sites, stylistic differences among human groups, and/or sampling factors. The objective of the work was to

FIGURE 3.1.   Map of southwest Europe showing research areas mentioned in the text: the northern Meseta, Cantabria, Gascony, Alentejo, Algarve, Estremadura, and Catalonia.

control for as many variables as possible and to try to explain Upper Paleolithic variability, using the Solutrean as a test case. Choosing the Solutrean made sense because, in the absence of radiometric controls, I felt that it represented a fairly narrow time slice, usually easily recognizable even (especially?) in old artifact collections because of the distinctive foliate and shouldered stone points. I made no a priori assumptions about the Solutrean as a "culture" or "ethnic unit" of any kind. The existence of Solutrean points merely served as an approximate temporal indicator. Sampling vagaries could in some cases be partially controlled for by the fact that old excavations often covered very large areas of the sites, thereby homogenizing the residues from different lateral activity areas and from different individual occupations (lenses) in the caves. Style would be approached by analysis of the points themselves, as objects representing a considerable investment of time, energy and—possibly—social identity. Function would be studied by comparing artifact assemblage composition with faunal assemblage composition and site location characteristics. My research in Spain was especially aided by the wise, experienced counsel of J. González Echegaray and J. Altuna, as well as by the enthusiastic collegiality of my peers M. González Morales, M. C. Marquez, V. Cabrera, F. Bernaldo de Quirós, J. A. Moure and J. Fernández-Tresguerres. The inter-paradigmatic discussions have been fruitful!

After analysis of all the whole collections and critical study of the original excavation reports and subsequent exegesis, I concluded that there was no convincing evidence (stratigraphic or otherwise) to subdivide the Solutrean into temporal phases (i.e., Lower, Middle, Upper), at least in Cantabrian Spain. Assemblage differences did not pattern temporally. There were, however, definite assemblage groupings (facies), measured particularly in terms of percentages of points, scrapers, burins, denticulates, backed blade(let)s, and truncations. Raw material variation in locally available rocks was thought to be partly responsible for some of this variability (e.g., scrapers and denticulates are predominantly made on quartzite, the main lithic raw material in the west [Asturias]).

I relocated and visited all the known Solutrean sites (some long lost). Their geographic distribution clearly seemed to consist of a series of alignments along the region's river valleys between the northern slopes of the Cantabrian Cordillera and the present coast, suggesting a pattern of (seasonal?) transhumant movement. There are striking differences between sites chosen for their shelter qualities (large, low, south- or west-facing, coastal zone location) and those chosen for specialized activities presumably including hunting (mountainous interior locations, strategic situations, panoramic views, not necessarily "comfortable" or easily accessible, often small). The extant faunal collections from sites in the rugged relief of the Basque Country were dominated by ibex and chamois, as well as small fur-bearing carnivores, whereas the sample of collections for Santander and Asturias was biased in favor of sites on the narrow coastal plains, and these were dominated by red deer, horses, and bovines. There were correlations between types of faunal assemblages and types of artifact assemblages which suggested some sort of direct or (more likely) indirect functional relationship (probably linked to the different topographic settings/habitats of the sites).

The search for genuine stylistic differences among site groups was frustrated by the fragmented nature and skewed distribution of the Solutrean points (i.e., most pieces were small fragments and were from a few sites—notably the large coastal zone locations such as Altamira, Cueto de la Mina, El Pendo, La Riera, etc.). These facts in themselves were interesting from a functional standpoint (e.g., the points were returning to sites broken after use and a disproportionately high number of them were being discarded at only a few sites). On a larger geographic scale than the river valley basins among which I had hoped to observe microstylistic differences, there are some clear patterns in point style (e.g., concave base points are almost all found in western Santander and eastern Asturias; there is a distinctive "Cantabrian" type of shouldered, dorsally invasively retouched point; a few "nonlocal" types do appear, such as "Montaut" points in northern Spain and concave base points in the Basque Country and Pyrenees, perhaps through social contacts) (Straus 1975a, 1983a with refs.).

In short, despite the difficulties of using old collections, I was able to demonstrate regular patterning and to suggest that much of it had to do with the functions of sites in an organized settlement-subsistence system operating under full glacial conditions in the diverse but structured habitats of north coastal Spain. Indeed, the most controversial aspect of my dissertation research (followed by additional analyses of "Lower Magdalenian" collections in 1975) was my suggestion that, without Solutrean points, it would be difficult or impossible to distinguish some "Solutrean" assemblages rich in burins and backed bladelets from "Gravettian" assemblages, or others rich in thick endscrapers, denticulates, and notches from "Cantabrian Lower Magdalenian" assemblages, since the tool "substrate" would vary from site to site because of *functional* (rather than temporal/ethnic) factors (e.g., Straus 1975b). It remained to collect modern-quality chronometric evidence and data on paleoenvironments, technology, seasonality, subsistence, and structural features for the Last Glacial Maximum time interval. (In fact, during my dissertation fieldwork I had participated in excavations at Tito Bustillo, Chufín and Rascaño—sites that would make significant contributions to the Solutrean and Magdalenian records from Santander and Asturias.) Up until this time (1975), I was mainly involved in lithic analysis.

When hired to teach at the University of New Mexico in 1975, however, I was asked by Lewis Binford to contribute to *For Theory Building in Archaeology* (1977). I chose to approach another key problem in processual archaeology: the explanation of change. The article, which appeared a couple of years later (Straus 1977), dealt with changing subsistence in paleolithic Cantabria and built on the earlier work of J. Altuna (1972) and L. G. Freeman (1973). I saw in the data a trend toward subsistence intensification based on both overall diversification (to include the collection of shellfish, fishing, and hunting of difficult or dangerous game) *and* on the specialized hunting of already familiar resources (red deer) beginning in the Solutrean time period and accelerating through the terminal Paleolithic and Mesolithic. This trend coincided with a rapid increase in site numbers, arguably reflective of a growing regional human population and, given the topographically confined nature of this coastal strip, population pressure. In short, this article, which dealt fundamentally with the question of change through time in a causal framework, argued for a "broad spectrum revolution" *before* the onset of Holocene conditions, and posed the question of what had perturbed the early Upper Paleolithic adaptive system in this region—environmental or demographic change.

The La Riera Paleoecological Project

La Riera cave in eastern Asturias was known to contain a deep, rich Upper Paleolithic-Mesolithic stratigraphy, with well preserved faunal remains. Indeed it had been a key site for the development of the Cantabrian regional sequence in the first decades of this century (Obermaier 1924, Vega del Sella 1930) and provided important Solutrean and Asturian collections for analysis by myself (Straus 1975a, 1983b) and by Geof Clark (1976a, 1983a; Clark and Richards 1978). Thus the opportunity to excavate the remaining archaeological deposits in La Riera, proposed to me by Clark, provided a superb chance to test some of the ideas I had developed in the Solutrean project and in the faunal article, as well as to contribute to the modern-quality data base for Cantabrian Stone Age prehistory. Here was a site where time could be controlled by radiocarbon; paleoenvironments monitored through sedimentology, palynology, and paleontology; site function, technology, and subsistence practices followed through time; seasonality ascertained through analysis of mammalian dentitions (and where, we thought, site structure could be revealed and analyzed). As with the Solutrean project, an opportunity could be pragmatically exploited as a theoretically significant and timely research effort.

The aims and results of the La Riera Project are well known (e.g., Clark and Straus 1977, 1983; Straus and Clark 1978, 1986; Straus et al. 1980, 1981), so only a few reflections on it will be made here. From my perspective on the nature of Upper Paleolithic interassemblage variability, the La Riera sequence not only clinched the argument, but it also brought us closer to an explanation of the observed differences and similarities. At La Riera supposed *Upper* Solutrean fossil directors occurred at the *bottom* of the long succession of Solutrean-point bearing levels and were radiocarbon dated to ≥ 20 kyr B.P. More recent levels lacked these shouldered and concave base types and some of the sixteen "Solutrean" levels yielded *no* Solutrean points. Indeed some deposits above and below the "Solutrean" group of levels could be

"Solutrean" as well, as their radiocarbon dates fall into the same time range (ca. 20.5–17 kyr B.P.). Aside from the variability in point representation, there are significant differences in the composition of the artifact assemblages (tools and unretouched debris) *among* the "Solutrean" levels and great similarities between some of those assemblages and overlying ones normatively labeled "Cantabrian Lower Magdalenian."

The systematic collection and analysis of lithic debris (cores plus débitage) and faunal remains at La Riera permitted us to understand at least part of the variability among the assemblages of "formal" tools by showing how the function of this cave as a locus of different human activities changed situationally through time. Some of these changes cross-cut while others coincided with normative culture-stratigraphic units. La Riera, the place, could alternatively be a specialized location for ibex hunting parties, a multipurpose residential base camp, or a bulk garbage dump. Indeed, as I argued in a polemical article in *Quaternaria* (Straus 1979a), the difference between two early Holocene "cultures" in northern Spain—the Azilian and the Asturian—may have to do with different suites of activities, which left behind different archaeological signatures. These activities may have been conducted by the same people at different places, La Riera being the only place where "poses" are securely represented in stratigraphic succession.

La Riera was also a crucial test case for the argument about subsistence change. Not only did its stratigraphic sequence contain clear evidence for the beginnings of marine resource exploitation at around 20 kyr B.P., for *over*-exploitation of shellfish by the end of the Pleistocene, and for intensive hunting of red deer, but it also provided a climatic record which did not usually show correlations with subsistence developments. Most aspects of the subsistence trend seem to have continued inexorably despite fluctuations in climatic conditions. The specialized hunting of red deer (a notably adaptable creature [Straus 1981]) took place under a wide range of Pleniglacial, Tardiglacial and Postglacial conditions, for example. The non-coincidence of climatic changes and subsistence trends would seem to reinforce the hypothesis that population pressure was the basic cause for the intensification of the food quest outlined above. Although just one site, La Riera, provided powerful evidence for change through time, it seemed to confirm in detail what was probably a regional pattern. Indeed other modern excavations also point in the same directions. La Riera prompted a review of the regional prehistory from a new perspective. The shift in focus returned to a broader, comparative scale based on the lessons learned at that cave.

Models for Late Ice Age Cantabrian Adaptations

By the end of the 1970s the masterful syntheses for the Lower, Middle and Upper Paleolithic of western Europe, developed fundamentally by F. Bordes and D. de Sonneville-Bordes in the 1950s and 1960s were becoming a bit "frayed around the edges." This was altogether natural, as they had primarily been based on a few key excavations conducted before World War II. The accumulation of new sequences and the application of new methods (notably oxygen isotope analysis, radiocarbon and other dating methods) led to the discovery of increasing numbers of anomalies (cases of assemblages which did not fit the "typical" culture-stratigraphic schemes) and it has become clear (to some, at least) that the traditional archaeological taxa (e.g., Mousterian, Solutrean, etc.) were useful at best in only a general, heuristic sense. While the new methods (slow to be appreciated in typologically-dominated European prehistory) lessened the absolute status of the traditional taxa, they provided the tools needed for independently building site, regional, and interregional chronologies and correlations. Without reliable relative and absolute chronologies, it is impossible to do any sort of specific or general comparisons. Time must be controlled for in order to do synchronic studies of inter-site or inter-regional variability in technology, activities, subsistence, etc., or to do diachronic studies of environmental and adaptive change in any given region.

In this spirit, I decided in the early 1980s to take stock of the state of Upper Paleolithic affairs in France and Spain and found that my experiences with the Gravettian, Solutrean, Magdalenian, Azilian, and Asturian of Cantabria were indeed not isolated. I was able to enumerate many similar anomalies, especially cases of supposedly "typical" assemblages appearing at the "wrong" radiocarbon age or in the "wrong" stratigraphic position (Straus 1987a). In my opinion, the accumulated evidence suggests that the phylogenetic paradigm, built up over three-quarters of a century by G. de Mortillet, H. Breuil, D. Peyrony and D. de Sonneville-Bordes, is ripe for replacement, which is not to say that it did not play an absolutely crucial role in the study of the Upper Paleolithic or that many of its empirical contributions are not and will not continue to be valid. While, in principle, I agree that Thomas Kuhn's model of scientific revolutions does apply (at least symptomatically) to much of what happened in archaeology—particularly in Anglo-American archaeology—in the 1960s, I am firmly convinced that scientific "progress" (or development) does have a significant component that is cumulative—despite revolutions in majority thinking ("paradigm shifts"). I believe the old paradigm to be lost in terms of its once universally accepted (albeit often implicit) general goals for prehistory, but I fully acknowledge the factual contributions (notably in terms of basic methodology, typology, and stratigraphy) of its many, often brilliant practitioners. This personal ambivalence, this acceptance of a philosophical paradox ("data do not speak for themselves" and "there are no data without a theoretical context of relevance," but "knowledge is cumulative") is perhaps the result of my background, training, and experiences (Straus 1988a). Perhaps it is a reflection of the conservative "atheoretical" nature of European students of the Paleolithic—far greater, I would say, than, for example, that of British or Continental scholars of the Neolithic or Metal Ages.

Prehistoric archaeology is, for me, a branch of paleoanthropology: the holistic study of the biological and cultural adaptations and evolution of pre- and early modern hominids. It is fundamentally concerned with both sociological and biological issues and derives much of its theoretical underpinnings from ecology. It depends substantially upon specialized applications of numerous natural sciences, notably geology, paleontology, botany, and physical chemistry. However, it seeks to describe and explain not only "man-land" relations but also "man-man" relations in time perspective. What it lacks in ethnographic detail (despite the pretensions of the reconstructionist "paleoethnography" school), prehistoric archaeology makes up in terms of its unique potential for studying long term processes of change. Whether derived from American "Processual Archaeology" or British "Economic Prehistory," it is unabashedly functionalist in outlook, while recognizing that human evolution has consisted in the long term of both successful and unsuccessful adaptations. Prehistoric archaeology is eminently eclectic in its pragmatic methods and in the sources of its hypotheses and theories of causation. It exploits all opportunities and techniques to rediscover, document and attempt to explain the past. It necessarily sacrifices concern for the individual human and for idiosyncratic behaviors, while trying to elucidate regularities in the behavior of humans as members of social units adapting to environmental and demographic conditions, which are themselves not unique, but patterned.

Although the prescribed hypothetico-deductive epistemology of certain "new archaeologists" (e.g., Fritz and Plog 1970, Watson et al. 1971) has justifiably been criticized for its rigidity, narrowness, and inappropriateness to the archaeological enterprise (see e.g., Clark 1982, 1987a), I continue to believe that archaeology is a peculiar kind of experimental science (albeit with genuine elements of humanism, such as justifiable recourse, on occasion, to the methods of art history). By this I mean that we seek to *test* ideas (by digging, surveying, or analyzing extant collections) which have *material consequences*. The trick, as

was discovered in the period of disillusionment with the "New Archaeology," is to assess accurately the possible links between original behavior (the ultimate goal of our studies) and the physical residues
which constitute the fragmentary archaeological record—our reality.
Each archaeological research project is a semi-replicative experiment
for those of us who believe in the general regularity of human behavior. The most difficult part of designing and conducting such experiments comes in the specification of the relevant factors *conditioning*
the prehistoric behavior. The probability of a valid test of any hypothesis lies in the completeness and accuracy of the empirical controls we
have developed for those conditioning factors. In that regard I whole-
heartedly agree with Binford's (1977a) concept of "Middle Range Theory." Prehistoric archaeology, if it is to be anything other than an
exercise in armchair speculation, based on criteria of empathy and the
psychic unity of humankind, must anchor its explanations in carefully
justified, uniformitarian principles derived from observations of the
present world. In this regard, we are a science like geology, although
our uniformitarian principles are likely to be somewhat more controversial than those of the earth sciences, since they concern humans and
their behavior as well as physical facts and processes. In my own work,
those aspects of middle range research which have to do with site
formation/disturbance processes have been and are crucial (Butzer
1982, Wood and Johnson 1978, Schiffer 1987).

Experience has taught me, however, that excavations are full of
surprises; they may yield classes of data that were unexpected, and data
that were expected may be absent. While it is true that data do not exist
in a theoretical void (a key tenet of the New Archaeology), it is equally
true that archaeologists have an ethical obligation to try to collect
excavation data (objects and observations) which may not be strictly or
directly related to their initial research hypotheses. This means that
they must keep as widely informed as possible about new research
problems, new methods, and newly recognized classes of data. Indeed,
this is more than an ethical imperative; it is a practical necessity as well.
Even if one approaches a "dig" as an experiment designed to test some
particular set of propositions, when things turn out differently, a project can be legitimately enlarged by having taken the trouble to collect
and record other classes of data than those originally prescribed by the
experimental protocol. Naturally, however, all "digs" have to be conducted with the limits of available funding, personnel, and time.

Preferring the concrete to the abstract and believing in the patient,
cumulative nature of archaeological investigation, I have concentrated
my research on a relatively limited (albeit crucial) period of time in human evolution (the Upper Paleolithic-Mesolithic) in a relatively small

(albeit rich and varied) geographic region (the Atlantic facade of south-west Europe). Recently I sought to take stock of what I believed we had learned in the last few years about the adaptive systems of the Upper Paleolithic in Cantabrian Spain, including uniting strategies, settlement patterning, and the relationship of cave art sites to the overall pattern of human exploitation of the region. The specific models I proposed (Straus 1985b, 1986a, c, 1987b, c), based on significant numbers of new surveys, discoveries, and excavations throughout the region (as well as a reanalysis of older materials), sought to apply some of the general theories of hunter-gatherer butchering options and mobility strategies developed by Lewis Binford (e.g., 1978, 1980, 1982b) and some of the ideas concerning hunter-gatherer locational and social relations and territoriality set forth in recent years by Edwin Wilmsen (1973), Martin Wobst (1976), and Michael Jochim (1983). These and other theoretical perspectives on hunter-gatherer survival strategies are highly relevant to the Cantabrian situation. My models were presented as first approximations, subject to testing by further excavations and analyses. Archaeological science proceeds by hypothesis formulation (preferably explicitly), data collection, model building, further testing, and either model readjustment or replacement. Such a cycle has characterized my original (1973) hypothesis of altitudinally transhumant seasonal migrations in Upper Paleolithic Cantabria, rejected after direct testing at La Riera and, indirectly, by the accumulation of seasonality data from other sites.

The Abri Dufaure Prehistoric Project

A series of theoretical and practical considerations led me to expand the focus of my research to the pre-Pyrenean region of extreme southwest France. This work would be centered on the Abri Dufaure, one of a cluster of terminal Pleistocene sites at the foot of a strategic cliff in front of a permanent ford, just upstream of the confluence of two major rivers. I had read the monograph on another one of these "Pastou Cliff" sites, Duruthy, by Robert Arambourou (1978) and was intrigued by some of his conclusions. He hypothesized that the site (and the whole cliff base) represented a major cold season residential base camp of hunter-gatherer bands (an "aggregation" site) that moved transhumantly between summer highland pasture areas and this lowland region of the southern Aquitaine Basin in pursuit of migratory game (bison, horses, and especially reindeer, as well as salmon). Duruthy, with its long, chronometrically dated stratigraphic sequence, its slab and cobblestone pavements, postholes, and enormously rich faunal, lithic and bone artifact assemblages (and collections of mobile art works) was clearly a major, repeatedly occupied place on the Magdalenian landscape, no doubt because of the favorable topographic situation of the Pastou Cliff (shelter, solar exposure, view, position *vis à vis* the ford and the valley axis of communication between the Pyrenees and the Aquitaine lowlands and coast). The paleoenvironmental, radiometric, faunal, and archaeological analyses done at Duruthy were up to the standards of the early 1970s. Excavation of the smaller, nearby rockshelter of Dufaure could test the ideas developed by Arambourou and his colleagues at Duruthy by controlling for topographic situation (Dufaure and Duruthy are essentially the *same* place) and time (radiometrically), and by searching systematically for differences and similarities in site function (artifacts, fauna, structures, seasonality, etc.) Specialized analyses at Dufaure (e.g., site formation and site structure analyses made possible by exhaustive recording techniques, lithic microwear, faunal anatomical element analyses, dental cementum and other seasonality analyses, accelerator radiocarbon dating, lithic debitage and petrographic analyses, etc.) can extend the information base from the Pastou Cliff beyond the results presented in the Duruthy monograph (Straus and Spiess 1985; Straus 1988b; n.d.e, g; Straus et al. 1988). In short, the excavation of Dufaure comes close to being a replication of the Duruthy "experiment," albeit on a smaller scale. Thus the first objective of the Dufaure Project was a "controlled comparison" (to borrow Fred Eggan's phrase) between two adjacent sites.

Beyond the confines of the Pastou Cliff, the Dufaure excavation was designed to contribute to an understanding of hunter-gatherer adaptations during the terminal Pleistocene and initial Holocene in the Pyrenean region, by providing controlled data on the lowland "pose" of the settlement subsistence system under a variety of environmental conditions (stadial, interstadial, and interglacial). These data could be (and have been) compared with the penecontemporaneous data from modern excavations of sites in the foothills (e.g., Enlène) and in the high Pyrenees (e.g., Les Eglises). Thus Dufaure, like La Riera, was to contribute to the construction of a *regional* prehistory of mobile hunter-gatherer adaptive systems through time, beyond the typological concerns of the phylogenetic paradigm until recently dominant in this region. The empirical bases for *regional* reconstructions of mobility and subsistence strategies by hunter-gatherer groups are the excavations and analyses of individual *sites* of different sizes and types—as well as intelligently evaluated survey results (given the great biases of differential preservation and visibility).

Ultimately one of the goals of the Dufaure Project is to compare the Pyrenean regional adaptive system with the Cantabrian one during the same Tardiglacial and early Post-Glacial climatic phases. It is at the scale of the geographical region, after all, that hunter-gatherer systems, with their more or less high mobility and extensive annual exploitation ranges, must be studied and compared. Such comparisons can hopefully bring out the distinctive features of each system, as each amounts to a somewhat different set of articulations between people and nature (physical environment and resources) and among people (demography and social organization). The comparisons which I have begun to sketch out between Cantabria and Gascony (e.g., Straus 1983b, c; n.d.e) are logical ones: both regions lie on the same parallel of latitude (43°N), along what is essentially the same east-west mountain chain (Pyrenees-Cantabrian Cordillera) and abut the same Atlantic gulf (Bay of Biscay/Gulf of Gascony/Cantabrian Sea). In addition, considerable paleoenvironmental work (notably palynology) indicates that basically the same Last Glacial and Holocene climatic phases are represented in both regions. The lithic and osseous artifact industries of both regions are essentially similar, as is the cave and mobile art. These two regions (together with Périgord-Quercy) have by far the richest Upper Paleolithic cave art ensembles in the world. The Upper Paleolithic-Mesolithic archaeological records of both regions are also very rich, and many new excavations are providing a wealth of modern-quality data on technology, subsistence and settlement patterns, as well as a quickly growing list of radiocarbon dates that permits objective control of time in all comparisons among sites and regions.

Given these similarities, it is interesting from the analytical standpoint that some of the basic topographic facts of the two regions are different (e.g., the vast Aquitaine Plain versus the narrow Cantabrian coastal strip; the now inundated Aquitaine Glacial coast versus the little changed Cantabrian littoral) and that some of the key food resources of the Last Glacial were different (reindeer versus red deer, different in body and herd size, migratory behavior, and habitat). Marine resources became important to the subsistence of late Ice Age Cantabrians, but they are not apparent in at least the surviving sites of Gascony. Ibex was hunted in the hills and mountains of both regions; however, although bison and horses were hunted in Cantabria, they were far more significant resources in Gascony. The lithologies of the two regions are different, making for differences in available raw materials for tool manufacture (e.g., Straus n.d.h). The differences in topography and resource structure are likely to have significantly affected the scale and nature of human territories, social groupings and networks, mobility strategies and subsistence practices and trends. Indeed, there are *detailed* differences in the industries and in the industrial sequences of Cantabria and Gascony which should have long ago led prehistorians to suspect some important systems differences worthy of investigation.

Instead, under the normative, phylogenetic paradigm, Spanish pre-historians often were content to force their materials into the Périgord-based French scheme for the Upper Paleolithic.

What I am suggesting here is that, while the data of prehistoric archaeology still must be gathered at individual sites (and in these cases they are mostly caves and rockshelters, since erosion and burial in these mountainous regions have effectively eliminated most open air sites), the most appropriate scale for the analysis of hunter-gatherer adaptations is regional and an excellent way to gain insight into the operation of such extinct adaptive systems is by doing inter-regional comparison. This is the approach persuasively advocated by Soffer (1985), Gamble (1986), and others in recent years with respect to the Upper Paleolithic of Europe. Thus, while our analyses of individual sites become more detailed (to include microhabitat reconstructions and studies of site formation and site structure), sites, which are the data bases for much regional analysis, must be understood in regional contexts. The Du-faure Project, like the La Riera Project, was conducted from this per-spective. In that spirit, a recent survey of late Upper Paleolithic subsis-tence strategies throughout western Europe (Straus 1987d) presented a broad overview of the interregional comparative scale, and high-lighted some interesting differences and similarities.

Change Through Time

Much of my research has focused on relatively narrow time slices (e.g., Soffer and Gamble 1990; Straus 1990b), making synchronic compari-sons between sites of regions, although the subsistence studies of La Riera in particular and Cantabria in general were clearly concerned with changes in human adaptations through time. Recent interest has focused on "transitions" in paleolithic prehistory, which is our inade-quate, categorical way of trying to deal with processes of evolutionary change in the record. A number of symposia whose papers are either in press or published (e.g., Trinkaus 1983, Straus 1986b, Ronen 1982, Nitecki 1987, Mellars and Stringer 1989, n.d.) have addressed the Lower to Middle, Middle to Upper, early to late Upper, and Upper to Post-Paleolithic "transitions." Archaeologically, I have tried to deal with differences *and* similarities between traditionally defined time slices such as the Mousterian and Early Upper Paleolithic (Straus and Heller 1988; Straus n.d.d), Mousterian and Magdalenian (Straus 1983d), early and late Upper Paleolithic and Mesolithic (Straus 1977, 1985c, 1986b, n.d.f) by comparing and contrasting such subsystems as settle-ment pattern and density, technology, subsistence, artistic activity, etc. One of the main conclusions of several of these studies has been that change has been *mosaic* in nature. For example, changes in human anatomy and in certain aspects of technology after around 35,000 B.P. did not mean instantaneous changes in subsistence strategies or even a ubiquitous "explosion" in artistic activity. Many of the supposed hallmarks of the Upper Paleolithic (e.g., specialized mass hunting of herd species, elaborate compound weapons such as the atl-atl, darts, bow-and-arrow, the most spectacular art works) did not develop in southwest Europe until the second half or even end of this period (i.e., ≤ 20 kyr). Not even all the changes traditionally thought to coincide with (and "caused" by) the Pleistocene-Holocene climatic "transition" are necessarily congruent with it. Some, such as the "broad spectrum revolution" in subsistence in Cantabria occurred well before, as did the development of the "Azilian" in France. Others, such as the shift from Magdalenian to the Azilian in Cantabria, took place after the P-H boundary. In some regions of the world that boundary seems to have had specific environmental impacts that really did quickly and dramatically cause change in human adaptations (e.g., the reforestation, coastal plain flooding and extinction of reindeer in southern France). But in other regions, like Cantabria, the changes were far more gradual and subtle in their effect on humans (e.g., red deer remained the dietary mainstay under Glacial and Postglacial conditions due to the broad adaptability of this cervid species).

While trying to address change through these comparative studies, and while demonstrating that the picture is far more blurred and the problems far more complex than traditionally believed, I must admit that we are far from really understanding *process*, far from satisfactorily demonstrating actual *courses* of change. In the last analysis, however, that goal remains valid and depends on both theory construction and data gathering.

The Capellades Paleolithic Project

I am convinced that many fundamental surprises await us even in the understanding of such basic facts as the chronology of phenomena supposedly marking our "transitions" (witness the effects of the discovery of the Saint-Césaire Châtelperronian Neanderthal or of the TL/ESR "dating" of Qafzeh and Skhūl). My current research is designed to explore, document, and hopefully understand the implications of J. Bischoff's (Bischoff et al. 1988, 1989; Cabrera and Bischoff 1989; see also Straus 1989a) U-series and AMS C14 dating of the terminal Mousterian and initial Aurignacian to 40 kyr in northern Spain. Excavations of long sequences of rapidly deposited, travertine-rich rockshelter deposits in Catalonia should provide a wealth of detailed chronostratigraphic and paleoenvironmental data, as well as specific cultural information on the MP-UP "transition" from short-term, high-resolution occupation residues. In short, I wish to try to replicate Bischoff's results *and* to provide data and analyses on the context and nature of the supposed changes in human adaptations, that may or may not have been related to the appearance of anatomically modern *Homo sapiens* and/or of blade-based, bone point supplemented technologies in southwestern Europe. Again, this is a multi-national, multi-disciplinary research project, based on the collaboration of Catalan researchers E. Carbonell and R. Juliá, as well as Bischoff and other American and French specialists.

The Portuguese Upper Paleolithic Project

With the data gathering phase of the Dufaure Project completed, preliminary reports published, and the monograph and other studies in press, I wanted to expand the scope of the interregional comparative approach outlined above. Following a visit to Portugal in 1986, I decided to begin exploratory research in that country. Again, pragmatic and theoretical reasons for this venture converged. Upper Paleolithic-Mesolithic research in Portugal is undergoing a renewal in activity and perspective with the work of prehistorians such as V. O. Jorge, F. Real, Luis Raposo, T. Gamito, João Zilhão, and José Arnaud, part of a general archaeological renaissance in the country. Much needs to be done in terms of finding new sites, building chronostratigraphies, developing paleoenvironmental and resource data bases, analyzing artifacts independently of the traditional schemes based on the Périgord sequence, etc. From the theoretical perspective, Portugal presents the possibility of fascinating variety and contrasts in Last Glacial adaptive systems, since one of the steepest temperature gradients anywhere in the world existed in the North Atlantic between northern and southern Portugal at 18 kyr, according to CLIMAP (1976). Portugal can ideally provide a transect of terrestrial environments and human adaptations across that gradient. Southern Portugal may have been very different from southwest France and even Cantabrian Spain in the late Upper Paleolithic, thus, it may provide very provocative comparative data if sites can be found and thoroughly researched.

In 1987 and 1988, under the auspices of Zilhão's Portuguese Estremadura Project and of Arnaud's and Gamito's Alentejo and Algarve Projects respectively, I conducted three regional surface surveys and tested 18 caves and two open air sites (e.g., Casa da Moura, Bocas, Buraca dos Mouros, Goldra, Soidos, Vidigal, Escravelheira) (Straus

1987e, 1988c, 1989b, n.d.c; Straus et al. 1988, 1990, n.d.; Carvalho et al. 1989). The results for a study of the central and southern Portuguese Upper Paleolithic have so far been largely negative, but they did raise (and help a bit to resolve) some problems involving the passages (evolutionary adaptations) from Epipaleolithic to Mesolithic to Neolithic to Chalcolithic in these archaeologically rich regions. We are faced with the problem (as in Burgos and elsewhere in Spain) of explaining the spotty distribution of Upper Paleolithic sites in Portugal. And yet, from a theoretical perspective, the development of the famous Mesolithic shell middens of the estuaries of Estremadura and Alentejo and the apparently late adoption of agriculture in those regions (as opposed to other areas of Portugal and Iberia) *requires* an understanding of the Upper Paleolithic. A complex mosaic of local adaptations is suggested by our admittedly scanty, possibly geomorphologically "biased" data base. Radiocarbon dates, stable isotope analyses of human skeletal remains, and faunal and paleoenvironmental analyses are all contributing to the unravelling of the Portuguese puzzle. Initial observations suggest significant population increase in Portugal at the time of the Last Glacial Maximum, as in the other coastal regions of the Iberian Peninsula—coinciding with the Solutrean. Each region shows evidence of considerable subsistence intensification well before the Mesolithic. Why it is in south-central Portugal (as in southeast Spain) that spectacular evidence of complex forms of social and economic organization should have arisen in the late Neolithic-Chalcolithic is obviously a burning issue for processually oriented prehistorians. But even here such basic issues as chronology have yet to be satisfactorily resolved.

Thus, this present research involves basic archaeological exploration, testing and dating, as well as more elaborate, albeit preliminary, analyses of aspects of human adaptive processes. Although the goal has been to find and study Upper and Epipaleolithic deposits, archaeological ethics require the documentation and analysis of the more recent materials which may overlie the Stone Age levels. The cave of Goldra near Faro, for example, yielded a wealth of artifactual, botanical, faunal and human skeletal evidence, dating (by ceramics and radiocarbon) to the middle Neolithic. Threatened by the surrounding construction of villas, unfortunately, our test pit might be the only archaeology done at this rich site (Straus et al. n.d.) On the other hand, our intensive surface and subsurface sampling of the late Mesolithic open air shellmidden site of Vidigal (near Sines) yielded excellent site structure data, as well as evidence for different lithic reduction sequences, subsistence and seasonality indicators, and interesting clues to the successful late survival of foraging economies along the coast of southern Portugal (Straus et al. 1990, Straus n.d.c). So problem-oriented research and basic exploration and "salvage" must go hand-in-hand. Such are the realities of fieldwork.

Conclusions

My vision of the kind of prehistoric archaeology that I practice is the product of a somewhat unusual background for an American archaeologist of my generation: an Old World family tradition of prehistory and natural science and an interest in history; a long, diverse series of fieldwork experiences; and an early, first-hand exposure to major proponents and principles of Processual Archaeology. Within paleoanthropology, prehistoric archaeology discovers and provides detailed documentation of the residues of past human cultural adaptations and attempts to explain variability and change. It is an eminently materialist discipline whose methods are fundamentally comparative. While heavily dependent on geology and the other natural sciences, prehistoric archaeology is ultimately concerned with the definition and explanations of collective human cohesion in specific environmental and social contexts. It can expand the purview of anthropology through its capacity to study long term evolutionary change. It is also a humanistic discipline in the same way that social history may be so classified. Ultimately, my approach to doing prehistoric archaeology of the moderately remote past is eclectic and pragmatic, while holding to long term theoretical goals that are comparative and explanatory, as well as documentary.

Postscript

It is an interesting experience to be attacked simultaneously as being a misguided, naïve, American radical by D. de Sonneville-Bordes (1989) and as an overly cautious, backsliding, neoconservative by I. Davidson (this volume). Madame Bordes, whose contributions to Upper Paleolithic prehistory have been seminal and enduring, tries to dismiss almost all the empirical cases cited by me (Straus 1987a) that violate her normative phylogenetic scheme, as instances of mechanical mixture of deposits. I respectfully disagree. But I do believe that—whatever their meaning in terms of technological traditions, regional adaptive systems, connubia, exchange networks or macrobands—some of the larger formal typological groupings of the Upper Paleolithic do seem to have consistency and practical analytical utility. At differing scales, such phenomena as the taxa we archaeologists have called "Aurignacian" and "Gravettian" or "Solutrean," "Upper Magdalenian," and "Azilian" serve as useful shorthands for talking about broad patterns (albeit all with internal variations due to activity and raw material differences, seasonality, archaeological sampling, etc.).

Davidson, who has contributed much to our knowledge of chronology and paleoeconomies in eastern Spain, is critical of my continued use of such terms to describe swatches of time in particular regions of the Upper Paleolithic world. He—like me—believes in the application of *independent* measures of chronology, namely radiocarbon. With radiocarbon we can, in theory, compare and contrast synchronic and diachronic assemblages in our attempts to explain variability and hence to understand the operation of prehistoric adaptive systems. The systematic application of radiocarbon dating was and is, after all, a major goal of the La Riera, Abri Dufaure, Portugal and Catalonia projects. However, as Davidson well knows, radiocarbon, particularly in the Upper Paleolithic—prior to the period with dendrochronological calibration—is no magic bullet. Radiocarbon time is quite relative and can mislead. It is not yet—even with the accelerator-mass spectrometer method—*the* solution to all our chronological problems. (For that reason a key aspect of the Capellades Project is to try to "calibrate" AMS ^{14}C dates on charcoal and on individual bone amino acids with U-series dates on travertines having demonstrated equilibrium conditions.) I admit that the La Riera situation, with several inverted dates (among a total of 28) due to vertical sample movements and inter-laboratory differences or errors, was disquieting. On the other hand the 14 Dufaure dates (both conventional and AMS) gave astonishingly coherent results for embarrassingly "normative" assemblages. And, as Davidson well knows, many sites and many more old collections can still only be "dated"—however approximately—"by their artifacts." In the end, radiocarbon has shown the *general* chronological validity of such major Upper Paleolithic entities as the "Cantabrian Solutrean" or the "Pyrenean Middle Magdalenian"—often marked by such diagnostic (though unfortunately not omnipresent) artifacts as foliate/shouldered points or *contours découpés*, respectively. Why is Davidson so upset? These are archaeological facts.

Whether we choose to call the artifact assemblages of the period between around 20,500 and 16,500 B.P. "Solutrean," "folipointian," or "UP Stage 4" seems to me to be irrelevant. The real task is to document and explain variability and similarity in human behaviors and adaptations in regional environmental contexts. Semantics are a separate and less important issue. Assemblage typologies are indeed sterile, when they are the "be-all and end-all" of archaeological research (usually of a normative, phylogenetic nature). But *as tools*, they are useful, descriptive instruments—just as are artifact typologies. What is important is the questions asked, the reasons for classification. Naming is a trivial matter, if it is kept in proper perspective.

I work actively in the world of European prehistory with European colleagues. These names are part of a descriptively valid 120-year-old tradition begun by G. de Mortillet. In order to be understood and to participate in the development of the large, active, powerful discipline of paleolithic prehistory, it only makes sense to try to respect a language which can be understood by the majority of its practitioners. Perhaps I am too ambivalent for Davidson's tastes, but he can take comfort in the ire my modest views have raised in some quarters in Europe, if not in Australia. There are problems enough having my theoretical points of view understood, let alone adopted by European colleagues, without causing problems by refusing to speak their language!

Chapter 4
A Paradigm is Like an Onion: Reflections on my Biases

Geoffrey A. Clark

Introduction

A degree of introspection, a sense of humor, and a thick skin are required to make explicit the paradigmatic biases that underlie archaeological research designs. In this essay, I attempt (1) to outline some of the main features of the paradigms that appear to govern "indigenous" Old World paleolithic research; (2) to describe the fuzzy, half-formed, and poorly integrated concepts and ideas that make up my own theoretical orientation (i.e., identify the paradigmatic biases that characterize my work); and (3) to illustrate the contrasting perspectives with a discussion of Pleistocene biocultural evolution and the "modern human origins" question.

Like the other contributors to this volume, I am an Old World prehistorian actively involved in field work on Upper and Post-Pleistocene hunter-gatherer adaptations in the Mediterranean Basin. I have what might be called "an American preparation," but am also more or less familiar with the work of European-trained scholars who share my research interests. Over the past few years, I have taken part in a number of international conferences concerned mainly with various aspects of hunter-gatherer research and human evolution in the circum-Mediterranean region. What struck me most about these meetings were the enormous differences in the assumptions that different workers brought to the resolution of problems thought to be held in common. These differences were often so great that any meaningful discussion of issues was precluded. There also seemed to be variable — usually little—appreciation that such epistemological questions existed, with some workers evidently subscribing to the notion that "the facts speak for themselves," and that in consequence theoretical issues were largely irrelevant.

While these remarks might seem self-evident to many American workers, they are by no means self-evident to the many Old World scholars who are responsible for producing the archaeopaleontological records that we both interpret. This, in my opinion, is because "critical self-consciousness," as David Clarke (1973) put it, is a feature almost entirely confined to the Anglo-American research traditions. I can think of no better example of paradigms in conflict than the recent conferences on the origins of modern humans, and the related question of the nature of the Middle/Upper Paleolithic transition. These debates, conducted as much in the media as in the scholarly press, are marked by major differences in (1) assumptions about the nature of culture and past human behavior, (2) differences in the systematics invoked to address these problems, (3) different perceptions of the archaeological and paleontological records, (4) different views of the diagenetic processes that have transformed them, and (5) different opinions about how pervasive change is and what causes it to occur. These biases in turn determine which biological and cultural variables are regarded as significant to monitor and how much difference "makes a difference" (that is, how much difference is significant in phylogenetic or behavioral terms). In short, I believe that there are several discernible "indigenous" paradigms for Old World prehistory at the level of the metaphysic, and that they tend to part company with their American counterparts along the lines of national research traditions. As is evident from other contributions to this book, not everyone agrees that it is possible to characterize regional or national archaeological paradigms at the metaphysical level.

As Binford and Sabloff (1982) recently expressed it, a (metaphysical) *paradigm* is a "worldview," a statement about the way the world (or some portion of it) is perceived to be. A *theory* is an argument invoked or constructed to explain *why* the world is as it appears to be. Metaphysical paradigms are sometimes represented as closed logical systems; and, in a sense, all sociological and construct paradigms are derived from them (Kuhn 1970b, c, Clark 1987a). However, the fact that paradigms exist at levels other than that of the metaphysic can cause problems (Masterman 1970). Whether or not distinct metaphysical paradigms overlap to a significant degree, and whether or not lower level paradigms are appropriate to more than a single metaphysic, are what this book is all about. Some think that an inverse relationship exists between the level of paradigm and the extent to which it is shared (the lower the level of paradigm, the more likely it is to be shared by more than one higher order paradigm). I cannot completely agree with what is probably a majority view, however. Except perhaps at the most fundamental level of universal analytical procedures and techniques (those common to all scientific endeavors), the metaphysical paradigm determines what variables are significant to measure. Since perception of variability is theoretically infinite, limited only by the precision of the measurement instrument, paradigms focus attention on a smaller part of the spectrum of perceived variability which is thought to be relevant to a particular problem or research domain.

On the Positivist Infrastructure of Western Science

One of the hallmarks of the Old World paradigm, and one of the more irritating things about it, is a near-total failure to confront the subjective quality of pattern. This is sometimes embodied in the assertion that pattern (whether archaeological or paleontological) is an inherent quality of an archaeopaleontological record, and that it can be perceived directly and understood by any informed observer. For more than a century, however, what is essentially a strict empiricist view ("the facts speak for themselves") has been thoroughly discredited. There is no such thing as an "objective observer" who can apprehend the qualities of the natural world directly and thus "discover" facts latent in nature (see, e.g., Hempel 1966, Hanson 1961, Kuhn 1962). Meaning comes from humans and is not an intrinsic feature of an external reality. In a philosophical sense, data have no existence apart from the conceptual frameworks that define them, a point to which I will return.

By around 1900, logical positivist philosophies of science—the infrastructure for the unparalleled scientific advances of the twentieth century—had made the distinction between the process of discovery (gathering facts, generating theories) and the process of evaluation of theories (see, e.g., Dunnell 1982, Clark 1982, Watson et al. 1984). In the best-established, "big science" fields, efforts were made to develop methodologies for the evaluation of theories that had a deductive component to them, embodied in the concept of prediction— identifying beforehand the probable causes of observable phenomena (or the consequences of those causes) and checking them empirically. Archaeology was slow to adopt this point of view. It was not until the late 1960s/early 1970s that some archaeologists began to question the credibility of the strict empiricist tradition (e.g., Clarke 1973). There is still no evidence of a deductive element in the research designs of paleoanthropology (Clark 1988, 1989a).

If nature does not dictate the meanings we assign to it (Hanson 1961), and if we can never "observe" a true, objective natural world, there is a paradox: since the source of ideas about nature is subjective, how do we assess the credibility of these subjective ideas? Sir Alfred Ayer, whose book *Language, Truth and Logic* (1936) was the first exposition of logical positivism in the English language, proposed that for a statement to mean anything at all, it must be verifiable by experience or analysis and, if that is not possible, then the statement is merely an expression of opinion (this led him to atheism, for which he was often criticized). Thomas Kuhn's answer was similar: we determine the credibility of the subjective by developing objective methods of evaluation based on experience (1962, 1970a, 1977). This viewpoint is practically universally accepted today, especially in the physical sciences (see also Blalock 1972, Binford 1981b, Clark 1982).

As noted, however, the objective evaluation of ideas by reference to experience is problematical because the methods for evaluating experience are ultimately determined by the paradigm—the description of the world or problem domain. Kuhn recognized this and concluded that the direct testing of theory is probably impossible since such tests would, perforce, be constrained by the subjective nature of the paradigm, an idea which has found its way into the New World literature through the writings of Lewis Binford (esp. 1981b). The paradox cannot be resolved. What actually seems to take place in physics, chemistry, etc., is that a kind of consensus emerges as to the general features of the paradigmatic "landscape," which in turn gives rise to a series of conventions at the sociological and construct (methodological) levels that (1) recognizes certain variables as "legitimate" or "essential" to monitor within a particular problem domain (and denies that recognition to others) and (2) authorizes certain analytical procedures as the "appropriate" ones to use in evaluation (and denies that authorization to others) (e.g., Feynman 1985, Kitchener 1988). Apart from the near-universal adoption of probabilistic models at all levels, the extent to which methods are transferable from one domain to another is debated.

The Kuhnian model of "scientific revolution" characterized paradigm change at the level of the metaphysic as relatively abrupt and disjunct, irrational and largely unpredictable. Science advanced through the discard of outmoded paradigms, and by generational replacement, rather than cumulatively, through the evaluation of ideas by means of tests using empirical data. This disjunction had consequences for the acceptance or rejection of theory, which was regarded as paradigm-dependent. Characterized almost immediately as an oversimplification of a more complex reality, this perspective on change has been extensively criticized by philosophers and historians of science (e.g., Masterman 1970), and Kuhn has modified some of his views (e.g., 1970b, 1974). In archaeology, there is presently a diversity of opinion about the appropriateness of Kuhn's scientific revolutions as a model for the discipline (e.g., Meltzer 1979, Binford and Sabloff 1982, Dunnell 1982, Watson et al. 1971, 1984; Clark 1982, 1987a). The main point, though, in regard to the empiricist biases of the Old World paradigm, is that science can develop either through changes in paradigms or theories, but it *cannot develop solely through the acquisition of data.* Thus, to assert that new discoveries of hominid fossils combined with "theoretical" advances like cladistics (e.g., Foley 1987) or "methodological" advances like TL-dating (e.g., Valladas et al. 1987, 1988) are bringing about radical changes in our perceptions of human biocultural evolution is naive in the extreme. To make these assertions is to argue for a strict empiricist interpretation of both the archaeological and human paleontological records. Whether archaeological paradigm change is abrupt, cumulative, or whether it combines elements of both (Clark 1987a, b; see also Straus, Harrold, Bietti in this volume), there is a perception that it is possible to characterize a paradigm on a national or regional scale in terms of the research traditions operative in a particular country or geographical area (see, e.g., Binford and Sabloff 1982, Soffer 1985, Gamble 1986).

Binford and Sabloff's Characterization of the Metaphysical Paradigm of Old World Prehistory

To illustrate the impact of paradigmatic biases on archaeological systematics at all levels, Binford and Sabloff (1982) have recently described the basic elements of a paradigm that they believe has governed much archaeological research in the United Kingdom and on the Continent since the 1920s. The starting point is a view of culture that contrasts sharply with its American counterpart.

In the Old World, they suggest, cultures are usually perceived to be the material expressions of particular peoples, a tenacious idea that can be traced back at least to V. Gordon Childe in the UK and to the Abbé Breuil in France (see, e.g., Bailey and Callow 1986). On a regional scale, cultures are differentiated packages of traits materially expressed, and are held to be isomorphic with ethnically differentiated peoples, societies, "tribes," or "civilizations" (especially France). The perpetuation of cultural distinctiveness over time is assumed from the operation of internal social factors embodied in the Continental notions of *esprit* or *volk* (that is, ideational factors that are coextensive with a particular, identity-conscious social entity). Cultural continuity is thought to be documented by pattern among the materials left at archaeological sites; the formal distinctiveness of artifact assemblages is attributed to the ethnic characteristics of their makers, who share similar norms, values, etc.—in short, an ideational definition of culture but one which supposedly has direct material correlates.

The Old World view of culture is exemplified in the writings of the late François Bordes, whose work, they allege, is based on the notion that similar packages of artifacts (or, more precisely, retouched tools) equal ethnically distinct cultural groups. This definition of culture allowed Bordes to postulate the existence of ethnically distinct groups of people living side by side over millennia in the same region (e.g., the Mousterian *facies* in the Périgord, the early Upper Paleolithic in general). Within these units, culture was seen as essentially static over long periods of time. In place of the continuity emphasized in the New World research tradition, when change occurred, it was abrupt and conclusive because actual population replacement—the only process mechanism generally recognized—was postulated to have brought it about. Again, Old World construals of modern human origins are an excellent contemporary example (e.g., Stringer and Andrews 1988).

Binford and Sabloff (1982) make the point that the Old World view of culture is a (metaphysical) paradigm. It summarizes Old World prehistorians' expectations about what culture is "like." To be sure, it perceives or constructs a "reality" but, since that reality is different from its New World counterpart, descriptions and explanations of pattern in cultural phenomena are different. Cultures equate with ethnic groups, change little, mix less, and are modified only gradually (if at all) with the passage of time. There is no acknowledgment of the possibility that aspects of a single cultural system could appear as different "cultures" at different places and times (cf., e.g., Clark and Clark 1975, Clark 1987b, 1989a, b; Straus 1975b, 1979a; Straus and Clark 1986, Clark and Straus 1986). The definition of culture itself rules this out (cultures must change *en bloc* if they change at all). These paradigmatic biases affect Old World systematics from top to bottom and, while there are acknowledged differences between the research traditions of the United Kingdom and those of the Continent (and differences within the Continent), in the aggregate they result in archaeologies that (1) are often very "artifact oriented" (the widespread use of *fossiles directeurs* to identify cultures and their subdivisions is a case in point); (2) de-emphasize context and the spatial characteristics of cultural systems (because of historical links with geography, the UK is an exception [Clark 1978a]); (3) ignore overarching similarities in assemblage composition, site layout, settlement patterns, subsistence practices, etc., by concentrating on index fossil tool types and/or normative summaries of the retouched tool components of lithic assemblages (see, e.g., Clark and Lindly 1989a, b); and (4) ignore or minimize the relational aspects of particular categories of artifacts (e.g., the

French proclivity to study harpoons, bone points, plaquettes, etc., as isolated problem domains is a good example—Julien 1982). The result is that the organizational properties of past cultural systems, as manifest in the relational aspects of things and places, are obliterated because of preconceptions about culture that destroy the conceptual integrity of the dynamic systems that produced these artificially segregated pieces of the archaeological record.

A Reaction

Readers will, of course, match their perceptions of the Old World paradigm with those of Binford and Sabloff (1982). It is my opinion, based on some twenty years' experience doing archaeological research in France, Spain, Turkey, Cyprus, and Jordan, that it is a fairly accurate rendition, although clearly more on the mark in respect of the biases that underlie Continental (especially French, Spanish, Italian) research than that conducted by British or German scholars. It also has a somewhat "dated" quality in respect of recent French work, which is experiencing a departure from the traditional phylogenetic model that so dominated the field up until the early 1980s. Defections from the traditional model are most evident in an increasing willingness to look for causes of patterning in factors outside of and not necessarily related to ethnically bounded, ideational conceptions of culture (e.g., raw material variability, debitage analysis, core and reduction sequence reconstructions, site functional variation). These changes are very recent phenomena, however, and are mainly the work of younger scholars who have (1) attempted to react to the near-total collapse of the normative type site/sequence-based systematics that have been in place since the 1920s, and (2) been influenced by the functionalism evident in the work of many American and English writers (Clark 1983b). There is still relatively little concern with survey data and the regional aspects of past systems, and there is still a general absence of an holistic perspective. Influence has been mostly "one-way," reflecting a predominance of anglophone theoretical views that are sometimes explicitly acknowledged (e.g., Gallay 1989).

Economic Prehistory

It is, however, in regard to the United Kingdom that I take strongest exception to the Binford and Sabloff characterization. British paleolithic archaeology has been strongly molded by the "products" of a single institution, Cambridge, which has supplied most of the archaeologists currently working on hunter-gatherer adaptations in the Mediterranean Basin (and elsewhere). Two individuals, Grahame Clark and the late Eric Higgs, and a large, long-standing, interdisciplinary research effort, the British Academy Major Research Project on the Early History of Agriculture (organized and directed by Higgs) together make up the nucleus of what has become known colloquially as the "Cambridge Paleoeconomy School" or "the economic prehistory approach." The biases of the Cambridge School, which lacks any conception of culture, are completely distinct from those of Continental scholars. The most important one is the assumption that the economy is the primary determinant of much human behavior in general (and of site location in particular—site catchment analysis is a Higgsian invention). The approach, outlined in three edited volumes (Higgs and Jarman 1972, Higgs 1975, Jarman et al. 1982), and in approximately seventy-five published articles, entails reconstruction of past environments in order to assess the availability and energetics of potential and actual food resources within the "economic range" of a site or site cluster. Fundamental is the notion that relationships between plants, animals, and humans had been too narrowly conceptualized by archaeologists in their quest for the origins of domestication, and that new insights could be gained by examining the literature of animal ethology and by expanding inquiry beyond documenting evidence of morphological changes in those species presently important in domestication economies. An important entailment of this perspective is the idea that complex relationships involving plant-animal manipulation and control extend well back into the Pleistocene, and that the impetus for directed, linear change in paleoeconomies is to be sought in the examination of demographic variables, especially those that give rise to imbalances between populations and their established or traditional resources. The *raison d'être* for economic prehistory is the derivation of law-like general principles of economic behavior that are stable over time and that have evolutionary significance. It should be noted again that culture plays no part in any of this. It is regarded as a kind of epiphenomenon which is determined by the structure of the paleoeconomy and which, in any event, is probably not accessible to the archaeologist in most situations (a viewpoint many American workers might find objectionable).

It is of some interest to note that Higgs (1975) attempted to elevate economic prehistory to the level of a paradigm (or at least a major theory) of long term human behavioral change. He contended that, despite the rhetoric of the "new archaeology," modern archaeological research is "cast in a traditional mould" (1975:2) and the paradigms that govern what he called artifactual explanation, paleoethnography, systems approaches, and paleoecology were all considered inadequate on various grounds. Only paleoeconomic studies, concerned with "those aspects of human behaviour which appear in the archaeological time perspective to have been of long-term significance" (1975:4) supposedly offered the promise of generating the natural laws that he assumed to underlie human behavior. This was because of the time depth inherent in archaeological data and "because the primary human adaptation to the environment is the economy" (1975:4). Higgs considered the study of human economic behavior to be a special kind of ethology, since the focus of many of the "concerns, concepts and even language of animal ecology and ethology is that of simple economics" (1975:4). Economic behavior was in turn determined by "natural selection" operating on the level of the group in a loosely structured biological evolutionary paradigm that owed more to Lamarck than to Darwin. Much of this was simply asserted or weakly argued, and many scholars reacted to it by ignoring the theoretical justification for the approach while retaining much of its methodology (see Clark [1984b] for a brief overview of the Cambridge approach to economic prehistory).

Given its Continental origins, it is puzzling that epistemology has been, and continues to be, almost wholly confined to the anglophone research traditions. Why an explicit concern with paradigmatic bias, and with archaeological theory, should be so marginal on the Continent is not at all clear to me. One of the reasons probably has to do with the fact that non-theoretical, "empirical" approaches are practiced with considerable success by many archaeologists in both hemispheres, and the successful practice of archaeology does not require one to make one's biases explicit. It also might be the case, in countries where the cadres of professional archaeologists are both small and "products" of one or a very few institutions, that biases are shared by all or most practitioners and are therefore implicit and not much discussed (see Bietti, this volume). Characterizations of American archaeology prior to the enormous expansion and "democratization" of the field following World War II come to mind (e.g., Willey and Sabloff 1974). It is paradoxical that, in one of the few French works explicitly devoted to an exposition of theory (Gallay 1989, see also Gardin 1987), the view is presented that, in contrast to the English, French "logicism" has kept faith with positivism, whereas the British are characterized as abandoning it in the rush to be "post-processual"! While I can see little in this particular, rather confusing essay that I would consider linked to positivism, the point is simply that there is so little concern with epistemology in the Continental research traditions that it is difficult to find any awareness that such a thing exists. I also wonder how widespread endorsement of "post-processualism" is in the United Kingdom (see, e.g., Bell 1987, Binford 1987a).

The Origin of Bias: Aspects of my Formal Education

The University of Arizona (1963–1967)

My formal education (1963–1971) happened to coincide with the rise of the "new archaeology," and I was fortunate to have participated in programs staffed partly by "first generation Binfordians" at both Arizona and Chicago. An early interest in southwestern archaeology brought me into contact with William Longacre, whose arrival at Tucson coincided with my own. Longacre was a stimulus for many exciting new perspectives on the prehistoric Southwest. His courses were taught not so much as culture histories as histories of concepts and ideas (i.e., although we learned the basic "facts," the "facts" were represented as context dependent). Functionalism was not the pejorative term that it sometimes is today, and, from my point of view, the department appeared to have a strong British structural-functionalist orientation which revolved around the singular figure of Edward Spicer, regarded as the intellectual leader of the social anthropologists. In those days of holistic, "four-fields" curricula, there were many liaisons between social anthropology and archaeology (more, I suspect, than at present) and I came out of my undergraduate years with what I regarded as a credible background in a number of regional or topical "archaeologies" (e.g., Old World, Southwest, North and South America, Historical), a hefty dose of anthropological theory (also taught by Spicer, with Edward Dozier) with an emphasis on comparative social organization (Spicer), some exposure to statistics (a rarity in those days), and a latent (although tenacious) interest in human evolution (Hulse).

There was also a memorable year-long course sequence on the geology of New World "early man" sites, taught by Vance Haynes. Haynes, whose position on the "peopling" issue is well known, emphasized stratigraphic analysis, geomorphology, and geochronology (i.e., glacial chronologies, alluvial cut-and-fill sequences, the properties of soils, sedimentology, what would now be called archaeozoology, absolute dating methods, etc.) as he systematically dissected and dismantled *every single claim* for "*early* early man" (i.e., pre-15 kyr B.P.) in the New World. It was all very convincing and, although it was my only exposure to Pleistocene archaeology, it left me with the conviction that the approach had real potential for even more ancient Old World sites.

In 1964 I was chosen to attend the UA archaeological fieldschool at Grasshopper Pueblo, returning in 1966 as a member of the staff. These were my first sustained exposures to fieldwork. Under the able direction of Raymond Thompson, a man with superb organizational skills, the two summers under the Mogollon Rim firmly convinced me that a career in archaeology combined aspects of the physical and the intellectual that were unrivalled in any other profession. Like many young people (I was 19 at the time), I really enjoyed the fieldwork; but one of the virtues of Grasshopper was that the intellectual ramifications of what we were doing physically were constantly being reinforced. Reinforcement took the form of nightly lectures by the professional staff; trips to other sites, fieldschools, and research projects in Arizona; and many visitors, including the legendary Binford himself, accompanied by his equally legendary wife, Sally.

The work at Grasshopper eventually led to a Master's thesis on the 200+ human burials uncovered through 1966 in which I tried to show (by ransacking the mortuary data for evidence of sodalities, kinship, post-marital residence, age and sex markers, and status ascription) that the inhabitants of the pueblo exhibited some characteristics of chiefdoms (i.e., ranking or incipient stratification—patterns not found in ethnographically known Pueblo societies) (Clark 1967, 1969). Marshall Sahlins, Elman Service, and the "neo-evolutionist" paradigm were much in evidence; and archaeologists had begun to look for ways to identify, in the residues of the past, the various levels of sociocultural integration (bands, tribes, etc.) postulated by those workers. Mortuary analysis was regarded as especially promising because of the relatively direct linkage (compared to other categories of evidence) between the archaeological context and the organizational characteristics of extinct societies. My thesis caused something of a debate, since it raised the possibility that social organizations more complex than those observed in the ethnographic present might have existed in the Southwest prior to European contact, and called into question some of the "levels of sociocultural integration" proposed by Service (especially those of the tribe and chiefdom). While, in the intervening years, the rigid stage models of the neoevolutionist paradigm have either been discarded as oversimplifications or extensively modified (e.g., Earle 1989), it is interesting to note that the smaller issue of Southwestern social complexity is still not resolved, with discernible UA (complexity up to but not exceeding that of the ethnographic present) and ASU (complexity sometimes greater than that known ethnographically) positions much in evidence in the current literature (e.g., Graves et al. 1982, Neitzel 1985, Upham and Plog 1986, Douglass 1987).

The University of Chicago (1967–1971)

Although I enjoyed my UA stint immensely and felt that I had learned a great deal from it, my primary interests remained in Old World hunter-gatherer archaeology and, when I was awarded an NSF Fellowship (which, in those days, guaranteed *entrée* to almost any graduate program), I applied to the University of Chicago. Chicago in the late 1960s was the fountainhead of the American version of social anthropology, but the archaeology faculty included such luminaries as Robert Braidwood, F. Clark Howell, Karl Butzer, and Robert McCormack Adams, as well as a young assistant professor, Leslie Freeman. Since I professed to be interested in European paleolithic archaeology, and since Freeman was currently working on a paleolithic cave site in Spain, it seemed natural that I be assigned to him as my advisor. Chicago also had an illustrious cadre of committed, articulate graduate students (e.g., Chuck Redman, Jane Buikstra, Meg Conkey, John Fritz, Fred Plog, Greg Possehl, Larry Straus, Don Johanson, Jody Hopkins, Dan Bowman) who, while initially quite intimidating in the aggregate, were in more congenial settings to become friends and, eventually, colleagues.

My years at Chicago were interrupted by lengthy field projects in France (at Solvieux, with UCLA's Jim Sackett), Spain (Cueva Morín, with Freeman) and Turkey (Çayönü, with Braidwood)—work that exposed me for the first time to European Middle and Upper Paleolithic archaeology. In between these field stints, I took a number of anthropology "history" courses, courses on social and cultural anthropological systematics (from Schneider, Yalman), and immersed myself in hunter-gatherer ethnographies. I also learned the basics of European typological systematics (the Bordes, LaPlace systems) and began to get some indications about what they were supposed to be telling us about pattern. Perhaps most valuable were courses by Freeman and Butzer which dealt in varying degrees with hunter-gatherer adaptations (what would now be called paleoecology) and geomorphology, sedimentology, paleoclimatology, and palynology—concepts and methods that allowed one to pursue "environmental archaeology" (e.g., Butzer 1971). I was also fortunate to get hold of copies of the complete texts of François Bordes' paleolithic archaeology, human paleontology, and paleoethnology courses at the University of Bordeaux—works that, in my estimation, remain the definitive statements of his biases (and, by extension, those of most French prehistorians in the 1960s and 1970s). An interest in quantitative analysis fostered by Longacre continued at Chicago under the tutelage of Tommy Muller, a professional statistician who was almost unique in the late 1960s in being a full-time consultant in the employ of the department.

These diverse intellectual strands coalesced to some extent in my dissertation research on the mesolithic Asturian of Cantabrian Spain (Clark 1971a, b; 1976a, 1983a). In it, I tried to show that global characterizations of the Mesolithic (e.g., Waterbolk 1962) were at best only partly valid and that different kinds of adaptations were demonstrable for mesolithic societies that could not be correlated neatly with specific geographic regions, topographical settings, vegetational configurations, or episodes of climatic change. Generalizations summarized by Binford (1968) about population growth and distribution, changes in lithic industries ("microlithization"), greater geographical variety in stone tool assemblages, increased exploitation of aquatic resources (especially shellfish), and a trend toward the hunting of small and medium-sized game all proved either to be difficult to substantiate in the Asturian case or were demonstrably "out of synch" (i.e., first became apparent in Upper Paleolithic or post-Asturian contexts). While I used the conventional typological systematics (and some I invented myself) to describe patterns of lithic variability, it soon became evident that there was little in the Asturian that was unique to it (not even the supposedly "diagnostic" unifacial quartzite cobble "picks"). I eventually came to the conclusion that the Asturian was "incomplete," and that it probably was only a part of a regional adaptation of considerable antiquity (see, e.g., Straus 1979a).

One of the puzzling aspects of north Spanish prehistory is the very partial, late appearance of ovicaprine/wheat domestication economies. The dissertation research also showed that the regional Mesolithic was an extremely flexible adaptation that exhibited trends in resource exploitation, site placement, and lithic technology that extended well back into the Pleistocene and that showed no correlations with episodes of climatic change (and, therefore, were apparently little affected by it, at least directly). This has led in subsequent work to a de-emphasis on climatic change as a significant causal factor, and to a view of forager adaptations that is at some variance with the perspectives of many Continental prehistorians.

Throughout this work, the bias was a broadly-defined systemic ecological one, in that economic variables were regarded as primary (and perhaps most visible archaeologically) and prehistoric economies were considered to be intimately adjusted to, although not determined by, the distributions of perceived natural resources. The perspective was diachronic in that an effort was made to define a distinctive Asturian configuration and examine it in relationship to adaptations that bracket it in time. I felt that more behavioral information could be extracted from the archaeological record if a systemic, diachronic perspective was adopted than if archaeological evidence was "simply regarded as a means for identifying groups of people or periods of time," as is so often the case in Old World prehistoric research (J. G. D. Clark 1975:7). It was a "broadly-defined" study because archaeological monitors of subsystem components (technology, economy, habitats, settlements, demography, etc.) were not adequate to permit a more sophisticated, thoroughly quantified investigation. Overall, the data were quite bad; and only in isolated cases were they likely to improve in the foreseeable future. Although I recognized that in *any* systemic model, the relationships among the various component subsystems are multiple, reciprocal, and complex, and that only a first approximation had been made toward limning in the outlines of a peculiarly Asturian adaptation, it was nevertheless possible to suggest a principal determining factor for the subsistence and settlement transformations observable at the Pleistocene-Holocene boundary in the Cantabrian archaeological record. That principal factor, explored more thoroughly in subsequent work, was long term regional population growth.

Putting Biases to Work: Research Designs

My dissertation research excepted, I have directed three major, long term collaborative archaeological projects that were organized endeavors requiring substantial external funding and explicit formulation of research designs. Two of these were located in Spain: (1) the North Burgos Archaeological Survey (1972–79) and (2) the La Riera Paleoecological Project (1976–86), the latter co-directed with my friend and colleague, Lawrence Straus (see Straus, this volume). Since 1983, I have been working (3) in west-central Jordan, on a series of Upper Pleistocene rockshelter and open-air localities in the southern tributaries of the Wadi Hasa, a major wadi system that drains into the southeast corner of the Dead Sea depression near As-Safi (the Wadi Hasa Paleolithic Project, 1983–). This work is still in its preliminary stages (Clark et al. 1987). Because the research designs for these projects encapsulate my expectations about pattern and causality in the archaeological record, a brief review of one of them, the NSF-funded La Riera proposal (Clark and Straus 1975), might bring into sharper focus my attempts to "put biases to work" in the context of an actual field research project.

The La Riera Paleoecological Project

The La Riera project was focused on the "paleoecology" of the site, and on that of other Upper Paleolithic and Mesolithic sites in northern Spain. Papers published in the early/mid-1970s by Freeman, Altuna, Straus, and myself described patterns of apparent selectivity in the hunting and gathering practices of the prehistoric Cantabrians from ca. 45,000 to ca. 5,000 B.P. These models, derived in large part from the literature and based on both qualitative and (some) quantitative data, were expressed in terms of a typology of biotopes. Shifts in the intensity of exploitation of one biotope over another were noted through time and were thought to equate with decisions by the prehistoric inhabitants of the region. Evidence independent of faunal data had begun to accumulate that detailed macroclimatic change in temperature and moisture regimens over the interval corresponding to the Pleniglacial, Tardiglacial, and early post-Würm. We sought to develop paleoecological models using quantified measures of (plant and) animal species exploited and to try to relate stone tool and debitage characteristics to patterns of faunal exploitation, controlling for climatic change to the extent possible, given the near-absence of a large corpus of "modern quality" paleoenvironmental data. Primary variables were (1) climate, (2) vegetation, and (3) human activity at the site. Time was regarded as a "reference variable" controlled by radiocarbon dating and stratigraphy. Locational parameters were, initially, held constant; but we hoped eventually to be able to test the generality of our conclusions at La Riera against similar, "modern quality" data from other, contemporary Cantabrian sites.

The proposal was written during the "high tide" of confirmatory data analysis (i.e., hypothesis-testing approaches—Clark 1982), and, in keeping with the times, was rather rigid in the initial formulation of the research design. Four "nested" (hierarchically organized) hypotheses were to be tested; test implications were deduced, in each case, from the hypotheses. The first hypothesis sought to examine the relationship between biotope selection and macroclimatic change, and was to be an empirical test of the models for prehistoric subsistence practices developed by Freeman, Altuna, Clark, and Straus. The second hypothesis attempted to resolve the question of seasonal versus perennial occupation/use of the site during any given "cultural" unit represented in the sequence. The third sought to determine whether or not a covariant relationship existed among artifact and faunal debris categories, with the objective of assigning gross "functions" to the various levels in the cave. The fourth hypothesis sought to isolate adaptive shifts in what we believed to be an 11,000-year-long record of site use, and to determine whether or not these adaptive shifts could be correlated with the classic, prehistorian-defined culture/stratigraphic analytical units used by most French and Spanish workers. Each of the hypotheses was discussed at some length in terms of the assumptions that underlay it, the kinds of data required to put it to a test, and the "quality" of the data likely to become available in order to do that. Detailed test implications were generated in every case that would, theoretically, allow us conclusively to "accept" or "reject" the hypothesis. In some cases, generalized versions of hypotheses were also developed, in the event that the data actually obtained in excavation fell short of our expectations.

Ultimately, we hoped to be able to undertake a "processual" study of change in the subsistence aspects of a prehistoric economy, and to elucidate behavioral regularities in human adaptation in the Cantabrian region, by comparison of assemblages from similar periods but different locales and by comparison of assemblages from different periods at La Riera and at other sites. Skeptical of many of the biases in the "indigenous" paradigm, we postulated that many differences and similarities in artifact assemblages currently "explained" by recourse to temporally-sequent cultural or ethnic differences are more likely to be related to differences and similarities in recurrent human activities at particular places and moments in time. The argument was essentially a functionalist one, but without the implication of a harmoniously integrated, homeostatically regulated system. We also thought that these modal activity sets might vary independently of the classic culture/stratigraphic units to which these assemblages were customarily assigned (i.e., we recognized that such units were prehistorian-defined, and were not demonstrably socially or behaviorally "meaningful" in their own right). We pretentiously concluded that these were significant anthropological questions and issues (in case this was somehow lost on a reviewer!) that lay at the roots of an understanding of the recurrent behavioral regularities and changes in adaptation suggested by the descriptive models that we had outlined earlier. In short, it was a very "contemporary" research design, and contained all or most of the conventions adopted by Americanist "scientific archaeology" in the mid-1970s. It is worth remarking that, while Straus and I had our differences over the course of a ten-year collaboration, the fact that we are both products of the same (or similar) intellectual tradition(s) no doubt immensely facilitated working together. While there were disagreements about analytical and procedural matters and field methodology, the basic paradigm for the investigation of past human behavior embodied in the shared concept of "adaptation," and how it might be studied, remained intact throughout the long and exceedingly productive collaborative effort.

The work at La Riera has been extensively published in more than thirty articles and a monograph by Spanish, French, British, and American workers. The research showed that patterns in the abundant archaeological and faunal remains recovered from the thirty-six levels in the site were multiple and usually independent of the analytical units defined by conventional European typological systematics. We also found few correlations between episodes of climatic change and the composition of either the lithic assemblages or the subsistence base. Close correspondences between economic faunas and episodes of climatic change are perhaps expected under most European paradigms that (1) use poorly dated and coarse-grained "cultural" units as the basis for analysis, (2) hold that the ungulates that make up the bulk of the economic faunas accurately reflected the composition of the animal population in the site vicinity, (3) hold that the archaeofaunas were due largely or exclusively to human predation, (4) hold that the animals involved were tied to more or less restrictive sets of environmental conditions, and (5) hold that the topography of the region itself was largely undifferentiated. We also came to the conclusion that the situation at La Riera was hardly unique and that what we were witnessing at the cave were instances of region-wide, general phenomena visible (albeit with lower "resolution") in many north Spanish Upper Paleolithic and Mesolithic sites. This led us to question the credibility of the standard systematics and the conventional analytical units that resulted from them. By the late 1970s, problems with the temporal integrity of the conventional units could also no longer be ignored. The proliferation of absolute dates was bringing about a near-total collapse of the type-fossil based unilineal sequences first defined in France and used as a basis for most Spanish prehistory. Taken together, these "anomalies" resulted in a loss of faith in the explanatory potential of the Continental paradigm for paleolithic archaeology—a skepticism shared by most American and many British, but few European workers. Skepticism about the Continental paradigm was, of course, part of the original La Riera research design; but it was strikingly confirmed by the results of the actual fieldwork.

Biases Generalized

Americans working in the Old World often find themselves in conflict with or puzzled by the "conventional wisdom" of the Old World paradigms they encounter—the normal science practices of Old World archaeology as conducted from European perspectives (see Simmons, this volume). Like my European colleagues, I see my own biases (if an individual can have paradigmatic biases) as the combined result of three things: (1) my formal education as an anthropological archaeologist (see above—my degrees are from the universities of Arizona [1966, 1967] and Chicago [1971]); (2) the general kinds of problems and questions in which I have been interested over the long term (that is, the biological and cultural aspects of Pleistocene hunter-gatherer adaptations); and (3) the necessity for modifying these intellectual components to satisfy the requirements of actual field situations and data sets.

A Materialist Strategy

I am a cultural materialist in that I seek to account for differences and similarities in sociocultural phenomena by trying to understand the general material conditions that determine the economic infrastructure, which I take to be primary in the ancient time frames and relatively simple societies with which I work. However, I am a wishy-washy cultural materialist because I am also an archaeologist, have a strong pragmatic bent, and see little hope for the fully-integrated theoretical perspective that, for example, Marvin Harris (1979) envisions when dealing with the realities of archaeological data sets. I am forced to be eclectic, which means that I have opted for a set of theoretical principles derived from middle-level paradigms that are useful in problem contexts with which I must repeatedly come to terms.

It should be noted that the latter statement is the sort that would give Harris apoplexy, since he would see in it nothing more than a proliferation of potentially contradictory middle-range theories. However, I submit that eclecticism is an honorable anthropological tradition; and I see no real alternative to it, given the present lack of progress in *archaeological* theory building and the general disintegration of the parent discipline. I would hope that the problems and questions that make up my research interests would cohere to the extent that, if anyone were foolish enough to try to summarize my published work, the result would not be too internally contradictory. Nevertheless, I see evidence of considerable schizophrenic behavior in respect of attempts, including my own efforts, to reconcile the theoretical with the pragmatic aspects of doing field research. I consider fieldwork to be crucial in the sense that no idea, no matter how intellectually beguiling, has value unless its credibility can be tested empirically. Given my interests and orientation, this effectively rules out most "post-processual" archaeology, which usually cannot be subjected to any conceivable kind of empirical verification. I will have a few more nits to pick with the post-processualists later on.

Another aspect of the Marvin Harris brand of cultural materialism that I find appealing is his emphasis on the forces of production (rather than on the relations of the producers, as is typical of the marxist variant). I suggest that this emphasis is appropriate for hunter-gatherer archaeologists because the forces of production can usually be monitored or controlled in the archaeological context, even in ancient situations. As Trigger (1984) has pointed out, the experience of biology and the physical sciences indicates that *some* kind of materialist research strategy is essential for the construction of overarching scientific theories. In fact, I cannot see how any prehistoric archaeologist could fail to subscribe to materialist biases, given the nature of the data base, and still expect to subject theories to some kind of empirical verification. That the acceptance or rejection of theory must ultimately rest on probability statements—a fact that some might find objectionable—doesn't bother me a bit, probably because my own statistical background predisposes me toward explanations couched in probabilistic terms and because deterministic models are notoriously inadequate except in situations where causality is simple, linear and direct. The latter has been recognized for a long time even in the quintessentially experimental discipline of physics (see, e.g., papers in Kitchener 1988).

Some readers are probably thinking that it is exceptionally difficult to quantify archaeological data on a scale grand enough so that patterns become evident and amenable to testing. While I acknowledge this to be true, I think that we must make the attempt. We have to get away from the restrictions inherent in confirmatory approaches, a legacy of the 1970s effort to be "explicitly scienterrific," and make greater use of more flexible exploratory methods, which were themselves developed to avoid the constraints of the classic Neymann-Pearson statistical models that underlie hypothesis testing as it is usually construed in laboratory science. Put another way, if we want to be scientific at all (which from some recent perspectives is an arguable proposition), we should spend some time worrying about what *kind* of science we want to be. There are several different "kinds" of science. As Dunnell (1982) has observed, it is very likely that the archetypal "big science" model of physics, promoted with such enthusiasm by "explicitly scientific" archaeologists in the 1970s (e.g., and especially, Watson et al. 1971), is structurally inappropriate to a "time-like" discipline like archaeology (see also Gingerich 1985).

The recipe for my theoretical perspective also includes selected aspects of optimal foraging theory, especially diet breadth models, which I think have generalizable explanatory properties and which can often be operationalized in archaeological contexts. An emphasis on the demographic and environmental variables that constrain the forces of production is also part of my work, as is a commitment to a quantitative approach, and a picture of the Upper Pleistocene archaeological record that is probably at variance with that of many other workers (Clark 1989b, c). I recognize that this eclecticism precludes theory building at its highest, most abstract levels and that a quantitative perspective can only produce probabilistic (and because of the eclecticism, middle-range) theories. I am content with these limitations, however, and I regard them as a compromise forced on me by the nature of the archaeological data in the time ranges and areas in which I work. I think such compromises are inevitable in the absence of cohesive, overarching general theory for any archaeologist who seeks to test his or her ideas against actual data sets.

Arguments for the utility of a cultural materialist paradigm for prehistoric archaeology have recently been published by Kohl (1981), Trigger (1984), and Price (1982). All that a materialist paradigm really claims is that the causes of behavior are best sought in relation to the material conditions of life (that is, the technoeconomy of production). A materialist paradigm can comfortably accommodate the systems perspectives that are so much a part of contemporary research designs (that is, there is no need to postulate a prime mover or single factor model of causality). Cultural materialist explanations also rely upon a relatively small number of causal parameters and are, therefore, easier to operationalize. Finally, because of the emphasis on the technoeconomy of production, those causal parameters are precisely the ones that can be monitored most effectively in ancient hunter-gatherer contexts.

A Critique of the Radical Critique

The last few years have witnessed a reaction to the creation of a "scientific" archaeology, with the positivist underpinnings of processual archaeology being assailed on various fronts by "post-processualists," "neo-structuralists," "structural marxists," symbolic and contextual archaeologists of various persuasions (e.g., papers in Hodder 1982; Hodder 1985). While several philosophically and historically distinct perspectives are represented in these assaults, its critics seem to be agreed that processual archaeology has been a failure, that the scientific method and the quest for "laws" have produced few significant generalizations in our understanding of the past, and that we should look instead to symbolic anthropology for rules and principles that would help us make sense of an archaeological record. Archaeology is redefined as an historical discipline, in which meaning and sense are ever-changing, contextual, and dependent upon the symbolic order. Interpretation is considered a direct, intuitive process and is substituted for verification.

While I think that there is substance to some of the criticisms levelled at the *results* of processual archaeology (especially the notion that, with its concentration on the environment and on ecology, social factors are minimized), it also seems to me that the radical critique has utterly rejected any notion of a disinterested evaluation of the credibility of its precepts and ideas. It is a cornerstone of western philosophy of science that there is an empirically verifiable reality that exists apart from our perceptions of it. Our perceptions of that reality might be faulty or incomplete, and they certainly are paradigm dependent, but that does not obviate the existence of the external world (Commins and Linscott 1947). It is one thing to argue that because science is paradigm dependent, the results of scientific enquiry must therefore always be subjective. It is quite another to assert, as Hodder has done, that we should eschew explanation and verification altogether and essentially become humanists, interpreting—or, better, creating—a past of our choosing, out of our view of our culture and/or our culturally conditioned perceptions of the ethnographically recorded cultures of others (Binford 1987).

It has not escaped the attention of its critics that the radical approach is always most successful when reliance is placed on historical and ethnographic data (e.g., Earle and Preucel 1987). I submit that an "archaeology of mind" (Leone 1982) is totally unworkable in the absence of ethnographic or historical sources against which individual motivation and the symbolic order of things can be identified and checked. In default of a written record, the archaeologist has no mechanism for getting into the minds of people long dead. To claim that we can somehow intuit the principles according to which past individuals organized and constructed their cultural worlds is a cop-out and a charter to redefine the discipline along humanistic lines (and, in some deplorable cases, to use it as a vehicle for the promotion of a sociopolitical agenda). So long as we wish to be scientists, however, we cannot create any old past we choose. It seems to me that much post-processual archaeology is to varying degrees anti-scientific and has turned its back on the quest for the explanatory and predictive principles that are the foundation of all western science.

This stance is most emphatically *not* a call for a return to the "age of innocence" (Clarke 1973). It is simply an acknowledgment of the fact that western science, with all of its imperial warts, is *solely responsible* for the unparalleled growth of knowledge that characterizes the contemporary world. The alternatives offered by post-processual archaeology are not scientifically viable because, in the absence of written records or living informants, there is no way to evaluate objectively the credibility of its knowledge claims. As Trigger (1983) has noted, controlling for cognitive processes in the formation of an archaeological record is a great deal more complex than most workers would have realized (and, if we owe anything at all to symbolic archaeology, it is the realization that this is so). But do we need to control for them? From a strict materialist perspective, the answer is no: cognitive processes are epi-phenomenal and are largely determined by the relations of produc-tion. They could be argued to have only a limited influence over the rest of the sociocultural system. On the other hand, if cognitive pro-cesses do in fact play a major role in determining the form of a so-ciocultural system, then the potential contribution of prehistoric ar-chaeology to the explanation of social process questions would be correspondingly limited. The relative importance accorded to cogni-tive processes by different workers is bound up with issues of paradig-matic bias. I prefer to think, since the problems with verification are, so far, insurmountable in the post-processualist camp, that prehistoric archaeologists have no real alternative to materialist biases. No doubt Hodder would disagree.

Paradigms in Conflict: Modern Human Origins in the Levant

The debate over the biological and cultural origins of modern humans in the Levant and western Asia is a superb example of paradigm conflict, not only because cleavage planes have tended to coincide with national research traditions, but also because the debate involves rela-tively clear-cut positions in human paleontology and molecular biology that archaeologists have invoked to support their views about the nature of the cultural transition between the Middle and the Upper Paleolithic. Despite occasional assertions to the contrary (e.g., Bar Yosef and Meignen 1989), the evidence from one of these fields clearly has implications for the findings of the others and, while it is reason-able to expect that some linkages would be apparent, those linkages are not necessarily linear or direct. Paradigmatic biases about the nature of biological and cultural evolution underlie many of the differences of opinion expressed in the literature and in public forums and affect choices of evolutionary models, which in turn determine the variables considered significant to monitor. These are "paradigms with a capital P"—paradigms at the level of the metaphysic that tell us, from quite distinct perspectives, what biological and cultural evolution is sup-posedly "like."

Much of my recent work, and that of my students John Lindly and Nancy Coinman, constitutes a reaction to the idea, heavily promoted in the media, that morphologically modern humans evolved only in Africa and replaced either archaic *Homo sapiens* or "neandertals" throughout their range with little or no admixture. This is the major implication of the mitochondrial DNA scenario for an African origin for moderns promulgated by Rebecca Cann and her colleagues (1987) and too readily accepted by archaeological "replacement" advocates (e.g., Gowlett 1987, Foley 1987, 1989; Mellars 1989—all Brits, interestingly enough).

Hypotheses

Two opposing hypotheses have been offered to describe (and supposedly explain) the transition between archaic and modern humans in the Levant. Hypothesis No. 1 states that moderns appeared early there, and coexisted with archaic *Homo sapiens* (AHS), who arrived at a later date. Hypothesis No. 2 states that moderns evolved there, as elsewhere, from the local archaic *Homo sapiens* stock. The recently published thermoluminescence dates for supposedly modern humans at Qafzeh Cave in Israel (Valladas et al. 1988), and the later TL determinations for alleged neandertals at nearby Kebara Cave (Valladas et al. 1987), have led to claims that Levantine neandertals are later immigrants from Europe and are unrelated to modern human origins in the Levant. While the Qafzeh and Kebara dates are provocative, what they mean is open to question.

Supporters of Hypothesis 1 might be called *replacement advocates*. They make a distinction between AHS and "neandertals" and postulate a series of adaptive radiations out of Africa, rather than a single prolonged one. They typically ignore grade/clade distinctions, emphasize cladogenic over anagenic speciation, invoke "splitter" taxonomies and dendritic phylogenies. They seek support for a particular construal of the fossil evidence by invoking a chronology implied by a particular construal of the mitochondrial DNA evidence (Cann et al. 1987). They suggest that archaic *Homo sapiens* was displaced or extirpated by moderns in the Levant (and elsewhere), and that there was little or no admixture between them. This is the replacement without gene flow position advocated by many Continental and Israeli scholars (e.g., Bar Yosef et al. 1986, Bar Yosef and Meignen 1989; see also Stringer and Andrews 1988, Stringer et al. 1984, Lévêque and Vandermeersch 1980).

Supporters of Hypothesis 2 might be called *continuity advocates*. They consider neandertals to be the European and west Asian clades of AHS and postulate a single prolonged hominid radiation out of Africa corresponding to the *Homo erectus* grade in human evolution. They emphasize grade/clade distinctions, anagenic over cladogenic speciation, "lumper" taxonomies, and reticulate phylogenies. They claim that moderns evolved from AHS throughout the range originally colonized by *Homo erectus*. They see many indications of morphological (hence genetic) continuity in the fossil evidence and invoke a chronology implied by another construal of the mtDNA evidence, that of Masatoshi Nei (1985, 1987). They suggest that admixture was not only likely but inevitable (assuming, for the sake of argument, the presence of "immigrants") and that local continuity and gene flow, rather than replacement without admixture, characterized the evolution of modern humans in the Levant and elsewhere. This is the multiregional continuity position first advocated by Schwalbe, Hrdlička and Weidenreich more than fifty years ago (Wolpoff 1980, Spencer 1984). While the replacement advocates have garnered most of the publicity so far (cover articles in *Newsweek, Time* and so forth), a coordinated response is gathering momentum on the archaeological, human paleontological and molecular biological fronts.

Archaeology

The continuity position in archaeology is being pushed by me and Lindly (1988, 1989a, b), Sackett (1988), Simek (Simek and Snyder 1988, Simek and Price 1990), Straus (1990a, Straus and Heller 1988), Marshack (1988a, b; 1989) and others—mostly Americans. The argument is simply that if one looks at anything more comprehensive than the retouched stone tools emphasized by traditional systematics, there is continuity in human adaptation over *both* the Middle/Upper Paleolithic transition *and* the biological transition between archaic and modern *Homo sapiens*—that is, vectored, clinal change in the major technological characterists of lithic industries, faunal exploitation (can't say much about plants), raw material procurement, and settlement patterns—in short, all of the things archaeologists use to monitor human adaptation. Even in the hopelessly inadequate (although time-honored) systematics of European paleolithic archaeology, there is evidence for continuity. Supposedly "diagnostic" Middle and Upper Paleolithic tools often do not assort themselves in time the way they are supposed to according to French type sequences and, further, are often produced on similar kinds of blanks, indicating technological continuity crosscutting or operating independently of typological discontinuity. Although research is more preliminary in western Asia, anomalies with normative Middle and Upper Paleolithic type sequences underscore similar problems with Levantine systematics (e.g., Lindly and Clark 1987, Coinman 1990).

Human Paleontology

So far as human paleontology is concerned, the chief modern advocates of continuity are Milford Wolpoff (1980, 1989) and, of course, the intellectual father of the multiregional continuity model, C. Loring Brace (1964, 1967, 1988b; Brace et al. n.d., see also Smith and Trinkaus n.d.). The adversaries are either Brits (Stringer, Andrews) or Continentals (Vandermeersch, Hublin, Brauer) with a few Americans thrown in (Howell, probably Klein). Continuity advocates insist upon grade/clade distinctions, emphasize anagenesis (over cladogenesis) and "lumper" over "splitter" taxonomies, and contend that there was only a single, prolonged hominid radiation out of Africa between about 1.7 and 0.7 million years ago, corresponding to the *Homo erectus* grade in human evolution. Substantial gene flow between *Homo erectus* and *Homo sapiens* is postulated and, therefore, local continuity between archaic and modern populations throughout the geographical range originally colonized by *Homo erectus*.

Figure 4.1 shows a reticulate phylogeny for the later phases of human evolution of the type supported by Brace and Wolpoff. It is based on the idea that the human evolutionary record is characterized by broad and very roughly contemporaneous similarities in organizational level (grades) and by characteristics indicating common descent within a region that are superimposed on grade features (clades). Grade features are most convincingly defined in terms of functional morphology (e.g., Trinkaus 1986) and are only meaningful in relation to features characteristic of bracketing taxa.

Advocates of the replacement position typically ignore grade/clade distinctions, emphasize cladogenesis (over anagenesis) and "splitter" over "lumper" taxonomies, and appeal for support to the Cann construal of the mtDNA evidence. They contend that *Homo erectus* and archaic *Homo sapiens* were replaced throughout their ranges by moderns sometime between 200,000 and 400,000 years ago. Figure 4.2, taken from a recent article by Rob Foley (1987), shows a typical dendritic phylogeny of the kind supported by Leakey, Walker, Stringer, and Vandermeersch. Notice that a series of adaptive radiations are postulated, rather than a single unilinear, multiregional process. All but one of the "branches" end in extinction.

A Levantine Example

To illustrate the contrasting positions with an example from the Levant, replacement advocates allege that the founding population of anatomically modern people from Africa had already reached Qafzeh Cave in Israel by about 90–100 kyr B.P. (Valladas et al. 1988). The apparent "fact" that neandertal remains at nearby Kebara date to a more recent time interval (Valladas et al. 1987) suggests to them either (1) that morphological moderns and neandertals lived side by side for

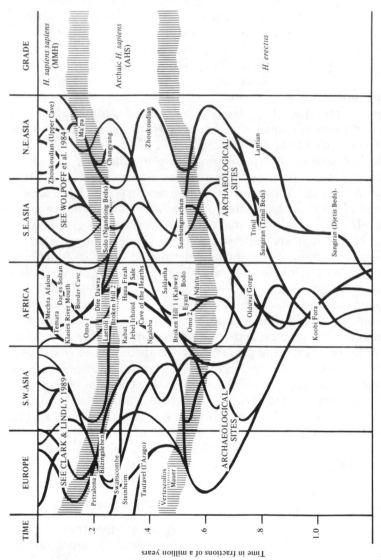

FIGURE 4.1. A reticulate grade model for the later phases of hominid evolution. A single, long term adaptive radiation corresponding to the *Homo erectus* grade is assumed, with substantial gene flow between the colonizing *Homo erectus* population and subsequent populations of archaic *Homo sapiens*.

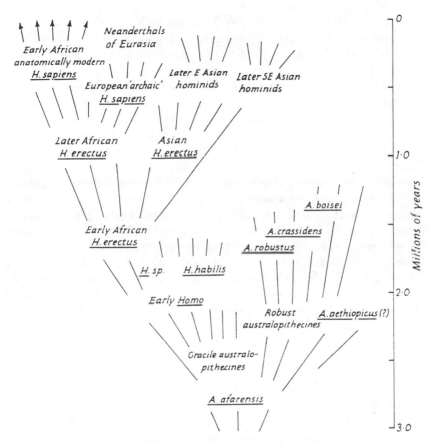

FIGURE 4.2.   A dendritic model for hominid evolution. A series of adaptive radiations is assumed, and a series of replacements, with little or no gene flow between colonizing and subsequent populations (except in Africa) (after Foley 1987, used with the author's permission and the permission of *Antiquity*).

more than 50 kyr without interbreeding or (2) that neandertals moved southward into the Levant from Europe around 60 kyr B.P. where they coexisted with modern people until the latter began to colonize Europe about 25,000 years later (Bar Yosef et al. 1986, Bar Yosef and Meignen 1989, Bar Yosef n.d. a, b). The 92 kyr B.P. TL dates for alleged moderns at Qafzeh have often and vociferously been invoked by replacement advocates in support of their position. They constitute an anomaly which, replacement advocates contend, cannot be satisfactorily explained by the tenets of the continuity paradigm. The dates are only anomalous, however, if it is accepted (1) that paleoanthropologists can really distinguish a "neandertal" from a morphological modern,

(2) that the differences between them are differences at or near the "species" level, and (3) that a plausible explanation is forthcoming as to how on earth two allegedly different hominids (i.e., neandertals, moderns) could have coexisted for nearly 50,000 years in an area about the size of Indiana without interbreeding (thereby implying that they are indeed different species) and without showing any archaeological differences in adaptation. To anyone well grounded in evolutionary ecology, the idea is preposterous on the face of it. Yet this is exactly what some Continental and Israeli scholars are arguing. Although my objections to this point of view are not based just on the lithics, most Levantine prehistorians (including, ironically, some of the replacement advocates) would acknowledge that the industries associated with neandertals at Kebara and moderns at Qafzeh are in general and in most details alike. In short, not what one would expect from a replacement scenario! Bar Yosef and Meignen (1989) have asserted that the contemporaneity of AHS and MMHs in Israel is an indication of no direct relationship between them and their cultural attributes (i.e., their archaeological assemblages). I think instead that it is much more likely that the validity of the biological taxonomic units themselves is suspect.

Molecular Biology

With respect to molecular biology, the sticking point with the Cann mtDNA scenario has always been that no admixture could be accommodated. This means that differences between moderns and other earlier hominids *had to be at the species level*. Replacement advocates picked up on the rapid base substitution rate published by Cann (2–4%/myr), which indicated a modern human origin somewhere in Africa at about 300,000 years ago. There was little realization by archaeologists and paleoanthropologists that, first, other base substitution rates were published and defended—especially that of Nei (0.71%/myr, which implies a hominid radiation out of Africa ca. 800,000 years ago corresponding to the *Homo erectus* grade). These other rates can be reconciled much more easily with the fossil and archaeological records than can that of Cann (Wolpoff 1989, Spuhler 1988). Second, most people didn't realize (initially, at least) that the Cann rate implied an absurdly late hominid/ pongid split, at about 3.5 million years ago, for which there is no fossil evidence whatsoever. Finally, there seemed to be little realization by archaeologists and paleontologists that, just like any other field, molecular biology has an internal dynamic characterized by the same kinds of controversy and debate found in other disciplines. In short, replacement advocates jumped on the Cann bandwagon because it supported their biases about the course of human evolution, and without having the foggiest notion of just how incompatible her arguments were with the fossil and archaeological records (Clark and Lindly 1988, 1989a, b). In fact, the whole field of DNA clock models is becoming increasingly problematical, as indicated by a number of recent exchanges in the journal *Science* (Lewin 1988b, c). Because they are relatively new, mitochondrial DNA clock models suffer from these conceptual and methodological drawbacks to an even greater extent than nuclear DNA clock models, which have a much longer history.

Summary of Biases and Conclusions

To try to pull all this together a bit, the points we continuity advocates are trying to make are these. First, preconceptions about human biological evolution have real consequences for interpretations of the archaeological record. Things that are "reasonable to conclude" under one set of paradigmatic biases are "not reasonable to conclude" under another. A second point is that biological replacement without admixture runs counter to *any* construal of the archaeological evidence. Third, we contend that cladistics (in fact, cladogenic speciation models), on which replacement advocates rely, has major practical and conceptual problems (Gingerich 1984, 1985; Clark 1988, 1989a, b). Fourth, we believe that the archaeological record over both the biological transition from archaic to modern humans *and* the cultural transition from the Middle to the Upper Paleolithic shows overwhelming evidence for continuity on any and all archaeological monitors of adaptation. Discontinuity would clearly be expected under all the replacement scenarios published so far. Fifth, we argue that the two transitions did not coincide in time and were, therefore, probably not directly or immediately related to one another. Sixth, we think that the archaeological time/space grid, because it is more complete than that of the fossil evidence, can sometimes stand as a sort of proxy for monitoring (or at least generating test implications about) biological evolution. Seventh, we recognize no correlation whatsoever between archaeological industries and particular hominid taxa, as has recently been claimed by some British workers (e.g., Foley 1987). Finally, we think that archaeological evidence for fully modern behavioral patterns post-dates the Middle/Upper Paleolithic transition by at least 15,000 to 20,000 years. In other words, the advent of the Upper Paleolithic at ca. 40 kyr B.P. does not also mark the appearance of biological moderns equipped with a fully modern behavioral repertoire (*contra* White 1989; cf. Clark and Lindly 1989a, b). That happens later, between 20,000 and 15,000 years ago. In terms of cultural evolution, the boundary between the early Upper Paleolithic and the late Upper Paleolithic at about 20 kyr B.P. is beginning to look like a more significant behavioral "Rubicon" than the traditional boundary between the Middle and the Upper Paleolithic at about 40 kyr B.P. In a recent issue of *Archaeology*, Rob Foley (1989) predicted that, by AD 2050, neandertals will have been shown to be doomed to extinction without issue, to have played no role in modern human origins. I am, of course, inclined to take exactly the opposite position. As C. Loring Brace recently put it, so far as Europeans are concerned, "we have met the neandertals, and they are us"![1]

Note

1. Discussion at the 87th annual meeting of the American Anthropological Association, 16–20 November 1988, Phoenix, Arizona.

Chapter 5
Straight Archaeology French Style: The Phylogenetic Paradigm in Historic Perspective

James R. Sackett

Introduction

Paleontologists tell me they doubt that the existence of the dinosaurs, at least the more spectacular ones, could ever have been inferred from a knowledge of extant reptiles alone. And even though dinosaurs are now so richly represented in the fossil record, there is much about them that remains inexplicable in terms of modern reptilian anatomy and physiology. The same can be said of the manner and extent to which historically documented hunter-gatherer cultures inform upon the more spectacular achievements of Stone Age times such as the Upper Paleolithic of western Europe. So much about this key stage of culture history seems alien and beyond the imaginative grasp of even an ethnographically sophisticated prehistorian. This fundamental ambiguity in particular envelops what might be regarded as the basic anatomy that structures its archaeological record, that is, the formal patterning displayed by Upper Paleolithic stone industries over space and time—a realm that can be termed interassemblage variability or, as I prefer, *industrial variation*. The tools may rival in abundance and degree of patterning those artifacts with which archaeologists of later periods ply their trade. Yet in comparison they seem silent and even defiant, possessing a special power to frustrate the prehistorian who aims to unveil the paleoethnological world of peoples and life-ways that lies behind them.

In the opinion of many Americans who have enjoyed the privilege of working in France and its west European neighbors, the problem is compounded by the manner in which lithic systematics itself is practiced. French systematics (in this broader geographic sense) gives the appearance of being self-contained and inward looking, a confined and even scholastic enterprise. More important, it seemingly fails, at least in any explicit fashion, to order industrial variation in what an anthropologically oriented prehistorian would regard as culturally meaningful terms. Instead it generates classificatory schemes that often seem to suggest an essentially paleontological model of the archaeological record more in keeping with a branch of natural, rather than cultural, history. Many of us have consequently found ourselves at one time or another referring to French systematics as being "phylogenetic" in nature. However, by right of possession earned through their numerous and provocative writings on the topic, the term now properly belongs to Lawrence Straus and Geoffrey Clark, who have given it a quite specific meaning. In their view, the weaknesses of French systematics, at least insofar as it concerns Upper Paleolithic times, stem from being grounded in the *phylogenetic paradigm,* which supposedly has dictated the assumptions and practices of researchers throughout most of the present century.

A reading of the sources in which Straus and Clark develop their views suggests they are actually looking toward the future, and to a considerable degree use the phylogenetic paradigm as a foil against which to contrast new ideas and approaches which they hope will lead to a paradigm more attuned to modern trends. Nonetheless, their thesis is couched in historic terms and warrants being dealt with in kind. What follows will review somewhat more than a century of French Upper Paleolithic research, comparing their views regarding the historic development of its logic of inquiry to my own. It will be seen that we arrive at quite different conclusions. But it will also be seen that there is more than antiquarian interest in knowing how and why our largely forgotten predecessors came to pose the questions with which we still struggle today. For there is one point on which Straus, Clark, and I heartily agree: we should have a better idea of where we are going if we have a clear idea of where we came from.

The Phylogenetic Paradigm

The notion of the phylogenetic paradigm emerged in the 1970s during the course of work Straus and Clark were pursuing in Cantabrian Spain, research that culminated in their joint excavations at La Riera (1986a). It was forged in the conflict of their own ideas and findings with the more conventional views held by many European archaeologists working in the region. But by extension it quickly became applied to what they regard as the received opinion that guides Upper Paleolithic archaeology in the greater French sphere as a whole. Let it be stressed that I greatly admire the innovative research of Straus and Clark. La Riera, for example, justly deserves recognition as one of prehistory's key resources, and the ideas generated there are playing an important role in the revisionist movement now taking place among Late Paleolithic archaeologists throughout Europe (for one account of which see Sackett 1988a). My disagreement is rather with the general thesis of the phylogenetic paradigm, with which Straus and Clark's work is associated and in whose terms it is often framed.

Attempting to comprehend the shape and thrust of the Straus-Clark thesis requires collating several sources, as no single one offers a complete picture. My understanding of it stems largely from a reading of Straus and Clark 1978, 1986b; Clark 1987a; and Straus 1986c, d; 1987a. These differ somewhat from one another in detail and emphasis; they also give the impression that Clark may regard the paradigm in somewhat less doctrinaire terms than does Straus (see especially Straus 1987a). In any event, I believe a reasonable characterization of the thrust of their thesis might read as follows.

The phylogenetic paradigm was initiated by Henri Breuil in his classic publication of 1913 and continued to guide the work of two major figures who have in turn dominated Upper Paleolithic archaeology in the Périgord—Denis Peyrony and Denise de Sonneville-Bordes. (It is occasionally referred to as either the "Breuil" or the "Breuil-Peyrony-de Sonneville-Bordes" paradigm.) It has four basic tenets. First, the industrial sequence derived from the key sites of the Périgord has essentially universal validity throughout western Europe; in other words, regions such as the Pyrenées or Cantabria can for classificatory purposes be regarded as appendages of southwest France. Second, classifying the Upper Paleolithic calls for establishing a taxonomic scheme comprising a unilineal temporal succession of industrial phases whose sequencing is inherently directional in nature and is based upon preconceived, a priori, vitalistic notions of technological evolution. Third, these phases are construed in a highly stereotyped or "normative" fashion, a practice that has two important consequences. One is that, since normatively defining phases is an inherently restrictive, variety-reducing procedure, it discourages researchers from recognizing novel or anomalous industrial variability in a time slot already occupied by an established phase in a taxonomic scheme. The other is that, when such variability does happen to receive notice, it is unlikely to be incorporated within (and thereby broaden) that phase's definition; instead, in keeping with the second tenet, it is more likely to be given special temporal significance of its own. The paradigm's fourth tenet is that industrial phases are assumed to be culturally significant in the sense of constituting material expressions of specific ethnic groups. An important corollary of this, which probably could be listed as a fifth tenet in its own right, is that variability in the archaeological record is to be explained in cultural (i.e., ethnic) terms, to the exclusion of other possible sources of variability such as functional differences arising from the activities in which the assemblages were made and served.

Gaining a full grasp of the Straus-Clark thesis is impeded not only by the inconsistencies in the basic sources noted above but also by certain omissions. One is that several key terms, such as "vitalistic," "normative," and even "phylogenetic," are never clearly defined. Another is that the thesis is largely presented as a series of assertions rather than as an organized argument that explicates the logic and specific historical circumstances that account for and give coherence to its individual tenets. It sometimes fails to suggest, in other words, either immersion in the original sources or an attempt to view the researchers who preceded us empathetically in the context of their own time. Finally, it remains unclear just how the thought of Straus and Clark may have been influenced by others. Although he is rarely cited, one seems to hear echoes of Lewis Binford in many of their terms and much of their method. A Binfordian chord is surely struck by their gratuitous equation of "cultural" with "ethnic," which serves to restrict a general term essential for anthropological discourse to a specific meaning for which a perfectly adequate word already exists. And one finds their thesis actually being referred to as the "normative paradigm" and even attributed to a "normative school." The matter will only be touched upon in this essay, as its detailed consideration might easily have an effect opposite that of clarifying the issues at stake. Yet noting it should serve to remind the reader that what follows is only a preliminary sally into broad and controversial territory, that it may beg as many questions as it addresses, and that its success will in part depend upon eliciting further discussion from Straus and Clark regarding the very real issues they have directed to our attention.

Some History

Now, the Heroic age of French archaeology ended shortly after 1859, with the scientific world's recognition of a Paleolithic Age based upon the claims of Boucher de Perthes and his colleagues for the association of human remains with extinct Pleistocene animals. French paleolithic research subsequently passed through three stages, which began respectively in the early 1860s, shortly after 1900, and around 1950 (Sackett 1981). These may be termed respectively the Formative, Traditional, and Bordesian eras. The first of these saw paleolithic research established as a scientific discipline, and therefore deserves some attention. Although Straus and Clark ignore it, it is the only era in which French research was conducted in terms that to my mind recall the phylogenetic paradigm. The second began with Breuil and was dominated, at least insofar as the Périgord is concerned, by Peyrony. For better or worse, it defined how French prehistorians were to regard the culture-historical significance of the Upper Paleolithic, established the ground rules for attacking its archaeological record, and created the scientific idiom in terms of which that attack would be conducted. This era then is of key importance and will receive the bulk of our attention. The third era is of course named after François Bordes, whose approach continues to dictate most conventional archaeology right down to the present. The Bordesian approach in effect governs Stone Age research throughout western Eurasia. But it is closely allied with the Périgord, where research has been dominated by the Bordes school at the University of Bordeaux, of which his wife, Denise de Sonneville-Bordes, has been the leading Upper Paleolithic specialist. The Bordesian era will be dealt with only briefly, as it carries us away from times that can be viewed with historic perspective into the very lively and tangled issues which preoccupy contemporary archaeology. Their detailed consideration is best deferred for another day.

A word is in order regarding my use of certain terms in what follows. "French" refers not only to France itself but also to neighboring countries, such as Spain, whose research evolved more or less in tandem and has entailed essentially the same outlook. "American" refers to researchers who, with some exceptions, come from North America and whose intellectual orientation is strongly influenced by American anthropological archaeology. (Given that some British prehistorians fall into this category, it might not unreasonably bear the label "Anglo-American.") The term "Périgord" is used rather broadly but still with archaeological integrity to refer not only to the Department of the Dordogne but also adjoining departments, particularly Corrèze and the Charente. Finally, because the Straus-Clark thesis places such a narrow construction upon the word "cultural," I follow French practice and employ "paleoethnological" in many instances where American usage would normally call for the former term.

The Formative Era

The 1860s saw congresses, journals, exhibitions, and even university chairs established in France to promote research into the new field of paleolithic archaeology. Glyn Daniel's review of the successive classificatory schemes it generated for ordering Stone Age times is a useful chronicle (1975:99–109, 122–128). But it fails to hint at the complex mixture of thought, approach, and more than a touch of irony that lay behind these schemes.

Edouard Lartet

The eminent paleontologist Edouard Lartet (1801–1871) attempted to subdivide the paleolithic into temporal stages based upon the succession of certain major Pleistocene mammals (1861). But allied with this patently geological approach to archaeological systematics was one of the most ambitious attempts at paleoethnology the field has seen. This was the great *Reliquiae Aquitanicae* which grew out of Lartet's joint work in the rockshelters of the Perigord with the London banker Henry Christy, a highly capable amateur archaeologist and collector of ethnographic materials. Published serially over a decade (1865–1875) and completed only after the deaths of its principal authors, the book's many contributors sought to illuminate Lartet and Christy's archaeological results with information on such diverse topics as the habits of reindeer and game birds and the fishing and hunting techniques of native Canadian tribes. A particularly modern note is struck by Lartet's interpretation of the quite dissimilar artifact assemblages from Laugerie-Haute (essentially Solutrean) and La Madeleine (Magdalenian), which his faunal scheme indicated to be quasi-contemporary. Their differences might as easily be attributed to the contrasting practices of neighboring groups of different ethnic composition as to local specializations in site use by one and the same group. Here we see an open-minded appreciation of the two fundamental kinds of information paleoethnology attempts to wrest from industrial variation—what was going on and who was doing it, in other words, the complementary issues of activity and ethnicity. It is the same question that François Bordes and Lewis Binford were to debate in more doctrinaire terms a century later with respect to Mousterian interassemblage variability.

Gabriel de Mortillet

Considerable contrast marked the thought of Lartet's pupil and successor, Gabriel de Mortillet (1821–1898), with whose name the Formative era is most closely associated. He was the first to classify the Paleolithic in what his age referred to as "archaeological" terms—even though their obvious kinship to geological practice was acknowledged (de Mortillet 1867). Its successive "epochs" were named after archaeological sites (e.g., Magdalenian from La Madeleine), and each was identified in terms of its diagnostic index types, the *fossiles directeurs*.

Thanks to de Mortillet's prolific and authoritative writings, this epochal classification soon became the standard frame for paleolithic research throughout Western Europe.

Yet, though the terms in which it was cast are familiar to the modern ear, Mortilletian systematics was grounded upon assumptions that to us seem alien indeed. Instead of constituting discrete artifact complexes, the epochs represented vaguely delimited temporal phases within a unilinear succession of paleolithic technological evolution that was seemingly held to be valid for Western Europe as a whole. In a manner never made specific, this industrial stream was regarded as the behavioral concomitant of a similarly unbroken, if largely hypothetical, line of hominid evolution indigenous to France, beginning with the highly simian makers of Chellean hand-axes and culminating in the still not fully human possessors of Magdalenian culture. (De Mortillet never accepted the validity of Upper Paleolithic burials, maintaining that true human beings only subsequently entered France as intruders bearing Neolithic culture.) Hence, while only the prelude to truly human history, the Upper Paleolithic nonetheless constituted the fundamental point of departure in man's evolution and progress—notions that were essentially interchangeable in de Mortillet's enthusiastic if vague brand of nineteenth-century vitalism.

At a more prosaic but crucial level, what appears most disconcerting to us about Mortilletian systematics, and indeed the entire era it represents, is the thinness of the empirical base upon which it rested. De Mortillet's publications are richly illustrated with both archaeological and ethnographic objects, between which the reader is invited to see piecemeal points of similarity. But they betray no rigorous knowledge of artifact variation apart from the obvious *fossile* types. As Hallam Movius has shown, the basic technology and range of form making up burins, the single most numerous Upper Paleolithic tool family, was not really appreciated until after the turn of the century (1968). Equally important, the stratigraphic basis of de Mortillet's scheme was even less firmly established than that of the fauna-based one it had replaced. Logic, in the form of simple-minded notions of technological evolution, had usurped stratigraphy as the basis of temporal ordering. This is tellingly illustrated by the fate of what Lartet originally identified as the Aurignacian, which we now recognize as the complex Aurignaco-Perigordian block of industries that occupies the entire first half of the Upper Paleolithic. De Mortillet, following his mentor's lead, at first correctly placed it as a distinct epoch preceding the Solutrean and Magdalenian (1867). But it was soon redefined as the initial phase of the Magdalenian by virtue of the fact that, unlike the Solutrean, it possessed bone and ivory work, whereas the Solutrean exhibited bifacially chipped stone tools supposedly reminiscent of Mousterian technology (de Mortillet 1873). Shortly afterward even the term Aurignacian itself disappeared from de Mortillet's publications.

In its universal unilineal sequence, narrowly defined *fossile*-based industrial phases, vitalism, preconceived notions of technological evolution, and silence on the causes of variability in the archaeological record, the modern reader would have little difficulty seeing much of Straus and Clark's phylogenetic paradigm in de Mortillet's thought. (They themselves, however, ignore him, apparently as a result of holding Breuil responsible for its invention.) But there seems little else to arrest one's attention. By the mid-1880s, paleolithic research had entered a period of stagnation. For one thing, the rejection of unilateral cultural evolutionism by ethnologists had taken away the promise of reconstructing Stone Age life-ways through the search for straightforward ethnographic parallels. It in fact helped doom serious paleoethnological research for three generations, thereby contributing much toward breaking paleolithic archaeology's tentative alliance with cultural anthropology and simultaneously reinforcing its traditional ties to geology. For another, advances in the quality and grasp of purely empirical research slowed to a crawl (see Smith 1966:13). And industrial systematics itself relaxed into the arms of received opinion. Nowhere is this more pronounced than in the later publications of de Mortillet, whose scheme continued to enjoy widespread acceptance even though it had come to assume a dogmatic rigidity not unlike that which had overtaken the man himself. His popular *Le Préhistorique,* which first appeared in 1883, reminds one of a well organized but too perfect museum case, whose exhibits and labels convey a sense of clarity and order that quite belie the ambiguities and complexities of the archaeological record they supposedly characterize. As Marcellin Boule was later to comment, the book provides the strange spectacle of a fervent evolutionist giving the most perfect example of scientific immutability (1910:428).

The remainder of the formative era offers only occasional points of interest, such as Emile Cartailhac's rumblings about the weaknesses of the Mortilletian scheme and Edouard Piette's successive classifications of the Upper Paleolithic sequence of the French Pyrenées, which— despite their complexity and progressively bewildering terminology— indicated the region might prove to rival the Périgord in the wealth and variety of its archaeological record. But shortly after the opening of the twentieth century there took place a revolution in Upper Paleolithic research that could not help but evoke the interest of any student of Thomas Kuhn.

The Traditional Era

Henri Breuil

Its most visible manifestation was the extraordinary *bataille de l'Aurigna-cien,* which Cartailhac spurred a young and soon famous Henri Breuil (1877–1961) to wage against the partisans of de Mortillet, who were led by Gabriel's son Adrien (Breuil 1906). Breuil's task was threefold. He first had to demonstrate what Lartet had claimed—the existence of a stratigraphically well defined Aurignacian stage preceding the Solu-trean. Second, in the process of doing so, he had to show how de Mortillet's refusal to recognize its existence on both logical and empiri-cal grounds revealed the irretrievably flawed nature of his approach. Third, he had to offer a new approach in its place.

The battle's turbulent course, which soon led to the complete rout of the Mortilletians, would make an excellent case study in the sociology of science. But of much greater importance to us here was the more fundamental change it both reflected and helped catalyze in the con-duct of paleolithic research during the Traditional era. This saw the emergence of a new generation of researchers, freed from the precon-ceptions of the nineteenth century and dedicated to wrestling with the empirical content of the archaeological record insofar as possible in its own terms. Their achievements in excavation, artifact classification, and industrial systematics—which define the domain I have referred to as *straight archaeology* (Sackett 1981)—were truly impressive. Equally impressive is how their work was shaped and given direction by Breuil in a classic succession of papers (1906, 1907a, 1907b, 1909b, and 1913). The last is his remarkable synthesis, *Les Subdivisions du Paléolithique supérieur et leur signification,* one of the cornerstones of prehistoric research in our century.

Les Subdivisions was, first of all, a classificatory scheme—or, better, system of schemes—and established the terms in which Upper Paleo-lithic systematics would be framed even down to the present day. The system itself was not in any narrow sense Breuil's own creation, but rather a masterful collation stemming from many *voyages comparatifs* during which he methodically tracked the progress of the new breed of regional prehistorians. Even its sixfold subdivision of the Magdale-nian, based largely upon Breuil's interpretation of bone and ivory artifacts from Le Placard in the Charente, in part followed the lead of earlier work by his mentor, Piette, in the French Pyrenees. In any event, it is not so much the substance of *Les Subdivisions* that concerns us here as the thought that drives it. This I believe departed significantly both from that of the Formative era and from what the Straus-Clark thesis holds it to have been. It is not overly difficult to reconstruct, because of the clarity of Breuil's exposition and also because he took pains to lay forth his position in fairly explicit terms in both the 1913 masterpiece and the earlier papers that laid its groundwork.

To begin with, he regarded the Upper Paleolithic as a virtually self-contained stage of culture history, as distinct from the Lower Paleolithic (to which he assigns the Chellean, Acheulian, and Mousterian) that preceded it as it was from the Neolithic that followed. He in fact employed the term *Paléolithique supérieur* only reluctantly, preferring Lartet's *Age du Renne* (Reindeer Age); in his subsequent writings he often used Piette's term *Leptolithique,* which refers to the supposedly gracile nature of its blade industries. Its evolutionary break from the Lower Paleolithic was complete. The Upper Paleolithic was produced by diverse races of fully modern human beings, all of whom were intrusive into Western Europe and bore no apparent evolutionary relationship to the decidedly more primitive Neanderthals who preceded them there (several specimens of which—at La Chapelle-aux-Saints, La Ferrassie, and La Quina—had appeared in indisputable Mousterian contexts in the years just preceding *Les Subdivisions*). Further, the complexity of the Upper Paleolithic of western Europe was due not to its having been a center of cultural development but rather to the fact it was a cul-de-sac at the extremity of the great Eurasian landmass that saw a continuous infiltration and mixture of outside peoples and influences.

From these premises certain key conclusions followed regarding the nature of patterning in the archaeological record for the Upper Paleolithic of France and its neighbors. First, the record ought not be expected to show directional cultural evolution in any but the broadest sense, as in the case of the overall (if by no means continuous) perfection of art and of bone and ivory artifacts. Second, even though temporal changes within any given industrial tradition might give the appearance of continuity, they in fact represent successive contacts and mutual influences between several groups and, not infrequently, even wholesale replacement of some by others. In short, in Breuil's view a given Upper Paleolithic tradition could not be regarded in any meaningful sense as representing a culture-historically distinct unit of ethnicity. Third, neither could it be assumed to constitute a unilineal sequence to any significant degree.

One cannot help but note in this connection Straus's claim that Peyrony's subsequent reorganization of the Aurignacian complex into parallel industrial phyla was "of fundamental importance in questioning the straightforward, unilineal explanation of interassemblage variability envisaged by Breuil" (1987a:157). For reasons noted above this claim appears to be invalid in the general case; and in the specific instance of the Aurignacian Breuil himself quite explicitly rejected it. He argued that, along with its relative paucity of characteristic Middle Aurignacian forms, the appearance of an evolved backed blade (Gravettian) element in his Upper Aurignacian stage, reminiscent of the primitive (Châtelperronian) one in his Lower, indicated a direct historic affinity between the two that neither shares with the Middle. He suggested that the Old Caspian of Tunisia may represent a transition in the development of backed blade industries that took place while the Middle Aurignacian prevailed in Europe, which in its advanced form returned to the continent to dominate the Upper Aurignacian. In short, the French Aurignacian complex might express itself archaeologically as a lineal temporal succession, but it in no way represents a unilineal evolutionary sequence.[1] The distinction is crucial.

A fourth conclusion to be drawn from Breuil's premises is that in comparing regional sequences like those, say, of the Périgord and the French Pyrenées, one should expect to find significant disparities. Major blocks of a given tradition represented in one may be missing from the other; the diagnostic artifacts they share may (due to diffusion or independent convergent invention) be seen to associate with quite different assemblages of *banal* stone tools; and—even when they assume essentially the same form—the blocks ought not necessarily fall in the same time period. All of these points concerning the regional differentiation of the Upper Paleolithic archaeological record are illustrated in *Les Subdivisions* by several concrete examples, which—it is interesting to observe—often give as much attention to the *banal* artifacts as to the supposedly diagnostic ones.

Breuil's views on industrial variability as such were equally sophisticated and departed radically from the tenets of Mortilletian systematics (and, it might be added, from those of the phylogenetic paradigm). He of course recognized that specific technologies have their own inbuilt logic, so to speak, and that some amount of directional sequencing of form is to be expected. It is not unreasonable to suppose, for example, that single-row barbed Magdalenian harpoons appeared before those with double rows. (Breuil also illustrated, but without textual comment, hypothetical *formes de passage* akin to the typological series seen in the era's books in all branches of archaeology, showing how one form of stone tool might have evolved into another.) But he stressed that, overall, the industrial succession in any given region is necessarily neither logical nor progressive. The overall tendency toward refinement in Upper Paleolithic technology is halting and occasionally even reversed; progress seen in one aspect of industrial change is more likely than not accompanied by collateral regression in another. Moreover, the detailed industrial subdivisions he recognized within a given tradition are to be regarded as relative and plastic rather than indicative of a rigorous succession, and have no more than general utility. Quite early in the century he was noting that industrial change is always influenced by *retards, survivances, regressions,* regional *idiotismes* (idiosyncracies), and even more localized special site uses and economic activities (Breuil 1907a:346). Finally, Breuil was careful to emphasize the provisional nature of his taxonomies, and *Les Subdivisions* as a whole gives no hints of schematic dogmatism. Even forty years later, by which time Breuil had indeed become dogmatic in many matters, he retained much of his flexibility with respect to Upper Paleolithic systematics. He was not unknown to state that parts of his 1913 scheme continued to hold up better than he had a right to expect given the quality of the data upon which they had been based (e.g., Breuil 1954:60).

It should be clear from the above that Breuil's approach fails to conform to the tenets of the phylogenetic paradigm. The ground for such a paradigm had indeed been prepared by de Mortillet, but Breuil refused to cultivate it. To read his pre-World War I writings is to encounter a sophisticated view of the culture historical background and dynamics of Upper Paleolithic industrial variation that has seldom if ever been rivalled in France before our own age.[2] The origins of his sophistication were manifold. He had been trained as a Dominican scholar-priest, and by the time *Les Subdivisions* appeared he was already ensconced in French intellectual and academic life. He had entered archaeology as a Neolithic and Bronze Age specialist, well versed in the perspective being brought to these fields by contemporary scholars like Joseph Dechelette, who were culture historians rather than natural scientists. And he applied this knowledge to the Upper Paleolithic, being convinced that it had left the primitive state of humanity behind it and should be treated in essentially the same terms as later prehistoric and protohistoric periods.

To be sure, Breuil was by all accounts a fine typologist and he enjoyed a nearly universal acquaintance with the fieldworkers of his day. But he never undertook a sustained excavation program himself and he possessed neither the inclination nor the mentality of a journeyman archaeologist. Nor did he have much to say about how, and even whether, industrial systematics might be guided by an awareness of the complex dynamics he saw at work in the Upper Paleolithic. He never attempted to show how paleoethnology was to be translated into the idiom of archaeological taxonomy, and he may not have been convinced that it could. *Les Subdivisions* shook off the preconceptions that had so restricted the Mortilletian world and furnished the impetus and a coherent frame for French Upper Paleolithic research in the Traditional era. But the nature of its actual impact upon that research must not be misunderstood. Breuil's sophisticated views regarding the culture historical background of industrial variability in Western Europe as a whole were never operationalized into a workable program for attacking it in detail at the regional level.

Denis Peyrony

The actual conduct of day-to-day research in the Traditional era was determined not by Breuil but by the new generation of regional prehistorians who emerged during the decade preceding World War I (and upon whose work Breuil based his great synthesis). They were not sophisticated culture historians, but instead straight archaeologists—journeyman fieldworkers whose mundane, data-loaded, and often cryptic articles filled the pages of the *Bulletin* of the newly formed Société Préhistorique Française (Figure 5.1).

By all accounts, the era's greatest fieldworker was Denis Peyrony (1869–1954), who made his living as a schoolteacher at Les Eyzies and ultimately built his National Museum there. This prodigious excavator of rockshelters dominated Périgord research from virtually the beginning of the century through World War II, combining a bent for independent thought with a command of field techniques that were matched by few if any of his contemporaries. To the world at large he is often regarded simply as someone who "modified" Breuil's scheme (and, so depicted, receives but two lines in Daniel's authoritative history of archaeology [1975:240]). In reality, a great deal of the stratigraphic evidence Breuil used to fight the Aurignacian *bataille* was provided by Peyrony, as was much of the overall depiction of the Périgord sequence found in *Les Subdivisions*. Subsequently Peyrony went on to subdivide the region's Solutrean and Magdalenian traditions on more solid stratigraphic and industrial grounds than Breuil had been able to provide them. And most important of course was his fundamental reorganization of Breuil's Aurignacian complex (Peyrony 1933, 1936). Instead of representing three intergrading temporal blocks, it constituted two distinct industrial traditions—the Aurignacian *sensu stricto* (Breuil's original Middle stage) and Perigordian (Breuil's Lower, Châtelperronian, and Upper, Gravettian, stages)—which evolved as parallel phyla over more or less synchronous series of temporal phases.

This parallel phyla model was to become a consuming *idée fixe* that led Peyrony to some excesses of amateurish enthusiasm. But it was a triumph of straight archaeology which serves to remind us that solid theory does not always promote solid fieldwork. Breuil's very sophis-

FIGURE 5.1.   French prehistory comes of age. Allegorical illustration appearing in the program for a fête which the Société Préhistorique Française held in November 1910, to celebrate the official decree of its *utilité publique* as a scientific enterprise. The society had been founded seven years earlier. In addition to numerous discourses, the fête included *tableaux vivants* depicting life during various epochs of prehistoric times as well as a presentation (*exquise et tout artistique*) by Adrien de Mortillet on the subject "Woman and Beauty Across the World." (Redrawn by Nancy Pendleton after the quite murky original.)

tication in some respects may actually have retarded its development. His recognition of the multiplicity of historic factors entombed in the archaeological record seemingly had as a corollary the notion of developmental intergradation. Diffusion, migration, and hybridization, along with variability arising from special site use and activities, could be expected to blur the transition from one phase of a cultural tradition to the next. Fair enough. But not all prehistorians were quick to realize that it was often inadequately segregated assemblages rather than the structure of the archaeological record itself that accounted for the paucity of sharply delineated breaks in their regional sequences. Peyrony did, and therein lay one of the keys to his success.

This is not the place to review the Byzantine complexities which his argument ultimately assumed nor the still hotly debated question of the industrial composition and historico-genetic integrity of the Perigordian. But it is pertinent to consider a few points raised by Straus that are germane to the subject of this essay (1987a:157). That Peyrony's model of the parallel phyla was a "patchwork of partial sequences" is indeed true. Nonetheless, the patchwork represented something of a methodological tour de force, being based upon simultaneously seriating stratigraphic, industrial, faunal, and—perhaps for the first time (see Peyrony 1939)—sedimentological data. It might fairly then be considered the prototype from which our modern approaches to chronostratigraphy have evolved. It bears noting as well that Peyrony might never have appreciated the industrial cleavage upon which his parallel phyla scheme was based had his patches not been obtained from the clearly segregated stratigraphies noted above.

Also deserving comment is Straus's contention that Peyrony's seriation was based upon an "*a priori* theory of technological change" and constituted a "cultural evolutionary scheme" (1987a:157). I find it difficult to see much here or elsewhere in Peyrony's thinking that is evolutionary at all beyond the everyday and fairly ambiguous sense with which the term is still used by prehistorians. The bulk of the actual directional temporal industrial shifts he reported were solidly grounded upon stratigraphy, such as the frequency changes displayed within the Aurignacian at La Ferrassie—which were independently observed by prehistorians of the Brive school at Correzian sites like La Columba-del-Bouitou (Bardon et al. 1907). In passing from Aurignacian stage I to stage II, for example, the diminution over time of pieces bearing scaled marginal retouch is accompanied by an increase of muzzled carinate scrapers at the expense of broad rounded ones. But neither evolution, let alone any form of a priori theory of technological change, would seem to account for the fairly brisk rise and fall of busked burins in Aurignacian II or the temporal changes in form exhibited by bone sagaie points over Aurignacian stages I through IV.

For the rest, insofar as technological change is concerned, the only assumptions called for by Peyrony's parallel phyla scheme were that industries belonging to the Aurignacian line should possess Aurignacian *fossiles* like carinate scrapers and lack Perigordian *fossiles* like backed knives and points; that the reverse should hold true of industries in the Perigordian line; and, finally, that the key hinge industry uniting Breuil's original Lower and Upper Aurignacian (the Perigordian III in Peyrony's scheme) should have fewer and less elegant Gravette points than those seen in the Perigordian IV, and also presumably lack the special *fossiles* (truncated elements, Font-Robert points, and Noailles burins) seen in Perigordian V. It should be obvious, by the way, that the last mentioned types fall into no logical evolutionary sequence regardless of what temporal order one might put them.

Two additional aspects of Peyrony's failure to conform to the tenets of the phylogenetic paradigm may be touched upon. First, as Straus is fully aware, Peyrony's belief in the parallel phyla ran counter to the straightforward unilineal treatment of industrial variation the paradigm supposedly demands. In fact, he was not adverse to seeing non-lineal overlaps between other traditions as well. For example, he at one time argued that the Upper Perigordian and Lower and Middle Solutrean were synchronous within the Périgord itself, as were the Upper Solutrean and Lower Magdalenian (e.g., Peyrony 1932). Furthermore, as a result of recognizing the distinctiveness of the Mousterian of Acheulian Tradition, Peyrony became the first to establish the presence of synchronous, interstratifying industries within the Middle Paleolithic.

The second aspect concerns whether or not Peyrony viewed the industrial succession recognized for the Périgord as having in some sense general validity for France as a whole. It is true that in the twilight of his career he attempted to trace the basic elements of his Aurignacian-Perigordian scheme all the way across Europe and into Palestine (1948)! But, as a reading of his argument clearly shows, this reflects little more than special pleading for the obsession that had come to take hold of him regarding his cherished parallel phyla. His Perigordcentrism was actually of a quite different sort. Peyrony was of local peasant stock, in some respects as unpretentious and provincial as he was intelligent, and never gained the recognition given professionals like Breuil. (The reputation Peyrony's name enjoys today was only posthumously created, largely through the writings of the Bordesian school.) His world was circumscribed by a fifty-kilometer radius drawn around Les Eyzies; he seems to have traveled little apart from attending congresses; he never excavated a site outside the Périgord; his few publications that touch upon the world beyond always carry the reader back to strictly regional concerns. And his only work of a general nature, *Eléments de préhistoire* (which went through five editions between 1923 and 1948), essentially treats the outside world along the lines established by Breuil and later modified by other regional archaeologists. In short, Peyrony was very much a Perigordcentric, but to no significant degree was he a Périgord imperialist.

We have so far seen little to show that Peyrony's work and thought conform in any obvious manner to the tenets of the phylogenetic paradigm. But the business has not been disposed of entirely. He was as silent on matters of assumption and theory as Breuil was explicit, and considerable immersion in his publications and some amount of reading between the lines are called for if one is to grapple with the non-methodological aspects of his approach. The effort reveals a constellation of factors in his work and thought that is indeed relevant to issues raised by Straus and Clark's thesis, even though I myself believe they lend themselves to a somewhat different interpretation.

One factor is that Peyrony defined his industrial taxa in a highly stereotyped, presumably normative fashion. Although he collected remarkably complete assemblages by the standards of his day, his typological descriptions of them tend to be perfunctory. And they are based nearly exclusively upon piecemeal consideration of *fossiles directeurs*, often taking the form of idealized accounts written years if not decades after excavation. Another factor is that, while Peyrony may have rejected unilineal sequencing along the lines postulated by de Mortillet (and the phylogenetic paradigm), he very much embraced it in a specific and rather special sense. The industries making up his parallel phyla were ordered into rigid sequences whose stages in turn correlate fairly narrowly with what he seems to have regarded as specific regional chronostratigraphic zones. Aurignacian I industries, for example, are usually described as belonging to highly cryoclastic rockshelter deposits (*éboulis sec*) and dominated by reindeer, whereas both sediments and fauna associated with Aurignacian II industries indicate a milder and wetter climatic phase. Occasionally, the need to see a rigid, essentially lock-step correlation between archaeological sequencing and the natural stratigraphic succession appears to have overridden even industrial considerations. Thus the upper Aurignacian horizon at Abri Castanet seems to have been assigned to Aurignacian II more because it occupied a distinct stratigraphic context overlying that of the lower (Aurignacian I) than because of its typological make-up (Peyrony 1935a). Although this interpretation received some amount of support from *fossile* bone points, the two lithic assemblages involved are in fact essentially identical to each other and at the same time quite distinct from most regional Aurignacian I and II industries. (In terms of Bordesian systematics, they belong to a single industrial taxon which may be as likely to represent a lateral as a temporal facies of Aurignacian I.)

The third member of the constellation of factors is Peyrony's "biocultural" explanation of industrial variation. He regarded Aurignacian and Perigordian not simply as distinct cultures in some undefined sense but actually as behavioral expressions of distinct races of *Homo sapiens* (respectively Cro-Magnon and Combe-Capelle). The ramifications of Peyrony's biocultural model can sometimes be unsettling. For example, it requires his postulating that Combe-Capelle people manufacturing the Perigordian III industry occupied Laugerie-Haute at essentially the same time that Cro-Magnons producing Aurignacian II assemblages were heavily installed only a few kilometers away at sites like Abri Cellier, La Faurelie, and La Ferrassie (Peyrony 1935b). Seemingly to his mind, regionalism could express itself at as fine a level as the individual *commune*. It was, among other things, scenarios like the above that prompted Breuil to dismiss Peyrony's parallel phyla as a *vue de l'esprit* (1935). Now, if taken at face value, biocultural interpretations along these lines seemingly approach what the phylogenetic paradigm regards as cultural, that is, ethnic explanations of the archaeological record. However, their very naïveté—especially when viewed in combination with his oversimplified notion of chronostratigraphic zoning and his stereotyped industrial phases—suggests that rather different, and deeper, forces were at work in Peyrony's mind.

The Traditional Paradigm

Let us examine what these forces might have been. The exercise should not only throw light on Peyrony specifically but also afford an opportunity to outline some of my own views about the evolution of the logic of inquiry that has guided French prehistoric research during the present century. While I reject the specific tenets as well as the overall thrust of the phylogenetic paradigm, I agree with Straus and Clark on the key importance of many of the issues they stress. At least my interpretation of them may more clearly illuminate the historic facts as they are summarized here.

Around the time *Les Subdivisions* appeared, there emerged a paradigm for pursuing Upper Paleolithic research that was to dominate the Traditional era and that continues to influence French research even today. It was the product of the new breed of regional prehistorians of whom Peyrony was perhaps the most notable member. As we have seen, they were not general culture historians, but instead journeyman fieldworkers who practiced straight archaeology. This entails a craft-like involvement with the empirical dimension of the archaeological record to the exclusion of nearly all other considerations. It is narrowly preoccupied with the tasks of defining the structure and content of archaeological deposits, of classifying the formal variation contained in their artifact assemblages, of comparing these assemblages to ascertain their industrial similarities and differences, and, finally, of summarizing the results of such comparisons in terms of regional taxonomic schemes. These tasks are essentially equivalent to what is known as space-time systematics in New World archaeology. However, in contrast to their American counterparts, archaeologists working in the French tradition have cultivated an artisanal-like empiricism much more reminiscent of certain branches of natural history than of anthropological archaeology.

The essence of the paradigm is seen in its approach to the complementary tasks of classifying stone tools, that is, lithic artifact typology, and of classifying the assemblages into which the tools archaeologically segregate, that is, industrial systematics. Stone tools and industries tend to be regarded as actors or agents in their own right. They are seen as possessing a kind of life and logic unto themselves that to a considerable extent can be investigated without direct reference to the people who made them or the techno-economic systems within which they served.[3] Artifact typology may constitute a fairly refined enterprise with reasonably explicit canons of terminology and observation, and its sophisticated pursuit calls for the trained eye demanded of a good mineralogist or botanist or pathologist. But it is nonetheless *morphological typology* (*typologie morphologique*), which restricts its purview to the formal anatomy of stone tools and the lithic technology in which this is grounded. Industrial systematics is approached on equally straightforward empirical grounds. It rests upon the principle that, all things being equal, the degree of similarity in artifactual make-up between assemblages is an index of their relatedness. Thus highly similar assemblages are generalized into industrial facies, and facies sharing enough artifactual similarity to suggest kinship are in turn grouped into industrial phases, traditions, and so forth. Since such classification is essentially a matter of assessing kinds and degrees of formal similarity without explicit regard to larger considerations, it can by extension be referred to as *morphological taxonomy*.

Now, morphological taxonomy in the Traditional era more often than not took on phyletic overtones reminiscent of those given fossils in paleontological systematics. It was pursued in terms of, and mutually reinforced by, what I have termed the *organic* model or, perhaps better, metaphor. (This notion, along with some of the argument of this section, was first developed in Sackett 1981.) The taxa into which assemblages were grouped were conceived of as essentially *natural* units in both the philosophical and the everyday senses of the term, which—like paleontological taxa—could assume but a single form at any given time and place. Two closely interrelated corollaries followed. One was that any given taxon, say a specific industrial facies like Aurignacian I, was expected to display a highly stereotyped aspect. The other was what might be termed the *principle of exclusion*, which in turn expressed itself in two different but complementary ways. First, industries which exhibited obvious differences yet shared enough similarity to be considered genetically related necessarily had to be assigned to different time (and/or space) loci in the archaeological record. Second, conversely, industries which significantly differed from one another but which seemingly occupied one and the same space-time locus necessarily had to be assigned to different taxa.

The similarity of these taxonomic rules to certain tenets of the Straus-Clark thesis should be obvious and is by no means accidental. I agree with them in seeing parallels between the format of Traditional industrial classification and the phyletic organization given fossils in paleontological systematics. Where we disagree is that I maintain that the archaeological taxa were being treated as if they were in fact natural units, whereas Straus and Clark argue that they were somehow nonetheless being conceived in cultural terms. We shall return to his point.

The reasons why Traditional French archaeology adopted morphological taxonomy grounded in an organic metaphor are presumably numerous but are not entirely clear. The field's long-standing alliance with geology and paleontology was surely a factor, particularly when reinforced by its estrangement from anthropology following the collapse of nineteenth-century cultural evolutionism. Traditional prehistorians had little familiarity with, or interest in, anthropology as we know it. Nor could they have easily gained more, given the state, theoretical bent, and institutional arrangements of the field in France at the time (see Mercier 1966). Behind the Traditional paradigm lay not only an ignorance of anthropology but also the complementary conviction that paleoethnological interpretation was in any case mere speculation and could only distract attention from the more pressing concerns of straight archeology. Invoking the principle of unripe time, one could safely defer wrestling with it until some unspecified point in the future, "once the data are in." Art, burials, and similar remains did of course warrant special if piecemeal attention, and there was no reluctance to draw broad paleoethnological conclusions that could be easily paraphrased from the more obvious contents of archaeological levels (e.g., Magdalenians hunted reindeer, whose meat they ate cooked). But none of this was seen as having any direct relevance to the interpretation of industrial variation exhibited by stone tools and assemblages, which was dealt with in all of its formal immediacy along straightforward empirical lines.

Another factor contributing to the organic cast given Traditional systematics was the simple matter of efficacy, which can play as strong a role in dictating the form assumed by scientific paradigms as do prevailing notions of truth themselves. No knowledgeable prehistorian ever believed that stone tools could actually be understood in the same terms as organic fossils (Balout 1955:153 illustrates the point well). However, given the alien, dinosaur nature of lithic industries and the great complexity of their archaeological contexts, treating stone tools as if they *were* fossils introduced a highly useful element of reductionism that at least allowed prehistorians to get on with their work in a situation which otherwise might easily have promoted intellectual paralysis. It is altogether possible that organic analogues have particular appeal in the human sciences precisely at those times when the data seem most subtle and the methodologies weak.

Unfortunately, the literature of Traditional archaeology does little to clarify matters. As Peyrony's oeuvre effectively illustrates, being almost invariably preoccupied with the specific details of specific regional sequences, the writings of straight archaeologists possess a strongly arcane and parochial element that puts them beyond the grasp of a reader unfamiliar with the specific data involved. Moreover, possessing the mentality of artisans who have learned their trade as much by insinuation as by instruction, and at the same time writing for colleagues who share essentially the same experience and assumptions, their publications seldom if ever treat issues of method and theory explicitly: assumed to be understood because they are familiar, these go unstated. In science, as in everyday life, habit crowds out consciousness.

To compound the problem, Traditional prehistorians adopted a terminological practice that can seriously mislead modern readers, particularly Americans. They saw no inconsistency in referring to their industrial taxa as "cultures" and even attributing them to "tribes" (*tribus*). A close reading of the literature reveals this to be little more than a convention of labeling. It was not meant to imply that the industrial taxa were to be equated with units of ethnicity in any anthropologically meaningful sense, but rather simply to convey the fact that the empirical data which they organized fall into the domain of *Homme* rather than of *Nature*. (It bears noting in this connection that, despite its specific connotations when translated literally into English, *tribu* as they used it suggests little more than that the particular slice of Man's domain concerned with a relatively primitive state of cultural development.) In short, when we encounter such terms in the writings of Traditional archaeologists, we are dealing not with culture history in any meaningful sense but rather simply with an idiom of taxonomic description and thought.

Back to Peyrony

It should now be clear why Peyrony's approach fails to conform to the tenets of the Straus-Clark thesis. Given the canons of the Traditional paradigm, there is no logical necessity to believe that the Périgord sequence should have validity beyond the region's frontiers, or to assume that industrial evolution should necessarily involve directional unilineal sequencing of phases based on a priori, vitalistic notions of technological evolution. One was free to believe such things, and for all I know some Traditional prehistorians may have. But one was not logically required to—and Peyrony did not.

Examining Peyrony's thought in the light of the Traditional paradigm clarifies an additional point that is somewhat obscured by Straus's treatment of the man. As was noted above, Straus seems to argue that dismantling Breuil's original Aurignacian complex into distinct Perigordian and Aurignacian parallel phyla implies a more sophisticated view on Peyrony's part of the cultural dynamics behind industrial variation. In fact, regardless of its intrinsic importance to regional systematics, the business intellectually entailed no more than a logical use of morphological taxonomy guided by the organic metaphor. It was a matter of employing the principle of exclusion in a situation where considerable interassemblage variability seemingly cross-cut a succession of regional temporal loci. In order to obtain satisfactory "natural" taxa, Peyrony found it necessary to draw as many lines of industrial demarcation in the horizontal, synchronous dimension of his taxonomic scheme as the vertical, diachronic one. That the idea of parallel industrial phyla resulting from this essentially taxonomic operation continues to enjoy wide acceptance is a tribute not to Peyrony's culture-historical insight but rather to his acuteness as an empirical observer, the quality of his artifact assemblages, and, to some extent, the accuracy of his stratigraphic inferences.

To my mind the important question lies elsewhere: why did he recognize such highly stereotyped and seemingly invariant taxa in the first place? In part the answer lies in the inherently reductionist nature of the Traditional paradigm itself. But in addition it bears stressing that the paradigm was not simply a set of guidelines but also a model of expectations, expectations that were generated by (and in turn helped perpetuate) the analytic methods of the day. These deserve examination.

Even the best excavators of the Traditional era tended to concentrate on archaeologically rich deposits, which were subdivided only in terms of their major and most obvious stratigraphic divisions. The artifact assemblages recovered from such excavations rarely represented what a modern prehistorian would regard as meaningful episodes of occupation. They were instead ensembles that globally sampled thick palimpsests of occupation in which numerous discrete archaeological lenses were mixed. As a result, what was likely very often a quite variable and even disparate succession of discrete artifact complexes got averaged out, and the excavator's view of the nature of the archaeological record became distorted in two important respects: diachronic change was exaggerated at the same time that synchronic variation was suppressed. Thus the archaeological record seemed to present itself as a succession of clearly defined, homogeneous industries whose abrupt artifactual changes lent themselves to ordering in terms of clear-cut industrial stages. This accounts for the fact noted previously—despite the illusory taxonomic flexibility suggested by Peyrony's parallel phyla, the industries making up any one of them are defined and ordered into highly rigid sequences.

To compound matters, systematics depended heavily upon the supposedly diagnostic *fossiles directeurs*. The notion itself was a fluid one, and in the hands of sophisticated typologists like those associated with Jean Bouyssonie in the Brive school could mean a carefully defined collective representation of a fairly broad block of distinctive typological intergradation (e.g., Bourlon et al. 1912). But the *fossiles* stressed by most Traditional prehistorians, including Peyrony, were discrete, specialized types which made seemingly abrupt entrances and exits in a regional sequence and which could be dealt with in essentially qualitative terms. Ignoring the greater body of common and supposedly banal forms, these *fossiles* were taxonomically employed in such a manner as to define simultaneously both the significant formal content of artifact assemblages and their genetic industrial affiliations. The analytic circularity inherent in this procedure inevitably fed back into the sampling procedures involved in excavation itself. Often it was only the *fossiles* that consistently found their way into the laboratory, which of course served to restrain and even to a considerable extent predetermine how a researcher visualized technological evolution. This practice, in tandem with the coarse resolution of the era's stratigraphic segregation of site deposits, meant that prehistorians literally created in an empirical sense an archaeological record that did in fact mimic the paleontological record in consisting of formally discrete taxa that over time evolved in straightforward successions of invariant stages, which could be simultaneously identified and defined by a series of index *fossile* forms.

There remains the question of whether these taxa were somehow normative cultural constructs in the sense of Straus and Clark. My depiction of the Traditional paradigm suggests they were not. Yet

Peyrony's biocultural explanations of industrial variability could be construed as an attempt to translate the parallel phyla into something at least approaching ethnic terms. To some extent the issue remains obscure because the argument has no parallels in the thinking of other regional prehistorians of the Traditional era so far as the Upper Paleolithic is concerned. In other words, the answer may be unique to Peyrony himself. Perhaps he saw no reason not to apply to Upper Paleolithic times a kind of explanation that Breuil himself had carefully restricted to the Lower Paleolithic (see note 2). Or perhaps we are dealing with the penchant for overschematization of a turn-of-the-century provincial French schoolteacher. Or, again, with a kind of lawyer's brief for the *idée fixe* of parallel phyla, drafted on the assumption that its validity could somehow be measured by the number of interdependent variables that could be invoked in its favor. Or, finally, with an example of a kind of libido for closure that afflicts many immature sciences, whose researchers feel a compulsion not seen among their brethren in more sophisticated fields to tie up all the loose ends.

However, my own view of the matter is that Peyrony's thinking was essentially void of significant anthropological content. As we have seen, the naïveté of the cultural scenarios he wrote is itself striking. Even more important is that his attempt to see one-to-one correlations between industrial phyla and human races was accompanied by an equally strong desire to see one-to-one correlations between cultural and natural stratigraphy. Stone tool industries, human biology, and natural environmental succession appear to have intertwined so closely in Peyrony's thought that one wonders whether he ever could, or cared to, draw the line between *Homme* and *Nature* in Upper Paleolithic times. It is not unlikely that we are dealing with someone to whom the organic metaphor actually assumed the form of a model.

The Bordesian Era

François Bordes

With the Bordesian era we enter modern times. It appears to me as a period of great complexity, not simply because I have happened to see much of it unfold, but because of its own peculiar dynamics in which conscious innovation and implicit conservatism seem to mix in no logical fashion. The work and thought of its individual researchers, let alone the period as a whole, defy easy generalization. I sometimes think of the Bordesian era as a kind of amphibian period that began the transition from the Traditional era to one which still lies in the future and whose form we can only dimly perceive. At any rate, I shall deal with it in only perfunctory fashion. One reason is that future debate over the issues will largely focus on this era, and I shall consequently have ample opportunity to discuss it in detail later. Another is that informed readers should have sufficient knowledge of recent archaeological history to weigh the merits of the Straus-Clark thesis and my own views with respect to Bordesian times with only a minimum of prompting.

The Bordesian era saw a significant leap in the degree of resolution with which prehistorians were able to exercise control over the empirical contents of the Upper Paleolithic archaeological record. Excavation took on the character of stratigraphic dissection aimed toward segregating artifact assemblages with reference both to specific occupational lenses and to the individual sedimentological components observable in site deposits. Essentially all lithic materials were now saved, along with representative samples of faunal, palynological, and sedimentological data. Techniques were devised to use these paleoenvironmental (especially sedimentological) data in conjunction with the artifact industries to seriate site stratigraphies holistically, thus recasting regional taxonomic schemes into the form of "chronostratigraphies" (e.g., Laville 1975), which eventually came to be supplemented by a time line of radiocarbon dates.

As a result of its fine-grained depiction of the archaeological record, Bordesian chronostratigraphy forced the abandonment of Peyrony's tenet that industrial and natural successions should necessarily equate in an obvious lock-step manner. This had introduced a great deal of inflexibility into Traditional systematics at the same time it reinforced the confusion between the natural and cultural worlds fostered by the organic metaphor. Even more important, the greater resolution provided by refined excavation called for two major revisions of Peyrony's depiction of the tempo and mode of industrial evolution itself. For one thing, it became clear that members of the classic suites of *fossile* types recognized by Traditional prehistorians do not necessarily replace one another in a straightforward temporal fashion. Instead, they overlap in such a manner as to suggest that whatever temporal significance they possess lies in their relative frequencies rather than sheer presence or absence; indeed, in some instances these *fossiles* may not be narrowly time dependent at all. For another, enhanced resolution brought an increased appreciation of synchronic industrial variation, especially of the polymorphism of specialized variants any given regional industry might display in one and the same block of time and space. It should be noted that major industrial novelties brought to light by open-air research, which only began to be pursued aggressively in the Bordesian era, have done much to promote an appreciation of polymorphism in the Upper Paleolithic archaeological record (see Sackett 1988b, Lenoir 1988).

Complementing these major advances in empirical realization of the archaeological record have been equally profound changes in the methodology of describing and classifying lithic assemblages. Belief in the potential diagnostic value of *fossiles directeurs* was by no means abandoned. But a significant shift of emphasis from qualitative to quantitative thinking took place, based upon the notion that a sophisticated appreciation of industrial variation requires that at least as much attention be paid to the proportional representation of all tool types in assemblages as to the piecemeal occurrence of whatever diagnostic *fossile* types they may contain. Many prehistorians of the Traditional era had provided tool counts of one sort or another, but it was François Bordes who first saw clearly that translating the notion of diagnostic into quantitative terms required introducing two new methodological elements into systematics. One is that defining a given assemblage's artifactual make-up must be operationally distinguished from defining its industrial status, that is, its taxonomic affiliations to other assemblages. We have seen how this distinction was blurred by Peyrony and his contemporaries, who used *fossiles directeurs* in an inherently circular fashion so as to define simultaneously an assemblage's formal content and assign it to a taxon. The second is that meaningful quantitative inventorying calls for *comprehensive typologies* in which all retouched tools, including the supposedly banal forms, can be assigned to a specific category of a type-list and subsequently be counted. Without this criterion of comprehension, which was only occasionally appreciated in Traditional systematics, quantitative statements about relative tool frequencies lose most of their meaning.

Armed with its comprehensive type-lists and some relatively simple techniques of statistical description, such as the cumulative frequency graph, Bordesian systematics has greatly refined the business of industrial taxonomy. It has also led to enhanced taxonomic flexibility, as is exemplified in its classificatory translation of industrial polymorphism into *faciès latéraux,* a perhaps awkward but still quite serviceable taxonomic device for ordering specialized variants of a given industry that happen to occupy the same time-space block but nonetheless exhibit significant artifactual differences. Recognition of lateral facies requires one to accept that a given regional industrial tradition need not assume the form of a simple unilineal sequence of stereotypical phases, but can instead express itself as a continually ramifying flow of technological change which at any given time may display considerable synchronic variation. Perhaps not surprisingly, this ramifying model received the paleontological term of *évolution buissonante* ("bushy" evolution). But its acceptance marked the repeal of what I have termed the law of exclusion, and with it the assumptions that industries are somehow natural categories and that, as a consequence, only one essentially invariant industrial taxon can occupy any given time-space locus. All this means in turn that the Bordesian era, wittingly or not, gave up the practice of phyletic taxonomy itself even though it retained much of the idiom.

Denise de Sonneville-Bordes

The above discussion should serve as a sufficient point of departure for readers who wish to trace the impact of the Bordesian approach upon Upper Paleolithic research in the Périgord. If they have access only to general sources, the exercise might profitably begin with de Sonneville-Bordes (1960), which redefined Peryony's world in Bordesian terms, and culminated in Laville et al. (1980), which documented the considerably more complex world of industrial flux with which a prehistorian today must contend. They may not encounter a great deal that brings to mind the phylogenetic paradigm. However, they will find—freed of the organic metaphor and vastly strengthened in its empirical reach, methodological control, and taxonomic flexibility—a straight archaeology that retains much the same character as that practiced by the journeyman archaeologists who laid the foundations for *Les Subdivisions*. This is not to deny there has been a kind of renaissance of concern with the paleoethnological dimension of the archaeological record. But it remains true that those who pursue it still stand with one foot solidly planted in the Bordesian era. The reason of course lies in the formidable problems of an immediate empirical nature that remain to be overcome by straight archaeology before industrial variation loses the dinosaur quality attributed to it at the start of this essay (see Rigaud and Simek 1987 for an informed discussion of this point). If paleoethnology is to be grounded in stone tool industries, its pursuit must necessarily begin with stratigraphy and systematics.

The Contemporary Era

One additional stage—the Contemporary era—might be recognized. It would be characterized by a general restlessness with respect to conventional method and theory and by the opening of new lines of investigation designed to realize more of the paleoethnological potential of the Upper Paleolithic archaeological record. This partly results from new trends within France itself, such as the emergence of a highly viable Paris school centered upon the imposing figure of André Leroi-Gourhan (Audouze and Leroi-Gourhan 1985:172–173). Equally important, it reflects scientific hybrid vigor stemming from growing collaboration between French and American scholars (see Jelinek 1985–86). The Contemporary era might be said to have begun a decade or so ago. But the date is arbitrary, both because the roots of these new developments extend deep into the Bordesian era and because an essentially Bordesian outlook continues to dominate quotidian French archaeology. The richness and variety of the contemporary scene are well documented by the other chapters in this volume. It is also tellingly illustrated by the on-going research of Lawrence Straus and Geoffrey Clark, which stands as a model of what Franco-American hybridization can achieve. I may disagree with them about the paradigm of the past, but I regard with enthusiasm their contribution to the paradigm of the future.

Epilogue: Taxonomy and Meaning

Many of the issues dealt with in this essay are matters of fact that can be resolved by direct appeal to the literature of French prehistoric research. Others are matters of interpretation that call for a considerable amount of reading between the lines. One of the latter proves to be particularly elusive. Not surprisingly, it may be the most interesting of the lot, and its interest extends considerably beyond the immediate question of the phylogenetic paradigm itself. At stake is the meaning of the taxonomies produced by French Upper Paleolithic archaeologists. According to Straus and Clark, the taxa one encounters in these schemes are normative—not simply in the sense of being stereotyped but, more importantly, in the sense that they partition industrial variation along what are purportedly cultural, that is, ethnic lines. As should be clear from earlier discussion, this notion lacks conviction to my mind. I also believe it represents a perspective from which it may be difficult to gain an empathetic understanding of the logic of inquiry behind French straight archaeology. A few additional comments may be in order.

What do the industrial taxa generated by French prehistorians actually mean? What do they explain? The specific answer may vary somewhat among individuals and from one era to the next. However, insofar as French straight archaeology in general is concerned, the answer in short is "nothing"—at least in the sense that most American archaeologists seem to conceive of meaning and explanation. French straight archaeology is an essentially descriptive and classificatory science of the archaeological record, grounded in extreme positivism and uninformed by any larger agenda. At first glance, its reification of stone tools and industries as active agents in their own right might suggest an attempt to embue them with meaning. But in fact they act only within the narrow confines of taxonomic schemes, and what meaning they may possess does not extend beyond the schemes themselves. Such reification actually serves to abrogate the need to refer them in any systematic fashion to a paleoethnological domain that would provide them with meaning in some broader sense.

We have seen why the terms "culture" and "tribe" perhaps ought not to be taken too literally when used by a French prehistorian. The same holds true for "style" and "function." Such usage is equally loose and seldom betrays a rigorous attempt to relate formal variation among artifacts to the cultural setting of ethnicity and activity that gave rise to them. Often, in fact, style is simply equated with diachronic variation and function with synchronic: thus *fossiles* that have lost the specific temporal significance originally attributed to them are often referred to as possessing "functional" significance instead. That diachronic variation might be functional, and synchronic stylistic, never seems to be entertained. And industrial systematics is equally mute about the specific nature of the kinship that unites the assemblages making up its taxa. It might seem reasonable to assume that historico-genetic, or ethnic, relation of some sort are implied when two or more assemblages are placed in a given taxon. But in fact formalistic classification of the kind used by French straight archaeologists begs the question. It does not argue that the members of a taxon are similar because they are related for some specified reason, but instead simply holds that they are related in some manner because they are similar—which is quite a different thing. Relatedness might actually refer as easily to similarities arising from activity as from ethnicity. In any event, one must be cautious in inferring that French industrial systematics necessarily involves a conscious attempt to map the paleoethnological domain.

I suspect that confusion over the issue of taxonomy and meaning stems from a kind of myopia with which American scholars regard French prehistoric research, one born of preconceptions grounded in the rather different form taken by straight archaeology in the New World. At the level of technique and methodology it of course shares many similarities with French practice. But the rules of the game are entirely different. This is in large part due to the nature of the New World archaeological record, which contains very few cultural dinosaurs indeed, but instead refers to kinds of lifeways and technologies that are well documented ethnographically. This fact historically accounts for the integration of New World archaeology with anthropology, and means as well that considerable ethnographic sophistication is part of the scientific commonsense of any trained American researcher.

As a result, artifacts are not regarded as actors in their own right, but rather simply as shadows or reflections of culture. At the same time, an archaeologist is likely to be able to make plausible guesses about the nature of their stylistic and functional variation. Hence the passage from straightforward morphological observation of archaeological variability to the assignment of cultural meaning to that variability takes place quickly and largely unconsciously. The task of ordering assemblages into taxonomies, that is, the practice of *space-time systematics*, is not an exercise in pure morphological taxonomy as such but rather one in actual culture-historical modeling. Taxonomic schemes are viewed more or less automatically as skeleton culture histories, if not even more. In the thinking of some theorists, the jump from ordering to interpretation is at once so great and so blurred that space-time systematics itself is claimed to be a form of paleoethnological explanation. It is of course this jump that underlies so much of Lewis Binford's thought, which in this instance would seem to be echoed in the Straus-Clark thesis. Typical would be Binford's long-standing claim that what I would presumably regard simply as conventional Americanist straight archaeology actually constitutes a "normative school" committed to a specific theoretical stand regarding the terms in which the archaeological record is to be given cultural interpretation (e.g., Binford 1965; Sackett 1986:632–633).

What this boils down to, as David Meltzer (1979) argues, is that American archaeologists have no paradigm apart from that furnished by anthropology itself (see also Clark 1987a). Indeed, the anthropological paradigm is so ingrained in their outlook that they find it difficult to believe that a field of prehistoric research could logically have any other.[4] This of course is why so much of French taxonomy is puzzling, if not incomprehensible, to American eyes. If one takes its references to cultures, tribes, styles, and functions literally in the American sense, French systematics does indeed seem anthropologically naïve. What to the French is largely the idiom of systematics appears to the American mind as an attempt to invest it with meaning, to explain the archaeological record in some sort of cultural terms. Given their adherence to the maxim that "archeology is anthropology or it is nothing," Americans often seem unwilling to cultivate the informed empathy needed to perceive that the French are neither third-rate anthropologists nor (seemingly the only alternative in some American eyes) naive empiricists. They are instead prehistorians who have devised an approach that sharply demarcates straight archaeology from culture-historical modelling and explanation. It provides serviceable techniques for ordering the archaeological record in terms of taxa which constitute empirically demonstrable congeries of industrial variation, regardless of the fact their paleoethnological significance is decidedly ambiguous. The approach may not seem exciting to some, but it does allow highly skilled researchers to get on with the task of grappling with a highly intractable archaeological record.

Acknowledgments

It is a pleasure to have the opportunity of acknowledging a long-standing debt to M. Elie Peyrony, former Conservator of the National Museum of Les Eyzies, who some three decades ago helped kindle the interests reflected in this essay by giving me access to the museum's archaeological collections and archives. His kindnesses were many and his memories evocative.

I also wish to thank Louise Jackson for some astute editing of the manuscript.

Notes

1. The gist of Breuil's thesis actually strikes a rather modern note, since even those researchers who believe today in the unity of the Perigordian find it necessary to seek evidence for the transition from Châtelperronian to Gravettian well outside the Périgord itself (e.g., Bordes 1968b; Rigaud 1988).

2. The reader would be more than justified in observing that depiction of Breuil's approach to the Upper Paleolithic clashes with his starkly robotic Lower Paleolithic scheme that emerged in the 1930s (well if briefly summarized by Movius 1953:163–164. This postulates flake tool and core-biface traditions alternating with one another in direct linkage with distinct paleoanthropic and neanthropic lines of hominid evolution. The matter is especially intriguing because Victor Commont's work early in the century had clearly demonstrated the falsity of the archaeological distinction and because there are many hints in Breuil's writings that his thought was not untouched by certain theologically based preconceptions regarding the origins of human beings. It is also of interest that Breuil's Lower Paleolithic scheme enjoyed much greater popularity in England than it ever did in France. It is tempting to see its continuing legacy in Mary Leakey's inclination to attribute the Acheulian and Developed Oldowan to distinct phyletic lines (1971) and even in Robert Foley's recent claim that stone tool typologies were essentially "hard-wired" among hominids prior to the emergence of *Homo sapiens* (1987; see also Clark 1989b).

3. This presumably accounts for the fact that the Traditional literature often seems to depict stone tools and industries interacting as if they were capable of sexual reproduction or at least, as Movius would have it, entering into matrimonial alliances (1953:188).

4. Nonetheless, attempts to identify an anthropological source for "normative" thinking in French archaeology have not proved convincing. For example, Binford and Sabloff (1982:141–142) attribute it to the legacy of Emile Durkheim. Yet it was the leader of the Durkheim school throughout most of our Traditional era, Marcel Mauss, whose study of seasonal variation among Eskimos must be regarded as one of the classics of non-normative thought (1904–05).

Part II: Paradigms for the Franco-Iberian Paleolithic and Mesolithic

Chapter 6
Retouched Tools, Fact or Fiction? Paradigms for Interpreting Paleolithic Chipped Stone

C. Michael Barton

Introduction

Chipped stone artifacts form the most ubiquitous material record for hunter-gatherers, not only in the circum-Mediterranean region but throughout the world. While few would argue with the idea that they represent only a portion of prehistoric technological systems, lithics were, in all probability, of considerable economic importance. This importance plus their durability over extremely long time periods makes them the primary database for reconstructing and explaining paleolithic lifeways. For this reason considerable study has been devoted to these artifacts. These range from studies of prehistoric lithic assemblages that include innumerable descriptive reports (see Dennell 1983, Gamble 1986), the development of classification systems (Bordes 1961, Brézillon 1968), and statistical analyses of the distribution of types (Binford and Binford 1966, 1969; Freeman 1964) and morphological attributes (Barton 1987, 1988; Baumler 1987; Dibble 1981, 1983; Fish 1979, 1980; Jelinek 1982) to replicative and controlled experiments (Dibble 1981, Newcomer 1971, 1972) to ethnoarchaeological studies of modern stone artifact users (Gould, Koster and Sontz 1971, White and Thomas 1972, Gallager 1977).

In spite of this concentration of effort, however, many questions remain about the behavioral significance of lithic variability. This is especially true for the early Upper Pleistocene assemblages assigned to the Middle Paleolithic, where uncertainty about the extent of biocultural differences between these hominids and modern humans leaves analogies with recent hunter-gatherers open to question. Chipped stone artifacts are often the only reliable, surviving record of behavior for the

Middle Paleolithic. For this reason, the Middle Paleolithic of the western Old World has become an arena for continuing investigation and debate on the relationships between lithic variability and human behavior.

Much of this debate has centered around whether such variability is primarily stylistic or functional in origin. Those maintaining a "culturalist" position (e.g., Bordes 1973, 1981a; Bordes and de Sonneville-Bordes 1970, Butzer 1981, Collins 1970, Laville et al 1980:208–215) interpret variability in relative frequencies of artifact types in assemblages as primarily stylistic, resulting from differences in cultural tradition of the makers. Those taking a more "functionalist" position (e.g., Binford 1973; Binford and Binford 1966, 1969; Freeman 1964), on the other hand, see the same variability as deriving from the different uses for which artifacts were intended. These different views of the interpretation of lithic variability, which have come to be called the "Mousterian debate," have yet to be adequately resolved.

While there are certainly a number of historical/theoretical reasons for these different interpretations (see Binford and Sabloff 1982, Gamble 1986:1–27), it is not the intent here to present yet another detailed methodological and theoretical critique of these positions. Rather, it is argued that the difficulties in convincingly relating lithic variability to past behavior may be due, in considerable part, to an underlying paradigm that structures not only the way in which both sides of this debate view lithics, but pervades most interpretations of chipped stone artifact assemblages. This paradigm is derived from implicit analogies with the industrial technology of our own society in which most tools essential for modifying the environment are made of metal. In the sections which follow, an attempt will be made to outline this paradigm and illustrate the ways in which it has been applied to the interpretation of lithic assemblages. Subsequently, an alternative paradigm for interpreting chipped stone is presented that is derived, in part, from recent studies of Middle Paleolithic assemblages.

The Industrial Paradigm

Production

Although metal technology is complex, it can be broadly divided into several categories of production activities. The initial activity is the obtaining of raw material, metal ore. While this may have once been a more opportunistic process of collecting ore-bearing rocks from the surface, today it involves systematically locating ore deposits and mining them as a distinct and specialized set of activities. Ore is then processed to obtain metal through another set of distinct and specialized activities that may or may not be spatially associated with mining operations or each other. Such intermediate processes include milling and smelting, which generally produce large amounts of waste material (e.g., tailings and slag) relative to desired end products such as metal ingots, bars, or sheets. The transformation of metal into usable implements requires the creation of molds into which molten metal is poured. These molds, in turn, require that the finished form of the object be planned in advance. Finally, most metal objects used today require at least a minimal amount of processing in the form of finishing (e.g., polishing or removal of burrs) and some assembly (addition of a handle, for example).

Several features of this process are especially notable in their application, by analogy, to lithic technology. With respect to production technology in general, the production of metal implements involves a series of distinct activity sets that are often performed in separate spatial contexts. Additionally, the location of use of such artifacts is usually spatially distinct, and often distant, from the location(s) of production. Finally, this process involves the transformation of raw material into morphologically (and chemically) very different products through a series of distinct, intermediate stages, many of which are characterized by the production of a large amount of waste material relative to the desired end product.

In the transformation of metal into usable implements, the nature of the casting process as well as the amount of effort required for the production of metal implements encourages planning the form of the end product (i.e., "mental templates"). It also encourages a close, and often very specific, relationship between form and function. Within the limits proscribed by function, it also permits the incorporation of stylistic design elements that reflect "cultural traditions" or "ethnic identity." Because they only have to be executed once for each mold, these design elements can be quite complex with a relatively small amount of effort expended per piece over the life of the mold. Finally, casting both permits and encourages the mass production of populations of implements that exhibit minimal within-group variability and considerable between-group variability. The amount of between-group variability is primarily related to either the intended function(s) of the implements or the stylistic features.

Use

In addition to the production of metal implements, aspects of use are also worth considering in their application to lithic technology. In modern western, industrial societies, most metal implements undergo little if any morphology-altering maintenance during their use life. Significantly, the use life of metal objects is often quite long and may even exceed the lifespan of the original user. This lengthy use of life also affects production by encouraging detailed planning of artifact morphology to ensure its long-term functionality. Similarly, it encourages the incorporation into the artifact of more meaningful (and often more labor-intensive) stylistic elements (Bamforth 1986).

When these pieces eventually are worn or broken they are often discarded and replaced by new ones. One reason for this is that the form of the implement is so closely associated with its function that any alteration of its morphology would render it useless for its intended original purpose. Another factor relates to the economics of replacement. In modern society, much to the disdain of the "shade tree mechanic," replacement is often more economical than repair even for complex mechanical objects. Obviously there are exceptions to this tendency, one example being the general class of cutting tools, many of which are regularly resharpened. Implements may also be reused for purposes other than their originally intended function—reusing a broken automobile leaf spring for a chisel, for example. Most often, however, reuse of metal implements involves melting down scrap metal for recasting into new objects.

Behavioral Residues from Industrial Sites

Based on these general observations about industrial, metal technology, a set of relationships can be postulated between these processes and their potential material correlates. As exemplified below, these relationships are applicable to interpretations of variability among sites and of variability within and among assemblages of artifacts.

Sites

1. Sites having both a source of raw material (ore) and large amounts of initial production debris (such as tailings) often represent specialized resource extraction loci—mines.
2. Sites having no source of raw material but with production debris (tailings, slag, clinkers, shavings, etc.) represent specialized manufacturing loci such as mills, smelters, and foundries.
3. Sites with finished implements usually represent use sites (or discard areas associated with use sites). Production of such finished implements, even those discarded at mining and manufacturing sites, usually took place at localities other than the site of use and discard.

4. Sites with mixed characteristics indicate localities at which more than one of the above-described activity sets took place. Hence, a site with ore, tailings, and finished metal implements would be identified as a combined mine and use site. In reality, most sites will be of a "mixed" character, of course. However, the specialization associated with industrial metal technology ensures that it is usually possible to classify a site according to the primary activity that took place there.

Assemblages and Artifacts

1. In an assemblage of objects that include metal ore, tailings, smelted ingots, and finished metal artifacts, the pieces with the greatest degree of modification, from the raw ore, are usually the desired end products.
2. Waste from production is much greater in both mass and volume than finished end products.
3. Discrete artifact classes or types were produced, the members of which were intended to be identical or very similar by the makers because they were designed for the same tasks and/or to represent the same style.
4. Within-group variability is much less than between group variability.
5. Between-group variability is primarily a function of intended use (function) and/or culturally favored design (style). Thus, there is generally a close relationship between at least some aspects of form and function, and some aspects of form and style. Correct classification of such artifacts will provide information about the activities for which they were used and/or the ethnicity of the makers.
6. When broken or worn to the point of uselessness most metal artifacts are discarded or melted down to be recast into a different form. Hence, morphology tends to be relatively stable throughout the use life of such artifacts. At the end of its use life, the morphology of a discarded artifact tends to be either quite similar to its original form or lost altogether in recasting.

The Industrial Paradigm Applied to Lithic Assemblages

As a source for middle range theory that describes a variety of relationships between process and product, or behavior and material culture, the "industrial paradigm" can aid archaeologists in the interpretation of residues derived from metal technology. However, archaeologists often implicitly assume that very similar relationships also obtain between prehistoric behavior and archaeological residues consisting of chipped stone, rather than metal, artifacts.

Sites

For example, sites having both a source of lithic raw material and large amounts of production debris in the form of cores, flakes, and shatter are usually interpreted as specialized quarry and primary manufacturing sites (e.g., Binford and Binford 1966, Bordes and de Sonneville-Bordes 1970, Burton 1980, Gamble 1986:276–284, Howell et al. 1962, Isaac 1977:109, Marks and Freidel 1977). This is especially true if retouched tools are rare or absent at such sites. In these cases, partly finished artifacts are thought to have been taken elsewhere for finishing, and finished artifacts are taken elsewhere for use. The lack of retouched tools at such sites is felt to support the interpretation that they were specialized raw material extraction/manufacturing sites.

On the other hand, sites having no immediate source of raw material but with considerable amounts of debitage are interpreted as lithic manufacturing sites (Burton 1980, Fish 1979:85–135, Jelinek 1976). It is assumed that raw material extraction took place elsewhere. Again, if retouched pieces are rare or absent, it is further assumed that artifact finishing and use also took place elsewhere.

Finally, sites with retouched artifacts are interpreted as use sites (Binford and Binford 1966, Fish 1979:85–135, Jelinek 1976, Marks and Freidel 1977). If fine screening was employed during artifact recovery and small flakes were recovered, interpretations of site function may also include such activities as tool finishing and maintenance.

Sites with combinations of these characteristics are interpreted as sites where more than one of these activity groups took place (Bordes and de Sonneville-Bordes 1970, M. Collins 1975). For example, sites with debitage and retouched tools, but no apparent immediate source of lithic raw material, are interpreted as mixed manufacturing and use sites.

Assemblages and Artifacts

It is my contention that inferences about the significance of variability within and among lithic assemblages often seem drawn from the industrial paradigm. In most interpretations of chipped stone, those artifacts which exhibit the greatest degree of modification and tend to be numerically few in assemblages, the retouched pieces, are considered to be the most desired end products. Conversely those pieces which are more numerous and least modified, unretouched flakes for example, are often considered to be either production waste or blanks (analogous to metal ingots) with an unrealized potential to be transformed into useable tools (Binford and Binford 1966, D. Collins 1970, M. Collins 1975, Kleindienst 1962).

Particularly in typological studies of lithics, a fundamental assumption is that assemblages can be divided into distinct classes whose members show considerably less within-group variability than between group variability (e.g., Brézillon 1968, Bordes 1961, D. Collins 1970, Laville et al. 1980:32–41). These classes represent stages in the sequence of tool manufacture, tools designed for specific tasks or task sets, or functionally equivalent artifacts that exhibit different, culturally determined styles.

It is also widely implied in most interpretations of lithic variability that chipped stone tools are preconceived and are the end product of goal oriented production (or, more accurately for lithics, reduction) sequences that transform them from naturally occurring rocks to finished implements (e.g., Bradley 1975, M. Collins 1975, Isaac 1977:174, Kleindienst 1962). Hence, retouched pieces are considered the most informative of chipped stone artifacts because they exhibit intentional modification. Such modification is taken to indicate a maker's intent to create a tool whose form was shaped by the task for which it was intended and/or the maker's traditionally inspired concepts of how this particular tool should be made (see Jelinek 1976). The further implication is that variability is deviation from the desired form due to the differences in knapping skill, constraints of the raw material, and available or utilized technology.

Finally, built into most interpretations is the implicit assumption that the morphology of finished tools remained relatively static throughout their use lives. Hence, the discarded tools found at archaeological sites should reflect to a large degree the maker's intended form. This means that it should be possible to identify morphologically distinct tools or tool classes associated more or less exclusively with specific activities or activity sets. Morphological differences between such tool classes are then attributable either to their being associated with different activities or, if associated with the same activities, to being derived from different, culturally influenced concepts of the "proper" form for that tool.

This "industrial" view of lithic manufacture and use leads to several implications about the kinds of information that can be derived from lithic artifacts. Variability in unretouched debitage (including flakes, cores, and debris) primarily provides information about stages in the process of tool manufacture that took place at sites or about the different types of manufacturing processes utilized for tool manufacture. Variability in retouched tools, on the other hand, provides information about the nature and range of (primarily economic) activities that took place at sites or about social structure, ethnicity, or time (through diachronic stylistic changes in morphology).

An Alternative Paradigm

There may well be aspects of the industrial paradigm that are useful for interpreting lithic assemblages, especially when chipped stone artifacts are produced in the context of a specialized industry in a complex society (see Spence 1981, for example). However, a variety of evidence suggests that the wholesale application of this model to the production and use of chipped stone is both inappropriate and misleading. This is apparent in a number of recent studies of Middle Paleolithic assemblages which are based on an alternative paradigm that may be more useful for the interpretation of lithic variability. Several of these studies are briefly summarized below to exemplify this interpretive structure at different levels of analysis, including morphological variability in artifacts and edges, traditionally defined artifact classes or types, and the broader level of assemblages and industries.

Morphological Variability in Artifacts and Edges

In the first study, the retouched pieces from the sites of Cova del Salt and Cova del Pastor in eastern Spain, and Gorham's Cave and Devil's Tower in Gibraltar, were examined in detail from the point of view of their edges (Barton 1987, 1988, 1989). Features such as edge angle, edge length, edge shape, and invasiveness of retouch were measured in order to characterize quantitatively the edge morphology of these "tools."

For almost all attributes studied, variability is continuous and often normally distributed. With one exception, the distribution of attribute variability is unimodal and, thus, does not support the existence of distinct artifact classes. As more than a single type of task was performed during the Middle Paleolithic, this indicates a lack of function-specific edge morphologies and suggests that many retouched edges were multi-functional rather than designed for specific tasks or task sets. Edge shape is the only attribute that shows an exception to this pattern, with a minor, secondary mode for those comparatively rare edges with distinctively concave shapes—primarily notches.

Not only do these attribute data fail to provide evidence for a variety of distinct "types" of retouched edges, they also suggest that retouched edges may not be qualitatively different from unretouched edges. Edge angles, measured for both retouched and unretouched edges, are especially interesting in this respect (Figure 6.1). Figure 6.1a displays angles for all retouched edges and the combined group of retouched plus unretouched sharp edges. In Figure 6.1b, these edges are further broken down into unretouched sharp edges, marginally retouched edges (those with retouch extending less than 2 mm into the piece), and scraper edges (representing edges with more intensive retouch). While marginally retouched edges tend to have steeper edge angles than unretouched edges, and scraper edges have the steepest edge angles, there is considerable overlap in the distributions of these three edge groups (Figure 6.1b). Combined as a single group, however, (Figure 6.1a), they display a continuous normal distribution (mean = median = mode = 55°, σ = 14°). This situation suggests that the distinctions of unretouched, marginally retouched, and invasively retouched edges are simply arbitrary divisions of a single continuous distribution of edge morphology. It also implies that differences between debitage and retouched tools also may be more quantitative than qualitative—that is, retouched pieces do not represent a group of artifacts distinct from unretouched pieces.

If edge attribute data do not indicate the existence of a suite of morphologically distinct tools, then what accounts for variability in the amount and configuration of retouch on Middle Paleolithic chipped stone artifacts? A model to explain this variability is suggested by the pattern of relationships between edge attributes. Among edges with minimal retouch, edge angles can vary greatly. However, increasing amounts of retouch are associated with steeper minimum edge angles and a decreasing range of variability in angles. Edges with the most intensive retouch always have edge angles that are equivalent to the steepest angles on minimally retouched edges. Similarly, edges with minimal retouch occur on pieces with a wide range of relative widths (width/thickness), while intensively retouched edges occur only on relatively narrower, thicker pieces (Barton, 1988:66–71). In part, these patterns appear to represent mechanical relationships between attributes, based on the degree to which use, resharpening, and consequent edge reduction has taken place. As an edge is resharpened, the minimum edge angle that can be maintained becomes steeper and the flake it is on becomes relatively thicker and narrower (Figure 6.2).

However, these patterns also seem to be affected by discard behavior. With respect to edge angles, edge rejuvenation will only be taken to the point that the angle becomes too steep to be considered usable, at which time the edge will be abandoned. Subsequently, another edge may be used or the piece may be discarded. For pieces with initially

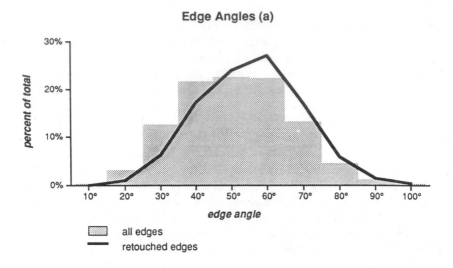

Edge Angles (a)

percent of total

edge angle

all edges

retouched edges

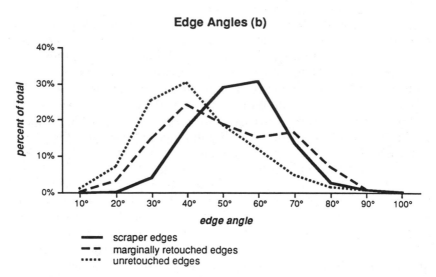

Edge Angles (b)

percent of total

edge angle

scraper edges

marginally retouched edges

unretouched edges

FIGURE 6.1.   Edge angles of Middle Paleolithic artifacts from Cova del Salt, Cova del Pastor, Gorham's Cave, and Devil's Tower rockshelter. (a) Frequency distribution for all retouched edges, and combined group of retouched and unretouched sharp edges. (b) Frequency distribution for sidescraper edges, marginally retouched edges, and unretouched edges.

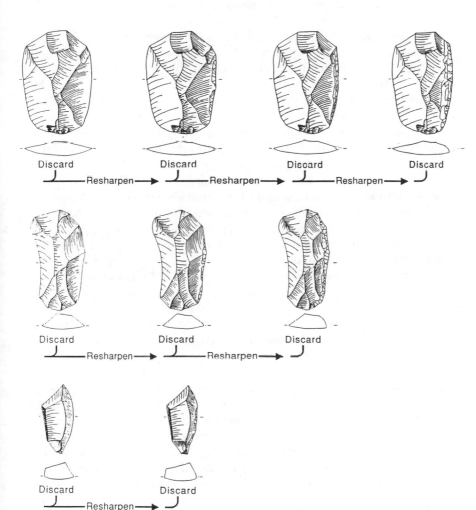

FIGURE 6.2. Schematic representation of relationships between artifact morphology, intensity of utilization, and edge resharpening. The top row represents relatively wide flakes with acute edges. These can undergo considerable edge rejuvenation, but may also be discarded prior to experiencing the maximum resharpening possible. The bottom row represents narrow, thick flakes with steep edges. With only minimal edge rejuvenation, such pieces become too narrow and their edges too steep to be used further. The center row represents flakes intermediate in width and edge angle. The maximum edge angle permitted is equivalent on all pieces.

steep edge angles, this point will be reached with only minimal re-sharpening, while pieces with initially acute edges can undergo consid-erable edge maintenance before reaching this point. However, these pieces with a potential for considerable resharpening also may be discarded before their edge angles reach such a discard-controlled limit. The more these edges are resharpened, of course, the closer they approach the maximum edge angle considered usable. This results in a wide range of variability for the angles of minimally retouched edges, an increasingly restricted range for more intensively retouched edges, and a maximum value for edge angles that remains constant regardless of the amount of retouch edges experience (Figure 6.2).

Likewise, pieces initially close to the minimum width or maximum thickness usable will be only, at most, minimally resharpened. While wider and thinner flakes have the potential for undergoing consider-able edge rejuvenation, they too may be discarded prior to experien-cing the maximum resharpening acceptable. The result, again, is a wide range of variability in relative width and thickness for minimally retouched edges, more restricted variability for heavily retouched edges, and a constant minimum value of width/thickness.

Finally, relationships between edge length and other attributes sug-gest a dichotomy in the way that edges were used. With one pattern of edge use, the more intensively an edge was used, the greater the linear extent of an edge that shows evidence of modification or resharpening. Edges characteristic of the class of artifacts termed scrapers would ex-emplify this pattern of edge use. Alternatively, on other edges, greater intensity of use is associated with an increasingly restricted area of retouch. Notches would typify this pattern of edge use. This dichot-omy also appears to be reflected in the distribution of edge shape discussed above, in which notches formed a secondary mode of shape (Barton 1988:71).

In sum, then, attribute data indicate that variability among re-touched edges is predominantly continuous; the data do not support the existence of a suite of distinct tools whose forms might be attributa-ble to specific intended functions or styles. Edges can be divided into only two broad groups, one consisting of edges in which use and subsequent modification was linearly extensive and shape is generally convex, and the second consisting of edges in which the linear extent of use and modification was restricted and shape is often concave. Furthermore, retouched artifacts seem to form a continuum with un-retouched artifacts. This suggests that the functional distinctions be-tween unretouched "debitage" and retouched "tools" may be consider-ably less significant than is usually implied. Finally, the intensity with which edges were used and rejuvenated may be a more important determinant of variability in retouched edges than the tasks to which edges were put or culturally determined edge forms.

Typological Variability

Besides characterizing morphological variability in Middle Paleolithic retouched artifacts, the processes described above can be used to explain the differences among traditionally defined artifact types. The class of artifacts termed side scrapers make up a third of Bordes's 63 Middle Paleolithic tool types and comprise 20–80% of the retouched artifacts in most Middle Paleolithic assemblages. The 21 side scraper types can be grouped into those with only one retouched edge (simple scrapers and transverse), those with two non-adjacent retouched edges (double scrapers), and those with two retouched edges that converge to a point (convergent and déjeté scrapers).

From studies of assemblages from the sites of Tabūn (Israel), Bisitun and Warwasi (Iran), and La Quina (southwestern France), Dibble (1987a, b, 1988) has argued convincingly that morphological differences among simple, double, transverse, and convergent scrapers are attributable to the degree to which edge resharpening took place. The degree to which edge rejuvenation took place is controlled, in turn, by the original dimensions (especially width) of the flake used.

He found that double scrapers show evidence of more intensive retouch than simple scrapers, and that convergent and transverse scrapers display the most intensive retouch. Using platform width to estimate the original widths of unretouched flakes, Dibble compared widths of scrapers with the original widths of the flakes on which they are made. While the mean widths of simple, double, transverse, and convergent scrapers in each assemblage differed little, the original widths of the flakes on which they were made varied considerably. Convergent and transverse scrapers were made on the widest flakes, simple scrapers on the most narrow flakes, and double scrapers on flakes of intermediate width.

To explain these data, Dibble postulates two pathways for scrapers to follow during their use life. Both begin with a simple scraper on which retouch occurs along one edge. If the piece is wide enough, it can continue to be used with edge rejuvenation. Following one pathway, the single edge is continually resharpened and consequently reduced. For pieces with sufficient initial width, the resharpening will cause the edge to retreat to a point that the scraper becomes typologically a transverse scraper by the time it is discarded. Alternatively, instead of continuously resharpening only one edge, the opposite edge also may be used producing a double scraper. If the piece is wide enough to permit continued resharpening of both edges, they may eventually meet, forming a convergent scraper at the time of discard.

In other words, differences among these significant Mousterian tool types are attributable to the degree to which flakes were resharpened rather than to differences in tool design based on considerations of function or style. Moreover, variability in the frequency of scraper types and scrapers as a whole are responsible to a large extent for differences between the industrial variants of the Mousterian initially defined by Bordes (i.e., Quina and Ferrassie variants of the Charentian, Typical, Acheulean Tradition A and B, and Denticulate) (Dibble 1988, Rolland 1977, 1981). The "meaning" of these industries has been a primary focus of the previously mentioned "Mousterian debate." Dibble's work and the edge analysis discussed above permit new questions about Middle Paleolithic assemblages to be asked and may render the "Mousterian debate" considerably less relevant. To ask why "Quina Mousterians" were resharpening their flakes so much more than "Typical Mousterians" will hopefully prove more fruitful, as exemplified below, than to ask whether "Quina Mousterians" were doing different things than "Typical Mousterians" or were different groups of people.

Assemblage Variability

In a pioneering study, Rolland (1977, 1981) re-examined the nature of typologically defined Middle Paleolithic industries. In so doing, he looked at the distribution of broad artifact classes within assemblages (all scraper types combined, all notches, all denticulates, and debitage, for example) in relation to a variety of contextual information, especially paleoenvironmental. He identified two general types of assemblages: (1) those that have both a high percentage of scrapers among retouched pieces and a high percentage of retouched pieces in the entire assemblages and (2) those with a high relative frequency of denticulates and/or notches among retouched pieces but in which retouched artifacts make up a much lower fraction of the entire assemblage.

Rolland also found that scraper rich assemblages, and assemblages of many retouched pieces, tend to occur, both temporally and geographically, in association with more rigorous environments characterized by open vegetation and seasonal temperature extremes. Scraper-poor assemblages, on the other hand, tend to be associated with more mesic, wooded environments having less extreme seasonal temperature fluctuations. Rolland postulates that industries with high scraper frequencies were a result of the resharpening of flakes due to a need to economize on lithic raw material. He further suggests that denticulates and notches may have been associated primarily with woodworking, while scrapers were simply reused flakes that served a variety of functions. He also argues that the association of industries with relative high frequencies of scrapers among retouched pieces, and retouched artifacts among all lithics with rigorous environments, reflects seasonal sedentism necessitated by climatic extremes. This would have had the effect of limiting movement and access to raw material sources. Such conditions would lead to a need to economize on raw material already available at a site by reusing pieces as often as possible. If notches and denticulates are associated with woodworking, they might be rarer in these environments with their open floral communities, lacking in trees. However, even if these latter artifacts were made in consistent quantities, the high absolute numbers of "scrapers" produced by the regular reuse of flakes would result in a low relative frequency of notches and denticulates among all "tools."

Conversely, Rolland suggests that the association of scraper-poor and notch/denticulate-rich assemblages with mesic environments results from more mobile settlement patterns that permit regular replenishment of raw materials. Given such conditions, there is less need to economize on raw material through reuse of flakes. Hence, "scraper" relative frequencies would be lower and notch/denticulate frequencies concomitantly higher among retouched artifacts. Furthermore, there would be fewer retouched pieces in assemblages. Finally, if notches and denticulates are associated with woodworking, the forested communities of these environments would permit more opportunity for manipulation of this medium and, hence, higher frequencies of these artifacts.

An Iberian Case Study Compared

An analogous study of Iberian peninsula sites reveals a slightly different pattern (Barton 1988, 1990). Here, assemblages from upland sites tend to have higher frequencies of scrapers among retouched pieces, but lower frequencies of retouched pieces relative to unretouched pieces compared with assemblages from lowland sites. Also, the density of artifacts per cubic meter of sediment is much higher in upland site deposits, even when differences in sedimentation rates are taken into consideration. While assemblages from lower elevation sites are considerably more variable than those of upland sites, there is still a general trend toward lower scraper frequencies and higher frequencies of pieces with restricted edge use and distinctive edge shapes (e.g., notches, burins, and piercers) among retouched pieces, higher frequencies of retouched pieces overall, more intensive retouch on those pieces that are modified, and lower artifact densities in site deposits.

As with Rolland's study, these data seem to represent differences in Middle Paleolithic settlement strategies. In a settlement model that accounts for observed variability in the lithic assemblages, upland sites represent short term occupations by relatively mobile groups. Lithic raw material could be regularly replenished, reducing the need to economize on this resource. This tendency toward the production of new flakes rather than resharpening of used ones, along with repeated visits to the sites, would encourage the deposition of denser quantities of lithic debris, relatively little of it modified. Finally, mobility associated with short, relatively unspecialized occupations, typical of a "forager" strategy (Binford 1980), might encourage the use of fewer multipurpose edges (e.g., "scrapers" and marginally retouched flakes) rather than a larger number of more specialized edges.

Lowland sites, on the other hand, represent less frequent but longer occupations in this model. Lithic raw material would be replenished less often, encouraging conservation through edge maintenance or resharpening, and would produce lower overall lithic densities in site deposits but more evidence for intensive use of the pieces that are present. The need to use sub-optimum pieces (e.g., broken flakes and shatter) in order to conserve lithic resources might also be expected to produce a wider diversity of edge configurations. Finally, these sites may represent more of a "collector" strategy (Binford 1980). If so, the greater variability in edge morphology, apparent in assemblages from these sites, may be indicative of the more specialized and more widely varied activities that took place.

The upland and lowland sites may only represent different, possibly seasonal, aspects of a single type of settlement pattern rather than two different strategies. It is interesting to note, however, that the assemblages at the lowland sites become more similar to those at the upland sites through time, exhibiting trends toward lower amounts of retouch in assemblages, higher lithic densities, and less morphological variation with a focus on extensively retouched edges. These temporal trends in lowland site assemblages occur during the transition from an interglacial to a glacial regime, associated with changes in temperature and precipitation and a concomitant altitudinal descent in life zones. During this transition, the environments of lowland sites became more like the interglacial environments of upland sites. The changes in lithic assemblages may be an indication of the way in which human groups adapted their settlement strategies to cope with the environmental changes that accompanied the approach of the full glacial.

Both studies focus on the interpretation of assemblage level variability in terms of such factors as mobility, intensity of occupation at sites, pressure on lithic resources, and overall settlement strategies. This exemplifies an alternative approach to that of the "industrial paradigm" which tends to emphasize the classification of sites on the basis of specific activities performed there or the ethnic affiliation of the inhabitants. This is not to say that information about settlement strategy is inherently more interesting than prehistoric activities and social organization. However, the database of chipped stone artifacts seems a better support for the preceding interpretations than those of the "Mousterian debate."

Discussion

Although the studies summarized above differ in their approaches to Middle Paleolithic chipped stone assemblages, they paint a consistent picture that is quite different from that derived from the previously described "industrial" paradigm. These studies bring out several characteristics of chipped stone artifacts of considerable significance to interpretations of lithic variability. Notable is the lack of more than a very few distinct artifact classes that can be associated with different functions or styles. Rather, morphological variability is generally continuous and reflects the amount of work performed by artifacts more than it reflects the type of work performed.

The use life of lithic artifacts is very short, compared with metal tools. This tends to discourage any significant investment of labor to execute or maintain a predetermined, standardized form. Also, many retouched pieces are multifunctional over the course of their use life, and both use and maintenance tend to alter their morphologies markedly (Bamforth 1986). The result is that lithic morphology is initially quite variable and subsequently dynamic during use. Hence, the form of a chipped stone artifact will often reflect only the last of a variety of uses. Jelinek (1976) has termed this latter characteristic the "Frison effect" after Frison's (1968) study of lithics from a North American Paleoindian kill site.

This means that, in many cases, the forms of chipped stone artifacts in archaeological assemblages are the cumulative result of a combination of many factors that affected their morphology during use life rather than intentional shaping to match a mental template. Such factors can include flake dimensions, extensiveness of margin use, intensity of edge use and associated edge maintenance, availability and character of raw material, and intensity of site occupation as well as the tasks for which artifacts were used and any culturally influenced choices affecting their production, use, and modification. Obviously, these factors are often closely interrelated. For these reasons, re-touched lithic artifacts will tend to have complex life histories from which specific functions or stylistic elements may be difficult to extract. Differences in frequencies of retouched pieces may relate more to the intensity with which a site was occupied or re-occupied than to specific activities carried out there or the ethnicity of the inhabitants.

In Middle Paleolithic flake industries, the regular, extensive reuse of edges for a variety of tasks appears to lead eventually to pieces that are usually classed as scrapers. Alternatively, use may repeatedly focus on the same section of edges, often resulting in artifacts classified as notches. If denticulates are considered to be multiple notches (see Dibble 1988), these processes produce the majority of the retouched "tools" on Bordes's type list (types 4, 6–29, 42–43, 51–52, and 54) and the majority of retouched artifacts in Middle Paleolithic assemblages. In other words, flakes that are repeatedly used will tend to produce typical Middle Paleolithic tools.

These same processes operating on different "blank" forms (such as blades and bifaces) also might be expected to produce characteristic "tool types," but not necessarily side scrapers and notches. This would mean that "blank" production technology alone could be responsible for an important part of what appear to be significant morphological differences between the artifact types of different industries. In this respect, it would be interesting to examine the extent to which differ-ences in core reduction technology affects the apparent differences be-tween Middle and Upper Paleolithic assemblages. The primary direc-tion in which long, narrow pieces like blades can be resharpened (thereby producing "retouched tools") is longitudinal, from the dis-tal or proximal end. Such reduction would produce end scrapers, piercers, truncations, and burins. While the lateral margins of blades might be used, the narrowness of these pieces would preclude signifi-cant edge rejuvenation. Hence, laterally retouched pieces (except for pieces with edge backing for hafting), or side scrapers, should be relatively infrequent.

It may well be, then, that many chipped stone "tools" simply repre-sent varying degrees of use of the initially produced "blanks," not the preconceived implements implied by the industrial paradigm. This is not to say that there was no planning or forethought involved in the manufacture of lithic artifacts. However, in many (perhaps most) cases, the "tools" that were planned and desired by prehistoric knappers may not have been the retouched pieces that archaeologists have generally considered the most important, but the unretouched debitage that is usually minimally analyzed at best, and has often been discarded.

If this is so, the great majority of lithic artifacts at sites are likely to be desired end products, rather than production waste or unfinished tool blanks. Also, instead of being desired end products, many of those pieces with the greatest degree of modification may simply be the most worn-out pieces. This means that debitage, largely ignored in much previous work (especially studies with a primarily typological focus), is not only more numerous but may also be potentially more interpretable than the retouched tools, with their more confused life histories, on which reconstructions of activities and social organization usually have been based (see, e.g., Clark et al. 1986, Straus and Clark 1986c). This stands in contrast to the implications about the significance of debitage derived from the industrial paradigm. Furthermore, it calls into question site classifications based on this paradigm—in particular, distinctions between quarry sites, manufacturing sites, and use sites. Thus, while an abundance of raw material and "debitage" with rarity or lack of "tools" might signify a lithic procurement and primary manufacturing site, it might equally indicate simply that a local abundance of raw material permitted the continuous creation of fresh flakes to replace those dulled by use rather than encouraging the rejuvenation of edges through retouching (e.g., Barton 1988:102–103).

Finally, virtually all lithics found at archaeological sites are discards. Some pieces were discarded after minimal use, while others experienced considerable reworking prior to discard. The recognition of factors influencing the point at which used lithic artifacts are discarded should be an integral part of interpreting variability in lithic assemblages.

Although these processes have been discussed primarily in the context of Middle Paleolithic assemblages, they may have wider applicability to other prehistoric societies in which chipped stone artifacts constitute a significant part of the technological system (see, e.g., Clark et al. 1986, Straus and Clark 1986a–c, Clark 1989c, Hayden 1987). This application may not simply be limited to flake industries like those of the Middle Paleolithic. For example, the various bifacial implements from Upper Paleolithic and later industries, in both the Old and New Worlds, appear to represent exceptions to the processes described above. They seem to be objects with planned, carefully executed morphologies, primarily determined by functional and/or stylistic constraints. However, several studies indicate that variability among even these artifacts may be more strongly affected by factors such as intensity of use and maintenance than would initially seem to be the case (Goodyear 1982, Hoffman 1985, Flenniken and Raymond 1986, Flenniken and Wilke 1989). This is not to say that the Middle Paleolithic should serve as a model for the interpretation of all lithic assemblages. Still, the paradigm presented above seems a more useful starting place

for understanding the meaning of lithic variability in prehistoric societies than a paradigm based on western industrial technology.

Conclusions

An attempt has been made here to outline a usually implicit paradigm
commonly applied to the interpretation of lithic residues of prehistoric
behavior. Subsequently, an alternative paradigm was presented based
on several recent studies of Middle Paleolithic assemblages. It is felt
that this alternative more realistically models behaviors associated with
the manufacture, use, and discard of chipped stone artifacts than the
interpretive approach here termed the "industrial paradigm." The title
of this paper reflects the fundamental differences between these approaches to chipped stone artifacts.

While retouched lithic artifacts most certainly exist, these models
lead to very different views of their significance. Based on the "industrial paradigm," these artifacts would be viewed as distinct tools, analogous to those in a modern toolbox, whose forms were planned to
correspond with their intended uses and with stylistic considerations
determined by cultural tradition.

Within the alternative paradigm presented above, however, these
artifacts would represent a group of multipurpose implements, generally homogeneous both functionally and stylistically, whose morphological variability reflects to a large degree the intensity with which they
were used. If they have analogies in modern society, it is perhaps more
with an assemblage of Marshalltown trowels in the equipment closet of
a long-running archaeological field school than those artifacts we normally consider tools. Recent purchases would have large blades with
dull, convex edges. Among those that have been used, variability in
blade morphology might include size (ranging from original size to
very short or narrow), edge sharpness, and the shape of lateral edges
(which could be convex, straight, or even concave) and tips (which
might vary from round to pointed). Trowels are used for a wide variety
of activities by archaeologists. Also, students attending the field school
over the years might come from a variety of cultural backgrounds.
However, most observed variability in these artifacts is better attributed
to such factors as the texture of the deposits in which they were used,
the frequency with which rocks were encountered, the diligence with
which the blades were resharpened, and the frequency with which the
field school could afford to replace worn trowels with new ones than to
the specific uses to which they were put or the ethnic affiliations of the
students.

Not even the archaeologist's trowel is a truly accurate analogy for chipped stone artifacts, however. In fact, it is difficult to identify any implements in modern western, industrial society that would serve as useful analogies for these most common items of material culture for prehistoric hunter-gatherers. Yet this does not mean that lithics must defy interpretation. In fact, although many forms of behaviors and social organization common to Pleistocene populations may have no modern analogs, even among remnant hunter-gatherer populations, one of the challenges of paleolithic archaeology is the reconstruction and explanation of such lifeways. The interpretive model presented here is an attempt to account for a set of such behaviors, once an integral part of daily life and now virtually extinct. Because lithics are the common artifactual evidence for the activities of Pleistocene hominids, developing better paradigms for interpreting these implements is essential to understanding this enormous part of the human past. It is hoped that the work presented here is a step in this direction.

Acknowledgments

I would like to thank E. M. MacMinn-Barton for her illustrations and critical reviewing of this manuscript. I would also like to thank D. Olszewski (University of Georgia), J. Lindly (Arizona State University), and N. Coinman (University of Tulsa) for reading and commenting on this manuscript.

Chapter 7
The Elephant and the Blind Men: Paradigms, Data Gaps, and the Middle-Upper Paleolithic Transition in Southwestern France

Francis B. Harrold

Introduction

In 1987, I attended the Cambridge symposium on the origins of modern humans (Mellars and Stringer 1989), which included much discussion of the archaeological transition from the Middle to the Upper Paleolithic. Like others, I was struck by the level of disagreement about what this transition actually meant in terms of ancient human cultural systems and its connection (if any) with the evolutionary origins of modern humans. It was also striking that after all the papers had been delivered and the discussions held, few minds seemed to have been changed. I was reminded of the Indian tale of the blind men encountering an elephant. Each touched a different part of the beast, and none could agree on its true nature.

In the wake of this experience I would like to explore an issue already raised by others, notably Clark and Lindly (1989a, b), Clark (1989b) and Straus (1987a): the extent to which the debates over the Middle-Upper Paleolithic transition are affected by paradigm differences. I use the term "paradigm" in the sense of the above authors; the term comes to us, of course, from Kuhn (1970a) through Binford (see especially Binford and Sabloff 1982). A paradigm is not a particular scientific theory, but rather a scientific frame or worldview. It is through a paradigm that an archaeologist perceives what sorts of things may be learned (and are worth learning) from the archaeological record and what sorts of evidence and analytical methods are relevant to learning them.

In this paper I will discuss paradigm differences and understandings of the Middle-Upper Paleolithic transition quite narrowly in terms of the area I know best, southwestern France. I will deal here primarily with archaeological paradigms and evidence, treating only tangentially the issue of the evolutionary origins of modern humans.

Un peu d'histoire

Some historical background is useful to begin this discussion, since the controversy is due in part to our use today of some theoretical constructs (e.g., "Aurignacian") formulated long ago, when research preoccupations (and paradigms) were different from today's. It is important to recall that prehistory in France began in the last century in an attempt simply to establish the geological antiquity of mankind—to prove the very existence of "early man" (Grayson 1983, Sackett 1981; Bordes, Rigaud and de Sonneville Bordes 1972). Only later did the focus shift to learning something about ancient humanity from the archaeological record.

In a manner roughly paralleled in the history of American archaeology (Willey and Sabloff 1980, Rigaud 1982:34–38), the focus of de Mortillet and his contemporaries around the turn of this century was on space-time systematics—the demonstration of the ways in which artifacts (primarily stone tools) varied over space and time. Stratigraphic ordering (and lithic seriation based on it) were the main dating tools. The "fossil director" approach borrowed from paleontology was used to construct a sequence of prehistoric stages, recognized by the key artifact types which were supposedly unique to them. Culture-stratigraphic units (or industries) began to be recognized and arranged in a culture-historical sequence. Behavioral interpretation of these units tended to be intuitive. It was clearly shaped by the unilineal evolutionism and "doctrine of progress" characteristic of anthropology at the time. The prehistoric past was seen as a series of stages of cultural evolution documenting mankind's rise from simple savagery to agricultural sophistication.

More than anyone else, Henri Breuil (1913) established the culture-stratigraphic unit sequence in use today in southwestern France. In winning the "Battle of the Aurignacian," he demonstrated that the Solutrean, despite its supposedly archaic bifacial retouch, was not the earliest Upper Paleolithic industry. Breuil placed the Middle-Upper Paleolithic boundary more correctly between the Mousterian and the Aurignacian (Breuil called "Lower, Middle, and Upper Aurignacian" the industries known today as Châtelperronian, Aurignacian, and Upper Perigordian). He also exemplified a trend toward interpretation of industries less as evolutionary stages than as representing "cultures" or "peoples." Thus, rather as ancient Gauls had left Gaulish pottery and other artifacts in their sites, while Romans left Roman pottery in theirs, the Aurignacians had left Aurignacian tools (most importantly, fossil directors) in their caves.

Related to this shift in interpretive emphasis was a change from a prior position on the nature of the Middle-Upper Paleolithic transition (Breuil 1909a). Earlier, it had been seen simply as a passage from a lower to a higher cultural stage, with no elaboration as to how it happened. But by 1913 Breuil was explicit; the Aurignacians (anatomically modern people) had replaced the Mousterians (Neanderthals), their mental and cultural inferiors. Marcellin Boule's (1911–13) unflattering interpretation of Neanderthal anatomy and phylogeny may well have influenced this shift (though Narr [in Brace 1964:29] sees the influence running the other way).

Breuil established the basic paradigm in French prehistoric research, with its emphasis on time-space systematics, recognition of "cultures" through fossil directors, and use of cultural or ethnic identity to explain most variability in the archaeological record. Important changes in this basic paradigm were to occur in the ensuing decades, but not through paradigm crises or clashes. Rather, a process of gradual paradigm shift, or what might be termed "creep," ensued, in which new methods of excavation and analysis led to successive modifications of the existing paradigm. Rarely, though, were the basic premises of Breuil's paradigm (the analytical primacy of ancient cultures and their accessibility through lithic assemblages) questioned.

One important shift was due mainly to the work of Denis Peyrony (1933). On the basis of more excavations and finer stratigraphic distinctions that had been available in 1913, he reformulated Breuil's "Aurignacian" into two parallel cultural traditions or "phyla." Each consisted of five numbered stages based on the temporal succession of stone and bone fossil directors, stratigraphically confirmed at a few key sites, and assumed to be generally valid in and around the Périgord. One phylum was the Aurignacian, the other the Perigordian (in which Peyrony joined the Châtelperronian, or Lower Perigordian, to the Upper Perigordian on the basis of the backed pieces in both industries).

For Peyrony, the Middle-Upper Paleolithic transition (hereafter, simply "the transition") involved the rapid replacement of Neanderthals by the Combe-Capelle race of modern man, who made Perigordian tools.[1] Later, the Aurignacians (the Cro-Magnon race) entered the Périgord and pushed the Perigordians to its periphery, only to be themselves ousted later by the resurgent (Upper) Perigordians (Peyrony 1933, Peyrony and Peyrony 1951).

In introducing the notion of parallel cultural phyla, and tying them to particular "races" of fossil man in a way which seems to modern readers like a just-so story, Peyrony went beyond Breuil's culture historical framework, but he did so by interpreting a more detailed and nuanced data set, not by questioning basic principles. For Peyrony, patterning in the archaeological record which had not been visible earlier was apparent, simply because of improvement in its quality and quantity, not because it was to be perceived in a fundamentally different way.

Further significant interpretive change occurred after World War II, mainly in the form of the incorporation of new lines of evidence. The modern natural-science orientation of French prehistory emerged, as geology, palynology, and faunal analysis all came increasingly to be used as means to date archaeological levels more exactly and to describe the environment in which ancient people had lived.

Of equal importance were the developments summed up as *la méthode Bordes*, whereby lithic assemblages were characterized no longer primarily by their fossil directors, but by an inventory of all retouched tools, classified according to standard typologies for the Middle and Upper Paleolithic. This innovation allowed the discrimination of previously unrecognized dimensions of variability within and between assemblages. Combined with increasingly refined techniques for relative dating of cave and rockshelter occupations (culminating in achievements like Laville's chronostratigraphic sequence—Laville et al. 1980), it allowed far more sensitive assessments of time-space systematics.

With more and better-excavated collections and the new methodology, prehistorians were able to find weaknesses in Peyrony's scheme—for instance, when de Sonneville-Bordes (1955) showed that stages II and III of the Perigordian did not really exist. But the two-phylum theory itself was still widely accepted. So was the primacy of the cultural interpretation of variability, as when Bordes interpreted the new-found Mousterian facies in cultural terms. It is significant, though, that he also considered (and ruled out) climatic and other factors as possibly underlying facies differences (Bordes and de Sonneville-Bordes 1970).

Another effect of Bordesian methodology was the conclusion that much gradual vectored temporal change had occurred in paleolithic assemblages which had previously gone unrecognized. For instance, Bordes (1958, 1972) inferred a gradual evolution in the Mousterian of Acheulean from type A, to type B (with some blades and Upper Paleolithic types), to the Lower Perigordian (or Châtelperronian) with many Mousterian types, and so on through the Perigordian sequence. Thus the Middle-Upper Paleolithic transition involved cultural continuity—and probably biological continuity as well: Bordes (1968b,

1972) strongly suspected that this artifactual continuity paralleled the local evolution of Neanderthals into *Homo sapiens sapiens*. An element of abrupt change was retained in the transition, however, for the Aurignacian was still seen as intrusive in southwestern France (e.g., Bordes 1984:424).[2]

Thus in this review we have seen the standard French interpretation of the Middle-Upper Paleolithic transition change from in situ transition to abrupt replacement in a simple, then complex form; and finally to gradual transformation followed by abrupt entry. While the archaeological record's interpretation underwent considerable shifts, the underlying paradigm changed mainly incrementally. The basic proposition that typological and technological differences between assemblages are explicable primarily in terms of culture did not change from Breuil to Bordes, though Bordes did acknowledge a significant role for factors like raw material variation and site specialization (e.g., *ateliers de taille*) in conditioning assemblage composition (e.g., Bordes et al. 1972). It is also true that by Bordes's time more attention was devoted to the interaction of humans with their environment—though such interaction was usually judged to have had little or no effect on assemblage makeup, since there was no correspondence between climatic phases and changes in industries (Bordes et al. 1972, de Sonneville-Bordes 1980). In sum, new lines of evidence were incorporated as important to the prevailing paradigm, but were mainly used to give more precise traditional answers to questions posed in traditional ways. One lesson to draw from this is that very different interpretations of the archaeological record may be undergirded by very much the same paradigm.

An indisputable paradigm clash did occur in the 1960s as French prehistory collided with American processual archaeology, most memorably in the Bordes-Binford dispute over the nature of Mousterian variability. Here indeed were such different conventions for asking and answering questions about the past that "settling" the argument was all but impossible. The facies issue is far from resolved today, though there is a consensus that neither opposing paradigm was able at that time to encompass the complex nature of Mousterian lithic variability (e.g., Rolland 1981, Sackett 1988a). A period of paradigmatic conflict and confusion ensued as North American archaeologists and students crossed the Atlantic to work and argue with their European counterparts. It was not, however, a paradigm crisis in Kuhn's classic sense. It was generated, not internally through increasing dissatisfaction with the old paradigm, but through confrontation between two existing ones.

In the wake of the conflict, ideas on the Middle-Upper Paleolithic transition were affected. Lynch (1966), critically viewing the Lower

Perigordian data base, argued that the Châtelperronian industry did not actually exist, being the result of incorrectly interpreted assemblages mixed by excavators or geology (see Harrold 1978 for an opposing view based on more complete data). To more lasting effect, Brace (1964, 1966) and Brose and Wolpoff (1971) contended on archaeological and fossil grounds that both the biological and cultural transitions in France had been gradual and continuous. Interestingly, a different paradigm had in this case produced an interpretation not far from the standard French one. However, the two-phylum aspect of the French interpretation was often rejected (or at least viewed askance) by New World workers. S. Binford (1972), for instance, suggested that the Aurignacian and Perigordian could represent seasonal or other activity variants of the same cultural system, a point reprised by Ashton (1983) and Clark and Lindly (1989a). Klein (1973:111–114) presented another variant of the two-phylum theory. He accepted the Aurignacian as intrusive and associated with modern humans, while the Châtelperronian represented the temporary and partial acculturation of Neanderthals.

All of these developments affected the interpretations and paradigmatic biases of French researchers, but, except for Bordes and de Sonneville-Bordes (e.g., 1970, Bordes 1973), they did not generate many lengthy rejoinders or discussions in the French literature. A general reason for this is that French paleolithic prehistorians were and are less given than their New World counterparts to epistemological debate. They tended, especially at first, to regard processual archaeologists from overseas as full of grand theoretical schemes which went beyond what the data could confirm (e.g., Bordes et al. 1972), as not always sufficiently familiar with the data,[3] and as sometimes uncongenially patronizing.

There was little controversy at this time in the French literature specifically over the Middle-Upper Paleolithic transition, due to widely-acknowledged inadequacies in the data base. It was recognized that many of the archaeological sites and human remains relevant to the period were poorly dated or otherwise dubious. For instance, the two assemblages critical in the early formulation and interpretation of the Châtelperronian, La Ferrassie E and Le Moustier K, were known to be badly mixed by cryoturbation with material from underlying Mousterian levels (de Sonneville-Bordes 1972).

Despite the lack of explicit discussion of the transitional period, the late 1960s and the 1970s were important, for much information of generally high quality was added to the archaeological record. New sites were excavated and/or reported with modern methods of data recovery and analysis (for details see Harrold 1978, 1983) and fitted into regional stratigraphic schemes (e.g., Laville et al. 1980). In Upper Paleolithic studies generally, it came to be realized that the numbered stages of the industries had limited temporal validity and that tool type proportions within a given industry might vary greatly from site to site (e.g., Rigaud 1982). Furthermore, as we will see below, the research paradigms of workers in the area were indeed being affected by the meeting of Old and New World approaches.

The catalyst for renewed interest in the transitional period was the discovery in 1979 of Neanderthal remains in one of a series of Châtelperronian levels at Saint-Césaire, Charente (Lévêque and Vandermeersch 1981, Vandermeersch 1984). This find was important because, for the first time, diagnostic human remains were associated unequivocally with the Châtelperronian.[4] A Neanderthal was now linked with the earliest Upper Paleolithic tradition in the region (albeit one widely seen as deriving from the local Mousterian), while anatomically modern humans (AMH) were associated with the penecontemporaneous Aurignacian. As the most recent known Neanderthal, Saint-Césaire also had implications for the proposition that regional AMH populations had evolved from Neanderthals, thought to date at Saint Césaire to roughly 34,000–35,000 B.P. Did it leave enough time for the morphological shift to the condition seen in the AMH Cro-Magnon remains of roughly 30,000 B.P.?

The Saint-Césaire discovery coincided with increased preoccupation among researchers in the worldwide question of the origins of AMH (e.g., Spencer 1984) and the nature of the relations among biological evolution, behavioral change, and the archaeological record of such change. The dispute between proponents of regional continuity models and those of restricted origin (or "Out of Africa II" [Gowlett 1987]) models was joined by archaeologists and, eventually, molecular and DNA researchers. Saint-Césaire and the Châtelperronian were often cited as evidence of abrupt population replacement and cultural change (or of how such inferences could be wrongly drawn!).

Current Views

Thus the Middle-Upper Paleolithic transition in southwestern France has become a controversial issue. Current interpretations vary widely. A number of researchers, including Dibble (1983), Harrold (1983, 1989), and in Cantabria, Butzer (1986), have proposed that the transition in this region was primarily a matter of replacement; the Châtelperronian, associated with Neanderthals, was a relatively short-lived "bow-wave" acculturation phenomenon related to entry of AMH and the Aurignacian.[5] This is consistent with the model of biological replacement of Western European Neanderthals by AMH advanced by Stringer et al. (1984), Trinkaus (1986), and Howell (1984).

Other workers interpret the record very differently. Clark and Lindly (1989a, b), Clark (1987b, 1989b), Straus (1987a, n.d.d), and Simek and Price (1990) argue for continuity and gradual change across the Middle-Upper Paleolithic boundary. They see lithic change as gradual and directional and propose, especially on the basis of faunal studies in northern Spain, that patterns in evidence for human subsistence show no significant shift until much later in the Upper Paleolithic. They are supported here by Chase's (1987, 1989) analyses of a number of Périgord faunas as well. They relate such archaeological continuity to the biological continuity between Neanderthals and AMH inferred by Wolpoff (1980, 1989) and Smith (1984; Smith et al. 1989). For these workers, there was no drastic shift or replacement, biological or cultural, at 30,000–35,000 B.P. in southwestern France or elsewhere in Europe.

Other opinions differ yet again. Working with material from Arcy-sur-Cure, Farizy (1990) suggests an abrupt emergence of the Châtelperronian from the local Mousterian, via unspecified processes. Bahn (1982, 1983) sees no evidence for subsistence-settlement changes until long after the transition, but does agree that the addition of bone artifacts and items of decorative and symbolic import to archaeological inventories at the beginning of the Upper Paleolithic is an important change. Rigaud (1989) sees abrupt change at the boundary in some respects (e.g., population replacement and artifact change) but not in others (e.g., raw material acquisition patterns).

Several authors, including White (1982, 1989), Wobst (1976), and Gilman (1983) focus on the appearance in the Upper Paleolithic of stylistically variable items like pendants and beads, with symbolic or decorative implications, as the key development of the transition. They attribute their appearance to sociocultural innovations (related to maintenance of mating networks or social boundaries) which were in turn triggered by increasing subsistence efficiency and population crowding. White (1982), though, allows that the sociocultural developments may have been the prime movers in the process (as opposed to demographic stress).

Binford (1982a, 1982b, 1989d) suggests great discontinuity across the transition, with Upper Paleolithic sites showing far greater evidence of logistically-organized subsistence, planning and foresight, and curative tool use. However, he sees it as premature to specify the nature or tempo of the transition or its possible relationship to human evolution.

Other authors (e.g., Laville et al. 1980, Bricker 1976, Mellars 1973, Lévêque and Miskovsky 1983) refrain from detailed proposals as to how or how quickly the transition occurred, or its evolutionary implications. They do recognize a role for local Mousterian-Châtelperronian continuity, and (usually) see the Aurignacian as intrusive. Most French workers fall into this category. Generally, they seem to think available data are insufficient to resolve things further.

After this brief survey, one can agree with Gilman's (1983:121) unenthusiastic assessment: "The available literature on the Middle to Upper Paleolithic transition, so far as it transcends a purely descriptive level, does not contain a satisfactory account of the nature of the processes involved." Those authors who are clear about identifying the nature of the broad patterning in the archaeological record (e.g., the gradualist and abrupt-change positions first cited) are vague about the specifics of the processes of change—what ancient cultural systems were like and how they came to change.[6] Others propose certain processes as crucial to the transition (e.g., Gilman, or S. Binford's [1970] suggestion relating subsistence change to the transition in the Near East), but do not show how the suggested explanation fits a regional data set. Still others are noncommittal because of insufficient information.

This state of affairs is partly due to the fact that discussions of the transition are often in fact *en bloc* comparisons of "Before" and "After," with little or no attention given to the crucial transitional period itself. We are also hampered by the lack of specification (i.e., operational definitions) of some key terms and concepts. When we argue about whether the transition was "abrupt" or "gradual," I am not sure we all have in mind the same temporal scale. Would a transition which took a thousand years from beginning to end be abrupt or gradual? The answer could be either, depending on one's choice of temporal scale. Confusion can also arise about "continuity." Most of us who favor a model of abrupt change nonetheless argue for significant cultural continuity between Mousterian and Châtelperronian. How much change, of what sort, and at what rate qualifies as abrupt or discontinuous? This terminological issue must eventually be addressed, but it is secondary here. When one compares the views of authors at opposite ends of the spectrum of opinion presented above, there are clearly other reasons for disagreement.

Paradigms Today

Are differing paradigms for paleolithic research the basis of current disagreements? A useful basis for discussion of this issue is Clark and

Lindly's paper (1989a; see also Clark 1989b), which strongly contrasts two paradigms outlined for researchers dealing with the transition.

According to Clark and Lindly, the first paradigm (not named, but characterized as an Old World one) is based on a normative notion of culture as a set of beliefs and practices characterizing a people or ethnic group. Culture is manifest in the archaeological record, in this characterization of the (or "an") Old World paradigm (or OWP), through typological (and to a lesser extent, technological) variation in stone and other artifacts. The main task of archaeologists is to order such variability in time and space so as to trace the evolution of ancient cultures. The OWP is described as centered on artifacts, especially fossil directors, and little concerned with their contexts and associations. Its typologies are designed to emphasize certain kinds of lithic variability (notably that of fossil directors), while obscuring much variability related to subsistence, raw material, or (sometimes) technological factors. Separate Middle and Upper Paleolithic typologies ensure that discontinuity is perceived between the two stages. The OWP is naively empiricist; under its terms, archaeology "progresses" by means of discoveries and post-hoc rationalizations rather than scientific method.

In contrast stands what might be called the New World paradigm, or NWP. Clark and Lindly do not describe it so explicitly as the OWP, but its main features are clear. It is like Gamble's (1986) and Straus's (1987a) "culture as adaptive system" paradigm and is explicitly derived from Binford and Sabloff (1982). This paradigm is strongly oriented toward cultural ecology. Artifacts are regarded merely as elements in ancient cultural systems, which were variable over space and time, even among people of the same "culture." Artifactual variability is comprehensible only in light of context—spatial, faunal, technological, etc. With this approach (e.g., Straus and Clark 1986a), it is becoming apparent that much variation once considered "cultural" was in fact ecologically conditioned. An explicitly scientific process of attributing meaning to archaeological observations through theory-building is espoused.

According to Clark and Lindly, the difference between these two paradigms underlies the interpretive disputes over the Middle-Upper Paleolithic transition (and in parallel fashion in paleoanthropology, the biological transition to AMH). Those committed to the OWP embrace abrupt transitions (both culturally and biologically), while those with the NWP accept gradual transitions (or transitions with different aspects developing at variable rates). Presumably, the dispute will continue as long as there are two competing paradigms.

But does Clark and Lindly's account accurately describe the distribution of paradigmatic biases and interpretive theories regarding the transition, and the relationship between them? My answer is, "not entirely," for two reasons. First, when one tests this analysis—at least for southwestern France—by comparing various workers' paradigms (expressed or inferred) with their interpetations of the transition, the expectations noted above are not found. Most of the French pre-historians do not take a position on the nature or tempo of the transition, though one would expect that, given their presumed paradigm, they would espouse a model of abrupt change. Yet nearly all French prehistorians stress some degree of Mousterian-Châtelperronian continuity. Furthermore, following Bordes, they do not necessarily see the development of the Châtelperronian as a "bow wave," but rather as an autochthonous development. If we then look at who does explicitly favor an abrupt-change model (with the Châtelperronian as a side effect), we find mostly American archaeologists—who we might expect to share a New World paradigm, and in consequence a continuity model. Interestingly, the individual most closely identified with the sort of paradigmatic approach described by Clark and Lindly, Lewis Binford, has not adopted a gradualist model; and, given his emphasis on contrasts in inferred human behavior between Middle and Upper Paleolithic, one could not automatically assume that he will.

This discordance between expectation and outcome is consistent with my own impression, based on both the literature of the transition in the Périgord and my interactions with many workers in the field. I believe that Clark and Lindly's characterization dichotomizes what is better described as a spectrum of paradigms among researchers in this area (at least among archaelogists). The scientific worldview represented by Clark and Lindly is indeed at loggerheads, as they describe, with those of some senior members of the French archaeological community. However, I find the paradigms of most workers, French and otherwise, to be somewhere between these extremes and with a greater region of potential agreement than is sometimes recognized.

I think that the degree of mutual paradigm influence which has occurred in the two decades since the initial clash has been underestimated. Each side has come to see that the other had something to offer, a way to enlarge the sphere of understanding of prehistory. Most New World workers have gained a healthy respect for the difficulties of working with such a long and complex archaeological record and, rather than dismissing traditional typology, have come to think that it monitors a significant axis of behaviorial variability (e.g., Sackett 1975). Their French counterparts have in turn begun to pay systematic attention to the multiple sources of variability that are unrelated to cultural variation. An exemplar of such a synthetic approach is Rigaud (see especially Rigaud 1982, Rigaud and Simek 1987), who, while still arguing for the significance of traditional systematics, hardly exemplifies the OWP in method and theory. He and French colleagues provided most of the excavations and analyses showing that the spatiotemporal variability of Périgord Upper Paleolithic industries simply cannot be described in neatly numbered stages (Rigaud 1982, 1985).

Most French and American workers investigating various aspects of this transition use largely the same body of techniques, in both excavating or other data-gathering, and in data analysis. This body includes not only traditional typological analysis, but also raw material source analysis (e.g., Morala 1984, Demars 1982), lithic reduction sequence study (work currently underway by J. Pelegrin and others), and microwear polish analysis (e.g., Beyries 1987, Anderson-Gerfaud 1990). Paradigmatic overlap extends from analytical methods to criteria (at least general ones) for interpreting evidence behaviorally. In the case of the transition, I submit that there is a good deal of agreement on just what evidence would support a gradualist model versus one of abrupt change.

I have outlined elsewhere (Harrold 1989) what sorts of patterning in the data different models would predict; but let us suppose for purposes of argument that it could be shown that paleoenvironmental, faunal, and tool-function analyses were consistent with the proposal that contemporary Aurignacian and Châtelperronian occupations were in fact functionally complementary—winter versus summer sites, say, or occupation versus special purpose sites (cf. Ashton 1983; on the basis of available information, I doubt this, but readily agree that the analyses necessary really to test such a proposal have not been done). I think most workers on both sides of the Atlantic would agree that the "parallel phyla" interpretation had been dealt a serious blow. Or to turn to fossil evidence, suppose that several adequately dated future finds of human remains in the region fit the pattern suggested by Saint-Césaire—that is, of morphologically typical Neanderthals slightly antedating or overlapping temporally with AMH, with no fossils interpretable as intermediate forms. Once again, most researchers would interpret that evidence as favoring a biological discontinuity model. Despite our differences, there is a broad if often implicit consensus concerning the patterning in the data expected for competing models of the transition. One can see something of this implicit acknowledgment, for instance, in Clark and Lindly (1989a, b), Simek and Price (1990), and Straus and Heller (1988), in which the authors argue for lithic typological continuity over the transition. It could be asked why, if traditional typological studies are of such dubious value, one should take the trouble to do them? Furthermore, if typological continuity is found, so what? After all, the main trouble with the old paradigm was its dependence on traditional typology. The answer, I believe, is that NWP archaeologists think that traditional typologies are still telling us something of interest about behavior during the transition.

But if we agree on so much about seeking and evaluating patterns in the archaeological record, then why do some workers perceive paradigm clash? I think that there are several reasons. One is historical. To many North American workers, the OWP is mainly defined by the work of Bordes and de Sonneville-Bordes, whose work is not fully representative of French researchers today. More important is the existence of different national research traditions which lend a particular format and vocabulary to the work of those sharing them. The formation of most French (and other continental) prehistorians is not in anthropology or American processual archaeology, with its self-conscious search for reliable means of archaeological inference. Instead, they are trained in a natural-science-oriented perspective (Rigaud 1982:38) in which inference is cautious and careful, but not reflexively self-questioning. Something seldom questioned is that "cultural" variation exists in assemblages, though exactly what shared toolmaking methods imply in cultural terms is seldom detailed. A French archaeologist may refer to the "Magdalenians" who occupied a site, but does not *necessarily* thereby refer to an ancient identity-conscious social unit, though he may seem to be doing so to many readers.

The problem of misunderstanding terminology used differently in different national research traditions is not limited to the case of "culture." When a French archaeologist writes of using typological indices to trace the "evolution" of the Aurignacian "civilization" through several superimposed levels at Cave X, a NWP reader may grind his teeth. However, my reading of and conversations with French prehistorians have convinced me that, in most cases, a "literal" reading of this standard, received terminology would be misleading. Usually, such statements are the functional equivalent of a North American worker's observations that certain typological indices of the Aurignacian culture-stratigraphic unit were found to show vectored change over time. Terms can have different meanings over time and between cultures, and it is my experience that some of the terminology of the French paleolithic research tradition is more noncommittal than it might at first appear to be.

Differences of vocabulary and procedure associated with national research traditions clearly do separate American and French archaeologists. The latter tend to be less explicit about their presuppositions and definitions and about the process of formulating and testing hypotheses. They tend to be more oriented toward studies that produce space-time systematics and empirical generalizations, and more cautious and less explicit about interpreting such patterning in terms of human behavior (recall how few French workers have strongly espoused a specific scenario for the transition). Many have a keener—to their minds, more realistic—sense of the limitations of the archaeological record than do their North American counterparts. Thus, while most French prehistorians share overlapping biases with New World counterparts, they do tend to cluster toward the more conservative end of the spectrum—especially senior members of the profession.

When paradigm differences are discussed, most of the disagreements revolve around one issue, that of traditional typology, about which a few remarks seem appropriate here—once again on the theme of unexpectedly shared suppositions. I think it is now widely recognized among workers on both sides of the Atlantic that traditional typologies measure only one axis of variability in the archaeological record, one without special pre-eminence. We are also generally aware that lithic assemblages are not merely collections of deliberately produced end products, but complex constellations conditioned by site function, raw material, knapping technology, and patterns of re-use and discard. Few workers any longer have a naïve sense that "culture" is reflected directly in stone tools.

If so, then why still use terms like "Aurignacian," which for some carry unwanted symbolic baggage? One reason is that, at the very least, they are handy labels, convenient shorthand descriptions for assemblages characterized by certain similarities in material culture (e.g., Straus 1987a). Beyond that, however, I think (with others) that morphological variation as measured by traditional systematics monitors variation in cultural behavior which is valuable for us to study and try to understand. I agree with NWP proponents that the equation of industries with ancient cultures is wrongheaded and imposes a particular construct of the recent ethnographic record on the distant past (Wobst 1978). However, I do not agree that such a naïve approach necessarily accompanies a concern with typological analysis.

Such analysis will not tell us much about ancient "tribes" or identity-conscious social groups. However, studies of stylistic artifact variation do have potential ("style" being used here in Sackett's [1982] sense of a particular way of doing things specific to a block of time and space). The implications of spatiotemporally bounded, shared craft norms in prehistory are yet to be systematically drawn, but they may be related to large-scale networks and boundaries of social interaction. If so, links might someday be established with such sociocultural phenomena as language groups or the mating networks proposed by Gamble (1986) and Wobst (1976). In this respect, ethnoarchaeological work like that of Wiessner (1983) and Larick (1985), relating variation in projectile points to sociocultural variables, offers interesting possibilities for middle-range theory eventually to bridge lithic variability with possible explanations. As Lenoir (1975) has pointed out, Upper Perigordian, Solutrean, and Magdalenian shouldered points seem to have had equivalent uses, yet were produced in quite different ways. Understanding such variability is as worthy an analytical goal as understanding variability in archaeological faunas.

A related issue deserving brief discussion is that of the Bordesian Middle and Upper Paleolithic typologies (Bordes 1961a, de Sonneville-Bordes and Perrot 1954–56). As noted above, using two different systems of classification ensures a descriptive gulf across the transition. However, that point having been made, it seems useful to ask why there are two typologies in the first place. Implied in some of the criticism over this issue seems to be the point that if only a unified taxonomy had been originally established, then Middle-Upper Paleolithic contrasts would correctly have been perceived as underwhelming. In my experience with Périgord materials, such an assumption is unwarranted and, indeed, incorrect. Bordes and his colleagues devised their typological systems, not a priori, but a posteriori,[7] on the basis of vast experience in examining variability in lithic assemblages. I think that the two typologies differ primarily because they are monitoring different sorts of variation. Upper Paleolithic variability, from the beginning, involves well-differentiated types, both "banal" ones like ordinary endscrapers or burins, and fossil directors more restricted in spatiotemporal occurrence. The de Sonneville-Bordes-Perrot typology is devised to detect them.

The Middle Paleolithic, however, is rather poor in such types, and Bordes's typology reflects this fact. My own attempts to type several Mousterian collections in the Upper Paleolithic system (Harrold 1989) did not work very well, serving to underline rather than diminish the differences between Middle and Upper Paleolithic. Recent work such as Dibble's (1987a) on Mousterian scraper reduction heightens the contrast with Upper Paleolithic variability by showing that several scraper "types" are probably one generalized type in successive stages of reworking and, ultimately, exhaustion. Despite typological continuities across the transition, the available information justifies the use of separate Middle and Upper Paleolithic typologies. Understanding this shift in lithic variability is one of the major challenges presented by the transition.

To sum up, I am not sure that a model of gradual change necessarily follows from a New World paradigm, or an abrupt change model from an Old World paradigm. I am sure that, at least in southwestern France, paradigm variation is intergraded rather than dichotomous, and that paradigm incompatibility is not the main explanation for the disputes over the Middle-Upper Paleolithic transition.

Then What Is the Problem?

If incompatible paradigms are not the main source of our difficulties, then what is? In my opinion, it is the quality and quantity of the base of analyzed data available for testing our ideas about the transition. Most arguments, whatever model of transition they support, take the form of attempts to show that the patterning in relevant variables fits that predicted by one's own model, rather than an opposing one.[8] However, if the available data are sufficiently ambiguous, no proposed explanations (no matter how sophisticated) can be either falsified or confirmed to the exclusion of others. Even within a broad paradigm, researchers may arrive at different positions, based on their reading of the evidence and influenced by their own experiences and the vocabulary and methodology of their research traditions. Predictably, participants in this dispute tend to stick to their established positions, less from paradigm incompatibility than from inertia. Neither "side" can yet amass a strong enough evidentiary case to change many minds on the other side or among the uncommitted.

For a multitude of reasons often cited in the literature (old excavations, geological and human disturbance, the slow pace of data recovery and reporting), the archaeological record for the transition is poor. Several of these reasons merit discussion. Dating is a crucial one; this period lies near the effective extreme range of the radiocarbon method, and even with an increasing sample of dates (Mellars et al. 1987), we still must grapple with the difficulties of calibrating the transition process on the basis of a few dates with large error ranges. It is essential for understanding the transition to know how long it took, which can be difficult if sites actually several centuries apart in age can appear coeval through the lense of our dating techniques.

The worst shortcoming is that a host of methods with much to tell us have been applied to the transition only barely or not at all. Yet their systematic application to the later Mousterian, Châtelperronian, and Aurignacian is exactly what we need. These methods include spatial analysis (e.g., White 1985, Simek 1987). They also include zooarchaeological studies oriented less toward climatic indicators and faunal evolution than toward human subsistence patterns (here Chase's work has made a good start; see also Clark 1987b for Cantabria). They further comprise studies of lithic reduction practices, raw material procurement and use, and microscopic traces of artifact function.

Those critical of past overemphasis on typological methods and cultural explanations for the transition correctly emphasize the error of sole reliance on traditional approaches. However, the task of applying the newer methods to the period of the transition has barely begun. As long as this is the case, we will simply not know whether the overall patterning in the archaeological record matches the predictions of various transition models. For instance, Clark and Lindly (1989a) point out that many archaeologists are reluctant to consider "parallel phyla" (in our case the Aurignacian and Châtelperronian) as possible seasonal or activity variants of the same cultural tradition. Elsewhere I have explained why I think such interpretation is not supported by the data at hand (Harrold 1989). But to resolve the question we need to test rival hypotheses. And to do that we need to analyze data (indicators of seasonality, site and artifact function, and so on) which for the most part are not yet collected. Until we do this, the "functional variant" explanation must remain an intriguing suggestion with somewhat less going for it than the traditional explanation.

Unfortunately, the analytical methods just mentioned are specialized and time consuming. But we must learn in some detail how technology, artifact and site function, and faunal exploitation patterns varied across the transition in order to have reliable bases for accepting or rejecting current explanatory models—and to assess the role of stylistic change as measured by traditional typology. Even in the latter well-worn area there is much to do. As I have noted, very basic typological and technological information that one might suppose to be easily available for excavated assemblages (such as blade indices for early Upper Paleolithic collections) is often unpublished (Harrold 1989). And as Sackett (1988a) and Clark and Lindly (1989a, b) have pointed out, much of the "conventional wisdom" concerning Middle and Upper Paleolithic typological variability is misleading. Not all Upper Paleolithic assemblages are dominated by blades, for instance, nor do their fossil directors necessarily represent the most carefully made or curated tools.

My point here is that the status quo is not primarily a creation of paradigm clash (though that is a factor). With available methods and interpretive frameworks, applied carefully, quantitatively, and systematically to both newly excavated and old materials, we can vastly reduce the controversy and confusion over the Middle-Upper Paleolithic transition everywhere. I echo the stress placed by Straus (1987a) and others on the importance of detailed regional studies. The "Big Picture" of the transition obviously concerns us all, but our best chance for an accurate Big Picture is through synthesis of a series of solidly based "Little Pictures," rather than premature extrapolation from one or a few.

The foregoing is not a plea for "rabid empiricism," nor a cheerful hope that if we amass enough data they will start telling us directly what happened 35,000 years ago. It is a contention that we collectively share enough paradigmatic biases to be able to agree—if we systematically apply tools whose interpretive potential is widely accepted—on at least the broad outlines of the process under study. Nor am I claiming that all our problems are solved if only the large analytical task before us is undertaken. With our current tools I believe we can isolate the main outlines of the transition, but not the details of the nature of past cultural systems. This is partly because of the coarse grain of the archaeological record, and partly because the middle-range theory has yet to be developed—relating stylistic variation to sociocultural variation, for instance, or interpreting the accumulation of archaeological *couches* in both behavioral and geoarchaeological terms. Rather like a historian who could not begin an analysis of the American Civil War until he could establish first that it lasted four years (as opposed to four weeks or a century) and ended in a Yankee victory, we are very far from posing detailed models of cultural systems and their change during the transition. I think that our first priority in the task of working toward such models is to recognize (while giving due regard to paradigmatic issues, which are real) how much we have in common in our approaches to the past, and to see how far systematic application of our current *armamentarium* of methods will take us. Such work, properly synthesized, could (in the terms of the Indian fable) sufficiently reduce our blindness to allow consensus on the outlines of the beast we are examining.

Notes

1. Like Breuil, Peyrony (1922) originally espoused a view of the Middle-Upper Paleolithic transition as a gradual in situ evolutionary stage progression, but by 1933 he had changed his mind.
2. The suggestion has been made, but never developed seriously, that the resemblance between Aurignacian retouch and Quina Mousterian retouch may indicate a southwest French origin for the Aurignacian (Laville et al. 1980:267, Harrold 1989). Generally, the typological discontinuity between Aurignacian and either Mousterian or Châtelperronian is emphasized (e.g., de Sonneville-Bordes 1966).
3. François Bordes is said to have wondered aloud how many of the American students who argued so enthusiastically about the Mousterian facies would know a biface from a burin.
4. Bordes (1981b) was dubious about the usual interpretation of Saint-Césaire (i.e., that Neanderthals manufactured Châtelperronian artifacts), but not because he doubted regional Mousterian-Châtelperronian or Neanderthal-AMH continuity. His belief was that the biological transition had already

occurred during the time of the Mousterian of Acheulean Tradition type B. Thus the "Châtelperronians" would have been AMH, and the best fossil candidate was the AMH Combe-Capelle skeleton excavated in 1908 by the notorious antiquarian Hauser. Bordes (in litt. 1979) acknowledged Hauser's atrocious excavation methods, but pointed out that Denis Peyrony, who witnessed some of the excavation, accepted Hauser's attribution of the remains to the site's Châtelperronian level, rather than to the overlying Aurignacian one. As an ethical archaeologist and patriotic Frenchman, Peyrony despised Hauser and would certainly have disputed Hauser's attribution had he seen reason to. However, we will never know the provenience of Combe-Capelle Man or, since the skeleton was destroyed in World War II, any more about him than we do now (Harrold 1978).

5. But almost certainly not related to the much later Gravettian or "Upper Perigordian" (Harrold 1981, 1983).

6. For instance, it is one thing to argue that the transition involved cultural and biological discontinuity, but another to specify what competitive advantages the cultural systems of AMH immigrants would have had over those of the local Neanderthals to allow replacement. Or one might ask a "continuity" advocate what selective pressures shaped the biological evolution of local Neanderthals into AMH in the absence of archaeological documentation for significant changes in subsistence or other behavior.

7. The rival typological scheme of Laplace (1966) is to some extent an a priori one (Hemingway 1980:3–4). Used in parts of Italy, Spain, and southern France, it is more cumbersome than the de Sonneville-Bordes system, and not notably more successful at describing assemblages; it tends to minimize inter-assemblage differences. It attempts to avoid the pitfalls of the fossil director approach, but, as Rigaud (1982:75–77) ironically notes, nonetheless ends up using fossil director names (e.g., "fléchette") in type descriptions. One unfortunate effect of its use is to hamper communication between users of the two systems.

8. All too often in these cases, the argument takes the form: "Opposing models should be discarded because I can supply examples of data inconsistent with them. On the other hand, my model should be adopted for a priori reasons (e.g., simplicity, theoretical elegance, similarity to models adopted elsewhere), and also because it is not inconsistent with selected data."

Chapter 8
Issues in Biological and Behavioral Evolution and the Problem of Upper Pleistocene Subsistence

Philip G. Chase

Introduction

The editor's objective for the papers in this collection was to have "workers active or recently active in circum-Mediterranean hunter-gatherer research . . . 'make their biases explicit' . . . to try to articulate the basic, fundamental premises under which they conduct the research enterprise" (Editor's letter to contributors). Since to do so in detail would require far more space than is available, I would like instead to discuss, in the context of a particular research question, one part of my overall epistemological worldview—two attitudes toward the relationship between data and explanation that have resulted from my attempts, as a zooarchaeologist, to grapple with the connections between biology and behavior in the Upper Pleistocene.

The first of these concerns the limits imposed on research by the nature of the available evidence. I share the generally held view that relevant data are not forthcoming until a problem has been defined and archaeologists set out deliberately to find those data. However, the archaeological record is by its very nature incomplete, especially in the Paleolithic, and not all gaps in the data can be filled simply by asking the right questions. This means that although we may ask whatever questions we wish, possible ways of answering them are necessarily limited. This is not a surprising conclusion, but I believe that it is all too often overlooked, with the result that Paleolithic archaeologists are tempted to draw unjustified inferences from inadequate data.

Secondly, I believe strongly that the process of inference demands that one consider alternative explanations. Ideally this is true even when the archaeologist's goal is simply to produce a model to account for a given set of phenomena. As Chamberlin (1890/1965:754) put it, "the re-action of one hypothesis upon another tends to amplify the recognized scope of each, and their mutual conflicts whet the discriminative edge of each." However, when theory is used not for modeling but as the basis for inference, it becomes crucial to consider alternative explanations. In such a case, the role of theory is not to enlighten but to serve as "truth," as a given upon which one can rely. The fact that taphonomic agent X may produce pattern P in the faunal record does not alter the insight that a given set of human economic activities Y may produce the same pattern. However, the archaeologist who attempts to *infer* Y from a given faunal assemblage runs a serious risk of error if he fails to consider alternative X. Although such taphonomic alternatives are now well recognized, there is still a strong tendency to make inferences without considering other, non-taphonomic possibilities.

Neither of these arguments is novel—in fact, stated in such general and abstract terms, they might be dismissed as truisms. However, by discussing them in the context of a specific, concrete research problem, I hope to show why they are so much at the forefront of my attention as a paleolithic zooarchaeologist.

The Research Question

Determining whether behavioral change was causally linked to biological evolution is one of the most important problems facing Upper Pleistocene prehistorians. There is general consensus that hominid bioevolution *as a whole* contributed to an increase in problem-solving ability, in versatility of communication, in planning ability, and probably in overall flexibility of behavior. There is no such consensus about biological changes during the Upper Pleistocene. It therefore becomes relevant to ask whether or not changes in economic behavior observable in the archaeological record can be cited as evidence of advances in the inherent, biologically determined capacities of hominids.

The subject is a complex one with many ramifications. It is not my purpose here to try to answer it. However, in the context of this question, the importance of the two epistemological issues I raised above may become clearer:

- First, although theoretical and practical issues involved in inferring behavior from the archaeological record have been much on the minds of zooarchaeologists during the past two decades, one relevant shortcoming of the Upper Pleistocene archaeological record has rarely been discussed—the limitations imposed by our inability to demonstrate economically functional links between assemblages from different sites.

• Second, inferring biological evolution in hominid mental capacities from changes in economic behavior requires that the latter be the result of the former. If new subsistence patterns were the outcome of other factors, then they do not imply genetic change.

The Limitations of Data: Inferences Based on Data from More than One Site

Reconstructing Subsistence Systems

Perhaps the most direct way of understanding a prehistoric adaptation is to reconstruct a subsistence system from the archaeological record. If one can do this, then one understands a key part of that adaptation. Unfortunately, in the case of hunter-gatherers, reconstructing a subsistence system involves using data from more than one site.

I have discussed this problem in some detail elsewhere (Chase 1986b:1–4), but it is worth summarizing the discussion here. By a subsistence system I mean the set of activities by which a single group of people make their living. It is difficult to define the limits of such a system, but in practical terms I mean the set of activities that would have contributed to the survival of a single individual, if not in one year then during the course of at most a few years.[1]

It is probable that paleolithic peoples were more or less migratory in their habits. Even if at certain times and places some populations were semi-sedentary, this must have been at most a matter of returning to a primary settlement from trips elsewhere in the environment for economic activities not directly represented at the main site. This means that no single site can give us a complete picture of a subsistence system. Yet our dating methods, absolute or relative, operate on a geological time scale, while subsistence systems operate on an annual or at most generational scale. We cannot, therefore, be certain that any two archaeological assemblages belonged together functionally; and instead of seeing an entire subsistence system, we are merely looking through archaeological windows (individual sites) onto very limited parts of what may well have been unrelated systems.

There are therefore very restricted options for reconstructing subsistence systems. First, one might *assume* that certain sites were actually parts of the same subsistence system, but given the paucity of assemblages and the huge amounts of time involved in paleolithic archaeology, this is probably unwarranted.

Second, one could proceed as if paleolithic subsistence behavior was so persistent that a set of archaeological assemblages, even if not strictly contemporaneous, may be taken as representing different parts of a long-lived economic pattern and may be treated as if they were functionally related. This involves the assumption that the minor features of subsistence behavior (such as exactly where and when people obtained particular resources) were remarkably constant. If one is used to thinking in geological terms, sampling behavior over a period lasting centuries or millennia may seem logical; but when one thinks in human terms, this is a very long time indeed. It may be that Middle Paleolithic peoples were too inflexible or too uncreative to change even the details of their yearly round more rapidly than this, but to assume so would be to presume what one should be investigating.

A third way of approaching the problem is to study the topographic and environmental data to reconstruct what would have been a reasonable subsistence system (a sort of site-catchment analysis on a broader scale). This, however, means imposing our notions of reasonable behavior on others—and when the goal is to determine if different groups of hominids behaved differently given similar circumstances, the method is of no use whatsoever.

Recognizing Subsistence Strategies

Although we are probably unable to reconstruct subsistence *systems* because we cannot demonstrate functional links between archaeological assemblages, we may still be able to recognize different subsistence *strategies*—different overall approaches to the problem of obtaining nourishment, such as year-round dependence upon a single species versus a more or less opportunistic exploitation of a wide range of species.

To a large extent, however, the recognition of such strategies is also hampered by our inability to relate archaeological assemblages. Although different strategies may leave recognizably different patterns in the archaeological record, this is true only at the level of the subsistence system. At the site level, two contrasting strategies may leave identical records. For example, exploiting different animals at different places and in different seasons will produce a number of sites each dominated by a single species, while depending year round on only one kind of animal will also leave a number of sites dominated by a single species. Without being able to determine whether or not sites are related, the archaeologist cannot determine if several specialized systems or a single diversified system is represented.

I have attempted elsewhere to solve this problem on a probabilistic level (Chase 1986b). I argued that the European Middle Paleolithic record contained too many specialized assemblages to infer a *universal* pattern of more or less random, opportunistic hunting of whatever animals one happened to encounter, although it was certainly impossible to argue that such a pattern was *absent* or even *rare* in the Middle Paleolithic. By the same token, I argued that the absence from any one part of the continent of a preponderance of assemblages all dominated by the same species made it *unlikely* that year round dependence on a single species was the *universal* or even the *most common* Middle Paleolithic strategy. Rather, I concluded that the pattern of specialized and generalized faunal assemblages in the archaeological record was *most consistent with* a purposeful exploitation of different species at different times and in different places as the *most frequent* of Middle Paleolithic subsistence strategies.

The use of italics in the preceding paragraph is intended to indicate just how probabilistic my conclusions were. I found and still find no way of justifying an argument excluding any of these patterns in the Middle Paleolithic in Europe. Moreover, even my guesses concerning their relative frequency were necessarily couched in probabilistic terms. Until we find a way to link different sites as part of a single subsistence system, we cannot be more precise than this because the problems of equifinality at the site level are too severe.

I do not foresee that the application of new dating techniques will solve this problem in the near future. A standard deviation of a thousand years may seem small in geological terms, but in human terms it represents some forty or fifty generations. It is more likely that techniques such as lithic raw material analysis will permit us to connect a site to surrounding parts of the landscape without requiring chronological correlation, thus providing some clues about patterns above the site level.

Inference and Alternative Explanations

Even if we were able to reconstruct subsistence systems or to identify clearly changes in subsistence strategies, it would still be necessary to eliminate other explanations before inferring biologically based increases in hominid capabilities from changes in subsistence behavior. Yet although considerable effort has recently been expended to identify changes or continuities through time in Upper Pleistocene subsistence behavior and sometimes to explain them (e.g., L. R. Binford 1984, Butzer 1986, Chase 1987, Clark and Yi 1983, Freeman 1973, 1981, Klein 1977, Mellars 1973, Simek and Snyder 1988, Soffer 1987, Straus 1977, 1985b, White 1982), attempts to evaluate competing hypotheses have been almost non-existent.[2]

It is assumed by foraging theory (see Bettinger 1980, Winterhalder 1981, and Stephens and Krebs 1986 for summaries) that, because of the pressures of natural selection, all species must move toward optimization of subsistence behavior (although theorists in this field are well aware that, particularly for a species as behaviorally plastic as humans, there are other considerations as well; see for example, Durham 1981, Stephens and Krebs 1986: chapters 4–6). Although there is room to criticize the approach (see below), there are two important points that paleolithic archaeologists must accept: (1) that organisms must be at least minimally efficient, and (2) by approaching subsistence from this point of view, foraging theorists have made it very clear that optimal behavior is situation-dependent.

Thus, for example, the number of species a group of people will exploit depends in part on the amount of time required to find, kill, and process each (see Bettinger 1980, Winterhalder 1981), variables that are not absolute but change with circumstances. A shift from generalized to specialized hunting may therefore reflect nothing more than an alteration in the distribution of resources in the environment such that the time required to locate less important species increased (in relative terms) and concentration on one or a few species became more profitable. On the other hand, the size of the human population relative to the resource base may affect the number of species exploited as well by forcing populations either to concentrate on a few species at a higher level of technology (Straus 1985b) or to utilize a broader range of species (Straus 1985b, Clark and Yi 1983). Certainly the number of species available in the environment will affect the number exploited. Thus the decrease in the faunal diversity in Solutrean and Magdalenian sites in the Périgord found by Simek and Snyder (1988) is probably due simply to a decreased diversity of fauna in the environment due to climatic conditions.

All of this means that before a change in subsistence behavior can be accepted as evidence of increased capacity for problem solving or foresight, one must first demonstrate that the earlier behavior was not more nearly optimal—given existing conditions—than the later behavior would have been under same circumstances.

Examples and Implications

The implications of all this can perhaps best be illustrated by discussing certain specific examples of recent research in terms of these two issues. In all of them, I find the research strategy promising because there is no need to assume functional links between sites. Instead, subsistence behaviors can be identified either at the site level or using data from a large number of quite possibly unrelated sites. At the same time, I find that there has perhaps been less attention given to alternative explanations than is necessary.

Lewis Binford (1984, 1985), in his studies of the Klasies River Mouth and of the European Middle Paleolithic, has suggested that scavenging rather than hunting was used to obtain meat from large animals. Others, including myself, have disagreed (Klein 1986, Grayson 1985, Chase 1986b, 1988). The point here is not to recapitulate or continue this debate, but to analyze what is involved in Binford's research strategy.

Behaviors such as scavenging can potentially be recognized without establishing functional links between sites, and have important implications for our understanding of the Middle to Upper Paleolithic transition. The recent work of Blumenschine (1986a) has demonstrated, by empirical observation of modern carnivore behavior, that there is a set of archaeologically observable criteria that can be used to recognize scavenging.[3] There include such variables as where on the skeleton marks of stone tools and carnivore teeth appear and which portions of the skeleton are best represented. These criteria have only recently been used to examine the archaeological record (Blumenschine 1986b, Chase 1988), but their existence demonstrates that the question is one that can be answered archaeologically.

The case of scavenging is an interesting one, since its implications for hominid capabilities seem clear. Binford first discussed the notion in the context of the early Lower Paleolithic (L. Binford 1981b), where it had obvious importance as a refutation of the hypothesis that hominid evolution had been shaped in large part by hunting (e.g., Dart 1953, Washburn and Lancaster 1968). In the Upper Pleistocene, a demonstration that hominids were not hunters would be even more unsettling for traditional concepts. However, two points must be kept in mind.

First, accepting the scavenging of a species as evidence of inability to hunt that species means rejecting the alternative explanation, that these animals were not hunted because exploiting other species paid off better per unit of time or energy, and that scavenging reflected merely the opportunistic exploitation of carcasses encountered in the course of other economic activities (much as a thief specializing in expensive jewelry might casually pocket a few coins found on the dressing table, even though he would never consider risking prison by burglarizing a house just for loose change).

Second, it is crucial to remember that negative evidence must be used with caution. When one infers that a biological population was genetically incapable of a certain behavior, the implication is that they *never* behaved in this way. However, failure to observe such behavior at one site or in one area does not, in itself, indicate that it was absent from the repertoire of contemporary hominids. For example, even if we were to accept Binford's (1985) argument that the animals at Swanscombe were scavenged rather than hunted by humans (cf. Chase 1988), we would nevertheless not be justified in concluding that Middle Pleistocene hominids did not hunt ungulates. The same could be said of the apparent lack of exploitation of very large animals such as rhinoceri and mammoths in Western Europe in the Middle Paleolithic. There is a strong temptation to draw conclusions based on the site or area with which one is most familiar. When one's results are positive, when one has recognized a phenomenon such as large-game hunting, then it is justifiable to conclude that it was a part of the behavioral repertoire of at least part of the population living at the time. Negative conclusions, however, require more broadly based evidence.

Another of Binford's suggestions, that Middle Paleolithic subsistence behavior was characterized by a lack of planning depth, can also be approached archaeologically—at least in a limited way—using data from a single site. Evidence that animal parts were transported from one site to another and that lithic raw materials were carried into a site from sources elsewhere has important implications concerning planning, and perhaps sharing and social cooperation as well. While recognizing the transportation of animal materials from their archaeological remains is not simple—primarily because taphonomic factors tend to distort the faunal record—it is not impossible and has in fact been a standard part of zooarchaeology for years (cf., e.g., Perkins and Daly 1968). The *importance* of the role of storage and transportation in a subsistence system is difficult to determine at the site level, but its *existence* can be recognized.

However, the presence or absence of a behavior such as the logistical organization of subsistence (L. Binford 1980) may still be explainable, as Binford pointed out, without invoking bioevolutionary change. Indeed, both situations are known ethnographically. The long-range planning and co-ordination of subsistence requires human as opposed to hominid mental capacities, but it also requires us to specify circumstances that make such a strategy advantageous. The shift from one subsistence strategy to the other may thus reflect no more than altered circumstances. Only if there is no evidence of this level of organization anywhere before a given point in time can one argue that biological change was involved. A shift from foraging to logistically organized collecting (in Binford's [1980] terminology) might indicate an increase in the capacity for foresight and for social co-ordination of activities, but it might also indicate a change in the number, seasonal availability, distribution, and mobility of resources.

A final example can be drawn from the apparent failure of European Middle Paleolithic populations to exploit small animals, even such sessile and easily obtained species as shellfish. Straus (1977:67) has remarked that they evidently lacked the "knowledge, skill, technology, and/or motivation" required to exploit these species. It has been suggested that Middle Paleolithic hunters concentrated on large game because this was more efficient than exploiting small animals, since the return per animal is higher (see Ackerly and Bayham 1984). Yet at least on occasion Middle Paleolithic peoples did exploit small animals (Freeman 1981, Chase 1986a, b). When both hypotheses presented by Straus—lack of knowledge, skill, or technology on the one hand, and lack of motivation due to the relatively poor returns from small animal exploitation on the other—are examined in light of this fact, then the weight of evidence shifts toward a non-biological explanation (see, e.g., Clark 1987b).

The fact is that even major alterations in subsistence behavior can often be explained without recourse to biological evolution. The most obvious example is the shift from hunting and gathering to farming. It would be foolhardy, therefore, to explain lesser phenomena—such as exploiting a narrow rather than a broad range of prey species—in terms of biological evolution without first considering the alternatives.

Conclusions

I have not, obviously, fully discussed either my own theoretical and epistemological worldview or all the topics relevant to the behavioral evolution of Upper Pleistocene hominids. Instead, I have attempted to clarify two procedural issues in Paleolithic zooarchaeology, issues that in my eyes are crucial because until they are recognized a major problem in Upper Pleistocene research cannot be tackled successfully. This does not mean that the relationship between biology and behavior is the only important problem in Upper Pleistocene subsistence studies, nor does it mean that the only important issues in investigating that relationship are the ones discussed here. However, they do have important implications for how research on this problem can be done.

I see only three ways of overcoming our inability to relate paleolithic sites to one another as parts of the same subsistence system: (1) we can develop methods for demonstrating such links, (2) we can focus on behaviors identifiable at the site level, or (3) we can concentrate on behaviors inferable using evidence from multiple sites without assuming they were related. (In this last context, Gamble's [1986] suggestion that behavior be correlated to environmental variables measured on a regional scale is of particular interest.)

On the other hand, changes in behavior must be explained, and the process of explanation must include choosing among competing hypotheses. This will be difficult and time consuming. For example, although I cited the occasional exploitation of small game in the Middle Paleolithic as evidence that its rarity was not due to biologically determined lack of capabilities, I might also have argued that the species involved could not have been exploited on a major scale without the complex "cord" or "string" based technology required for nets and snares, technology that may have been beyond the capabilities of archaic *Homo sapiens*. (For example, the few fish found in Middle Paleolithic sites are often salmon that may have been trapped in shallow waters after spawning.) Finding a way of testing such assertions may not be easy.[4]

A final example will illustrate just how imposing the task really is. Klein (1977:122–124, 1987:33–38) inferred that Middle Stone Age peoples of southern Africa were less capable hunters than those of the Holocene on the basis of a number of observed differences in the faunal assemblages they left behind. He rejected alternative explanations of the kind discussed above on the grounds that the environment was essentially the same at the two time periods. Thus he cannot be accused of violating either of the premises I have presented above.

However, this example uncovers a new, although related, problem. Theory available to zooarchaeologists does not always meet the standards demanded by inference. For example, although foraging theory has done much to clarify the factors underlying the subsistence strategies of all animals, it does not yet constitute a comprehensive model of foraging behavior. Rather, it is a corpus of often quite diverse models that share certain assumptions and procedures. While any or all of them may have explanatory value, they have not been subjected to the kind of systematic comparative testing that would permit a "user" such as Klein to choose among several alternatives. Nor have these diverse models undergone the kind of adjustment and consolidation into a single coherent whole that would permit an archaeologist to determine just *how* similar two environments must be, and in what respects, before environmental change may be rejected in favor of neurological evolution. An inference such as Klein's may, therefore, be perfectly reasonable given the current state of our knowledge; but our knowledge is woefully inadequate. Until relevant theories are developed and tested in such a way as to produce a solid basis for inference as well as a source of insight, theoretical deficiencies will continue to hamper research.

Acknowledgments

I would like to thank John Speth and Harold Dibble for their very helpful comments on an early draft of this paper.

Notes

1. The fact that paleolithic economic or social units may have been more or less open ended merely increases the severity of the problems discussed here.

2. Changes in subsistence behavior have of course been used to explain changes in other phenomena (e.g., Binford 1968, Orquera 1984).

3. More correctly, he provides criteria for rejecting scavenging as the mechanism that produced a zooarchaeological assemblage, since hunting may produce similar patterns under certain circumstances.

4. My own preference is still for a non-biological, non-technological explanation, partly because even sessile, intertidal shellfish were only rarely exploited (as mentioned above) and because there is evidence of the deliberate removal of tendons from carcasses, presumably for use as cords (Chase 1986b:66–68, 72–74).

Chapter 9
A Great Thick Cloud of Dust: Naming and Dating in the Interpretation of Behavior in the Late Paleolithic of Spain

Iain Davidson

> While Don Quixote and his squire rode on . . . our knight saw a great thick cloud of dust approaching . . . and, seeing it, he turned to Sancho and said: ". . . Do you see that dust cloud rising over there, Sancho? It is all churned up by a prodigious army of various and innumerable nations that is marching this way."
>
> "In that case there must be two armies," said Sancho, "for in the opposite direction there is a similar cloud of dust rising as well."
>
> Don Quixote . . . rejoiced exceedingly . . . for every hour his mind was full of those battles, enchantments, adventures, miracles, loves, and challenges which are related in books of chivalry; and everything that he said, thought or did, was influenced by his fantasies. As for the dust cloud he had seen, it was caused by two great flocks of sheep . . . but owing to the dust cloud they were not visible until they drew near.
>
> Cervantes, *Don Quixote de la Mancha*

Introduction

The story from Don Quixote can be thought of as a metaphor that contrasts culture historical approaches to prehistoric events and processes with economic ones. My own work in Spain had been concerned primarily with the opposition between these two points of view about the archaeological record. I argued that the culture historical approach was a convenient way of organizing the available data at a time when there were no means of providing a chronology independent of the materials for which a chronology was required. When radiocarbon dating became available, this approach was no longer appropriate, since the central objective of archaeology is to understand the variability of archaeological materials in terms of human behavior in the past. The culture historical approach tended to assume that the major determinant of variability was time, and an unstated, untested assumption about the relationship between regularities in the materials and "various and innumerable nations." In contrast, I sought to account for the archaeological material in terms of the activities of people as real as the shepherds with their "great flocks of sheep."

My work in Spain (see Davidson 1974, 1976, 1983, 1986, 1989; Bofinger and Davidson 1977; Bailey and Davidson 1983; Davidson and Estévez 1985; Fortea et al. 1983) was centered on the region of Valencia, with special concentration on the cave of Parpalló (Pericot 1942, Fullola 1979). This site was first reported by the geologist Vilanova (1893—one of the first champions of the authenticity of Altamira) and visited by Breuil and Obermaier (1914), who found a stone plaquette engraved with a picture of a lynx. The cave was completely excavated in three seasons by Pericot (1942) between 1929 and 1931, with methods which have proved unusually meticulous for their time.

Before the excavation of Parpalló there had been a long controversy about the chronological relationships of the artifact sequences in eastern Spain. In contrast to the Upper Pleistocene sites of France and Cantabrian Spain there seemed to be no evidence for the cold-adapted fauna that could provide simple stratigraphic markers for the changing climate of the last glacial stages. This was recognized at the time of the earliest attempts by foreign scholars to authenticate the discoveries of prehistoric artifacts in Spain (Casiano de Prado 1864, Verneuil and Lartet 1863). At about the same time the hypothesis was tested and falsified that African species might have crossed the Strait of Gibraltar (Busk 1877). Garrod (1928) tried to date the Mousterian site of Devil's Tower, in Gibraltar, by reference to the faunal sequence at Grotte du Prince, on the south coast of France, despite the fundamental environmental differences between the two regions. We now know that there was no such evidence to be found (see Fortea et al. 1983).

Parpalló and Typological Approaches

Parpalló stands in the historical literature as fundamentally important in the culture-stratigraphic approach to the Upper Paleolithic because it provided the first evidence that some of the stratigraphic divisions defined by artifact typology in France could be applied in eastern Spain, as they could in northern Spain. But there was actually no proof that they were contemporary sequences. This was only confirmed when the first radiocarbon dates for Parpalló showed near identity in age for artifacts which Pericot (1942) called Solutrean with the Solutrean dates previously established at Laugerie Haute, in France (Davidson 1974). In addition, the artifact sequence at Parpalló showed some discrete stratigraphic distributions of artifacts that could possibly be used as regional chronological markers (see, e.g., Davidson 1986, Bofinger and Davidson 1977). The application of these markers, however, was questionable given the scarcity of sites which repeated the sequence of artifact assemblages found at Parpalló (see, e.g., Fortea and Jordá 1976), although attempts have been made to define a Mediterranean province for some of the artifact types.

Parpalló and Regional Perspectives

Despite the importance of Parpalló for an approach based primarily on artifact sequence, my own approach was different (Davidson 1980). I sought to define the economic changes (Davidson 1981) which had taken place in the Valencia region by studying the animal bones and site catchments (Davidson 1983) and the site exploitation territories (Bailey and Davidson 1983) for a range of sites in the region. In the course of this work I confronted a relatively simple anomaly. The culture historical approach would predict that once the change from Middle to Upper Paleolithic had taken place, then the Upper Paleolithic, and its stone industries, would occur in all regions. But almost all of the Upper Paleolithic sites with stone industries are found in the northern coastal region of Cantabria, or along the Mediterranean coast. There are a few claims from other regions, but Upper Paleolithic artifacts seemed to be almost completely absent from the high plateaux of central Spain. And this is not due to sample bias. In the two areas where systematic surveys for paleolithic sites have been conducted (by Clark and his collaborators [1979] in Burgos province, and in Albacete province while I was excavating the Upper Paleolithic painted cave of Cueva del Niño [Davidson 1980]) no Upper Paleolithic sites were found. Although there are only a few Upper Paleolithic decorated caves outside Cantabria, several occur in both the northern and southern high plateaux of central Spain, despite the scarcity of Upper Paleolithic artifacts. In addition there are decorated caves of this period in southern Spain, south of the Sierra Nevada; and Parpalló itself is a major "art" site with more than 6,000 plaquettes engraved or painted with animals or other designs (Pericot 1942, Villaverde 1988, Davidson 1989). The evidence does not support a clear separation between Upper Paleolithic stone industries and decorated caves. Thus the plateaux, contrary to expectation from the culture historical paradigm, seem to have Upper Paleolithic decorated caves, but no Upper Paleolithic industries.

I suggested previously (Davidson 1986) that there were several possible explanations for this.

1. There may have been too few surveys.
2. The sites may be there but the geomorphology of the region prevents their easy detection.
3. The sites may be there but we have failed to recognize them.
4. The absence of sites represents a real absence of people.

Why the Conflicting Interpretations?

For a variety of reasons I preferred the third hypothesis (Davidson 1986). Large numbers of surface sites are known in central Spain with industries made of readily available quartzite cobbles. Such industries are generally attributed either to the Middle or to the Lower Paleolithic (Santonja and Villa 1990). I suggested that they were actually undated, but that industries of this type occurred in later sites including Upper Paleolithic stratified deposits (see, e.g., Clark and Richards 1978:124, 125). Little importance was attached to these artifacts because they were not "typical" of the artifact lists derived from French studies and used in Spain (cf. Straus 1980).

I suggested that some of the sites where the only artifacts were made on quartzite cobbles were created during the Upper Paleolithic. At issue here were two points of view almost diametrically opposed to one another. In my view the traditional artifact typologies were dominated by the artifact sequences recorded from stratified cave sequences in France. We know remarkably little about the effects on our knowledge of lithic variability of concentrating on cave sequences. We do, however, know quite a lot about the influence of raw material on artifact variability (e.g., Straus 1980). Although there is now some recent evidence about raw material sources for Middle and Upper Paleolithic sites in the "classic" typological heartland of the Dordogne and Vezère river valleys (e.g., Geneste 1988), those materials are almost all flint or chert. Our current understanding of stone technology is sufficient to realize that there may well be different artifact types and different reduction sequences for flint and chert, on the one hand, and quartzite on the other.

In addition, Gould (1979) demonstrated in Australia (though he otherwise missed the point—Gould 1980:141–159, cf. Davidson 1988), that for modern mobile people, artifacts will be made in different ways depending on the nature of access to raw material sources and forms in which these might occur. In situations of shortage, or restricted access, there are curating strategies where a whole technology is based on specialized tools (such as *tula* adzes) and on the production of cores which will enable resupply during movements away from suitable raw material sources. In situations where there are no problems of supply,

expedient tools may be produced which have none of these characteristics. Hayden (1979), for example, worked with groups of desert
Aborigines, to whom he supplied stone so they would make tools. He
was surprised (although we were not, in light of Gould's [1979] observation) to learn that they made expedient tools without any evidence
for deliberate patterning of artifacts into recognizable artifact "types."
In the situation I have described for the *plateau gar* regions of Spain,
quartzite cobbles are readily available, and flint and chert are relatively
scarce. It is to be expected that artifacts would be made which differ
from the French typological sequences because of the nature of the raw
material, because of the contexts in which it was used, and because of
its availability.

This analogic argument about causes of stone artifact variability
underscores the issue in Spain, as elsewhere. Some believe that artifacts
and assemblages of artifacts varied systematically through time, so that
artifacts and assemblages are a clue to chronology. I believe that other
factors also determine the variability of artifacts and assemblages. I
have chosen to point to raw material and rationing here, but I might
also have discussed function as revealed through usewear and edge
damage (e.g., Vila 1984, 1985, 1987). The extraordinary thing is that
so little needs to be changed. We might portentously observe, by analogy, that Newtonian mechanics are such a good approximation to the
world as predicted by Einstein that we all play pool on the assumption
that they were correct. But to conceive of the universe as a pool table,
and the stars and planets as balls, is not adequate. If you attempt to
understand mechanics and motion at the smallest (subatomic) or largest (astronomical) scales, then the Newtonian paradigm is no longer
sufficient (e.g., Hawking 1988).

We can, of course, achieve something by assuming that artifact variability changes regularly through time, but we might discover much
more if we do not assume it. And we do not need to make such an
assumption since we have truly independent means of dating. I am not
referring to stratigraphic correlations, using sedimentological or palynological results since these are not independent of the archaeology:
"sedimentology and palynology depend on industries for relative chronology . . ." (Leroi-Gourhan 1986:62). Such is the force of the dominant paradigm for artifact variation that this has not been seen as the
problem that it is. The tragedy is that at the same time the potential of
pollen or sediment analyses to explore the causes of variability in
archaeological assemblages have been mostly overlooked. I have even
heard it said by archaeologists in Spain that the radiocarbon chronology is of no relevance because other methods are more accurate (e.g.,
Leroi-Gourhan 1986:59–64). Just such a battle was fought in the 1960s

over the relative accuracy of the chronologies based on radiocarbon and the historical sequence in Egypt (e.g., Renfrew 1973). We hardly need to acknowledge that the independent chronology was supported and the result was the emergence of new ways of looking at the relation between those regions with direct historical chronologies and those with inferred ones.

The La Riera Project

It is unfortunate that the most ambitious attempt to give precedence to the radiocarbon chronology in Spanish paleolithic archaeology has not been entirely successful, due to unexplained reversals in the strati-graphic sequence of dates (Straus and Clark 1986a). This study also presents one of the most audacious challenges to what the authors refer to as the phylogenetic approach to cultural stratigraphy—an approach which holds that stone "assemblages of each culture-strati-graphic unit conform to a standard relative frequency distribution" (Straus 1986d; see also Clark 1971a, 1976a, 1983a—Clark coined the term "tool type phylogeny"). The authors correctly emphasize the vacuity of the reasoning process that defines a limited number of frequency distributions and "explains" those patterns by giving them labels. But the dominance of the phylogenetic paradigm is very strong, especially in France where it originated. Spanish archaeological paradigms have typically followed those of the French.

Although Clark and Straus have done much to argue against the phylogenetic paradigm, they do not escape its clutches entirely, either in the La Riera report or in subsequent papers that for the most part demonstrate the fragility of the scheme (Clark 1987a, b; Straus 1987a). Such is the dominance of a paradigm that, even in an attempt to show anomalies which do not fit the current version of normal science, observations must be made which actually derive almost entirely from that approach to the material. Thus the statement that

Many Cantabrian Solutrean assemblages, were it not for the presence of foli-ate points, closely resemble Cantabrian Lower Magdalenian ones. . . . On the contrary, some assemblages *without* foliate points date to the Solutrean time range . . . (Straus 1987a: 159)

is derived entirely from the phylogenetic paradigm, however much it may be argued that the demise of the paradigm must be couched in terms which its practitioners can understand. Why not suggest that some Lower Magdalenian assemblages have foliate points? Why emphasize foliate points (or retouched pieces) at all, or was it not possible for people during the "Solutrean time range" to knap stone until after they had left a foliate point at the knapping place?

The Notion of Paradigm

The difficulties I have outlined are real enough. They are part of the reason why Kuhn's (1970a) notion of paradigm change required a revolution to move from one paradigm and its normal science to another. It is possible to identify an assemblage of stone artifacts as similar to another and give these assemblages a name, such as "Solutrean." It is possible to show that an entity defined in this way has a restricted distribution in time and space, and, using an independent dating method, it is possible to show that similar assemblages occur at similar times in different places. All of this is appropriate archaeological practice. In these circumstances, it is possible to use the tight time definition of an assemblage to define the time of creation of unstratified or otherwise undatable assemblages. The problem arises in the use of the characteristics of whole assemblages to provide such a chronology, because many factors create variation in whole assemblages.

In the cases I have been discussing, European Upper Paleolithic assemblages require the presence of blades (at least), so that no assemblage without blades could be called Upper Paleolithic and by extension could not belong to the "Upper Paleolithic time range." Similarly, certain kinds of foliate points are fundamental to the recognition of Solutrean assemblages; therefore, an assemblage with those foliate points must be called "Solutrean," whatever the nature of the rest of the assemblage. But then it becomes an anomaly that some assemblages contemporary with Solutrean assemblages do not have foliate points (Clark 1987a).

The simple way out of this is to emphasize the formation processes of stone artifact assemblages. If we accept that raw material, rationing, reduction sequence, and use are major causes of variability in stone artifact assemblages, then we should move away from defining chronostratigraphic units based on assemblages. We should expect that some aspects of assemblages changed as people moved away from sources of supply of raw material and as they used their artifacts (see, e.g., Marks 1989). It is not, therefore, reasonable to suppose that whole assemblages should change only because of chronology. It might be the case, however, that distinctive artifacts, such as foliate points, have a restricted distribution in time (though they should not be expected to occur in all sites of that time period because of sampling error and uncertainties about the reasons for deposition of artifacts at sites). The relations between the Cantabrian Solutrean and the Cantabrian Lower Magdalenian are complex in this regard, since the stratigraphic boundary between the two is a boundary between an industry with distinctive foliate points and an industry which can be named "because of an absence of Solutrean and Upper Magdalenian diagnostics and because of a certain incidence of quadrangular-sectioned bone/antler points" (Straus and Clark 1986b:139), although fragments of these bone/antler points occurred in earlier layers (Hemingway 1980, González Morales 1986:213). The Lower Magdalenian, therefore, occurs between two industries with distinctive artifacts and is really defined by this characteristic (i.e., absence of distinctive types). All these assemblages are given names of equal value; and entities with these names are then able to be compared or counted (e.g., Clark and Straus 1986a:362), despite the fact that their "recognition value" is not equal. It would presumably be relatively difficult to identify a Lower Magdalenian open site, a little easier to find one of the Upper Magdalenian (if bone/antler harpoons were preserved), and relatively easy to identify a Solutrean open site.

"Naming" is clearly part of the problem. All analysis depends on our ability to name entities we consider to be comparable. We want to tell a story, but some of the words predetermine its outcome. Once we have decided that there are entities called "Solutrean" and "Magdalenian," we tend to treat them as if they had a reality which maps onto the entities which ethnographers define in modern groups of people. This is part of our failure to understand the importance of ethnography for its ability to inform us about the formation processes of the archaeological record rather than for the detail of the social and symbolic relationships between people (Davidson 1988).

For two reasons, the problem cannot be resolved simply by a return to a type fossil-based systematics. The first is because the approach I am advocating would only use type fossils as a start to the analysis. Much more attention should be given to formation processes, raw material, rationing, reduction sequences, and use. Definition by type fossils is just a traditional activity capable of doing a more limited version of the job assemblages are currently forced to do in our storytelling. The second reason is more fundamental and conjures up the spectre of long-forgotten papers with titles like "What are types?" Davidson and Noble (1989) have recently presented a detailed theoretical argument, with supporting archaeological evidence, that the early part of the Upper Pleistocene was the period which saw the origin of language—a reflective form of communication capable of reference in which words or signs function as symbols for things in the presence and the absence of such things, and in which meaning can be assigned by agreement between communities of language users. As part of this theory we find it impossible to believe that Oldowan choppers were tools made with the intention to create Oldowan choppers. Rather, the form of a cobble from which several flakes were struck in the simplest fashion was determined by the rock type and the mechanics of rock fracture. They become types because of the propensity of archaeologists to classify into types (i.e., they are analytical categories defined by prehistorians).

Nevertheless, Acheulean handaxes are a problem. We suggest that their long dominance of the archaeological record results from the advantage to hominids without language in learning to make artifacts by imitation. The skills involved in toolmaking, among other things, had a strong selective effect on the evolution of those areas of the brain important in motor control and sequencing which are also involved in the production of syntax and speech. Not until language emerged was it possible for hominids, now human, to conceive of types of artifacts. Dibble (1987c) has shown that many of the artifacts given discrete type names in Middle Paleolithic assemblages in the Bordes (1961a) type list result from discard at particular stages of a single generalized reduction sequence. Again the insistence on calling them types is a result of the classificatory habits of language-using archaeologists employing the methods of Bordes.

The implication of this line of reasoning is that the creation of types is part of the process of archaeological analysis, not necessarily part of the process of production of stone tools (cf. Dibble 1989). We might restrict our interest in types to those that seem to be restricted in time like Solutrean foliate points. The analysis of the remaining (overwhelming) parts of assemblages might eschew typological description in favor of an analysis of reduction sequences in relation to the factors that affect the supply of raw material. In this way, with a chronology supplied by radiocarbon dating or the strict definition of time-restricted type fossils, we might be able to study artifact variability in the way that we now discuss faunal remains: in terms of the likely availability of resources, the selection from those resources, the butchery or knapping of the selected portion (Witter 1988), and the processes which led to materials being deposited in or deleted from the archaeological context. Let us abandon the pretense that entities like the Solutrean mean anything in terms of "prodigious armies," for they are "fantasies." To do this will mean abandoning the old paradigm completely, not just in terms of abandoning the status of the Solutrean as a culture, but in terms of the need to restrain our habitual methods of classifying stone artifact assemblages. We can then move on to the interpretation of the activities of the people who created assemblages of artifacts much as we do with the interpretation of faunal assemblages, seeing those "armies" as shepherds with their "flocks of sheep." That will not be easy for some archaeologists, but that is what happens when a paradigm is replaced.

Acknowledgments

I must acknowledge my debt to Geoff Clark and Lawrence Straus. My paper may seem critical of their work, but in reality it is a tribute to the remarkable detail and honesty with which they have consistently published the results of their work at La Riera. I must also acknowledge their generosity in continuing to provide, by sending reprints and by the invitation to contribute to this volume, an opportunity to make comments which others would avoid. I feel certain that, if my paper has contributed in any small way toward the further decline of the phylogenetic paradigm, then they will be happy. I also thank Peter Hiscock, Dan Witter and Stephen Sutton for making me understand what was wrong with traditional typological approaches to stone artifacts. The opinions expressed in this paper are of course my responsibility.

Chapter 10
From Hunter-Gatherers to Food Producers in Northern Spain: Smooth Adaptive Shifts or Revolutionary Change in the Mesolithic

Manuel R. González Morales

Introduction

In keeping with the general theme of this book, I wish to emphasize a specific aspect of paradigmatic bias, which I will illustrate by making reference to the specifics of the transition from the final Upper Paleolithic to the Neolithic in the northern part of the Iberian Peninsula. I hope to determine to what extent we are conscious of our perceptions of specific change processes, and to show how our perceptions of change are strongly influenced by previous theoretical and ideological components of our training and experience. Although a classic theme in the literature of prehistory (and the example to which I will refer—the end of the Upper Paleolithic and the transition to the Neolithic—is also a classic in the western European literature), I nevertheless think that some insights might be gleaned from scrutiny of these issues as they are reflected in the north Spanish archaeological context as perceived from Spanish and American points of view.

Specifically, I want to show how, depending upon the point of theoretical departure adopted (and that point of departure is always strongly determined by "ideological" factors), the very process of the transition, and its results, can be analyzed and described in radically different ways. Semantic issues, and the near total lack of unambiguous definitions with explicit empirical referents, can also alter our perceptions of pattern and negatively affect our capacity for analysis and understanding.

Historical Antecedents

The historical antecedents of European prehistorians' efforts to understand the nature of the Paleolithic-Neolithic transition go back to the early years of this century (see also Sackett, this volume). The general paradigm that served as a reference point for the west European Upper Paleolithic for most of this century was first developed by Henri Breuil in 1912, and was based on his analyses of changes in the character of lithic and bone/antler artifact industries, changes that he attributed to ethnic differences on the part of their makers:

Il devient de plus en plus évident que ce qu'on a pris d'abord pour une serie continue, due à l'evolution sur place d'une population unique, est au contraire le fruit de la collaboration successive de nombreuses peuplades réagissant plus ou moins les unes sur les autres, soit par une influence purement industrielle ou commerciale, soit par l'infiltration graduelle ou l'invasion brusque et guerrière des tribus étrangères. (Breuil 1913:169)

The end of the Upper Paleolithic in Breuil's scheme was explained in the same way, but with one novelty: the Azilian represented, to a considerable degree, a genuine *revolution* in art and technology when compared to the preceding Upper Paleolithic:

Révolution, l'Azilien en est une: Plus d'art animalien, seulement des peintures sur galet et sur paroi d'éléments schématiques ou géometriques. Révolution dans le travail de l'os et de la corne de cerf . . . , les précédents semblent dériver directement de l'outillage appauvri des aurignaciens, et il en est de même pour les silex. (Breuil 1913:216)

The Neolithic, however, was conceptualized as the result of an exogenous process, without any continuity with the earlier industries of western Europe. In respect to Cantabria, the first synthetic works for the region tended to identify, in the various sites being excavated in the last quarter of the nineteenth and in the early years of the twentieth century, the phases described by various French authors and, after 1912, those of Breuil's scheme.

A significant departure from French systematics appeared in Cantabria in the path-breaking investigations of the Conde de la Vega del Sella after about 1914, with the discovery of industries of novel aspect and the subsequent definition of a new "culture" indigenous to the region: the Asturian of Cantabria (Vega del Sella 1916, 1923; Obermaier 1916). The term, which was actually coined by Hugo Obermaier (1916), carried with it the implications of ethnicity found in the works of French writers of the period.

The initial definition of the Asturian as a Mesolithic culture, interposed between the Paleolithic and the Neolithic, was based on a specific set of criteria; it should be noted that this definition fitted perfectly into the research traditions currently in vogue at the time in western Europe (especially France). The Count was to develop the topic of the nature of the local transition to the Neolithic in subsequent publications (e.g., 1925).

Specifically, Vega del Sella defined the Asturian (1) on the basis of a lithic and bone industry distinct from those of the final Upper Paleolithic and the Neolithic; (2) by an equally distinctive *habitat* criterion (i.e., occupation sites in the entrance to, outside of, or immediately in front of the mouths of caves and rockshelters); (3) by a form of exploitation in which shellfish gathering assumed an exceptional importance vis à vis earlier periods, so much so that it determined the kind of site characteristic of the Asturian—a shell midden or *conchero;* and (4) by a particular chronological position defined stratigraphically in some key sequences (as can be seen, for example, in his interpretation of the deposits in the Cueto de la Mina rockshelter or, definitively, in the results of his excavations in nearby La Riera cave between 1917 and 1918 [Vega del Sella 1923, 1930]).

Thus, the Asturian came to occupy an intermediate chronological position between the Upper Paleolithic and the Neolithic in the regional periodization schemes. However, and again in keeping with the paradigm accepted at the time, Vega del Sella retained the notion of a *hiatus* (i.e., an actual population vacuum between the final Upper Paleolithic-Epipaleolithic and the Neolithic), in such a way that he understood and defined his Asturian as a *preneolithic* culture, indicating thereby that he did not consider continuity to be established in the local transformation from the Upper Paleolithic to the Neolithic. The Count's formulation of the Asturian had, then, all the components of a "culture," defined according to the ruling paradigm of the era, including the theory of the *hiatus* and the related notion that the local Neolithic was of external derivation.

After Vega del Sella's work in the 'teens and '20s, some thirty years elapsed before Spanish prehistorians turned once again to the "Asturian question," and to its possible relationship with the Upper Paleolithic-to-Neolithic transition in central Cantabria. Toward the end of this interval, an argument was mounted based exclusively on the characteristics of the lithic industry, and ignoring all other categories of evidence, that the Asturian was in fact a kind of "pebble culture" and was of very great antiquity (i.e., Middle or even Lower Paleolithic in age—Jordá 1957, 1958, 1959; especially Crusafont 1963). Although the Count had previously taken up the issue of the crude appearance of Asturian quartzite "picks" and had reaffirmed a mesolithic age for the assemblage, his completely logical, stratigraphy based arguments fell on deaf ears as Jordá and his colleagues sought to make this anomaly in the classic local sequence "disappear" by emphasizing formal morphological relationships between Asturian retouched tools and Lower Paleolithic assemblages from diverse parts of the Old World (especially the north African littoral—Biberson et al. 1960). Few were convinced, mainly because Jordá never directly addressed possible change mechanisms, or the nature of the relationship between the Upper Paleolithic and the Neolithic in Cantabria once the Asturian was "extracted" from the sequence.

More Recent Work

A serious restudy of the Asturian had to await the initial fieldwork of G. A. Clark (beginning in 1969) in Asturias and Santander in order to arrive at new conclusions about this crucial moment in the regional prehistory. In fact, one of the questions raised by previous authors (including, in the extreme case, Jordá with his assertions about the great antiquity of the lithic industry) was the apparent *lack* of a relationship between Asturian industries and those of the bracketing Upper Paleolithic and Neolithic. In the late 1960s and early 1970s, the early Neolithic (in fact, the Neolithic in general) was also very poorly known in Cantabria, being represented only by a very few levels in a few sites dug long ago.

All this taken together made the establishment of a coherent culture historical sequence difficult or impossible and contributed significantly to the perception of a rupture, or sharp break, between the end of the Upper Paleolithic and Asturian. Clark's works (1971a, b; 1972, 1975a, b; 1976a, 1977, 1983a–c), which laid the foundation for an Asturian radiocarbon chronology and contributed significantly to an improved understanding of Asturian adaptations, constituted a first attempt at demonstrating possible continuity in the lithic industries of the Upper Paleolithic and Neolithic, entailing comparisons of the supposedly Asturian open-air site of Liencres (Clark 1975a, 1979) and the Azilian of the caves and rockshelters (e.g., Levels 1 and 2 from Liencres [Asturian?], Level 1 in Cueva Morín [Azilian]—González Echegaray and Freeman 1971, 1973). Although limited to a few sites and levels, Clark's statistical comparisons nevertheless indicated many compositional similarities between some open air sites (e.g., Liencres) and some Azilian cave and rockshelter industries (e.g., Cueva Morín) (see also Clark 1989c, d).

However, it is interesting to note that, through all of Clark's publications over the course of the past twenty years, and despite the detailed elaboration of the data, the descriptions of his test excavations, and especially the clear theoretical stance he takes on his work (guided by a systems ecological perspective), there is no in-depth discussion of the topic of *continuity per se*, and, therefore, of the kinds of changes that can be observed over the Upper Paleolithic-Neolithic transition (however, cf. Clark 1987b, 1989d). Like many Anglo-American publications, Clark's works (e.g., 1983; Clark and Lerner 1980, 1983) are grounded in a functionalist perspective and often include relatively sophisticated statistical analyses of Asturian resource catchments, site territories, site placements, and industries. He provides a relatively fine-grained static description of a "moment in time" (or a time interval—9000–6000 yr B.P.), but what is lacking is an account of the transformation of that system (i.e., its dynamic aspects). It could be argued that his approach is an *ahistoric* one that, while "anthropological" in terms of its biases (at least as that term is commonly understood in the Anglo-American research traditions), stands in some opposition to an historical perspective. It gives the impression that the temporal variable lacks importance except as a reference variable for framing the analytical context of the descriptive process mentioned above. In fact, both Clark and Straus often describe time as a "reference variable," used to monitor changes due to other causes (e.g., 1983).

More recently, in a series of post-1979 publications, L. G. Straus makes reference to the same problem, but attempts to integrate it into a broader theoretical perspective. Straus's works on the north Spanish Mesolithic have some aspects of essential interest that underscore problems that can result when an ahistorical perspective is applied to a transformation process or interval and the difficulties that can arise when this point of theoretical departure is applied to his, and others, consideration of these data.

In his 1979 article, Straus directly confronts the issue of possible contemporaneity between the Asturian *concheros* and the Azilian of the caves:

Many of the *concheros* themselves represent centrally-located spots from which hunters could exploit the main protein sources (deer, goat, boar) either seasonally or at various times of the year. At other times, entire human groups of specialized teams exploited terrestrial (and riverine) resources, often in the interior, depositing residues which are recognized archaeologically as "Azilian." Efficient, lightweight "Azilian" hunting (and fishing) gear (armatures, or points; harpoons, knives, scrapers, burins etc.) could be used (and are found) both on the coastal plain and in the hill country, but they are not likely to have been disposed of in *concheros*. (Straus 1979a:321–322)

This opinion is supported by the supposed overlap of Asturian and Azilian radiocarbon dates in the interval between ca. 9500 and 8500 B.P.

However, if one carefully examines Straus's Table 1, it is evident that the overlap is confined exclusively to a restricted series of rather problematic determinations: (1) Urtiaga C, pertaining to a group of very controversial dates from this site, all considered anomalous; (2) the post-Azilian travertine at Cueva Morín, without any cultural ascription; (3) Lev 3.3 in my own excavations at Mazaculos, corresponding to the base of the *conchero* on the contact with the clay of the preceding level (and that dates, therefore, the *very earliest* phase in the Asturian occupation; the most recent Asturian stratum in the areas wc cxcavated dates two millennia later); and, finally, (4) the dates from the Azilian levels at Ekain and Los Azules. In the case of Los Azules, the date corresponds to the very top of the Azilian sequence in Lev 3 and is, therefore, the most recent in the entire site (whereas the other Azilian dates are more than a millennium earlier). Therefore the "clear chronological gap" cited by Straus is based upon a very restricted series of determinations, which represent the limits of the chronological series from which they are derived (i.e., the most recent Azilian dates, the oldest Asturian ones).

In a more recent work, Straus (1986a) returns again to this theme, treating the Asturian *concheros* as probable trash middens associated with nearby (but never located) coastal habitation sites, probably occupied during the winter months, according to the oxygen isotope data from the shells (see also Clark and Straus 1983). Complementing these winter occupations is a probable "hunting facies," represented by inland Azilian sites, located by preference in interior valleys during the summer months (Straus 1986:358, 369; Clark 1983c, 1989d).

Underlying these arguments is a functional bias and a theme that is tacit but nearly unavoidable when dealing with the Asturian: the character of its lithic industry. If this particular functional explanation is accepted, it is possible to suggest that the Asturian *concheros* are simply a depositional facies of the Azilian, comprising great quantities of shell and other debris, but they were not utilized as habitations. From this point of view, the presence of the distinctive Asturian picks in them "may have, in fact, no functional significance, if it is simply a product of disposal behavior" (Straus 1986:320). Since he rejects a functional relationship between the picks and shellfish collecting (as has been suggested from time to time by Madariaga [e.g., 1973]), Straus prefers to consider them tools used for the collection of roots and other vegetal products.

In his latest publication on the subject of the relationship between the Azilian and the Asturian, Straus (1987d) proposes explicitly that the overpopulation in the coastal areas of Cantabria is the basic explanation for the changes in exploitation strategies that occurred in the area around 10 kyr B.P., and that these were largely independent of climatic changes. This aspect of the argument had already been discussed at length by Clark and Straus (1986), in respect of the data from the late Upper Paleolithic and Mesolithic sequence at La Riera cave (see also Clark and Straus 1983, Clark and Yi 1983, Clark 1987b).

A Critique of Straus and Clark's Functionalist Perspective

We have in the above-cited publications all of the elements necessary for an evaluation of the credibility of the overpopulation argument of Clark and Straus, and we should be able to assess how the paradigmatic biases of these authors "slant" their analyses in a particular direction. First, they appear to assume that observed changes in the makeup of these Mesolithic archaeofaunas are to be analyzed in terms of adaptive adjustments, which appear to them to be gradual. They seem to reject a priori even the possibility of any abrupt break. Second, because of a bias in favor of gradual change, the clearly disjunct character of the Asturian lithic industry vis-à-vis earlier phases tends to be discounted or ignored. In consequence, they tend to reject the possibility of temporal discontinuity, converting the clearcut differences in assemblage types into a "depositional facies." When the Azilian and the Asturian are identified, their essential differences are simultaneously denied. Finally, the adaptive mechanism to which Clark and Straus appeal is justified by reference to a general demographic model regarded as acceptable from their initial premises: demographic pressure (differentials in population density and imbalances between population and resources) is seen as the cause of the adjustments (Cohen 1977).

It is striking to me how their initial premises determine which data are to be taken seriously and which are to be ignored or deemphasized. The data available to these workers are the same as those found in all western European Upper Paleolithic and Mesolithic sites: stratigraphic sequences, series of radiocarbon dates (La Riera has produced more coherent ^{14}C dates than any other site in Iberia), and complementary analyses of fauna, flora, and industrial remains. It is difficult for me to accept, when the phenomenon is seen from a different perspective, that (1) the "Azilian" could persist as a recognizable entity much beyond 5500 B.P. (the date of some of the latest "Asturian" *concheros* with typical material); (2) intensification in the use of marine resources beginning in the Magdalenian, and the consequent, rapid decrease in limpet size because of overexploitation (Clark and Straus 1986:365) could have permitted this kind of economy to have remained relatively stable over millennia; and (3) lithic industries of "Azilian tradition" appear to be systematically absent from all recent mesolithic excavations in the region.

One more aspect stands out in recent "functionalist" analyses of the transition from the final Upper Paleolithic to the Mesolithic and Neolithic in the Vasco-Cantabrian region—an aspect that, from my point of view, underscores the importance of functionalist biases in structuring a problem. I am referring here to the systematic omission of references to paleolithic art, especially *arte parietal*. Traditionally, the end of paleolithic art has been approached in a formalist or idealist manner, with the understanding that its disappearance after the splendor of the Upper or Final Magdalenian obeyed the same processes of efflorescence and subsequent decay that were thought to characterize the lithic and bone industries. However, from the perspectives of Straus and Clark, it would be more reasonable to approach the problem in such a way that the disappearance of the art could be explained as one more in a series of adaptive changes (see also Lindly and Clark 1990).

Neither Straus nor Clark usually pay much attention to art. If we analyze in detail the above-cited works, we find only tangential references to paleolithic art or to the character of the sites that have produced this kind of evidence (Straus 1986b:347, 360; 1985c:117; however, see Straus 1987c). Sometimes their analyses focus on detailed discussions of "economic" aspects of the evidence (e.g., kilograms of meat provided by individual animals, proteins or calories yielded by each type of resource, vitamin content, etc.) or on "ecological" implications, which lead to a mechanical causality in the calculation of resources, the size of local groups involved in site formation, or the generation of general hypotheses about settlement patterns on either side of the Paleolithic/Mesolithic boundary, without breaks or discontinuity, as we have already seen. To omit evidence of paleolithic art in this context produces, in my judgment, one more manifestation of their ecological, economic, and functionalist theoretical premises; and these premises tend to structure all the subsequent argument (i.e., that the "art" can be analyzed independently from the economic and social aspects of a human community, or not analyzed at all). It could be the case that the context in which the art functions is ideological and varies independently of the socioeconomic contexts which are the targets of Straus and Clark's analyses. Whatever its function might have been, the disappearance of the art at the end of the Upper Paleolithic remains a significant "fact" that demands some kind of explanation.

The Disappearance of Paleolithic Art: Observations on Materialism and the Role of Ideology

Obviously, from a materialist perspective, it is not possible to uncouple, in the study of primitive societies, the economic aspects of the social structure from its ideological manifestations (like art). All form part of an integrated whole, without the compartmentalization or functional specialization that is so much a part of the modern world (Godelier 1974, 1977:155–179; Sahlins 1972). Because of this, it simply *does not make sense* to avoid the problem of the disappearance of the art when studying the Upper Paleolithic-Mesolithic transition in Cantabria since the disappearance of material evidence for a very long-standing ideological subsystem, present throughout most of the Upper Paleolithic, is a datum that cannot be ignored. Because the changes in the art are probably linked to changes in the forms of production (both the material conditions of production and the relations of the producers), from my perspective it makes little sense to postulate so radical a change in so short a period of time without implying a whole series of other changes in the social organization of production.

Recently, González Sainz (1989a, 1989b:254–264) has addressed some of the issues related to the disappearance of paleolithic art coincident with the end of the Upper Paleolithic. For this author, the increasing rarity and final disappearance of paleolithic art can be attributed to:

... la perdida del sentido original de unos temas y formulas de composición parietal, mantenidos durante casi todo el Paleolítico Superior, pero cada vez más en contradicción con las bases económicas de los grupos humanos.

Tendencias a un menor grado de interrelación cultural de los grupos humanos, por el menor papel de los movimientos a larga distancia y la nueva orientación del aprovechamiento económico, más intensivo y diversificado, desde finales de la época magdaleniense. (1989b:264)

... the loss of the original sense of some themes and formulas of wall-art composition, maintained throughout most of the Upper Paleolithic, but more and more in conflict with the (changing) economic bases of these human groups.

Tendencies toward decreasing interaction amongst human groups, due to the decline in long distance movement and a novel economic orientation, which became more intensive and diversified after the end of the Magdalenian. (1989b:264)

We can see how, in this case, there is an attempt to link the disappearance of the wall art to changes in the paleoeconomy, although a relationship is not fully articulated on a theoretical level.

A final deficiency in functionalist approaches to the analysis of this period in Cantabrian prehistory is a failure to project pattern searches into the Neolithic period: the key transition of the initial appearance of food production is viewed simply as one more adaptation in the system (e.g., Clark and Yi 1983, Clark 1987b). We find ourselves faced once again with the hoary question of whether the initial phases of the Cantabrian Neolithic should be viewed as a gradual process or as a revolution, in the archaic terminology of V. Gordon Childe (e.g., 1942).

There can be little question that biases introduced by implicit or explicit theoretical positions act to determine the entire course of an investigation. In this case, it is clear that, from an historical materialist perspective, the analysis of these data takes on a very different character from that of a functionalist perspective. Recent studies of the final phases of the Cantabrian Upper Paleolithic, like those of González Sainz (1989a, b), seek to identify and correlate changes in exploitation which are necessarily linked to transformations in the use of territories, in the organization of the forces of production within and between groups, and in ideology.

Regionalization and Its Consequences

The process of *regionalization* which is so evident in the European Mesolithic in general is also clearly discernible in the Cantabrian final Upper Magdalenian and Azilian. It entails the progressive substitution of specialized hunting (already detectable in the Solutrean, according to Straus 1977) in what were previously large, unbounded territories, due to population growth and the spatial restriction of exploitation and linked to a parallel diversification in resources as new sources of raw materials and foods located in close proximity to habitations were increasingly utilized. Reduction in the size of group territories, in group movements and, in consequence, long distance contacts are also part of the scenario (González Sainz and González Morales 1986:260–285). A tendency toward a reduction in the typological variety of tools, already noted by Fernández Tresguerres (1980) in respect of the Azilian, points in the same direction. These trends probably have functional explanations, but might also be related to changes in the procurement of raw materials (Binford 1979).

This process is not, of course instantaneous; but if we "scale" these changes to the passage of time, there is no doubt that, at least in Cantabria, these transformations become accelerated around 10,000–9000 yr B.P. (as a ballpark estimate). Because of these dates, one cannot avoid the possibility that climatic change coincident with the end of the

Pleistocene might have had some effect on the processes analyzed here. In respect of productive forces, one of the most striking is the increase in the collecting component of the economy, especially evident in the intensive, systematic collection of marine and estuarine shellfish, and new developments in fishing technologies. There can be little doubt that the rapid rise in early Holocene sea levels in Cantabria created a drastic reduction in exploitation territories in present-day littoral zones, while at the same time it reduced the distance from habitation sites to the resources of the encroaching shore. The extension of marine exploitation practices as a basic part of the economy must also have necessitated changes in the technology of production: (1) a progressive simplification of the "classic" tools of the paleolithic, (2) the development of new tool types designed specifically for detaching shellfish (especially limpets) from the estuarine and intertidal rocks to which they adhere, and (3) the appearance of toolkits for marine fishing (fish hooks) and the simultaneous disappearance of the traditional tools of riverine fishing (harpoons).

In light of the close linkage between foragers and their environments, the social structure of these hunter-gatherer groups must have undergone fairly abrupt transformations over a relatively short period of time. In primitive societies, social organization is coextensive with, and inseparable from the organization of production; they typically lack the neat separation that we can sometimes establish in more advanced societies between the economic infrastructure and the juridical-political superstructure (Service 1978). The decrease in mobility resultant from the geographical circumscription mentioned above, and the less-extensive contacts with neighboring groups which would have resulted from it, must have produced changes in kinship structures, mating networks and the like, at the same time that the social organization of labor in a "broad spectrum economy" (Flannery 1969), and an apparent reduction in traditional hunting practices, must have been quite distinct from those of the Upper Paleolithic.

Aspects of Ideology

One final element in this analysis is the ideological component in the form of myth and ritual, which also cannot be considered in isolation, divorced from their social and economic contexts. André Leroi-Gourhan (1968) already underscored some time ago the role that certain signs appear to play as "ethnic markers;" other authors have dealt with the topic of paleolithic "sanctuaries" as aggregation sites where dispersed local groups periodically came together for a variety of reasons (e.g., Conkey 1980). But, during times or intervals of dispersion of these social units and against a backdrop of increasing regional-ization, myths and rituals (as manifest in paleolithic art) linked to a particular mode of production and to an already outdated social struc-ture, would no longer have been maintained. The contradictions that emerge in the Cantabrian Magdalenian between the parietal and the mobile art indicate how supposedly ritualized art forms (those found in sanctuary contexts) retain a more conservative expression of content, while others, related to the mundane (e.g., objects in daily use in hunting and gathering contexts) seem to reflect much more directly their thematic (in good part, productive) content.

In sum, we have to try to understand the abrupt disappearance of paleolithic art at the end of the Magdalenian from a materialist per-spective as evidence of the culmination of trends in the subsistence economy and in social structure that go back to the Upper Paleolithic. Although our example refers exclusively to the situation in Cantabria, there is little doubt in my mind that this analytical perspective can be applied successfully to many west European contexts, although later developments were extremely variable from place to place (and across time) because of the regional fragmentation mentioned earlier.

Concluding Remarks: The Transition to the Neolithic

In respect of the character of the transition to *food producing* economies (in the traditional sense of the term), I have already noted that, in my opinion, Cantabrian mesolithic studies of a functionalist persuasion lack a clear statement of problem; in fact, the food producing transi-tion is located *outside* the problem domain recognized by functionalist theoretical orientations (but cf. Clark and Straus 1986, Clark 1987a, b). However, a materialist perspective can very comfortably accommodate the problem of the appearance of food production. From my point of view, the comprehension of the regional Mesolithic in its totality de-mands an understanding of the transformation processes that marked both its beginning and its end.

In this case, and in many others, the habitual lack of adequate archaeological documentation is often invoked to avoid an in-depth treatment of problems. In a recent publication, we refer to the neces-sity for integrating data relating to the appearance of first regional, megalithic phenomena in order to acquire a more adequate under-standing of process (González Sainz and González Morales 1986:295–310). The reader is referred to this work for an expanded discussion of the problem. Our idea is, in brief, that the expansion of neolithic economic territories associated with megalithic construction into the moderate and high elevations of the Cordillera Cantábrica is correlated with new forms of exploitation and distinct kinds of social structures, involving the organization of communal labor over much wider areas than the restricted economic territories of earlier periods, and that these changes brought with them changes reflected in new forms of collective funerary ritual—ideological novelties that brought the infrastructural economic transformations full circle and are manifest in new kinds of ritual and art. We submit that it is only through this kind of integrated perspective that the transition—revolutionary in its consequences—can be adequately understood (González Sainz and González Morales 1986).

In conclusion, it is my hope that this essay, although poorly supported empirically and intentionally polemic, might serve as a basis for discussion of the paradigmatic biases that underlie and are inextricably woven into our research designs, our methodologies, and the conclusions that result from our investigations.

Acknowledgments

This essay was translated from the Spanish original by G. A. Clark and L. Antonio Curet S. (Arizona State University), and proofread by the author.

Chapter 11
Paradigmatic Differences in a Collaborative Research Project

Harold J. Dibble and André Debénath

Introduction

When archaeologists from different nationalities work together, either on different sites in the same region or, as is becoming much more frequent in the Old World, in collaborative research projects, paradigmatic differences can become apparent. This is because different intellectual traditions often exist between countries, which in turn can lead to dissimilar research methods, goals and, of course, conclusions. An example of such paradigmatic differences exists for the two authors of this chapter, who work jointly in France at the Middle Paleolithic site of La Quina. One of us (AD) has a doctorate in Natural Sciences from the Université de Bordeaux, where paleolithic prehistory falls under the Department of Geology. The other (HD) has a Ph.D in Anthropology from the University of Arizona, a department well known for the breadth of anthropological training given its students (see Clark, this volume). What is interesting is that, in our case, the different backgrounds and theoretical orientations have not only *not* had a detrimental impact on our work together but, ironically, have resulted in considerable agreement between us in terms of fieldwork and analysis.

Debénath's approach to paleolithic prehistory is founded in natural history, particularly paleontology and geology. The basic goals of his research involve the documentation of the evolution, distribution, and behavior of humans through time, as evidenced by the remains of artifacts analyzed in the context of the prehistoric environment (see Debénath 1987). For him, the basic units of archaeological analysis (whether they are lithic attributes, types, or industries) are taken as discrete, modal categories that reflect real behavioral units in the same way that paleontological species are defined to reflect biologically meaningful units. It is a largely inductive approach, wherein all of the observations taken on each site and artifact provide some evidence for the larger research goal of documentation and classification. Thus, while some observations may contribute more information than others, it is Debénath's view that a coherent and comprehensive picture of human prehistory depends on the observation and collection of as much information as possible from the prehistoric record. This is essentially a classificatory paradigm (Audouze and Leroi-Gourhan 1981).

Dibble's background is in anthropology, and thus his goals are to understand the processes of human evolution and change. In his view, lithic and other artifacts are not necessarily discrete units, but can reflect continuous variation resulting from several factors operating simultaneously to affect different aspects of their morphology. Thus, if different attributes reflect different external factors, then the basic analytical units must vary depending on which factor is being currently explored. Moreover, his approach to science is focused more on the testing of hypotheses (a hypothetico-deductive paradigm), whereby only those aspects of the material that serve as test implications of the hypotheses in question (i.e., that are relevant to particular problems) are seen as important at any given time. Because many of the same processes presumably operate both in present human populations and in extant non-human populations, the data, models, and analogies drawn from ethnographic and even ethological sources make significant contributions beyond the prehistoric record alone.

Fortunately, both of us agree in terms of many of our research techniques, in spite of these two completely different research goals and, especially, the scientific approaches used to reach them. This is ironic, since as will be shown below, we agree for essentially different reasons. What follows, then, is not an argument for one approach or the other, but rather an attempt to describe each of our views and to show how they come together.

The Goals of Excavation: Data Recovery, Documentation, and Testing

In terms of both his general goals and scientific approach, it would follow that Debénath's primary goals in excavation would be to recover the maximum amount of data. For Dibble, emphasis would be given to the recovery of only those artifacts and features that have the most direct bearing on the hypotheses being investigated. However, both agree that techniques oriented toward near-total recovery of artifacts and their provenience are to be used whenever possible.

André Debénath

In French systematics, especially those used in France itself, a major emphasis is placed on acquiring detailed familiarity with a small number of restricted geographical regions. Much of the role of a prehistorian is to document or catalog the prehistoric activity in those regions. Within a geographic specialization, there is considerable breadth of familiarity with the varieties of archaeological materials found there. Thus, it is not uncommon for a French paleolithic researcher to be at home with the Lower, Middle, and Upper Paleolithic (and, perhaps, the Neolithic and even the Metal Ages) within his particular region.

For example, Debénath has specialized in the Lower and Middle Paleolithic of the Charente and in the entire paleolithic sequence of Morocco. In his lab in Bordeaux there are others with specializations in other geographic areas, such as the departments of the Gironde or the Dordogne, and often with a secondary geographic specialization as well. It is not uncommon for an individual to spend most of his active career working in just a few restricted geographic localities, with the aim of documenting most, if not all, of the paleolithic sequence there.

Again, the major goal is to gather as much information as possible on the known occurrences of paleolithic materials in order to arrive, eventually, at a good understanding of the natural history of that area. Periodically this documentation is published, together with regional catalogs of prehistoric occurrences, in periodicals like *Gallia Préhistoire,* or the comprehensive *La Préhistoire Française* (de Lumley 1976).

Harold Dibble

A different perspective is taken by Dibble. What draws him to a particular country or region is the potential there for obtaining evidence bearing on a particular research question. In his case, these questions concern Middle Paleolithic lithic technology and behavior. The prehistoric record of France offers significant potential for investigation of these problems, and it is for this reason that he is interested in working in that country and at sites that are particularly well suited to test specific hypotheses about prehistoric behavior and processes of change. Perhaps this is typical of most archaeologists when they work outside their own national boundaries: a shift in emphasis occurs away from a documentation of local history to questions of broader concern.

Methodology: A Common Ground

For both of us, however, the need for exhaustive documentation exists during the excavation of a site. It is generally agreed that the French are leaders in the development of precise and detailed excavation techniques, pioneered by people such as François Bordes and André Leroi-Gourhan. For example, the latter's work at Pincevent is a model for the detailed recording of artifact distributions over a large area (Leroi-Gourhan and Brézillon 1983). In many cases, artifacts and features are not only mapped and/or photographed in place, but life-sized casts are produced of entire occupation surfaces. Where occupation surfaces are not as clearly preserved, excavators rely on measuring the three-dimensional Cartesian coordinates of virtually all observable artifacts and natural features, often complemented by hand-drawn field maps and plans. These methods were used in all of the excavations by Debénath at La Chaise, Sidi Abderhamman, Dar-es-Soltan, and other sites. In fact, the influence of these methods extends throughout the world and beyond the paleolithic period.

For the French, this emphasis on near-total recovery and proveniencing stems from a need to preserve permanently the original status of the site and thus its contribution to the regional prehistory. This seems to be the primary objective of most casting projects, for example, which forever preserve paleolithic occupation surfaces. Beyond simply preserving the finds, from a research perspective this attention to detail reflects the need for accumulating as much data as possible in order to arrive inductively at a comprehensive explanation (or perhaps better, interpretation) of prehistory. As expressed by Audouze and Leroi-Gourhan (1981:174), this represents a "science of observation" that underlies the French archaeological paradigm. The maxim is that "the most accurate archaeological reconstruction requires the maximum amount of data recovery." Typically such information includes the entire spectrum of natural phenomena with preserved traces in the archaeological record. Thus, excavation is *pluridisciplinaire*, and involves collaboration of many specialists, including sedimentologists, geomorphologists, palynologists, and paleontologists.

The French emphasis on total data recovery might seem at first to be in conflict with an hypothesis testing approach, in which only those data that serve as test implications are considered to be important. However, amicable collaboration between us is possible because the French approach is not only useful for maximal data documentation, but also because it creates data on archaeological context, or the relationships among artifacts and between them and their surrounding matrix. In a hypothesis-testing approach, this information is important because research questions are constantly changing and new analyses of already excavated material depend on the availability of original contextual information. Of course, the recording of this information must be done at the time of excavation, since the act of excavation permanently destroys it.

This, then, is a major point of agreement between us regarding excavation procedures. That is, we believe that the archaeologist's primary role in the field is to preserve information that will be lost as soon as the artifact is removed from its context. As they are as vital for accurate interpretations as the artifacts themselves, these contextual data must be archived along with the artifacts. It is, therefore, the excavator's responsibility to guarantee their accuracy and integrity. Our use of detailed recording techniques reflects the view that as much information as possible about the context of archaeological material should be recorded and that techniques of excavation can be somewhat independent of the intellectual problems being pursued by the excavator. Thus, the use of the most comprehensive recording techniques available satisfies the requirement of documenting and preserving the original status of the site, as well as providing basic contextual data that will be useful for future analyses of the recovered material. The computer methods developed for use at La Quina (and which are now being extended to Combe-Capelle and La Chaise) are, in fact, simply a refinement of traditional means of documentation, but with enormously expanded analytical capabilities (Dibble 1987d, Dibble and McPherron 1988, McPherron and Dibble 1988).

This raises an important point regarding the publication of field provenience data. Although the importance of artifact context is widely acknowledged, no adequate means of managing or disseminating these basic (but voluminous) data is widely used. Most site reports present finished results based on context, either as interstratigraphic comparisons or as trends and intrastratigraphic spatial analyses. But, it is becoming apparent that no analyses are ever truly finished so long as research questions keep changing; and problems often arise when the material needs to be restudied. While the artifactual material itself may be available for use by other researchers, the equally important contextual data often are not, except in the form of major stratigraphic unit proveniences. Thus, the ability to carry out further work with data on exact three dimensional co-ordinates is often limited. Computer technology will be of crucial importance here, too, since it provides a permanent association between "fine-grained" contextual (and other) data and individual artifacts that is both efficient to distribute and may be easily incorporated into the research designs of other workers.

The Analysis of Lithic Types and Assemblages

Both of the authors have major research interests in Middle Paleolithic typology and technology and both use what is called the "Bordesian Method." This method, based on the lithic typology developed by

François Bordes (1961a), is considered the standard typology for the Lower and Middle Paleolithic in most of the western Old World. Bordes's views on technology, based on his pioneering replicative experiments (see, e.g., Bordes and Crabtree 1969), have also been fundamental to understanding lithic variability and to modern interpretations of paleolithic assemblages. Through our training we have each been heavily influenced by both the man and his work, and so it follows that we would share some common approaches to dealing with lithic artifacts. Specifically, we each support the use of Bordes's types and observations in paleolithic research, though with some modifications. We have, however, different ideas about the *meaning* of those categories and their possible relationships to particular kinds of prehistoric behavior.

The Debénath Perspective

Debénath's views closely parallel those of Bordes, stemming in large part from his geological and paleontological training. Just as paleontological species are defined to reflect real, biologically meaningful units (see, e.g., Gingerich 1985), lithic types reflect intentional end products that were behaviorally and cognitively meaningful. The important stress here should be on the word "intentional"—lithic types are real because they are what the prehistoric flintknapper wanted to make (see Bordes 1969). This means that the morphology of stone tools was, to a large extent, premeditated, and that they reflect in their design discrete units conceptualized by their makers. This is basically what Sackett (1982) calls an "organic" model, though we do not here mean to imply that specific types necessarily act as *fossiles directeurs* (archaeological index fossils) characteristic of specific paleolithic cultures. In fact, it was Bordes who replaced this notion with a method that relies upon the analysis of the *total* retouched tool component of an archaeological assemblage. But that aspect of his method concerns the level of the assemblage; at the level of the individual artifact, a certain reality analogous to biological taxonomic units is assumed.

While variability is acknowledged *within* individual type categories, it is less important than variability *between* types and more often than not this intratype variability is seen as deviation from a conscious norm. Thus, variations from ideal forms are either errors, ad hoc accommodations to specific circumstances, such as blank morphology, or due to other outside factors, such as the use of raw materials with different flaking qualities (cf. Brace 1988a, Clark 1989b for an enlightening comparison with French paleontological paradigms). Intertype variability, on the other hand, relates to differences in style (different peoples or cultures with different desired end products) or to different activities that required specific tools.

This view carries over to major technological categories (e.g., Levallois, disk core, and bifacial techniques) and to individual typological and technological attributes (e.g., Quina retouch, platform faceting, or surface preparation). A common assumption in viewing any of these categories or attributes is that they were intentionally produced (i.e., that flintknappers wanted to make Levallois flakes at a particular place or time, wanted to produce Quina retouch, etc.). The corollary is that if a particular attribute is absent in an assemblage, then the prehistoric flintknappers either did not *want* to make it, did not *have* to make it, or did not *know how* to make it. It is assumed throughout that prehistorians are capable of (even adept at) identifying technotypological variables that were "meaningful" to prehistoric peoples in the distant past.

Building upon these defined types and attributes, the Bordesian Method organizes Middle Paleolithic assemblages according to differential frequencies of the various types, type groups, and major technologies exhibited (see also Sackett 1982). This has led to the recognition and definition of several Mousterian assemblage groups (facies) based on different typological compositions. While there is debate over whether assemblages variability reflects different cultures or activity variants of the same group of people (Bordes 1961b, 1973; Binford and Binford 1966, Binford 1973), this is not a controversy over the reality of the types used to define the facies. The two points of view simply represent two hypotheses about the interpretation of those types and therefore the interpretations of assemblages that are aggregates of those types.

The assumption of the reality of the types, and the assemblage groups based on them, has become so ingrained that the types and facies constitute the major analytical units of paleolithic research in Europe and the Near East. Thus, major current research questions focus on the relationship of one or more of them to the environment (Rolland 1981), to economic resources (Gamble 1986, Chase 1986a, b), chronology (Mellars 1969, 1988) and raw materials (Geneste 1985, 1988). If patterns are found, then those patterns are thought to reflect intentional behavioral responses on the part of the Middle Paleolithic peoples. There are also suggestions that some of the major typological categories may reflect prehistoric linguistic categories (Holloway 1981).

The Dibble Perspective

An alternative approach, one taken by Dibble, is the view that the Lower and Middle Paleolithic types do not necessarily have any cognitive reality, other than that for modern archaeologists. In large part this perspective develops from difficulties in recognizing modalities in the artifacts due to the dynamics of flintknapping itself. Lithic artifacts are much more amenable to significant reworking, with resulting changes in their morphology, than are other kinds of material culture, such as ceramics. Furthermore, many factors simultaneously influence lithic morphology, including aspects of raw materials, technology, function, and style. To a large extent, these factors can be intentionally controlled by the flintknapper. But in the case of Middle Paleolithic industries, the question is whether external factors contributing to artifact morphology are overriding the effects of intentionality. At any rate, such factors become the principal focus of investigation rather than the perceived modalities. Of course, this view also has French intellectual roots, notably in the work of Leroi-Gourhan (1964a, b).

The Dibble perspective is not just an alternative interpretation of the types defined by Bordes: it represents a completely different viewpoint on the nature of typological variation. First, it holds that the lithic types recognized today are *modern categories* imposed on what is essentially continuous variation and, therefore, that the types do not represent modal categories, with only incidental intratype variation. Second, it sees these types not as the imperfect material manifestations of ideal forms or desired end products, but simply as pieces that were no longer useful or desired and so were discarded and thus incorporated into the archaeological record. So, while flakes were undoubtedly deliberately retouched to achieve a suitable working edge, the overall morphology of the final piece is not, in this view, intentional. Even at an assemblage level it has been suggested that raw material availability, intensity of occupation, and technology used to produce flake blanks are major sources of interassemblage typological variability and, therefore, that an assemblage taken as a whole is not a direct reflection of intentional behavioral responses (Rolland and Dibble 1990, Dibble and Rolland n.d.).

A Comparison

There is, then, a contrast between our views on the nature of lithic types and artifact variability, but agreement about the use of Bordes's typology. This might appear contradictory: assuming that types have no prehistoric cognitive reality, why should Dibble continue to use them in the course of his research? The answer is that to deny the native reality or intentionality of types is not to deny the usefulness of a typology. This notion can be traced to the famous Ford-Spaulding debate that took place among American archaeologists in the middle part of this century (Ford 1952, 1954; Spaulding 1953, 1960). From this debate arose the consensus view (in America, at least) that archaeological type categories are analytical constructs defined by contemporary archaeologists. Thus, they need not bear any necessary or demonstrable relationship to mental templates, ideal types, or desired end products in the minds of people long dead. The validity of a typology should be judged on its usefulness for particular questions of prehistoric research, not on its prehistoric "reality" which, from an American perspective, cannot be known.

So, whether Mousterian peoples made convergent scrapers for a particular task or according to a cultural norm, or whether they represent only an end point in a sequence of resharpening, is a question of the *interpretation* of that type, not a question of its validity or its usefulness for archaeological research. In fact, since Dibble (1987a–c) argues that the various scraper types reflect stages in a reduction process, Bordes's types have become extremely useful to him as a measure of reduction and intensity of utilization of the lithic resources. The interpretation may be different, but the usefulness of the typology remains, at least for certain questions. If anything, this shows the power and general utility of Bordes's typology for the description of assemblage variation. It is, therefore, perfectly logical that we both use Bordes's typology in basic descriptions of Middle and Lower Paleolithic assemblages. In this way we can agree completely on the basic nature of a particular assemblage, however much our interpretations of those assemblages might differ (cf. Binford and Sabloff 1982).

On the other hand, paradigmatic differences do lead to slight differences in how we might choose to make other observations. For many, archaeology is an "observational" (or at least a "non-experimental") discipline (Clark 1982). In an inductive approach there is much more focus on the understanding and description of each individual artifact, which is often considered interesting for its own sake. This leads to important concerns about techniques for making observations. The problem is that any description inevitably provides a less-than-perfect image of the original artifact, and this is especially true if the description is to be generalized. There is a continual impetus to develop new techniques which preserve more of the original quality of the artifacts and at the same time remain analytically manipulative. This is not so much a matter of concern for "deductive" approaches (i.e., those based on hypothesis testing), since these focus only on attributes that are relevant to particular questions and there is little interest in describing the artifact as a whole. From this viewpoint, carefully chosen observations will, in the context of a specific research question, be more useful than an overall description of the artifact itself because they reduce the amount of "noise" and therefore throw into sharp relief the relationship under investigation.

Conclusions

While paradigmatic differences between the authors are both apparent and real, we are fortunate that they do not impede our collaborative efforts. The reason for this largely stems from the fact that we both require the same basic kinds of data, contextual and typological, for our own particular research objectives. The larger goals are the same: we are both interested in understanding prehistoric human behavior in its own settings and contexts. We do not feel that one or the other's approach is intrinsically "better," or that there is such a thing as "good" or "bad" archaeology—only good and bad archaeologists. In fact, we think that our views are complimentary since the more behavioral "American" perspective often depends on the context provided by the natural historical "French" paradigm. Where we agree completely is in the desirability of maximal recovery of contextual information. The destructive aspect of archaeology is unique among the scientific disciplines and forces a certain measure of responsibility on us to collect basic data vital for other researchers working on questions beyond those of primary concern to the original excavators. If there is a paradigm common to all archaeology, it must at least have this basic characteristic.

Acknowledgments

The authors wish to thank various people who have read this manuscript and offered comments, especially Philip Chase and Simon Holdaway. Funding for the La Quina Prehistoric Project has come from the Universities of Arizona, Pennsylvania, and Bordeaux; the Wenner-Gren Foundation for Anthropological Research; the National Geographic Society; l'Action Thématique Programmée d'Archéologie Metropolitaine, and private donations.

Part III: Paradigms for the Paleomesolithic of Italy and Cyprus

Chapter 12
The Community Ecology Perspective and the Redemption of "Contaminated" Faunal Records

Mary C. Stiner

Introduction

The identification of hominid foraging adaptations is a pressing concern in evolutionary studies of our species. The most proximate records of *Homo* foraging behaviors available for this time range are faunal remains in archaeological sites. Unfortunately, the likelihood that faunal assemblages are biased by the actions of other, non-human agencies increases as one searches farther back in time. Two groups of processes contribute to this problem, geological and biological. The probability of geological disturbance is more or less cumulative as a function of time. No less significant, although relatively instantaneous, are the ecological and behavioral contexts of bone deposition attributable to the hominids themselves. The possible importance of scavenging in the Lower and Middle Paleolithic, for example, and the frequent association of cultural- and carnivore-generated debris in cave sites, implies that the foraging niches of archaic *Homo sapiens* interlocked with those of other large predators in ways not typical of moderns.

While biased records present some difficult methodological challenges to archaeologists, disturbance by biological agencies need not be viewed as disadvantageous to scientific research. Community ecology provides a diverse body of theory appropriate for dealing with faunal records created by multiple agencies because it emphasizes interaction among trophically related species in any given environment. Applications of the community ecology approach are relatively new in paleolithic archaeology and, as argued below, are uniquely suited to many of the practical problems posed by early hominid sites. In the absence of any sort of direct behavioral analogs, the general principles of foraging ecology and community structure provide a solid framework for investigating changes in hominid foraging adaptations.

The community ecology approach to studies of human evolution focuses on human relations with coexisting species rather than the exclusive study of man, and it effectively expands the scope of archaeology as a discipline. It has gained this position very recently due to a revolution in our perceptions of how archaeological records come into being.

Paradigms in Paleolithic Archaeology of the Mediterranean Region

By way of background, there are at least three paradigms used by paleolithic archaeologists in the Mediterranean region. The most traditional of the three focuses on culture history and chronology. Vertical excavations are the rule and follow the geological tradition of using distinctive artifacts as *fossiles directeurs* or, in the case of *la méthode Bordes,* lithic assemblage composition, to date deposits. This perspective testifies to the long history of intellectual exchange among the interpretive sciences of geology, paleontology, and archaeology. This geology-based view is the foundation for defining regional cultural sequences throughout the Old World.

The cultural chronology paradigm has fallen from favor in many circles, having given way to one or two alternative paradigms that emphasize human behavior. For purposes of discussion, I will call these the "behavioral reconstructionist" (*sensu* Binford 1981a) and the "evolutionist" paradigms. The "reconstructionist" and the "evolutionist" perspectives differ in the ways archaeologists conceive of behavior and the processes of culture change. Apparent overlap in these two perspectives, both of which allude to behavior, is largely superficial and may relate to an overly generous use of the term *evolution* in the place of *change.* Everyone agrees that cultures changed between 2 million years ago and the present, but only some researchers are genuinely concerned with the mechanisms of change in hominid adaptations and how change should be measured against other, independent phenomena.

Important differences between the reconstructionist and evolutionist paradigms also are evident from the scale at which archaeological patterns are considered relevant for describing hominid behavior. The difference is apparent from the variables chosen for study (e.g., frequencies of tool forms, species representation, spatial dimensions used for comparisons, and so on) and what an investigator is willing (or not willing) to invest in order to establish reliable connections between cause and effect for a given variable.

Finally, differences in view are evident from where data presentation stops in project monographs. Do the elegant vertical and/or horizontal maps produced by modern excavation methods require analyses of a higher order to understand behavioral systems, or are they the primary pictures to be assembled together as the final document of prehistoric life? It is clear, at any rate, that proponents of each view make some distinct requirements of the archaeological record that center on the question of site "integrity." As I argue below, such a requirement may not be realistic and could even get in the way of learning about the past.

Taphonomy: Harbinger of Conflict

While I obviously prefer the "evolutionist" view in my own research, it would be unfair simply to rate one paradigm against the other two. In fact, one has grown from the foundation of another in such a manner that an historical sequence beginning with the culture-chronology view, shifting to the "reconstructionist" view and, in a few cases, to the evolutionist view can be traced through the course of the twentieth century. In Italy, the culture history-chronology view guided most or all work up to about 1970. It is responsible for major advances in understanding geological conditions of site formation and relative dating of regional sequences in that country (see, in particular, Blanc and Segre 1953, Segre 1976–77, Segre 1984, province of Latium).

Today, most archaeology in the Mediterranean region, and in Italy specifically, falls under one of the two behavioral paradigms. Archaeologists have not lost interest in the chronological associations of vertical sequences, but have shifted much of their attention to the horizontal dimensions of site structure. While spatial relationships among objects are the basic concern of all archaeologists, we nevertheless differ in our concepts of what these data can mean.

Behavioral reconstructionists seek small but clear apertures into the past. The view is one of paleoethnological history and originates largely from the work of Leroi-Gourhan (see Audouze and Leroi-Gourhan 1981 for an insightful review of this perspective). Each aperture is a well preserved, more or less undisturbed archaeological site; and the discovery of "living floors" is eagerly anticipated at the outset of each new project. Because accurate observations of the spatial distribution of artifacts and site contents are the keys to visualizing the past, this view is largely responsible for a revolution in primary data collection and artifact recovery (see Dibble and Debénath, this volume).

Archaeologists have long been fascinated with pure records of the past. Like the other branches of anthropology, archaeology is traditionally bounded by an interest in people; and undisturbed cultural deposits naturally seem the optimal sources of information for any fine-grained behavioral reconstructions of prehistoric lifeways. I think that there is something of the reconstructionist in all of us, since the attractions of a well preserved site are undeniable. Yet one cannot escape the fact that undisturbed sites are difficult to find. The reality suggested by recent work in taphonomy is even more jarring: pristine records may not exist.

The subdiscipline of taphonomy has changed what many researchers are willing to believe about the heuristic potential of archaeological records (e.g., see Behrensmeyer and Kidwell 1985, Gifford 1981). Taphonomic applications in archaeology have illuminated a philosophical conflict, particularly in research on earlier forms of *Homo*, by showing that site formation normally is complicated by the actions of non-human agencies. Something about the very nature of the hominid activities involved permitted this to be so.

Taphonomic studies in circum-Mediterranean archaeology are rather belated compared to like research in North America, Africa and Western Europe (e.g., Binford 1981b, 1984, Blumenschine 1986, Brain 1981, Bunn 1981, Bunn and Kroll 1986, Lindly 1988, Potts 1982, 1984), but applications of these methods present essentially the same conflicts that have been experienced elsewhere. In the case of Middle Paleolithic shelter sites in Italy, recent analyses indicate that carnivores exercised strong effects on some faunal records that originally had been attributed to hominids alone (e.g., Stiner 1990a, 1991).

What can be done with the imperfect archaeological records which constitute the bulk of the paleolithic record? Some biases may actually yield valuable information about the hominid foraging niche and changes therein, provided that archaeologists can meet the challenge of sorting out who did what. Such exploration must precede inferences about hominid activities. Taphonomic investigations aid in the effective exploration of ecological relationships between hominids and their prey, and between hominids and other coexisting predators. While it prepares the way, however, taphonomy will not provide the interpretive structure for understanding hominid adaptations.

Biased Records, Evolutionism, and the Community Ecology Approach

The view that archaeological records can be ranked on a scale of purity precludes the possibility of finding ways to render "contaminated" (biased) records informative. The biologically based approach known as community ecology provides a graceful exit from the current imbalance between expectations of site pristinity and the realities of site formation. Community ecology is a potentially powerful means for researching evolutionary questions about human prehistory in the absence of unbiased records of the past. It can make use of the alternating (or even mixed?) effects of hominids and other biological agencies in shelter deposits. The community ecology approach is a logical extension of the view that selection pressures faced by pre-modern hominids were not unique, while allowing for the possibility that the specific adaptational solutions were (Foley 1984a). As is the case for "evolutionism" in general, community ecology is simply a point of view.[1]

Theory of Adaptational Change in Animal Communities

The notion that organisms evolve in response to external pressures is fundamental to the community ecology approach and has fostered the development of niche theory. My research on paleolithic faunas in Italy is organized primarily under the guidelines of this theory: a set of ideas about inter-specific relationships, species "packing" in animal communities, and the rules of niche assembly (Diamond 1975, MacArthur 1968, 1972, MacArthur and Levins 1967, May and MacArthur 1972, Roughgarden 1983, Schoener 1974, 1984).

Niche theory represents a means for predicting and testing hypotheses about how hominid adaptations were structured relative to coexisting species. The law of *limiting similarity* (also called mutual exclusion), the main principle of niche theory, states that no two species can occupy the same niche space. The rules of community assembly are of evolutionary importance, because they may condition the opportunities as well as the potential directions for change in any given species.

Applied niche theory assumes that animal communities have a general structure that is inferable from regularities in the relationships among species in a food web. A community is comprised of multiple resource niches, each occupied by one species. The niche spaces have *form*, the abstract dimensions of which can be mapped as places in the community structure. Most ecologists assume that there are few if any holes among animal niches, such that they are densely packed together in an ecosystem.

The structure and content of an ecological community can change. New species arrive via colonization or through divergence toward a qualitatively distinct adaptation. Recruitment of new species is thought to occur most often at the level of resource *guilds*. Guilds are comprised of trophically related species that depend on the same general set of resources, irrespective of the phylogenetic histories of the member species. The scavenger guild in southern African communities, for example, may include raptorial birds (especially vultures), certain species of beetles, brown hyenas, and spotted hyenas.

Resource guilds, such as the one centering on ungulate prey, are thought to represent potential arenas of evolutionary change. Each member must meet its own needs while reducing competition with other member species that depend on the same resources (Root 1967, Pianka 1978). Competitive exclusion fixes and stabilizes the boundaries between niche spaces (Walter et al. 1984).

The relationships among guild members are modeled as bonds for which a limited range of unions is possible. Some bonds are almost inviolable, based on their persistence in evolutionary history, while others appear less stable. Recruitment of species into guilds proceeds in a conservative fashion, with new species attaching themselves to weak links in the structure or by quickly filling any temporary opening. However, opportunities for addition do not occur entirely at random. They are governed by the contingencies of fit and, therefore, history. For this reason, generalist feeders are thought to enter in the early stages of community formation (when there were fewer limitations on the dimensions of niche spaces in the ecosystem) while specialists enter late.

Members of a predator guild respond to niche boundaries of other, trophically similar predators in addition to the limits set by food supply. This idea provides an essential premise for my comparisons of hominid- and carnivore-generated faunas in Italy. The niche boundaries of sympatric guild members should be particularly useful for evolutionary studies of a "neighbor" undergoing change within a particular chronological period—as was certainly the case for *Homo* during the Middle and Upper Pleistocene (e.g., Foley 1984a, b, Turner 1984, 1986).

Large carnivores (the other members of ungulate predator guilds) underwent evolutionary changes too, but most of this process took place during the Miocene or Pliocene (Eisenberg 1981, Kurtén 1971). The adaptations of large carnivores were *relatively* stable by the Middle and Upper Pleistocene. Hence, for the purposes of my study, many of the basic features of carnivore adaptations can be inferred from the habits of modern counterparts. Identification of the strategies and contexts of resource use by non-human predators and hunter-gatherers permits the development of a general framework in which to compare the predator niches of modern and archaic *Homo sapiens*.

Niche Comparison of Middle and Upper Paleolithic Hominids in West-Central Italy

My research in west-central Italy poses the following questions. Did the subsistence adaptations of Middle Paleolithic hominids fall somewhere within the range of fully modern humans *as a subspecies*? Did they occupy similar ecological niches, and did they respond in similar ways to particular environmental challenges?

The Mousterian technological data, vague as they are with regard to foraging, suggest that the answer to each question may be negative. My study of shelter faunas investigates hominid foraging adaptations in Italy independently of the chronological boundaries defined by hominid skeletal biology and technology in Western Europe. The investigation reveals how Mousterian hominids[2] obtained prey (e.g., selective hunting, non-selective hunting, and scavenging), the degree and character of strategic diversity in the overall subsistence system, and the scales of land use.

The study sample consists primarily of museum collections from a series of stratified Mousterian caves along the Tyrrhenian coast of Italy. These are Grotta Guattari, Grotta Breuil[3] (Monte Circeo), Grotta dei Moscerini, Grotta di Sant'Agostino (near Gaeta), and a stratified hyena den complex known as Buca della Iena (north of Pisa). The Mousterian deposits in these sites collectively span a time range of 120,000 to 35,000 years ago. The comparative sample for the Italian late Upper Paleolithic ranges between 15,000 and 10,000 years B.P.

The study sample represents resource use by several carnivore species in addition to Middle and Upper Paleolithic hominids, and the analyses capitalize on the natural alternations of hominid and other predator components in the caves. Two general types of resources (ungulate prey and natural shelters) linked hominids, sympatric spotted hyenas, and wolves into a single resource guild in Pleistocene Italy. Overlapping use of resources in this region implies close, although not necessarily competitive, ecological and evolutionary relationships among these ungulate predators (also see Gamble 1983, 1984, Straus 1982, Turner 1984).

The study involves two major stages. (1) The first problem is determining through taphonomic and related analyses which faunas actually represent hominid feeding activities at shelters and which represent the activities of other predators. (2) Once the authorship(s) of each assemblage has been established, the second problem is to determine what the culturally associated faunas reveal about hominid foraging behavior throughout the time frame examined. Some of the main results of this hierarchical investigation are summarized below.[4]

The ecological comparisons necessitate the development of a framework (or map) of niche relationships among large predators that effectively calibrates adaptational differences as *distance* and *direction*. Once established, it should be possible to evaluate how modern and archaic *Homo sapiens* fit within this larger framework. The degrees of difference would provide a reliable, independent means for interpreting the ecological significance of any shift in resource niche. I approach this problem by first investigating some of the basic variables used in foraging models through inter-specific comparisons of modern predators. (It should be noted, however, that none of the variables are sufficiently well controlled to be articulated within a single equation.)

The Mousterian patterns are compared to those for late Upper Paleolithic humans, spotted hyenas, and wolves in a limited geographical area of coastal Italy, as well as to some modern carnivore and human cases from other parts of the world. Four classes of results prove particularly interesting with regard to hominid foraging niche in Upper Pleistocene Italy. These are (1) the array of and relative emphasis on prey species consumed, (2) the anatomical parts of ungulate prey carried to shelters, (3) prey age selection (mortality patterns), and (4) the general seasons of shelter use. These data are reviewed below.

1. I find no significant differences in the range and the relative proportions of large (ungulate) prey species consumed by each type of predator at shelters. Mousterian hominids and late Upper Paleolithic humans emphasized the same prey species in this region. The lack of any significant differences between the diets of either hominid and spotted hyena is more interesting still, as it testifies to the overreaching effects of natural prey abundance on ungulate selection by large predators! A minor exception is found for denning wolves in paleolithic Italy, consistent with what is observed for modern wolves (Stiner 1990a). While wolves generally depend on large prey, they are known to shift to smaller species when tethered by immobile young in dens each year.

I find more variation in transport of small prey, such as mollusks and turtles, because these items are present in certain Mousterian cases only. However, small prey contributed only a minor fraction of the overall diets of hominids at shelters. The overall comparisons of animal species in predator diets at shelters show that *species representation (particularly of ungulates) is not a suitable criterion for evaluating evolutionary trends in hominid adaptations during the Upper Pleistocene.*

2. Because ungulate remains occur inside shelters and taphonomic analyses indicate biological agencies of accumulation, it is reasonable to assume that the assemblages represent food transported by predators. In general, biases in anatomical representation in transported faunas relate to the general methods of food procurement, natural food abun-

dance, and the nutritional quality of food (particularly fat content). Comparisons of transported faunas created by each of the four types of predators reveal significant differences among them. *The range of variation exhibited by each predator can be linked to the number of qualitatively distinct strategies incorporated by its general adaptation.* The maximum potential variation expresses the difference between a heavy emphasis on hunting and a heavy emphasis on scavenging, as established by modern control data. While each class of predator may have engaged in both strategies to procure ungulates, only spotted hyenas and Mousterian hominids placed strong emphases on *both* in coastal Italy. Only the procurement tactics of the Mousterian hominids were segregated by site, however. Most or all ungulate parts brought to Grotta dei Moscerini and Grotta Guattari by hominids came primarily from scavenged sources. The ungulate components of these faunas consist almost exclusively of head parts, and they associate with mollusk and turtle exploitation. In contrast, ungulates—all meaty parts, and often whole carcasses—brought to Grotta di Sant'Agostino and Grotta Breuil were certainly hunted by Mousterian hominids. Late Upper Paleolithic humans and wolves of the same geographical area displayed much less strategic diversity overall, and emphasized hunting as the primary tactic for obtaining ungulate prey.

3. Modern wildlife data, basic principles of prey demography, and the life history characteristics of prey species provide the analytical framework for interpreting mortality patterns in death populations. Comparisons of the ungulate mortality patterns (based on tooth eruption-wear data) attributed to modern and Pleistocene predators effectively map the niche spaces of predators, the major methods of procurement, and their long term exploitive relationships with prey populations (Stiner 1990b). Like the data on anatomical part transport, comparisons of mortality patterns in ungulates reveal greater variation in the procurement habits of Mousterian hominids than for those of late Upper Paleolithic humans in Italy and modern humans in general. Again, Mousterian tactics for obtaining ungulates *vary by site*. The late Upper Paleolithic faunal record appears more specialized by comparison, as I only find evidence of hunting in this area.

4. The nature of the study sample severely limits the possibilities for seasonality analyses, yet the results obtained supplement the observations outlined above in a very interesting way. The full cycle of seasons appears to be represented in the Italian Mousterian sample if all sites are considered together. Data on juvenile tooth eruption wear and the absence of antler relative to the high incidence of deer crania suggest spring-summer occupations at Grotta dei Moscerini and Grotta Guattari by Mousterian hominids. Grotta di Sant'Agostino and Grotta Breuil

represent fall-winter occupations, possibly extending into the early part of spring. The seasonality information available for the late Upper Paleolithic sample indicates fall-winter (and early spring?) occupations only.

Because the study sample represents a relatively small geographical area, the greater range of seasons evident for the combined Mousterian sample than for the late Upper Paleolithic could imply significant differences in the scale and strategies of territory use between periods. Mousterian hominids in this coastal area invariably made do with local flint pebble sources obtained near the caves—definitely obtained within a 50 km radius, and usually obtained less than a few kilometers away. There is the problem that Upper Paleolithic humans did not necessarily use natural shelters throughout the year, but Kuhn's (1987, 1990) data on lithic raw material transport also indicate greater geographical movement by Upper Paleolithic foragers. These people arrived in the area "geared-up" with tools made of non-local flint, apparently in anticipation of an extended (albeit seasonally restricted) stay. They also made use of local lithic raw materials while in the coastal area, perhaps as the transported tools were exhausted and replaced (Kuhn and Stiner n.d.).

If these interpretations are correct, then the Mousterian sample is generally more representative of the full scale of land use in this part of Italy than the late Upper Paleolithic sample. In other words, the annual territories of Mousterian hominids may have been smaller than those used by Upper Paleolithic peoples. These data do not necessarily imply that the study area is equivalent to Mousterian home range, however. The strategic variation in the Mousterian was expressed at a relatively smaller geographic scale. It therefore stands to reason that Mousterian foraging responses were governed by more local, or more immediate, exigencies than was true for Upper Paleolithic foragers.

To summarize, three dimensions of resource exploitation reveal significant differences in food niche and land use between Mousterian hominids and late Upper Paleolithic humans of west-central Italy. The Mousterian sample displays greater strategic variation than the Upper Paleolithic sample within the limited geographical area examined. It is unlikely that any of the specific foraging methods were entirely unique to one or the other of these closely related hominids, but the rules of strategic combination were quite different. Mousterian hominids were capable hunters of ungulates, for example, but they did not exercise this option with the intensity typical of Upper Paleolithic foragers in the same region several thousand years later. Instead, Mousterian hominids turned to scavenging relatively small amounts of ungulate parts (nearly always the head), mollusk gathering and probably (most importantly?) plant use[5] while at some shelters.

The fourth dimension of comparison, prey species selection, does not distinguish hominid adaptations from one another or from certain other species of large predator. This class of faunal data identifies the importance of ungulates in the diets of all these predators and, therefore, the trophic affinities that bound them all into a single resource guild.

The results of this study unequivocally demonstrate greater variation in Mousterian foraging practices than for late Upper Paleolithic ones in west-central Italy (and probably modern hunter-gatherers in general). The results of this research also raise a series of new questions of a specific and testable nature: it is not clear, for example, if the level of strategic variation, the actual character of that variation, and the geographical scale at which it occurs would be the same for the Mousterian record of one major geographical region versus another. Perhaps the range of variation was more characteristic of Mousterian adaptations than the actual foraging practices involved.

It is interesting that the traditional data sets on Mousterian tool typology show Mousterian cultures to be less diverse than Upper Paleolithic industries in general. This is certainly true for the Pontinian Mousterian according to formal typological criteria. On the other hand, Kuhn's (1990) technological studies of the Pontinian Mousterian show little transport of raw material by these hominids, but considerable variation in strategies of core and tool reduction among the sites examined. Mousterian hominids altered their methods of lithic reduction to cope with raw material availability in a more confined area, while late Upper Paleolithic peoples apparently enjoyed the option afforded by tool (or raw material) transport. Hence, the major differences in the Mousterian and late Upper Paleolithic samples in Italy are really about the scale of land use.

Finally, some chronological separation among Mousterian foraging practices may also be indicated by the Italian data. It is not clear if this represents linear change in Mousterian lifeways or simply a problem of sampling. If the latter situation is true (and I suspect that it is, to some degree), the variation would be explained by seasonal differences in site use by Mousterian hominids using a relatively small foraging area. Comparisons of the Italian data to information for other regions are needed to resolve these questions.

Conclusions

Taphonomic studies reveal that the search for undisturbed Pleistocene archaeological sites is a simplistic, even inappropriate, notion about human life in the past and illuminate a conceptual conflict between what I have called the reconstructionist and the evolutionist paradigms in archaeological research of recent decades. While both paradigms concern human behavior, they are comparable only in some of the more basic aspects of data recovery. They differ greatly in how the archaeological record is perceived, explored, and (from conservational and analytical perspectives) evaluated.

Insights about the processes of site formation are essential to evolutionary studies of the genus *Homo*. The combined records of coexisting predators and the sequence of depositional events can provide valuable, and *new*, information about hominid adaptations. The community ecology approach allows archaeologists to recognize some of the boundaries of hominid resource niche through interspecific comparisons of the schedule and sequence of place use, prey choice, food transport, and food processing.

Such an approach calls for a rather different way of framing problems in hominid behavioral ecology. Some of the most compelling sources of controls for interpreting the archaeological data come from outside the traditional boundaries of the discipline. As paleoanthropologists focus more and more on problems of behavioral ecology of pre-modern hominids, they come to depend on general ecological principles based on studies of other species.

The results obtained from this research were enhanced by consideration of non-human predators, both in Pleistocene Italy and in modern ecosystems throughout the world. Moreover, much of the data on sympatric non-human predators in Italy come from the same cave sites as the data on hominid economies. Such mixing (or alternation) of hominid and carnivore records is ordinarily treated as a bad thing, a source of disruption to be isolated and eliminated—metaphorically if not literally. Yet coexistence was an important part of hominid life, and to study hominid foraging adaptations apart from the world that defined them is detrimental to the best interests of evolutionary research.

I concur with Rigaud and Simek (1987) that behavioral theories cannot be tested without previous commitment to taphonomic research on site formation processes. I also believe site pristinity is not a prerequisite for doing rigorous and fruitful research—a point upon which there is considerably less agreement among archaeologists (see Binford 1981a).

The full potential of the community ecology approach for addressing questions about human evolution can only be realized as cross-regional comparisons become more feasible. The paleolithic records of western Europe and a few regions of Africa and the Near East are relatively well known, while equally rich sources of information from other parts of the Old World have not been as thoroughly explored.

Acknowledgments

I am indebted to Lewis R. Binford, Erik Trinkaus, Lawrence G. Straus, Diane Gifford-González and Steven Kuhn for their insights, guidance, and support throughout the course of my research. Special thanks go to Steve, whose work on raw material economy in the Italian Mousterian and late Upper Paleolithic complements my study of the faunal remains from the same region. I also thank my Italian colleagues, A. Bietti, A. M. Bietti-Sestieri, P. Cassoli, D. Cocchi, A. Radmilli, A. G. Segre, E. Segre-Naldini and C. Tozzi, for their assistance, kindness, and encouragement during the data collection phases of the project. My research was made possible by grants from the American Association of University Women (Educational Fellowship Program), the Institute of International Education (Fulbright Program), the National Science Foundation, the L.S.B. Leakey Foundation, and the Sigma Xi Scientific Research Society of North America.

Notes

1. The archaeological perspective on evolution is seldom a theory. The archaeologist's framework embodies a series of vague notions about evolution—not so much how it works, but that it happened. The concept of "evolution" instead functions as a paradigm, because it does not pose testable mechanisms for how change occurs. This need not be seen as a shortcoming of the discipline, as general evolutionary theory has become much more complex since the time of Darwin. The subfields of biology and anthropology are partitioned according to the scales and contexts in which theories are proposed and tested. In each subfield, the vagaries of the general evolutionary paradigm are mitigated through more explicit propositions of how one phenomenon of interest relates to another.

2. All of the faunas in the study sample dating between 120,000 and 35,000 years ago are associated with Mousterian tool industries. The human fossil associations for the end of this cultural period are ambiguous, such that I prefer the terms "Mousterian hominids" or "Middle Paleolithic hominids" rather than neandertals. Several neandertal fossils are known from open and cave sites of west-central Italy (Latium), but none of the finds coincide with the end of the Middle Paleolithic cultural period as defined from lithic assemblages. The most recent, unambiguous neandertal fossil material of this area comes from Grotta Guattari and is no younger than 51,000 B.P. (Schwarz et al. n.d.). Fragmentary hominid remains have been recovered from recent excavations at the late Mousterian site of Grotta Breuil, but the material does not supply the level of morphological detail required to distinguish neandertals from fully modern *Homo sapiens*.

3. Materials from modern excavations at Grotta Breuil complement information gained from studying the old collections.

4. All of the issues and results described in this section are presented in detail in the author's doctoral dissertation (Stiner 1990a) and related publications (Stiner 1990b, 1991), to which the reader is referred for data and full descriptions of controls used.

5. Exploitation of mollusks, turtles, and rarely monk seal is documented in the many strata of Grotta dei Moscerini (Stiner 1990a), although the actual quantity of these remains is small per vertical provenience. The rates at which ungulate parts (and any other animal resources) were introduced into the shelter relative to the rates of lithic accumulation were also quite low. These patterns of exploitation suggest that Mousterian economic activities focused on something other than ungulate procurement during the many occupations of this shelter. The seasonality data based on ungulate material point to warm weather occupations, and plant use may have been quite important during the Mousterian occupations at Moscerini (and possibly at Guattari as well).

Chapter 13
New Problems, Old Glasses: Methodological Implications of an Evolutionary Paradigm for the Study of Paleolithic Technologies

Steven L. Kuhn

Paradigms Past and Present

The culture-historical paradigm has dominated paleolithic archaeology since the nineteenth century (Gamble 1986:8). This point of view is founded upon the assumption that historical causality, the interaction of human groups, populations or ethnic units, stands behind the development of the modern world. The primary role of archaeology is to reconstruct and chart the geographic history of human groups (Leroi-Gourhan and Audouze 1981:171–172). Overwhelming emphasis is placed on the study of variation in the forms of artifacts and features as indicators of culturally imposed biases, "mental templates," or styles. Adherents to the culture historical paradigm have tended to adopt a non-generalizing stance, in which the history of an area or an archaeological "culture," and not general patterns of historical change, is the primary object of study.

Binford and Sabloff (1982) have argued that archaeology is currently in the process of redefining its paradigmatic position. At present there is no single unifying paradigm in paleolithic studies, and research is pursued along several divergent intellectual paths. With the exception of those who continue to adhere to the culture historical paradigm, however, most paleolithic researchers (including the author) have adopted or would advocate some form of behavioral approach to the study of evolutionary or adaptive processes.

Even within that portion of the archaeological community which advocates an evolutionary perspective, there is a diversity of opinion as to the nature of the evolutionary process and the proper methods for studying it (e.g., the review in Leonard and Jones 1987). What sets apart the nascent evolutionary paradigm in archaeology is an emphasis on approaching the archaeological record as the by-product of human populations making a living within their natural and social environments. In a sense, this represents a shift from the study of human *motivation* to the study of human *behavior*. Motivation, in its most abstract sense, is treated as a constant: what "motivates" adaptive behavior and evolutionary change is survival and the perpetuation of local populations. The phenomena of interest relate to how variation in the behavior of prehistoric humans was linked to the environmental and social conditions within which these past human populations existed.

If the conceptual basis of modern, behaviorally oriented "evolutionist" archaeology is not easily defined, there is some agreement about the kinds of questions which most readily lend themselves to scientific methods of investigation. Two themes which dominate modern evolutionary/ecological approaches to paleolithic hunter-gatherers are *resource procurement* (foraging) and *land use* (settlement and mobility) (Gamble 1979:35, 1986:13–24). Because of the uniformitarian character of the energetic and material processes which underlie human ecology and community dynamics, questions about the ways in which prehistoric populations extracted energy from the environment and the manner in which they used the landscape in pursuit of their livelihood have the potential to be addressed using a scientific methodology.

This chapter is not intended as a defense of a behavioral/evolutionary approach to the Paleolithic, nor as a criticism of other perspectives or paradigms. Once the research "agenda" of the evolutionary (or any other) paradigm is fairly widely established, however, changes in how the archaeological record is studied should follow. Yet the methodological and theoretical ramifications of changing paradigms have yet to be systematically implemented in the study of prehistoric technologies. Artifact taxonomies formulated under the culture historical paradigm, and the observational units derived from their application (i.e., assemblage types), continue to be the focal points of most studies of the Paleolithic. Until the analytical "instruments" used to calibrate and partition the archaeological record are brought into line with the prevailing research issues, the goals of a new paradigm cannot be fully realized.

Systematics and Views of the Past

The dominant "measuring instruments" in paleolithic archaeology were, and continue to be, typologies for the classification of stone tools.

The most widely used typological methods for studying the Mousterian and earlier periods result mainly from the pioneering work of
François Bordes (Bordes 1950, 1961). The only major challenge to *la
méthode Bordes* in Europe came from Georges Laplace (1968). Laplace's
typological system, which enjoys greater popularity in Italy and Spain
than in northern Europe, differs structurally from that of Bordes. It
responds to the same paradigmatic directives, however, seeking to
monitor changes through time in the cultural identity of the makers of
stone tools through study of the shared conventions of artifact design
(Bietti 1978).

La méthode Bordes represents a rational response to a particular set of
goals and problems. Bordes argued against the method (borrowed
from paleontology) of using so-called *fossiles directeurs* to create divisions within the French Paleolithic. Instead, he pursued the strategy
of examining variation between assemblages in the relative proportions of different artifact forms (Sackett 1981:95). Relatively "coarse-
grained" geological criteria were used to define assemblage boundaries.

In creating his typological system, Bordes attempted to describe the
culturally imposed conventions of tool makers (Bordes 1967:25, Bietti
1978:3) in an explicit, replicable manner. The system he developed for
describing Middle Paleolithic tools focuses on idealized artifact forms,
defined largely in terms of the morphology, the orientation, and the
number of retouched edges. The central focus is on seemingly arbitrary choices in the form of manufactured items. The means by which
tools were produced were seen as simply one of a number of practical
alternatives, while the form of the final product was taken to be the
ultimate expression of cultural biases and tendencies (Bordes 1961).
The original form of the retouched blank is consequently of little
importance in the typology, and different strategies of core reduction
or flake production are taken into account only in the computation of
certain technological indices.

Bordes's exhaustive system for describing stone tools has for years
been seen as the most rational system for describing the design choices
made by Middle Paleolithic populations. More importantly, the typology seems to do what it was intended to do. In applying the typology
Bordes succeeded in isolating discrete typological entities, the four
major "facies" of the French Mousterian. These empirically defined
entities have dominated research on the European Mousterian since
the 1950s. There has been considerable discussion about Bordes's
interpretation of the Mousterian facies, most notably the Binfords'
"functional arguments" (Binford and Binford 1966, Binford 1973) and
Mellars's discussions of possible temporal sequencing (e.g., Mellars

1969, 1986). New tool types have also been added (e.g., Crew 1976, Valoch 1967) and new facies proposed as the geographic range of the Middle Paleolithic data base has expanded. Still, most arguments, pro or con, center on the empirical relevance and interpretation of results obtained from *la méthode Bordes* for particular cases.

Systematics as Tools for Learning

Archaeological typologies are conceptual instruments for measuring the material results of past human behavior. While we generally conceive of measurement in terms of continuous variables, most archaeological typologies are simply frameworks for assessing variation in non-continuous variables or in discrete states of configuration among continuous variables.

In any science, the ways in which the world is described must be responsive to theories about how that world works, if the descriptions are to aid in explanation (Lewontin 1974:8). There is no advantage to relying on a single typology to answer all questions about the past. Typologies are created by archaeologists, and there is no one "true," all-encompassing typology for a particular class of data or time period. The selection of attributes in a classificatory system and the means by which types are defined should instead be responsive to the particular problems to be investigated (Vierra 1982, Whallon 1982:137).

Typologies can be evaluated in a number of ways. Some account for more variation within a particular set of dimensions than others, and some classifications are more easily and reliably replicated than others. But these are simply comparisons of the relative merits of alternative typologies designed for the same purpose. One can also ask whether a particular system of classification is appropriate for a given set of research goals. The typological system developed by Bordes for the Mousterian was certainly consistent with the goals of a culture historical paradigm. The question remains as to the degree to which Bordes's approach to analysis, and the patterns which it has produced, are consistent with the goals and biases of the evolutionary paradigm followed by many paleolithic researchers today.

One of the most serious problems which traditional paleolithic typological methods pose for a behavioral approach are the means by which assemblages, the indivisible unit of analysis, are defined. Rigaud and Simek (1987) have critiqued the use of geological criteria as a means of partitioning archaeological assemblages. As the focus of archaeological attention shifts from cultural identity (a presumably stable phenomenon) to behavior (an inherently variable phenomenon), the level of resolution with which we approach the record must change as well. They argue that, unless we are prepared to assume that human behavior and sedimentary conditions are somehow directly correlated, there is no reason to expect that the archaeological record will be uniform within a particular geological stratum. The fact that the contents of one stratum differ from those of another is significant, but such facts can only be addressed by fine-grained studies of the processes responsible for assemblage formation and not through simple inter-assemblage comparisons.

A second difficulty with adopting Bordes's classifications of stone tools to current research issues has to do with the focus on idealized tool forms and, by implication, tool design. The form of a tool that ends up in the archaeological record may be quite different from its original, "designed" morphology. The combinations of attributes observed on archaeological specimens are the result of a period of *use* and not exclusively of the "original form" of things. It has been argued that many or all alternate forms of Mousterian scrapers (Dibble 1987a, b), as well as Great Plains flake-knives (Reher and Frison 1980), and Australian stone adzes (Cooper 1954) are actually progressive reduction variants of one another. The discarded slug or stub-end of an artifact may in fact be the form most likely to be seized upon by the analyst as a consistent artifact "type."

In reality, contrasts between the tool forms that make up the Bordes typology may well reflect varying duration of use, reduction intensity, blank form, functional design considerations, and even arbitrary cultural conventions. The problem is that the results of a large number of such behaviors and processes are inextricably combined or summarized in the typology. Questions about tool function, raw material economy, artifact "curation" and the duration of use, and the *existence* of tool design as a technological behavior (e.g., Wynn 1985) have assumed paramount roles in current research. These new research orientations require techniques for looking at artifacts and assemblages which allow researchers to study these individual behavioral processes in isolation.

In spite of its rather indefinite relevance on modern research issues, the Bordes typology continues to be one of the dominant "instruments" used for the study of the Mousterian. In some cases, the typology itself has become the focus of research. For example, testing hypotheses about the functional specificity of Mousterian tool types has motivated micro-wear research (e.g., Beyries 1987, 1988). Given the widespread use of *la méthode Bordes* as a descriptive convention, it would indeed be helpful to be able to relate Bordes's tool forms and assemblage types to phenomena which concern contemporary researchers. Dibble's "reduction" arguments imply that some aspect of typological variability might be used to monitor reduction intensity within lithic assemblages. Clearly, however, it is both possible and desirable to address new research issues directly, rather than framing all analysis in terms of the traditional typological categories.

Alternative Approaches

The shift from researching cultural identity to researching foraging behavior and land use has been accompanied by major changes in the kinds of data collected and the ways that they are used. Faunal remains have recently come to assume a position of much greater importance in archaeological investigations of prehistoric human foraging adaptations (e.g. Binford 1981b, Chase 1986b, Gamble 1979, 1983, Klein 1979, 1981, Stiner 1990a, Straus 1983c). Analyses of intra-site spatial patterning and its relation to larger-scale systems of land use represent another, productive new focus in paleolithic studies (e.g., Simek 1984, 1987, Hietala 1983).

The problem of how to integrate the study of lithic artifacts into new research programs has been less completely resolved, in part because archaeologists are so accustomed to thinking about stone tools in terms of old conventions (Meyers 1987). It is insufficient simply to impose new interpretive conventions on the units of analysis and patterns inherited from the previous paradigm. For the study of stone tools to become relevant to the research issues arising out of new paradigms, major advances are required in inferential and analytical methods for linking technology to foraging, land use, and other behaviors and processes of interest.

As the focus of archaeological attention shifts from "cultures" to past behavior and even behavioral "events," studies of the composition of archaeological assemblages will become less central to paleolithic research. Even with very precise modern excavation techniques, the relevance of the behavioral associations between the components of an assemblage becomes increasingly problematic. As the basic units of provenience designation shrink from geological strata to finely delimited "living floors" or horizontal subdivisions within them, assemblages must also become smaller and less tractable.

Although variation in assemblage composition will remain an important source of information about prehistoric technologies, the issues arising from new paradigms require that we delve more deeply into variation within assemblages. Ultimately, the finest-grained and most securely linked behavioral data on stone tools come from the associations of attributes on a single artifact. Behavioral perspectives on the archaeological record therefore beg a more intense analytical focus on variation in the characteristics of individual artifacts, viewed within some larger theoretical/interpretive framework. Studies of variation in the associations between attributes on individual artifacts also have the potential to render data from coarse-grained "palimpsest" deposits more useful for addressing problems of past human behavior, since these associations are not affected by recovery techniques or excavation strategies.

Rather than approaching technologies as the *expressions* of culturally driven people, the research priorities of an evolutionary paradigm require that they be studied as the *results* of adaptively linked behavior in an evolutionary context. In the study of human bio-cultural evolution, technology can be viewed as a strategically organized set of tactics for meeting both immediate and anticipated needs for tools and raw materials. Behavioral tactics, as used here, are equivalent to techniques of, inter alia, artifact manufacture and renewal and raw material procurement. The salient functional characteristics of different tactics of tool manufacture and husbandry—their costs and benefits in terms of time, energy, and raw materials—can be investigated through experiments and comparative analyses of archaeological cases. Once these characteristics are established, their adaptive significance may be addressed by studying the contexts in which different tactics appear archaeologically and their relationships to independent indicators of mobility, site use, and resource procurement patterns. In this way, it is possible to address the strategic integration of technology within a larger subsistence and settlement system.

Archaeological and ethnographic studies of the ways technology is linked to subsistence and land use are still in their infancy. Yet, work done to date does at least point to the dimensions of technology most likely to reflect such relationships. Studies have tended to focus on two major sets of strategies, one of which relates to the *design* of tools and weapons. Torrence (1983, 1989), Oswalt (1976) and others (e.g., Bleed 1986, Meyers 1987) have argued convincingly that the diversity and complexity of artifact forms provide evidence of the varying pressures prehistoric populations faced in making a living.

Design-based approaches to technology as an adaptive phenomenon appear to be best suited to the study of weapons and implements used in high impact, low tolerance situations such as hunting. In contrast, most paleolithic assemblages consist primarily of tools (scrapers, burins, denticulates, and the like) used to process or modify other materials. Middle Paleolithic assemblages may contain nothing *but* manufacture and processing tools (Holdoway 1989, Kuhn 1989a, but cf.

Shea 1988). Aside from some general associations between edge form and tool function (not always borne out by microwear research), the importance of overall "design" is not at all clear for tools used in manufacture and processing activities.

This is not to say that aspects of technology not directly involved in resource procurement carry no information about the nature of the larger adaptive system. Non-subsistence activities are linked (indirectly) to foraging and land use primarily through a shared time and energy budget. The scheduling of resource procurement and patterns of movement about the landscape determine both the temporal and spatial scheduling of manufacture activities and the opportunities to make and replace tools used in such activities (Kuhn 1989b, Torrence 1983). To examine the linkages between this kind of non-procurement technology and subsistence, it is necessary to turn to studies of what might be called the "technological delivery system," or those strategies which serve to bridge the spatial and temporal gaps between needs for tools, on the one hand, and opportunities to procure raw materials and work them into tools, on the other.

Strategies for making tools and raw materials available as needs for them arise have been addressed through studies of several different technological phenomena. A number of researchers have presented convincing arguments linking the use of alternative tactics of core reduction with needs for tools and raw material arising in different mobility and land-use contexts among modern human hunter-gatherers (e.g., Goodyear 1982, Johnson 1986, Kelly 1988, Parry and Kelly 1987). Artifact transport and resharpening are also closely linked to subsistence and land use. The transport of tools and raw material is one strategy which permits tool manufacture and use where it might not otherwise be possible. Resharpening prolongs the useful life of artifacts. Not surprisingly, patterns of raw material exploitation, artifact transport, and reduction/resharpening have variously been linked to mobility and general subsistence organization among modern foragers (e.g., Binford 1977b, 1979, Goodyear 1989, Kelly and Todd 1988, Lurie 1989, Shott 1989).

The possible relationships between technology, foraging, and land use have by no means been completely explored or explained; and a number of issues, such as the importance of raw material availability and distribution (e.g., Bamforth 1986), have yet to be resolved in a satisfactory way. Nonetheless, the studies cited here provide a number of indications of both the technological variables which might be profitably studied and the kinds of typological instruments needed to study them.

An Alternative Typology in Action: The Middle Paleolithic of West-Central Italy

The use of one kind of alternative typology in the study of variation in Mousterian assemblages illustrates some of the arguments presented above. The archaeological case in point involves Mousterian assemblages from a series of cave sites and open-air locations on the Tyrrhenian coast of the region of Latium, Italy (southwest of Rome). These assemblages have all been assigned to the so-called "Pontinian" facies of the Mousterian (Bietti 1981, Blanc 1937, Taschini 1970), found only in coastal west-central Italy.

Materials from four coastal Mousterian cave sites are included in the study: Grotta Guattari (Taschini 1979), Grotta di St'Agostino (Tozzi 1970), Grotta Breuil (Bietti et al. 1988, Taschini 1970), and Grotta dei Moscerini (Vitagliano 1984). Guattari and Breuil are located on Monte Circeo, while the other two sites are situated about forty kilometers to the south, near Gaeta. With the exception of Grotta Breuil, all collections come from excavations conducted in the late 1940s and early 1950s. An artifact sample derived from controlled collections of paleolithic open-air locations on the marshy Pontine plain around Monte Circeo (Voorrips et al. 1983) is also included in the sample.

Pontinian Mousterian assemblages are noted for the small size of the tools (maximum dimensions are generally less than 3.5 centimeters), and for the scarcity of denticulates and corresponding abundance of simple and transverse scrapers. From a typological perspective, there is little or no significant variation among the subject assemblages. Most researchers attribute the size, and at least some of the formal characteristics of the Pontinian artifacts, to the reliance on very small, locally available flint pebbles as the primary source of raw material (cf. Taschini 1972, Piperno 1984, Bordes 1968:119). These pebbles are the only usable flint found within at least fifty kilometers of the coastal caves containing the Mousterian deposits.

The primary questions addressed in this research revolve around the role of technology in larger Middle Paleolithic adaptive systems, more specifically how Mousterian technology was related to the energetically primary concerns of subsistence and mobility. It is difficult to demonstrate that any of the Mousterian artifacts studied (predominantly sidescrapers) were used *directly* in food procurement or foraging, so they are treated as general purpose tools for manufacture or the processing of other materials. The most important links with subsistence behavior are expected to be through tactics related to making tools or raw materials available when needed, and analyses focus on technological behaviors which affect the *utility* of tools and cores. Three technological phenomena are of particular interest: flake production techniques, artifact transport, and resharpening or reduction of stone tools.

Investigations proceed from a study of variation in techniques or tactics of core reduction. The way tool makers produce flakes and tool blanks from cores determines the utility of both raw materials and the tools made from them. Different reduction techniques will produce varying numbers of flakes with contrasting functional attributes (size, edge characteristics) from similar raw materials. Control over the productivity of cores and the sizes of flakes should be especially important where raw materials are both scarce and of small size.

In spite, or perhaps because, of the limitations imposed by raw material size, there are a number of distinctive manufacture techniques represented in the flakes, cores, and retouched tools from the subject assemblages. Reduction techniques fall into three basic groups, each of which has somewhat different consequences for the utility of tools and cores. Their economic characteristics are summarized in Table 13.1. One distinctive type of reduction found in many Pontinian assemblages involved splitting small pebbles by bipolar, or hammer and anvil, technique (e.g., Laj Pannocchia 1950). This technique allows one to maximize the *size* of flakes produced relative to the size of the pebble, and permits the production of usable blanks from very small pebbles. The resulting flakes are thick and mostly cortical, and are most suitable as "supports" for steep edges. Bipolar technique can here be seen as a measure for producing the largest possible (but few) flakes or supports from available pebbles.

A second group of reduction tactics involved the use of the centripetal reduction techniques more typical of Mousterian industries throughout the world. Experimental and archaeological data suggest that centripetal reduction of the small pebbles available locally in coastal Latium is relatively "wasteful" of raw material, but allows the production of relatively large flakes or "supports" with long, sharp edges. Rather than being an economizing measure, centripetal reduction in these assemblages is likely to be related to obtaining flakes with specific functional properties.

The third group of techniques involved the use of cores with one or two (usually opposed) platforms of percussion (see, e.g., Bietti et al. 1988, Kuhn 1990, Laj Pannocchia 1950). Platforms may be either plain or faceted: in the former case, resulting cores often resemble crudely made prismatic blade cores. Platform cores tend to produce small, rather elongated flakes, some of which are naturally backed. Experimental and archaeological data indicate that the use of platform core

TABLE 13.1: Characteristics of Major Flake/Blank Production Techniques

		Reduction Technique	
	Bipolar	Centripetal/ Levallois	Single/opposed platform
Number of flakes per pebble	Low	Low	Moderate
Minimal pebble size	Very small	Moderate	Small
Flake size	Moderate/large	Large	Small
Sharp edge per flake/blank	Low	High	Moderate

reduction permits the production of a somewhat larger number of flakes per core than other types of reduction: where raw materials are small, any such advantage may be significant. As such, these techniques are potential measures for maximizing the *number* of flakes and supports produced, at some sacrifice in flake *size*.

Because the subject assemblages were derived from excavations conducted in the 1940s and 1950s, proveniences are subdivided at no finer level than the geological stratum or arbitrary level. It is necessary to approach links between technology and subsistence behavior in terms of general patterns of association between different forms of behavior within these coarse-grained assemblages. In order to study how the use of alternative core reduction techniques is related to independent evidence for subsistence and land-use patterns, it is necessary somehow to measure the frequency with which different reduction tactics were used.

One very direct approach to investigating the reduction techniques used by prehistoric tool makers is to conduct detailed refitting studies (e.g., Cahen 1984). To be truly effective, however, refitting requires relatively complete samples obtained from spatially extensive excavations. The subject assemblages are derived from relatively small trench excavations, and, although sediments were sieved, it is clear that a major portion of the small-sized debris fraction (< 1.5 cm) is missing.

Although cores are a common element in these assemblages, the frequencies of different core forms are also not ideal measures of the use of different reduction techniques. Core form changes with progressive reduction, and the final form of a core may be quite different from its form during most of its lifetime. This problem is particularly acute where raw materials are large, but cannot be ruled out even for the small pebble cores characteristic of the Pontinian.

For the purposes of this study, variation in the forms of flakes and tool blanks is the most appropriate measure of the frequency of use of different reduction techniques. Since the raw materials are small and reduction sequences are short, flake and core forms should be closely linked. Moreover, the forms of tool blanks do not change during their lifetimes such that a flake produced by one technique would be taken for something else: at worst, fracture or extensive reduction makes it impossible to reconstruct the manufacture technique at all.

In order to monitor core reduction tactics through flake form, a typology of flakes and tool blanks was constructed using two variables—dorsal scar pattern and platform treatment. A summary of the expected attributes for flakes produced by the three principal reduction techniques is presented in Table 13.2. The typology of flakes and blanks is relatively straightforward, with one exception. Specimens with parallel/longitudinal scars plus lateral scars from one side were attributed to single/opposed platform core reduction because abandoned cores occasionally exhibit a second or third platform oriented at 90° to the other platform(s). It is clear that not all possible combinations of attributes are included in the typology. Many pieces with cortical butts, most flakes with only laterally originating dorsal scars, and broken specimens for which either the platform and/or dorsal scar pattern are unrecognizable, cannot be reliably assigned to a particular type of reduction.

Unlike taxonomies intended to monitor stylistic variables, the efficacy of this typology of flake and tool blank forms can be subject to an empirical test. In a preliminary blind test, flakes produced experimentally from centripetal and single/opposed platform cores were classified by two analysts using the criteria presented in Table 13.1. The success rate for correct identification was approximately 90% (Bietti et al. n.d.).

The simple fact that this system of classification accurately monitors the use of different tactics of reduction does not mean it is archaeologically useful. Most archaeological typologies are first evaluated in terms of their ability to summarize or partition observed variability with regard to other dimensions (usually chronology or geography) (e.g., Close 1989:8): with explicitly "non-functional" typologies, this is the only kind of evaluation possible. Although the three sets of core reduction techniques vary in terms of their "economy" and the properties of the flakes produced, the question remains as to whether Mousterian tool makers actually took advantage of these contrasting characteristics in order to fill different needs for tools.

Variation in the "use histories" of flakes and blanks can be used to gain insight into the nature of the roles played by different reduction techniques and the kinds of needs they filled. If alternative techniques

Table 13.2: Reduction Techniques and Expected Flake/Blank Attributes

| | | Reduction Technique | |
	Bipolar	Centripetal/ Levallois	Single/opposed platform
Platform types	Acutely angled, split/negative bulb	Plain, dihedral, faceted	Plain, faceted
Dorsal scar patterns	None, lateral opposite platform	Radial, semi-radial	Longitudinal/ parallel, with or without lateral scars from 1 side

were employed in different contexts, the resulting tools and flakes should show contrasting patterns of use. If variation in reduction technique represents a simple response to raw material form or some other variable, regardless of context, there should be no differences in the ways different flake types were transported, retouched, or reduced.

Analyses of tool production, resharpening, and breakage patterns (Kuhn 1990) demonstrate strong contrasts among the flake-blank forms associated with different tactics of manufacture. These contrasts are summarized in Table 13.3.

The cortical flakes produced by bipolar technique exhibit both the highest frequency of retouch and the greatest intensity of reduction. Large cortical artifacts appear to have been transported infrequently. Flakes and blanks produced from platform core reduction techniques show significantly less frequent retouch and less advanced reduction. The high frequency of pebble cortex and very strong correlations between related core, tool, and flake forms suggests in situ production at the coastal cave sites. Flakes and tools produced from centripetal cores exhibit a frequency of retouch and extent of reduction midway

Table 13.3: Summary of Characteristic Use Patterns for Different Types of Flake and Support

| | | Reduction Technique | |
	Bipolar	Centripetal/ Levallois	Single/opposed platform
Frequency of retouch	High	Moderate	Low
Extent of reduction	High	Moderate	Low
Frequency of transport	Low	Moderate	Low

between the two other forms. Although "exotic" raw materials are surprisingly rare, the unusually large size of some specimens, the distinctive mix of raw materials represented, and the weak associations between centripetal cores and the corresponding tool and flake forms indicate that this last group of artifacts was transported relatively frequently, both within and from outside of the coastal pebble zone.

Contrasts in the treatment of different flake and blank forms suggest that alternative reduction techniques were in fact often used in different functional contexts to fill varying needs for tools. These results also show that the typology of flake forms is a useful way of monitoring variation in tactics of tool production and use. In investigating the linkage between technology and other forms of adaptive behavior, the frequency of different classes or types of flake and tool blank appears to be a reasonable measure of "technological response" to varying requirements for tools or raw materials.

Variation in the frequency of different classes of flakes and tool blanks in turn exhibits strong relationships with variation in the use of places and the procurement and treatment of game animals in these Mousterian assemblages (Kuhn 1990, Stiner 1990a). The lithic and faunal data together point to several contrasting patterns of foraging, site use, and technological response. One group of assemblages seems to represent land-extensive foraging and very restricted use of ungulate resources. Associated reduction techniques (bipolar pebble splitting and centripetal reduction) emphasize the production of large tools, which were relatively heavily reduced. Within these assemblages, variation in the use of bipolar versus centripetal reduction appears to be linked to the frequency with which animal resources were exploited. In a second group of assemblages, there is an undeniable focus on hunting, provisioning cave sites with meat, and more intensive use of places. In such situations, people brought local raw materials to places to produce tools for immediate use using single and opposed platform reduction techniques, and there was little transport and renewal of tools (Kuhn 1990).

Conclusions

As paradigms change, the compelling research problems in a field change with them. When the idea that diseases were caused by microbes rather than "humors" or evil spirits first gained credence, physicians began to take a very different approach to diagnosis. Similarly, archaeologists need to adapt the "glasses" through which they view the archaeological record to the kinds of phenomena they seek to observe. Paleolithic archaeology is in the midst of a major paradigm shift, from an essentially culture-historical perspective to a behaviorally oriented, evolutionary approach. As views of the past have been modified, the questions researchers ask of the archaeological record have changed radically. As the questions change, so should the ways in which researchers subdivide and measure the archaeological record.

In the case of stone tools, this second step has yet to be actualized completely. Bordes's typological system for the Mousterian has continued to dominate research. The Bordes type list is a remarkably exhaustive set of descriptive conventions. It will (rightly) continue to have a role in paleolithic studies, perhaps not as the lingua franca but certainly as one of a number of alternative tongues. Attempts to translate Bordes's tool and assemblage types into units meaningful for current research issues will also be valuable, if only because so many data have already been organized according to the system. Yet there is no reason that Bordes's type list should remain the single, central organizing principle in studies of the Mousterian. There are other ways to look at the paleolithic technological record. Alternative typologies, formulated with specific goals in mind, can be expected to produce results that are more relevant to the changing research priorities of the field.

Typologies for monitoring reduction technique through flake and tool blank morphology are not argued to represent a universal solution to the problem of how more appropriately to classify lithic materials to deal with current research problems. There is a nearly infinite variety of ways that lithic assemblages can be partitioned and scaled, according to what one wants to learn. When different goal-oriented systematics are applied to the same data base, they should produce contrasting, and hopefully complementary, results. Understanding of the past can only be enhanced by the contrasting results obtained using different, problem-oriented classifications of the archaeological data.

Acknowledgments

This paper has been greatly improved by discussions with Lewis R. Binford, Lawrence Straus, Erik Trinkaus, Amilcare Bietti, Mary Stiner, and Jim Enloe. The faunal analyses referred to in the text are part of Mary Stiner's research on hominid-predator niche relationships in the central Italian Mousterian. Access to collections was generously provided by Prof. A. Segre and Dressa. E. Segre-Nardini of the Istituto Italiano di Paleontologia Umana (Rome), and Prof. C. Tozzi of the University of Pisa. My research in Italy was made possible by generous funding from the L.S.B. Leakey Foundation and the Institute for International Education (Fulbright Collaborative Research Program).

Chapter 14
Normal Science and Paradigmatic Biases in Italian Hunter-Gatherer Prehistory

Amilcare Bietti

Introduction

A developed scientific community, according to Thomas Kuhn (1962, 1970a), is characterized by a group of scholars sharing a common general perspective or research framework, called a "paradigm." These scholars, as a consequence, practice their everyday activity according to a set of common rules, or conventions, which define what may be called a shared scientific language. This activity, which has the goal of a better understanding of the phenomena predicted and anticipated by the paradigm through a system of particular theories and models, is essentially what Kuhn defines as normal science. Normal science sometimes produces anomalous results, which can become the basis of a "scientific revolution" and which, in turn, eventually results in the establishment of a new paradigm.

Practical illustrations of these processes are taken from developed sciences such as chemistry and physics, whose "scientific" status has been well documented in Europe since the Renaissance. Examples of paradigms are Lavoisier's combustion theory, Newtonian classical mechanics, or Einstein's theory of special relativity. The normal science activities related to these paradigms are represented, of course, by the numerous experiments performed and the particular theories and models proposed by the scientists actively working in the various research subfields. In respect of prehistoric archaeology, Kuhn's ideas were enthusiastically accepted by a number of English speaking archaeologists in the early 1970s. The existence of paradigms in prehistoric archaeology was vigorously affirmed (Clarke 1972, Sterud 1973), as was the possibility of discipline-wide scientific revolutions (Martin 1971).

As I have pointed out, however, the present status of scientific research in prehistoric archaeology does not in fact allow for analogies with the situation of the more developed sciences (Bietti 1976–77:376, 1978; Bietti and Bietti-Sestieri 1985). There is not, in my opinion, a scientific methodology commonly shared and accepted even *within* a given archaeological paradigm. The debate on the relative merits of the typological systems of François Bordes and Georges Laplace (both belonging to the same "chronotypological" paradigm) in western Europe in the late 1960s is an example. In other words, there is no real "normal science," *sensu* Kuhn; and this probably means that we are still in a "preparadigmatic" situation, somewhat similar to that of pre-Copernican astronomy, where a true scientific community, following a commonly shared paradigm and requiring scientific rules and procedures, is still lacking.[1]

The paradigms (or, more properly, *protoparadigms*) in prehistoric archaeology are not yet, in my opinion, *constellations of group commitments* or *shared exemplars* as defined by Kuhn (1970a); and I think this situation holds for Italian prehistoric archaeology generally. In this chapter I will try to illustrate a particular case of "pseudo-normal science" activity: the usual kind of Italian hunter-gatherer research, which generally stems from a cultural-historical and hence "chronotypological" protoparadigm. This protoparadigm represents the views and orientations of Italian traditionalist researchers.

I could also present the aims, proposals, and first practical results obtained in the Italian paleolithic and mesolithic according to an emergent "new" paradigm,[2] but no consistent data set is available for a reasonable discussion on paradigmatic biases from the new perspective, since the traditionalist protoparadigm essentially determines more than 90% of current Italian research. In what follows I will try to sketch the main features of the traditionalist paradigm in Italian hunter-gatherer research. I will then illustrate in more detail the direct influence of this protoparadigm on practical research work, from data collection procedures through data analysis and, finally, the general interpretation of the results.

The Traditionalist Protoparadigm in Italian Hunter-Gatherer Prehistory

It is difficult to obtain information on the general characteristics of the Italian cultural-historical protoparadigm directly from the researchers who share it. In fact, as is often the case with traditionalist perspectives, the basic issues and propositions of the research are largely implicit; no attention is paid to issues of theory and/or methodology, so that it is customary to think that "data speak for themselves." It happens, therefore, that the only explicit discussion of the characteristics of this protoparadigm are to be found in papers written by critics of the traditional research orientation (see, e.g., Bietti and Bietti-Sestieri 1985). It is impossible to understand the nature of the Italian traditionalist protoparadigm without first knowing something of the historical circumstances of the development of paleolithic and mesolithic research in Italy over the past sixty years.

Italian hunter-gatherer prehistoric studies stem from two distinct sources: (1) the naturalist perspective of French paleolithic prehistory, present in Italy since the beginning of the century (e.g., the work in the Balzi Rossi caves in Liguria), and (2) the humanistic-historical influence of classical archaeology, particularly important in a country like Italy where the remains of classical antiquity are to be found everywhere. In contrast to the situation in Anglo-Saxon countries at that time, the influence of anthropological and ethnological studies is practically absent in the Italian research tradition, with the exception of a few studies, mostly in the first quarter of the century, based on the well-known Graebner-Schmidt diffusionist perspective (the so-called Vienna school).[3] Classical archaeology has traditionally been considered in Italy as art history, with a sound chronological basis derived from written sources, whereas the traditional French perspective is based on Quaternary geology and chronostratigraphy without any real connection to anthropological studies in the modern sense of the term. At first glance, one might think that there would be many contradictions between the chronostratigraphic-geological and the humanistic-historical aspects of this protoparadigm. Actually a closer examination of Italian paleolithic and mesolithic research shows how well the two perspectives have been integrated.

The concept of culture is derived directly from the humanistic branch; cultures are *archaeological facies,* characterized by particular kinds of archaeological remains. Cultures equate with one (or several) industrial assemblage(s). Culture is thus something drastically different from the standard anglophone anthropological definition; and the industrial assemblage, as is customary for a humanistic discipline, is characterized by a set of *types,* which represent the "normative" ideas and mental templates of extinct people. The notion of an archaeological record as a *behavioral* record is practically unknown in the traditionalist perspective. On the other hand, cultures are also considered to vary through time, whence the merging with the geological chronostratigraphic perspective: the aforementioned *types* assume the same values that index fossils have in traditional geological studies. The traditionalist paradigm, thus, may very well be called *chronotypological*.

The influence of the natural sciences is also reflected by the importance given to evolution, but evolution is not considered a property of whole *systems*, as it would be from any modern evolutionary perspective, but is applied only to the evolution of "cultural facies." Changes through time are monitored by changes in the industrial assemblage, marked both by the presence/absence of index types and by the percentages of and ratios between kinds of tools. Faunal remains, as we shall see later, do not participate directly in this kind of evolutionary scheme. Their importance is mainly related to making inferences about paleoclimates and is (in that sense) chronological, but without any connection to the human behavior manifest in the archaeology.

It should be stressed that a true "systemic" perspective, found in any anthropological protoparadigm, would be inconceivable for the traditionalist protoparadigm, mainly because the traditional geological and humanistic-historical perspectives do not consider evolution as a *whole process* of living entities, but rather as a chronological sequence of events organized in static records documented by paleontological remains or lithic industries. Another characteristic of the chronotypological protoparadigm is the persistence of the concept of "cultural facies" through time. By this I mean that traditionalist prehistorians still recognize a "pebble culture," a sequence of Acheulean "cultures," eventually subdivided into "inferior," "middle," "evolved" or "superior," without any reference to the biological characteristics of the human types that supposedly produced them! An informed reader of European prehistory will note that most of the characteristics of the Italian traditionalist protoparadigm also occur in French traditional paleolithic and mesolithic prehistory. There are salient differences, however, that seem to have a "regional" character.

In Italy, the concept of evolution is strictly unilinear, whereas chronologically parallel phyla are rather common in French prehistory. A good example is the case of the Mousterian facies. In France, according to the classic theory of Bordes (1953, 1981a), there are four main groups of Mousterian: (1) the Mousterian of Acheulean tradition, (2) the typical Mousterian, (3) the Charentian, and (4) the denticulate Mousterian, which supposedly represent independent and contemporary cultures (actual groups of people), with frequent cases of interstratification amongst them. However, in Italy, the concept of interstratification is essentially unknown. According to Palma di Cesnola (1987), for instance, we have several local unilinear sequences unique to and characteristic of different regions. In middle-southern Italy (Latium, Campania, and Apulia) we have a general sequence starting with a Quina Mousterian, developing into another Quina Mousterian variant with a very high percentage of sidescrapers, and followed by a typical Mousterian with fairly large levallois debitage (mainly in Calabria, Campania). In northern Italy (Liguria, Veneto), we have a typical Mousterian with consistent levallois debitage, followed by an "oriental Charentian" rich in sidescrapers. Palma di Cesnola considers these sequences to be independent of one another, so that the typical Mousterian of southern Italy, for instance, bears no resemblance and is not related to the typical Mousterian of Liguria (Palma di Cesnola 1987:140).

The Italian emphasis on unilinear evolution, with a continual search for chronotypological sequences that can be "parallelized" among the various regions is probably derived from the influence of Laplace (1959, 1964, 1966). This is particularly true of the Upper Paleolithic. In Italy the standard Upper Paleolithic sequence parallels that of France. First we have the Uluzzian, which corresponds to the French Châtelperronian, then the Aurignacian, followed by the Gravettian, which corresponds more or less to the classic French Upper Perigordian, and finally the Epigravettian, divided into Ancient, Evolved and Final, which equates more or less to the French Solutrean, Magdalenian and Azilian. In contrast to the French situation, there is not, according to Italian scholars, an interstratification between the Aurignacian and the Gravettian. I will return to the ideas of Georges Laplace, who represents in some respects an extreme example of the French chronotypological protoparadigm and whose influence is particularly strong in the "marginal" areas of this protoparadigm, such as Italy or Spain (e.g., Muñoz 1976). This unilinear evolutionary bias is grounded in the recognition and definition of a *reference or type site*, that is, a site whose sequence is the standard for the correct chronological ordering of the sequence from any other site. For the Italian late Upper Paleolithic, Palma di Cesnola believes that such a site is represented by Grotta Paglicci in northern Apulia (Palma di Cesnola and Bietti 1983:185), while in a situation of more marked regional differences, as is the case with the Mousterian, one should look for several local reference (type) sites. Needless to say, the idea of a *site de réference*, also common in the traditionalist French literature, is completely at odds with any behavioral or contextual interpretation of archaeological variability.

Another point of contrast with French traditionalist classifications is the de-emphasis by Italian researchers on the local denominations of the cultural facies. This again depends on a particular construal of the unilinear evolutionary scheme of Laplace. This attitude stems, in my opinion, from the greater emphasis that a unilinear scheme devotes to the time properties of a cultural facies as opposed to its space properties. As a matter of fact, old denominations like "Grimaldian" or "Romanellian" were abandoned, under Laplace's influence, in favor of more neutral terms like "final Epigravettian of the northern Tyrrhenian zone," "final Epigravettian of the southern Adriatic zone," etc. A. M. Radmilli, perhaps the only true representative of the old diffusionist school, still maintains the term "Bertonian" for a particular facies of the Abruzzian (Radmilli 1954, Radmilli in Bisi et al. 1983: 252–263), while the "official" denomination places the Bertonian in the "final Epigravettian of the northern and middle Adriatic zone." Such definitional contrasts are widely understood by workers *within* a given paradigm, but they might not always cross the boundaries of different research traditions (or cross them completely). A good example of this is provided by the debate on the denominations of the Ligurian Epigravettian, which has been subdivided by French researchers into "Arenien," "Protobouverien," and "Bouverien" facies (Onoratini 1983), while the Italians consider these same entities to be the Ancient, Evolved, and Final Epigravettian of the northern Tyrrhenian zone (Palma di Cesnola 1983).

It is clear that the basic perspective is exactly the same in both cases: both groups of researchers are primarily concerned with establishing chronological sequences and both define the cultural facies in terms of diagnostic lithic types or type groups. The fact that such a debate still exists is typical, in my opinion, of a "pre-Copernican" situation, and therefore, justifies the use of the term "protoparadigm."

This outline of the main features of the Italian chronotypological protoparadigm is probably too brief, but I hope that it has provided a general impression of the main issues of the traditional research model for hunter-gatherer prehistory in Italy. More details will emerge from the examples of paradigmatic biases in practical research work that I illustrate in the next section. Most of the examples will be taken from the Upper Paleolithic and Mesolithic, but a few cases of Lower and Middle Paleolithic will also be presented.

Biases in Data Collection Procedures

What I mean by "data collection" is archaeological field work, analogous to "experiments" in the professional activities of laboratory disciplines. The subsequent activity of data analysis can be compared to the "phenomenological" data analysis of the developed sciences. A peculiarity of the archaeological sciences compared to physics or chemistry is, of course, the impossibility of repeating an experiment (a characteristic which, however, does not preclude a scientific status for them, as has been stressed repeatedly by many scholars).

For traditionalist archaeologists, this "experiment" phase of the research has always been considered the most "objective" and the least subject to problems of different interpretations. What is required, to this end, is that any researcher should employ a well-defined and standardized procedure of excavation, according to the more refined and modern techniques, marked by careful collection of all possible information (faunal remains, lithic and bone industries, samples for pollen and sediment analysis, adequate recording of every possible archaeological feature, such as burials, hearths, etc.). At this point it is commonly assumed that methodological biases (more properly called "systematic errors" in an experiment) have been avoided and that there is at one's disposal a data set comparable to any other collected according to the same rules and following the same procedures. Moreover, this data set is held to be independent of the a priori perspective or paradigm of the individual researcher. I do not want to belabor this discussion of "objectivity" since many comments and observations have been made on this point, mainly by American "new archaeologists" beginning around 1970. I will only note that data collection consists at least of two parts: (1) the first, which deals with what might be called the *planning* of the experiment, and (2) the second, concerning aspects of practical fieldwork, such as how to excavate a cave. Biases may be present in both aspects of this process.

Examination of the Italian literature of the last thirty years shows that most planned fieldwork consists of the excavation of caves. There are some reports concerning open air sites, but they are mostly surface finds, lacking in stratigraphic context. Furthermore, only professional researchers dig in caves and rockshelters (or, at least, publish the results of their excavations), while many amateurs are involved in the publication of surface finds. Thus, there are "first class" data, represented by caves and rockshelter digs, and "second class" data, represented by surface finds. There are some "objective" reasons for this rank order, caves and rockshelters almost invariably provide the best (most reliable) stratigraphies; faunal remains are most frequently preserved in caves and rockshelters, and surface finds are often mixed because of agricultural works. This is generally the case for Middle and Upper Paleolithic sites; in the Lower Paleolithic, on the other hand, most of the sites are open sites, and only some of them have any kind of stratigraphic context.

There are, in contrast, very few examples of systematically planned surveys of a territory or a portion of a territory, and those that are accomplished are mostly done by northern European workers.[4] A notable exception is the systematic survey of mesolithic mountain sites in northeast Italy, initiated by B. Bagolini in the early 1970s (see, e.g., Bagolini et al. 1983). Aside from the aforementioned "objective" reasons for digging in caves (see also Straus 1979b), the Italian preference for working in caves and rockshelters essentially stems from the characteristics of the chronotypological protoparadigm: if the main task of research is to establish chronological sequences, it is natural to look for the sites that provide reasonably unproblematic stratigraphies. Thus the preference for open air sites in the Lower Paleolithic results from the fact that there are no cave deposits of that period, and not from a particular sense of "problem."

The chronotypological perspective does not consider at all the *potential complementarity* of cave and open-air sites; thus isolated surface finds can be "inserted" in the chronological sequence of cultural facies originally established through cave excavations.[5] When complementarity is recognized, as it was in the mesolithic sites of northeast Italy, the combined results of the rockshelter excavations and the surveys (and subsequent tests) of open sites produced a considerable shift in perspective. In fact, although Broglio (1980) was accustomed to refer all mesolithic sites to the standard lowland rockshelter sequences (such as Romagnano III, in the Adige valley near Trento), new interpretations aimed at more detailed understanding of the subsistence and settlement strategies of these mesolithic hunter-gatherers are now beginning to emerge (see, e.g., Lanzinger 1985).

However, the chronotypological protoparadigm not only produces biases in the planning of data collection, but also in the resultant excavation procedures. In fact, since the main interest of research lies in the definition of chronological sequences, the only kind of variability that is generally recognized in archaeological data is that which can be derived from vertical stratigraphy (i.e., change due to the passage of time). As a consequence, excavation focuses mainly on digging test trenches as deeply as possible in order to encompass the maximum possible time span and, therefore, the best definition (i.e., longest sequence) of cultural facies. Since horizontal variability is considered of secondary importance, most paleolithic excavations in Italy deal only with a very limited portion of the surface area of sites, so that we are in most cases basing conclusions on nothing more than deep *sondages* (the "telephone booths" of American writers). Moreover, excavations follow essentially an artificial stratigraphy, according to arbitrary levels or spits, and the natural stratigraphic sequence is only reconstructed at the end of the field season. Even if the stratigraphic sequence is expanded by enlarging the test trench or by opening new test trenches in successive field seasons, the net result is very often that only a single stratigraphic profile is drawn for the whole site.[6] As an example, Figure 14.1 gives the schematic stratigraphy of the Upper Paleolithic site of Grotta Paglicci, in northern Apulia, taken from a review article on the Italian late Upper Paleolithic (Bartolomei et al. 1979). The profile (no indication is given of its orientation) is drawn from the superimposition of two profiles: the first one, from level 1 to level 18a, was produced by three field seasons in the early 1960s (1961–1963) (Mezzena and Palma di Cesnola 1967) and the second, from level 18b to level 22, from two additional field seasons some ten years later (1971–72) (Mezzena and Palma di Cesnola 1972).

It is rather surprising, in my opinion, that for an important site such as Grotta Paglicci the possibility of drawing more than a single profile, even after five field seasons, was never considered. I think that treating the site stratigraphy only in geological terms, where all that was required was a schematic overall sequence of the various strata with no reference to horizontal variations in stratigraphy, strictly depends on the chronotypological perspective chosen by (or implicit in the work of) the researchers. In the case of Grotta Paglicci a single stratigraphic profile might be thought to be adequate since the strata shown in Figure 14.1 are essentially horizontal, so that the figure presents all the strata that have been recognized during the successive excavations. In some (perhaps most) cases, however, a single stratigraphic profile would clearly not be sufficient.

This is the situation at another important Italian site, Grotta della Cala near Salerno, in Campania, whose schematic stratigraphic section is represented in Figure 14.2 (Palma di Cesnola 1971). From the drawing it is evident that the stratigraphic sequence is rather complex, and, moreover, two levels (P, O) are not indicated on the illustration, although they are described in the article. They were present only "in some sectors of the excavations, between layers Q and N" (Palma di Cesnola 1971:263). Even if a more complete schematic section has been published (cf. Bartolomei et al. 1976), I think that Grotta della Cala is a classic example of a site where several profiles, together with horizontal maps of the cave and of the test trenches, are of paramount importance. On the other hand, since most of the industrial assemblages (more precisely the ones from layers beta (β) to F in Figure 14.2), that were the real object of interest of the chronotypological protoparadigm, had been fully published (Palma di Cesnola 1971: 264–313, Martini 1978, 1981), perhaps the investigators thought that the schematic sections would suffice. The presentation of a single stratigraphic section is rather common not only in the south but also in other Italian regions such as Liguria (for the Mousterian sites see

PAGLICCI

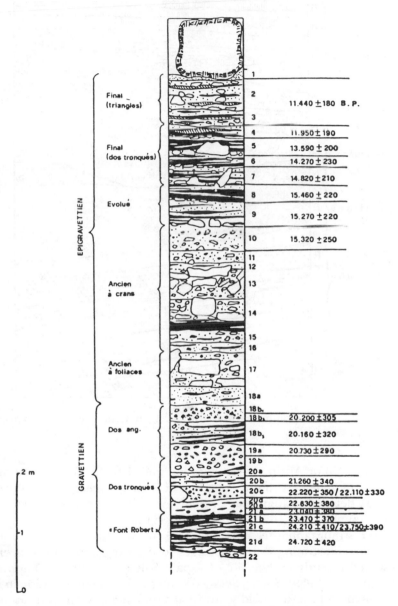

FIGURE 14.1. Stratigraphic section of Grotta Paglicci (from Bartolomei et al. 1979).

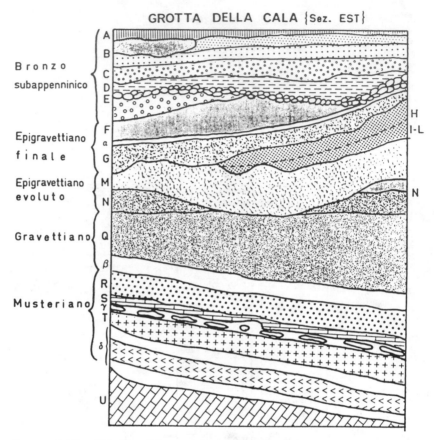

FIGURE 14.2. Stratigraphic section (east wall) of Grotta della Cala (from Palma di Cesnola 1971).

Lumley 1969) or Abruzzo (see, e.g., Radmilli 1977). The same thing happens in Veneto, with the exception of Riparo Tagliente, for which two very detailed stratigraphic profiles, extended over several meters, have been published (Bartolomei et al. 1984).

Three stratigraphic sections (one frontal and two transverse) and two maps, illustrating different stages in the excavations have been presented recently for the site of Riparo Salvini in southern Latium (Avellino et al. 1989). Such a detailed stratigraphic documentation in a preliminary report (five field seasons) of a rockshelter with a surface of only ca. 30 m², is probably due to the fact that at least one of the authors cannot be considered an orthodox follower of the traditionalist proto-paradigm.

The concept of intrasite variability is, understandably, somewhat alien to the strict chronotypologist, who typically assigns a priority to depth rather than to extension in an excavation. However, differentiated spatial distributions are of course the norm, and not only in the cases of genuine high resolution/integrity (very few in Italy, in my opinion). At Riparo Salvini, where the deposit most probably represents an accumulation of archaeological material through time due to the particular shape of the bedrock, there is strong quantitative variability both in industry and faunal remains even 2 m apart (Avellino et al. 1989). At the C shelter of the Cipolliane caves, a late Upper Paleolithic site in southern Apulia, the percentages of tools found in the 1962 field season are quite distinct from the ones collected in a different trench in 1964 (Gambassini 1970:170–172). The same thing also happens at Grotta Paglicci where the 1972 excavation resulted in tool percentages very different from those of the previous years (Galiberti in Palma di Cesnola et al. 1983:276–277). These differences, however, are often ignored in the definition of the cultural sequences (see below).

Very recently, there have been signs of an increasing interest in horizontal distributions and in more extensive excavations. In particular, there are some very interesting results from excavations of *Lower* Paleolithic sites, partly due to the rarity of stratified sites of this period, and partly due to the influence of the well-known African "occupation floors" (Leakey 1975). "Paleosurfaces" of major importance have been discovered in southern Italy at Isernia La Pineta, Molise (Cremaschi et al. 1984), Venosa (Segre and Piperno 1984) and at Castel di Guido, near Rome (Mallegni et al. 1984).

As regards the Upper Paleolithic, some interesting results have been reported from Veneto. At Riparo Tagliente, an area devoted exclusively to flint knapping has been identified in an Epigravettian level (9) (Guerreschi and Leonardi 1984). The Aurignacian open site of Monte Avena has been interpreted as a raw material procurement locality (Broglio 1984, Lanzinger 1984). The most systematic results come from mesolithic sites in the northeastern Alps. Several sites show evidence of more or less discrete activity areas (Bagolini et al. 1983), and the first interpretations of this kind go back to the early 1970s (Bagolini et al. 1975). It seems, therefore, that some kind of paradigmatic shift is taking place in current mesolithic research, especially in northeastern Italy. This is apparent both in research planning and excavations strategies.

Biases in Data Analysis and Interpretation

According to the chronotypological protoparadigm, of the different kinds of data collected in excavations, the study of the lithic industries has the highest priority. Almost all the papers on the (mostly Upper) Paleolithic published in *Rivista di Scienze Preistoriche* in the last twenty years have what might be called a standardized organizational structure: (a) an introductory section with general information on the site and essential stratigraphic information, (b) a classification of the lithic industry according to the Laplace (1964) typology, (c) remarks and comments on the industry, again following observations deemed important in the Laplace system, (d) comparison with other sites (in particular the "reference" sites), and (e) attribution of the industry to one or another of the already identified cultural facies. In some cases there are appendixes, mainly on the faunal remains and on absolute dates, when they are available.

The traditional lack of sedimentological analyses is due to the lack of specialists in this field who are also interested in prehistoric archaeology. This circumstance might also be explained, at least partially, by the humanistic-historical component of the traditionalist protoparadigm, and therefore by the limited interest of archaeologists in this kind of analysis. In the last few years, however, some very good sedimentology of prehistoric sites has been published. The same situation holds for palynological studies. Until some years ago, pollen analyses were done only in the context of Quaternary geological research, without interest in or applications to archaeological problems. A few good pollen series have been published recently, mainly in northern and central Italy.

The situation with faunal analysis is different. A concern with faunal remains has been from the beginning an important component of Italian prehistoric research. There is, however, great variability in the sophistication of paleontological studies. They range from the simple listing of the presence or absence of species up to lists of percentages of the different species represented in the various strata of a site. Calculations of the minimum number of individuals or complete listing of anatomical parts are, however, almost unknown. Studies of anatomical parts include a preliminary analysis of the fauna of Riparo Salvini (Cassoli and Guadagnoli 1987) and the work of F. Scali and A. Tagliacozzo (in Piperno et al. 1980) on the mesolithic and neolithic layers of Grotta dell'Uzzo, in Sicily. As regards the Mousterian, there is the analysis of the faunal sample from Grotta San Agostino in Latium (Tozzi 1970). In Lower Paleolithic sites where faunal remains have great paleontological interest as indicators of evolutionary processes through the occurrence of species now extinct, faunal studies are essentially ecological-climatological in character. The main objective is to correlate archaeological strata with the climatic oscillations of the glacial periods; and, therefore, their relevance is essentially chronological. These goals are evident even in the most detailed work, such as the classifications of bird remains from the late Upper Paleolithic site of Arene Candide in Liguria (Cassoli 1980), as well as in several excellent review articles (e.g., the work of B. Sala [1983] for the late Upper Paleolithic). True archaeozoological studies, together with taphonomic analyses, are completely unknown in Italy. To my knowledge, the only existing study of seasonal patterning and bone modification caused by human behavior is Stiner's work on the Mousterian of Grotta Breuil in southern Latium (see Bietti, Brucchietti and Mantero 1988; Stiner, this volume).

It should be stressed that the climatic-chronological study of faunal remains, particularly when correlated with good stratigraphic data, with sound analyses of sediment and pollen, and with absolute dates is of the utmost importance, regardless of *any* set of paradigmatic biases, as a way to establish a correct chronostratigraphy *independent of* and prior to the analysis of the industrial assemblage. Some good examples of this approach are the study of the Visogliano shelter near Trieste (Bartolomei and Tozzi 1978) and the analysis of the Anagni complex in Latium (Biddittu et al. 1979—both Lower Paleolithic) and work at Grotta Romanelli in southern Apulia (Cassoli et al. 1979—late Upper Paleolithic). It is unfortunately true, though, that these kinds of analyses are often considered *ancillary* to the study of the industries. They are regarded as a kind of a posteriori "check" of the accuracy of the chronological subdivision established by the typological analysis of the flint industries. This is also true as regards absolute dates. In the case of the Upper Paleolithic, where a large number of ^{14}C dates are available, when an absolute date of a site or of a stratum is in contradiction with its chronotypological classification, it will immediately be considered doubtful or even discarded.[7] The "ideal" situation is of course the one shown in Figure 14.1: there is a good correspondence between typological chronology (on the left) and absolute chronology (on the right). One could even imagine an almost linear process of sedimentation and "interpolate" the dates for layers 17–11 from it.

In many situations, however, real contradictions exist. This is the case, for example, with the late Upper Paleolithic site of Taurisano, in southern Apulia. The whole Epigravettian stratigraphic sequence (23 artificial levels) is ^{14}C dated around 15,500–16,000 B.P. In the first typological classification (Laplace 1966—at that time no absolute dates were available), a Lower Complex (levels 23–6) and a Final Complex (levels 5–1) were identified, essentially because the tanged points, characteristic of the Lower Epigravettian, are absent from levels 5–1. Following Laplace, Palma di Cesnola (et al. 1983:285) does not accept the absolute date of levels 5–1, and therefore assigns the industry to the final Epigravettian. Two important elements, obviously relevant to the relative chronology of the site but not taken into account, are (a) the stratigraphy and the faunal distribution which do not vary appreciably across all 23 levels and (b) the limited area of the test trench, which may well cause sampling bias effects (Bietti 1979, Bietti in Palma di Cesnola and Bietti 1983:211).

The discrepancy that often exists between the chronotypological and the ^{14}C attribution of an Upper Paleolithic industrial assemblage is illustrated by Figure 14.3, which shows a summary of the absolute dates for the Italian Epigravettian (Bartolomei et al. 1979). It is obvious that there are a number of sites, or of layers in a single site (e.g., Paglicci, Palidoro, Taurisano), which are attributed to different "phases" of the Epigravettian (Ancient, Evolved, and Final) even if the absolute dates coincide within two standard deviations.

Figure 14.3 refers to the Italian situation up to about 1977. However, more than ten years later there are only a few minor changes. In particular, in the period around 15,000 B.P. we have two dates from Grotta della Cala: $16,320 \pm 850$ B.P. for layer N and $14,780 \pm 850$ B.P. for layer M (see Figure 14.2 for the stratigraphic context). The industry in both layers (which span the Ancient Epigravettian of Taurisano, the Evolved Epigravettian of Palidoro and Paglicci, and the Final Epigravettian of Ugento, Taurisano 5–1 and Paglicci 7—see Figure 14.3) has nevertheless been attributed to the Evolved Epigravettian (Martini 1978). I might say that, personally, I do not object to defining the Ancient, Evolved, and Final Epigravettian as *conventional* chronological phases (say ca. 20,000–16,000 B.P. for the Ancient, 16,000–14,000 B.P. for the Evolved, and 14,000–10,000 B.P. for the Final Epigravettian). The problem is that the definition of these phases is based only on the characteristics of the industrial assemblages (cf. Figure 14.3).

In respect of the classification of industries, practically all the industries of the Italian paleolithic and mesolithic have been studied by means of typological lists (i.e., according to a morphologic-stylistic point of view, as is customary for a chronotypological perspective). Functionally oriented studies (including microwear analyses) are essentially ignored or are considered complementary to morphologic-stylistic analyses, although there are some good examples of type-fossils (in the chronotypological sense) which are quite probably only functional variants of other types (see, e.g., Bietti 1989). For the Lower and Middle Paleolithic most workers use Bordes's (1961a) typology.[8] Such a difference in typological lists might seem surprising, but is essentially due to the fact that systematic typological analyses only began around the early 1960s, when Laplace was at the "Ecole de Rome" and was engaged in the study of Italian Upper Paleolithic complexes. No tradition of typological analysis existed in Italy before

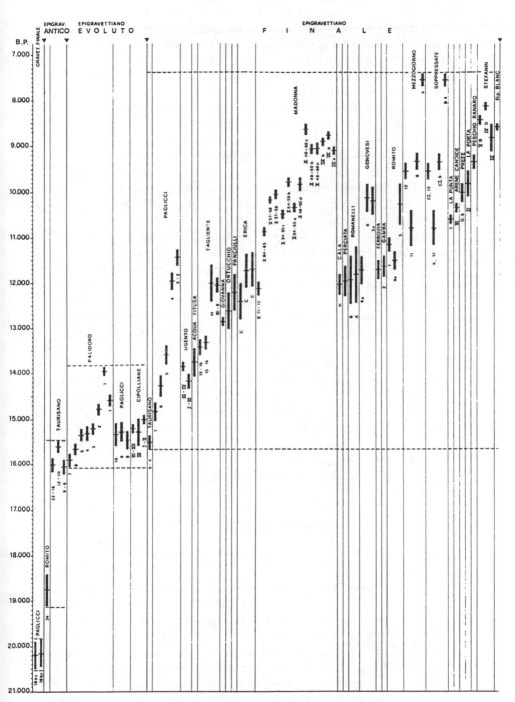

FIGURE 14.3. Radiocarbon dates for the Italian Epigravettian (from Bartolomei et al. 1979).

that date. The most prominent Italian researchers of the 1950s, men like A. C. Blanc and L. Cardini, were oriented to a geological-ecological perspective that de-emphasized typology.

I will not describe the characteristics of Laplace's "analytical typology" here (see Bietti 1978). In my opinion, it can be considered a special case, an extreme variant of the classic French typological method represented by François Bordes and his school. Its "extreme" character results from the fact that it is strictly dependent on Laplace's (1959, 1966) "Synthétotype" model of evolution. According to this model, industries such as the Aurignacian and the Perigordian in France developed by specialization from an undifferentiated base complex (i.e., the "Synthétotype"—the Châtelperronian in France, the Uluzzian in Italy). The "analytical typology" thus considers some "primary" types *véritables thèmes typologiques* common to all industries regardless of geographical distribution (Laplace 1966:29). A more refined level of analysis is then attained with the "secondary" types, which result from more specific definition of some attributes. These supposedly define specialized cultural facies in continuous evolution. Applications of the Laplace typology are, in my opinion, a sort of "pseudo-normal science" activity, in which the common rules and methods of scientific research do not depend on a general perspective or paradigm, but rather on a particular model of evolution, such as the "Synthétotype" model. However, it doesn't quite work the way Laplace had intended. Actually the evolution of cultures and their definitions are almost invariably determined by the analysis of the "primary" types. The "secondary" types are more or less epiphenomenal. This is particularly true in Italy, where primary types play a role similar to that of the traditional Bordesian types, with the same kind of percentages, indexes, and so forth—a role that should instead be reserved for the "secondary" types. In any case, all the relevant attributes of the artifacts are frequently listed by Italian researchers, but with no attempt to quantify correlations among them. It may well be the case that a quantitative attribute analysis will produce results that are puzzling or contradictory from a morphologic-stylistic point of view, but more interesting from a functional perspective (Bietti 1989).

Another main difference with the French traditionalist perspective is the almost total lack of interest by Italian researchers in problems of lithic *technology*: typology, in agreement with Laplace's indications, is the main object of research. To my knowledge, the first complete listing of debitage characteristics is the one given for the Palidoro industry (Bietti 1976–77). In almost all the other works done under a traditionalist perspective, studies of technology are confined to "lithometric" analyses: studies of the distributions of blank length, widths or

thicknesses, without any further indication of technological procedures or reduction processes.

Traditionalist Italian researchers also subscribe to the idea of continuous evolution of industrial assemblages. The major objective of their
work is to slice and subdivide the cultural facies into finer and finer
"phases" and "subphases," all defined according to tool percentages or
ratios and even according to the percentages of some characteristic
tools, which then assume the role of the type fossil types in the traditional French systematics. As an example, Figure 14.4 gives a tentative
seriation of the mesolithic complex of Romagnano III in the Adige
Valley near Trento (Broglio 1975). This is considered a "reference" site
for the northeastern Italian Mesolithic. The sequence starts at ca. 9,900
B.P. (layer AF) and extends up 6,500 B.P. (layer AA, where the first
potsherds appear). Five facies have been recognized on the grounds
of the data shown in Figure 14.4 (Broglio 1975:11): (1) a "Lower"
Sauveterrian complex (layers AF–AE), characterized by three-sided
retouched triangles (Number 8, Figure 14.4); (2) an "intermediate"
Sauveterrian complex (layers AC8–AC4), characterized by a high incidence of crescents (No. 9, Figure 14.4), triangles (No. 10, Figure 14.4),
and Sauveterre points (Number 5, Figure 14.4); (3) a "recent" Sauveterrian complex (layers AC2–AC1), characterized by double-backed
points (Number 3, Figure 14.4) and the "Montclus" triangle (Number
7, Figure 14.4); (4) a "transition" level (layer AB3); and, finally, (5) a
"Castelnovian" complex (layers AB2–AB1, AA) with a high incidence
of trapezes and rhomboids (Numbers 11, 12 in Figure 14.4). Actually,
the only evident differences are between the "Castelnovian" levels
(AB2–1, AA) and the Lower Sauveterrian complex with the triangles
retouched on three sides (layer AF–AE).

If some kind of chronotypological trend can be recognized at Romagnano III, the situation of several paleolithic complexes is much
worse. Following the suggestion of Laplace, who recognized in the
industry of Palidoro a classic example of "internal evolution of an
industrial assemblage" (Laplace 1966:129), Martini (in Bietti et al.
1983:334–337) subdivided the eight artificial levels at Palidoro (which
date from $13,950 \pm 100$ to $15,900 \pm 150$ B.P.) into three "subphases" of
the Evolved Epigravettian, even though the limited surface exposed by
the excavation (about 1 m^2 !) should have constituted a serious warning
against any attempt at fine chronotypological subdivisions (cf. Bietti
1976–77, Bietti et al. 1983: footnotes 2 and 3). In this case too, problems of sampling bias have been overlooked in efforts to establish a
refined chronotypological sequence. Martini did the same thing with
the Final Epigravettian of the middle and southern Tyrrhenian region.
It covers a time period twice as long as that of the Evolved Epigravet-

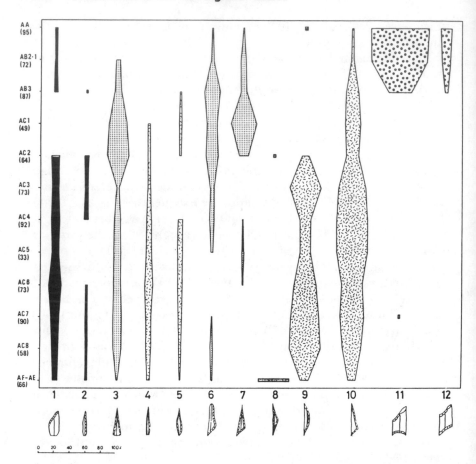

FIGURE 14.4.   Chronotypological seriation of the Romagnano III rockshelter (from Broglio 1975).

tian (ca. 14,000–10,000 B.P.) and has been subdivided into six subphases, always on the basis of the characteristics of the retouched pieces (Martini in Bietti et al. 1983:338–341).

After the first analyses done by Laplace (1966), the Ancient Epigravettian was traditionally defined as coextensive with the whole of Italy, with two phases *à foliacés* and *à crans* being somewhat parallel to the French Solutrean (Bartolomei et al. 1979). The Evolved and Final Epigravettian, however, were divided into "regional" facies: northern Tyrrhenian, middle and southern Tyrrhenian, northern and middle Adriatic, southern Adriatic and Sicilian. The characteristics of these facies, phases, and subphases have been defined by the presence and frequency of fossil types (e.g., the *foliacés* and *crans* of the Ancient

Epigravettian) or by percentages and ratios of various retouched tool groups.

It is interesting to observe that every single quantitative analysis performed on Italian Upper Paleolithic and Mesolithic assemblages is in contradiction with the qualitative traditional chronotypological classification. The first quantitative analysis was done by Ammerman using 27 industrial assemblages of the Italian Epigravettian, analyzed by the method of multidimensional scaling (1971). The data were Laplace's (1966) tool percentages for these sites. No geographical or chronological trends were observed. A second attempt, using constellation analysis on 35 Epigravettian assemblages produced similar results. Some evidence of time trends is apparent, especially if restricted tool groups such as endscrapers or denticulates are used (Ammerman and Hodson 1972). Similar "non-results" were obtained for a sample of 40 Final Epigravettian and Mesolithic assemblages using a cluster analysis with average linkage and percentage distance coefficients (Bietti 1981). A further quantitative classification of Italian Epigravettian industries, again using cluster analysis and percentage distance coefficients, has been done recently by Coverini et al. (1982). Once more, however, there is a complete contradiction with the qualitative results. In contrast with the Laplace classification, faithfully followed by the Italian chronotypologists, the Ancient Epigravettian exhibits clear-cut regional differentiation (Coverini et al. 1982:25–27). On the other hand, the Evolved and Final Epigravettian show little of the regional subdivision proposed by Laplace (1966) and subsequently followed by most Italian researchers (e.g., Bartolomei et al. 1979). In the face of these obvious anomalies with the established view, it was surprising to note the conclusion that "this result confirms the observations of Laplace and his concept of subdivision of the final Tardigravettian in regional 'facies,' with different local evolution (1966) as well as the results of more recent studies of the Epigravettian industries (Bartolomei et al. 1979, Martini 1981)" (Martini and Sarti in Coverini et al. 1982:31).

A more recent quantitative classification of Epigravettian industries uses Student's T-test and a linear stepwise discriminant analysis on the traditional retouched tool types (Bietti and Burani 1985). One hundred twenty-four industrial assemblages (limited to continental Italy) were analyzed, and Figure 14.5 displays the scatterplot according to the first two principal axes (which account for 64.4% of the total variance) of a principal components analysis. Once again, no clear structure emerges from the data. The only reasonable geographical clustering is a group of northern Adriatic Final Epigravettian assemblages on the right (label G), while on the bottom there is a cluster comprising two layers of a Ligurian site (Arma del Nasino, label F) and

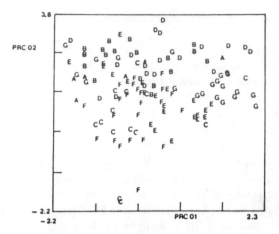

FIGURE 14.5. Scatterplot on the two principal axes of Italian continental Epigravettian assemblages. A: Ancient Epigravettian à *foliacés;* B: Ancient Epigravettian à *crans;* C: Evolved and Final Epigravettian of the northern Tyrrhenian zone; D: Evolved Epigravettian of the middle and southern Tyrrhenian zone; E: Final Epigravettian of the middle and southern Tyrrhenian zone; F: Evolved and Final Epigravettian of the southern Adriatic zone; G: Evolved and Final Epigravettian of the middle and northern Adriatic zone (from Bietti and Burani 1985).

an Apulian site (Grotta Romanelli, label C), all attributed to the Final Epigravettian.

Discussion: Is There any Possibility for a "Scientific Revolution"?

The contradictory statement by Martini and Sarti quoted above (in Coverini et al. 1982:31) is a good starting point for a discussion of what I have called "pseudo-normal science" in Italian paleolithic research. This apparently is a case in which evidence arising from data analysis (usually pattern searches) has been overlooked. Moreover, as we have seen in the previous section, contradictions between qualitative chronotypological assessments following Laplace and the results of subsequent quantitative analyses are *absolutely independent* of the particular method employed to make comparisons. Multidimensional scaling, constellation analysis, cluster analysis with several linkage procedures, T-tests and linear stepwise discriminant analyses, principal component analysis: *all* these procedures give results that contradict the qualitative classification. It seems, therefore, that there is a strong bias against the possibility of recognizing anomalies resultant from ransacking the data, so that the very idea of looking at data with "different glasses" is excluded beforehand by some of these scholars: traditional classification is the only sound framework within which new data can be arranged. It is quite clear that, starting from these premises, there will be no possibility of a "scientific revolution."

What, then, are the possible sources of a paradigmatic shift, a radical change in perspective, in Italian hunter-gatherer research? I have already mentioned a few examples of research oriented toward viewing the past through "different glasses": Mesolithic sites in the northeastern Alps, Riparo Salvini for the Upper Paleolithic, and Grotta Breuil for the Mousterian. The reexamination of Pontinian faunal complexes and industrial assemblages in Latium by M. Stiner and S. Kuhn, respectively, are also noteworthy exceptions (see their contributions to the present volume). Another interesting departure from the traditional perspective is Donahue's functional analysis of layer 4a of Grotta Paglicci, traditionally studied within the confines of the chronotypological approach (Palma di Cesnola et al. 1983). Donahue's work is based on microwear analyses on the flint implements and on the anatomical element distributions in the faunal remains (1986).

Despite these innovative approaches, no new perspectives are evident from recent Lower Paleolithic research. As noted earlier, this is independent of the generally high quality of the field work. The main difficulty lies in a kind of "modernism" in the interpretation of the results. The substantial lack of interest in modern anthropological studies so characteristic of the Italian traditionalist protoparadigm most often results in naïve extensions of modern hunter-gatherer behavior to biologically different hominids in the remote past. Faunal remains associated with industrial assemblages are almost automatically interpreted as remnants of hunting activities, without any real control of bone modification features. The famous site of Isernia La Pineta (dated to ca. 700,000 years B.P.) thus exhibits "a complex and articulated social structure, a complex living structure in its building technique and in the organization of space, a perfect knowledge and mastery of the territory, and a consequent development of activities of group hunting and gathering" (Peretto and Piperno 1984:101–102)! Piperno also re-proposes the old diffusionist arguments for the Italian Acheulean: the peopling of these "cultures" may be seen as a series of successive migratory waves (Piperno 1982:43). Furthermore, differences among Acheulean facies in Latium can allegedly be explained in terms of "ethnicity," so that it is possible to identify real "cultural provinces" (Piperno 1984:43–44). Putting it mildly, it seems unlikely that new, soundly based results and interpretations could arise from such "sensationalistic" outcomes, whatever the quality of the field work. In fact, the main objective of most Lower Paleolithic research continues to be the isolation of "occupation floors" and "habitation units" similar to the ones claimed in East Africa or in southern France. Warnings on the stratigraphic integrity of these living floors have of course been published (Bordes 1975, Villa 1983, Binford 1985) but have so far been ignored. Once again, we are in presence of a kind of "pseudo-normal science." A real "contextual" study of the archaeological record seems to be lacking in these interpretations, which, in the end, are not very different from the chronotypological classifications illustrated for more recent periods.

Accurate fieldwork and a continuous refinement of data collection procedures are certainly required for a better interpretation of the archaeological records. However, I think that there will be no substantial progress, in the sense of a Kuhn-like "scientific revolution," in Italian paleolithic archaeology unless a drastic change in mental attitudes takes place and the need for establishing a *methodology* for the conduct of prehistoric research is acknowledged. In other words, as the history of the developed sciences has shown, there is an absolute need for a commonly shared sense of problem, for agreement about data collection and analysis, and a commonly shared scientific language. The various biases illustrated in this paper show very well, I think, that "scientific revolutions" are impossible in the absence of true "normal science."

Acknowledgments

I wish to thank my wife, A. M. Bietti-Sestieri, for a number of fruitful discussions of these topics and for a critical reading of the text.

Notes

1. As a matter of fact, astrologers were pretty soon excluded from the scientific community of the astronomers, while clandestine diggers and local amateurs can easily write (at least in Italy) papers for scientific journals, be invited to international conferences, etc.

2. I hope that, in what follows, it will be clear that my research perspective is oriented toward an "anthropological-behavioral" protoparadigm, even if my formal studies were in the traditionalist French chronotypological perspective.

3. Interpretations based on this strict diffusionist perspective are still evident in a few papers in paleolithic archaeology (for a discussion on this point, see Bietti 1980–81:180).

4. Most of these surveys are concerned with more recent periods (i.e., the Metal Ages, classical, and medieval archaeology). Notable amongst the surveys oriented toward hunter-gatherer prehistory are the work of the University of Amsterdam in the Agro Pontino (Latium) (Kamermans et al. 1985), the survey

of the territory of Rome (Bietti-Sestieri and Sebastiani 1986) and of the Fondi basin (province of Latina) (Bietti et al. 1988b).

5. It must be stressed, however, that the chronotypological protoparadigm is not the only one which denies such a complementarity. On the opposite end of the spectrum, in the "landscape" approach of some British workers (see, e.g., Barker 1981), the importance of cave deposits is largely underestimated compared to that of open-air sites (which, for later time ranges, would probably give a better picture than caves of settlement patterns in a given territory).

6. It is interesting to observe that, in many cases, the lithic industry and stratigraphic sequence of a site are published rather quickly, following two or three excavation campaigns. Extensive monographs, published after several regular field seasons, are practically unknown in the Italian paleolithic and mesolithic literature. One exception is the work published of A. M. Radmilli (1974) on the Upper Paleolithic site of Grotta Polesini near Rome. Excavated under rather difficult conditions from 1953 to 1956, it presents only one general and very schematic stratigraphic profile for the whole site (Radmilli 1974:20).

7. A. Palma di Cesnola (personal communication) says that the correct procedure for studying a site is to analyze the industry first and assign it to a chronological cultural facies. *After that* one can look at the absolute dates to determine whether they fit into the scheme. Taking into account the absolute dates from the beginning may be dangerous, because one can thereby be influenced in the attribution and chronological definition of the industry.

8. Only quite recently have Mousterian industries been classified using Laplace's method, and with rather confusing results. As an example, Levallois flakes, or any other kind of predetermined debitage, are unclassifiable with Laplace's "analytical typology," since it was originally designed for the study of the "leptolithic" industries of the European Upper Paleolithic.

Chapter 15
One Flew Over the Hippo's Nest: Extinct Pleistocene Fauna, Early Man, and Conservative Archaeology in Cyprus

Alan H. Simmons

Introduction

Paleolithic archaeologists working on the Mediterranean Islands are few and far between. The reason for this is obvious: there is very little clear evidence for human occupation of most of these islands prior to the Neolithic. A few claims have been made for pre-Neolithic, even paleolithic, antiquity; but more often than not, these have been based on very insecure data. In this paper, I examine a recently investigated site in Cyprus that has shaken the paradigmatic structure of the way prehistory is viewed in the Mediterranean. This site, Akrotiri-Aetokremnos (Eagle's Cliff, or simply Site E), is located on the southern tip of Cyprus and is significant for two reasons. The first is that it represents the earliest site on Cyprus and, indeed, one of the oldest well-documented sites on *any* of the Mediterranean Islands. The second reason is that it is associated with a Pleistocene fauna—primarily pygmy hippopotamus (*Phanourios minutus*)—thought to have been extinct long before people ever set foot on the island.

Following the theme of this volume, this is not a data paper. By way of essential background information, however, it is necessary to summarize the scant knowledge of endemic Pleistocene faunas on the Mediterranean Islands and the state of early island prehistory. Following this, I provide a summary of the two short seasons of test excavations at Akrotiri-Aetokremnos in 1987 and 1988, along with a discussion of the site's significance. I then conclude with a discussion on the professional reaction to the work at Akrotiri-Aetokremnos.

Although the title of this contribution is somewhat whimsical, its content is not. I became involved with Akrotiri-Aetokremnos precisely because I was *not* a Cypriot expert and was perceived not to have a pre-formed bias toward what is a very controversial locality with implications reaching far beyond the Mediterranean Basin. The findings from Akrotiri-Aetokremnos have caused some researchers working in the area to push archaeological canons of evidence beyond what is normally regarded as "convincing." The resulting controversy has been interesting to watch, for it has provoked some rather unconventional behavior from some normally very conventional scholars, whence the title of this contribution.

Island Biogeography in the Mediterranean: The Quaternary Faunal Record, Extinct Island Fauna, and the Role of Humans

Islands have often been viewed as controlled laboratories for the study of cultural and ecological processes (cf. MacArthur and Wilson 1967, Evans 1973, 1977; Terrell 1977). A considerable literature exists on island biogeography, and in recent years the explanatory potential posed by these environments has been recognized by many archaeological researchers (Keegan and Diamond 1987). The endemic fauna of the Mediterranean Islands and their unique adaptations have fascinated scholars for years. Both dwarfed and gigantic forms of mainland species are well documented (Sondaar 1986), and of particular interest to this paper is the presence on several of the islands of extinct pygmy hippos and pygmy elephants.

Cyprus is the third largest Mediterranean Island and, despite its size, is one of the geologically and biogeographically most isolated. Contrary to earlier assumptions and despite the difficulty of reconstructing paleo-coastlines in regions of tectonic instability (such as Cyprus), current consensus favors the view that even at times of minimum sea levels during Pleistocene glacial maxima, the island remained separated from the mainland by at least 30 km (Held 1989a:12, Swiny 1988:1–3). It therefore seems unlikely that endemic species could have arrived on Cyprus or any of the Mediterranean islands by a means of a land bridge, despite suggestions to this effect by some researchers (Audley-Charles and Hooijer 1973, Kuss 1973). Sondaar (1977:673–679) presents a convincing argument against this, noting that the land bridge theory does not account for the composition of island faunas. Instead, the so-called *Island Sweepstakes* model proposed by Simpson (1940, 1965) seems a more probable scenario for colonization (Sondaar 1986). This phrase refers to instances in which animals may venture far from the coast, reach an isolated island from which they cannot return, and are forced to settle there. The actual mechanism by which fossil mammals found on the Mediterranean Islands (e.g., deer, hippopotamus, and elephant) initially *got* to the islands probably was by swimming. Improbable as this might seem, these species are known for their swimming abilities (e.g., Carrington 1962, Johnson 1980).

In Mediterranean Quaternary faunal assemblages, two salient features are a pronounced lack of species diversity and the presence of evolutionary dwarfism. The dwarf species found on the Islands were considerably smaller than their mainland counterparts, and most researchers believe that the dwarfism was an evolutionary response both to the lack of predators and to the limited resources available (Sondaar 1977). In Cyprus, Pleistocene fossil and subfossil sites consist almost exclusively of the remains of two terrestrial mammals, pygmy hippopotamus (*Phanourios minutus*) and pygmy elephant (*Elephas cypriotes*).

Although largely ignored by archaeologists until the investigation of Akrotiri-Aetokremnos, sporadic paleontological research since the beginning of this century has produced a respectable body of knowledge about the occurrence and osteology of these animals (Bate 1903a–c, 1904a–c, 1905, 1906; Boekschoten and Sondaar 1972, Faure et al. 1983, Houtekamer and Sondaar 1979, Reese 1975a, b; 1988, 1989 n.d.; Swiny 1988) and analysis suggests that large numbers of pygmy hippos roamed Cyprus during the Pleistocene (Sondaar 1977:687). The demonstrable absence from Pleistocene Cyprus of carnivores and other terrestrial megafauna indicates the island's hippo and elephant populations were subject neither to predation nor probably to resource competition, thus contributing to their persistent ability to survive—now documented archaeologically—into the early Holocene.

The presence of pygmy hippo and/or elephant is now documented at 32 confirmed bone-bearing faunal localities throughout Cyprus (Held 1989a:17, Reese 1989:24–25), with assemblages weighted heavily in favor of the hippos. Many sites occur in caves or rockshelters, as well as near rivers or ponds and on alluvial fans. Nearly all the remains are in brecciated deposits and are heavily fossilized. Most of these deposits are exposed bone beds with little or no stratigraphy. Significantly, none of these fossil sites displays the abundance of bone seen at Akroitiri-Aetokremnos.

The causes for extinction of these species probably were multiple. Overpopulation is one possible scenario. The role of man is problematic (e.g., see Sondaar 1987, Martin and Klein 1984 and references therein). Despite occasional claims to the contrary (e.g., Sondaar 1986:55–56, Sondaar et al. 1986), the association of cultural remains with extinct fauna in the Mediterranean was not well documented until the test excavations at Akrotiri-Aetokremnos. If there was a temporal overlap between human populations and extinct fauna, it was invariably short and associated with Neolithic or later occupations. In most cases, though, the assumption is that these species were extinct before man's relatively recent arrival on any of the Mediterranean Islands (although see Martin 1984:390–391). If man was responsible for the extinction of endemic island faunas, either (1) he hunted the fauna, resulting in overkill, and/or (2) he changed the habitat of the indigenous animals by the introduction of cultigens and the importation of potential animal competitors (Boekschoten and Sondaar 1972:336, Davis 1987:124–125).

Prior to work at Akrotiri, there never had been a clear association of humans with extinct pygmy hippo or elephant in Cyprus or *any* of the Mediterranean Islands. The only associations reported consisted of *one* pygmy hippo metacarpus at the aceramic Neolithic site of Cape Andreas Kastros (Davis 1984) and *one* modified shaft bone from Akanthou Arkosyko (Reese 1989:28–29). These, however, do not necessarily imply direct relationships. As Davis (1987:125) has suggested, isolated bones "might have been collected as a fossil by some keen Neolithic paleontologist" (Davis 1987:125). Barring the possibility of an overlap between remnant populations of Pleistocene fauna and the aceramic Neolithic culture of Cyprus *as it is currently defined* (Dikaios 1962, Held 1982, 1989b, Le Brun et al. 1987), the absence of pygmy hippos and elephants from the Neolithic faunal record supports the argument that these "mini-megafaunas" were hunted into extinction earlier by the island's first occupants during what may tentatively be called the "Akrotiri Phase" (Simmons et al. n.d., Simmons 1989:2).

The Initial Colonization of the Mediterranean Islands: Archaeological Evidence

Consensus opinion holds that the initial occupation of all of the Mediterranean Islands, including Cyprus, was relatively late, occurring during the Neolithic (e.g., Stanley-Price 1977a, b; Cherry 1979, 1981, 1984, 1985). Over the years, however, there have been some claims for pre-Neolithic remains, but most are poorly supported (Vigne 1983, 1987). These claims include Maroula in the Cyclades (Honea 1975), presumed Upper Paleolithic skeletal remains in Crete (Facchini and Giusberti 1988), three localities in Corsica (Lanfranchi 1967, 1974; Lanfranchi and Weiss 1973, 1977; Bonifay 1983); Corbeddu Cave in Sardinia (Sondaar et al. 1986), and alleged Lower Paleolithic finds in northern Sardinia (Arca et al. 1982, Martini and Pitzalis 1981, 1982). The Upper Paleolithic *is* well-represented in Sicily (Garcia 1972:23), but this island is extremely close to the mainland and a landbridge existed during the Upper Pleistocene (Sondaar 1987:162).

Most of these claims do not stand up to critical archaeological scrutiny, and many of the more serious researchers working in the region have rejected them as unfounded. The majority are represented by unstratified surface finds, which are notoriously difficult to date precisely. Indeed, some of the supposed earliest sites in the Mediterranean, located along the Rio Altana and at Pantallinu in the Perfugas district of Sardinia (Arca et al. 1982, Martini and Pitzalis 1981, 1982), consist of huge lithic scatters (or chert fields). One of these, located in a plowed and burned agricultural field, was visited by several scholars as part of the International Conference on Early Man and Island Environments held on Sardinia in September 1988. Discussion of the Perfugas finds is worth a brief digression, since they reflect a major paradigm or, more properly, the lack of a paradigm, in examining evidence for claimed early sites. Many of the conference members were not archaeologists, and many seemed to accept, with very little critical examination, the claim that the Perfugas materials possibly date to the Lower Paleolithic.

The Perfugas situation illustrates a problem in presenting controversial archaeological data to a well-educated, but non-archaeological, audience. We often tend to view the results of our research as "facts," much as other scientists do. However, given the nature of archaeological data, one scholar's "facts" are not necessarily another's. This seemingly obvious point is frequently lost on non-archaeologists, who often assume that we know what we are talking about and thus accept at face value what we tell them. This was clear during the visit to the Perfugas district. However, even a casual examination of the "facts" of Perfugas led several of us on that site visit to question its "interpretation." The site has been dated to the "Lower Paleolithic" by the presence of "Clactonian-looking" implements (i.e., large, hard hammer-struck flakes). While such flakes could indeed represent a Lower Paleolithic assemblage, they could also represent specialized activities of much later groups. Furthermore, the presence of these objects in a plowed chert field raises the spectre of post-occupational disturbance and, indeed, the possibility of a very recent "manufacture" of these implements by modern agencies. Despite such problems, Perfugas is now enshrined as an integral part of the Sardinian archaeological "paradigm" of early pre-Neolithic occupation. In the Sardinian museums we visited, the Perfugas finds are presented as examples of Lower Paleolithic occupation without mention of possible distorting factors.

During that same conference, one of the more credible localities for pre-Neolithic occupation also was visited. This is Corbeddu Cave, initially examined for its paleontological interest. However, cultural materials also have been found there, and some are claimed to represent pre-Neolithic occurrences (Sondaar et al. 1986, Spoor and Sondaar 1986). It is only recently that professional archaeologists have become associated with the project, and, although an impeccable excavation was conducted, the evidence I saw is far from convincing support for the pre-Neolithic claims. However, continued research at the site promises to yield better evidence, and the jury is still out on Corbeddu Cave's presumed pre-Neolithic human usage.

The point of this digression is simply to observe that it is by no means an easy task to document precisely early hunter-gatherer remains. When an association with an extinct Pleistocene fauna is claimed, the task becomes even more difficult. One must be cautious of jumping to conclusions based on sparse or equivocal data, and alternative scenarios for presumed associations must be considered.

Let me now return to the situation on Cyprus. The Neolithic is well documented on the Island. The earliest sites pertain to the aceramic Neolithic, and date to ca. 6000 B.C. The two oldest sites are Kalavassos-Tenta (Dikaios 1960, Todd 1978, 1982:37–50) and Khirokitia-Vouni (Dikaios 1953, LeBrun 1984, Stanley-Price 1977b, Stanley-Price and Christou 1973). Other sites include Cape Andreas-Kastros (LeBrun 1974, 1981), Petra tou Limniti (Gjerstad et al. 1934), Troulli (Dikaios 1962), Kataliontas-Kourvellos (Morrison and Watkins 1974, Watkins 1979), Phrenaros (Gjerstad 1926), and Dhali-Agridihi (Lehavey 1974). Few of these, however, have been systematically investigated and are documented only by test excavations or surface collections. Most appear to represent relatively ephemeral limited occupation sites; only Khirokitia, Cape Andreas, and Kalavassos are considered major villages. Of significance to this paper, however, is that *all* these sites are considered by Cypriot archaeologists to be habitation sites; the concept of specialized activity stations of limited duration is *not* a common feature of Cypriot archaeological paradigms.

There have been claims in Cyprus for pre-Neolithic occupation. The two most widely cited are Vita-Finzi (1973) and Stockton (1968). Critical examination of both shows them to be less than convincing. Vita-Finzi believed that several flint artifacts were of pre-Neolithic age, but these were surface finds with little or no context and were not "diagnostic" of any known early assemblages. Stockton's claim of early flint artifacts near Kyrenia is equally tenuous. His illustrated "tools" (Stockton 1968:17–18) are questionable. In my experience, much of this material is of questionable human origin. Adovasio et al. (1975, 1978), in their survey of the Khrysokhou River drainage, also note some possible pre-Neolithic spot finds. Most of these were artifacts eroding out of gravel deposits and were not associated with other lithics (Ado-vasio et al. 1978:42–44). Other surveys, however, have failed to locate indisputable pre-Neolithic sites (e.g., the Cyprus Survey, Rupp et al.'s Palaipaphos project (1984, Fox 1987) or Todd's (1982) Vasilikos Valley study). Nonetheless, it is important to keep in mind that such occurrences would undoubtedly be represented by low-visibility archaeological remains, since it is unlikely that they were major settlements.

While true paleolithic occupation of Cyprus may, in fact, be unlikely, the possibility of antecedent Neolithic groups should be considered, especially since the Neolithic appears with little or no suggestion of developmental phases. Both Watkins's (1981, Morrison and Watkins 1974) concept of a "para-Neolithic" and Held's (1982:6, 1989a:8) suggestion of a "proto-Neolithic," pre-Khirokitia phase, deserve attention as possible precursors. Such adaptations might not represent orthodox Neolithic patterns and could be difficult to characterize archaeologically. It is hard to evaluate Akrotiri-Aetokremnos' role in these debates. Does it represent an unrelated, pre-Neolithic occupation? Is it ancestral to later developments? Is it an early, previously undocumented variant of the aceramic Neolithic? Whatever the answer, the site represents a well-dated ninth millennium B.C. occupation and constitutes clear-cut evidence for an early human presence on the Island.

Akrotiri-Aetokremnos (Site E)

Akrotiri-Aetokremnos is situated at the extreme south end of Cyprus on the Akrotiri Peninsula (Figure 15.1), a massive sandstone and marl outcrop roughly 12 × 9 km (ca. 108 km²) in area. It is flanked by Akrotiri Bay to the east and Episkopi Bay to the west. The southern portion of the Peninsula rises from the shallow waters of the Mediter-ranean in cliffs reaching a height of ca. 70 m (Heywood 1982:162–164, Bear and Morel 1960, Swiny 1982:1–2). The site is located on a parcel of land called Royal Air Force-Akrotiri, part of the British Western Sovereign Base Area in Cyprus. It sits on a narrow talus slope of a precipitous cliff approximately 40 m above current sea level. At one time the site was a rockshelter that has since collapsed. Much of it is rapidly eroding into the sea.

The history of the discovery of Akrotiri-Aetokremnos is an interesting example of how important archaeological sites often come to be known. The existence of Pleistocene faunal remains on the Akrotiri Peninsula was first noted in 1961 by a fourteen-year-old English boy named David Nixon, who was spending time with family or friends stationed at the Akrotiri R.A.F. base. While exploring the Akrotiri cliffs, he came across fossilized bones, marine shell, and fragments of

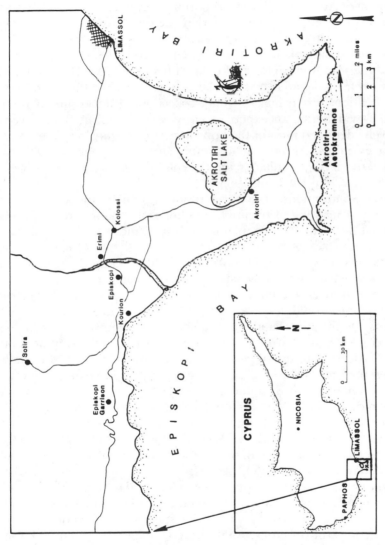

FIGURE 15.1   Location of Akrotiri-Aetokremnos on the Akrotiri Peninsula of southern Cyprus.

chipped stone. Nixon took some of this material back to England, and in 1966 showed it to the late Dr. Kenneth Oakley of the British Museum, who identified the bones as pygmy hippo and the chipped stone as possibly Neolithic. In 1971, this information was reported to the Department of Antiquities, but the report was never acted upon. Then, in 1980, a British officer named Lt. Brian Pile rediscovered the site when he was conducting an archaeological survey of the Peninsula. Pile made his findings known to Dr. Stuart Swiny, director of the Cyprus American Archaeological Research Institute (CAARI). Swiny and other professional archaeologists subsequently visited the site on several occasions, often making small collections. During one of these visits, David Reese, an expert in early Mediterranean faunas, conclusively identified most of the bone as that of pygmy hippopotamus. I first examined Akrotiri-Aetokremnos in the summer of 1985. Although these visits resulted in limited collections, no excavations were undertaken until 1987 and 1988.

Surface indications of cultural residues at Akrotiri-Aetokremnos are scant, consisting of pygmy hippo bone, shell, and a few chipped stone artifacts. In 1981, samples of both shell and bone were collected from the surface of the site for radiocarbon dating (Table 1). The results caused a good deal of controversy. Although the dates indicated considerable antiquity, they also presented some problems. If the shells dated to ca. 10,500 B.P. represented a cultural event, Akrotiri-Aetokremnos would be some 2,000 years older than any other site on Cyprus. On the other hand, the bone dates were equivocal in verifying the site's antiquity. Furthermore, the paucity of clearly associated artifacts led many to question whether Akrotiri-Aetokremnos actually represented an archaeological site or simply another of the several pygmy hippo bone beds found on the Island.

To recapitulate, if this evidence could be verified, Akrotiri-Aetokremnos would represent an extremely significant site from at least two perspectives. First, it would be the earliest evidence of a human presence on Cyprus and, indeed, one of the earliest known occupations in the Mediterranean. Second, because pygmy hippo is generally believed to have gone extinct prior to man's arrival in Cyprus (or shortly thereafter), if a direct association could be demonstrated, the circumstances surrounding extinction of this species would have to be reevaluated. Akrotiri-Aetokremnos offered tantalizing evidence of a situation unknown until that time in the Mediterranean, but the archaeological context of this controversial locale was not confirmed until excavations were undertaken in 1987, 1988 and 1990.[1] These have demonstrated both the site's antiquity and the association of cultural materials with a huge Pleistocene faunal assemblage, although, as will be shown later, there has been an amazing reticence to accept the archaeological evidence.

The first professional archaeological work at Akrotiri-Aetokremnos was undertaken during a brief testing season in 1987 during which surface collections were made and 3 m² were excavated (Simmons 1988a, b). Less than two weeks of excavation at the site recovered data strongly suggesting that the site was, in fact, what initial impressions had indicated. Additionally, and despite the limited surface indications, the presence of stratified remains resembling a midden was documented. A well preserved and large faunal assemblage was recovered, as were numerous associated chipped stone artifacts. Several radiocarbon dates were obtained from buried and stratified deposits (Table 15.1). These new dates have at least partially resolved the chronological problem: by eliminating the three *surface* samples (i.e., those taken in 1981) as contaminated, a remarkably consistent series of 12 dates is obtained from the *buried* specimens, providing a weighted average of 8080 ± 35 BC (uncalibrated).[2]

After the 1987 season, the controversy surrounding the site became more pronounced. There were several who felt that the test excavations did not clearly establish an association between the faunal remains and the artifacts, and that I was being precipitous in claiming this to be the case. Certainly, there are numerous variables to consider in dealing with a situation like this, and my colleagues and I attempted to examine objectively every scenario that would *not* indicate such an association. We readily acknowledged the problems of dating bone and shell. We also considered the obvious possibility that a much later human occupation might have been responsible for the cultural remains (i.e., a camp site fortuitously located on top of a Pleistocene bone bed).

Given the novel implications of the site, we also had to consider taphonomic processes that could have accounted for the natural accumulation of the bone. There are at least three scenarios for a non-human accumulation: (1) a natural death site with some considerable temporal duration, (2) accidental falls over the cliffs or into a sinkhole, or (3) a single mass-death site. After analysis of the excavation results, these possibilities can effectively be discounted. Briefly, the bones are far too concentrated to reflect these natural occurrences. Furthermore, the lack of lateral spreading of bones along the cliff faces precludes an accretional-death site, whereas the lack of vertical spreading precludes a mass-death site. Additionally, the geology of the Akrotiri Peninsula is not conducive to sinkhole formation (Bear and Morel 1960, Mandel 1987). The lateral and vertical concentration of bones at Akrotiri-Aetokremnos cannot be attributed to any combination of natural pro-

Table 15.1: Radiocarbon dates from Akrotiri-Aetokremnos[a]

Date (B.P.)	Laboratory	Material	Provenience/comments
3,700±60	Pta-3435	bone collagen	surface
6,310±160	Beta-3412	charred bone	surface
8,330±100	Pta-3281	charred bone	surface
9,040±160[b]	TX5976A	bone apatite	N95E88, Level 1/top of Level 2
9,100±790[c]	ISGS 1743	total organics from bone	N95E88, Level 1/top of Level 2
9,240±420[d]	TX5833C	humins fraction[e]	Feature 1, ca. 60 cm. below present ground surface; N98E88/87, Level 2
9,250±150	Pta-3128	charred bone	partially exposed beneath shell layer
9,420±550	TX5976B	bone collagen	N95E88, Level 1/top of Level 2; same sample as TX5976A
9,490±120	TX5833A	bulk organic carbon	Feature 1
10,120±110[f]	Beta-22811	shell	N95E88, Level 2; in dark midden-like matrix containing bone and artifacts below exposed shell layer
10,150±60[g]	SMU-1991	shell	N98E88/87, Level 2; outside of midden area; associated with bone, artifacts, and Feature 1
10,150±130	TX5833B	humic acid fraction[h]	Feature 1
10,280±100[i]	Pta-3322	shell	exposed shell layer
10,310±100[i]	Pta-3112	shell	exposed shell layer
10,340±130[f]	Beta-28795	shell	N98E89, Level 2
10,840±270[j]	Beta-40655	charcoal	N96E90, Level 2B
11,720±240[k]	Beta-40380	charcoal	N97E89, Level 2, Feature 11

a. All the Pta dates, as well as Beta-3412, were obtained prior to the 1987 test excavations, thus exact provenience information is not known. The exposed surface specimens are likely to have been contaminated due to their long exposure; this may well account for the wide range in dates. All of the bone dates presented here are from pygmy hippopotamus. All dates except Beta-3412 are ^{13}C adjusted.

cesses. There is no evidence for major water transport; and carnivores, which could have created such a deposit, are absent on Cyprus. Moreover, the presence of abundant burnt bone indicates cultural deposition.

With these considerations in mind, and with the results of the 1987 excavations indicating a strong likelihood (if not a thoroughly convincing case) for the association of cultural materials with extinct fauna, a more comprehensive, but still limited, excavation was undertaken over four weeks in 1988 (Simmons et al. n.d., Simmons 1989). These investigations confirmed the earlier findings. An additional 23 m² were excavated (although not all units were excavated to sterile), and indicated that the midden deposit extended over an area of (minimally) 30 m². The 1988 excavations also documented at least two separate cultural and fauna-bearing occupations, again toward the back of the shelter (Figure 15.2). These are stratigraphically separated by a sterile sand layer, although this separation disappears toward the front of the

---

b. This date is from 7 pygmy hippopotamus bone fragments from the same excavation unit and level.

c. As with TX 5976, this date also is from 7 pygmy hippopotamus bone fragments. These are from the same excavation unit and level as were the TX 5976 specimens. The large sigma is due to the small amount of total organics, including collagen, present in the sample (0.2 grams from a total sample weight of 400 grams).

d. All three TX5833 dates are from the soil matrix of Feature 1.

e. The humins fraction is a very small sample consisting of the insoluble humate fraction.

f. There is some question as to how many years need to be subtracted from shell dates to account for the "reservoir effect," which is an estimated correction for surface ocean water contamination; 400 years frequently is used (Vogel and Visser 1981); Stuiver et al. (1986) marine calibration curve allows calibrations up to about 8500 B.P. The local ¹⁴C correction, which compensates for upwelling and evaporation effects, has only one point listed for the Mediterranean Sea, off the coast of Algeria. With this information, a calibrated age of 690 years older than the ¹⁴C age is calculated by Stuiver's calibration program and speculative studies for ages beyond the established calibration curve indicate corrections of the same size or larger of 10,000 years B.P. (H. Hass, Southern Methodist University Radiocarbon Laboratory, personal communication). Accordingly, all of the shell dates presented here have had 690 years subtracted from the ¹⁴C age. It should be realized that this correction is an estimate.

g. See note f.

h. The greater age of this sample compared to the other TX5833 specimens may be due to the presence of old carbon in the humic acid fraction.

i. Both of these dates are from the same specimen; inner and outer fractions; also, see note f.

j. This sample is from a composite of three separate small samples, all collected from the same quadrant and at the same elevation. Due to the small size, the sample only received an acid wash in pre-treatment. An extended count was used in processing to minimize the standard deviation.

k. This sample is from a "casual hearth"; the sample was very small, with only 0.53 g of pure charcoal present. Due to the small size, the sample only received an acid wash in pre-treatment. An extended count was used in processing to minimize the standard deviation.

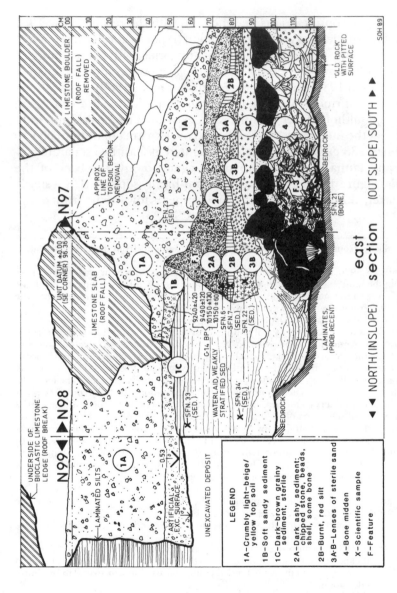

FIGURE 15.2. Akrotiri-Aetokremnos: stratigraphic section of the east face of Units N 99-98-97/E 87-88, showing the two cultural strata (Levels 2, 4).

shelter where mixing has reworked the cultural deposits into a single archaeological unit ca. 50 cm thick. This latter was the midden deposit identified during the 1987 test excavations.

The artifact assemblage has been augmented considerably, with an assemblage size of over 1,000 chipped stone artifacts (Table 15.2). Significantly, the presence of thumbnail scrapers now seems to be a diagnostic of what we have labeled the "Akrotiri Phase." Additional tools include burins, notches, and continuously retouched pieces. This assemblage has no documented counterparts in Cyprus, and is not immediately comparable to other Mediterranean or Near Eastern assemblages. Other artifacts include numerous shell and serpentine beads (over 50 individual items), some worked igneous pieces that might have been ground, and two hammerstones. Over 75 percent of the chipped stone assemblage comes from subsurface contexts. We also can now identify twelve features. Ten of these are hearths or casual hearths, while one is a shell concentration and the other an extensive concentration of burned bone.

In addition to the artifacts, well-preserved faunal remains are abundant. Akrotiri-Aetokremnos has produced an enormous quantity of animal bones and shell, especially when the limited area surface collected and excavated is taken into account. Over 250,000 bones (including undiagnostic fragments) have been recovered. Some of the bone is encrusted with calcium carbonate while much appears to be as "fresh" as modern bone. Over 95 percent is referable to *Phanourios;* the pygmy hippo is represented by all body parts. An estimated 200 individuals are present; all ages from fetal to very old individuals are found. Many limb bones are complete, and a number of skulls are restorable. Specific areas of the midden produced abnormally large numbers of cranial remains, vertebrae, and ribs. Very few pieces are articulated. Numerous bones are burnt, although they are not in a majority; burnt bone is represented by all body parts, including skulls and foot bones. Definitely butchered bones have not been positively identified. The lack of cut marks does not concern us greatly. A scarcity of cut marks is frequent in many assemblages, since soft tissues often shield bones from being incised (Shipman and Rose 1983:86). This may be especially true on an animal with as much meat and fat as a pygmy hippo, particularly if it was not butchered efficiently or thoroughly—a possible scenario since the supply was apparently abundant. All this evidence indicates differential discard of these parts rather than a natural "die site" or deposition by natural causes.

Pygmy elephant is rare at Akrotiri-Aetokremnos; this, as noted previously, is a common pattern at other, non-cultural fossil sites. There are, however, remains of at least three subadult individuals repre-

TABLE 15.2: Chipped Stone Assemblage Recovered from Akrotiri-Aetokremnos

Class	Surface	Subsurface (Levels 1-4)	Total N	%	R%[a]
Tools					
Scrapers					
Thumbnail scrapers	4	32	36		28.1
Side scrapers		8	8		6.3
End scrapers		3	3		2.3
Scraper/plane	1		1		0.8
Scraper/knife		1	1		0.8
Burins	2	17	19		14.8
Backed pieces		2	2		1.6
Truncations		3	3		2.3
Unifaces		2	2		1.6
Pièce esquillée		1	1		0.8
Notches		3	3		2.3
Axe	1		1		0.8
Retouched blades	1	15	16		12.5
Retouched flakes	4	18	22		17.2
Microliths					
trapezoid		1	1		0.8
truncation		1	1		0.8
lunate		1	1		0.8
retouched bladelets		3	3		2.3
Subtotal			128	12.6	100.0
Debitage					
Core trimming elements		4	4		
Core tablet		1	1		
Cortical flakes	2	10	12		
Secondary flakes	13	65	78		
Tertiary flakes	17	148	165		
Secondary blades		12	12		
Tertiary blades	8	56	64		
Bladelets		42	42		
Subtotal			378	37.3	
Burin spalls		16	16	1.6	
Microflakes	8	168	176	17.4	
Debris	15	280	295	29.1	
Cores	3	18	21	2.1	
Total			1014	100.0	

[a]R% refers to tools only

sented. A variety of birds are also present in small numbers, including great bustard, geese, and dove (Mourer-Chauviré 1989). Some of these are also burnt. All bird bones have a similar color and matrix when compared with the associated hippo bones. Six samples of eggshell have also been found, and one example of a tortoise carapace. The most common marine invertebrates present are topshells (*Monodonta turbinata*), followed by limpets (*Patella spp.*), both generally broken and frequently burnt. Rarer are marine crabs and sea urchins. All these forms suggest collection from shallow waters on a rocky shore. Some marine shells were used as beads.

In summary, the excavations at Akrotiri-Aetokremnos have demonstrated that: (1) it is unequivocally an archaeological site; (2) the association of extinct Pleistocene fauna, notably pygmy hippo and elephant, with cultural material seems apparent; (3) far more intact deposits are preserved than initially thought; and (4) a distinctive stone tool assemblage, dominated by thumbnail scrapers, is present. We presently have a general idea of the composition of the site, but, until final analysis is completed, our knowledge of its exact configuration and function remains unclear. Based on currently available information, Akrotiri-Aetokremnos might have functioned as (1) a kill and butchering site; (2) a dwelling site where carcasses obtained elsewhere were brought in and processed; (3) a camp established at a kill site, where a full range of activities pertaining to butchering, processing, and domestic tasks occurred; or (4) a bone "cache." The large number of individual animals present further suggests that they might have been killed by being run over the cliffs in some sort of "hippo drive," as comical an image as that scenario might conjure up. Confirmation of this, of course, will require additional analyses.

The Implications of Akrotiri-Aetokremnos for Mediterranean Prehistory: Paradigms Versus Facts

Akrotiri-Aetokremnos's significance transcends Cypriot, and even Mediterranean, archaeology. The site has produced intriguing evidence relevant to a variety of contemporary archaeological, paleontological, ecological, and biogeographic research issues. Man's adaptations to insular environments are a topic of considerable recent interest (cf. Sondaar 1988), and Akrotiri-Aetokremnos promises to stimulate discussion on how and when humans first colonized the Mediterranean and the effects of this colonization on the endemic fauna and flora.

One of the most tantalizing aspects of Akrotiri-Aetokremnos is the light it sheds on Pleistocene extinction processes. As noted earlier, both pygmy hippos and elephants were believed to have been extinct prior to the arrival of man in the Mediterranean. Akrotiri-Aetokremnos has shown that this was not the case, at least for Cyprus. There have been claims for human associations with extinct fauna elsewhere in the Mediterranean, especially on Mallorca and Sardinia (Arca et al. 1982, Burleigh and Clutton-Brock 1980, Sondaar et al. 1984, 1986; Sondaar 1986, 1987; Spoor and Sondaar 1986), but in many cases, these are tenuous, and, where well documented, involved later, Neolithic populations. There are, of course, other examples of more recent extinctions of endemic island fauna by colonizing human groups, such as the moa bird in New Zealand (Anderson 1989). What Akrotiri-Aetokremnos does, however, is to provide a time depth to extinction processes and events set against the backdrop of late Pleistocene/early Holocene climatic change.

The presence of pygmy hippos and elephants with cultural remains at Akrotiri-Aetokremnos represents one of the best documented cases of this association. The *nature* of this relationship, however, is presently unclear, but the role of man in the extinction of these species must be re-evaluated. These extinctions almost certainly involved a complex interaction of both human and natural agencies, including man's impact on the supporting environment (cf. Sondaar 1987, Burney et al. 1988). Clearly, excavation of one site will *not* support (or refute) a model of Pleistocene overkill, but it will certainly add to the limited data base and support Martin's (1984:391) claim that the " . . . Mediterranean islands appear to be especially strategic places to study extinction as well as evolution of insular forms." It may be that pygmy hippos were already on the verge of extinction in Cyprus (cf. Sondaar 1986) and that man's presence accelerated this process. The introduction of competing animal species by man might also have been a variable. In any event, it is likely that hippos, a "naïve" fauna unused to any predators, would have been easy prey for human hunters.

Another significant aspect of Akrotiri-Aetokremnos is its chronology. Based on the presently available dates, the site is important for models of the initial colonization of Cyprus and subsequent cultural development. It also has wider implications for island settlement and would contradict the relatively late colonization model for the eastern Mediterranean posited by Cherry (1981). A late Epipaleolithic or "proto-Neolithic" interval might be appropriate. Such a development has not been documented previously on Cyprus, and the presence of a proto-Neolithic could help to explain the relatively "developed" and apparently sudden initial appearance of the Khirokitia aceramic culture.

While it is of interest that the site represents one of the earliest colonizations of a Mediterranean island, the dates alone are not its most significant feature. Of greater importance is the capability of apparently pre-Neolithic groups to settle an island that has a relatively low biomass. Consensus opinion has held that the Mediterranean Islands are too impoverished to have supported long term hunter-gatherer occupation (Cherry 1981, Evans 1973, 1977). Akrotiri-Aetokremnos appears to argue against this *unless* its inhabitants were, in fact, members of Neolithic groups. If this were the case, Akrotiri-Aetokremnos would push back the Neolithic on Cyprus by some 2,000 years. At this point, however, there is no evidence whatsoever to link Akrotiri-Aetokremnos with the Cypriot Neolithic in terms of artifacts, site configuration, or chronology. It is possibly significant, however, that at about this time the surrounding circum-Mediterranean mainland was experiencing the so-called "Neolithic Revolution," and there is no reason why the inhabitants of Akrotiri-Aetokremnos could not have had knowledge of Neolithic economies.

Akrotiri-Aetokremnos also constitutes one of the earliest documented cases of sea travel in the Mediterranean, although seafaring ability is assumed to have existed ca. 50,000 years ago, when man first made his entry into Australia (Glover 1973, Mulvaney 1975:144–147, White and O'Connell 1982:42–50). In any case, Akrotiri-Aetokremnos is not the oldest evidence of seafaring in the Mediterranean. That distinction belongs to Franchti Cave on the Argolid of Greece, where obsidian in stratigraphic context dating to ca. 10,000 B.C. has been traced to the Island of Melos, in the Cyclades, some 150 km distant (Jacobsen 1976, Perles 1979).

Associated with the colonization issue is the distinction that Cherry (1981:45–64) makes between actual colonization of an island, resulting in permanent settlement and potential "founder populations," and mere utilization of an island's resources on a temporary or seasonal basis. He notes that "colonization" is a potentially misleading term, since it implies well-planned expeditions by groups intending to establish a permanent base. A more realistic perspective, in his view, sees early Mediterranean seafaring as "many, tentative, impermanent, short-distance reciprocal movements by mere handfuls of individuals . . ." (Cherry 1981:60). Such groups, he continues, would in all likelihood have produced ephemeral, low-visibility sites, if indeed they could be archaeologically detected at all. Akrotiri-Aetokremnos's limited visible surface remains fit well into this scenario.

Another significant issue is related to site function. Previous archaeological research on Cyprus has concentrated on habitation sites, resulting in a research bias that scarcely recognizes the existence of specialized or limited-activity sites. Akrotiri-Aetokremnos appears to represent just such a site, perhaps the first one identified on the Island. Its study has added dimension to our understanding of economic diversity in early Cyprus.

Finally, archaeological considerations notwithstanding, there is no doubt that Akrotiri-Aetokremnos is an extremely significant paleontological resource. Most instances of pygmy hippos and elephant in Cyprus (and elsewhere) consist of deposits of often-poorly preserved fossilized bone with limited depth. At Akrotiri-Aetokremnos, approximately half a meter of "intact" bone is present. In summary, Akrotiri-Aetokremnos appears to be the earliest site known on Cyprus, representing a site type previously unrecognized on the island. It seems very likely that pygmy hippos were indeed exploited by prehistoric man there. Whether or not these animals became extinct because of the effects of human predation cannot be determined on the basis of excavation of any single site, but the implications are intriguing. Research at Akrotiri-Aetokremnos represents a significant contribution to Mediterranean prehistory. On a global scale, it also is important to the study of Pleistocene extinctions.

Discussion

More research is required at Akrotiri-Aetokremnos to obtain a better understanding of the full significance of the site. It is, nonetheless, clear that the site has tremendous implications for the colonization issue, for a variety of problems in island biogeography, and for the existing "Neolithic colonization" paradigm. Realizing this, how did Akrotiri-Aetokremnos fit into the way prehistoric archaeology is viewed on Cyprus? Not well, I am afraid. The remainder of this essay will discuss the professional reaction to the site, and by doing so will examine some of the biases in the paradigms that govern Cypriot (and by extension, Mediterranean Island) archaeological research.

Despite meeting papers, public lectures and publications (Simmons 1988a, b, 1989), the work at Akrotiri-Aetokremnos has met with considerable skepticism. This is not an unforeseen reaction given the initial lackluster impression of the site. Skepticism is healthy in archaeology, and the initial rejection of the suggestion that Akrotiri-Aetokremnos might be the oldest site on Cyprus, while not appreciated, was probably deserved. Prior to our investigations, the site simply was not a convincing example of anything beyond a bone bed with some problematic artifact associations. It posed some interesting possibilities, but lacked secure documentation. What I found surprising, however, was the general unwillingness even to consider the possibility that Akrotiri-Aetokremnos could be what it appeared to be. To understand this reluctance, one must examine the background of early prehistoric research in Cyprus. Prior to the discovery of Site E, the consensus view was that the earliest convincing materials were prepottery Neolithic, dated to about 6,000 B.C. Relatively few Cypriot archeologists work with Neolithic materials, however, preferring to concentrate on the later remains of classical antiquity. Thus, there is little general appreciation of the value of Neolithic research compared to those regions (e.g., the Levant) that have a longer tradition of prehistoric research.

As noted earlier, there have been a few claims for paleolithic materials on Cyprus. By and large, however, these claims have *not* been made by members of the "Cyprus Club," having originated instead with part-time amateur archaeologists or with relative newcomers to the Island. They do not come from the mainstream group of professional archaeologists working on Cyprus. I attribute the reluctance of the Cypriot archaeological establishment to accept Akrotiri as a credible archaeological site to this latter fact. I was a newcomer to the Island (but not to Near Eastern archaeology), and that may have caused some Cypriot researchers to be even more skeptical of the site than they might otherwise have been.

Furthermore, since previous claims for early materials on Cyprus have not stood up to critical scrutiny, the initial, skeptical reaction to Akrotiri-Aetokremnos was understandable. Even after the excavations, however, there were still those who were unwilling to consider the possibility that Akrotiri-Aetokremnos could be a genuine pre-Neolithic archaeological site. Particularly intransigent were the French who, perhaps not coincidentally, have been working for years at one of the earliest sites on the Island, the aceramic Neolithic village of Khirokitia.

It is not my intention here to examine the paradigmatic and methodological differences that govern French and Anglo-American archaeology. Suffice it to say that there are substantial differences in how archaeological remains are perceived and what they are thought to represent (see Clark, this volume). There is, of course, no "right or wrong" way to do archaeology, and, in my opinion, linking disciplinary biases to national research traditions explains relatively little (cf. Binford and Sabloff 1982). However, the fact remains that some metaphysical differences do exist that cleave along national lines; and they cannot be ignored, for they affect the way that archaeology is conducted and interpreted (Clark 1989a, b).

Why this unwillingness to accept something apparently novel yet well documented? One reason, I believe, is that small, limited activity sites simply do not exist as conceptual categories in early Cypriot archaeology. In consequence, they have not been dealt with on Cyprus in any satisfactory way. There is an unfamiliarity with the kinds of information that can be gleaned from sites that do not, for example, contain architecture. In just about any other context, I think there would be little question that Akrotiri-Aetokremnos has a substantial "cultural" component. Its *interpretation* (what it "means" behaviorally) is open to question, but that is another issue. While I regard it as a credible archaeological site, I remain open to the possibility that I am wrong in my interpretation, and that the constellations of modified bone, artifacts, and early dates could conceivably be "explained away" in some mysterious fashion. But, by standard canons of evidence in use in American archaeology, the results of the excavations have provided more than adequate cause for the site to be accepted as a legitimate, primarily "cultural" occurrence.

Most of the controversy about Akrotiri-Aetokremnos relates to its claimed antiquity. In Cyprus, there is a marked disinclination to place much faith in chronologies based on radiocarbon dates (see also Leroi-Gourhan 1986). We all know that radiometric techniques are not perfected, but if one acknowledges their limitations they are extremely useful dating tools. From my point of view, this is a somewhat amusing attitude to take for a group that relies strongly on less robust forms of dating, such as ceramic seriations or the styles of hairdos on templeboy statues. Certainly the first dates from Akrotiri-Aetokremnos were suspicious, but the amazing consistency of the dates from buried and sealed contexts should have been convincing to even the most hardened skeptic.

Even among those who are intrigued by the site, and who regard it as more or less credible, there seems to be developing a rather unfortunate tendency to view it as "paleolithic." By examining the dates, to call Akrotiri-Aetokremnos "paleolithic" is stretching things considerably. Using mainland Levantine terms, it would probably be considered proto-Neolithic, or late Epipaleolithic, possibly contemporary with the later Natufian. Related to this "Paleolithic Perception" was the initial requirement, imposed by the Cypriot Department of Antiquities, that the excavation have on staff as a consultant a "real paleolithic archaeologist," whatever that is. In other words, despite more than fifteen years of working with Neolithic and earlier materials in the Near East, I was not considered to be a legitimate paleolithic specialist. What this "means" is that I had not worked with "classic" European paleolithic cave sites, a telling comment on the French influence on paradigmatic biases in Mediterranean research.

What I find more intriguing than the site's antiquity is the association of an extinct Pleistocene fauna with cultural materials. Surprisingly, this has not generated as much controversy as the dates, which indicates the general conservatism afflicting much of Mediterranean archaeology. Yet the association has tremendous implications. Consensus opinion has it that the first Cypriots were full-fledged herder/agriculturalists, possessing both domesticated plants and animals. However, for me, at least, the idea of fledgling Neolithic seafarers transporting both domestic *and wild* (e.g., deer) animals on Neolithic "Arks" requires a considerable leap of faith (cf. Le Brun 1984). Certainly Akrotiri-Aetokremnos indicates that there was another, non-domestic, economic focus on early Cyprus. Furthermore, the site is one of the few instances in the island archaeological record where we appear to have a good association of cultural materials with extinct vertebrate fauna at the time of their extinction. Although I personally have remained skeptical of a general human role in Pleistocene extinctions, Akrotiri-Aetokremnos is a case in which the human element might have been particularly important and which, for that reason, deserves particularly careful scrutiny.

Acknowledgments

Individuals too numerous to mention have contributed to the success of the Akrotiri-Aetokremnos project. I would, however, like to single out several. First, Dr. Vassos Karageorghis, former director of the Cyprus Department of Antiquities, is to be thanked for his cautious, yet entirely reasonable, support of the project. A. Papageorghiou, present director of the Department, has continued support. Dr. Stuart Swiny, Director of the Cyprus American Archaeological Research Institute (CAARI) in Nicosia deserves special mention for his tireless efforts to try to get someone to investigate the site. CAARI's support of the project greatly facilitated both field and laboratory phases. My profound thanks to all those individuals who volunteered their time on the project. These include Bonnie Bazemore, Geoffrey Clark, Susan Dolczal, William Farrand, Alexandra and Steve Held, Susan Horne, Gerald Hemmings, Rolfe Mandel, Deborah Olszewski, Catherine Perles, David Reese, the Swiny Family, and many others. Special thanks go to Corporal Gavin Muir and Sergeant Phil Simkin of the Royal Air Force for their tremendous logistical and other support. Several other members of the Royal Air Force-Akrotiri base made the project a delight. I also wish to acknowledge the support of the radiocarbon labs that have cooperated with the project. Finally, I owe a considerable debt of gratitude to the numerous, and sometimes critical, archaeologists working on Cyprus who gave freely of their opinions. I did not always agree with them, but they all kept us thinking. The project was sponsored by the American Schools of Oriental Research with principal funding by the National Geographic Society and the National Science Foundation. Supplemental funding was provided by a grant to the Desert Research Institute by the National Science Foundation's Experimental Program to Stimulate Research (EPSCoR), by the Leakey Foundation, by the Lindley Foundation, and by the Desert Research Institute.

Notes

1. Since the original draft of this manuscript was prepared, another, more comprehensive excavation season was undertaken during the summer of 1990. To incorporate most of the data from that season, which still are under analysis, would have required major revisions to the present paper, and publication schedules did not allow this. I have, however, included some of the more significant findings in the present work (e.g., updating the radiocarbon dates, artifacts, features, bones). The weighted average of radiocarbon dates presented in the text includes the newest dates obtained from the site.

2. In an effort to obtain more geochemically defensible dates, we attempted isotopic analysis on multiple individual amino acids, instead of total collagen residues (Belloumini and Bada 1985, Stafford et al. 1988). The first step in such an analysis is to test for nitrogen content, which is indicative of the state of preservation of the amino acids. Unfortunately, on the samples submitted to Dr. T. Stafford, the nitrogen content was too low to warrant further analysis. However, I am still confident of the suite of dates presently available, since the context and the *patterns* revealed by radiocarbon determination on widely different materials (e.g., bone, shell, and soil) are strikingly consistent. Certainly clarification of the chronological situation remains a priority in future studies, but the number of dates already available far exceeds what is usually considered adequate for dating an archaeological context.

Part IV: Paradigms for Levantine Epipaleolithic Research

Chapter 16
Paradigms and Politics in the Terminal Pleistocene Archaeology of the Levant

Steven A. Rosen

Introduction

In the past 25 years, the Terminal Pleistocene cultures of the Levant have been the focus of intensive research which has resulted in the systematic survey, collection, and excavation of hundreds of sites. This wealth of new data, along with new analytic tools and methods, has brought about continual refinement in the scale at which we can document these adaptations. Recent syntheses have been able to suggest, if not demonstrate, the isolation of groups on the level of individual tribes (*sensu lato*), or even subtribes, in very restricted time periods. Convincing models of group seasonal movement, cultural successions, and environmental change and its resulting human adaptations have been presented. In short, the achievements have been impressive.

The debates and arguments engendered during the course of this work have concentrated on the details of the prehistoric record. Although discussions of substantive issues such as the origins of agriculture, the interpretation of seasonality, or the nature of relationships between different cultures and complexes have been lively, few have addressed questions concerned primarily with differences at the level of paradigm. Biases stemming from the political polarities of the region also affect our interpretations, even if on an apparently subconscious level. Some might claim that such questions are peripheral to the fundamental concerns of prehistoric archaeology, and that hypotheses and models can be evaluated on the strength of the data alone. However, this ignores the issue, for any evaluator cannot fail to be biased by perceptions external to the particulars of the archaeological record.

It could be claimed that prehistory is a more subtle discipline in respect of biases than other branches of archaeology. The stress on "objective" methodologies serves the valuable purpose of culling out the cruder manifestations of political and personal bias. The scale of bias evident in segments of South African archaeology (Hall 1984), nineteenth-century Palestinian archaeology (Silberman 1982), and the archaeologies of Mexico, England, and China (Fowler 1987) is too extreme to serve as a model for the Levantine Epipaleolithic. From the perspectives of Marxist or "radical" critiques (e.g., Leone et al. 1987), Levantine prehistoric archaeology is too far removed in time, and too esoteric a discipline (especially as practiced by some workers), to play an active role in fashioning trends of thought among the non-archaeological public. There are, for example, only some 100 members of the Israel Prehistoric Society, whose only active functions are a yearly convention and the publication of the journal *Mitekufat Haeven* (total circulation ca. 300). In contrast, the circulation of *The Biblical Archaeology Review* is greater than 100,000.

Our biases are more in the realms of geographical interpretations, emphases on particular data sets, and in the semantic nuances of professional jargon. In some ways, these "minor" tendencies are more problematic than the cruder cases mentioned above since they are not so obvious. The definition of discrete industries along a modern national border, when it coincides with an apparently geographic one, may be legitimate. The characterization of a specific region as a "culture core" area, and outlying regions as "peripheral," might be justifiable. However, in both cases we must pause to consider the authors' assumptions in their definitions and characterizations, and then consider our own in evaluating theirs. The data themselves are only rarely unambiguous.

The analysis of these perceptions can be undertaken on two distinct levels. On a more active level, we are all products of particular intellectual traditions, or schools of thought, bringing specific analytic tools and perspectives to bear on the data sets we are investigating. Evaluating these different approaches is not particularly difficult. We can easily distinguish a culture-ecologist from a typologist from a structuralist, or comprehend when a researcher has combined several of these approaches. This level could be labeled that of the "scientific paradigm." Although some archaeologists would claim that specific approaches (even specific paradigms) are inherently unsatisfactory (e.g., Binford 1962, Hodder 1986, Watson et al. 1971), this dissatisfaction is often evident only to one side of the polemic. In my opinion, most approaches are complementary rather than exclusive.

The second level is more passive. Our interpretations are unconsciously guided by events and perceptions external to the study of prehistory. The mere fact that we tend to view prehistory as external to the present reflects the contrast that exists between prehistory and historic archaeology in the Levant. The archaeology of the Israelite or Islamic periods, or even the Canaanite period, can hardly be defined as external when national myths are built on perceptions of those periods. By contrast, in prehistory biases are more likely to consist, for example, of implicit assumptions regarding the open or closed nature of a system, more reflective of modern situations and bearing little relation to the past. This is especially true when access to primary materials might be restricted for reasons of modern national politics. In many places, especially in the Americas, this contrast between the historic and the prehistoric seems to be much less evident. Explanation of the development of this schism (which roughly divides in the Levant at the Chalcolithic, ca. 4000 B.C.) is beyond the scope of this paper, but clearly resulted from different stimuli at the historical origins of the subdisciplines (cf. Glock 1985, Rosen 1983:1–10, Bar-Yosef 1980). Furthermore, the scientific paradigm adopted might be tied implicitly to political perspectives. For the later periods, it is not difficult to pick out the relationship between the culture-historic approach and the generation of national myth, even if most archaeologists are themselves not particularly interested in this connection. Sources of funding are often more explicit in their philosophies and biases.

In prehistoric archaeology, there is often an unconscious conflict between schools of thought, which on a deeper level may reflect political or ideological subdivisions. The celebrated Bordes (1967)–Semenov (1970) exchange certainly reflected national ideologies as well as scientific outlooks. Binford and Binford's (1966) early functionalist interpretations of the Mousterian facies can also be viewed as reflecting dominant American utilitarian (and anti-culturist) ideologies. Much of the archaeological concern with demography and ecology in America can be traced more or less directly to larger trends in American society. In Israel, some of these conflicts can also be viewed against a general background of local-foreign competition, not to mention the ever-present Arab-Israeli conflict.

The interpretation of an individual scholar's motivations is a speculative endeavor, and is not the intent of this chapter. Nor is it my objective to provide a comprehensive review of Levantine Epipaleolithic research (e.g., see Perrot 1968, Bar-Yosef 1980). Instead, I will try to characterize the features of the major research trends, examining them for possible correlations with modern Levantine politics and ideologies. Recognizing such effects, we will perhaps be in a position to better evaluate the prehistoric record.

The Early Framework

Garrod's (Garrod and Bate 1937:113) and Neuville's (1934, 1951:261) early frameworks place the Terminal Pleistocene cultures of the Levant, referred to collectively today as the Epipaleolithic, into two separate categories: the latest Upper Paleolithic (Upper Paleolithic VI) and the Mesolithic (cf. also Rust 1950). For Garrod, the Mesolithic was comprised exclusively of the Natufian (in the Levant), whereas Neuville seems to have incorporated the Khiamian (from the terrace site of El Khiam, in the Jordan Valley) as well, although there is some terminological confusion over his intent (Gopher 1985:2–5). Buzy (1928) also defined the PPNB Tahunian as Mesolithic, but his suggestion was not adopted in later syntheses. These approaches were strictly unilineal and viewed the archaeological record as comprised of a sequence of industries ordered in time, each replacing the previous one. In some cases replacement was seen as gradual and in others, abrupt, reflecting either culture evolutionary change (or perhaps better, techno-evolutionary change) or the influx of new people with different material culture assemblages.

The geological paradigms are clear. Cave sites were more or less the only ones excavated, and they provided the chrono-stratigraphic sequences which were allegedly only partly preserved elsewhere. Cave stratigraphies were gross, and corresponded to large scale geological units. Industries were arrayed in chrono-stratigraphic succession, and artifacts were seen as index fossils of particular industries and layers, not as residues of prehistoric cultural behavior. Geographic variability was neither recognized nor sought, nor were changes in human behavior or adaptation (with the exception of the "quantum leap" that marked the appearance of the Natufian).

The framework established was imported directly from France, even to the point of *nomina* such as Châtelperronian (e.g., Perrot 1968:355), Magdalenian (Buzy 1929), and Aurignacian (Garrod and Bate 1937). Although local names for some industries were also suggested (e.g., Kebaran [Turville-Petre 1932], Atlitian [Garrod and Bate 1937]), scholarship was so weighted toward French paradigms that even as late as 1960, Bordes (1960) suggested that the pre-Mousterian blade industries discovered at Yabrud and Tabūn (later termed Amudian by Jelinek [e.g., 1981]) were chronologically equivalent to the French Aurignacian, and that the entire Levantine sequence was in consequence "retarded." Perrot (1968) and Bordes (1968), as well as Garrod and Neuville, consistently used French artifact terminology with loaded geographic associations in reference to specific tool types (e.g., Gravette points, Châtelperron points, *lamelles Dufour*, etc.). While understandable on a certain level, this terminology served to underscore the "secondary" or "dependent" status of Levantine assemblages with respect to those of western Europe. With European names attached to the retouched tool types, there was a tendency to assume a European origin for the industries as well. Thus, even when Terminal Pleistocene industries were given local names (e.g., Nebekian, Antelian), they often continued to be regarded as adjuncts to the European framework and were seen as equivalents of the latest Upper Paleolithic industries in the West.

The Natufian, however, was recognized from the start as something different and unique (see especially Perrot 1966, 1968), and both Garrod and Neuville realized the significance of the culture for understanding the origins of agriculture. Nevertheless, the European Paleolithic-Mesolithic-Neolithic trinity was so well entrenched that both classified the Natufian as a Mesolithic industry; this despite recognition that the Natufian was a Pleistocene culture and that it represented an adaptation which was to evolve independently (of developments in the Near Eastern uplands) to agriculture. In both of these features it contrasted significantly with the European Mesolithic (cf. Price 1983).

Explaining the pervasive European perspective on Levantine prehistory at this early stage in the history of the field is not difficult. Europeans were doing the first professional archaeological research in the region. The only framework available to them for comparison was the European one. However, in Europe a completely independent, original framework had been developed by the early/mid-nineteenth century (of necessity, since none had really existed before); and one might have expected that the Levantine sequence, which only vaguely resembled the European one, would have very quickly taken on its own distinctive flavor. That was not to be the case, essentially because of historical reasons.

A strong European presence in the Levant was the direct result of the British Mandate in Palestine and the French Mandate in Syria following World War I. In a physical sense, the imposition of a European framework was the result of European political control. It is perhaps expecting too much to think that the prehistorians of the period would have been any more free of Eurocentric perceptions than others of their time. Nevertheless, in evaluating this stage in the history of prehistoric research, it is important to recognize these influences.

Discussion of the inadequacies of the unilineal European framework is beyond the scope of this paper. Even during the earlier stages of research, however, the proliferation of assemblage and industry names that attended each new excavation hinted at a complexity greater than that expressed in the synthetic framework. In Europe as well, the unilineal scheme was early on revised significantly to incorporate facies changes and the notion of parallel phyla (e.g., Peyrony 1932).

The Later Frameworks

The proliferation of research and researchers in the Levant in the 1960s and 1970s, from essentially four countries (France, England, the United States, and Israel), engendered a widening range of approaches to the study of later prehistory. It is correspondingly difficult to characterize this period as reflective of any single scientific framework. Nevertheless, one can trace general directions influenced by different schools of thought. Although there is a risk of oversimplification in identifying a scholar or group of scholars with a particular intellectual "niche," the intent is to be roughly representative. It is not possible to classify precisely most workers in the absence of detailed discussion of their work.

On the most general level, it is important to note that the European bias in terminology and in terms of culture origins has all but disappeared, replaced by a clear comprehension of the independence of local sequences. This is most directly reflected in the adoption of local industrial and cultural designations (e.g., Mushabian, Harifian, Qalkan, Hamran, Ramonian, etc.) and emphasis on local terminologies for retouched pieces (e.g., Kebara point, Harif point, Qalkan point, etc.) even when virtually identical European types have also been defined.

American Perspectives

On a more detailed level, scientific approaches differ in both their objectives and their methodologies. Henry's (1982, 1983, 1985a) work is a good example of research geared toward a particular school of thought—what might be called an "American" perspective. It falls under a broadly defined culture-ecological paradigm, and the overall intent is to improve understanding of the Epipaleolithic sequence by understanding how social and technological changes contributed to adaptation over the long term. In fact, much American work shows a similar emphasis on environment and environmental adaptation (e.g., Marks 1976b, 1977b, 1983b; Clark 1984a, Clark et al. 1987b). This tendency can perhaps be attributed to (1) Binford's (1968) post-Pleistocene adaptations paper, which stimulated a whole new set of hypotheses concerning the origins of agriculture (the roots of which are clearly to be sought in the terminal Pleistocene), and (2) the research stimulated by the Aswan Dam project in Egypt, which Marks (1976a) indicated was a direct influence on his work in the Negev. Phillips (e.g., 1972, 1975) also did much of his early research on Egyptian materials. The influence of Butzer (1975, 1976; Butzer and Hansen 1968) on this perspective, and also on later Levantine studies, is evident.

French Perspectives

In contrast, the French emphasis seems to be more one of description and typo-technological analysis, especially as exemplified in Valla's (1984) research on the Natufian, but also in the works of Hours (1974, 1976; Hours et al. 1973), M. C. Cauvin (1966, Cauvin and Stordeur 1978) on the Neolithic at Mureybet, and Calley (1986) and Lechevallier on the Neolithic (1978). There is also a tendency to be skeptical, if not outright critical, of models espoused by the "new archaeology" (e.g., Valla 1988). The roots of this approach can be traced to the work of Tixier (1963, Tixier et al. 1980) on the North African Epipaleolithic, and more generally to other French typo-technological schools (e.g., and especially Bordes 1961a, de Sonneville-Bordes and Perrot 1954–56, G.E.E.M. 1969, 1972, 1975). In contrast to the American school, whose initial geographical orientation seems to have been toward the southern Levant (Egypt, Israel), French research has been more northerly oriented, toward Syria and Lebanon, although there has certainly been a substantial presence in Israel as well. The reasons for this are probably to be found in historical political connections (i.e., the League of Nations mandates).

British Perspectives

Recent work by British scholars can be divided into two phases. The earlier phase was stimulated by Higgs and the Cambridge Paleoeconomy School (Higgs 1972, 1976, Vita-Finzi and Higgs 1970), especially in conjunction with the work at Nahal Oren and Rakefet (Noy et al. 1973, Legge 1972). This research shows a clear emphasis on paleoeconomy and subsistence (also Saxon 1974, 1975; and for Syria see Moore et al. 1975, Moore 1982). British work in Lebanon (Copeland 1975, Copeland and Hours 1971, Newcomer 1972, Bergman 1987) has focused on materials from the Ksar Akil rockshelter (paradoxically excavated originally by an American expedition [Ewing 1947]) and a few other caves, and has been conducted in collaboration with French researchers (e.g., Tixier 1970). A more recent phase has focused on Jordan's Azraq Basin, but so far has appeared primarily in the form of preliminary reports (e.g., Garrard et al. 1985, 1987; Betts 1982, 1985) and is therefore still difficult to place within a larger scientific framework. Be that as it may, there is a continued emphasis on environmental analysis, perhaps at the expense of the paleoeconomy, and strong parallels with American research.

The current near absence of research in Lebanon needs little explanation. The British exodus from Israel might be a reflection of (and reaction to) the colonial legacy and international politics, but this is difficult to evaluate objectively. A British presence is still evident in neighboring Jordan.

Israeli Perspectives

The origins of the Israeli school are clearly eclectic. Prior to the late 1960s, Stekelis, whose background was Russian, was the only professional (i.e., formally-trained) Israeli prehistorian (although, in fact, he devoted little effort to this period). In terms of "native" Israeli contributions, the works of Noy (1970, Noy and Schick 1973, Yizraeli 1967) in the Negev and of numerous amateurs (e.g., Burian and Friedman 1973, 1975; Olami 1973) provided much of the data later incorporated into surveys and other, more synthetic works. Direct access to the work of amateurs published in Hebrew (especially in *Mitekufat Haeven*, until 1985 published either with English abstracts or in Hebrew only), and the consequent broadening of the data base has been another contribution of the modern Israeli school. When compared to foreign expeditions, easy access to sites and materials has facilitated much Israeli archaeology. Threatened destruction of archaeological remains by the military has also been a major stimulus to work in the country, especially in Sinai (Bar-Yosef and Phillips 1977: foreword) and the Negev (Goring-Morris 1987:9, Rosen 1987). Development of the Negev over the past fifteen years has provided large quantities of new data, mainly from salvage operations (e.g., Goring-Morris and Rosen 1986), and important opportunities to revise, refine, or replace earlier frameworks.

Israeli research on the Terminal Paleolithic entered its modern phase with the doctorate of Ofer Bar-Yosef (1970), whose thesis was the first synthetic systematization of the period. He first detached the Epipaleolithic from the Upper Paleolithic, and incorporated the Natufian as the final Epipaleolithic culture. He then divided the period into cultures and subcultures, which he outlined geographically as well as chronologically, in essence laying to rest all of the unilineal development schemes. His students, especially Goring-Morris (1987) and Gilead (1981), have amplified and refined his approach, and Gilead

(1984) has recently suggested an alternative paradigm which stands in dialectical opposition to that of his mentor.

Modern Borders and Prehistory

The effects of modern world politics are evident in many aspects of our perceptions of prehistory. Many of these effects are subtle and, therefore, can be interpreted in many ways. While some specifics are derived more or less directly from non-political sources, the regional geopolitics are, at one level or another, all-pervasive.

At a most basic level, international political alignments affect who works in Israel and in other Levantine states. While the absence of Israeli scholars in Arab countries comes as no surprise, the French influence is most evident in Syria, Lebanon, and to some extent Israel; the British were initially important in Israel, and more recently in Jordan; and American workers (especially Marks) have had an impact and are now becoming important in Jordan. Although there is some scholarly movement between Jordan and Israel, there is virtually none between Syria and Lebanon, and Israel. The fluid political situation in the Near East makes any kind of one-to-one correspondence between research areal emphases and politics difficult; however, the relatively complementary British, American, and French regions of research emphasis probably reflect underlying political structures and alliances more than anything else. This is even more evident if the Upper Paleolithic and Neolithic are examined as well, and if Lebanon and Syria are viewed as separate spheres. The American presence in Israel and Jordan and its near absence in Syria clearly mirrors the character of foreign relations among these countries. This is also true of later periods (e.g., Chalcolithic, the Bronze and Iron Ages). The immediate practical consequences of these political alignments are that Israeli scholars are effectively limited to the study of their own collections (or those stored in European or American museums) and that researchers working in Syria and Lebanon have no direct access to collections excavated in Israel.

Since different theoretical frameworks and research methods are correlated with different schools of thought associated with different countries, these alignments also have an effect on the type of research conducted in each region. While scientific communication sometimes tends to break down differences in research protocols, physical separation and the antagonistic political stances of these nations also tend to encourage the scientific modalities characteristic of national archaeologies. For example, in their respective articles on the Natufian in the *Préhistoire du Levant* volume (Cauvin and Sanlaville 1981), the Frenchman Valla (1981) cites the American Henry only twice, both in direct reference to Hayonim Cave, and Henry (1981) does not cite Valla at all. M.-C. Cauvin (1981a, b), in an article on the Epipaleolithic (including the Natufian) at el-Kowm and its environs, cites neither Valla nor any of the Epipaleolithic research conducted by Henry (although one of the latter's articles on the Upper Paleolithic is mentioned). The Israeli Bar-Yosef (1981a) is more even-handed; he cites Henry five times, and Valla four. Another example of these "quoting circles" is the Southern Methodist University conference on North Africa and the Levant (Wendorf and Marks 1975). This was a conference dominated by Americans, and the near absence of reports on the northern Levant and Syria by French scholars must at least partially reflect the southern Levantine orientation of much American research.

When working in a specific region, there is an inherent tendency to concentrate only on that region, to the near exclusion of regions perceived as "peripheral." However, the very definition of what constitutes a region is generally dependent on preconceived notions. A research proposal to conduct a regional analysis in effect identifies the region beforehand on the basis of modern perceptions, before the credibility of the notion can be tested against data. Once such assumptions are made, testing them is all the more difficult. Obviously, a major source of this sort of sampling bias is modern political boundaries.

Problems of bias in sampling strategies on the level of regional survey have been discussed by many scholars (e.g., Redman 1982, Flannery 1976, Schiffer et al. 1978, etc.). In the Near East, some of these biases can be linked tentatively to modern borders. The Geometric Kebaran and Mushabian complexes are cases in point. Unlike the Kebaran and Natufian, both initially defined during the British Mandate period by foreigners working in Palestine (Turville-Petre 1932, Garrod 1932b), the Geometric Kebaran was defined in post-1948 Israel by Bar-Yosef (1970, 1975) and the Mushabian in Israel-controlled Sinai, in the context of an American-Israeli project (Bar-Yosef and Phillips 1977, Phillips and Mintz 1977, Bar-Yosef 1981a, b). To that extent, and in contrast to preceding and succeeding cultures, they are distinctively "Israeli" formulations. The definitions of these complexes are fairly robust. The Geometric Kebaran has been identified all over the coastal Levant and Sinai (e.g., Bar-Yosef 1981a, 1986) and in west-central and southern Jordan (MacDonald et al. 1982) and in Syria (M-C. Cauvin 1981a), and the Mushabian over much of the Negev and Sinai (Bar-Yosef 1986, Goring-Morris 1987) and southern Jordan (Henry 1989). Nevertheless, they are conspicuously absent from some areas in Jordan, notably the bleak expanses of the Eastern Desert (but see Cauvin 1981a). Goring-Morris (1987:142) has suggested that Henry's (1982) Hamran industry falls into the general Geometric Kebaran class. Also, plates and data presented in preliminary reports by Garrard et al. (1985, 1987) (especially the microburin index and the relatively high proportion of La Mouillah points and arched-backed bladelets) from surveys in the Azraq Basin (north-central Jordan) show pronounced similarities to Mushabian industries in Sinai (especially UW 14; Goring-Morris [1987:199] indicates that Wadi Jilat 8 shows affinities to the "Nizzanan" [a subdivision of the Mushabian]). However, Garrard does not attribute any of these Epipaleolithic sites to named culture-stratigraphic units. The better-known Geometric Kebaran is almost universally recognized as the precursor to the Natufian (Bar-Yosef 1975a, Henry 1981, Kaufman 1989), and its absence in some of these Jordanian areas is all the more striking given the acknowledged presence of Natufian assemblages in southern Jordan (Henry 1989).

Ascribing this apparently limited distribution of the Geometric Kebaran and Mushabian to the influence of modern political boundaries is clearly somewhat of an oversimplification. Nevertheless, there is no reason to assume that the southern Jordan Rift served as a barrier to these prehistoric cultures, since it clearly did not do so in the succeeding Natufian. In addition, it might be noted that the Arava Valley (Wadi Araba) does not seem to have served as a border in later prehistoric or early historic times. These problems might reflect in part the relatively advanced state of Israeli archaeological research when compared with that of Jordan (Clark 1984a).

The issue of changes in culture areas or territory during the Epipaleolithic has been discussed by Bar-Yosef (1981a, b, 1986), especially in reference to the Mushabian and its relationship to the Geometric Kebaran and the Ramonian (Negev Kebaran) (see also Goring-Morris 1987:253–255, 430–433). Of interest here are its apparent North African affinities (Phillips and Mintz 1977) which Bar-Yosef (1981a, b; 1986, 1987) thinks might indicate a North African geographical origin. Given this, the total absence of detailed comparison with North African industries is striking. A similar absence of comparative research is evident for other cultures and periods as well (e.g., the Upper Paleolithic, Geometric Kebaran), and is even more significant in light of numerous references to the importance of the Levantine land bridge between Africa and Asia in prehistory (e.g., Marks 1976b, Bar-Yosef 1987c).

The Egyptian-Israeli cease-fire line along the Suez Canal provides a possible explanation for these conceptual "blind spots." Although it might be claimed that Egypt along the Nile constitutes a natural geographic unit, this "natural unit" has also tended to incorporate the

Western Desert, the geographic proximity of which cannot be claimed to be greater than that of northern Sinai. In light of the later traditional Egyptian border at El-Arish, the tendency to separate Sinai from Egypt in the Epipaleolithic can be attributed at least partially to the recent history of border disputes.

Beyond imposing artificial limits to the delineation of culture areas, modern boundaries negatively affect the location and interpretation of fieldwork. This is particularly problematic in light of the relative scarcity of Jordanian, Syrian, and Lebanese scholars working in later prehistory. One example of the near absence of fieldwork and its effect on interpretation can be seen in the distribution maps of sites from various Epipaleolithic complexes presented by Bar-Yosef (1981a, b). The dearth of sites in the Central Hills region of Palestine, excluding the Galilee, is telling, since these regions were inaccessible to Israelis from 1948 to 1967 (e.g., Fig. 16.1). Bar-Yosef's distribution maps, based for the most part on his 1970 dissertation, mostly reflect work conducted in Israel from 1948 to 1970, but also include Palestinian sites discovered prior to 1948, such as those investigated by Neuville in the Judean Desert. Exceptions are in the Jordan Valley, where several surveys have been conducted since 1967 by Israelis and foreign collaborators (e.g., Goring-Morris 1980, Bar-Yosef et al. 1974, Schuldenrein and Goldberg 1981, Noy et al. 1980, Hovers and Bar-Yosef 1987). There is still a dearth of research in the central regions. Although it might be claimed that this imbalance in site distributions reflects real settlement patterns or differences in site visibility or preservation, the presence of sites in the highlands of the Galilee, as well as in the Jordan Valley, suggests that this is not the case. Although Bar-Yosef (1981b) has suggested a bipolar, seasonal model for Kebaran transhumance, the skewed nature of the distributional data preclude any empirical tests of general patterns. We simply lack data on the upland regions with which to test the models. This deficiency is clearly related to the perturbing effects of modern borders.

A similar problem arises with models of seasonal movement presented by Vita-Finzi and Higgs (1970) for the Natufian of the Mount Carmel region. Although east-west movement from the Coastal Plain and Carmel range inland to the Galilee uplands was proposed, the distance from Wadi Mughara, or Nahal Oren, southwest to the 1949 armistice line (Green Line) is only some 25 km (Fig. 16.1). Data are available for comparison in the Galilee and Upper Jordan Valley, but are absent from Samaria. No less significant, the 1949 armistice lines "create" an integral unit comprising the Galilee and Carmel, which are, in turn, distinct from areas south of the "Green Line." Figure 16.1 is a distribution map of Epipaleolithic sites according to Bar-Yosef (1981a);

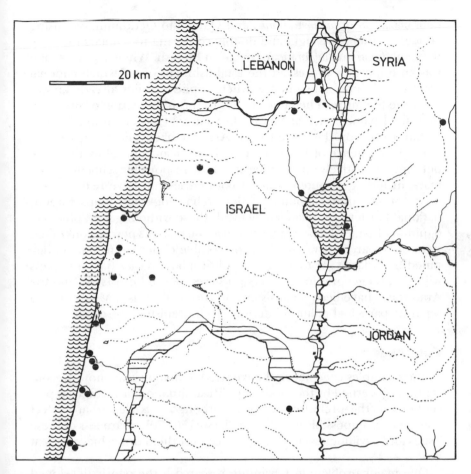

FIGURE 16.1.   Distribution of Epipaleolithic sites (Kebaran through Natufian) in the region of northwestern Jordan, southwestern Syria, northern Israel, and southern Lebanon according to Bar-Yosef (1981a, b). The shaded area indicates the Israeli border security zone prior to 1967, to which access was somewhat restricted. It should be noted that the area within Israel proper (i.e., within the security line) on this map is approximately 4,200 km², in contrast to areas outside, totaling ca. 6,100 km². The difference in site distribution is obvious.

it also includes the 1949 armistice line and Israeli security zone. The effects of these artificial "borders" are clear enough with respect both to site distributions and perceptions of "natural" geographic units. The Syrian border to the east and that of Lebanon to the north have much the same effect.

Another peculiarity of the Near East is the politically motivated renaming of archaeological sites. Two prominent examples are the

hebraicization of *tabūn* to *tanur,* and Qafzeh to Qedumim, confusing
enough in their own right and doubly confusing to scholars unaware
that both *tanur* and *tabūn* mean "oven" in English. While hebraicization
was an important process in the establishment of an Israeli national
identity, it is a dubious practice when applied to sites already known
from the literature. The same applies to the arabicization of sites with
published names, such as Sha'ar Hagolan (el-Qahwaneh in Arabic—
Kafafi 1987). By the same token, Arab archaeological maps which
erase the existence of Israel not only have clear political motivations,
but reflect negatively on the integrity of the responsible scholar.[1] While
maps including disputed political boundaries can have real implications for our understanding of the archaeology and maps without
national borders are relatively neutral, those without geographic recognition of Israel deliberately prejudice the reader's perceptions of the
state of research. It would seem preferable either to include all disputed boundaries, or to delete all political boundaries (i.e., use maps
with natural geographic markers [or cities] only). Both Israel and the
Arab states have been inconsistent on this issue. It is perhaps time to
separate parochial political interests from prehistoric research.

Conclusions

In the examples cited above, I have tried to demonstrate how preconceptions governed by the modern political situation have affected perceptions of the prehistoric record. Although it is clear that perfect
objectivity is impossible (cf. Hodder 1986:156–70), awareness of these
issues and a willingness to attempt to correct them can achieve a great
deal.

One major problem in Levantine research is the poorly developed
state of its systematics. Non-rigorous definitions allow vagueness to
affect our understanding of the range of variability. To a degree this is
unavoidable since, as data accumulate and variability increases, initial
definitions based on more limited samples become inadequate. For
example, Belfer-Cohen (1989) has recently noted that the definition of
the Natufian has tended to become extended to include any industry
with Helwan lunates. She has suggested a more rigorous polythetic
definition, incorporating sets of tool types, architecture, bone tools,
burials, and other components of Natufian culture as known from the
"core area" of Mount Carmel and the Galilee.

Goring-Morris (1987:416–17) has also noted what might be called a
"hierarchical" discrepancy between different entities of the Levantine
Epipaleolithic. For example, the Kebaran is a different order of phenomenon than the Harifian, the Kebaran qualifying, in Clarke's (1968)

terms, as a techno-complex or complex, and the Harifian as a culture. Appropriate comparisons of the two require either (1) comparison of one of the subclusters of the Kebaran with the Harifian, or (2) comparison of the general terminal Natufian/Khiamian/Harifian cluster with the Kebaran. The same might also be said of the Natufian (Goring-Morris 1987). Helwan lunate-bearing assemblages are clearly "related" in some way to the "true" Natufian, but our systematics do not allow explication of that relationship.

The same is true of the Geometric Kebaran. Henry (1982) clearly states that according to some of his parameters, part of the Hamran falls into the Geometric Kebaran, but according to others, it does not. Our current approach to systematics leaves us with very few options—in effect a "yes" or "no" proposition. Thus, explicit definitions of each of these analytical units is not enough. To avoid some of these problems, a "neutral" (i.e., non-Israeli) hierarchical scheme like that proposed by Clarke (1968) might help. At a minimum, technocomplexes and cultures should be terminologically and conceptually differentiated. If, for example, the Harifian is a kind of late Natufian, perhaps this should be denoted as Natufian-Harifian, or, in the manner of biological taxonomic nomenclature, as N. Harifian. Such a system might allow for greater local variability to be expressed terminologically, while still acknowledging the more pan-Levantine aspects of these analytical units. My intent here is not to present a new terminological framework (which I leave to those who know the material far better than I), but to point out the shortcomings of the present system. Its lack of rigor and of a clear-cut hierarchical structure results in an untidy vagueness that can be influenced by irrelevant (especially political) factors. I do not claim that such a framework would solve all scientific problems; however, it might mitigate the effects of some of the problems caused by issues external to the archaeology.

Acknowledgments

I am grateful to O. Bar-Yosef, G. A. Clark, I. Gilead, A. Gopher, A. N. Goring-Morris, and P. de Miroschedji for commenting on this manuscript. I stress again that my intent has only been to raise issues, and not to question the integrity of any scholar. I am, of course, solely responsible for all errors of comprehension and fact.

Note

1. However, it is the policy of many Arab governments not to publish maps which identify Israel as a political state equivalent to other political states in the region.

Chapter 17
Social Complexity in the Natufian? Assessing the Relationship of Ideas and Data

Deborah I. Olszewski

Introduction

Discovered and originally defined from excavation contexts in Palestine in the late 1920s and early 1930s (Garrod 1932a, b, 1942; Garrod and Bate 1937, Neuville 1951, Turville-Petre 1932), the archaeological manifestations of the Natufian "culture" have generated numerous interpretations concerning duration, presence of agriculture, and social organization for these prehistoric hunter-gatherers. Of these issues, only chronological placement has been resolved. Natufian sites range in uncalibrated radiocarbon years from about 12,500 to 10,300/ 10,000 B.P. (Bar-Yosef 1983:13, Henry 1982:437, Henry and Servello 1974:35–36).

As comprehensive summaries of Natufian material culture are available elsewhere in the current literature, interested readers are referred to these sources for an exhaustive treatment (e.g., Bar-Yosef 1970, 1983; Henry 1973a, 1981, 1989; Valla 1975, 1981). Briefly, the Natufian inventory consists of numerous areally small sites and several areally large sites. Characteristic of the large sites are thick occupational deposits, large quantities of chipped stone tools and debitage, numerous ground stone implements including mortars and pestles, as well as querns and handstones, a diversity of bone tools (some of which are carved into animal forms), art in the form of figurines of stone and designs on carved stone bowls, personal ornamentation (dentalium shells, paired gazelle phalanges, bone pendants), numerous burials, pavements, storage facilities, terrace walls, and circular stone-walled "dwellings."

The archaeological record of the Natufian thus presents what many have seen as an important contrast to earlier Levantine Epipaleolithic complexes (Kebaran, Geometric Kebaran, early Mushabian). The material record of this earlier period (19,000 to 12,500 B.P.) is characterized by numerous areally small sites, often with relatively thin occupational deposits, infrequent groundstone implements, little personal ornamentation, and few bone tools (Bar-Yosef 1987b; Henry 1983, 1989). However, it is probably significant that recent excavations have documented the sporadic presence of structures and burials in these earlier complexes. Neve David, a Geometric Kebaran site, is 1000 m² in extent and has yielded a burial and two structures (Kaufman 1986). Other sites with burials include the Kebaran contexts at Ein Gev I (Arensberg and Bar-Yosef 1973, Bar-Yosef 1987b:229), Kharraneh IV (Muhcisen 1985:150), and Kebara, where fragments of burnt bones were found (Bar-Yosef 1987b:229). There are also sites, other than Neve David, with structures, such as the Kebaran context at Ein Gev I (Bar-Yosef 1987b:229), and Geometric Kebaran contexts at Haon (Bar-Yosef 1975a, b) and Ein Gev III (Martin 1978). These occasional occurrences of structures and burials perhaps indicate the beginning of a trend toward intensive reutilization of favored localities.

The richness of the material inventory and the presence of various structures at a handful of Natufian sites has therefore been the focus of several types of explanation. Initial viewpoints saw the Natufian as either settled agriculturalists (Garrod 1957) or, when in environmentally favorable situations, as sedentary hunter-gatherers who collected, but did not cultivate (Perrot 1968). More recently, the notion of sedentism has been employed as a necessary component of a model which ascribes a high degree of social complexity to the Natufian complex (Henry 1981:428, 1983:144, 1985b, 1989). It is with this latter model that this paper is concerned.

Coloring the Paradigm

The important papers of the "Man the Hunter" symposium, and their subsequent publication (Lee and DeVore 1968a), essentially changed the orientation of archaeologists dealing with prehistoric hunter-gatherer groups. It has thus been known for some time that hunter-gatherers are able to spend some portion of their time on activities that are not tied to subsistence. In addition to this, most prehistoric hunter-gatherers probably lived in more amenable environmental situations (either larger quantities, or greater diversity, of certain food resources) than those situations in which modern hunter-gatherers are found.

These basic "facts" of hunter-gatherer life, in conjunction with certain instances of new or unusual features in the archaeological record, have been used in recent research to seek new ways to explain apparent changes in the organization of prehistoric hunter-gatherer groups. The past dozen or so years thus document a thrust in the direction of isolating social complexity in such circumstances (e.g., Albrethsen and Peterson 1976, various articles in Price and Brown 1985, O'Shea and Zvelebil 1984), particularly for the Mesolithic and/or Epipaleolithic periods (but also see Soffer 1985 for a discussion of this approach for the Upper Paleolithic).

Inferring Social Complexity

To initiate any discussion of social complexity, it is necessary to know the connotations carried by this highly loaded concept. On a very elementary level, there is a basic distinction between "socially complex" and "social complexity." The former is a characteristic of all human groups, almost by virtue of the fact that the presence of culture demands complex relationships between individuals and between groups of people (kin-based or otherwise). Few, if any, would argue that prehistoric hunter-gatherers were not socially complex in this sense.

However, social complexity is a beast of another stripe. At the very least, it represents an organizational structure "beyond" egalitarian, most often called ranked or socially stratified society (e.g., Henry 1985b:365, 1989 or Wright 1978:219). Less often, it is classified as somewhere between "egalitarian" and "ranked/stratified," in other words, a societal form that has never been observed ethnographically (e.g., one statement of this position is Soffer 1985:468). But, the implications of the term social complexity do not end with the notion of achieving a social organization that is something more than egalitarian. Social complexity is also intimately associated with population growth/population density, sedentism, storage to accumulate surplus resources for redistribution or trade, establishment of territorial boundaries, and, specifically for the Natufian, the development of matrilineal groups, matrilocal residence, and a "chiefdom" structure (Henry 1983:144, 151, 1985b:375–376, 1989).

These associated terms have, in turn, certain assumptions and implications that structure how the archaeological record is used to support the existence of social complexity. A closer examination of these concepts illustrates the fact that some of these terms are used quite generally, rather than precisely. Since general statements mask variability, the picture of the prehistoric past that emerges may be inaccurately colored. These considerations are used in a later section to assess whether or not the evidence of the Natufian archaeological record supports the model of social complexity for these prehistoric hunter-gatherer groups.

Burial data

The examination of burial data in the prehistoric archaeological record frequently provides evidence that is interpreted as presence of rank or social stratification. Here, rank/stratification is documented by one or more variables involving a large expenditure of energy in the construction of graves, the presence of wealth (either as rare items or as sociotechnic artifacts), or simply by abundance of grave furniture, as well as ascribed status inferred for burials of subadults with the above attributes (Binford 1971, Brown 1981:29, O'Shea 1981:44).

Evidently, rank can be isolated in some instances, as is shown by O'Shea's (1981:49) use of both ethnographic and archaeological sources for mortuary attributes at Pawnee and Arikara cemeteries. Kin-based social divisions (such as clans or moieties) were not recoverable from the archaeological context in this case. The use of burial evidence from strictly archaeological contexts (European Mesolithic), however, seems to indicate that horizontal social differentiation (age, sex, and personal achievement) is somewhat easier to document than the distinction of rank (Clark and Neeley 1987). If vertical differentiation (rank) does appear to be present, one of the interpretive problems is that the different ranks may actually have more to do with changes over time in mortuary behavior than with synchronic ranking (Chapman and Randsborg 1981:13, O'Shea 1981:51–52, Goldstein 1981:56). This is a problem amplified by the fact that the chronological resolution of radiocarbon dating is generally poor in establishing absolute contemporaneity of data sets within particular blocks of time.

Population density

The existence of ranked/stratified social organization is usually also associated with the presence of increased numbers of people, either in the sense of overall population growth or as increased population density at specific archaeological sites. In such situations, ranking is deemed necessary because larger numbers of people create problems in food redistribution and conflict solving that can no longer be adjusted by group fissioning (Henry 1983:144), which is the typical pattern for egalitarian groups (e.g., Lee and DeVore 1968b:9). As Johnson (1982) points out, however, population size is probably not the best measure of scale or scalar stress. In fact, unless a group is territorially circumscribed, responding to stress by group fissioning is common (Johnson 1982:408).

Measuring an increase in overall population or population density in the archaeological record is not an easy task. Most often, this is accomplished for population growth simply by counting the number of known sites for the region and contrasting this number with the number of sites from earlier periods of time, with the assumption that there is a correlation between the number of sites and the number of people present. This approach leaves much to be desired, especially since, in changes in settlement systems over time, a shift from residential mobility to logistical mobility (Binford 1980) or vice versa might produce increased or decreased numbers of sites without any dramatic change in overall population size.

Searching for increased population density avoids some of these problems, but assumes that greater numbers of people are living at certain sites. In the Natufian, increased population density is apparently documented by the appearance of hamlets ("villages"), where part-year to year-round sedentism occurred in a context involving several kin-based groups (Bar-Yosef 1987b:223, Henry 1981:422, although permanency at such types of base camps is not suggested or specified by Bar-Yosef 1983:12).

Base camps

For the Natufian, part of the poor resolution of the question of population density at hamlets has been due to the fact that the term "hamlet" has to some degree been used interchangeably with the term "base camp," which unfortunately has a variety of meanings. There are probably at least two types of base camps, those with structures, burials, and so forth, and those that are characterized simply as thick occupational deposits. This distinction, in fact, has been previously noted by Bar-Yosef (1970, 1983:12), who called these two types "base camps" and "seasonal camps," respectively.

In reality, there may actually be three types of base camps present in the Natufian archaeological record, base camps with dwellings, base camps with burials and/or structures other than dwellings, and base camps as indicated by thick occupational deposits. To subsume these sites, which may not be equivalent in structure, content, or function, under a blanket term such as "hamlet" or "base camp" without using a set of precise definitions, disguises potentially important archaeological information and leads to the description of a Natufian settlement system that is undoubtedly too simplistic.

If the term hamlet is defined as a base camp with dwellings, then the problem of identifying population density (and the assumed need for the development of ranking) is one closely tied to establishing the contemporaneity of the various dwellings, the number of such dwellings at any one time, and the number of people likely to have inhabited a dwelling. As previously discussed, the lack of chronological resolution of radiocarbon dating for short segments of time within a larger period to a large extent precludes the determination of the number of dwellings contemporaneously inhabited. Thus, for example, a hamlet with six dwellings might represent any point along the spectrum from contemporaneous habitation of all six structures to each structure inhabited sequentially over a period of one or several generations. The former would constitute evidence for increased population density over sites from earlier complexes. The latter would demonstrate the reutilization of a favored locality by a group of people and their descendants, but suggests nothing about overall population density. Short of finding conjoinable artifacts from floor contexts of different structures, refining the present radiocarbon dating methodology, or developing new dating techniques, this problem remains insoluble.

Local group size

Determination of the number of people inhabiting a structure or a site at a given time can also be fraught with difficulty. Although various formulas exist, for example, Naroll (1962) or Cook and Heizer (1968), these can often result in quite disparate totals (see, for example, the results of population size estimates calculated using several formulae in Soffer 1985:Table 6.29, 408). In an area such as the Levant, this problem is all the more acute since there are no ethnographically known hunter-gatherers whose environmental situation approximates that of the 12,500–10,000 B.P. interval in the Levant. Using ethnographic models from other areas of the world (e.g., the San of the Kalahari) may suggest certain population patterns. However, the use of ethnographically known hunter-gatherer groups from almost any environmental situation is potentially subject to revealing patterns of behavior that are the results of thousands of years of interaction between hunter-gatherers and other less nomadic groups (see also Mueller-Wille and Dickson, this volume). The resulting patterns may not be behaviors common to prehistoric hunter-gatherers (see, e.g., Denbow 1984 or Schrire 1984 for a discussion of this point).

Despite this, the hamlets of a complex hunter-gatherer group are assumed to indicate larger numbers of people living at such sites (than in earlier Levantine complexes), who supposedly need a controlling superstructure of ranked individuals to settle intragroup disputes and to redistribute surplus food resources. These communities are usually also thought to indicate part- or year-round sedentism. Sedentism in this context is documented by labor and time investment in the construction of dwellings and other structures, such as storage facilities, as well as by seasonality information retrieved through the study of animal bones and macrobotanical remains and, in some cases, the presence of human commensals (e.g., Bar-Yosef 1987b:232).

Storage

Critical to the development of social complexity in such sedentary situations is the potential for intensive storage as opposed to limited storage (Testart 1982). Intensive storage provides a surplus of food reserves that can be redistributed or used for other purposes like exchange (by the higher ranked individuals). However, the mere *presence* of storage facilities is not enough to assume *intensive* storage. Food resources must also have the potential to be accessed in large quantities and be storable for more than a few days or weeks. Natufian hunter-gatherers did have access both to large quantities and to a variety of storable food resources, most notably cereals and nuts (Bar-Yosef 1987b:223, Henry 1981:428). The crucial distinction thus becomes whether the storage facilities represent efforts to alleviate food shortages during the "lean" period of the year, or whether they represent efforts to overproduce or, in this case, to overgather (a point well made by Gould 1985:429–432). If storage facilities are "banks" against periods of the least quantity and variety in food reserves, then there is no need to postulate a redistributive mechanism or any form of tight control over such stored resources. There is also no need to postulate the existence of ranked individuals.

Territoriality

Finally, the use of the term social complexity for prehistoric hunter-gatherer groups can also involve the concept of the control of territories. One method used to suggest the existence of distinct territories controlled by corporate groups is the presence of cemeteries. However, as Goldstein (1981:60–61) points out, not all corporate groups will establish formal, bounded disposal areas. If there is such an area that is used *exclusively* for burial, then it probably constitutes *prima facie* evidence for a corporate group structure. Once again, however, one must be able to determine the sequence of use of an area, since Natufian burials often occur within deposits of occupational debris (e.g., as at el-Wad, Garrod and Bate 1937:14–19).

Another potential way to approach the documentation of territories is through the use of settlement pattern studies. The Natufian system is described as a radial pattern consisting of a residential home base (although the type of base camp is usually not specified) and nonresidential, exploitative satellite camps (Henry 1981:428). If the radial model is an accurate depiction of Natufian settlement/subsistence systems, and given that contemporaneity of home bases and exploitative camps can be demonstrated only in the broadest sense, the settlement patterns visible in the archaeological record may not represent territories in the sense of bounded units. These patterns could be something akin to what Binford (1982b:9) has called "complete-radius leapfrogging," in which, given enough time, one or a few groups are responsible for many/all of the radial patterns in a certain geographical range.

Assessing the Paradigm

Assessing the viability of the social complexity model as a paradigm for the Natufian requires the use of the distinctions previously discussed for the term base camp (hamlet). Here, the term hamlet is restricted to base camps with dwelling structures. In this way, the related connotations of the term social complexity (ranked society, population growth, population density, sedentism, food storage, and the existence of territories) are more easily reviewed, since features that may be related to these aspects are found at hamlets, but not necessarily at other types of base camps.

Hamlets: Base Camps with Dwellings

When hamlets are defined as base camps with dwellings, the number of such sites for the Natufian is quite small (n = 8), especially considering that the Natufian period lasts for at least 2000 years. This sample (Table 17.1) is further reduced when these hamlets are divided into the Early and Late Natufian, a division established on the basis of radiocarbon dates, average length of lunates, and presence/absence of Helwan backing retouch (Bar-Yosef and Valla 1979, Valla 1984). There are only three early hamlets: Ain Mallaha early phase (Perrot 1966, 1974, Valla 1981), Hayonim Cave B (Bar-Yosef and Goren 1973, Bar-Yosef and Tchernov 1966), and Wadi Hammeh 27 (Edwards 1986:224–226, McNicoll et al. 1984), and six late hamlets: 'Ain Rahub (Gebel and Muheisen 1985), Nahal Oren (Noy et al. 1973, Stekelis and Yizracly

1963), Ain Mallaha middle phase (Perrot 1966, 1974, Valla 1981), Hayonim Terrace B (Henry and Leroi-Gourhan 1976, Henry et al. 1981), Rosh Zin (Henry 1973b, 1976), and Rosh Horesha (Marks and Larson 1977). Future excavations will probably increase the number of hamlets for both the early and later periods.

There are two additional sites, Beidha and Jericho, that have been called hamlets (in the sense used here) but are not included in Table 17.1. As originally reported by Kirkbride (1968:264), an irregularly shaped, large pit floored with pebbles was described as a possible dwelling structure at Beidha. Kirkbride (quoted in Byrd 1987:78) has since decided that this pit is a natural feature. The structure at Jericho (Kenyon 1981:268) is more problematic. Described as a rectangular platform of natural clay that is surrounded by massive stones, of which three are pierced to form sockets, this structure is interpreted as a "sanctuary." If the Jericho structure is a dwelling of some sort rather than a "shrine," the different constructional features of this dwelling, compared to the circular stone-walled dwellings from other Natufian hamlets, make Jericho unusual.

Base Camps Without Dwellings

There are also six other sites (Table 17.1) that lack dwelling structures, but have one or more of the following features: burials, terrace walls, and pavements. These are el-Khiam (Neuville 1951), Khallat 'Anaza (Betts 1985:30–32), el-Wad (Garrod and Bate 1937:11–12), Erq el-Ahmar (Neuville 1951), Shukbah (Garrod 1942:5–6), and Kebara (Turville-Petre 1932:271). Since these sites lack dwellings, they are not, at this time, considered to be hamlets. They may or may not be a separate type of base camp. Base camps defined solely by thick occupational deposits and numerous artifacts, e.g., Wadi Judayid J2 (Henry and Turnbull 1985:49) are not examined here in terms of evidence for social complexity.

I want to make the point that these various types of base camps do not necessarily represent different levels in a hierarchy of base camps. Rather, they may document different types of settlement systems that co-existed during the Natufian period, even within the optimal Mediterranean forest environment of the Early Natufian. One model that might be of use here contrasts focal and diffuse adaptations (Cleland 1976). Focal adaptations occur when one or a few similar resources are intensively exploited. These must be high quality, abundant, and consistently available or reliable (i.e., they can be stored). The cereals and nuts of the Mediterranean zone are good candidates for such resources

TABLE 17.1: Natufian Base Camps

	Dwellings	Storage	Burials	Terrace walls	Pavements
Early hamlets					
Ain Mallaha	6–9	3	+	–	–
Wadi Hammeh 27	2	–	+	1	–
Hayonim Cave	3	1	+	–	–
Late hamlets					
Ain Mallaha	9–12	10	+	–	–
'Ain Rahub	2	–	–	–	1
Nahal Oren	1	2–4	+	1	–
Hayonim Terrace B	1?	1	–	1	–
Rosh Zin	4	–	–	–	1
Rosh Horesha	1	–	–	–	–
Other base camps					
el-Khiam	–	–	–	1	–
Erq el-Ahmar	–	–	+	–	1
Kebara	–	–	+	–	–
el-Wad	–	–	+	1	1
Shukbah	–	–	+	–	–
Khallat 'Anaza	–	–	–	2	1

during the Natufian. Focal adaptations can create an archaeological pattern of intensively occupied sites with some degree of permanency (perhaps Natufian hamlets organized in a radial settlement pattern with logistic mobility). Diffuse adaptations, on the other hand, generally result in sites that are extensively occupied, since they are repeatedly visited over many seasons of many years due to their proximity to certain resources. Natufian base camps without dwellings and, more specifically, those characterized by thick occupational debris and numerous artifacts, may represent these diffuse adaptations in a pattern of residential mobility.

Natufian hamlets (Fig. 17.1) from both the early and late periods tend to be concentrated in northern Palestine. With the exception of the late hamlets of Rosh Zin and Rosh Horesha, these sites are found neither throughout the area characterized prehistorically by a Mediterranean forest cover nor outside of this phytogeographic zone. Thus, they appear to be not only distinct in contrast to earlier Epipaleolithic

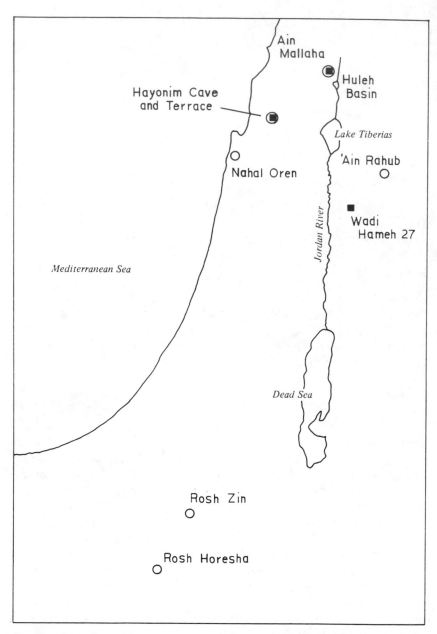

FIGURE 17.1. Natufian hamlets (square = early period, open circle = late period, square + open circle = early and late period occupation).

use of the same area, but also distinct from the rest of the other known Natufian sites (base camps of various sorts or otherwise). This distribution may reflect the fact that logistical mobility (Binford 1980), or a radial settlement pattern (Henry 1981), was possible or desired (Wiessner 1982) only within a very limited geographical region.

Evidence for Social Complexity at Hamlets

The archaeological data from these hamlet sites include many of the features that are often used to suggest the development of social complexity. Although it is difficult to establish year-round sedentism for these hamlets, there is some evidence that suggests that at least some of them were relatively permanent habitation sites. This evidence includes not only the time and energy required to construct the dwellings and other structures, but also the presence of human commensals at Hayonim Cave (Bar-Yosef and Tchernov 1966) and year-round hunting of gazelle at Hayonim Terrace (Davis cited in Bar-Yosef 1987b: 232). Natufian hamlets thus display evidence of the traits that are likely indicators of year-round occupation, such as house form (substantial construction), community planning (linear arrangement at Ain Mallaha, clustered at Rosh Zin), ceremonial structures (the "monolith" at Rosh Zin), heavy artifacts (e.g., ground stone implements), and storage facilities (Rafferty 1985:129–131), although not all of these traits are found at any one hamlet site. As Rafferty (1985:141, 146) points out, however, the development of sedentary communities is not necessarily followed by, or even related to, the development of social complexity.

Sedentism

If hamlets represent sedentary occupations, then one of the key components for the advent of social complexity is probably related to population density at any one hamlet at any one point in time, since control of the actions of greater numbers of people supposedly necessitates a higher level of authority. Based on hamlets with at least 8 percent excavation of the estimated site area, this aspect can be examined at the settlements at Ain Mallaha (Valla 1981), Hayonim Cave (Bar-Yosef and Goren 1973), Wadi Hammeh 27 (Edwards 1986, McNicoll et al. 1984), Nahal Oren (Noy et al. 1973, Stekelis and Yizraely 1963), Hayonim Terrace (Henry and Leroi-Gourhan 1976, Henry et al. 1981), and Rosh Zin (Henry 1973b, 1976). Both Rosh Horesha (Marks and Larson 1977) with less than 1 percent excavated and 'Ain Rahub (Gebel and Muheisen 1985) with only 1 percent excavated, probably have not yielded enough data to be properly assessed at this time.

Number of structures

Of the six hamlets that have greater than 8 percent of the estimated total area excavated, only Ain Mallaha has yielded more than four dwelling structures for any one time period. The absolute number of dwelling structures at hamlet sites thus appears to be quite low, with the extreme case perhaps being at Nahal Oren, where excavation of 50 percent of the site has located only one such structure. At Ain Mallaha, the early occupation appears to have been one in which a lineal arrangement of dwellings occurred along the foot of the slope of the terrace (Valla 1981:412). Six, or possibly nine, dwellings date to this period. However, as Valla (1981:412–415) amply documents in his study of the levels of occupation and the phases of construction, these units are not all contemporary. Once again, hamlet size seems to be in the neighborhood of four or fewer structures possibly occupied simultaneously. In the middle phase at Ain Mallaha (Late Natufian), nine, or possibly twelve, dwellings have been excavated. These are arranged in rows along the top of the slope, the middle of the slope and the base of the slope (Valla 1981:415). Superimposition of some dwellings reduces the total number of possible contemporary structures, and their location at different elevations along the slope complicates determination of relationships among them. However, this later settlement at Ain Mallaha may well have been somewhat larger than the occupation during the Early Natufian.

Dwelling size

Hamlet dwellings vary greatly in size, from 2.5 m in diameter at Rosh Zin to almost 10 m in diameter at Ain Mallaha. Within the same period of occupation at a site, size also varies considerably, ranging from 3 m to 10 m in diameter at Late Natufian Ain Mallaha, for example. This suggests that perhaps not all these structures were dwellings (Henry 1983:139). With that caveat in mind, the average size of these structures tends to be about 3–5 m in diameter, which yields around 7–20 m² of area per structure. The smaller dwellings could, therefore, scarcely contain more than a single small nuclear family, while the larger structures could possibly have accommodated a somewhat larger nuclear family or a small extended one.

Although the number of dwellings at Natufian hamlets is undoubtedly somewhat larger than the recovered sample, the fact that the number of possibly contemporary structures in this sample is low suggests that hamlet population size probably did not differ greatly from the size of an egalitarian hunter-gatherer group (that is, somewhere between 20–40 people). If population density at Natufian hamlets is equal to or less than 40 people, then there is a strong argument for the retention of nuclear family structure during the Natufian (Johnson 1982:401). Hamlets with populations of 20–40 people probably did not need to develop social stratification to settle intragroup problems. Despite the labor and time involved in building stone-walled dwellings, abandoning such structures as the result of group fissioning might still have been a viable alternative.

Storage and food surplus

If population density at Natufian hamlets was relatively low, so that disputes could be solved without the presence of ranked individuals, social stratification might still have arisen as a result of needs related to the distribution or redistribution of abundant stored resources. Although direct archaeological evidence for these sorts of plant foods at most hamlets is scarce due to poor preservation of macrobotanical remains, the higher temperatures and greater available moisture of the early part of the Natufian (12,500–11,000 B.P.) evidently allowed the areal expansion of nut-bearing trees of the Mediterranean park-forest and cereals from refugia (Bar-Yosef 1987b:222, Henry 1981:429, 1985a, b:378). Presumably, Natufian groups would be quick to exploit such regionally abundant resources.

That these sorts of plant foods were part of the Natufian diet can be supported by several lines of archaeological evidence. Numerous ground stone implements of various types are found at Natufian hamlets, and these have generally been linked to the processing of plant foods (Henry 1985b:372, Valla 1975:92–96). The presence of numerous sickle blades at some hamlets has been used by researchers (e.g., Garrod 1957:216; Henry 1981:428, 1985b:372; Sillen 1984:149, Smith et al. 1984:105) to suggest the harvesting of cereals. While this may have been the case, since even wild forms of cereals can be effectively harvested using sickle blades (Harlan 1967:197), microwear studies on glossed pieces from equivalent contexts at Mureybet and Abu Hureyra, in Syria, indicate that the primary use of such tools was to cut non-food plants such as reeds and rushes (Anderson-Gerfaud 1983). The context of sickle blade use is not completely resolved, however. For example, experimental and microscopic research by Unger-Hamilton (1989) suggests that sickle blades *were* used to gather cereals. Somewhat more direct evidence for plant food consumption can be seen by the dental attrition at Ain Mallaha and el-Wad, but, interestingly, not at Kebara (Smith 1972:236–237). Finally, the use of strontium-calcium ratios indicates that at *some* Natufian sites (hamlets and other types of base camps), the early Natufian is characterized by intensive cereal consumption (Sillen 1984, Smith et al. 1984:129).

Thus, it seems that some (but perhaps not all) early Natufian populations had diets with a high cereal content. Cereals (and nuts) are potentially storable commodities, and experimental work has shown that cereals harvested over a relatively short period of time (ca. three weeks) by a small number of people (e.g., a nuclear family) can provide enough to last a year (Harlan 1967:198). Such a yield would necessitate storage facilities, and these are, in fact, found at several of the hamlets (Table 17.1). It is unknown however, whether or not these facilities acted as a reserve for the portion of the year when other food sources were minimal, or were the reservoirs for overgathered resources that could be used for exchange or redistribution (by ranked individuals).

Number of storage facilities

One way to put this problem into sharper focus is to examine the number of storage facilities at hamlets. Except for Late Natufian Ain Mallaha, hamlets have four or fewer of these structures. At all of these hamlets, except Nahal Oren, the ratio of storage facilities to the number of dwellings averages one or less. This may suggest that these facilities are maintained by individual families rather than used as components of a redistributive network organized by ranked individuals.

Exotic materials

Current archaeological data suggest that, even if abundant excess food resources *were* available for trade, large scale exchange is not present during the Natufian period. The types of suggested trade materials found at Natufian hamlets and other types of base camps can include basalt for ground stone implements, obsidian from Anatolia (one piece at Ain Mallaha), greenstone from Transjordan or Syria, shells from the Red Sea, and dentalium shell from either the Mediterranean or Red Sea. As Bar-Yosef (1983:19–23) states, many of these materials are either few in number (obsidian, greenstone, Red Sea shells) or are found at sites relatively close to the sources (e.g., basalt from localities 30–50 km distant). The eastern Mediterranean orientation of the Natufian and a topographical situation promoting east-west mobility (Bar-Yosef 1987b:222) suggests that Natufian groups probably obtained dentalium shell from the Mediterranean rather than from the Red Sea, and that most procurement of raw materials was direct rather than through trade. The few exotics (greenstone, obsidian, and

Red Sea shells) that originate at greater distances may simply be the result of informal, down-the-line trade, a system of exchange that would have required no ranked middlemen.

Burial data

Thus, the existence during the Natufian of a ranked society (and therefore of social complexity, as the term is most often used in the context of the Levantine Epipaleolithic) appears to be poorly, if at all, documented by such features as population density, sedentism, storage, or trade. However, social differentiation has been suggested on the basis of an analysis of burial data from el-Wad (Wright 1978). In this study, Wright postulates the existence of two corporate groups, generating distinct collective-style burials, during the early Natufian (membership determined by burial in different parts of the site, presence of different types of burial goods, and other attributes). The groups are further said to demonstrate ranking because children and infants occur with burial goods (Wright 1978:215). Based on comparative data from other sites, collective burials are seen as the most frequent type during the Early Natufian (Wright 1978:217). It is difficult to assess the burial data from el-Wad in terms of how representative it might be for early Natufian groups, or if the postulated "vertical" social differentiation is genuinely present. As Wright (1978:221) himself points out, there is no reason to expect that all Natufian groups were necessarily similar in terms of social complexity. In fact, if early Natufian sites are canvassed for collective versus single burials, it is apparent that both burial modes are present in both the early and late periods, as well as in "contemporary" deposits at a site. Wright's general assumption that single interments are later in time may, therefore, mask other kinds of variability relating to contemporaneous differences in mortuary programs.

The presence of dentalium shell with some individuals possibly signals some kind of differentiation; however, this item of adornment was probably easily accessible to most individuals because of the relative proximity of the Mediterranean Sea to most sites, including those inland. The hypothesized corporate groups from el-Wad may simply reflect changes in burial customs during the early Natufian, since there is no a priori reason to view them as more than broadly contemporary, especially as most hamlets and other base camps demonstrate use of such locales over long periods of time. In fact, the successive reopenings of the collective grave in the cave as opposed to the apparent single event interment of several individuals in the collective graves of the terrace might be interpreted as such a change in burial customs.

Other aspects of social complexity

The remaining aspects of the postulated social complexity of Natufian groups are said to be the establishment of territories, a matrilineal structure with matrilocal post-marital residence, and the existence of chiefdom-level sociopolitical organization (Henry 1983:144–151, 1985b:375–376, 1989). Territories within the overall distribution of Natufian sites are extremely difficult to define. If cemeteries can be used as markers for territories, then their presence in the archaeological record might reflect distinct Natufian regions. The existence of more than one group utilizing the same cemetery at the same time, assumed by Wright (1978), would seem to negate the use of cemeteries as corporate group or territorial markers, unless population density in specific regions was so great as to warrant subdivision of the group. Such density of population is not, however, supported by current archaeological evidence. In addition, some hamlets (e.g., Ain Mallaha, Hayonim Cave) have burials under dwelling floors. Whether these can be considered cemeteries in the classic sense is open to some debate. The appearance of numerous burials in various contexts is more likely to be the result of increased sedentism among some Natufian groups than of an effort to legitimatize a claim of eminent domain over territory.

Undeniably, certain regions were used for long periods of time by groups of related individuals, as is documented by the findings of Smith (1973) at Hayonim Cave, where agenesis of the third molar (an inherited condition) occurs in greater than expected frequencies. This is the probable outcome of an endogamous mating pattern and would seem, once again, to reflect small population size for Natufian groups. Since this pattern is apparently restricted to the level of the community, it would also seem to contradict hypothesized male movement within a matrilineal, matrilocal society (Henry 1983:145), since movement of males from one community to another would promote gene flow between communities and thus reduce the frequencies of recessive inherited conditions like agenesis.

Prolonged absence of males from communities, due to long-distance hunting and trading activities, has also been used as further evidence for matrilineal, matrilocal settlements (Henry 1983:145, 1985b:376). The archaeological record of the Natufian shows both these claims to be unsubstantiated. Natufian hamlets are located in ecotones between wooded slopes and open country (Bar-Yosef 1987b:231, Henry 1981:427–428, 1985b:373). Since the location of hamlets in ecotones presumably maximizes access to resources, hunting of gazelle necessitating long-distance travel (and therefore prolonged absence from the settlement) would seem to have occurred rarely. As discussed above, there is no evidence for what Henry (1985b:376) has called "intensive trade." The small numbers of nonlocal materials, from sources at any great distance, that are present at Natufian sites were most probably acquired through an informal trade network as, for example, is demonstrated by the decrease with distance in numbers of Red Sea shells from their source (Bar-Yosef 1983:22). Without stronger evidence for social complexity and its assumed corollaries, it is not possible to claim a chiefdom-level sociopolitical organization for the Natufian.

Conclusions

Contrasted to earlier periods of prehistory in the Levant, the archaeological record of the Natufian apparently documents a series of changes in settlement and subsistence systems. These changes have been seen, in part, as a response to favorable climatic conditions that increased the abundance of storable food resources, primarily cereals and nuts. Because of the presumed abundance of such resources in the Mediterranean forest zone, there have been recent attempts to suggest that Natufian groups are representative of complex, rather than egalitarian, hunter-gatherers. The social complexity model encompasses several features. Briefly, these are increased population or population density, the appearance of sedentary "base camps" that are the focal points of a radial settlement system, presence of individuals of differing (hereditary) social status, storage facilities, and, for the Natufian in particular, bounded territories and matrilineal, matrilocal communities organized into a chiefdom-level society.

While it is true that there is some archaeological data that may be construed as evidence for these features, a careful examination of each of these concepts, as they are used in the context of the Natufian, indicates that they are not usually tightly defined and that there has been a general lack of effort in examining the associated issues and evidence. One example that illustrates this problem is the probable presence of more than one type of base camp. Thus, it may be erroneous to characterize the Natufian as a radial settlement system, when this pattern may be typical only of those few base camps that are hamlets (that is, that have dwelling structures). Another example of this problem is the evaluation of the presence of storage facilities. It should not be automatically assumed that the mere presence of these features at certain base camps (hamlets only) is evidence for storage of large amounts of excess food resources for later redistribution or use in trade, when, in fact, they may represent short-term storage to maintain an adequate food supply over the winter months.

When the archaeological record of the Natufian is examined in any detail with respect to the social complexity model, little supporting evidence can be found to validate blanket acceptance of this paradigm. The only data that suggest possible social stratification (and these are weak, at best), come from the burial study at el-Wad (Wright 1978). Here, ascribed status is inferred on the basis of children buried with grave goods. The simplistic description of Natufian hunter-gatherers as examples of social complexity (erroneous or not) may ultimately result in inadvertently masking a much more complicated set of subsistence and settlement patterns, occurring not only between the early and late periods, but also within each of the periods.

What is needed most urgently now is a re-examination of data from the various types of base camps and the spatial and chronological distribution of base camps by type. If Natufian hamlet type base camps are found only in relatively restricted geographical regions (such as northern Palestine), then careful analysis of archaeological data and the use of strictly defined terms may eventually yield evidence for social complexity in such relatively favorable locales. However, the Natufian data might only indicate that, in some regions, this was a period of intensification of trends already apparent in the earlier phases of the Levantine Epipaleolithic. As prehistorians interested in seeking anthropological answers to the questions posed by patterns in the Natufian archaeological record, it is essential that researchers not succumb to viewing a few unusual sites as "typical" of what then becomes, by extension, a homogeneous Natufian "culture."

Acknowledgments

I wish to thank Michael Barton (Arizona State University), Nancy Coinman (University of Tulsa), and John Lindly (Arizona State University) who took the time to read an earlier version of this paper and who contributed many helpful comments. It is the author's prerogative to be selective in dealing with critique, and so I accept full responsibility for the final product. Thanks also to the many people whose ears I bent in discussing this topic during the course of the preparation of this essay.

Chapter 18
Historic Biases in Modern Perceptions of the Levantine Epipaleolithic

Marcia L. Donaldson

Introduction

Research in the Levantine Epipaleolithic has been shaped by several factors since the first recognition of the period in the 1930s and 1940s (Garrod and Bate 1937, Neuville 1951). While the nature of the archaeological record affects our perceptions to a certain degree, the history of research also contributes significantly. Early research was strongly influenced by contemporary work in European prehistory and was undertaken by European prehistorians who often borrowed terminology, typology, and biases wholesale. An emphasis was placed on defining industries and culture groups, with a particular use of retouched stone tool typologies in these definitions. Even the label "Epipaleolithic" carries a certain connotation of affiliation with the Paleolithic despite evidence that the period might be more transitional between the Upper Paleolithic and the Neolithic. Such historic parameters may also affect our interpretations of the archaeological data in dealing, for example, with the tremendous variability present among Epipaleolithic assemblages.

We are all, of course, influenced by our educational backgrounds and the direction of previous research. The objective recognition of one's own paradigmatic biases is difficult at best. The outline of such biases becomes somewhat clearer when entering unfamiliar territory with a successful, established tradition already in place. This proved to be the case for me as I turned the focus of my studies from the American Southwest to the Levantine Epipaleolithic. Although worlds apart, the Levant and American Southwest share similar, semi-arid environments that experienced tremendous climatic flux during the last global warming period. Time scales certainly differ, but in both cases an independent transition was made from an essentially "paleo-lithic" mobile, hunting-gathering way of life to that of sedentary set-tlements dependent on domesticated resources. In both regions the presedentary period is represented by small ephemeral sites dom-inated by lithic tools and debitage, limited groundstone, and little evidence of domestic structures. Perhaps because of the lack of distinct tool types, with the exception of projectile points, the Archaic of the Southwestern United States is characterized more on the basis of subsistence and economic adaptations to various zones than by lithic industries. Data collection and research are heavily dependent on en-vironmental information as well as artifactual data. Many of my per-sonal biases therefore stem from studying the Archaic period from a perspective that emphasizes models of subsistence and environmental change with less attention paid to typology and the definition of cul-tural groups.

As a recent student of the Levantine Epipaleolithic, I find that several conflicting perspectives are implicitly accepted by many re-searchers. Among the most confusing are the definition of the Epi-paleolithic itself and the overwhelming role that lithic analysis has come to play in our understanding of the diversity within that period. These two topics will be discussed here, with an emphasis on the effect of distinct research traditions on current perspectives of the Epipaleo-lithic and how we view the variability present in the archaeological record.

What's in a Name? A Brief History of Epipaleolithic Research

Two main schools of thought have contributed to defining the Epi-paleolithic, with perceptions depending largely on the background and research interests of contributors. As Henry (1989) notes, the Epipaleolithic was essentially identified or "created" by paleolithic ar-chaeologists "working up" through time (Garrod 1932b, Garrod and Bate 1937, Hours 1973, Neuville 1951) and by neolithic researchers "reaching back" (Braidwood and Howe, 1960, Kenyon 1957). These two perspectives seem to have affected much of our thinking about the period, as well as the way in which it has been approached. In many ways the history of its emergence as a distinct conceptual unit and perceptions of the label itself reveal quite a lot about the various biases that have entered our thinking about the Epipaleolithic.

What is now called the Epipaleolithic was first recognized as a sepa-rate period in the first half of this century during the excavation of stratified, largely Natufian, cave deposits (Garrod 1932, Garrod and

Bate 1937, Neuville 1951). It was defined primarily on typological grounds, notably by the appearance of microliths as a dominant portion of the retouched components of lithic assemblages. While Neuville (1951) included these microlithic industries in the latter part of his sequence of Upper Paleolithic periods, Garrod (Garrod and Bate 1937) felt they represented something qualitatively different and labeled them Mesolithic, mainly because of their similarity to the microlith-dominated industries of Mesolithic Europe. The presence of a microlithic industry older than, yet distinct from, the Natufian was first detected during the excavation of Kebara Cave, in Israel (Turville-Petre 1932), and at similar non-geometric microlithic surface assemblages recovered throughout much of the Levant. The Kebaran was also defined primarily on typological grounds, with sub-groups created on the basis of the dominance of different kinds of non-geometric microliths and modes of retouch (Bar-Yosef 1970, 1981a; Hours 1973).

Garrod's Mesolithic label remained in use, especially in regard to the Natufian, at least until 1960 when two new research projects commenced. Perrot's (1966) work at Ein Mallaha (Eynan) revealed a Natufian settlement with a very low incidence of microliths in the retouched tool component, leading him to designate the industry "Epipaleolithic" (in Bar-Yosef and Vogel 1987). Second, Braidwood's publications on the work in Iraqi Kurdistan (Braidwood and Howe 1960) rejected labels like "mesolithic" and "neolithic" in favor of terms related to subsistence variables (e.g., food-collecting, incipient agriculture). These terms had no explicit temporal significance. Braidwood considered the Epipaleolithic period to represent the end of the Upper Paleolithic food-collecting era, with more tightly focused resource exploitation, seasonal movement, and the earliest visible social organization, as well as changes in artifact categories, primarily the appearance of microliths and ground stone tools (Braidwood et al. 1983). Practically immediately, however, there were differences of opinion as to how the period was to be defined. Some (especially workers trained in France) continued to define it almost exclusively on the basis of lithic typology, while others (especially Americans and Brits) invoked subsistence and social organizational criteria.

An emphasis on typology was maintained by Ofer Bar-Yosef (1970) in his seminal work on the Epipaleolithic and definition of the Geometric Kebaran. While other factors were recognized, lithic typology (and to a more limited extent technology) provided the means to distinguish several Kebaran and Geometric Kebaran subgroups based largely on the different proportions of microlithic categories. The subsequent definition of other Epipaleolithic industry variants found in Lebanon (Hours 1973), southern Jordan (Henry 1983, 1989), the

Negev (Marks 1973, Marks and Simmons 1977), and Syria (M.-C. Cauvin 1981a) all were founded on the presence and dominance of certain types of microlithics, in addition to limited technological (e.g., microburin technique) and stylistic (Helwan retouch, other types of backing) information. The importance accorded to technological studies has recently expanded (Calley 1984), offering a more objective view of *entire* lithic assemblages that often contradicts patterns derived exclusively from typological studies (Byrd 1988).

While typological definitions remain in place, an increasing effort is being made toward a greater understanding of subsistence and settlement patterns, particularly as they may have varied with environmental setting as well as through time. This is reflected in the increased collection of environmental and subsistence data (Garrard et al. 1988, Henry, Leroi-Gourhan and Davis 1981), including faunal, botanical, and pollen remains as well as geological information. Studies of changes in settlement patterns (Marks and Freidel 1977) also aid in detecting subsistence variability.

Yet, in a general sense, the Epipaleolithic continues to be defined as those industries dominated by either non-geometric or geometric microliths. Bar-Yosef and Vogel (1987), for example, advocate utilizing *only* the microlithic component of Epipaleolithic assemblages to monitor variability and to determine the existence of subgroups because the macrolithic component is allegedly affected by functional variation between sites. They assume that microliths all served the same function, a notion based on limited edge-wear analysis indicative of hunting and limited meat-cutting (Bar-Yosef and Vogel 1987, cf. Clarke 1978). Such an approach focuses analytical attention on a single, rather limited portion of the archaeological record that might, in fact, contain an unknown amount of variability unrelated to temporal, geographical, functional, or ethnic differences.

Although there is some variability, it is interesting to note that the *macrolithic* portions of these industries are basically Upper Paleolithic in nature, with many general tool types persisting throughout the Epipaleolithic. Because bladelets have been found in significant amounts in Upper Paleolithic assemblages dating back as far as ca. 30 kyr B.P. in various parts of the Levant (Lebanon, Sinai, the Negev), Gilead (1988) notes that the presence of microliths is not an adequate indicator of the Epipaleolithic. He suggests that changes in subsistence and settlement patterns are more important indicators of this period. A true shift in lithic industry seems to be found in the Pre-Pottery Neolithic, where the microlithic component practically disappears and tool typology and technology alter rapidly.

The Label "Epipaleolithic": Typological and Anthropological Approaches

The label "Epipaleolithic," while ironically first used in relation to a site with a low incidence of microliths (Ein Mallaha, Perrot 1966), has come to be equated with microlith-dominated industries representing the period between the Upper Paleolithic and the Neolithic (ca. 20–10 kyr B.P.). The Greek prefix "epi" means "next to," "in addition to," or "after"; the term "Epipaleolithic" is conceptually associated with the "Paleolithic." This association is supported by a typological approach to Epipaleolithic industries which are basically a continuance of Upper Paleolithic types with an added emphasis on microliths. The similarity is further reinforced by the recovery of microlith tools from Upper Paleolithic strata in southern Lebanon, the Azraq Basin, the Negev desert, and Sinai Peninsula (Gilead 1988).

While the label has a certain legitimacy from a typological perspective, it is rather confusing from a more anthropological point of view concerned not only with artifact variability but also with economic, social, and organizational systems. Although Garrod (1932a, b) certainly was aware of various "non-artifactual" characteristics of the Natufian, a real focus on paleoeconomy was first advocated by Braidwood as a consequence of his work in Iraqi Kurdistan (late 1940s–mid-1950s) (Braidwood and Howe 1960, Braidwood et al. 1983). This, combined with more theoretically sophisticated, less data-oriented studies (Binford 1968, Flannery 1969, focused attention on the Epipaleolithic as a kind of transition between more mobile Upper Paleolithic foragers and sedentary Neolithic villagers with full-blown domestication economies. The Epipaleolithic was variously seen as a "lifestyle," an "adaptation," rather than a collection of artifactual characteristics.

An anthropological perspective based on economic and social factors does not quite mesh with the typological approach outlined above. In part this is because the mobile foraging way of life associated with the Upper Paleolithic appears to have continued throughout much of the period now defined as the Epipaleolithic (ca. 20–10 kyr B.P.). Only sites from the last 2,000 to 3,000 years of this interval display evidence of a "transition" that suggests an increase in sedentism, greater dependence on plant foods (especially cereal grasses), increased use of ground stone, the appearance of structures and storage facilities, "long-range" interaction, formalized burial precincts, and possible social differentiation (Henry 1989). The differences between the early and late Epipaleolithic are identified by Moore (1983) in his scheme for

Epipaleolithic subdivisions, by Henry (1985a, b; 1987, 1989) in his discussion of complex hunting and gathering societies (i.e., the Natufian), by Valla (1987) who separates the Natufian from the rest of the Epipaleolithic, and by Bar-Yosef (1970, 1981a) in his Epipaleolithic periodization scheme (Kebaran, Geometric Kebaran, and Natufian). Despite labels there seems to be a consensus that a paleolithic-type, hunting and gathering way of life persisted at least through the first part of the Epipaleolithic. That is, most early Epipaleolithic sites are small, they generally lack architecture and storage facilities, have very little ground stone, have few exotics, and faunal exploitation seems to have concentrated on a few species (although cf. Edwards 1989). When these and other factors are taken into account, the "transition" event or process appears to have occurred only within the *later* Epipaleolithic, comprising the Natufian and contemporary industries. Henry (1985b), for example, makes a case for accepting the Natufian as a complex, short-lived, transitional adaptation between the foragers of previous periods and the subsequent Neolithic.

While these different perspectives affect how the Epipaleolithic is defined and while they are implicitly recognized by most Levantine archaeologists, they are rarely discussed in print (although see Gilead 1988, Henry 1983, Perrot 1983). It appears that the typological paradigm dominates in most formal presentations, largely because of the impact of European-trained scholars and the undisputed importance of lithic typology and technology. This importance stems largely from the fact that the "language" of lithic typology is understood by all and facilitates communication and some degree of comparison between assemblages from different sites and areas. It has even been suggested that two different typologies be used in the discussion of assemblages, one for detailed comparative research and the other for the easy dissemination of general information (Hours 1974). It is, of course, debatable whether and to what extent a period should be defined solely on the attributes of one material culture category.

The label "Epipaleolithic" and the emphasis on lithic typology, to my mind, lend an implicit bias to the consideration of this important transitional episode. The nature of that bias is not easily discerned, but it appears to be related to a higher-level paradigm that centers on our notions of process and change. Is change a slow, gradual, "evolutionary" process, or are transitions accomplished in steps between relatively stable plateaux (that is, by "punctuated equilibria")? Was the transition between Upper Paleolithic mobile foragers and Neolithic sedentary farmers a relatively slow process that took place over ca. 10,000 years, or was it fairly abrupt, requiring only the last 2,000 to 3,000 years of the Epipaleolithic? While the typological approach to the Epipaleolithic reflects a more gradual "evolutionary" perspective, a focus on subsistence, social organization, and interaction suggests that the change was relatively rapid and limited to the late Epipaleolithic. If this was the case, as is argued by some (e.g., Moore, Henry, Gilead), then it might be prudent formally to recognize differences between the "early" and "late" Epipaleolithic, or at least to arrive at some sort of consensus as to how the period(s) should be defined (e.g., like the recent Ksar Akil Conference on Upper Paleolithic systematics (Bergman and Goring-Morris 1987). While the early Epipalcolithic does indeed appear to be an extension of the Upper Paleolithic, the late Epipaleolithic is represented by a range of characteristics that separate it from "typical" Upper Palcolithic, hunting-gathering adaptations. Gilead (1988) suggests that the earlier period be regarded as the Late Upper Paleolithic, reserving the term Epipaleolithic for that period when economic, social, and organizational transitions are evident (i.e. the Natufian and contemporary, more complex societies). This division recognizes the greater similarities between the Upper Paleolithic and what is now considered to be the early Epipaleolithic, and treats the later Epipaleolithic as a separate entity.

The Question of Variability

The dominance of a normative typological approach to defining the Epipaleolithic and its major divisions seriously affects understanding of the variability present *within* these divisions. As noted above, this variability has been based largely on the differential occurrence of various categories of microlithic tools, limited technological attributes, and types of backing (or retouch) present. Typologies are indispensable for many research activities, but they remain the subjective constructs of modern archaeologists. The tremendous amount of detail present in many typologies (e.g., Hours 1974) has meaning only for the typologist and is not necessarily representative of any "real" differences to the prehistoric manufacturers. Any correspondence between typological and "real" patterns is based on the assumption that archaeologists can discover "real" patterns, and that options taken during manufacture are constrained by learning in a social context. Thus items made by individuals within a group tend to be more similar to each other than they are to analogous objects made by other groups. These assumptions overlook the possibility that manufacturing options vary contextually or situationally according to the availability of raw material, tool function, need for expediency, and individual skill and preferences. As Clark (1989c) notes, the success of typologies and the consideration of style in relation to these also assumes a certain fine temporal control that is seldom if ever achieved. Our grasp of temporal parameters is very coarse-grained, and often quite variable geographically. We also often find ourselves in the somewhat awkward position of using alleged directional change in typological analyses as the basis for relative dating schemes when absolute dates are not available, and, at the same time, using these same data to denote sub-groups and traditions. Obviously, some form of dating independent of patterns in artifacts and/or their attributes is required.

Lithic typology has recently been enhanced by increased interest in lithic *technology,* marked by studies of unmodified debitage in order to define reduction sequences and to determine the extent to which they were standardized (Marks and Volkman 1986, Calley 1984). Technological attributes are easily quantified, generally less subjective than retouched tool typologies, and as such are representative of a potentially more "objective" data base. Interestingly, the few Epipaleolithic technological data available so far do not reflect the fine-grained patterning seen from a typological perspective, but instead more general trends show some spatial variability within periods. For example, Byrd (1988) has recently noticed that the microburin technique, thought to have appeared ca. 12,000 B.P. (Henry 1987), seems to have occurred in the Azraq Basin much earlier, in an assemblage that does not resemble a known industry with a high incidence of microburins. Metrical studies also offer a more objective approach to the study of lithic variability (Valla 1981, Henry 1987), providing evidence of regional/environmental variability that cannot be accommodated by pan-Levantine labels (see Olszewski 1986b for a critique). The point here is simply that the more objective technological analyses do not generally reflect the many sub-groups formed on the basis of typological studies. Of course, it can be argued that technological studies are too coarse-grained to register such variability, and so do not reflect the manufacturing options that many regard as part of "style," however unintentional these might have been from the standpoint of the manufacturer (see Clark 1989c for a discussion of the different views on style and its definition in lithic assemblages).

Many of the subgroups defined within different Epipaleolithic periods are based on typological differences (i.e., variability perceived in the retouched tool component). Although the nature of such variability is usually neither articulated nor fully understood, there is an implicit equation of these subgroups with ethnic or identity-conscious social units such as bands (e.g., Henry 1989). In other words, variability displayed by hypothetical social entities "maps onto" that displayed by lithic assemblages and industries. This implies that typological and technological variability are patterned together, and in non-random ways (which, as noted above, is unlikely), and that the pattern is reflective of social and organizational variability. There are some problems with identifying ethnicity with lithic variation.

The identification of group boundaries and ethnicity are, or should be, of concern to archaeologists. Epipaleolithic settlement patterns and site contents suggest that for most of the period groups were generally small and mobile. Ethnographic data and computer simulations (e.g., Wobst 1974) suggest that such groups would have had to sustain some sort of interaction with adjacent groups both to maintain an adequate mating pool and for economic motives (e.g., spreading risk through reciprocal trade and through resource sharing, information sharing, etc.). Those boundaries were probably quite porous, and almost certainly constantly in flux. Archaeological evidence from the Near East, the American Southwest, and Australia indicates that rigid boundaries entailing the sort of group identification most often associated with ethnicity did not develop until populations reached a certain density, perhaps associated with sedentism and a corresponding reduction in birth spacing. With group mobility hypothesized for most of the Epipaleolithic, and the likelihood that group membership changed quite often, the definition of ethnic or cultural areas solely on the basis of patterned artifact variation is highly unlikely, particularly given the poor temporal control now available.

Although there have been many discussions of the sources of variability within Epipaleolithic industries, very little actual comparative work *between* assemblages has been undertaken. When undertaken, comparison usually takes the form of listing the proportions of (usually microlithic) tools present in various assemblages, and then noting differences and similarities among them. As mentioned above, this approach assumes that the subjective, fine-grained tool categories used for comparison reflect significant "real" differences, and that all microliths are, in a sense, functional equivalents. It would prove interesting to compare the variability displayed by typologically defined assemblages with that shown by technological and metrical studies. It would be even more meaningful to then try to discern whether there are any correlations with other behavioral and environmental factors. It may be, as suggested by Fish and Fish (this volume), that much of the variability evident among lithic assemblages is indicative of differences in adaptive strategies due to varied environmental conditions and/or methods of resource procurement. These patterns may be unrelated to ethnicity, or may be present within larger ethnic groupings.

Certain problems would naturally be encountered in trying to compare lithic variability with that of other factors. The most important of these, directly related to the dominance of lithic analysis, is the inconsistent recovery of non-lithic cultural and environmental data from Epipaleolithic sites. In many cases, lithics are the only abundant category of information available. Fine-grained control of prehistoric environments is also a stumbling block. Yet, modern excavation and recovery techniques, in addition to the increased number of sites that have been investigated, have greatly increased our knowledge of non-lithic data and are beginning to provide an independent source of information that can be utilized to evaluate hypotheses generated on the basis of patterns in lithic variability.

Where Do We Go from Here?

This discussion has centered around biases that I believe affect perceptions of the Epipaleolithic in the Levant. In general, it would seem that definitions of the Epipaleolithic are inconsistent and vary with the topic under consideration. On the one hand, the Epipaleolithic is defined typologically, with factors other than retouched tool variability being relegated to minor roles. This perspective is based partly on the dominance of lithics in recovered archaeological assemblages and partly on the historic background of prehistoric research in the Levant, which emphasized a typological approach to the definition of cultures. From an ecological or "adaptationist" perspective, the Epipaleolithic is seen as a transitional period between the Upper Paleolithic and the Neolithic; the transition is represented not so much by changes in lithic assemblages but by changes in economy, settlement pattern, social organization, and patterns of intergroup interaction. The former perspective basically views the Epipaleolithic as the tail-end of the Upper Paleolithic, while the latter considers it more as a separate entity. From a typological point of view, the entire Epipaleolithic is essentially an Upper Paleolithic industry with a significant number of (or sometimes dominance by) microlithic tools. From a more anthropological perspective, only the late Epipaleolithic witnesses significant, fairly abrupt (although uncorrelated) changes in subsistence strategies, settlement patterns, and social organization—changes that separate it conceptually from both the preceding Upper Paleolithic and the succeeding Neolithic. How are these two views to be reconciled, and is it desirable to attempt to do so?

It is time to consider redefining the Epipaleolithic, particularly given the growing body of data collected concerning not only lithic assemblages but other artifactual, subsistence, and settlement information. A progression of temporal changes in dominant microlith type is no longer as clear cut as previously thought. In addition, the recovery of backed bladelets from Upper Paleolithic contexts (Gilead 1988) reduces the importance of microliths as indicators of the Epipaleolithic. Excavation, settlement pattern studies, and subsistence research suggest that a mobile hunting-gathering (Upper Paleolithic) economy was maintained throughout most of the period in question, with rapid changes visible ca. 13–10 kyr B.P. This seems to warrant a reconsideration of defining factors by concerned researchers and a restructuring in our perceptions of the Epipaleolithic.

One of the most important features of the time period under discussion is the great amount of variability seen among the assemblages recovered. The variability is striking in comparison to the preceding Upper Paleolithic assemblages, and is evident mainly in the microlithic component. Until now microliths have been assumed to be functionally equivalent with variability, reflecting ethnic grouping or temporal trajectories of stylistic change. It may be that the role and function of microliths need to be studied in greater detail. On one hand they are considered to be reflective of hunting activities (e.g., parts of compound projectile points, perhaps knives), yet the recovery of lunates in a bone sickle handle (Garrod and Bate 1937) indicates they were not restricted to hunting activities, at least in the late Epipaleolithic. The unique property of microliths seems to be their considerable standardization within an assemblage; it is probable that they served as a generalized, partially formed "blank" requiring minimal retouching for fitting to a task-specific function. As Bar-Yosef and Vogel (1987) note, the final form of the microlith probably reflects the type of haft to which it was fitted. Perhaps the increase in diversity and average size of microliths recovered through time reflects an increase in types of compound tools of different function. What began as part of a compound projectile point may have been adapted into use as compound knives, sickles, or scrapers. The abundance of microlithic tools in sites dating between ca. 20–10 kyr B.P. is in sharp contrast to their almost total absence in succeeding pre-Pottery Neolithic assemblages, although hunting and related activities certainly continued. This sudden shift is notable and seems to require a more in-depth grasp on the role and function of microliths during the period preceding sedentary settlement.

Variability among Epipaleolithic sites is not limited to chipped stone assemblages. As Henry (1987) and others have noted, types of ground-stone recovered seem to vary with ecological setting, with mortars and pestles more common in forested areas and grinding stones dominant in open vegetation zones. The possibility that tool assemblages varied with ecological setting, and therefore different exploitable resources, requires continued investigation. This is particularly important considering that this period was one of considerable environmental flux, as climatic patterns and environmental conditions shifted over the millennia of global warming following the last period of glaciation.

As the amount of data collected on late Upper Paleolithic and Epipaleolithic occupation in the Levant increases, paradigmatic parameters that were suitable thirty years ago are not as appropriate today. The tremendous variability visible among Epipaleolithic assemblages can no longer simply be attributed to ethnic or temporal differences. The focus of research is broadening to include a range of factors concerned with subsistence strategies, settlement patterns, and environmental setting, as well as artifactual diversity. It is an appropriate time to reconsider the Epipaleolithic, in terms of both definition and research objectives.

Chapter 19
Foraging, Sedentism, and Adaptive Vigor in the Natufian: Rethinking the Linkages

Donald O. Henry

Over the last twenty years, the changes in our general understanding of the adaptive vigor of foragers and early agriculturalists has significantly influenced our interpretation of the archaeological record. While we have essentially reversed our views regarding the degree of success achieved on either side of this adaptive boundary, our perception of those sociocultural systems straddling the divide—the sedentary, complex foragers—remains little changed. Within the Levant, this transitional interval relates to the Natufian archaeological complex. It is argued here that our views on the origin and the adaptive success of the Natufian are partly shaped by our general perception of complex foraging and that they need rethinking.

Paradigmatic Origins

Our interpretation of the archaeological record is shaped in part by our "formal" exposure to the thinking of our discipline as found in its literature, lecture halls, and professional gatherings. Being aware of this, we tend to invest a certain amount of academic introspection examining how "theoretical movements" and "schools of thought" influence what we do as archaeologists. But I think we generally give little thought to another form of bias, a kind of ethnocentrism, that influences our perception of the archaeological record.

Ethnocentrism and Archaeology

Unlike most cultural anthropologists, archaeologists give little formal consideration to how their own culturally shaped world views enter into their interpretative equations. Although we of course recognize the economic and social distinctions of the cultures of the western industrialized world and separate them from the prehistoric societies that we study, we often incorporate our own world view in the interpretation of the material things of the past. Perhaps our greatest bias in this area is in using our own concept of adaptive success (i.e., more things mean greater security) to understand the archaeological record. While most archaeologists recognize that the abundance and diversity of material remains in foraging contexts is not necessarily indicative of successful adaptation or greater security, it is nevertheless difficult for us not to reach such conclusions when a deposit begins to yield rich and diverse artifact inventories.

Few foraging societies, either extant or extinct, have been associated with as much abundance and as great a diversity of material remains as the Natufian. And as an archaeologist, I grew up on the notion that this richness in material culture was in some way tied to the extraordinary stability and security enjoyed by the Natufians. When I later had the opportunity to excavate Natufian sites, the recovery of an incredible density and diversity of material remains drove home the idea that these prehistoric foragers must have lived very well indeed—that they might have been the original "affluent foragers." It really did not occur to me until a couple of years ago that there were a number of inconsistencies with the common practice of reading "adaptive success" from the material residues of the Natufian.

Formal Biases

As with other disciplines that focus on understanding extinct behavioral, biologic, and geologic systems, archaeology is greatly influenced by knowledge of extant, living systems. "The present is a key to the past" is more than a cliché, for our interpretation of modern baseline systems shapes the way we go about structuring questions and developing the answers in archaeological contexts. While we need not necessarily be held hostage to ethnographic analogies on specific, substantive problems, it seems nearly impossible for us to escape the influence of ethnographic interpretations of broader issues. The importance of understanding our biases is underlined by Binford's (1989c:20) recent comments that "all interpretations of archaeological observations are inductive arguments of some kind" and that such arguments are principally upheld by the "accuracy" of accompanying propositions and their "relevance" to the materials being interpreted. In this regard, I've always thought it a great irony that David Clarke (1968), perhaps the most articulate proponent of a theory distinct to archaeology, used an ethnographic parallel to distinguish between the successive scales within his basic organizational framework. The culture, culture group, and technocomplex labels (which he used to designate covariation in patterns of material culture, economy, environment, and social organization) would have equally well fit into the culture area concepts of Wissler (1917) and Kroeber (1939) as employed over a half-century ago.

When we examine how our perception of foraging has changed, it would seem that the collected readings published in *Man the Hunter* in 1968 mark the transition from viewing foragers as economically impoverished to affluent, in the sense that their wants and needs generally fall below their available resources. This certainly helped to reshape our interpretation of the archeological record and may even have led to a reevaluation of the adaptive success of early agriculturalists. Although ethnographic research raised the issue of the differences in energetics between foraging and agriculture, it is really paleoanthropological and archaeological studies that have reversed our opinion of the "Neolithic Revolution." Such studies consistently report that early farmers did not experience a marked improvement in their lifeways, but instead suffered from higher rates of infection and more frequent chronic malnutrition than their foraging predecessors (Cohen and Armelagos 1984).

Rethinking Adaptive Success

But how do we view the adaptive success of the in-between stage in this evolutionary succession, that is, sedentary foragers like the Natufians? In many ways our notions concerning such societies have not undergone significant rethinking in either ethnographic or archaeologic domains. From an archaeological perspective, the prevailing thinking is that such systems were "pushed" into place by an imbalance between population and resources (Flannery 1969, Cohen 1977, Hayden 1981, Moore 1985, Bar-Yosef and Belfer-Cohen 1989b). Although ideas about *why* complex foraging systems emerged differ in terms of the factors accorded most importance (i.e., population growth, decline in resources), most workers agree that stress on resources selected for a broadening of the economy and a reduction in settlement mobility (however, see Edwards 1989 for a different view). It is also argued that, once in place, these systems provided greater economic security through improved technologies, greater breadth in subsistence bases, and increases in the storage of foodstuffs.

Importance of Mobility

Ethnographic accounts provide little direct information on the evolution of simple to complex foraging, but they do suggest that foragers experiencing scarcity are more likely to increase than to reduce their settlement mobility (Jochim 1981:148, Kelly 1983:289–292). An exception to this relationship is argued to occur in cooler, less productive environments where the storage of foodstuffs acts to reduce group mobility during the cold season (Binford 1980, Kelly 1983). However, even in these cases the overall annual mobility levels tend to remain high unless aquatic resources form the subsistence base. These ethnographic observations suggest that those prehistoric populations dependent on land resources were unlikely to have been "pushed" into complex foraging by scarce resources.

I would argue that, once such complex foraging systems were in place, they did not experience greater stability but instead were destined to fail over the not-so-long run. This is principally because such systems sacrificed the fundamental means by which simple foragers maintain their security—namely their mobility. Sedentism and foraging are contradictory with respect to the long term success of a population, because the loss of mobility triggers progressive population growth that cannot be sustained by "fixed" natural resource ceilings (D. Harris 1978, Henry 1989). For simple foragers a decline in resources prompts greater mobility which in turn dampens fertility through several physiological mechanisms (e.g., lower fat:body weight ratios, higher prolactin levels, and elevated levels of other endocrine hormones tied to female energetics) (Lee 1979, Bentley 1985, Henry 1989). This acts to balance population and resources (Figure 19.1). In contrast, complex foragers would have disrupted this homeostatic relationship between resources and population by settling down.

Because of their lack of mobility, complex foragers adopted an economy that maximized the procurement of resources and storage in order to reduce risk. Binford (1980) has outlined some of the fundamental differences in the procurement strategies of "logistically positioned" sedentary foragers and "opportunistically oriented" mobile foragers who "map on" to resources (cf. Eder 1984). And Gould (1982) has contrasted food sharing behaviors among simple (Western Desert Aborigines) and complex (northwestern Californian Indians) foragers noting that the former shared to minimize risk, while the latter hoarded for the same reason. Along the same lines, but with a slightly different perspective, Woodburn (1979, 1980, 1982) distinguishes between those foragers with economies based upon "immediate-return" as opposed to "delayed-return" systems. What is important here is that mobile and

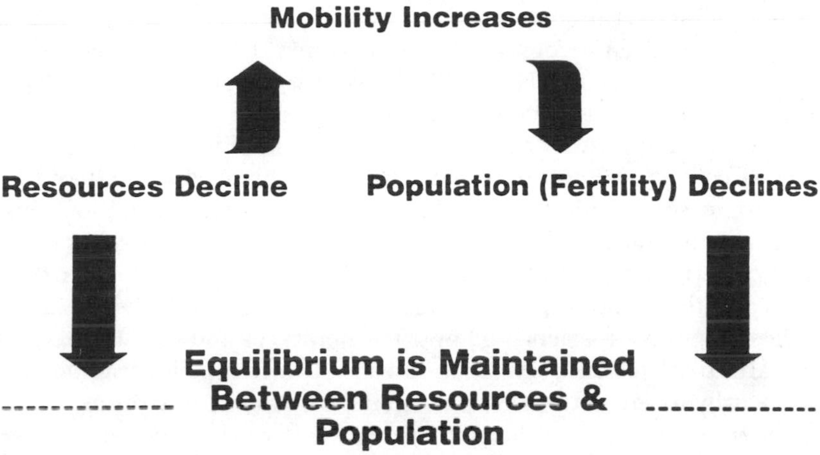

Mobility Increases

Resources Decline   **Population (Fertility) Declines**

Equilibrium is Maintained Between Resources & Population

FIGURE 19.1.   Diagram showing the linkages between resource levels, mobility, and population. Note that, when resources decline, groups tend to adopt higher mobility levels that in turn act to reduce fertility. These relationships help to maintain a balance between resources and population (after Henry 1989:44, Fig. 2.3, used by permission).

sedentary foragers have radically different ways in which they go about exploiting wild resources, insuring that they have adequate resources over an annual round, and reducing their risks. The key variable that appears to predict these different strategies is mobility.

Furthermore, I suggest that the strategy adopted by complex foragers more closely resembles that of food producers than that of simple foragers. That is because both complex foragers and food producers seek security through the intensified exploitation of resources and the development of surpluses. With this in mind, complex foraging could not have been developed without access to potentially storable resources (Kelly 1983:292) or sustained for very long in areas where resources were susceptible to depletion (Hayden 1981).

Distribution and Origin of Complex Foraging

Beyond the environmental factors related to the abundance and accessibility of resources, factors linked to the development of stored foodstuffs have to be considered in understanding the emergence of complex foraging. Murdock's (1967) *Ethnographic Atlas* lists 49 foraging societies that exhibit settlement patterns with a high degree of permanence (either semisedentary communities with fixed seasonal settlements or compact and relatively permanent settlements). These constitute a little over a quarter of the foraging societies included in the study. As has been recognized for some time, they are concentrated along the coasts of the North Pacific where about two-thirds of all complex foragers have been recorded.

In comparing Murdock's data on foraging mobility levels to associated "effective temperatures" (an indirect measure of the length of the growing season), Binford (1980) found a lack of correlation. From this he argues that mobility levels are responsive to "conditions other than gross patterns of food abundance" (Binford 1980:14). He points to one such condition in noting that storage among foragers tends to increase in those regions experiencing lower temperatures and greater seasonality. He attributes this correlation to a shift from a mobile foraging to a "logistically based" settlement pattern in "food-poor" environments in which foragers need to develop stores for surviving the winter. As previously mentioned, most of these groups are located along the shores of the North Pacific and rely upon aquatic resources.

In another study of 36 foraging societies, Kelly (1983:292) discovered a good correlation between the degree of group residential mobility (measured in the number of moves per year) and their associated primary biomasses (which he argues are indirectly related to the accessibility of resources). This seemingly contradicts the notion that residential mobility declines in food-poor settings. As noted by Kelly (1983:292), however, the direct correlation between residential mobility and biomass holds only when those foraging groups that are dependent upon aquatic resources (typically associated with very high biomasses) are removed from consideration (see also Shott 1986).

A review of the relationships between the annual residential mobility, winter mobility, and effective temperatures for Kelly's (1983) ethnographic sample (excluding groups dependent upon aquatics) shows an expected strong relationship between annual and winter mobility levels (Figure 19.2). But it also shows that those groups with the least mobility (i.e., 4–5 month residences) occupy settings with the highest effective temperatures. Furthermore, groups with low levels of winter mobility (i.e., 1–3 month residences) in areas of low effective temperatures nevertheless show fairly high mobility levels (i.e., some 10–15 camp moves per year).

The ethnographic data then suggest that neither a decline in resources nor the development of winter storage is a force likely to have promoted sedentism among foragers. The one factor that is consistently linked to ethnographic sedentary foragers is a dependence on aquatic resources. And while this connection between sedentism and aquatic resources is most pronounced along the North Pacific rim, it is also found in settings with high effective temperatures where winter

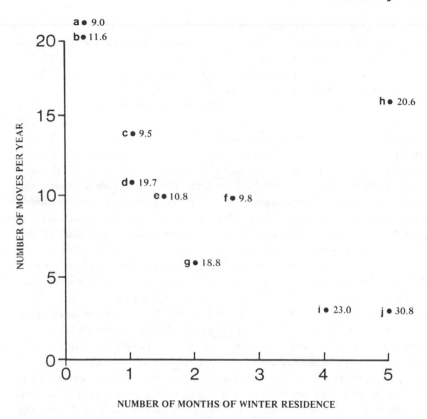

FIGURE 19.2. Number of moves per year plotted against number of months of winter residence for groups dependent on non-aquatic resources. Figures to the right of the point plots are effective temperatures (°C). Data are from Kelly (1983: Tables 1,4). a: Ona (60 moves per year); b: Montagnais; c: Netsilik; d: Birhor; e: Mistassini Cree; f: Nunamiut; g: Dobe !Kung; h: Siriono; i: Vedda; j: Chenchu.

storage would not be important. Some twenty years ago, Lewis Binford (1968) noted this connection and proposed that the emergence of complex foraging was due to the more intensive exploitation of aquatic resources at the end of the Pleistocene. Yesner (1980) has more recently emphasized the linkages between sedentism and the exploitation of marine resources (cf. Clark 1981).

Other ethnographic data reinforce this connection. The 49 sedentary and semisedentary groups listed in Murdock's (1967) *Atlas,* like most other complex foraging societies, show a distinct emphasis on fishing and other aquatic resources with an average 36–45 percent dependence on these foods in their economies. In fact, I could find only four complex foraging societies in the *Atlas* that showed a fishing dependence under 25 percent. Each of these displayed a "plant and small land fauna" dependence of 36–65 percent.

Sedentism among foragers then appears to be more strongly related to a *particular kind of food resource* than to the broader global environmental parameters that influence the abundance and accessibility of resources in general. With this in mind, it is my contention that complex foraging emerged because populations were attracted to or "pulled" toward the exploitation of certain resources that simultaneously allowed for and demanded a greater degree of sedentism. Such resources would have had to have been nutritious, easily and predictably procured, storable, resistant to depletion, and available over much of the year. They may also have required considerable monitoring and organization of labor for successful exploitation. Beyond aquatic resources, seeds and nuts satisfy these requirements.

Many scholars have argued that foragers were obligated to engage in the exploitation of such "poverty" or "non-preferred" resources because of scarcity due to population growth/expansion (Flannery 1969, Cohen 1977, Moore 1985, Clark and Yi 1983) or environmental perturbations (M. Harris 1977, Hayden 1981). These proposals have been criticized, however, on a number of points. Perhaps their greatest problem relates to timing and their inability to explain why it was that these resources only became intensively exploited with the onset of the Holocene (however, see Straus and Clark 1986a for an argument that resource diversification and intensification extend well back into the Late Pleistocene). Given the great potential for human population growth, imbalances would certainly have occurred much earlier in the Pleistocene had various biosocial mechanisms not been invoked (Hassan 1977). Furthermore, archaeological data from different parts of the world fail to show population growth preceding the intensive exploitation of such resources (Flannery 1986, Henry 1989).

In regard to those proposals that a climatically induced decline in resources would have pushed groups into complex foraging, one might again ask why earlier climatic/environmental perturbations during the Pleistocene did not produce similar results. As for the suggestions that the rise of complex foraging was linked to the massive faunal extinctions occurring at the end of the Pleistocene, we find that in many parts of the world faunal inventories remained unchanged across the Pleistocene/Holocene boundary (Flannery 1986, Bar-Yosef 1981a).

An alternative explanation as to why populations adopted those resources likely to give rise to complex foraging rests upon changes that occurred in the distributions of these resources at the end of the Pleistocene. Lewis Binford (1968) and Yesner (1980) have traced the intensive exploitation of aquatic resources to the formation of new habitats accompanying the post-glacial rise in sea level. This rise would have inundated continental shelves, drowned coastal plains, formed rocky platforms, and lowered stream gradients—all serving to increase the density and diversity of aquatic resources. Marine and anadromous fish, shellfish, and sea mammals might have become more attractive food resources as a result of these changes. Isolated evidence for the use of aquatics stretches back to the last interglacial and earlier, but it was not until the terminal Pleistocene that an emphasis on such resources became widespread. This is reflected in the direct evidence of aquatic remains and in an elaborate technology (harpoons, fishhooks, gorges, net-sinkers, etc.) devoted to their exploitation. Yesner (1980) has pointed out that it was not until the Hypsithermal (about 5,000 B.P.) that aquatic resources became intensively exploited on a world-wide basis. He attributes this to the effect that worldwide eustatic sea-level changes had on the formation of habitats for aquatic resources. Such habitats would have become most common between the initial slowing of a rising sea level at about 7,000 B.P. and final stabilization at modern levels about 4,000 B.P.

Changes in the distributions of other resources suitable for the support of complex foraging have also been tied to the global warming trend that took place at the end of the Pleistocene (Wright 1968, 1970, 1977; Henry 1973, 1981, 1989; Whyte 1977). It was only at this time that thermophile species, such as wild cereal grasses and nut bearing trees, began to colonize higher elevations and latitudes. Henry (1981, 1989) has argued that such a change in distribution had economic consequences beyond merely increasing the abundance of such food resources. With their enlarged elevational range, permitting the colonization of piedmont and montane settings, wild grasses and nut trees would have: (1) been less sensitive overall to short-term weather perturbations, (2) provided a harvest that was elevationally staggered over several weeks to months, and (3) created narrow, relatively closely packed niches in the form of linearly arranged elevational belts. Whyte (1977) has suggested that the generally warmer, drier settings of the terminal Pleistocene may even have selected for the replacement of perennial by annual grasses. His argument would mean that, besides a shift in distribution, annual cereal grasses with their economically attractive seed heads would have appeared in high densities only at the end of the Pleistocene. Each of these factors would have pulled foragers into the exploitation of cereals/nuts and indirectly into sedentary lifeways.

In sum, I do not think that the origin of complex foraging was simply a consequence of population pressure or a decline in resources. Instead it was more likely tied to an expansion of economically viable aquatic and plant resources that was triggered by a worldwide elevation in temperature beginning about 13,000 years ago. These changes in the distributions of key resources are thought to have prompted sedentism, population growth, intensification, social hierarchies, and ultimately the adaptive failure of sedentary foraging.

Complex foraging societies dependent on aquatic and plant resources are both terminal Pleistocene/early Holocene phenomena. However, those groups dependent on plant resources emerged and disappeared for the most part within the archaeological record, while their aquatic-based counterparts emerged during the late Holocene and persisted into the ethnographic present.

The apparent delay in the emergence and disappearance of complex foraging based upon aquatic resources may be related to: (1) the lag time between global warming and the stabilization of the sea level which generated rich aquatic habitats and (2) the greater resistance that aquatic, especially marine, resources have to over-exploitation and depletion.

This latter observation may well explain why most ethnographic complex foraging groups depend upon aquatic and not plant resources. The dependence on fishing by most modern complex foragers may well reflect the resistance of marine and anadromous fish to over-exploitation when compared to plants and land mammals. The concentration of complex foragers along the coasts of the North Pacific might be attributed to their greater survival in these areas due to the marine resources and to the unsuitability of the region for food production.

Adaptation and Changes in Social Organization

The shift from conservation to intensification of resources is accompanied by several changes in social organization that principally function to "close down" and formalize access to resources, and to intensify their procurement. With a growth in population coupled with the scarcity or depletion of resources, these mechanisms become more important. Thus in many ways the structure and dynamics of social organization in complex foraging societies mirror those of agricultural societies.

In distinguishing between "immediate-return systems" (simple foragers) and "delayed-return systems" (complex foragers), Woodburn (1982) points to several similarities in the social organization of the latter and that of agriculturalists. These parallels have prompted him to suggest that "to understand the development of agriculture from hunting and gathering, we ought to look at delayed return hunter-gatherers who have the values and the organization to facilitate the transition" (Woodburn, 1982:447). Woodburn (1982) sees relative equality in wealth, power, and prestige as differing greatly between foragers with economies based upon immediate as opposed to delayed return. He argues that egalitarian societies achieve their greater equality in these areas because of (1) direct, individual access to resources, (2) direct, individual access to coercion and mobility which limit the imposition of control, (3) practices that prevent saving and impose sharing, and (4) behaviors that allow goods to circulate without making people dependent upon one another (Woodburn 1982:431). In general, it would appear that each of these causal factors can be tied to the greater mobility and smaller group sizes of those foraging societies with "immediate-return" economies.

In regard to the social dynamics of complex foragers, it is instructive to look at the patterned covariation that exists among resources, demographic variables, and social organization of groups on the Northwest Coast of North America (Table 19.1). Along the coast there is a south-to-north cline of decreasing abundance and predictability of resources. Richardson (1981) notes that this gradient is paralleled by an increasing emphasis on descent-based groups and the ownership of resources. Ownership also follows a gradient of individually controlled resources in the south to kin-based, collectively owned resources in the north (Ames, 1985). Riches (1979) points to a gradient of replacement of local intra-group prestige in the south by inter-group ranking in the north. Ames (1985) describes larger households, villages, and home ranges (exploited territories) from south to north, but a corresponding decline in the numbers of villages. These correlations not only underline the adaptive significance of such social phenomena, but they also suggest their evolutionary trajectories given certain changes in the abundance and predictability of resources.

In those settings with fewer and less certain resources along the Northwest Coast, there has been selection for (1) more formalized control and transferral of resources (unilineal over cognatic descent), (2) more collective as opposed to individual ownership of resources, (3) greater control of and access to larger resource areas, and (4) larger economic units at both household and community scales. From an adaptive perspective, these clinal changes in social organization would have acted to reduce conflicts over resources in settings of increased competition. Similarly, the concentration of the population into larger villages and the control of resources from larger areas would have served to reduce the variability of available resources.

TABLE 19.1: Correlations of social and demographic variables with the south to north decline in resources among Northwest Coast groups of North America

South ⟶ North
Abundance and predictability of resources ⟶ decline
Descent-based groups and ownership of resources ⟶ increase (Richardson 1982)
Local intra-group prestige ⟶ heightened inter-group ranking   (Riches 1979)
Home range size ⟶ increase   (Ames 1975)
Mean household size ⟶ increase
Number of villages ⟶ decline
Size of villages ⟶ increase

To summarize the points made thus far, it is argued that:

(1) Complex foraging is most likely to have replaced simple foraging as a consequence of groups being "pulled" or "attracted" to resources that demanded and supported sedentary lifeways.

(2) Once in place, complex foragers would have experienced rapid community and regional population growth.

(3) Rising population would have resulted in the depletion of wild resources with the protein-rich K-selected species (most game animals) being affected first. For this reason those groups with access to marine resources would have been least affected by resource depletion.

(4) The social responses to sedentism, larger social units, and increasing scarcity and competition over resources would have been to intensify procurement (as mirrored by enhanced ranking and prestige), to bring tighter control over the resources (as reflected in more formalized descent-based groups and ownership), to concentrate resource controls within fewer, but larger population units (household and community), and to enlarge the areas of resource territories.

Archaeological Evidence from the Levant

So how do these, for the most part, ethnographically derived expectations fit the archaeological record as it relates to the Natufian?

Origin of the Natufian

All indications are that the Natufian emerged from a simple foraging base during a period of climatic-environmental amelioration some 12,000 to 13,000 years ago (Henry 1983, 1989; Henry et al. 1981, Leroi-Gourhan 1981, Dormon 1987). Palynological and zoological data point to an extension of Mediterranean woodlands well into the contemporary steppe/desert zone at this time (Tchernov 1981, Horo-witz 1979, Henry et al. 1985). This reconstruction is further reinforced by the intensive occupation of steppe and desert regions by the late Epipaleolithic groups that immediately preceded the early Natufian. In short, resource stress seems to be an unlikely explanation for the adaptive transition.

A more plausible argument, as initially advanced by Herbert Wright (1970), is that the increase in the earth's temperature at the end of the Pleistocene induced warmth-loving cereal grasses to expand from low elevation refuges in the Levant and to colonize their modern piedmont and upland habitat. The wild cereals (and nuts) thus provided an easily procured, nutritious, storable resource that was available for harvest at different elevational belts over three to five months of the year. As noted by Flannery (1969), however, such a resource demanded some degree of sedentism for processing, storage, and monitoring.

In the archaeological record we find that direct botanic evidence (pollen and carbonized grains) and indirect artifactual evidence (grind-ing stones, sickle blades, storage pits) are poorly represented and con-fined to low elevations outside of the modern natural habitat of cereals and nut-bearing trees prior to ca. 13,000 B.P. (Henry 1989). After 13,000 B.P., and associated with Natufian sites, we have abundant direct and indirect evidence for cereal collection and processing within the natural habitat zone at elevations up to 1,200 meters above sea level (Henry 1989).

The Degree of Sedentism

Recently scholars have questioned the degree to which Natufians were sedentary (Byrd 1987, Goring-Morris 1987, Olszewski, this volume). Although it is difficult to prove that Natufian basecamps or hamlets were occupied year-round, abundant and diverse evidence consistently points to the sites as having been occupied for most of the year. The presence of architecture, burials, human commensals, and exceedingly rich, thick cultural deposits all point to long-term occupations. Sea-sonal indications provided by certain faunal remains (e.g., reptiles and migratory waterfowl) and patterns in the age-sex compositions of ga-zelle remains (S. Davis 1983) also imply a multi-season or year-round residence at these sites.

As suggested by Byrd (1987), it may well be that there was some variability in the degree of sedentism of different Natufian groups. But in looking at the resources upon which they concentrated (i.e., cereals, nuts, and gazelles) and the locations where they placed their sites, it would appear that they had adopted a strategy of positioning themselves relatively permanently at the juncture of major resource zones (i.e., in ecotones). This contrasted sharply with the mobile strategies of preceding and even contemporary simple foraging groups that were not ecotonally situated. These fundamental differences in procurement strategies and settlement patterns are reflected in the differences in the distributions of Natufian sites and those of simple (Geometric Kebaran) foragers. Natufian sites are confined to the Mediterranean zone of the terminal Pleistocene and fall along the boundary of wooded uplands and level grasslands formed by broad interior valleys and the coastal plain. The sites are also tethered to strong water sources in the form of tributaries and springs. In contrast, Geometric Kebaran sites are distributed throughout various environmental zones and show no particular pattern of placement relative to resource boundaries. Also, many sites are found in settings that are likely to have had only seasonal water sources.

In regard to the question of sedentism, perhaps the most important observation to be made is that relative to the Geometric Kebaran: Natufian sites consistently yield a broad range of data that indicate a marked reduction in group mobility if not year-round settlement. The Geometric Kebaran site with the strongest parallels (i.e., burials, architecture, groundstone) to the Natufian is that of Neve David (Kaufman 1987). Dated to the very end of the Geometric Kebaran sequence (13,400–12,600 B.P.) and overlapping with that of the Early Natufian, it may well provide a glimpse into the transition from simple to complex foraging.

Population Growth

Natufian sites were some five times larger (1,000–2,000 m²) on the average than those of their simple foraging predecessors. Through time we can see an enlargement of Natufian sites and an expansion of Natufian communities from the Mediterranean woodland "core" to the margins of this zone. At Hayonim and Ein Mallaha, the two most thoroughly investigated Natufian sites, growth in settlement sizes during the course of their occupations can be seen (Valla 1981, Belfer-Cohen 1988). Finally, a comparison of site areas through time shows that Late Natufian sites are significantly larger on the average than Early Natufian occupations.

Dietary Changes

Osteological analyses of Natufian skeletal remains indicate not only that their diet contained significant amounts of stone-ground carbohydrates (most likely cereals), but also that stone-ground foods made up a progressively larger part of their diet through time. An examination of the skeletal populations from the sites of El Wad, Ein Mallaha, and Kebara for dental disease and attrition patterns showed that the El Wad and Ein Mallaha populations consumed a very high proportion of stone-ground foods, resembling in that respect early Neolithic populations (Smith 1972:236–237). Although the Kebara sample yielded relatively low dental attrition scores, strontium/calcium studies of the Kebara and El Wad samples point to equivalent high levels of plant food consumption (Schoeninger 1981). Other studies of strontium/calcium ratios from Natufian skeletal samples also point to a very high level of plant-food consumption (Schoeninger 1981, Sillen 1981, Smith et al. 1984), and indicate that it increased over that of earlier Late Glacial populations. Surprisingly, this research shows that plants comprised an even greater proportion of the Natufian diet than in the diets of later food-producing populations.

Responses to Resource Stress

Dental hypoplasia

Stress on Natufian populations can be seen in the relatively high frequency of enamel hypoplasia observed in skeletal populations. Hypoplasia frequencies provide a good indication of nutritional deficiencies experienced by infants and children (Goodman et al. 1984). In a study of the dental pathologies of samples from five sites, the incidence of enamel hypoplasia ranged from 10–61 percent (Smith et al. 1984). When these sites are arranged chronologically, a pattern can be seen in which the frequency of enamel hypoplasia increases through time (Table 19.2). This pattern is paralleled by a decline in stature between early (Ein Mallaha) and late (Nahal Oren) Natufian populations (Smith et al. 1984), but factors other than nutritional stress might have been responsibile for the latter trend.

Female infanticide

A social response to resource stress would appear to have taken the form of female infanticide. An examination of sex ratios for the skeletal populations from the four largest Natufian burial sites shows a consistent asymmetry in the favor of males, ranging from 57–75 percent (Table 19.3). These data, however, are restricted to adults because the skeletons of sub-adults cannot be sexed. Ruling out sampling bias, this could mean that, in order to achieve these adult ratios, a dispropor-

TABLE 19.2: Frequency of enamel hypoplasia for Natufian skeletal populations. The populations are ordered chronologically based on seriation schemes presented by Henry (1973) and Bar-Yosef and Valla (1981). The hypoplasia frequencies were published by Smith et al. (1984)

Site/phase	Frequency of hypoplasia	Time
Nahal Oren/Late	61	Late
Ein Mallaha/Early	27	
Kebara/Early	23	
El Wad/Late & Early	15	
Hayonim/Early	10	Early

tionate number of females would have had to have been removed from the population as sub-adults. The most likely explanation for their removal would be female infanticide or neglect, practices viewed as an important form of population control for many societies during times of resource scarcity (M. Harris 1977, Divale and Harris 1976).

Endogamy and matriliny

Interestingly, analysis of Natufian skeleton remains also provides a clue as to the nature of Natufian social organization. A recent study of 17 complete mandibles from Hayonim shows that third molar agenesis was present in 29.4 percent of the sample (Belfer-Cohen 1988). Although this is a much lower percentage of third molar agenesis than the 47 percent initially reported for the sample (Smith 1973), it still exceeds the 0–20 percent typically reported for other populations. Because the congenital absence of the third molar is a genetically

TABLE 19.3: Distribution of Natufian skeletal populations by sex. Note that all of the samples are skewed in favor of males and that all exceed the 56% threshold of a normal distribution

Site	Male		Female		Source
	N	%	N	%	
Ein Mallaha	9	75.0	3	25.0	(Ferembach 1977)
Hayonim	20	78.9	6	23.1	(Belfer-Cohen 1988)
Nahal Oren	11	61.0	7	39.9	(Crognier and Dupouy-Madre 1974)
El Wad	8	57.1	6	42.9	(Garrod and Bate 1937)
Combined mean/ percentage	48	68.6	22	31.4	

determined trait, inherited as a Mendelian recessive characteristic that occurs at relatively low frequencies, significant inbreeding or endogamy is indicated for the Hayonim population.

Universally, kin-group endogamy is quite rare, with only 67 of 862 (less than 8%) societies being listed in Murdock's (1967) *Ethnographic Atlas* as prescribing a form of endogamous marriage. When present, however, endogamy is almost always associated with sedentary, matrilocal communities (Murdock 1949, 1967; Levinson and Malone 1980). Matrilocal residence patterns are similarly highly correlated with matrilineal descent. The strong correlations between marriage, postmarital residence, and descent patterns in the ethnographic record therefore suggest that, given the evidence for endogamy, Natufian communities were most likely composed of one or more matrilocal groups that traced their descent matrilineally. This proposal also finds support in the inter-site differences in variability between male and female-related artifacts. As would be expected in a matrilocal system, male related artifacts (e.g., geometric microliths) show remarkable standardization between sites, while female linked artifacts (e.g., grinding stones) show little inter-site standardization.

Beyond being linked to the economic role of women and the periodic absence of males engaged in long-distance hunting, trade, and warfare, matriliny and endogamy also have been "functionally" related to the concentration of resource control by keeping heritable authority within the group (Hammel 1964, Goody 1976, Levinson and Malone 1980). In comparing Natufian and ethnographically derived evidence, Mussi (1976) also has argued for a social organization that promoted formal claims over goods and resources. This may well have become an increasingly important factor to Natufian communities as they experienced declining resources. Here it is important to recall that, among the Northwest Coast groups, the resource gradient was accompanied by a shift from cognatic to matrilineal descent and from intra-community to inter-community exchange.

Adoption of New Strategies

Within 2,500 years after the appearance of complex foraging strategies in the Levant, they appear to have been replaced by strategies characterized by incipient food production, on one hand, and a return to mobile, simple foraging on the other. The adoption of these alternatives seems to have been dependent upon differences in local environmental settings with food production emerging in better watered areas, while a return to simple foraging took place in the more arid regions (Henry 1989). The points that have been raised here, however, are not really related to the rise of agriculture *per se,* but instead they are linked to showing why complex foraging was destined to fail over the short term, and why it was a terminal Pleistocene-early Holocene phenomenon in the Levant. I suspect that this scenario might have some generalizable properties, in that non-aquatic complex foraging strategies might, always and everywhere, have been unstable and short lived. I recognize, however, that my own biases about what variables are important to measure (environmental change and its effects on resource distributions, resource stress, sedentism and its consequences for population growth, etc.) are not shared by all workers, and that these preconceptions must inevitably play a role in determining the plausibility of any explanation that might be proposed for the very distinctive Natufian adaptation.

Chapter 20
Stone Tools and Social Context in Levantine Prehistory

Ofer Bar-Yosef

Opening Remarks

In contrast to the early phases of prehistoric research in the Old World, when most prehistorians knew each other personally and when metaphysical paradigms were implicitly embedded in both field work and publications, we have since reached a point at which a personal statement concerning the fundamental assumptions held by a researcher might be regarded as desirable. This has resulted not only from a growing introspection in our discipline but also is the outcome of a period in American archaeology when "covering law" approaches tended to dominate the field (Watson et al. 1971, 1984; Lamberg-Karlovsky 1989). The recognition that it is legitimate to have different approaches to the study of the past makes it obligatory to try to express the basic assumptions that structure the research enterprise. In the case of the Levantine Epipaleolithic and early Neolithic periods, most of my biases concerning the nature and interpretation of archaeological residues were briefly presented in several previous publications (Bar-Yosef 1981a, b; 1983, 1987a, b, c; 1989). The editor's invitation to make these assumptions explicit in an independent essay is a good opportunity to explicate my approach to archaeology in general, and to the interpretation of the prehistoric sequence for the Late Pleistocene and Early Holocene Levant in particular.

Most of us are well aware of the diversity of approaches to archaeology, often located in different nations or at different universities. Clark refers to these as "national" or "regional research traditions." A shared paradigm is expressed by the expectation that certain kinds of data will be recovered in the field or the laboratory and that to do this, particular analytical techniques and classificatory systems are employed. Along with changing American approaches to archaeology (for a recent summary see Lamberg-Karlovsky 1989) there are other Old World research traditions that are sometimes poorly known or misunderstood by those who do not read French, Russian, or Chinese fluently (e.g., R. Davis 1983, Sackett 1981, Chang 1989).

I view the entire sequence of prehistory, for reasons detailed below, as divisible into two essential units: (1) the Lower and Middle Paleolithic and (2) the Upper Paleolithic, Epipaleolithic and Neolithic. I see archaeology as history and think that, in order to understand cultural evolution in a given geographic region, we need to know the history of social groups who played active and/or passive roles in the course of prehistoric events. Cultural changes were brought about by environmental and social stresses. Decisions made by humans during later prehistory can be decoded from the archaeological residues (in the broadest sense of this term) unearthed in the relevant sites. Not all groups were successful, of course; some made the wrong decisions and did not survive either biologically and/or culturally. The "history" of these groups can be learned through regional archaeological studies. If our objective is to define boundaries between groups, we should adopt a flexible definition of a region. We can easily imagine stress situations when intergroup social and cultural boundaries would have been well expressed, and situations when territorial maintenance and defense were less important and boundaries reflected in the archaeological records were very diffuse. In order to obtain the data necessary to allow us to reconstruct the "history" of such groups and to test our hypotheses concerning these processes, we adopt systematic approaches to data retrieval including excavation techniques and classificatory systems.

One such approach, which I believe to be of special relevance to Levantine prehistory, is the French paleoethnological school of André Leroi-Gourhan and his students (Leroi-Gourhan 1950, Audouze and Leroi-Gourhan 1981). This school combines a generalized ethnographic approach, accurate recording, and the use of simple spatial analytical techniques in order to achieve three-dimensional data sets. The excavation technique known as *décapage horizontale* (the simultaneous uncovering of large "horizontal" exposures) explicitly expresses the theoretical position of Leroi-Gourhan (Lavallé 1987). It was originally practiced in Middle and mainly Upper Paleolithic rockshelters in France, but is perhaps better known from the excavations of large, open-air Magdalenian sites there and in Germany (e.g., Leroi-Gourhan and Brézillon 1966, 1972; Bosinski 1988). *Décapage horizontale* has also been employed in rockshelters and caves in Europe, in South America and in the Near East (e.g., Rigaud and Simek 1990, Tixier 1974, Meignen et al. 1989, Valla 1988). This excavation technique aims at providing the information necessary to carry out the tedious work of refitting artifacts and bones (e.g., Leroi-Gourhan and Brézillon 1972) and thus to allow the description of a *chaîne opératoire* (see below). The next phase of analysis enables the archaeologist to propose an interpretation for the intrasite patterning revealed in terms of the domestic activities of hunter-gatherer groups and even to speculate (when certain aspects of faunal information are taken into account) on the length of seasonal or otherwise episodic occupation (e.g., Leroi-Gourhan and Brézillon 1972, Taborin 1987, Cahen et al. 1979, Cahen 1984). Although the particular model offered by Leroi-Gourhan was later challenged by Lewis Binford (1983a), more recent research indicates that both interpretations are in fact complementary (Audouze 1987). "Horizontal excavations" of open-air sites and refitting of artifacts are now quite commonly employed in the Levant (e.g., Marks 1983, Valla 1988b, Gilead 1988, Coinman et al. 1989).

Application of this approach to the excavation of stratified sites such as rockshelters and caves made it clear that there are certain problems with the interpretation of excavated units or visible thin layers. Site formation processes play an important role in the preservation of discrete stratigraphic units and often obliterate the presence of "living floors," both in caves and in open-air sites (e.g., Villa 1982, Villa and Courtin 1983). However, piece-plotting has its advantages even in cave sites (demonstrated, e.g., in the case of the cannibalized human remains from the French Neolithic levels of Fontbregoua cave [Villa et al. 1986]).

While I think there are problems with earlier periods, I believe that the data obtained through these field and laboratory techniques enable us to interpret the remains of Upper Paleolithic and later sites relatively unambiguously. We often assume that such late prehistoric occurrences, which represent only a minute fraction of a 2 my archaeological sequence, are simpler to interpret than those of the Lower or Middle Paleolithic because they contain residues left by modern humans, people like ourselves, who presumably behaved like us, and for which behavioral analogues abound in the ethnographic record. Modern humans, and especially hunter-gatherers, have been studied in order to discover rules governing their various domestic and public activities and the patterning of the material remains that result from those activities (e.g., Binford 1981b, Yellen 1977b, Hayden 1981, Gifford 1981). Of great importance are studies of hunter-gatherer territoriality (e.g., see Sampson 1988 for a full discussion of this neglected subject). However, these studies cannot be used without qualification as direct analogues to pre-agricultural prehistoric situations. Illuminating insights about site-formation processes can sometimes be gained through ethnoarchaeology, but the use of observations made by ethnoarchaeologists requires the same caution demanded of the users of any kind of reference collection. In other words, we need to evaluate the reliability of the informants, the possibility of recent cultural influence by state-level societies over the past few centuries, and sometimes even the outside influence caused by trade and exchange networks. The intricate mutual relationships between modern hunter-gatherers and neighboring farming and herding communities are illustrated by both field studies and summaries of ethnographic or historical records (e.g., Headland and Reid 1989, Eder 1987, Spielmann 1986). When the changing nature of these complex relationships is carefully examined, it becomes evident that more sophisticated approaches to ethnoarchaeology are needed, mainly because the recent prehistory of the indigenous peoples of Australia, New Guinea, the Philippines, and the Americas is poorly known (White and O'Connell 1982, Schrire 1984, Sampson 1988). We usually do not search for 1:1 correlations between the ethnoarchaeological samples and the archaeological residues, but rather hope to discover the organizational principles which govern the formation of those elements which survive through time.

Who Am I?

As someone who is a native of southwest Asia, I grew up in an intellectual tradition derived from various schools (Bar-Yosef and Mazar 1982). On the one hand was biblical archaeology (also known as Syro-Palestinian archaeology). This intellectual tradition combines the cultural-historical approach of William F. Albright (1943) with the excavation strategy of opening large spatial areas (first employed by the American archaeologist G. A. Reisner in Sechem [Tel Balata] in Samaria [Aharoni 1973]). On the other hand my formal training in prehistoric archaeology was in the tradition established by Dorothy Garrod and Réné Neuville (1928–1935) who together brought to the Near East the French approach of the 1920s and 1930s. This tradition emphasized lithic typology and the rather industrious excavations of caves in sections (which generally meant arbitrarily defined portions of the sites and not the metric grid systems used today). More accurate field recording techniques were introduced by Moshe Stekelis and Jean Perrot, who used grids in their excavations, recorded artifacts by arbitrary units and loci (a method also practiced in biblical archaeology), and conducted some basic dry sieving. I was directly trained by Stekelis, from whom I acquired an interest in ethnography which was part of his archaeological education in the Soviet Union. I also had the opportunity, like many of my generation, to work and study with François Bordes and his students.

In the Israel of my generation, the traditional view of Prehistory (with a capital P) was that defined by the European schools. The study of prehistory began in those institutions already involved in classical archaeology (from which biblical archaeology emerged). "Prehistory" meant everything earlier than the earliest documented historical period and, in the reality of academic life (i.e., in the structuring of university departments), it incorporated the paleolithic and the neolithic eras. However, the close relationship between the historically known periods and their archaeological remains, which last for at least 5,000 years in the Near East, caused the interpretation of prehistoric phenomena to become a simple extension of historical archaeology. Therefore, to someone who studies the last five millennia in southwest Asia, the identification of certain assemblages of material culture remains (sites, clusters of pottery types, or particular building plans) with a "people" is a common convention. The practice of identifying destroyed cities or burned villages with known historical or quasi-historical (biblical) events is, in the Near East, not only a legitimate scholarly activity but also in many cases a documented historical reality. For areas where there is no ancient historical past, such activities are, of course, more problematical.

Those who work in the Near East know quite well that the contemporary political situation can often provide useful historical analogies (see Rosen, this volume). The often antagonistic encounters among Near Eastern sociopolitical entities are easily traced on the landscape with the aid of common archaeological markers such as building types. For example, the distributions of the various kinds of sacred places—synagogues, mosques, churches—mark the location of definable religious communities. Similarly, Jewish, Bedouin, and Arab populations are architecturally recognizable from different types of house or apartment building plans, on the condition that acculturation or assimilation has not been profound.

Given my current research interests and the nature of my local archaeological training, the reader may understand my viewing of the Epipaleolithic and the Neolithic sequences of southwest Asia as representing *the continuous social history of groups that can be traced and defined in the archaeological record* within a framework explicitly defined by V. Gordon Childe (1951) and elaborated by David Clarke (1972). On the other hand, I can appreciate the position of certain Western schools, especially those dominant in the two or three decades after World War II, that are skeptical of or deny outright the ability of archaeologists to identify ethnic groups by using archaeological residues (Hodder 1982). Past examples of the abuse of archaeological investigations for political ends are well known and need not be repeated here.

The Early Prehistoric Periods: The Lower and Middle Paleolithic

At this point, it should be clearly stated that I do not consider the principles used for interpreting the contexts of *later* prehistory (Upper Paleolithic through Neolithic) to be the same as those employed as guidelines for explaining *earlier* periods. None of the analogies derived from modern hunter-gatherer research can easily be used to explain the remote past. Studies of non-anthropogenic natural formation processes, and the behavior of carnivores and scavengers, have proved valuable for understanding some of the processes involved in creating bone accumulations in Lower and Middle Paleolithic sites (e.g., Binford 1981b, 1983a; Brain 1981, Isaac 1984). None of these, however, have so far entirely clarified the behavioral processes responsible for the organizational attributes of Lower Paleolithic stone assemblages. In order to avoid confusion concerning the matter of lithic assemblages, I will explain my current approach to the interpretation of Lower and Middle Paleolithic sites. Nowadays such a statement is essential, since many of us are involved in modern human origins research; and there is a tendency to make sweeping comparisons between various aspects of the archaeological records of the Middle and Upper Paleolithic sequences from different regions, and to use those comparisons in order to argue for or against one or another position (e.g., Chase and Dibble 1987, Mellars 1989, Clark and Lindly 1989a).

It is trivial to remind ourselves that most of the artifacts of the paleolithic periods are lithics, only very rarely accompanied by accumulations of fragmented bone. Evidence for other aspects of material culture are either rare or totally absent due to poor conditions of preservation in most sites. Wooden objects are occasionally found in sites where conditions of preservation are exceptional (e.g., Kalambo Falls, Torralba, Clacton-on-Sea, Lehringen). Otherwise, no direct evidence is available, apart from microwear studies, concerning the possible use of other organic materials by early hominids during the Lower and Middle Paleolithic. We therefore cannot assume that these hominids used the same range of raw materials as modern humans did because this is exactly what we have to demonstrate. For example, cases in which bone was intentionally used as material for tool making are very few, and at Fontana Ranuccio (Segre and Ascenzi 1984) hominids evidently used fossil bones as raw material. In other cases, bones were manipulated without substantially altering the shape of the original piece. This situation is of course entirely different from that known in Upper Paleolithic assemblages. Similarly, the evidence for the use of fire and the discovery of credible "hearths" is equivocal, especially for most of the Lower Paleolithic. However, indisputable hearths are present in Middle Paleolithic sites, especially in the Near East and in South Africa (e.g., Perlés 1977, Clark and Harris 1987, James 1989, Straus 1989c, Meignen et al. 1989).

When site formation processes are adequately controlled (and in most cases it is impossible to do this), distribution maps of scattered remains together with micromorphological analyses (Courty et al. 1989) and microscopic examinations of the condition of animal bones and stone artifacts may serve as useful sources of information. By combining the results of these various studies we can sometimes determine whether humans and/or carnivores were responsible for the accumulation of bone in excavated assemblages, and to what extent natural agencies such as sheet wash, abrasion, and deflation have created a mixture of undecipherable patterns. In Lower and Middle Paleolithic research, we end up with generalizations about a "culture," "tradition," or "paleoculture" (*sensu* Jelinek 1977) which refers to the most abundant and indisputable human artifacts—the lithics. Therefore, those who accept the notion that "culture is man's extrasomatic means of adaptation" (White 1959:8) should wonder, first, what part of the cultural system is preserved in the lithics and fractured bones, and, secondly, what Lower Paleolithic archaeological remains (which, in the Levant, extend back at least 1.3 myr) can potentially tell us (Binford 1983a, b; 1987b; Isaac 1984).

Most studies of the Lower Paleolithic indicate that similar kinds of Oldowan and Acheulian tools, together with associated flake assemblages, can be found in sites stretching from temperate Europe across to the Deccan Plateau of India, throughout the Mediterranean Basin and into the subtropical environments of Africa and Asia. This suggests that the basic stone tool kits of *Homo erectus* do not reflect the range of possible environmental adaptations (or acclimatizations) that we might predict in such a variety of ecozones. Morphological variability among the core-choppers and the bifaces, as defined on the basis of several type list and attribute analyses (Leakey 1971, Bordes 1961a, Roe 1964), was found in most cases to correspond to the available raw material (Toth 1985) and to technological factors such as curation and resharpening which demonstrated that bifaces were used both as tools and curated cores (Jones 1979, 1980). In a few cases, such as the site of Gesher Benot Ya'acov in the Jordan Valley, numerous lava flake cleavers, made by the Tachengit/Tabelbalat technique common in the African world, testify to the preferences of a human group for a particular type of raw material, thus indicating their African origins (Bar-Yosef 1987c). I suggest that a change in the overall technomorphological picture is discernible among the Upper or Late Acheulian industries (ca. 80/60–15/11 kyr B.P.). In these industries, biface shapes are more regular and often were made by the removal of numerous flakes (including the stages of resharpening). The presence or absence of Levallois technique (also known in Africa as Victoria West) indicates some regional differences, although in some cases this may reflect the availability of raw material in nodules of sufficient size for Levallois flake production.

The overall picture of the Middle Paleolithic (or, in Africa, the Middle Stone Age) reveals a slightly different pattern from that of the Lower Paleolithic. By using the Bordesian classificatory system we are able to compare assemblages across the continents of the Old World. From time to time, American scholars have suggested that there are hidden assumptions behind Bordesian-based typological studies, yet they remain the best available descriptive procedure for recording Middle Paleolithic industrial variability. Even though Bordes took into account accepted or commonly used morphological definitions, Bordesian type lists, when combined with the results of metrical analysis, can provide new insights into the organizational properties of Middle Paleolithic stone industries (e.g., Dibble 1987a–c).

When a worldwide comparison is done, we find that the basic tool kits are quite similar across the various environments from the Cape region in South Africa through the Levant to the edges of the periglacial belt in Europe and the Indian plateaux. Differences in lithic technology are defined as Levallois and non-Levallois (Bordes 1961b) with a further subdivision of Levallois technique into several core reduction strategies for the production of flakes, blades, and points (e.g., Boëda 1988). Typological variability is often expressed in ranges of percentages per type, or group of types, which, together with the presence or absence of Levallois products, creates a general measure of interassemblage variability (e.g., Bordes 1980). However, the basic tool forms such as sidescrapers and Mousterian (or retouched Levallois) points are found in sites across the entire Middle Paleolithic world. Despite the role played by the availability and accessibility of raw material, the end products are basically similar throughout the entire Middle Paleolithic. However, in some regions and for some periods, particular tool forms demonstrate a restricted geographical distribution, such as the bifaces in the Mousterian of Acheulian Tradition in western Europe, the foliate bifaces (*blattspitzen*) in central and eastern

Europe, and the Aterian tanged points in North Africa (Ferring 1975, Wendorf et al. 1987).

The overall conclusion concerning the similarity of tool types across a wide variety of environmental zones is currently supported by lithic use-wear-based functional analyses following the methods first described by Semenov (1964) and directed toward a resolution of the Bordes-Binford debate on "cultural" versus "functional" interpretations (Bordes 1973, Binford 1973). Scholars who employ different microscopic techniques to interpret stone tool functions from lithic use-wear traces have reached essentially similar conclusions concerning the lack of a direct relationship between the morphological variability within Mousterian assemblages and the specific functions of the objects utilized (e.g., Beyries 1987, Shea 1989a). The same activities (butchery, woodworking, etc.) were accomplished using a variety of different artifact "types" including sidescrapers, knives, Levallois flakes; and the same artifact types were employed in a wide range of different activities. For some artifacts, however, there is a clear relationship between form and function (e.g., Levallois points, pointed flakes often served as projectiles and as hafted cutting tools in the Levantine Mousterian sites of Kebara, Hayonim, Tabūn and Qafzeh [Shea 1989b]).

In sum, when Middle Paleolithic assemblages are compared to Lower Paleolithic ones, a somewhat more geographically varied pattern of lithic variability emerges within a relative shorter time span (100–150 kyr). However, the rate of change, as demonstrated by the lithic artifacts, was very slow and probably does not reflect other, more important shifts in technology including the systematic use of fire or ephemeral use of red ochre in personal decoration or hide working. The lithic assemblages do not reflect the presence of two human morphotypes (i.e., neanderthals, moderns) in the Levant (Meignen and Bar-Yosef 1988, Bar-Yosef n.d.a). Social organization communication systems were perhaps improved or modified, but it is difficult to reconstruct them from the available evidence in the manner in which it is currently organized.

The Later Prehistoric Periods: The Upper Paleolithic, Epipaleolithic, and Neolithic

A major change occurred with the emergence of early Upper Paleolithic (EUP). What seems to be a slow rate of change for the beginning of the EUP becomes a rapid rate of change when compared to earlier periods. The literature on the Upper Paleolithic industries indicates the appearance of what seem to be relatively short-lived regional characteristics. For example, the Châtelperronian is not found in the Levant, nor are the assemblages with foliates (bifacially worked points) which typify the EUP in central and eastern Europe. Various archaeological "guide fossils" are found only in some regions and not in others (for details, see, e.g., Rigaud and Simek 1989, Kozlowski 1988, Otte 1989). In the Levant some tool forms, such as the distinctive *chanfreins* (chamfered pieces), subtypes of El-Wad points and nosed Aurignacian scrapers, have a restricted geographical distribution that seems real enough (see Bergman 1987, Marks and Ferring 1988, Bar-Yosef and Belfer-Cohen 1989a, b, Goring-Morris 1987 for additional examples). The lithic variability present during the Upper Paleolithic, which, in the Levant, also includes the Epipaleolithic (20,000–12,000 B.P.) (and, in Africa, the Late Stone Age), is greater than that of the preceding periods; and the changes are much more rapid when the length of the periods is taken into account. It is this lithic variability that we try to describe and then to interpret within a framework of social variability. It is important to emphasize, however, that although stone tools are elements incorporated within the system of extractive activities, they are not expected to reflect the entire array of subsistence activities. Almost none of the scholars working in the Old World have claimed that the technological and typological description of lithic assemblages can be the basis for reconstructing economic activities, and we all agree that lithic objects could have been tools in and of themselves, hafted as part of composite tools, artifacts for making other tools, and/or simply discarded "waste" products resulting from primary or secondary core reductions. However, it is a commonly held paradigmatic bias among scholars trained in the Old World that major typological and technological differences between chipped stone assemblages are assumed, either implicitly or explicitly, to represent social entities of some kind. In other words, we hold in common some basic assumptions about the existence of relationships between knapping techniques employed by humans and their participation in culturally defined social entities. Some of those assumptions are at variance with those held by scholars trained in the New World (see, e.g., Binford and Sabloff 1982).

Finally, in defining these social entities, whether we retain the neo-evolutionist terms "band," "macro-band," and "tribe" is, in my view, of little importance. Recent studies indicate that tribal-level organization might have emerged historically as a response to the needs of states and empires to exert control over nomadic groups. However, the way in which these terms are used in archaeology is so ambiguous that they might profitably be replaced by terms such as "small" or "large local groups," or small/large "social units." But before turning to a discussion of the paradigms for later prehistory (within which these terms are commonly employed), and in keeping with the efforts of other contributors, it might be worthwhile to examine briefly the academic environment of the Ancient Near Eastern studies that have shaped my basic viewpoints.

Identifying Archaeological Cultures in Historical Context

We all know that the archaeological past is often traced backward in a way similar to excavating a stratified site. Thus we begin with the recent past and, as we proceed, we find ourselves studying and trying to understand more and more remote time ranges. While examining past situations, we draw our analogies from recent history. This is a common practice in the study of archaeological sequences in both hemispheres. In both the Old and New Worlds, ethnographic records and travelers' diaries have frequently served as textual sources for observations considered relevant to the interpretation of certain large classes of archaeological observations. To cite a few examples, there are (1) similarities between Halafian domestic structures and traditional methods of house construction in present-day Syrian villages (Seeden 1982), (2) smudge pits in a prehistoric context and hide smoking in the ethnographic records (Binford 1972), (3) seasonal strategies of meat consumption by hunter-gatherers indicative of the dietary need for fats (Speth and Spielmann 1983) generated an explanation for the peculiar character of faunal remains at a fifteenth-century A.D. bison kill site (Speth 1983), and (4) ethnographic and ethnohistorical exchange patterns between hunter-gatherers and farmers which have served as a basis for a model simulation that was then used to explain archaeological patterns (Spielmann 1986).

Beyond the interpretation of discrete archaeological phenomena, textual sources are also used in the Near East for identifying foreign groups in archaeological contexts. Historical records and travelers' accounts (many of whom were pilgrims) provide detailed descriptions of Crusader towns and fortresses built during the 11–12th A.D. centuries in the Holy Land including their names in Old French (moreover, the present Hebrew or Arabic names are often corruptions of the archaic French). Several of these sites have been excavated; and their plans, the style of dressing stone, tombstones with inscriptions, etc., indicate that the actual fortresses can be accurately identified in the field. Most of these sites were constructed in accordance with architectural principles of Medieval European derivation, specific to fortifications, palaces, and hospitals. Thus the Crusaders as an archaeological entity can be identified in the field as well as in history and in collections of material culture. The dates these fortifications were destroyed are known historically, and archaeological contexts from destruction levels can often be placed in a refined and proper chronological order.

A somewhat similar example is furnished by the archaeological residues of an older allochthonous group known colloquially as the "Sea People." These groups came from the Aegean region during the twelfth century B.C. and settled on the Israeli coastal plain (Dothan 1982). The plans of their temples, private dwellings, and building arrangements within settlements are quite different from those of the autochthonous Canaanite tradition (Mazar 1985, 1986). Moreover, neutron activation analysis has revealed that certain decorated pottery types (Mycenean IIIC:1b) once considered imports were produced locally, replicating the same style as in their homeland (Gunneweg et al. 1986). The importance of this discovery will be understood if we take into account the fact that, during the previous three centuries, Mycenean and Cypriote imports were locally imitated without reaching the quality and refinement of these particular Mycenean IIIC:1b wares. The latter is therefore considered the best evidence for their being produced by potters who came from the Aegean world as part of a large influx of migrants. Most other material culture elements of the Philistines were not different from the local Canaanite culture (Bonimovitz 1986). Thus, if the combination of certain pottery types, house plans, and shrines is demonstrated to be a useful archaeological marker of ethnicity some 3,000 years ago, it is tempting to carry this procedure even further back in time in order to isolate, archaeologically, similar but unnamed people who lived in the more remote prehistoric past.

It is, of course, undoubtedly easier to identify a foreign population in the archaeological context if a sufficient number and variety of material culture elements is available. Pottery types by themselves, even if they have distinct forms and fabrication procedures, can hardly be considered to be unequivocal social indicators. A Levantine case in point is the presence of Khirbet Kerak (Beit Yerah) ware, dated to the Early Bronze III Period (ca. 2600–2300 B.C.). Khirbet Kerak ware is thought by one school to represent the migration of groups of people of eastern Anatolian origin, who came through Syria's 'Amuq Valley and who eventually settled in northern Israel, as far south as the Jezreel Valley (e.g., Albright 1943, Kenyon 1957). Alternative interpretations are possible. The Khirbet Kerak pottery in the southern Levant is a collection of types that includes a few domestic forms and many vessels that could be considered to have been prestige items (Stager n.d.). It is not inconceivable that all these were actually produced in the town of Beit Yerah and distributed from there around the central part of the Jordan Valley and up into the margins of the Galilee. One modest potter's workshop would have been adequate to produce all the pieces recorded to date in the excavations of various Early Bronze III sites.

Finally, it has been argued that the emergence of distinct "archaeological" cultures in southwest Asia first took place during the fifth through third millennia B.C. (e.g., Nissen 1988). The remains of these civilizations are reflected in both the archaeological and linguistic records and, in most cases, are considered to represent rather large social units. In this context, the founders of the early Mesopotamian and Egyptian states, and even those involved in the secondary wave of urbanization (as represented in Palestine), are considered by various scholars to have been the descendants of indigenous neolithic farming societies (e.g., Childe 1952, Braidwood 1975, Redman 1978, Nissen 1988). It might, therefore, be an interesting exercise to try to identify their ancestral social units. Urbanization was not a uniform process throughout western Asia, and evidently not all contemporaneous west Asians and northeast Africans participated directly in this major episode of cultural and political change. This is not to say that other aspects of this process are less important, but it was *clearly the history of particular groups,* such as the Natufians or the Halafians, who changed the face of the Near East. Understanding "how" these groups operated, and "why" and "when" they made the decisions that led to the establishment of increasingly complex societies, requires intensive study of the neolithic period.

The five millennia (ca. 12–7 kyr B.P.) during which farming communities established themselves over large parts of the Near East fall under the vague terms of "Early" and "Late" Neolithic, which, in the southern Levant, correspond to the Pre-Pottery Neolithic A and B (PPNA, PPNB) and Pottery Neolithic (PN, variously subdivided) following the taxa suggested by Kathleen Kenyon while digging in Jericho. These terms have only a chronological significance and bear no relation to the original European definition of the Neolithic, nor to the variable socioeconomic situations encountered in the Levant (see Mellaart 1975, Cauvin 1978, 1987; Aurenche et al. 1981, Moore 1985, Rollefson 1988, Rollefson and Köhler-Rollefson 1989, Rollefson and Simmons 1988, Simmons et al. 1987, Bar-Yosef 1981a, 1986, 1989; Bar-Yosef and Belfer-Cohen 1989a, b). The alternative taxonomic approach, long advocated by Robert J. Braidwood, employs a stage typology of terms with socioeconomic implications (e.g., level of incipient cultivation and domestication, level of primary village-farming communities, etc., Braidwood 1975). These definitions have no chronological meaning whatsoever, but refer instead to rungs on an evolutionary ladder through which a Near Eastern world of fully agricultural villages and urban centers has emerged. While there is a general consensus that the trend through time demonstrates the expansion of village farming communities at the expense of hunter-gatherer adaptations, there is considerable disagreement concerning the causes and linearity of this trend (cf., Smith and Young 1983, Moore 1985, Redding 1988, Henry 1989, Bar-Yosef and Belfer-Cohen 1989b).

The Near Eastern Neolithic is an intricate socioeconomic mosaic which, I believe, cannot be understood unless we trace the "histories" of the particular groups who inhabited the Levant since the late glacial maximum. The relatively extreme cold and dry conditions prevalent during most of oxygen-isotope Stage 2 (24/22–15/14 kyr B.P.) restricted the distribution of predictable, accessible resources in the Levant to a narrow, coastal "corridor," with a few "satellite" oases, and created some sort of a "bottleneck" in terms of local population continuity and biological stability. I think, therefore, that the later prehistory of this region "commenced" mainly with this time span and the ensuing period of climatic amelioration (14.5/14–13 kyr B.P.). I do not deny the apparent continuity with the Upper Paleolithic Ahmarian Tradition (Goring-Morris 1987, Gilead 1988). I only wish to caution against viewing the lithic bladelet industries (sometimes called Late Upper Paleolithic [LUP]) as representative of continuous local human evolution. Therefore, I will turn to the Levantine Epipaleolithic and, following a brief discussion of the archaeological methods which may allow us to identify the social units that inhabited the region during this period, I will proceed with a similar short survey of the Neolithic.

The Paradigm for the Epipaleolithic

The archaeological sequence of the Levantine Epipaleolithic industries is by now quite well known, although research in additional regions such as eastern Syria and Jordan will undoubtedly broaden the picture (Bar-Yosef 1981a, 1983, 1987a, b; Bar-Yosef and Phillips 1977, Bar-Yosef and Vogel 1987, Marks 1976b, 1977a, b: Henry 1983, 1989; Goring-Morris 1987, 1989; Valla 1984, 1987; M.-C. Cauvin 1987, Garrard et al. 1987, Garrard and Gebel 1988). Epipaleolithic archaeological remains can be seen to reflect human groups if the following assumptions are regarded as credible.

The identification of social units is accomplished on the basis of a selective analysis of artifacts and other archaeological traits. It is based on the assumption that, in most cases, the shapes of tools within one category of retouched pieces, such as the microliths, do not indicate different functions but instead convey stylistic variation. The lack of well preserved projectiles (with their wooden or reed shafts) is of course disturbing. It would be reassuring to know the actual hafting techniques of this period instead of being required to speculate about them (Bar-Yosef 1986). Use-wear studies point in the same direction (i.e., that the various forms are the result of stylistic variation and are not related to function—e.g., Anderson-Gerfaud 1983). Moreover, ethnographic studies (carefully selected to support our contention) demonstrate that stylistic differences among objects used for similar functions do in fact exist.

The reconstruction of group size is done on the basis of site size (the observed spatial distribution of the lithics and bones controlling for post-depositional effects). Three-dimensional attributes of excavated or surface collected Epipalcolithic sites indicate that most of them were 25–400 m² in area and are, therefore, considered to represent the distribution of garbage left by frequent residential moves (Bar-Yosef 1981a, Henry 1983, 1989; Clark et al. 1988). In every site the well-shaped microliths, which served as projectiles, were systematically produced, hafted, or re-hafted on older shafts. Therefore, their geographic distribution marks, in my view, the boundaries of a social unit. It should be stressed here that Neolithic projectiles were used in a much more complex social context and, therefore, do not convey, on the level of assemblage-by-assemblage analysis, the same social message—a point I elaborate below.

To argue that the analysis of lithic assemblages is our main source of inference about social information requires some justification. Generally speaking, lithic assemblages are analyzed and reported today on three levels. The basic knapping techniques are reconstructed on the basis of quantitative classifications of debitage (rarely through refitting), followed by a quantitative type list in which all formally "retouched pieces" are included. Attribute analysis of dominant debitage forms (the class of blades/bladelets) emphasizes scar pattern, platform shape, overall blank form, curvature of lateral profile, etc., as well as metric characteristics (e.g., Henry 1977, Goring-Morris 1987). A similar kind of attribute analysis is often employed in order to clarify and quantify the characteristics of certain tool groups such as microliths (e.g., Bar-Yosef 1970, Goring-Morris 1987). The overall quantitative and qualitative descriptions of each assemblage culminates in comparisons with other assemblages and the clustering of assemblages into industries (= cultures), cultural groups, and cultural complexes (cf. Clarke 1968).

Assemblages are considered to be the results of dynamic formation systems which encompass anthropogenic, biogenic, and other natural processes (e.g., Schiffer 1987, Courty et al. 1989). Human activities in sites (beside those which leave no archaeological trace—sleeping, mating, dancing, etc.) also include knapping and retooling (*sensu* Keeley 1982). This means that not all the objects made and used in situ were left behind. Depending on the duration of occupation and the range and nature of these activities, the resulting assemblages can be considerably different quantitatively from one another and yet remain the products of the same social group. Archaeological examples for different site types are easily found in the desert regions of the Levant, where groups rarely camped in exactly the same spot. Deserts were also less affected by subsequent human disturbance when more favored landscapes came under cultivation or were otherwise used more intensively by humans. Under these circumstances, it is only wishful thinking to expect that statistical comparisons would indicate similarity between assemblages retrieved from sites where accumulations resulted from repeated (seasonal?) visits of one group or alternate occupations by groups that possibly (but not necessarily) belonged to the same social unit (probably a "macroband"). Cultural and natural formation processes acted to modify and mix lithic assemblages in caves, rock-shelters, and open-air sites situated in optimal locations (e.g., and especially, springs), where groups returned many times or stayed for relatively long periods of time. This limits the utility of quantitative comparisons which, under these circumstances, can only indicate general cultural assignments. However, when treating the evidence from such sites, we should also consider the possibility that assemblages might be mixtures resulting from alternate occupations by different competing groups. These considerations suggest that quantitative comparisons should not be taken at face value and might sometimes be utterly meaningless. The only valid procedure for clustering Epipaleolithic assemblages might be through interassemblage comparisons of single groups of artifacts—namely the microliths. But, before dealing with this issue, I want to return briefly to the study of debitage which, since the days of François Bordes, has become a major field of enquiry in many Old World regions and time periods.

The debitage classification most commonly used in the Levant was introduced by Anthony Marks and his associates in the late 1960s while working in the central Negev. Since it is a lingua franca, its use is imperative for general recording; but the mere reporting of quantities of flakes and blades cannot be used as a scale for measuring social boundaries. While the number of potential core reduction strategies for obtaining blanks with laminar dimensions from Levantine flints is rather limited, comparisons between different Epipaleolithic entities using debitage variables did not disclose a clear pattern (Goring-Morris

1987). Therefore, we need to return to selective studies of certain debitage categories, aimed at discovering the *chaîne opératoire* (Lemonnier 1983) and examine once again the retouched pieces ("tools") which, through their form and size relations, convey non-functional information which I regard as "stylistic" in a very general sense (cf. Sackett 1982).

The Kebaran Complex

Using principles that combined core reduction strategies and selected typological analyses for identifying groups within the Kebaran Cultural Complex (19–14.5 kyr B.P.), the Geometric Kebaran or the Mushabian Complex (14.5–12.8 kyr B.P.) in the geographic region where these sites are found enable us to recognize particular prehistoric social territories (Bar-Yosef 1987b, 1989, Bar-Yosef and Vogel 1987, Goring-Morris 1987, Henry 1988, Hovers 1989). It should be stressed again that the study of the lithic artifacts is not expected to disclose direct information concerning the subsistence activities of its producers (except perhaps in the case of microwear analyses). These can usually only be gleaned from the plant and animal bone assemblages together with site locational data and the reconstructed paleoenvironment (based on pollen from lake cores, geomorphic features and paleosols—Hovers 1989).

On the basis of ethnographic principles underlying the possible culture-historical relationships between hunter-gatherers and their territories, I assume that the spatial distribution of human groups ultimately depends upon the carrying capacity of the region and the ability of those foragers to exploit available resources. It is therefore interesting and valuable to try to reconstruct the hypothetical size of Epipaleolithic socioeconomic territories and their potential resources, despite the often cited problems with quantifying carrying capacity (e.g., Winterhalder and Smith 1981).

Pilot studies show that, in the southern Levant, hunter-gatherer bands probably could have supported themselves in the Mediterranean phytogeographic zone in territories as small as 500–1000 km². Somewhat larger territories were required in the steppic Irano-Turanian belt and larger ones still in the true deserts of the Saharo-Sindian vegetational zone (Bar-Yosef and Belfer-Cohen 1989b). Such estimates are based on the seasonal availability of vegetal resources (seeds, nuts, fruits, and leaves) as well as what would have been the natural distribution of medium- and small-sized ungulates. Palynological studies of Upper Pleistocene cores from the Levant basically indicate that the same vegetal resources were available to Epipaleolithic gatherers as are present today (Bottema and van Zeist 1981, van Zeist and Bottema 1982, Weinstein-Evron 1986). Moreover, the pattern of seasonality was basically similar to that of today (Gamble and Soffer 1990). Although Holocene anthropogenic processes have partially altered the spatial distribution of the Mediterranean, Irano-Turanian, and Saharo-Sindian belts, the reconstruction of the late Pleistocene pattern is well grounded in the palynological evidence and by plotting the distributions of small relict plant populations (Horowitz 1979, Baruch 1986). With more information derived from carbonized macrobotanical remains like those recovered from Wadi Hammeh Sites 26 and 27 (northwest Jordan), Hayonim cave and terrace (Israel), and a cluster of PPNA sites in the Jordan Valley (Netiv Hagdud, Gilgal, Jericho), additional confidence can be placed in the above conclusions (Edwards et al. 1988, Edwards 1989, Hopf and Bar-Yosef 1987, Hopf 1983, Zohary and Hopf 1988, Bar-Yosef et al. n.d.). Thus we can try to simulate the impact of paleoclimatic changes on Levantine adaptations and perhaps ultimately test the various models offered as explanations for the cultural transitions that led to the establishment of farming communities there by about 10,000 B.P. Apparently abrupt climatic changes combined with a period of social stress might explain the Geometric Kebaran tendency to become more sedentary over time (and, *en bloc*, to be more sedentary than their mobile predecessors) (Bar-Yosef and Belfer-Cohen 1989a).

The Natufian

The emerging new social system in the southern Levant subsequent to the Geometric Kebaran is known as the Natufian culture. The lower layers in early Natufian sites are characterized by greater typological and technological (i.e., knapping techniques) heterogeneity when compared to those of the Late Natufian (Belfer-Cohen 1989). In our view, this means that flintknappers who were formally part of the residential movements of Geometric Kebaran foragers began to live together, and the social process of "homogenizing" the knapping techniques took place over a period of some time. Moreover, one can trace the general area from which these Geometric Kebaran groups moved to a more central place in order to form a semi-sedentary or sedentary Early Natufian community.

Group identity in the large Early Natufian settlements (e.g., Ein Mallaha, Wadi Hammeh 27) was maintained on several levels. For example, lunates were produced in every site; however, the distinctive microburin technique by which one may obtain the oblique snaps characteristic of many microlith blanks was practiced only in some sites and was apparently unknown (or not used) in others (Bar-Yosef and Valla 1979). Other means for maintaining group identity might have included different expressions in body decoration (combinations of jewelry made of marine shells, bone beads and pendants), and distinctive patterns of engraving on bone objects and limestone slabs. Given the fairly large and growing corpus of human skeletal material, it will be interesting to try to determine whether biological clustering can be detected—perhaps ultimately to test the hypothesis that some of the graves in Hayonim cave were those of communal family burials (Smith 1973).

In geographic terms, the Early Natufian "homeland" appears to have encompassed about 50,000 km^2, an area which easily could have supported a viable biological population (10–15 macrobands?). Its success was insured by the availability, accessibility, and reliability of the vegetal resources of the region (mainly cereal grasses). The new social organization is reflected in the variability amongst the burials, differences in house sizes, and the presence of special activity areas within sites like Ein Mallaha (Eynan) and Hayonim cave and terrace, and the proliferation in the production of bone objects and ground stone tools (Valla 1984, 1987; Perrot 1989, Belfer-Cohen 1989, Campana 1989). During the Early Natufian time range, hunter-gatherers continued to exploit other parts of the Near East (e.g., the Syro-Arabian desert, the Sinai, the Taurus and Zagros mountainous regions). Despite the paucity of archaeological documentation, sites like Abu Hureyra (Olszewski 1986) and some of the small cave sites in Turkey provide evidence which in the future might enable us to draw a better social map of the Near East during this period.

The Late Natufian (10,000–10,500/10,300 kyr B.P.) is undoubtedly the least-known phase of the Natufian sequence, as fewer sites have been tested or excavated than have been for the earlier phases. The general impression is that the Natufian economy responded to climatic deterioration (a drying trend) during this millennium by resorting to somewhat higher mobility. But the overall picture is far from clear, except in the Negev where intensive field work, first by Marks and his colleagues and later by Goring-Morris and his associates, revealed an interesting cultural sequence which documents the struggle for survival of later Natufian groups in this arid region.

The Harifian

The Harifian culture is a Late Natufian entity which occupied the Negev-northern Sinai region, an area of about 60,000 km^2. It was an adaptation to increasing aridity and dwindling resources (during the

Levantine equivalent of the "Younger Dryas"), and is recognizable by a distinctive settlement pattern based on seasonal transhumance with small, dispersed winter camps in the sandy lowlands and larger, summer and fall aggregation sites in the highlands. Summer and fall exploitation concentrated on the resources of the Har Harif plateau (whence the name) and its environs, which together comprise a scant one percent of the total area in which Harifian remains are found. A distinctive arrowhead type, the Harif point, was used in this territory; and one can find isolated examples in the vast sandy reaches of the northern Sinai and the western Negev. Subterranean structures with quantities of pounding tools were uncovered in the summer/fall camps, which also typically contain few examples of the Harif points. It is worth noting that these points were produced like other Natufian microliths by use of the microburin technique. Rare Harif points have been found outside their "home range" (e.g., in the terrace of el-Khiam in the Judean Desert) and, in my view, probably indicate some form of exchange of arrowheads—a practice most common in the Levantine Neolithic and a point of contrast with the preceding Epipaleolithic.

Although the fate of the Harifian social entity is unknown, it seems that they were unsuccessful in their efforts to survive in their semi-desertic territory. Intensive and extensive exchange or "gift giving" as practiced by the Harifians is documented in the wealth of marine shells uncovered in various sites, mostly of Red Sea (but some of Mediterranean) origin. The largest quantities of shell were found in camps on the Har Harif plateau, possibly attesting to seasonal aggregation and caching in sacred places. It is worth noting that, in contrast to earlier periods, the option of moving northward in order to escape the increasing aridity was blocked by other Late Natufian territories. In my view, a scenario in which the famine-stricken Harifians move out and join their Late Natufian relatives is not improbable, resulting in the abandonment of the Negev and northern Sinai.

The transition to the Early Neolithic occurred around 10,300–10,000 B.P. in the southern Levant and is marked by numerous economic and cultural changes. In what follows, I will only explore a selection of topics and mainly pursue the "history" of certain groups. Identifying them, if the effort is at all worthwhile, will be considered first.

The Paradigm for the Early Neolithic

The model employed for the early Neolithic is based upon the same set of assumptions as that of the Epipaleolithic, namely that socioeconomic changes result from an interaction between stress (both ecological and social) and success which could have been caused by several factors such as new technological innovations or the abundance of exploitable resources resulting from favorable climatic conditions. Change could also occur as a result of a failure to adapt to changing socioecological conditions. In order to identify which were the successful groups, and which were—from an evolutionary point of view—the "losers," we have attempted to reconstruct the socioeconomic map of the Levant during the PPNA and PPNB periods (Cauvin 1978, Bar-Yosef 1986, Rollefson 1988, Bar-Yosef and Belfer-Cohen 1989a, b).

Lithic assemblages of the Early Neolithic are studied in the same way as those of the Epipaleolithic. This means that debitage counts and quantitative type lists of retouched pieces are recorded and reported. However, to suggest that lithic assemblages occupied the same place in Neolithic technologies as they did during earlier prehistoric periods clearly is something that must be demonstrated, rather than assumed. Therefore additional categories of evidence are used to guide our search for interpretation. Among others, these include (1) the large size of some Early Neolithic communities (up to 12 ha); (2) the communal efforts involved in erecting large public buildings like the tower and walls at Jericho or the wall at Beidha; (3) the amount of energy invested in the construction of private houses; (4) the energy expended in quarrying for mud-brick, and the fabrication in quantity of standardized mud-brick types; (5) long-distance exchange indicated by the presence of obsidian and greenstone (malachite, dioptase, serpentine); (6) the evidence for cultic or ritual activities (e.g., stylized human statues found at 'Ain Ghazal, Jericho, and Nahal Hemar cave; the plastered skulls at Beisamoun, Tell Ramad and 'Ain Ghazal; the stone and clay human and animal figurines from Jericho, Netiv Hagdud, 'Ain Ghazal and almost every other PPNB site, etc.); and (7) a specialized mortuary program involving skull removal from adult skeletons in PPNA and PPNB contexts. If we limit ourselves to the lithic assemblages, the same criteria are used: the various debitage categories and their attributes, together with tool counts and the metrical and morphological attributes of the retouched pieces (e.g., Calley 1986, Rollefson and Simmons 1988, Simmons et al. 1987, Bar-Yosef and Alon 1988, Gopher 1989). However, other aspects of these archaeological sites and assemblages appear to be restricted to, or show up first in, Neolithic contexts. These include:

1. Considerable evidence in the Early Neolithic for the use of raw materials, such as flint, limestone, and basalt imported for the first time over distances as great as 50–100 km (although not so far as the central Anatolian obsidian—500 km).
2. "Heat treatment," used infrequently to improve the quality of

chipped blanks, and which may have required special expertise. The same is true of pressure flaking, which is a specialized skill not found in every Neolithic site.

3. New tool types, such as celts or axes with ground bits appear, and possibly reflect changes in scheduling and in the division of labor.

4. The appearance of an expedient industry as part of the lithic assemblage is already noted in some Epipaleolithic contexts. Its presence in Neolithic contexts becomes more evident, however, and clearer still during the subsequent Chalcolithic and early Bronze Age. It probably indicates, at some point along this trajectory, the emergence of lithic craft specialization.

The increased complexity of on-site and off-site activities probably testifies to the appearance of major changes in scheduling and in the division of labor. Some of the "art" or "cult" objects might indicate a change in the status of women in these early agricultural societies (Cauvin 1985). Changes also might have occurred in the neighboring desert groups, but, by their very nature, the archaeological evidence for them is ephemeral.

In conclusion, while the complete Epipaleolithic *chaîne opératoire* (from the retrieval of raw material to the final abandonment of exhausted tools) is almost always preserved in every site (except in the desertic regions), it is not the same as the *chaîne opératoire* in early Neolithic contexts. Neolithic lithic assemblages are far more "mixed" and are the results of many divergent and convergent activities and processes, involving the movement and exchange of tools, artifact reuse and resharpening, stratigraphic mixing caused by levelling operations, house building, refilling, trash pits etc. Those of the Epipaleolithic tend to be much more uniform in their technological and typological properties.

It is not surprising, therefore, that projectile points, exchanged among hunters, can be used as chronological markers and do not express social boundaries. Despite functional similarities with Epipaleolithic microliths, the role of microliths in Neolithic social circles was different (an issue which, I believe, was misunderstood by the North American archaeologist, James Brown [1987]). Moreover, with the aid of radiocarbon dates, we can observe a cultural diffusion from northeast to southwest, with the production of another distinctive arrowhead (the Helwan point) being documented first in Syria's Euphrates Valley and showing up eventually in the mountains of southern Sinai, a distance of nearly 1,000 km (Gopher 1989).

With these analytical tools in hand, we have tried to reconstruct a social map of the Levantine Early Neolithic "interaction sphere" (cf. Caldwell 1964), using available archaeological evidence. The main limitation on doing this for the PPNA was the relatively small number of reported and excavated sites (Bar-Yosef 1989b). It was easier and more successful to attempt it for the much better documented PPNB period (the seventh millennium B.C.), from which a wealth of data is available (e.g., Moore 1985, J. Cauvin 1978, M-C. Cauvin 1987, Simmons et al. 1987, Rollefson and Simmons 1988, Bar-Yosef and Alon 1988, and for interpretations, see Rollefson 1988, Cauvin 1987, Bar-Yosef and Belfer-Cohen 1989a, b, n.d.). The PPNB data point to the existence of an extended interaction sphere within the Levant but with distinct, sub-regional entities. The most obvious subdivision is between the various types of economic entities: the village farming communities in the "sown land" (i.e., the Mediterranean phytogeographic zone) and the foraging communities in the deserts. The evidence for village sedentism in the PPNB is very strong, as are the indications for mobile adaptations in the deserts (Moore 1985, Bar-Yosef 1984). Moreover, the archaeological data testify to various degrees of interaction between the two economic systems. Among these are the famous "desert kites," which are the tangible remains of large hunting drives used, no doubt, over millennia. Shaped like enormous keyholes (some are several kilometers in length), they were probably used by the desert groups to contain the movements of gazelle herds in order to provide the large quantities of meat required by sedentary farming communities, who typically would have depleted their nearby hunting grounds (Bar-Yosef 1986, Helms and Betts 1987).

Within the Neolithic world, we try to identify distinct groups of people by using archaeological markers—typically domestic tools which are either expediently made, or tools with limited geographic distributions. Most common are celts, axes or adzes, or particular scraper types. The distribution of arrowhead types, on the other hand, reflects what I believe to be evidence for long distance exchanges among hunters. Early Neolithic hunters would have been the most mobile members of these sedentary communities. Small, ephemeral camps of such Neolithic task groups are poorly documented archaeologically (and are, in fact, difficult to distinguish from those of earlier foragers). But when the uppermost layers in Levantine cave sites are examined carefully, a few arrowheads (broken, for the most part) can be recognized in what are usually mixed assemblages (e.g., at el-Wad, Kebara). I assume that a short stay of a few hours' duration, or a day, for retooling, meat processing, etc., would have resulted in only a very few artifacts left behind which, by the natural processes which are often concentrated in cave mouths, would have tended to become mixed with later archaeological remains.

Among the desert groups, where a high degree of residential mobility seems to have been the dominant settlement pattern, we expect periodic aggregation and dispersion cycles involving entire social entities (Bar-Yosef 1984, Tchernov and Bar-Yosef 1982, Dayan et al. 1986). Thus, I think that the boundaries of PPNB entities can be drawn; and there appear to be several relatively distinct "provinces": (1) the southern Sinai province, including the desert of southern Jordan; (2) the Negev and northern Sinai; (3) the central and southern hilly flanks of the Transjordanian plateau, the Jordan Valley, Judean Hills, and the Lower Galilee; (4) the Lebanese mountains; (5) the Damascus Plain and the areas around it; (6) central and eastern Syria; and (7) the southern flanks of the Taurus Mountains.

Concluding Remarks

Holding to the set of flexible assumptions described earlier, I believe that the life histories of unnamed Epipaleolithic and Neolithic groups can be reconstructed from the archaeological record which, despite its inadequacies, can be used as a kind of "fragmentary written document." When this is done (and we are only in the initial phases of doing it), we will find that only a few of these social groups were ultimately successful. Those who were resourceful knew how to exploit constantly changing situations to overcome the vagaries of abrupt climatic fluctuations, to deal successfully with their neighbors (either peacefully or aggressively) and, ultimately, to lay the foundations for the early states and what later became known as Western Civilization. As the descendants of these survivors, it is natural that we are interested to learn more about them, and why and how they made the decisions that shaped this cultural evolutionary trend. It is much more difficult to study the remains of the "losers," but at all times they were also part of the human career in the Levant. Being a "loser" is contextual. In the course of the prehistoric past, the "losers" in a particular event could have become successful during subsequent periods. What might have been a biological success can later turn into a cultural disaster. It is only by studying entire geographic regions and by paying attention to cultural boundaries that we will be able to achieve a complete picture of diachronic and synchronic changes in the geographic configurations of these social units.

When trying to reconstruct the past, we often make the systematic error of using examples from the present as analogies for past situations. One of the most common is, in my view, the use of what I refer to as "the western rationale"—a uniformitarian model for understanding human behavior. It seems to me that the religious tradition of Western Civilization over the past 3,000 years—monotheism (and in this domain, the Islamic world is part of the same tradition)—affects our ability to accept that there could have been other ways of reasoning. We often find it easy to resort to an ecological approach which, in some cases, can easily turn into a form of naïve or sophisticated environmental determinism. However, I do not think we can afford to ignore the role of the environment in influencing the process of decision making by these prehistoric foragers and farmers, but should simply keep in mind that different social groups could have coped differently with the same situation, using their varied experiences. The "tyranny of the ethnographic record" was already pilloried some time ago (Wobst 1978). While it serves as an important source of interesting ideas and models, we should try to do our best to understand the archaeological remains by constantly testing and re-evaluating our basic assumptions, our methods of inference, our models of lithic and faunal variability, and our understanding of site formation processes. This is not empty rhetoric but is instead my personal "philosophy" (if it is proper to dignify it with that term) in respect of the "doing" of archaeology. It explains why the reader who compares my papers of some 20 years ago with those of the present will find differences in the interpretations of the same archaeological records.

Acknowledgments

I am grateful to G. A. Clark who invited me to participate in the Society for American Archaeology symposium upon which this volume is based, who encouraged me to submit an expanded version of my paper, and who helped me with the editing of the final version. I would also like to thank my colleagues Z. Herzog (Tel Aviv University), C. C. Lamberg-Karlovsky, D. Lieberman, R. Preucel, J. Shea (Harvard University), A. Keene (University of Massachusetts, Amherst) and J. D. Speth (University of Michigan) for making useful comments on earlier drafts of this paper. Many of the ideas presented here were discussed during my years at the Institute of Archaeology, the Hebrew University, Jerusalem. In particular, I am indebted to Anna Belfer-Cohen with whom I have published a number of papers concerning these issues. However, I am solely responsible for the content of this essay.

Chapter 21
Comparative Aspects of Paradigms for the Neolithic Transition in the Levant and the American Southwest

Suzanne K. Fish and Paul R. Fish

Introduction

The paradigms that govern the prehistory of a region tend to become reified and attain the status of basic assumptions from which all further interpretations proceed. Parochial frameworks for reconstruction are countered in current archaeology through resort to concepts drawn from broader anthropological observations and theory. However, regional paradigms may come to relate even these concepts in such crystallized combinations or sequences that flexibility and rearrangement become unlikely. Interregional comparison of paradigms that structure similar spheres of inquiry therefore offer a source of fresh perspectives and identify common points of weakness.

We will examine some aspects of influential paradigms that shape our understanding of the origins of domestication economies in the Levant and the southwestern United States—Old and New World regions with which we are most familiar. Climatic, topographic, and other physical similarities in the two areas foster convergences in analytical approaches to the variables affecting the transition from hunting and gathering to food production. Parallels can also be seen in cultural patterns and trajectories attending this transition. Regional developments of a similar nature are disjunct in absolute time, but appear more synchronous in terms of elapsed time. For example, there are trends in both the Levant and the Southwest from earlier circular or oval pit house structures to later rectilinear, contiguous room complexes, culminating in aggregated settlements during the Neolithic and later prehistoric times respectively. It is probably not an accident that a number of circum-Mediterranean archaeologists studying the transition, including several contributors to this volume, have also worked in the Southwest.

Regional Contrasts

With regard to the establishment of domestication economies, an immediate contrast is between the Levant as a region of primary domestication and the Southwest as an instance of secondary acquisition of extra-regional domesticates. This disparity is critical only if the focus of inquiry is on circumstances surrounding the first appearance of the morphological changes producing domesticates. However, if domestication economies are viewed as alternatives adopted under certain ranges of natural and cultural conditions and with particular implications for practitioners, then indigenous or non-indigenous origin of domesticates is a minor issue (Earle 1980, Christenson 1980, Clark and Yi 1983). From this perspective, questions concerning combinations of variables under which agriculture was embraced and the nature of its consequences are equally appropriate for primary and secondary situations.

Distributions of wild ancestors generally encompass early domestication loci in the Levant, although localized development and later transport to adjacent zones figure in some reconstructions. Among these are models of Braidwood and Howe (1960) for cereals and Hole (1984) for sheep and goats. In the Southwest, botanical markers for cultivation have always been extra-local and clearcut, a benefit not without drawbacks. With cultigen status beyond dispute for even the earliest corn, beans, and squash, inadequate attention has been devoted to identifying environmental and cultural preconditions more compatible with initial adoption in some Southwestern locales than in others. Because domestication in the Levant has been expected to entail a temporal continuum from wild to domesticated forms, predispositions such as intensified foraging, dependence on a few productive species, and incipient plant and animal manipulation have been proposed, sought and analyzed in greater depth.

The presence of domesticated herd animals in the Levant and their absence in the Southwest is among the most portentous of regional contrasts. Animals provide an efficient means for harvesting the dispersed vegetative resources of arid landscapes—with the exception of turkeys in the Southwest, animal products were obtained directly by hunting. On an interregional scale, animals undoubtedly account for dissimilar organization of seasonal activity and divergences in pathways to sedentary and aggregated settlements (Redman 1978). The potential of animals for capturing energy, expanding human labor, and extending scopes of operation also must have generated regionally different rates of progression toward and beyond neolithic cultural configurations.

Nature and Rate of Change

A renewed scientific interest and dialogue on the role of gradual versus punctuated equilibrium models within evolutionary schemes of all sorts is echoed in the archaeology of the neolithic transition. Gradualist views are being supplemented in Old and New World studies by models based on chronologically compressed parameters of change. This tendency can be seen in recently advanced scenarios for the emergence of domesticate morphology from that of wild progenitors. Iltis (1983) has proposed a catastrophic genetic change to account for the differentiation of corn from ancestral teosinte. Likewise, Hillman and Davies (1990) use accumulating knowledge about wild cereals in the Near East to construct a model of successful human selection for a rare mutation within 20 to 200 years. They speculate that if the morphological changes creating domesticates occurred this rapidly and were rapidly disseminated thereafter, it might be impossible to find archaeological contexts encapsulating a botanical record of transition (Hillman and Davies 1990:200–201). Thus, the diffusion of cereals with domesticate morphology in the Levant, without a detectable prelude of intermediate types, may resemble the dissemination of exogenous corn in the Southwest to a greater degree than older reconstructions would suggest.

Refinement of archaeological data has also led to models of more punctuated change. In the Southwest, inaccurate dating of the presumed earliest corn created the appearance of up to 3,000 years during which this domesticate was present but created little visible effect on the economies or organization of Archaic populations. This impression encouraged perceptions that its introduction was a "monumental non-event" (Minnis 1985:310, also Irwin-Williams 1973, Ford 1981, Cordell 1984). These dates and their interpolations further pinpointed a prime highland environment from which agriculture was thought to have spread only gradually to less favored Southwestern locales (e.g., Haury 1962, Woodbury and Zubrow 1979, Ford 1981, Minnis 1985). Reexamination has now placed the anomalously dated corn later in time (Berry 1982, Wills 1988) and brought it in line with earliest instances in other parts of the region, including basin, plateau, mountain, and desert settings from central Utah to southern Arizona and New Mexico (e.g., Fish et al. 1986, Huckell 1990, Simmons 1986,

Wilde and Newman 1989, Wills 1988, Upham et al. 1987). Furthermore, where data are sufficient to judge representation in these earliest contexts, direct measures of diet such as coprolite contents and bone chemistry (e.g., Minnis 1989, Matson 1990) and indirect ones such as ubiquity among charred remains (e.g., Huckell 1990) have identified corn as a major resource.

The presence of domesticated cereals or livestock for any substantial period in the Levant prior to Neolithic horizons also has failed to be borne out by the archaeological record. Sickle blades, grinding implements, substantial houses, and other Natufian attributes considered to be probable indicators of a food producing society have not been associated with domesticates in subsequent analyses (see Henry, Olszewski, this volume). Indeed, a particularly promising set of botanical remains thought to represent residues of Epipaleolithic plant cultivation prior to the appearance of domesticates (Moore 1982, 1983), has since been reinterpreted as gathered resources (Hillman et al. 1989). The possibility exists for future evidence of cultivation, herding, or even domesticates in the poorly known latest part of the Natufian era. However, a pattern of relatively abrupt but geographically widespread appearance of cultivation and domesticates, lacking recognized precursors, now appears to characterize both the early Neolithic of the Levant and the Late Archaic of the Southwest.

Paradigms for Preceding Hunters and Gatherers

Concepts of social and economic modes characterizing sequential stages in cultural evolution enhance the comprehensibility of vast bodies of data and summarize meaningful trends, but at the expense of acknowledging or evaluating variability. In the basic schematization, innovations underlying food production appear, diffuse, and propel hunters and gatherers into a new neolithic stage in cultural development. Changes coincident with domestication economies are so dramatic that the temptation to overlook the significance of variability in both preceding and subsequent stages may be reinforced.

The tendency to regard hunters and gatherers as a primarily unitary phenomenon is inherent in the stage concept of cultural evolution, but is also fostered by a pervasive focus of current anthropological attention on a particular subset of hunter-gatherer behavior. According to a prevailing, generalized template for hunters and gatherers preceding the transition, small bands with seasonally mobile lifestyles "map onto" spatially discrete and sequentially available resources, most of which can support only modest group sizes in single locations. Although archaeological entities directly subsuming the transition, and particularly the Natufian of the Levant, are widely acknowledged to diverge to a lesser or greater degree from this model (e.g., Bar-Yosef 1981, 1983; Cauvin 1978, Henry 1985, 1989; Hillman et al. 1989, Moore 1982, Perrot 1966), its strictures are seldom seriously challenged for the immediately preceding Kebaran. Likewise, variants of this lifestyle are almost uniformly assumed for Archaic groups up to and usually including those possessing the earliest Southwestern domesticates (Wills 1988).

In both the Levant and Southwest, the predominant model for hunters and gatherers is heavily influenced by a few ethnographies of bands exhibiting highly mobile foraging economies. Descriptions of the Paiute Indians in the Great Basin of the United States and the Bushmen of the Kalahari Desert in Africa can be singled out as particularly influential in current perceptions (see Mueller-Wille and Dickson, this volume). Not only have foremost students of the Paiute and Bushmen, notably Julian Steward and Richard Lee, been instrumental in shaping anthropological theory concerning hunters and gatherers, but the arid environments of these groups invite comparisons with the Southwest and the Levant.

Problems of Analogy

In the last several years, questions have been raised as to the economic or political independence of modern groups still following a hunting and gathering lifestyle, and their representativeness of earlier hunters and gatherers (e.g., Wobst 1978, Bailey et al. 1989, Headland and Reid 1989, Schrire 1984). The Bushmen have been a particular target in this regard. It has been pointed out that Bushmen groups have maintained relationships with neighboring farmers and herdsmen for hundreds of years; individuals used to typify universal characteristics of hunters and gatherers participate on occasion in mixed economies (e.g. Wilmsen 1989).

The Paiute analogue is likewise derived from hunters and gatherers amidst an aggressive and ultimately dominant population of farmers and ranchers. Prior to the interval of ethnographic documentation, settlers had preempted better watered locations in Paiute territory, and their livestock were in the process of transforming the natural landscape and removing grasses and other vegetation important for human subsistence (Winter 1976:426). These pressures discouraged or diminished small scale plantings made by some bands. Many Paiute of the ethnographic interval interacted regularly with European colonizers and with adjacent groups of Native American cultivators. Portions of a broad belt between the Great Basin and Colorado Plateaus, inhabited historically by mobile Paiute, were occupied prehistorically by Anasazi agriculturalists.

While a case can be made that the Bushmen, Paiute, and other modern groups embody some essential qualities of hunters and gatherers (e.g., Solway and Lee 1990, Silberbauer 1981), arguments can also be advanced that the totality of ethnographic patterns do not duplicate the probable range of variability of the late Pleistocene and earlier Holocene, and may include some uniquely recent configurations. With the exception of Australia, the historically documented sample of hunters and gatherers is environmentally biased toward extremes limiting agriculture and other kinds of marginality, a caution noted by Leslie Freeman (1968) and others but sometimes disregarded in cross-cultural studies. Peoples with high latitude (cold), maritime, jungle, and desert orientations make up an overwhelming majority of the hunter and gatherer sample. There is a virtual absence of analogues from more desirable locations for food production, which might have constituted prime territories for prehistoric foragers.

Proximity to and ongoing relationships with food producers may in some cases affect the expression of variables such as population size and density, sedentism, and storage behavior that are cited as figuring in the transition to agriculture. The balance between population and resources is one example (Cohen 1975, 1977). It is difficult to judge the independent viability of desert bands following a seasonal round, when resort is made to agricultural neighbors and wage labor in years of pronounced scarcity, as among some Bushmen (e.g. Headland and Reid 1989, Denbow 1984, Wilmsen 1983, 1989). It seems possible that geographic adjustments, greater storage, different population distributions, or other alternatives might have been necessary to counter starvation in the face of recurring droughts in earlier times.

Rethinking Variation

If a probable breadth of variability among prior hunters and gatherers is acknowledged, questions regarding the emergence of modes that become more common during neolithic times can be framed in a manner other than as the departure from a previous norm. Rather than asking how triggering mechanisms might have pushed or pulled earlier groups away from "standard" hunter-gatherer behavior, it can be asked under what conditions such alternatives as greater sedentism or larger group size might have been advantageous and selected more frequently over time.

A continuum exists between residential duration in base settlements of foragers practicing mobility (Binford 1980) and a degree of sedentism conducive to harvesting cultivated plants. In spite of drawbacks including waste accumulation and fuel depletion, a variety of ethnographic hunters and gatherers have opted for this less mobile form of economic organization. A key variable in these patterns seems to be the availability of abundant staples that can be stored under given states of environment and technology. These are exemplified by the large game frozen by arctic hunters, the dried fish of Northwest Coast Indians, and the acorns of temperate California groups. It is not improbable that storable staples, capable of supporting localized subsistence economies of this nature, are represented by foxtail millet in the Tehuacán Valley (Callen 1967:287), mammoth at Dolni Vestoniče (Soffer 1985), wild cereals and acorns in portions of the Levant (Henry (1989:93–94), or Indian rice grass in the northern Southwest and riparian mesquite groves in the south (Fish et al. 1990). In drier regions, the combination of a storable staple, permanent water, and nearby topographic diversity should predict the location of prior patterns of logistical mobility, relatively greater sedentism, and subsequent early agriculture.

Along with sites consisting of more ephemeral remains, items such as residential architecture and storage pits appear sporadically in the Upper Paleolithic and earlier Epipaleolithic of the Old World and pre-agricultural Archaic of the New World. In the Levant, multiple instances of Kebaran settlements with dwellings are known, in one case co-occurring at Ein Gev with Natufian counterparts (Bar-Yosef 1980:122). While similar elements have frequently been invoked in reconstructions of sedentary life or more complex organizational forms for the Natufian, qualitative equivalence is seldom accorded to occurrences of these features in preceding times. If the model of hunters and gatherers as small mobile bands did not color perceptions so strongly, this variability in the archaeological record might better be interpreted to reflect the economic, social, and environmental variety among those populations who collectively gave rise to neolithic successors.

Paradigms for Transitional Entities

As with preceding hunters and gatherers, stage concepts also encourage monolithic treatment of archaeological manifestations that bracket the appearance of domesticates. The Natufian in the Levant and the terminal Cochise stages in the southern Southwest exhibit a number of elements typical of the ensuing neolithic periods. There are theoretical bases for understanding the origin and cohesion of these archaeological entities over their relatively broad geographic distributions. For example, sequential but overlapping interactions over wide areas among band and tribal peoples for mate acquisition, information exchange, and risk sharing have been discussed by Wobst (1974, 1977) and others (e.g., Johnson 1978, Sahlins 1976). Widespread interactions of these kinds have even been applied in contexts of domestication economies in the northern Southwest to explain the greater spatial extent of earlier (vs. later) design styles (Plog 1980, Braun and Plog 1982:513–515).

The Natufian is regarded as a unitary phenomenon at some level (e.g., Henry 1973a, Byrd 1987:246–247, 1989; Bar-Yosef 1980:124, 1983:24; Smith 1972), in spite of internal variability in terms of environmental setting (e.g., Henry 1985b, Cauvin 1978, Cauvin and Cauvin 1983:45), qualitative and quantitative assemblage characteristics (e.g., Henry 1973a, 1977; Olszewski 1984, Bar-Yosef 1981a, b), faunal remains (e.g., Cauvin 1978, Cauvin and Cauvin 1983:45; Edwards 1989), settlement pattern (e.g., Bar-Yosef 1983, Bar-Yosef and Goren 1973, Byrd 1987, 1989), and degree of sedentism (e.g., Henry 1985b, 1989; Bar-Yosef 1983, L. Binford 1968). Although relatively vast in size, the territorial magnitude of the Natufian is not so great as to preclude a quasi-ethnic conceptualization at implicit if not explicit levels of interpretation (see Bar-Yosef, Henry, this volume). In view of its distributional contiguity and shared stylistic and technological attributes, the unifying structure of the Natufian could also be compared to an interaction sphere or an environmentally based commonality in economic orientation.

An alternative to explication by reference to synthetic concepts is insight derived from analyses of ethnographic situations. The ability to envision Southwestern archaeological manifestations against a rich and varied ethnographic backdrop is a unique regional advantage. A greater range of cultural variables relevant to the transition can be observed among Native American groups than among peasant villagers and herders of the Near East. Hunters and gatherers, simply organized cultivators, groups with predominantly herding orientations, ones with mixed subsistence economies, and aggregated agriculturalists are represented in Southwestern ethnohistoric and ethnographic accounts. As analytical models for interaction among subsets of variables rather than as holistic patterns, these analogues can also enhance an understanding of archaeological manifestations beyond the Southwest. In particular, the spectrum of aboriginal societies in the Southwest offers an optimal vantage point for examining archaeologically tangible aspects of cultural variability.

Synchronic Models of Variation

An instance will be analyzed which might entail levels of both unity and variability similar to those embodied in the Natufian. By observing the synchronic distributions of variables of interest in Natufian research, some suggestions can be made concerning their articulation and the manner in which they might aid in posing future questions. Recurrent issues in the Levantine archaeological literature involve the degree of sedentism in the Natufian and the closeness with which Natufian subsistence practices approach incipient forms of cultivation. A Southwestern illustration of what can be termed a *subsistence mosaic* has implications for the pursuit of such problems. A Piman example from southern Arizona and adjacent portions of the Mexican state of Sonora serves not as a literal analogue for the Natufian phenomenon, but rather as a source of models for interrelationships among elements judged significant by archaeologists.

Anthropologists emphasize unity among Pimans primarily as a linguistic phenomenon (Miller 1982:120, Kroeber 1934, Sauer 1934). Mutually intelligible dialects were spoken within an overall territory of roughly 120,000 km² (Miller 1982:114, Figure 1). This territorial size compares closely to that encompassing the Natufian distribution according to Bar-Yosef (1983:33, Figure 1). Ethnographically recognized Piman subgroups include the Pima, Papago, Sand Papago, and Lower Pima (Figure 21.1). These peoples considered themselves to pertain to an inclusive Piman ethnic classification, although there were more separately named divisions than the four large ones noted here. Intermarriage from group to group was frequent. Trade in both consumable items and durable materials such as shell was routine. Risk sharing among large and small subdivisions was institutionalized to the extent that formalized procedures existed for initiating intergroup food donation and delayed reciprocation (Russell 1975:93–95, Underhill 1939:100–107). A degree of technological and artifactual unity among Pimans is exemplified by shared ceramic attributes including modes of vessel manufacture, certain shapes, and decorative treatments.

In spite of linguistic intelligibility and abundant social interaction, subsistence orientations and environmental settings could hardly have been more diverse. This diversity is of the nature of a *subsistence mosaic*, a series of somewhat overlapping but distinctive economic patterns forming a geographically contiguous network. The Piman subsistence mosaic encompasses almost the entire range of economic orientations documented for the Greater Southwest. The Lower Pima were high-elevation cultivators in the forested Sierra Madre of central Sonora. The Sand Papago emphasized a mobile hunting and gathering lifestyle

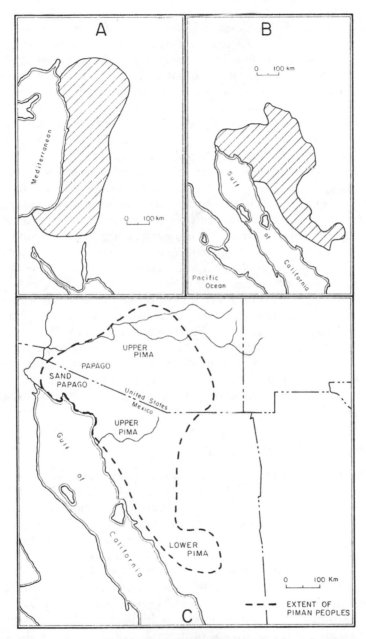

FIGURE 21.1. (A) Distribution of Natufian and Natufian-like assemblages in the Levant (after Bar-Yosef 1983:33, Fig. 1 and Byrd 1989:62, Fig. 1); (B) Distribution of Piman peoples in the Southwest (Miller 1982:120, Fig. 1); (C) Locations of Piman subgroups named in the text.

in small groups in the driest lowland desert of western Sonora and Arizona. The Papago subsisted by a combination of floodwater farming and intensive foraging in the more mesic desert zones of southwestern Arizona. Most favorably situated along perennial desert rivers, the sedentary Upper Pima practiced riverine irrigation as well as floodwater farming, with foraging a more supplemental endeavor.

The Piman analogy is not meant to imply that the element accounting for Natufian identity among contemporary Epipaleolithic peoples of the Levant was necessarily linguistic. Its relevance lies in insights concerning the articulation of variables at different levels of cultural commonality. Variables pertinent to sedentism and resource patterns tend to co-vary with divisions of what has been termed the subsistence mosaic, which exists at a more restricted demographic and geographic scope than the higher order Piman linguistic unity. The Piman model indicates a scale for questions concerning subsistence practices, and suggests that the Natufian manifestation as a whole might have produced a number of simultaneous answers.

The structure of a subsistence mosaic is likely to play a major role in shaping archaeological distributions because of the technological and economic nature of much preserved material culture. However, distributions for individual elements need not be isomorphic with one another or with subsistence modalities. Technological and stylistic commonalities in Pima and Papago water jars are among characteristics that extend beyond and cross-cut differing subsistence orientations of these two Piman subgroups (Fontana et al. 1962).

Diachronic Models of Variation

Synchronic variety within the Piman subsistence mosaic encompasses categories such as "hunter and gatherer" and "intensive agriculturalist" which are usually ordered sequentially (i.e., temporally) in evolutionary schemes. While current anthropological theory does not legislate that these categories or stages progress in mutually exclusive, unilineal series, regional paradigms influence perceptions toward that mold. The concept of a subsistence mosaic is also relevant to diachronic patterns in the Southwest, whether a cultural unit or a geographic area is the focus of interest over time. Southwestern instances of exceptions to unilineality in temporal progression are particularly instructive.

For an area as the analytical unit, the boundary between the Colorado Plateaus and Great Basin in the northern Southwest exemplifies an expression of a subsistence mosaic in the temporal dimension. Archaic hunters and gatherers and preceramic cultivators were succeeded by agricultural peoples of the puebloan Anasazi and Fremont ceramic traditions, and in turn were followed by the historic Paiute. These latest inhabitants were seasonally mobile foragers but included groups who tended stands of wild grasses or planted minor quantities of cultigens at more permanent bases. Subsistence reversals in this area occurred within highly abbreviated intervals relative to the Natufian timespan.

For a cultural category as the analytical unit, historic Athabascans illustrate fluidity in economic orientations and mobility over the short term. Affected by post-contact pressures and opportunities, economic lifestyles among various Apache groups frequently shifted from horticulture to mobile hunting and gathering and back again. Large segments of the Navajo switched to a herding emphasis after the introduction of sheep, often interacting with surrounding agriculturalists in a manner reminiscent of circum-Mediterranean mutualism. It is probably not coincidental that later arriving Athabascans rather than long-established Puebloans exhibited more pronounced flexibility in lifestyles in the historic Southwest.

The potential for subsistence shifts away from sedentary and intensified tendencies would likely be greatest among groups whose social and demographic patterns had been least shaped by long traditions of such experience. During initial portions of the transition to domestication economies in both regions, commitments to emerging food producer stances are likely to have been more ephemeral, and multidirectional shifts more commonplace. Donald Henry (1985b:380, 1989) suggests deteriorating climate as an impetus for such a reversal in Natufian subsistence trends. In the marginal Negev and Sinai deserts, intense involvement with cereal grasses during a mesic interval was replaced by more diversified hunting and gathering near the end of the Natufian period. Under such circumstances, remains of relatively sedentary groups could occur stratigraphically sandwiched between layers of mobile band occupations or be deposited in other unanticipated combinations.

Paradigms and Variability in Settlement Patterns

Aspects of archaeological settlement patterns are likely to diverge from expectations of uniformity evoked by stages in cultural evolution. Lithic scatters of limited size and density are commonly equated with extractive activities of temporary duration. Where diagnostics indicate chronological placement within the general time frame of transition, such remains and activities may more readily be attributed to mobile hunters and gatherers than to incipient agricultural groups, a convention and interpretational bias arising from regional paradigms.

In the northern Southwest, an automatic, traditional assignment of several modest lithic scatters to nonagricultural Late Archaic groups would have obscured some of the earliest evidence for cultigens. Three sites studied by Alan Simmons (1982, 1986) yielded lithic assemblages totaling between fifty and several hundred artifacts after excavation. Persistence in thoroughly investigating these sites beyond surface indications led to recovery of both pollen and macrobotanical indicators of corn. Initially, contradiction of paradigmatic expectations occasioned strong skepticism in the archaeological community that was overcome only with additional field investigation and confirmatory evidence (Simmons 1986). In the low deserts of southern Arizona, several unanticipated associations have likewise been found between remains of corn and similarly unimpressive Archaic sites (P. Fish et al. 1986, Dart 1986, S. Fish et al. 1990). It is significant that these Arizona sites are now known to be parts of preceramic settlement systems which also include sites with diverse artifact assemblages, varied trade goods, massive midden deposits, storage pits, substantial habitation structures, and cemeteries (Huckell 1990) comparable to Natufian counterparts at Hayonim Cave (Bar-Yosef and Goren 1973) or Ein Mallaha (Perrot 1966).

It seems easiest to misassign and misinterpret the small-scale elements of settlement patterns most apt to lack diagnostic artifacts. Assemblages in the small Southwestern lithic sites yielding corn were insufficient per se for assignment to settlement systems with or without agriculture; the presence of cultigen remains constituted the effective criterion. Wild resources are more strongly associated with models of hunter-gatherer strategies than with ones involving domesticates; a lack of diagnostics may particularly hamper recognition of extractive sites indicating important components of domestication economies. Problems of recognition loom larger in the Levant, where approximately 2,000 years of the Early Neolithic antedate the appearance of pottery as an abundant and highly visible marker. In terms of elapsed time following the initial appearance of regional domesticates, late prehistoric societies of the Southwest near the time of European contact would be roughly equivalent to ones in the Levant during the first several centuries of the ceramic Neolithic. Because Southwestern pottery appears from 1000 to 1500 years after cultigens, even small extractive sites with indistinctive lithics can routinely be linked to relatively early agricultural timespans, and often to particular ceramic phases.

Near Tucson, Arizona, remains of the most intensive extractive activity at a distance from water sources correlate with densest settlement during the Hohokam Classic Period between A.D. 1100 and 1350 (Fish et al. 1989). This agricultural period, marked by site size hierarchies and mounds as public architecture, is separated in time from the earliest local farming by an interval approximating that for the Pre-pottery Neolithic B in the Levant. Mobile or lower density populations in arid environments can emphasize hunting and gathering near water sources, but with increasing sedentism and population growth, con-veniently located wild resources may be depleted. It has been sug-gested by Cohen (1977), Hayden (1982:529), and others (e.g., Conklin 1969:229–230) that pressure on preferred or easily acquired and pro-cessed resources may lead to broader spectrum diets and generally intensified gathering among agriculturists, a process commensurate with this Hohokam example. In the absence of ceramics, misinterpre-tation of the chronological affiliation of such activities would reduce understanding of subsistence systems in both earlier and later portions of the cultural sequence.

Concluding Observations

Regional paradigms serve to organize results of previous study in a logical order and provide a basis for shared understanding. Influential synthetic concepts and analogues that structure our perceptions about the neolithic transition in the Southwest and Levant suffer from a common failure to provide frameworks for describing and evaluating variability at multiple scales. Not only can overly monolithic percep-tions hamper our detection and communication of the variation inher-ent in regional archaeology, but they can also circumscribe the field of inquiry and channel our questions into well worn pathways.

The nature and significance of variation should not be overlooked in the era of dramatic change in human history from predominantly foraging modes to ones based on food production. Among native peoples of the Southwest, the transition was long term, with persistent exceptions. Foraging remained a prominent component of subsistence systems, and nonagricultural lifestyles did not disappear. The mainte-nance of Southwestern variation can be approached in the context of alternatives or options followed under particular conditions, whether from negative standpoints such as environmental deterioration or pos-itive standpoints such as the energetic efficiencies of hunting and gathering when resources are abundant and populations are corre-spondingly low.

An eventually more comprehensive shift to domestication econo-mies was realized in the Levant, although multiplicity also emerged in these forms. The additional domestication of animals in the Old World is undoubtedly a critical factor in this regional contrast. Without live-stock, Southwestern Indians transformed the natural environment to a lesser degree, a process which accelerated rapidly in post-contact times. Progressive elimination of previous demographic and economic alternatives due to the historic introduction of herd animals must mirror similarly irreversible effects in the Neolithic Levant.

Interregional studies offer opportunities for conceptual cross-fertilization. Comparison of primary zones of food production as in Mesoamerica and the Levant are instructive; inclusion of secondary instances should reveal parallels and contrasts at scales above the outcomes of unique or localized domestication processes. Secondary acquisition of domesticates is unlikely to have been a process limited to singular classes of isolated elements. Other facets of early agricultural economy and organization influenced by donor groups may have affected the locations, timing, and rate at which those transitions proceeded. Comprehensive comparisons of elapsed time between initial appearance of domesticates and other economic and social thresholds in both primary and secondary contexts are particularly intriguing subjects for further study.

Chapter 22
Epilogue: Paradigms, Realism, Adaptation, and Evolution

Geoffrey A. Clark

Introduction

It has been my intention here to elicit from practicing, Mediterranean hunter-gatherer archaeologists what might be called their "logic of inquiry"—the biases, premises, and assumptions that each brings to the research endeavor in the particular geographical areas and problem domains in which they work. I submit that these nebulous, but no-less-real entities structure archaeological research in complex and subtle ways, and provide loosely defined conventions by which we attempt to give meaning to pattern. Depending upon one's own biases, of course, some of these conventions will appear more reasonable or defensible than others. I also think that paradigmatic biases exhibit a fuzzy but modal character, manifest geographically and temporally, that is essentially the product of the scholarly research traditions in which workers have received their training combined with the compromises they have learned they must make in order to come to grips with the realities of archaeological evidence in actual, "real world" situations. It is interesting to note that there are differences of opinion as to whether or not it is possible to identify the parameters of national or regional research traditions, and even whether such things exist (Clark 1989a, b, d). One might imagine that such differences would be most apparent at the level of the metaphysic, since it is reasonable to expect considerable overlap in lower level sociological and construct paradigms (Masterman 1970). However, whether metaphysical paradigms are in fact the closed logical systems that Kuhn (1962) originally thought they were is subject to debate (see below).

I asked the contributors to try to "make their biases explicit"—to articulate the fundamental premises under which they conduct archaeological research. I wanted "first person" accounts targeted at the level of the metaphysical paradigm—statements about what these workers perceived hunter-gatherer archaeological research to be "like." This turned out to be a good deal more difficult than I, and many contributors, had originally anticipated. As is evident from the book itself, what I often got instead were personal reactions to what contributors perceived to be the dominant theoretical (and sometimes methodological) biases operative in their particular research domains, which is not quite the same thing. However, in coming to grips with the preconceptions of the ruling paradigm, contributors were forced to confront their own; so, I believe, my objectives were accomplished, although in a round-about way. In these concluding remarks, I would like to exercise my editorial prerogatives and make some observations about what I take to be the major issues addressed in the book. In so doing, I hope to put the contributions into a somewhat broader intellectual context.

Paradigms, Theories, and Explanation

As might be expected, the notions of *paradigm* and *theory* are central to many of the papers, and there might be some point in trying to determine how these abstractions square with contributors' perceptions of them. The most widely accepted definition of a paradigm is a statement about the way the world (or some portion of it) is perceived to be. A paradigm is an assertion about the nature of reality; it comes to us through experience and is not directly subject to verification or falsification (in fact, to critical scrutiny of any kind). It just "is." Paradigms can exist at various levels, and level boundaries are never wholly impermeable either "horizontally" (between metaphysical paradigms) or "vertically" (between the metaphysical paradigm and its constituent sociological and construct paradigms) (Fig. 1.1). The historian of science Thomas Kuhn (1962) once tried to make the case that, in physics research, metaphysical paradigms are closed logical systems and that all lower-level sociological and methodological paradigms were derived from them. This notion, which was central to Kuhn's conception of "scientific revolutions," did not fare well in the experimental science contexts in which it was first proposed, and after the mid-1970s he jettisoned it (Kuhn 1974, 1977). In the present context, it seems singularly inappropriate since, however sharp the disagreements about the *meaning* of pattern in archaeology might be, there is an enormous amount of shared methodology and also much overlap at intermediate (i.e., sociological) levels (see, e.g., Dibble and Debénath, this volume). In my view this reflects major differences in complexity between the analytical units, relations, and processes modeled by experimental disciplines like particle physics (which tend to be few and, ultimately, simple) and the vastly more complicated units, relations, and processes which are the objects of scrutiny in non-experimental fields like archaeology (Clark 1982, 1987a). While I think that most contributors would agree that the particular kind of archaeology that is the subject of this book aspires to be "scientific," they would probably also reject the notion that a physics-type model of science is an appropriate model (see also Dunnell 1982).

Theories are juxtaposed with paradigms and are defined here as arguments invoked or constructed to explain *why* the world (or some portion of it) is as it appears to be (Binford and Sabloff 1982). Theories are the linkages between the paradigm and the world of experience, and provide a means of assessing the credibility of ideas about the experiential world. The distinction between theories and paradigms, and the recognition that both were essentially subjective, was another of Kuhn's important insights. He basically uncoupled the logical positivist notion that the unbiased perception of pattern in nature was an impossibility (the major tenet of strict empiricism) from the logical positivist conclusion that it was possible to have objective procedures for evaluating experience. To Kuhn, this meant that objectivity was not attainable in any absolute sense in science, and that criteria for attaining objectivity were ultimately determined by the metaphysical paradigm, which was itself subjective. Falsification and theory testing as conceptualized by logical positivism were thus an illusion, an idea that provided the springboard for his argument that paradigm shifts were unpredictable, relatively abrupt, comprehensive, and essentially irrational (although they conformed to some extent to the ideas floating around in the broader scientific milieu at any given point in time and space).

Kuhn's notion that theories are subjective originates from his conviction that metaphysical paradigms are closed logical systems; however, whether they are in fact such is open to question. While it is true that theories ultimately derive from the (metaphysical) paradigm, and are therefore subjective, it is also true that if paradigm boundaries are permeable (as they appear to be in many, perhaps all, fields), theories can be shared by or cross-cut distinct metaphysical paradigms—a point made by many contributors to this volume. In other words, whether or not one agrees with Kuhn's construal of "scientific revolutions," theory can vary independently of paradigm change. In a non-experimental discipline like archaeology, which is very poorly developed conceptually and in which epistemological concerns are shared by only a small number of practitioners (let alone accorded any importance), there is nevertheless a large amount of "low" and "middle range" theory attached to the construct and sociological paradigms that characterize the different segments of the field. That tends to leave "high theory" as something to be built "from the bottom up." In my view, the relatively recent and wholly commendable concern with middle range theory (e.g., Binford 1981 et seq.) has led to important new insights about the natural and cultural processes that contribute to the formation of an archaeological record, but it provides no guarantees that anything will cohere at higher levels of abstraction. If there is any coherence, it will come from a shared metaphysic that is essentially the product of a research tradition. For most American workers, the metaphysic is that of anthropology (Meltzer 1979). For many European scholars, the metaphysic is that of history (Bar-Yosef, Dibble and Debenath, Sackett, this volume).

It cannot be emphasized strongly enough that our knowledge of the past is wholly dependent upon the meanings that archaeologists give to observations on the archaeological record, and that those meanings will ultimately be determined by biases at the metaphysical level. It cannot be otherwise. To the extent that metaphysical paradigms differ (and I insist that, no matter how much is shared at lower levels, they *do* differ from one research tradition to the next), it is to that extent that what we think we know about the past will differ from one investigator to the next. However, I suggest that paradigms do not differ absolutely since, in archaeology at least, they do not appear to be the closed logical systems that Kuhn once thought they were in physics research. There is, in addition, the problem of strict empiricism in archaeology. Strict empiricism is alive and well in many research traditions and has a certain respectability in all of them, essentially because there is no mandate to make explicit, or justify, the inferential basis for knowledge claims. Strict empiricist viewpoints might be selected under certain kinds of historical paradigms, especially if historical process is regarded as particularistic and non-generalizing (see Bar-Yosef, this volume).

If we cannot use the archaeological record in any direct way to test the credibility of our knowledge claims, how can we determine whether our inferences about the meaning we attach to patterns are valid or not? There are two general, related kinds of answers to this question. Binford's (1981a, b) answer was by recourse to "actualistic studies" in which we monitor ongoing process, so to speak, and thereby hope to develop unambiguous empirical referents for analogous processes that we seek to understand in the past. Middle range research of the kind advocated by Binford is still in its infancy, however, and our empirical referents of process are anything but unambiguous (see, e.g., Lyman 1987, Lupo 1990—the same might be said of Schiffer's [e.g., 1987] efforts to model general kinds of cultural and natural formation processes). Binford (1981b) notes that our methods for *constructing* the past (actualistic studies, leading to middle range theory) must be intellectually independent of our theories for *explaining* the past (a priori ideas about the processes responsible for past events)—in other words, our general theory (which would, presumably, derive from the metaphysic). He thinks that, eventually, we might be able to test general theory using archaeological phenomena that can be completely comprehended through middle-range research. In the absence of sound methodology and a sophisticated observational language, however, building a hierarchy of inference on an inferential foundation that is itself not well justified is regarded as a very risky proposition.

While I would agree with Binford that archaeologists do tend to use the archaeological record (or an even more tenuous "inferred past") in a logically circular way to test premises and assumptions, I am skeptical of the extent to which we might eventually be able to build "grand theory" from the ground up, out of the conclusions of middle-range research. It occurs to me that (1) there are many processes of interest to archaeologists that would defy direct observation in the modern world, and in which uniformitarian principles cannot be assumed to hold constant (we will often be unable to "match the bear and its footprint," as Binford 1981b:29 put it), (2) the processes most amenable to middle-range research are likely to be trivial, or at least of limited interest to many workers (especially those who subscribe to an anthropological paradigm—this is also a frequent criticism of Schiffer's "behavioral archaeology"), and (3) those processes are likely to be "short term," observable only over relatively restricted time frames (and thus perhaps inappropriate for modeling "long-term" evolutionary processes). Since, in the opinion of many archaeologists, there is at present no exclusively archaeological "grand theory," nor much prospect of the emergence of one, and because of the disintegration of anthropology itself over the past twenty years, it seems optimistic to me to think that it will all somehow come together at the level of answering meaningful anthropological questions. But as we have seen, from some European perspectives, many meaningful questions are not anthropological in nature.

The other kind of answer complements the first and entails wider acceptance by archaeologists of some version of the general covering law (CL) model of scientific explanation (Hempel 1965; see also Dray 1957, and for archaeology, Watson et al. 1971, 1984). Most generally, the CL model of explanation involves subsumption of the particular phenomenon to be explained (technically, the *explanandum*) under one or more nomic (law-like) generalizations invoked to explain it. These law-like generalizations, and the particular circumstances under which they would apply to the *explanandum*, together constitute the *explanans*. Hempel contends that

All scientific explanation involves, explicitly or by implication, a subsumption of its subject matter under general regularities; . . . it seeks to provide a systematic understanding of empirical phenomena by showing that they fit into a nomic nexus. (1965:488)

Examples of efforts to include archaeological explanations under a general CL model are well known to most American workers and do not merit lengthy commentary here. There is a particularly lucid discussion of these issues in Watson et al. (1984:15–41), and an extensive literature over the different forms that CL models of explanation might take in order to best accommodate the particular nature of archaeological data (the statistical relevance [SR] model seems to be the hands-down favorite—Salmon 1967, Salmon and Salmon 1979, Salmon 1982). The point, though, is not what form CL models in archaeology should take, but rather that there are regularities to the logical structure of explanation in science and to the rationale of the quest for explanation that are applicable to archaeological research (and, arguably, to historical inquiry). Philosophers do not agree on the "correct" model of scientific explanation, but some form of CL model is ubiquitous in the justification phase of all scientific endeavor.

The generalized CL conception of explanation requires that explanations of particulars derive from theories (or sets of general relationships) that archaeologists think to be more or less adequately confirmed empirically. These general relationships should be made as explicit as possible, and some assessment provided as to the extent to which they are believed to be confirmed (Watson et al. 1984:40). In most archaeological research, explanations of general relationships typically remain implicit and are, at best, only very partially axiomatized. Whether we can use them to derive more specific law-like generalizations is presently questionable (Watson et al. 1984:39, 40).

If it could be shown to exist (or to have existed in the past), a fully confirmed body of archaeological theory would provide the discipline with a cohesiveness, and a unity of purpose—the commonly understood "paradigm legitimatized" objectives that structure scientific research in more fully axiomatized fields. I submit, however, that archaeological "grand theory" does not exist (indeed, never has existed). What we have now, and have always had, in place of "grand theory" is a partial and eclectic, at times even idiosyncratic, dependence upon selected aspects of anthropology and other social and natural sciences, that define and validate problems for different segments of the discipline. Adherence to these perspectives is partial at best, even within research traditions; and the penetrance of any one of them on the field as a whole is limited (Clark 1987a:31).

How do abstractions like paradigms, theories, models, and explanation square with contributors' accounts of them? Despite my injunction to direct their essays at the level of the metaphysical paradigm (and thereby hopefully throw major differences into sharp relief), many contributors in fact dealt with paradigms operative in particular and more restricted research domains. Although there appears to be a widespread conviction that archaeology is or should aspire to be scientific and generalizing (however, cf. papers by Bar-Yosef, Debénath), and at least tacit acceptance of a CL approach to explanation, many essays did not make a clear distinction among theories, models, hypotheses, and laws (or "law-like" generalizations). A certain amount of effort was expended on critiquing what writers perceived to be the paradigms of others (e.g., Davidson, Mueller-Wille and Dickson, Bietti, Sackett, González Morales). The perception of archaeological research that most frequently emerged does exhibit some modal characteristics, however, and in fact bears some resemblance to Christopher Carr's recent (1985b:18–41) description of the research process. My effort at depicting these regularities schematically is given in Figure 22.1. Carr should not, of course, be held accountable for my construal of his perception of the structure of archaeological inquiry. His is a highly formalized presentation which might be regarded as unrealistic by many practitioners, and which is also at some variance with contributors' accounts of the research process. The illustration is an abstraction that essentially tries to portray conceptual levels in scientific thought as these are relevant to archaeology. Some of these levels are more discrete and are more easily conceptualized and/or defined by consensus than others.

Some aspects of Figure 22.1 deserve commentary or emphasis. The model is both hierarchical and reticulate in structure, and proceeds from the more to the less inclusive, from the more to the less observable, and back again. If the entry point is at the bottom, at the level of "data," phenomena that are directly observable in the real world are involved (see below). "Facts," however, are abstractions, perhaps best conceptualized as measurements taken on data. Techniques like measurement, once applied to data, come to embody distinct assumptions about the structure of the phenomenon of interest. They relate data and facts to generalizations, which are derived inductively from data. Activities involving data and facts are common to all archaeological research and correspond to Masterman's (1970) "construct" or "methodological" paradigm concept (cf. Figure 1.1). Test implications are conditions that are expected to apply to patterns in data and are

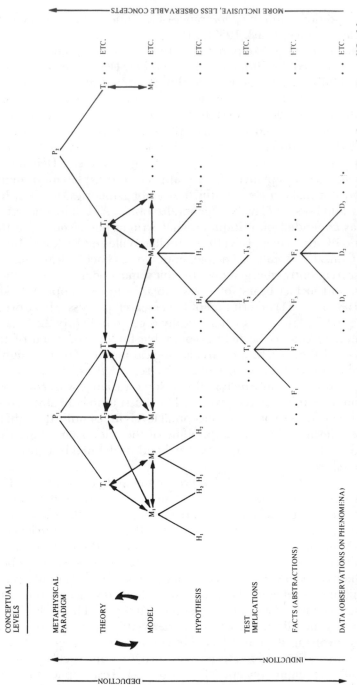

FIGURE 22.1. Conceptual relationships among paradigms, theories, models, hypotheses, "facts," and data, as exemplified by many (but not all) *Perspectives* contributors. The diagram bears some resemblance to Carr's (1985) conceptualization of levels of scientific thought in archaeology.

arrived at via deduction from a hypothesis, which can be defined as any unconfirmed but testable proposition (Hempel 1966:19). Hypotheses state that, in given circumstances, particular events are covered by (are particularizations of and thus explained by) suspected and/or confirmed laws or law-like generalizations (Watson et al. 1984:7).

Then things get very fuzzy conceptually, not only among the contributors but, I suspect, in the field at large. The reason is that archaeology lacks the body of confirmed, warranted, non-trivial laws or law-like generalizations that is characteristic of more fully axiomatized disciplines. Put another way, we don't have "theories" in the sense that physics has "theories." If there is an area of general confusion revealed by the essays in this book, it is at the level of "theories" and "models." While most workers appear to share a perception of what a metaphysical paradigm is (although they do not necessarily agree on the nature of the metaphysic), theories and models are used interchangeably throughout. Although theories have relatively precise definitions in more fully axiomatized disciplines, they are most generally viewed as the keys to understanding the empirical world. Hempel writes that theories

are normally developed only when previous research has yielded a body of information, including empirical generalizations about the phenomena in question. A theory is then intended to provide deeper understanding by presenting those phenomena as manifestations of certain underlying processes. (1966:244)

Personally, I prefer Binford's less rigorous, common-sense definition:

theories are the answers to the "why" questions of dynamics. They are concerned with understanding variability and how systems proceed from one state to another. (1981b:25)

Models, on the other hand, are more vague formulations that function at a number of levels to characterize or describe pattern, not necessarily "to provide deeper understanding" of it. Few archaeologists appear to make the distinction (and I, like many others, have often sought refuge in the comfortable ambiguity of "models"). Theories and models appear to occupy a position intermediate between that of the paradigm and that of the hypothesis (Figure 22.1). Whatever they are, they express relationships among non-observables (abstractions) of various kinds and, through hypotheses, relate diverse phenomena of interest to underlying causal processes. It is worth remarking that "facts" and "data" have a certain autonomy in archaeology, and observations are considered to be a better source of knowledge about the past than theories. Maybe we should think about turning that around.

While a constant interplay between the empirical and the theoretical is the hallmark of all "good" science, it strikes me that archaeology has tended to rely much too heavily on the strict empiricist notion that "the facts speak for themselves" and that structure in data is relatively self-evident. Nothing could be further from the truth.

Realism, Relativism, and the Radical Critique

Along with most of western science, and despite differences in respect of the nature of the paradigm, most *Perspectives* contributors appear to subscribe to what I would call "realist" biases. This is a philosophical position most often identified in recent years with the writings of Karl Popper (e.g., 1972, 1983). There are a number of different kinds of realism that have been identified in philosophy of science contexts (which, thankfully, need not concern us here!) and an historical treatment aimed at different construals of realism in archaeological theories by philosopher Alison Wylie (1981). At its most basic, realists believe that an objective reality exists "out there," apart from and independent of our perceptions of it. That reality is, at least in principle, discoverable through application of the methods of science; and there is the possibility of determining whether or not a theory is indeed really "true" or "false" (i.e., conforms with or is contradicted by objective reality) (Casti 1989:24, 25). Science in general would appear to demand a realist perspective of the world, although that realism is acknowledged to be mediated through the filter of the metaphysical paradigm. That we cannot know absolutely what the true nature of the real world is but must nevertheless postulate its existence is the paradox of what is called "hypothetical realism." Hypothetical realism has as its objective better and better approximations of reality through application of the methods of science. From the standpoint of hypothetical realism, all knowledge is contingent and preliminary, and "truth" is simply the best-supported current hypothesis (Flannery 1967, 1973). The realist perspective also assumes that the world "out there" is coherent, structured, orderly, and quasi-continuous and that it is at least partially knowable and can be comprehended through perception and experience (Vollmer 1987). Realist perspectives implicitly underlie most processual archaeology.

The objection has been made that if we cannot make sense of a reality that lies beyond our perceptions of it, if we cannot somehow specify what that reality would be "like," then the concept of an objective reality "out there" has no meaning or utility (Clark 1986, Ruse 1989). This is not a point of view that has found much favor in science, probably because of the implication that, if the world were ultimately subjective, inseparable from our thoughts about it, there would be no constraints at all on demonstrations of the credibility of our knowledge claims. It is worth remarking that this is a special case of what is known as the anthropic principle. The anthropic principle states that we tend to see the world the way we do because if it were otherwise, it (the world) would not satisfy the conditions necessary for our existence. We would not, therefore, be here to observe it! (Hawking 1988:124, 125)

Two other philosophical positions opposed to realism are instrumentalism and relativism (Casti 1989). Instrumentalism is the belief that theories are neither true nor false in any absolute sense, but are only instruments for predicting or approximating the results of measurements. In a sense, this is the ultimate strict empiricist position— the only things that are real and/or significant are the results of observations, and our capacity to apprehend that reality is limited only by the precision of our measuring instruments. It is a pragmatist viewpoint that is adopted essentially because it "works." It shows up in engineering and physics where there are many empirically-derived yet fundamental numbers that cannot be predicted from theory (in fact, efforts to develop a complete unified field theory in physics research are aimed, in part, at predicting these numbers [Feynmann 1985:124– 152]). Despite the well-known archaeological obsession with precision, instrumentalism has no conceptual or intellectual importance in archaeological epistemology.

Relativism is another matter entirely. Relativism denies the existence of a reality independent of our perception of it and depends, at least partly, on the social perspective of the person or group espousing a theory (Casti 1989:26). "Truth," instead of being the best current hypothesis, has no fixity, and changes from one generation, society, or theory to the next. Despite disavowals, relativist perspectives are implicit in much post-processualist archaeology (see below). However, relativism is a problem for science in general. His critics have pointed out that Kuhn's (1962) comprehensive "scientific revolutions," embedded as they were thought to have been in a larger social and intellectual matrix, comprise a relativist conception, as is his contention that paradigm shifts are essentially unpredictable and irrational (they were supposed to occur when anomalies accumulated to the extent that they could no longer be ignored). While he acknowledges their existence, Kuhn is silent on the social determinants of paradigm change. These observations led the philosopher Dudley Shapere (1971) to the conclusion that Kuhn's notion of science was nothing more than a series of fads essentially sustained by propaganda, and that there were no methods for evaluating the credibility of scientific theories. Kuhn (1974) responded by reiterating that rival paradigms cannot really be compared, although he did offer a set of criteria for characterizing the features of a good theory *within* a paradigm. According to Kuhn, a good theory must be (1) accurate (its consequences should be in agreement with experiments); (2) be consistent (no internal contradictions); (3) inclusive (the scope of the theory's consequences should extend beyond the particular subtheories, laws, or observations that it was created to explain); (4) simple (it should order phenomena that would otherwise be isolated); and (5) fruitful (it should disclose the existence of new classes of phenomena and/or previously unobserved relationships). It is important to note once again that, in a fully axiomatized science, these criteria of choice among theories apply to choice only under the aegis of a single metaphysical paradigm, and that the credibility of a theory results from its general acceptance by the scientific community defined by the paradigm (i.e., theories cannot be given objective justification). Kuhn is only a relativist, however, when it comes to paradigm shifts. During the "normal science" phase of his scenario, he advocates a realist perspective and basically subscribes to the Hempel or Popper-like process of conjecture, test, and falsification described above.

As I noted in the Introduction, the positivist legacy of western science that underlies most *Perspectives* contributions has become the target in recent years of some of the elements of the radical critique (see especially Hodder 1982a, b, 1983, 1989; Shanks and Tilley 1987, 1988). Arguing from both relativist and realist perspectives, critical theorists have claimed (1) that processual archaeology has been a failure, in that it has generated no new or better (i.e., inferentially more secure) knowledge of the human past than that produced by traditional (pre-1970) archaeology; (2) that processualists are largely oblivious to their own biases, especially to the behaviorism and/or functionalism and its derivatives that underlie their grounding theories; (3) that logical positivism has itself been misconstrued (as anti-empiricist) and is, in any event, not an appropriate philosophy for a "human science"; (4) that positivism is a product of the industrialized, capitalist west and that other (and by implication, better) paradigms are available (especially various forms of marxism); (5) that science cannot be disembedded from its broader social context and will always be influenced by prevailing social, political, and economic ideas; (6) that processualists believe the past to be directly accessible, and to be something that exists outside of our perceptions of it (i.e., it is "objectified"); (7) that processual archaeologists accept the existence of a permanent frame of reference (i.e., that of natural science, described above) for determining the nature of an objectified reality; (8) that they employ a model of economic rationality derived from western capitalism; (9) that they subscribe to adaptationist biases grounded in biosocial evolution (see below); (10) that processual archaeology is not in fact "processual" (i.e., it allegedly does a poor job of addressing process questions in both past and present); and (11) that, with its emphasis on material culture, the ideational sphere is ignored or deemphasized (and consequently dismissed as unattainable) (Yengoyan 1985, Bell 1987, Binford 1987a, Earle and Preucel 1987, Watson 1990, Meltzer 1990).

It is by no means easy to untangle distinct skeins of thought in critical theory, although Patterson has recently attempted to do so (1989, 1990). What emerges is a polythetic "fuzzy set" of three partly complementary, partly contrasting positions, all of which are grounded intellectually in French poststructuralism, various aspects of marxist social thought and, to some extent, symbolic anthropology. Patterson identifies a rapidly evolving variant, championed by Ian Hodder, that is realist but anti-positivist, materialist, and structural marxist and that, in its most recent incarnation (Hodder 1989), contends that social history affects our construal of pattern in past, present, and future; that different segments of society have different conceptions of the past (and thus create different representations of it), that our perceptions of the past reflect current power and authority relations and structures (and, more broadly, current social context), that the archaeological record has an objective reality (i.e., exists outside our perceptions of it) but is nevertheless a "text to be decoded," and that middle range theory (*sensu* Binford, Schiffer) is inadequate to model processes of any interest to anybody.

A second strand is identified with Michael Shanks and Christopher Tilley and receives its intellectual mandate from French structuralism, poststructuralism, and marxism (Patterson 1990). Presented as part of a rather glib, critical survey of the views of different processual and post-processual theorists, their own position acknowledges a realist view of the past (but, again, one that is accessible only through "reading" the material culture record as a text-analogue), contends that archaeology is an interpretive endeavor and is influenced by present ideological, sociopolitical, and economic realities, and asserts that there are alternative and equally valid "understandings" of the past which reflect contemporary relations of power and authority. Shanks and Tilley (1987, 1988) take the processualists to task for developing methods that seek to extract science from its social milieux (they maintain this is impossible to do). They advocate a kind of archaeological "activism" in which archaeologists join with other intellectuals to struggle against the established social order and all forms of knowledge and power that are used to "repress." Archaeological expertise is marshaled to empower the economically and socially disadvantaged victims of

western imperialism. An extension of that imperialism is the hege-
mony (one could almost read "tyranny") of the processualists' version
of the scientific method. Metaphorical Maoists, they wish to "let a
thousand flowers bloom" but at the same time eradicate a few noxious
capitalist weeds from the intellectual garden.

The third position is represented by the American historical archaeologist Mark Leone (1982, Leone et al. 1987), who argues that, while
archaeological practice and ideology are both part of the present, they
are nevertheless biased in terms of particular historical specifics (e.g.,
analytical frameworks, frameworks for justifying knowledge claims).
Like Hodder, he claims that processualists have been insufficiently
critical of their analytical frameworks and knowledge claims, and that
one cannot ignore ideology since it constrains human action in the past
and affects social consciousness (and lots of other things!) in the present. Ideology itself has a history; and it is necessary to examine it since,
by so doing, archaeologists can make better informed choices from an
array of alternative reconstructions of the past.

Faced with this assault based on what many of us take to be dated,
misconstrued, selective or mutually-conflicting versions of processual
archaeology, it is not surprising that a coherent response has not been
forthcoming. The attack itself is incoherent. As Patterson's summary
shows, there is considerable disarray in the post-processualist camp,
with as much intellectual energy expended on internecine disputes as
is directed at the opposition. In fact, it is sometimes difficult to tell just
who the opposition is. It is a little like fencing with a ghost in a surreal
landscape that is constantly shifting under one's feet. Nevertheless,
there has been a reaction, and, although it is still a partial one, there are
some recurrent features.

Perhaps the most damaging observation to come out of reactions to
various critical theory books is that post-processual accounts of the
methodology, inferential structure, and positivist underpinnings of
processual archaeology are often distorted, partly inaccurate, or sometimes simply wrong altogether (Bell 1987, Binford 1987a, b, Kristiansen 1988, Meltzer 1990, Watson 1990). There is a general tendency
to confound the role of deduction in verification with the inductive
context of discovery as if, somehow, the inductive, deductive, and
abductive aspects of problem solving could be neatly and absolutely
separated from one another (see also Clark 1976b, 1982, 1987a).

Shanks and Tilley (1987, 1988) also claim to reject quantification
because of the mistaken belief that processualists use it to produce
"value-free data." Since they deny the existence of value-free data (as,
of course, do processualists—Carr 1985b), Shanks and Tilley are similarly ill-disposed toward precision, prediction, and control; yet they

undermine their position by a heavy reliance on statistics in the famous beer can study which, Watson (1990:220) points out, accounts for about 30% of *Re-Constructing Archaeology* (1987). On the basis of other quantified pattern searches, they arrive at other post hoc accommodative arguments—explanations cooked up after the fact to account for pattern in data (Binford 1981b). Such explanation candidates are a weak form of empirical generalization, which Shanks and Tilley do not seem to recognize, asserting that they reject all efforts to generalize from data. Since they also reject, on a variety of flimsy grounds (Meltzer 1990:186), the whole concept of social evolution, time-transgressive patterns in data are due exclusively to the operation of historical factors, and history, to them, is particularistic and non-generalizing. The only explanation of change offered is "a full account of change" (Oakeshott 1933:43), which must by definition be particularistic, but their "full account of change" is rife with empirical generalizations (Watson 1990:220). And so it goes. Even ignoring what has been called "the crisis of historicity" (the problematic nature of historical "facts"—Young 1988), the problems for prehistoric archaeology are formidable and obvious.

Although there are clear differences between Hodder, on the one hand, and Shanks and Tilley, on the other, the British wing of the radical critique appears to be utterly lacking in a coherent research strategy that would allow independent assessment of the credibility of their "understandings" and "interpretations." In short, one either accepts these "understandings" and "interpretations" on faith (by acceptance of their biases) or one does not. There's nothing "in the middle" that might allow one to go from an assertion about "the way the world is" to empirical referents bearing on present construals of the nature of the (or a) past. They never make clear *how* one is to explain social transformations in the particular case (except as the unique outcome of an equally unique series of historical events) or in general, nor *why* social transformations are thought to have occurred in the first place. They reject any notion of a CL model for explanation, and with it any pretense to objectivity in the assessment of the credibility of their knowledge claims. The whole is embedded in a strident, 1960s-style rhetoric that advocates a "radical, value-committed archaeology" (Shanks and Tilley 1988:206) in which archaeologists are to employ their expertise in the fight against "the prevailing regime for the production of truth" (1988:204)—presumably the western, capitalist, positivist tradition. Non-western, non-capitalist, anti-positivist alternative archaeologies are advocated (marxist, post-structuralist, symbolic, etc.), but no compelling reason is articulated for choosing any one of them, or for choosing them over their positivist competitors. To someone who was a student during the turbulent 1960s, this confrontational approach "resonates" (yuk!) very well with my remembrances of my youth. It is a question of the pot calling the kettle black. Watson (1990:221) says it very well:

I also find quite telling a point made by Kristiansen [1986:481] and others about critical theorists such as Shanks and Tilley, who stress the importance of paying critical attention to the sociopolitics of archaeology as an expression of capitalism and imperialism, but do not indicate how their own critical position is situated within contemporary society. *What sociopolitical factors call forth and sustain their attack? What legitimates their authority as analysts and arbiters of archaeological (or any other) praxis? Are critical theorists somehow exempt from sociopolitical matrices? And are not the sociopolitical matrices to which they hark very like those general categories whose existence or analytic value they deny?* (1990:221, italics mine)

In reviews generally sympathetic to the radical critique, Patterson (1989, 1990) criticizes processual archaeology for its "largely implicit, empiricist, behaviourist, functionalist and logical positivist grounding theories" (1989:556), its obsession with technique, and its claims to objectivity. In contrast, post-processualists are supposedly more critically self-aware, employ broader conceptions of both history and culture, view history as a context-dependent human construction and archaeology as a "series of texts," also socially constructed, that cannot be "read" (in fact, do not exist) apart from the circumstances in which interpretations occur (1989:561). He calls for a dialectic between processual and post-processual archaeology in order to identify elements incompatible with the different theoretical perspectives of each (1990:197). The eclecticism characteristic of both sides is deplored (because it stands in the way of synthesis), and an appeal is sounded for critical assessment of their strengths, weaknesses, and implications for the study of process. Whatever the differences among them, the three kinds of post-processual archaeology he outlines supposedly (1) confront the empiricist, positivist biases of processual archaeology concerning structure, history, and change, (2) reject the notion that the past is directly knowable (i.e., has an objective reality apart from our perceptions of it), (3) view history as a human construction, rather than something handed down by nature, and (4) acknowledge the importance of contemporary sociopolitical influences in the construction of history (Patterson 1989:562). Is it possible to reconcile these allegations with the tenets of processualism? I would suggest (1) that some post-processualists (e.g., Leone) have in fact confronted the subjective element in history without abandoning independent verification of knowledge claims; (2) that most processualists would agree with the post-processualist assertion that the past is not directly knowable; (3) that processualists also see history (and archaeology) as human constructions (but nevertheless adopt a realist stance); and (4) that they would readily acknowledge the subjective element in history. In short, it seems to me that Patterson's points of alleged contrast are in fact wholly or mostly compatible with the position of processualist archaeology today. Moreover, it is the position taken by most *Perspectives* contributors, whether or not they formally identify themselves with a processualist stance (but cf. papers by Debénath, Gonzálcz Morales, Bar-Yosef). The processual archaeology that is the target of the radical critique is little more than a caricature of the processual archaeology of the 1990s.

I would also contend, despite assertions to the contrary, that the British wing of critical theory is, for the most part, a relativist archaeology in that "truth" itself changes according to the sociopolitical persuasion of the archaeologist. Not so, of course, for processualists, nor for the American post-processualist Mark Leone (1982, Leonc ct al. 1987) who, while he acknowledges the importance of the subjective element in the construction of history, also endorses a realist archaeology and the analytical strategy that goes along with it. Perhaps the most "processual" of "processual archaeologists," Lewis Binford has recently observed that our knowledge of the past is constructed *in the present* out of (1) the static material residues of once-dynamic processes now found in geological contexts (i.e., the archaeological record), (2) the observations we choose to make on the archaeological record, and (3) general contemporary knowledge about the world that guides our choices of observations and influences our interpretations of them (1989a:13). I suggest that many post-processualists would find this outline for a research agenda to be more or less compatible with their own. If there is a parting of the ways, it is because some of the more extreme post-processualists have abandoned any disinterested attempt at objective verification of their knowledge claims.

Adaptation, Ecology, and Systems Perspectives

Along with adherence to some form of positivism, and the conceptualization of the research process summarized in Figure 21.1, it appears to me that most *Perspectives* contributors endorse what I would call "adaptationist" biases which are, in turn, loosely grounded in some form of ecological systems perspective. Ecological systems perspectives constitute another polythetic set comprised of partly overlapping, partly discrete bunches of models and theories, the specifics of which are determined, in each case, by the conceptual filters imposed by the constraints of a given research tradition. Implicit in most such approaches is an adaptationist view of culture whereby the system representing the totality of human social behavior is composed of a relatively small number of constituent subsystems, some of which are more important (or at least more directly accessible archaeologically) than others (Binford 1962, 1964, 1965). A definition of *adaptation* that would probably be acceptable to most hunter-gatherer archaeologists is that of evolutionary biology:

[Adaptation is] any structure, physiological process or behavioural pattern that makes an organism more fit to survive and to reproduce. (Wilson 1975:577)

For "organism," one could substitute "group" (see below). Behavior can be viewed as "the dynamics of adaptation"—a strategy for survival and reproduction applicable at the level of the group (Binford 1972:133). It could be argued that an important goal for archaeologists involved in the study of ancient hunter-gatherers is to develop a perspective for the study of the past that emphasizes changing adaptive systems. While scarcely a novel idea from an Americanist point of view (see, e.g., Binford 1962, 1964, 1965; Flannery 1967, 1969, 1973), most Old World research traditions (1) tend to treat archaeological, subsistence, paleoenvironmental, and site distributional data as if these were more or less autonomous, largely independent categories of information, and (2) tend to concentrate on the characteristics of the retouched stone tool components of lithic assemblages, as if these were somehow "meaningful" in their own right (or more meaningful than other categories of data) due to the preconception that it is by examination of stone tool characteristics that one has the best chance to monitor or recover "ethnicity." Integrated systems perspectives are not common outside the anglophone research traditions, and the European tendency to compartmentalize aspects of the research gets in the way of a more unified approach to the study of behavior.

For all hunter-gatherers, adaptation is a *regional* problem and can be defined either biologically (in terms of inclusive fitness) or, in the present context, culturally, by identifying particular behavioral solutions from a range of possible solutions that would have allowed human groups to persist over time. Put another way, human adaptation is "the possession of a valid set of solutions to a variety of problems" (Jochim 1981:19). These solutions are developed in different contexts to meet different objectives (some specific, others general), only one of which need be reproductive success. Biological definitions of adaptation are practically impossible to test empirically since, in default of representative samples of biological populations, there is no way to measure reproductive success. Since it is more complete, the archaeological record can sometimes be used, as here, to generate test implications about aspects of biological evolution, always assuming that the creators of an archaeological record can be identified to genus and species (which, in light of the deplorable state of paleontological systematics, is an enormous assumption to make!). Studies cast in a broadly ecological, systems framework seek to understand the adaptive significance of different kinds of human behavior without making the assumption that all such behavior is "adaptive" (i.e., some [probably most] behaviors are adaptively neutral, some maladaptive, etc., over the long run). More important, adaptation has *specific empirical referents* that can be monitored using archaeological data and that can potentially inform us about the nature of change or process (i.e., whether change is directional, continuous or not; whether change is occurring at similar or different rates; whether patterns of change are correlated with one another across different variables; etc.). Analyses guided by these biases should be able to identify modal site and artifact functional categories and simultaneously monitor changes in function over time. Paleoclimatic fluctuations are controlled by the palynological, sedimentological and geomorphological studies that are so fundamental to European natural science research. Time, however, tends to be regarded differently in America and in Europe. In America, time is a "reference variable" against which to measure change attributed to other causes. Whenever possible, time is controlled by absolute dating methods and, in default of samples suited to such techniques, by paleoclimatic information—*never*, as in Europe, by the supposedly time-sensitive characteristics of the retouched tool components themselves.

A bewildering array of models underlie systems ecological approaches to adaptation, including (1) animal ecology-derived models of adaptation, (2) ethnographically grounded resource studies, (3) environmental models with various emphases and degrees of sophistication (usually aimed at describing the time-space distribution of resources), (4) optimization, risk-minimization, and "satisficer" models of human subsistence behavior, (5) decision models derived from game theory and linear programming, and (6) geodemographic models of settlement location (see Bettinger 1980 for an overview).

General models of hunter-gatherer adaptation rely on concepts and theories derived from animal ecology, economics, and geography, and are oriented mainly toward the elucidation of generalizable relationships between humans and their resource bases. Bettinger (1980:203–207) has divided these into environmental, subsistence, settlement location, and population models, of which the first two have received the greatest archaeological attention. Environmental models use concepts like diversity, stability, productivity, and patchiness to describe, and to an extent explain or predict, human behavior; but they operate at a general level and do not readily lend themselves to descriptions of specific cases. Subsistence models are much more widely used and base evaluation of adaptation upon the ability of a human group to produce an adequate food supply. Optimal foraging theory (e.g., Winterhalder 1981, Winterhalder and Smith 1981), hunter-gatherer goal satisficer models (e.g., Jochim 1976, 1981), game theory (e.g., Rapoport 1960), and linear programming (e.g., Reidhead 1979) are included here. Game theory is probably more valuable as a device for understanding the options available under a variety of general circumstances than as a given strategy for adaptation. As these examples indicate, subsistence models have been extensively formalized, but are, in each case, characterized by incompletely developed (and sometimes incompatible) theoretical justifications. They remain collections of methods with little basis for choosing among them, except insofar as choice would be dictated by the particulars of a given situation (i.e., some will be more appropriate than others given the kinds of data available to provide a test). Jochim's goal satisficer model has the advantage that it breaks down the subsistence system into a series of specific options that might obtain under a limited number of circumstances, rather than dealing with adaptive strategies as undifferentiated wholes. Applications of it can, therefore, be tailored to individual archaeological situations to a greater extent than is possible with some of the other approaches (especially game theory). All consider the costs and benefits of choices in subsistence behavior, but usually require higher resolution data than those typically attainable in Pleistocene hunter-gatherer contexts, thus limiting their utility in specific cases.

Hunter-gatherer models of settlement location are based on efforts to get at the complex nexus of decisions involved in the use of places in landscape as parts of an overall subsistence strategy. Included here are site catchment and site territorial approaches (e.g., Roper 1979, Dennell 1980, Jarman et al. 1982), gravity models (e.g., Jochim 1976), the optimal location model (Wood and Johnson 1978), and the "polythetic satisficer" location model of Williams et al. (1973). An outgrowth of a post-1975 concern with regional analysis, these approaches emphasize the importance of identifying (and usually ranking) the determinants of site placement in terms of the range of resources accessible from a given point once that point is known (rather than predicting site locations according to resource procurement cost/benefit ratios, as, e.g., Jochim 1976). They place some importance on the relationship of distance (or time) to resources recovered from sites, and the relative yield or incidence of resources, as determinants of site placement. The polythetic satisficer model considers distance only until certain thresholds are reached and not continuously. The satisficer criterion invoked here makes site placement dependent upon attainment of satisfactory levels of a certain number of "key" variables, rather than an assessment of the contributions of all of them. At the methodological level, there is a lot of variation in the algorithms used to monitor time and distance and to provide a rank order of economic resources.

Population models focus on the relationship of population growth and adaptive change. Two primary approaches are (1) those that consider population as a dependent variable, and (2) those that consider it to be independent of the overall subsistence system. Most hunter-gatherer archaeologists in both hemispheres (and practically all those concerned with more complex societies—Cowgill 1975) continue to favor the dependent relationship and consider the environment as a (perhaps *the*) primary determinant of population growth and stability. This bias is particularly evident in the research traditions of the Continent, with their strong natural science foundations. The approach is in direct opposition to that of workers who propose a more active role for long term population growth, and who argue that the tendency for population increases to approach regional carrying capacities creates population/resource imbalances and stress that drive change. These general kinds of relationships between population densities and resources are thought to underlie a host of significant adaptive shifts, including the "broad spectrum revolution" in the Levant (Flannery 1969, cf. Edwards 1989), the appearance of domestication economies in general (Binford 1968, Flannery 1973), and numerous other local subsistence changes (Cohen 1975, 1977; Clark and Straus 1986, Clark 1983a–c, 1987b). These models are diachronic and scale dependent, and require that changes in subsistence be monitored independently of changes in population density. It has been claimed that population models can also be used to examine other aspects of hunter-gatherer social organization, in particular demography and certain kinds of social (especially mating) networks (e.g., Wobst 1974, 1976). The problem with these applications is that it is often difficult, if not impossible, to provide an adequate empirical test of a model simulation.

Although written more than a decade ago, the general kinds of models reviewed by Bettinger (1980) constitute a fairly accurate appraisal of the range of choice currently available to hunter-gatherer archaeologists. However, as he points out, they are not all of equal descriptive or explanatory power. Environmental models tend to be favored by the indigenous Old World research traditions, but are usually either too "coarse grained" or too abstract to do more than provide very rough expectations of behavior. Location and population models, popular with many anglophone workers, are dependent upon rather detailed prior knowledge of adaptation (but can be very useful if such are forthcoming). Subsistence models perhaps have the greatest potential for developing adequate explanatory frameworks to the problem of hunter-gatherer adaptation, but their effective use is constrained by four limiting conditions or assumptions that should be reconciled if predictions based on the models are to have validity (Bettinger 1980).

The first condition is that credible subsistence predictions would seem to demand "perfect knowledge" of all subsistence items, including their "costs" and "payoffs," and some relatively defensible "currency" with which to measure these. Perfect knowledge is also sometimes postulated for the prehistoric groups involved, in order to reduce subsistence decisions to the sum total of economic decisions. This is unrealistic, of course, because criteria for perfect knowledge are difficult or impossible to ascertain (much less attain) since perfect knowledge is dependent upon a host of contingencies that cannot be controlled in any "real world" situation, past or present (a criticism often leveled at the highly axiomatized version of optimal foraging theory—e.g., Hespenheide 1980, Martin 1983). To postulate it for foragers involves a considerable leap of faith, and subscription to rigid "economic man" biases that are certainly not warranted or probably even appropriate. On the other hand, most archaeologists concerned with these issues make the assumption that foragers have a "reasonably good" working knowledge of resource types, yields, and distributions, and the capacity to rank them (at least approximately) in terms of expected cost/benefit ratios. Given particular (and specifiable) technological and behavioral means of procuring and processing resources, any effort to match prehistoric (or, for that matter, contemporary) patterns with subsistence predictions must relax the perfect knowledge assumption.

The second condition holds that the environment and its resources are stable over the interval of interest, so that individual resource yields can be described, or at least approximated, by mean values. It is also assumed that resource exploitation does not appreciably affect these values, which often is not the case (e.g., Ortea 1986). Variation in resource types and environmental regimes would certainly affect the utility of yield projections, and the challenge is one of determining how great those effects must be before they render the predictions of subsistence models invalid (Bettinger 1980:234).

The third condition involves the notion that problems of subsistence adaptations are resolved at the local level by means of "appropriate choices" among resources by minimum bands, and that no larger, extralocal economic interaction is involved. The reasoning behind this is that risk and time minimization are only meaningful considerations in the immediacy of local group contexts, and that extralocal economic associations would impossibly confound pattern empirically and also render these goals deferred in time (and, therefore, meaningless for local decision makers with their limited capacities to take future, long term contingencies into account). This condition is also contradicted by the literature, and Bettinger recognizes that it is probably always violated in ethnographic contexts which are, at best, only "moments in time" (1980:236, 237). Predictive subsistence models tend to assume that economic decision making is fundamental to understanding forager adaptations, but short term, quasi-economic decisions might be secondary to long term evolutionary processes; and it is probably a mistake to reduce the latter to the sum total of the former. At present, no grounding theory for this kind of long term selection has been developed (see below). Whether economic decision making assumptions are regarded as credible or not depends to some extent on the temporal and spatial frames of reference of a particular problem, but more generally on the importance of western, "economic man" biases in the paradigms that govern a regional research tradition.

The final condition is the assumption that, for a given environment and technology, there is only a single optimal adaptive solution and that the adaptive process among hunter-gatherers is sufficiently constraining that local groups will approximate that optimal solution. This assumption is obviously crucial for the optimal foraging, linear programming, and goal satisficer models, but it also pervades most other Americanist subsistence approaches. It is a simplifying assumption that archaeologists typically make in order "to get on with it" in a particular problem context, since it is probable that there are in fact multiple adaptive solutions, even under the same technoenvironmental circumstances, and that all foragers will not somehow "evolve" toward a single optimum adaptation. In regional, long term studies of hunter-gatherers, it has sometimes been possible to document changes in adaptation while holding technology and environment constant (e.g., Clark 1987b, Clark and Straus 1983, 1986; Straus and Clark 1986a, Clark and Yi 1983). However, the notion of optimality (or lack thereof) has proven elusive. What is, in fact, the "best" adaptive solution for any problem? Are there multiple alternative "best" solutions? More often than not, adaptive change appears to be driven by population/resource imbalances, and involves greater and greater investments of labor and energy to maintain adequate subsistence needs in the face of overexploitation caused by growing regional populations (e.g., Earle 1980, Christenson 1980, Clark and Yi 1983, Clark 1987b). It is probably more reasonable to use optimum adaptive solutions as theoretical abstractions or imaginary "baselines" against which to make relative comparisons of adaptative change at different places and over time.

No one would try to claim any intellectual integrity or coherence to archaeologists' ad hoc appropriation of parts of these models, nor has a unified grounding theory emerged that might subsume them all under a broad-based cultural ecology paradigm (a deficiency noted long ago by Schiffer et al. 1978). However, linkages between adaptation, ecology, and systems figure in many essays presented here and are part and parcel of most hunter-gatherer subsistence research. They appear to derive from a shared conviction that (1) foragers are particularly intimately connected via subsistence and settlement strategies to their physical environments (more than would be the case for more technologically complex forms of social organization), and (2) productive relationships might often obtain between general ecological principles and hunter-gatherer archaeological research, even in the absence of any kind of overarching theoretical justification.

There is a perception, widely shared by Anglo-American workers, that foragers are mainly food gatherers, small game hunters, and shell and/or shellfish collectors, and that large game is of minimal dietary importance. Women, rather than men, provide most of the food; and only a fraction of time is spent procuring and processing resources. Exploitation to satisficing levels is the normal objective of resource procurement, rather than maximization or risk minimization. These preconceptions arise from the historical impact of the *Man the Hunter* volume (Lee and de Vore 1968a) on the Anglo-American research tradition; taken together, they constitute a paradigm for much of the field as to what hunter-gatherer adaptations are "like" (see Mueller-Wille and Dickson, this volume). It is a view that has only recently come under attack, with the accumulation of archaeological evidence for "complex" hunter-gatherer adaptations that do not correspond to the normative characterization (e.g., Price and Brown 1985), and for "maladapted" foraging societies culled from the ethnographic literature (e.g., papers in Ortner 1983). The impact of this perspective on hunter-gatherer adaptations outside the anglophone world has been decidedly limited (cf., e.g., chapters by Sackett, González Morales, Debénath). If there is a general goal to this kind of research, it is to develop hunter-gatherer behavioral models that will allow prediction of adaptive responses, rather than just describing them. But, as we have seen, the models available so far are incomplete, partially contradictory in terms of basic assumptions, and lack a coherent theoretical framework. Given an absence of alternatives, and the enormous problems involved in putting these approaches to an empirical test, it is difficult to be very optimistic about the prospects for a more coherent, unified approach. Predictive subsistence models will continue to be applied to problems of regional scale in the eclectic, largely atheoretical way that they have been, in the hope that a broader, more inclusive theoretical perspective might eventually emerge.

Adaptation Again, Ecology, and Evolution

In the Introduction, I offered the opinion that, if there was a metaphysical paradigm that underlies the work of most of the authors represented here, it is probably some kind of ill-defined notion of human biocultural evolution. Even those workers who regard archaeology as a kind of history, projected back into the preliterate past, appear to be strongly influenced by evolutionary biases, concepts, and relationships, although these vary in importance from one research tradition to the next and are not usually made explicit in any of them (Brace 1988a, 1989; see chapters by Debénath, Bar-Yosef; the French paradigm described by Sackett). Since evolutionary biases figure prominently in the work of hunter-gatherer archaeologists in general (Dunnell 1980), it might be useful to try to identify some shared aspects of archaeologists' efforts to apply evolutionary theory to cultural evolution. Most such attempts conceptualize cultural evolution more or less along neo-Darwinian lines and involve selectionist explanations intended to account for non-teleological causal processes which result in the variably successful adaptations of local groups or populations to their environments. Thousands of such "experiments in adaptation" are recorded in the archaeological record, but archaeologists have not been notably successful at arriving at consensus descriptions of them, much less extracting general behavioral principles from them. Theodosius Dobzhansky once remarked that "culture is the most potent method of adaptation that has emerged in the evolutionary history of the living world" (1972:422). The paradigm of culture as an adaptive system is widespread and goes back to the 1930s, with the pioneering work of Julian Steward (e.g., 1938). While archaeology is perhaps the best situated of all the social sciences by virtue of its time-space frames of reference to explore human behavior from an adaptationist point of view, there is considerable disagreement as to *how* we might go about operationalizing the study of cultural adaptation.

The concept of adaptation has been used in biology in at least three different ways (i.e., in reference to a particular biological structure or organ, as a state of being, and as a process of change—Kirch 1980:103). Since about 1960, however, it has come to be linked more and more to evolution and to ecology. Evolution might be defined in a general way as a particular framework for explaining change as the differential persistence of variability under the selective pressures of the environment (Dunnell 1980, Kirch 1980). Differential persistence is a function of environmental constraints (and a number of stochastic factors). The continuity implied in "change" and "persistence" indicates that the phenomena in question are historically related to one another (Alland and McCay 1973). The natural environment is the province of ecology, and the objective of ecological research is to understand the functional integration of the physical and organic components of the environment as a total system (Hardesty 1980). The appearance of an "evolutionary ecology" paradigm over the past two decades is due to the realization that evolutionary change cannot be comprehended outside its ecological context, and that the functional integration of ecological systems is only comprehensible as the product of evolution and natural selection (Kirch 1980:102, 103).

Although the idea that living things had changed over the course of time was not new with Darwin, he was the first to conceive of evolution as a "two-step" process that involved the production of variation and the sorting of that variability by means of natural selection. By adopting the Malthusian perspective that populations reproduce, as a matter of course, to excess, and by applying the principle of natural selection (he called it "descent with modification"), Darwin was able to account for the phenomenon of adaptation without invoking goal-directed behavior or some form of guiding intelligence.

If it is assumed that an organism will always produce more offspring than the environment can possibly sustain, only those best fitted to a given set of environmental circumstances will survive to reproductive age. (Hahlweg 1989:49)

In biological evolution, selectionist explanations of adaptation are intended to account for how non-intelligent causal processes can result in the adaptation of organisms to their environments. If a satisfactory explanation of adaptation is to be achieved, there must be variability in both the environment and the gene pool; and that variability must be random in respect of any system trajectory (i.e., non-directional), and "non-purposive" sorting mechanisms must exist and operate on that variability. Empirically, however, it is possible to show that adaptation can occur in the absence of one or more of these conditions, and evolutionary change is not, of course, always adaptive. The implication is that natural selection cannot by itself account for all aspects of evolutionary change, especially when "intelligent" life is involved (see below).

There is no question that the development of a selectionist mode of explanation was a landmark in the history of the life sciences. The philosopher Ronald Amundson (1989) points out that the *only possible* naturalistic explanation of adaptation involves processes of variation and selection, and that no one has so far devised a satisfactory alternative. The claim is not that nothing can intervene between a selective process and what he calls an "end product adaptation" (since natural selection always works through intervening processes), but rather that the intervening processes by themselves cannot explain the "adaptedness" of the end result (p. 423). The distinction is that between "proximate" and "ultimate" causes (Mayr 1961); and a selectionist would argue that at some point in the historical explanation of an adaptation, Darwinian selective processes (ultimate causes) must be at work. For "cultural" organisms like ourselves, that point might be reached when we become *dependent* upon learned behavior for physical and social survival. The mode of transmission of learned behavior from one generation to the next is, of course, Lamarckian (i.e., it involves the "inheritance of acquired characteristics") although a predisposition toward a capacity to learn might be thought of as Darwinian. It is a question in evolutionary epistemology whether or not there is a Darwinian selectionist infrastructure whenever there is a Lamarckian surface structure (Dawkins 1983). Except to a radical sociobiologist, "culture," in the sense of learned behavior, would qualify as a "Lamarckian surface structure."

Archaeological approaches to adaptation constitute a special case of general selectionist models originally developed to account for biological evolution. Cultural adaptation is a process of alteration of a cultural system in response to changes in its coupled environmental systems, and these changes are brought about through the medium of behavior, which can be selected for or against. An exegesis of the theoretical basis for the study of behavior from an adaptationist perspective draws on this paradigm, and has been ably summarized by Patrick Kirch (1980:130, 131). Kirch identifies eight fundamental principles that constitute grounding theories for this approach, most of which are compatible with biological selectionist modes of explanation.

1. Variation is the ultimate source of adaptation.
2. Natural selection is the mechanism responsible for discriminating among variant behavior.
3. Heterogeneity and change in the environment are the primary sources of selective pressure.
4. Selection operates with regard to a specific environment and, as a consequence, is opportunistic.
5. Since the persistence of a group is determined by reproductive success, the ultimate criterion of selection is reproductive fitness.
6. For humans, the mechanism for selective retention and transmission of adaptive behavior is cognitive and symbolic, with consequences for the rate of adaptive response.
7. Selection of behavior operates not only on the individual, but also at the group level.

8. Since all human behavior cannot be reduced to the level of interaction with the environment, not all behavior is adaptive, or
explicable in an evolutionary framework (Kirch 1980:130, 131).

Probably the most controversial of these are numbers 5 and 7, and
potential objections to them have more to do with monitoring relevant
variables in archaeological contexts than they do with whether or not
group selection can be accommodated by neo-Darwinian notions of
"inclusive fitness." Most archaeologists invoke group selection models
rather than selectionist models that operate at the level of individual
behavior simply because the archaeological invisibility of individuals
compels them to do so. It is also widely held that the probability of the
survival of a group is, in some sense, the product of the probabilities of
survival to reproductive age of its constituent members. If we cannot
identify individuals in the past, but think that we can sometimes identify groups, we really have no alternative to group selection models so
long as there is an obligation to put our ideas to some kind of an
empirical test.

While I suspect that Kirch's principles would find favor with most
Perspectives contributors (and probably most hunter-gatherer archaeologists in general), the main challenge is using them effectively in
"real world" archaeological situations to learn something interesting
about adaptation. We need to come up with realistic archaeological
definitions of terms and concepts like "selection" that have unambiguous phenomenological referents, that are measurable, that will
allow patterns to be generated which can be subjected to empirical
verification, and that somehow still remain consistent with the general
theoretical framework of cultural adaptation. Kirch (1980:131–133)
outlines a hypothesis-testing research design that is compatible with
the general covering-law approach to the explanation given above, but
its successful application is contingent on the definition of temporal,
spatial, and behavioral analytical units appropriate to given problem
contexts. We have at our disposal an arsenal of independent techniques
to control for time, but space and behavior are far more problematical.
If adaptation is regarded as a process of interaction involving the
environment, human adaptive strategies, and demography, we need to
arrive at satisfactory monitors of this once-dynamic system in the static
residues of the past. But, how do we do it? How do we "test" adaptive
process? While answers will vary from one worker to the next, the
commonalities of the adaptive process itself and the nature of the
Upper Pleistocene archaeological record will tend to constrain those
answers to some extent.

Specifically, I think that (1) there is a need to focus on group selection, for the reasons just enumerated, even in the face of obvious

disagreement as to whether or not it is possible to identify groups prehistorically (cf., e.g., Henry 1989, Clark 1989c; see also Henry, Bar-Yosef, Bietti, Sackett, this volume). So far as archaeologists are concerned, the group is the effective unit of adaptation. (2) I believe we should try to get away from the basically inductive approaches characteristic of the European research traditions (i.e., build some kind of a predictive element into our research designs) in order to avoid the bewildering array of conflicting, post hoc accommodative arguments for pattern that presently afflict the field. One way to do this would be to set up alternative working hypotheses that are both mutually exclusive in terms of their test implications and empirically falsifiable (Chamberlin [1965]). (3) We should emphasize quantified, comparative approaches to testing grounded in a defensible operational language in order to relate specific behavioral responses to the operation of general selection mechanisms (Wilson 1975, Smith 1978). It seems abundantly clear that if we ever manage to explain anything in general, it is going to be in quantitative (probabilistic) terms. Finally, (4) we should pay more attention to ecology (Hardesty 1980). Relationships between general ecological principles and archaeological data are indirect, ambiguous, and complex, but constitute a means for linking behavior and evolution since they link the physical environment and the human behavioral response to it. However, ecology is only partly axiomatized (albeit much more developed in terms of its systematics than archaeology); and before successful integration can be attained, we need to come up with cultural equivalents for basic ecological analytical concepts like "species," "niche," and "population," upon which successful application of its systematics depends. Schiffer (1978) has criticized ad hoc archaeological appropriation of pieces of ecological models but, since ecology itself has no overarching metaphysic (is, in fact, in a state of paradigm flux), I see no alternative at present to this kind of eclecticism. General ecological principles can lead to novel insights in the study of long-term human adaptation, even in the absence of a metaphysical paradigm and despite a host of "equivalency problems" (e.g., whether or not human groups can be considered equivalent to biological species). It seems a shame not to take advantage of them.

Bibliography

Ackerly, N. W., and F. E. Bayham
  1984   Comment on "Specialization and the Middle/Upper Paleolithic Transition" (Orquera). *Current Anthropology* 25:85–86.
Adovasio, J., G. Fry, J. Gunn, and R. Maslowski
  1975   Prehistoric and historic settlement patterns in western Cyprus (with a discussion of Cypriot Neolithic stone tool technology). *World Archaeology* 6:339–369.
  1978   Prehistoric and historic settlement patterns in western Cyprus: an overview. *Reports of the Department of Antiquities, Cyprus* 1978:39–57.
Aharoni, Y.
  1973   Remarks on the "Israeli" method of excavation. *Eretz Israel* 11:48–53.
Albrethsen, S., and E. Peterson
  1976   Excavation of a Mesolithic cemetery at Vedbaek, Denmark. *Acta Archaeologica* 47:1–28.
Albright, W. F.
  1943   *The Archaeology of Palestine.* Baltimore: Pelican Books.
Altuna, J.
Alland, A., and B. McCay
  1973   The concept of adaptation in biological and cultural evolution. In *Handbook of Social and Cultural Anthropology* (J. Honigmann, ed.), pp. 143–78. Chicago: Rand McNally.
  1972   Fauna de mamíferos de los yacimientos prehistóricos de Guipúzoca. *Munibe* 24:1–464.
Ames, K. M.
  1985   Hierarchies, stress, and logistical strategies among hunter-gatherers in northwestern North America. In *Prehistoric Hunter-Gatherers: The Emergence of Cultural Complexity* (T. D. Price and J. A. Brown, eds.), pp. 155–180. New York: Academic Press.
Ammerman, A. J.
  1971   A computer analysis of epipaleolithic assemblages in Italy. In *Mathematics in the Archaeological and Historical Sciences* (F. R. Hodson, D. G. Kendall and P. Tautu, eds.), pp. 133–136. Edinburgh: University of Edinburgh Press.

Ammerman, A. J., and F. R. Hodson
  1972   Constellation analysis: a study of late paleolithic assemblages in Italy. *Rivista Scienze Preistoriche* 27:323–344.
Amundson, R.
  1989   The trials and tribulations of selectionist explanations. In *Issues in Evolutionary Epistemology* (K. Hahlweg and C. Hooker, eds.), pp. 413–432. Albany: SUNY Press.
Anderson, A.
  1988   The early human colonization of New Zealand. Paper presented at the International Conference—Early Man in Island Environments, September 25–October 2, 1988, Oliena, Sardinia.
  1989   Mechanics of overkill in the extinction of New Zealand moas. *Journal of Archaeological Science* 16:137–151.
Anderson-Gerfaud, P.
  1983   A consideration of the uses of certain backed and "lustered" stone tools from late Mesolithic and Natufian levels of Abu Hureyra and Mureybet (Syria). In *Traces de l'utilisation sur les outils Néolithiques du Prôche Orient* (M.-C. Cauvin, ed.), pp. 77–105. Lyon: GIS-Maison de l'Orient.
  1990   Aspects of behavior in the Middle Paleolithic: functional analysis of stone tools from southwest France. In *The Human Revolution: Behavioral and Biological Perspectives on the Origins of Modern Humans* (P. Mellars and C. Stringer, eds.). Edinburgh: University of Edinburgh Press.
Arambourou, R.
  1978   *Le Gisement préhistorique de Duruthy.* Paris: Société Préhistorique Française, Memoire No. 13.
Arca, M., F. Martini, G. Pitzalis, C. Tuveri, and A. Ulzega
  1982   Paleolitica dell'Anglona (Sardegna Settentrionale). Richerche 1979–1980. *Quadrani* 12:58.
Arensberg, B., and O. Bar-Yosef
  1973   Human remains from Ein Gev I, Jordan Valley, Israel. *Paléorient* 1:201–206.
Ashton, N. M.
  1983   Spatial patterning in the Middle-Upper Paleolithic transition. *World Archaeology* 15:224–235.
Audley-Charles, M., and D. Hooijer
  1973   Relation of Pleistocene migrations of pygmy stegodonts to island arc tectonics in eastern Indonesia. *Nature* 241:197–198.
Audouze, F.
  1987   Des modèles des faits: les modèles de A. Leroi-Gourhan et de L. Binford confrontés aux résultats récents. *Bulletin de la Société Préhistorique Française* 84:343–352.
Audouze, F., and A. Leroi-Gourhan
  1981   France: a continental insularity. *World Archaeology* 13:170–189.
Aurenche, O., J. Cauvin, M-C. Cauvin, L. Copeland, F. Hours, and P. Sanlaville
  1981   Chronologie et organisation de l'espace dans le Prôche Orient de 12000 à 5600 avant J.C. In *Préhistoire du Levant* (J. Cauvin and P. Sanlaville, eds.), pp. 571–601. Paris: Editions du CNRS.
Avellino, E., A. Bietti, L. Giacopini, A. Lo Pinto, and M. Vicari
  1989   Riparo Salvini: a new Dryas II site in southern Latium. Thoughts on

the late Epigravettian in middle and southern Tyrrhenian Italy. In *The Mesolithic in Europe* (C. Bonsall, ed.), pp. 516–532. Edinburgh: University of Edinburgh Press.

Ayer, A. J.
1936   *Language, Truth and Logic.* Cambridge: Cambridge University Press.

Bagolini, B., F. Barbacovi, L. Castelletti, and M. Lanzinger
1975   Colbricon (scavi 1973–1974). *Preistoria Alpina* 11:201–235.

Bagolini, B., A. Broglio, and R. Lunz
1983   Le mésolithique des Dolomites. *Preistoria Alpina* 19:15–36.

Bahn, P. G.
1982   Comment on White's "Rethinking the Middle/Upper Paleolithic Transition." *Current Anthropology* 23:177.
1983   Late Pleistocene economies of the French Pyrenees. In *Hunter-Gatherer Economy in Prehistory* (G. Bailey, ed.), pp. 168–186. Cambridge: Cambridge University Press.
1984   *Pyrenean Prehistory.* Warminster: Aris and Phillips.

Bahn, P. G., and J. Vertut
1988   *Images of the Ice Age.* New York: Facts on File.

Bailey, G.
1983a   Hunter-gatherer behaviour in prehistory: problems and perspectives. In *Hunter-Gatherer Economy in Prehistory* (G. Bailey, ed.), pp. 1–6. Cambridge: Cambridge University Press.
1983b   Economic change in late Pleistocene Cantabria. *Hunter-Gatherer Economy in Prehistory* (G. Bailey, ed.), pp. 149–165. Cambridge: Cambridge University Press.
1983c   Editorial. In *Hunter-Gatherer Economy in Prehistory* (G. Bailey, ed.), pp. 7–10. Cambridge: Cambridge University Press.

Bailey, G., and P. Callow (eds.)
1986   *Stone Age Prehistory: Studies in Memory of Charles McBurney.* Cambridge: Cambridge University Press.

Bailey, G., P. Carter, C. Gamble, and H. Higgs
1983   Epirus revisited: seasonality and inter-site variation in the Upper Paleolithic of northwest Greece. In *Hunter-Gatherer Economy in Prehistory* (G. Bailey, ed.), pp. 64–78. Cambridge: Cambridge University Press.

Bailey, G., and I. Davidson
1983   Site exploitation territories and topography: two case studies from paleolithic Spain. *Journal of Archaeological Science* 10:87–115.

Bailey, R., G. Head, M. Jenike, B. Owen, R. Rechtman, and E. Zechenter
1989   Hunting and gathering in tropical rain forest: is it possible? *American Anthropologist* 91:59–82.

Balout, L.
1955   *Préhistoire de l'Afrique du Nord. Essai de chronologie.* Paris: Arts et Métiers Graphiques.

Bamforth, D.
1986   Technological efficiency and stone tool curation. *American Antiquity* 51:38–50.

Barker, G.
1981   *Landscape and Society in Prehistoric Central Italy.* London: Academic Press.

Bardon, L., and J. and A. Bouyssonie
  1907   Station préhistorique de la Coumba-del-Bouïtou (Corrèze). *Revue de l'Ecole d'Anthropologie de Paris* 16:401–411.
Bartolomei, G., A. Broglio, L. Cattani, M. Cremaschi, A. Guerreschi, and C. Peretto
  1984   I giacimenti paleolitici e mesolitici. In *Il Veneto nell'antichità. Preistoria e Protostoria* (A. Aspes, ed.), pp. 169–199. Verona: Banca Populare.
Bartolomei, G., A. Broglio, and A. Palma di Cesnola
  1979   Chronostratigraphie et écologie de l'Epigravettien en Italie. In *La Fin des Temps Glaciaires en Europe* (D. de Sonneville-Bordes, ed.), pp. 297–324. Paris: Editions du CNRS.
Bartolomei, G., P. Gambassini, and A. Palma di Cesnola
  1976   Visita ai giacimenti del Poggio e della Cala a Marina di Camerota (Salerno). *Atti della XVII Riun. Scient. dell'Ist. Ital. di Preist. e Protostoria:* 107–140.
Bartolomei, G., and C. Tozzi
  1978   Nuovi dati stratigrafici sui depositi del Pleistocene medio a Ochotona del Riparo di Visogliano nel Carso di Trieste. *Accad. Naz. dei Lincei* 64:490–497.
Barton, C. M.
  1987   *An Analysis of Lithic Variability from the Middle Paleolithic of the Iberian Peninsula.* Ph.D. dissertation, University of Arizona. Ann Arbor: University Microfilms.
  1988   *Lithic Variability and Middle Paleolithic Behavior: New Evidence from the Iberian Peninsula.* Oxford: BAR International Series S-408.
  1989   Beyond style and function: a view from the Middle Paleolithic. *American Anthropologist* 92:57–72.
  1990   Stone tools and paleolithic settlement in the Iberian peninsula. *Proceedings of the Prehistoric Society* 56 (in press).
Baruch, U.
  1986   The late Holocene vegetational history of Lake Kinneret (Sea of Galilee), Israel. *Paléorient* 12:37–48.
Bar-Yosef, O.
  1970   *The Epipaleolithic Cultures of Palestine.* Ph.D. dissertation. Jerusalem: Hebrew University.
  1975a   The epipaleolithic in Palestine and Sinai. In *Problems in Prehistory: North Africa and the Levant* (F. Wendorf and A. E. Marks, eds.), pp. 363–378. Dallas, TX: Southern Methodist University Press.
  1975b   Les gisements Kébarien Géometrique A d'Haon. Vallée du Jourdain, Israël. *Bulletin de la Société Préhistorique Française* 72:10–14.
  1980   Prehistory of the Levant. *Annual Review of Anthropology* 9:101–133.
  1981a   The epipaleolithic complexes in the southern Levant. In *Préhistoire du Levant* (J. Cauvin and P. Sanlaville, eds.), pp. 389–408. Paris: Editions du CNRS.
  1981b   The "Pre-Pottery Neolithic" period in the southern Levant. In *Préhistoire du Levant* (J. Cauvin and P. Sanlaville, eds.), pp. 551–570. Paris: Editions du CNRS.
  1983   The Natufian in the southern Levant. In *The Hilly Flanks and Beyond* (T. C. Young, Jr., P. Smith, and P. Mortenson, eds.). Chicago: Oriental Institute Studies in Ancient Oriental Civilization No. 36.

1984   Seasonality among hunter-gatherers in southern Sinai. In *Animals and Archaeology, Vol. 2* (J. Clutton-Brock and C. Grigson, eds.), pp. 145–160. Oxford: BAR International Series S-183.

1986   The walls of Jericho. *Current Anthropology* 27:157–162.

1987a   Direct and indirect evidence for hafting in the Epi-Paleolithic and Neolithic of the southern Levant. In *Le Main et l'outil; manches et émmanchements préhistoriques* (D. Stordeur, ed.), pp. 155–164. Lyon: Maison de l'Orient.

1987b   Late Pleistocene adaptations in the Levant. In *The Pleistocene Old World: Regional Perspectives* (O. Soffer, ed.), pp. 219–236. New York: Plenum Press.

1987c   Pleistocene connexions between Africa and southwest Asia: an archaeological perspective. *African Archaeological Review* 5:29–38.

1989   The PPNA in the Levant: an overview. *Paléorient* 15:57–63.

n.d.a. Middle Paleolithic chronology and the transition to the Upper Paleolithic in southwest Asia. In *Continuity or Complete Replacement: Controversies in Homo sapiens Evolution* (F. H. Smith and G. Brauer, eds.). Rotterdam: Balkema Press (in press).

n.d.b   Upper Pleistocene human adaptations in southwest Asia. In *Corridors, Culs-de-Sac and Coalescence: The Biocultural Foundations of Modern People* (E. Trinkaus, ed.). Cambridge: Cambridge University Press. (In press)

Bar-Yosef, O., et al.

1986   New data on the origin of modern man in the Levant. *Current Anthropology* 27:63–65.

Bar-Yosef, O., and D. Alon

1988   The excavations in Nahal Heimar cave. *Atiqot* 18:1–30.

Bar-Yosef, O., and A. Belfer-Cohen

1989a   The Levantine PPNB interaction sphere. In *Peoples and Cultures in Change, Vol. I* (I. Hershkovitz, ed.), pp. 59–72. Oxford: BAR International Series S-508.

1989b   The origins of sedentism and farming communities in the Levant. *Journal of World Prehistory* 3:447–498.

n.d.   From sedentary hunter-gatherers to territorial farmers. In *Between Bands and States* (S. Gregg, ed.). Carbondale, IL: Southern Illinois University Press. (in press)

Bar-Yosef, O., P. Goldberg, and T. Leveson

1974   Late Quaternary stratigraphy and prehistory in Wadi Fazael, Jordan Valley. A preliminary report. *Paléorient* 2:415–428.

Bar-Yosef, O., and A. Gopher, E. Tchernov, and M. E. Kislev

in prep Netiv Hagdud: an early Neolithic site in the Jordan Valley. Manuscript in possession of authors.

Bar-Yosef, O., and N. Goren

1973   Natufian remains in Hayonim Cave. *Paléorient* 1:49–68.

Bar-Yosef, O., and A. Mazar

1982   Israeli archaeology. *World Archaeology* 13:310–325.

Bar-Yosef, O., and L. Meignen

1989   Levantine Mousterian Variability in the Light of New Dates from Qafzeh and Kebara Cave. Paper presented at the 54th Annual Meeting of the Society for American Archaeology. Atlanta.

Bar-Yosef, O., and J. L. Phillips, eds.
  1977   *Prehistoric Investigations in Gebel Maghara, Northern Sinai.* Qedem 7:
         Monographs of the Institute of Archaeology. Jerusalem: Hebrew
         University.
Bar-Yosef, O., and E. Tchernov
  1966   Archaeological finds and the fossil faunas of the Natufian and micro-
         lithic industries at Hayonim Cave, western Galilee (Israel) *Israel
         Journal of Zoology* 15:104–140.
Bar-Yosef, O., and F. R. Valla
  1979   L'évolution du Natoufien: nouvelles perspectives. *Paléorient* 5:145–
         152.
Bar-Yosef, O., and J. C. Vogel
  1987   Relative and absolute chronology of the Epi-Paleolithic in the south-
         ern Levant. In *Chronologies in the Near East* (O. Aurenche, J. Evin, and
         F. Hours, eds.), pp. 219–245. Oxford: BAR International Series
         S-379.
Bate, D.
  1903a Preliminary note on the discovery of a pygmy elephant in the Pleisto-
         cene of Cyprus. *Proceedings of the Royal Society of London* 73:498–500.
  1903b The mammals of Cyprus. *Proceedings of the Zoological Society of London*
         2:341–348.
  1903c On an extinct species of genet (*Genetta plesictoides* sp. n.) from the
         Pleistocene of Cyprus. *Proceedings of the Zoological Society of London*
         2:121–124.
  1904a On the ossiferous cave-deposits of Cyprus. *Geological Magazine*
         5:324–325.
  1904b Further note on the remains of *Elephas cypriotes* Bate from a cave
         deposit in Cyprus. *Geological Magazine* 5:241–245.
  1904c Further note on the remains of *Elephas cypriotes* Bate from a cave
         deposit in Cyprus. *Proceedings of the Royal Society* 74:120–122.
  1905   Further note on the remains of *Elephas cypriotes,* from a cave deposit
         in Cyprus. *Philosophical Transactions of the Royal Society* 197:347–360.
  1906   The pygmy hippopotamus of Cyprus. *Geological Magazine* 5:241–
         245.
Baumler, M. F.
  1987   *Core Reduction Sequences: An Analysis of Blank Production in the Middle
         Paleolithic of Northern Bosnia (Yugoslavia).* Ph.D. dissertation, Univer-
         sity of Arizona. Ann Arbor: University Microfilms.
Bear, L., and S. Morel
  1960   The geology and mineral resources of the Agros-Akrotiri Area and
         the Aspiou-Akrotiri Area. *Geological Survey Department Cyprus,* Mem-
         oir No. 7.
Behrensmeyer, A. K., and S. M. Kidwell
  1985   Taphonomy's contribution to paleobiology. *Paleobiology* 11:105–119.
Belfer-Cohen, A.
  1988   *The Natufian Settlement at Hayonim Cave: A Hunter-Gatherer Band on the
         Threshold of Agriculture,* Ph.D. dissertation. Jerusalem: Hebrew Uni-
         versity.
  1989   The Natufian issue—a suggestion. In *Investigations in South Levantine
         Prehistory* (B. Vandermeersch and O. Bar-Yosef, eds.), pp. 297–308.
         Oxford: BAR International Series No. 497.

Bell, J.
 1987   Rationality versus relativism: a review of *Reading the Past* by Ian Hodder. *Archaeological Review from Cambridge* 6:75–86.
Belluomini, G., and J. Bada
 1985   Isoleucine epimerization ages of the dwarf elephants of Sicily. *Geology* 13:451–452.
Bender, B.
 1978   Gatherer-hunter to farmer: a social perspective. *World Archaeology* 10:204–222.
 1981   Gatherer-hunter intensification. In *Economic Archeology* (J. A. Sheridan and G. N. Bailey, eds.), pp. 149–157. Oxford: BAR International Series S-96.
Bentley, G. R.
 1985   Hunter-gatherer energetics and fertility: a reassessment of the !Kung San. *Human Ecology* 13:79–104.
Bergman, C. A.
 1987   *Ksar Akil, Lebanon. A Technological and Typological Analysis of the Later Paleolithic Levels of Ksar Akil: Volume II: Levels XIII–VI.* Oxford: BAR International Series S-329.
Bergman, C., and N. Goring-Morris
 1987   Summary of the London Conference on K'sar Akil. *Paléorient* 13:125–128.
Berry, M. S.
 1982   *Time, Space, and Transition in Anasazi Prehistory.* Salt Lake City: University of Utah Press.
Bettinger, R. L.
 1980   Explanatory/predictive models of hunter-gatherer adaptation. In *Advances in Archaeological Method and Theory No. 3* (M. Schiffer, ed.), pp. 189–255. Orlando, FL: Academic Press.
Betts, A.
 1982   A Natufian site in the Black Desert, eastern Jordan. *Paléorient* 8:79–82.
 1985   Black Desert Survey, Jordan. Third preliminary report. *Levant* 17:29–52.
 1988   The Black Desert; prehistoric sites and subsistence strategies in eastern Jordan. In *The Prehistory of Jordan* (A. Garrard and H. G. Gebel, eds.), pp. 369–391. Oxford: BAR International Series S-396(ii).
Beyries, S.
 1987   *Variabilité de l'industrie lithique au Moustérien: approche fonctionelle sur quelques gisements français.* Oxford: BAR International Series S-328.
 1988   Functional variability of lithic sets in the Middle Paleolithic. In *Upper Pleistocene Prehistory of Western Eurasia* (H. Dibble and A. Montet-White, eds.), pp. 213–224. Philadelphia: University of Pennsylvania Museum.
Biberson, P., G. Choubert, M. Fauré-Mauret, and G. Lecointre
 1960   *Contribution à l'étude de la "pebble culture" du Maroc Atlantique.* Marseille: Bulletin Archéologique Marocaine No. 3.
Biddittu, I., P. Cassoli, and L. Malpieri
 1967   Stazione Musteriana in Valle Radice nel commune di Sora (Frosinone). *Quaternaria* 9:321–348.

Biddittu, I., P. F. Cassoli, F. Radicati di Brozolo, A. G. Segre, E. Segre Naldini, and I. Villa
  1979 Anagni, a K-Ar dated Lower and Middle Pleistocene site, central Italy, preliminary report. *Quaternaria* 21:57–71.

Bietti, A.
  1976/7 Analysis and illustration of the Epigravettian industry collected during the 1955 excavations at Palidoro (Rome, Italy). *Quaternaria* 19:193–387.
  1978 Alcune considerazioni sulla tipologia e sulle liste tipologiche per il Paleolitico Superiore in Italia. *Quaternaria* 20:1–27.
  1979 Le gisement Paléolithique supérieur de Taurisano (Lecce, Italie) et sa position chronologique et culturelle dans l'Epigravettien Italien. In *La Fin des Temps Glaciaires en Europe* (D. de Sonneville-Bordes, ed.), pp. 333–344. Paris: Editions du CNRS.
  1980/1 Un tentativo di classificazione quantitativa del 'Pontiniano' laziale nel quadro delle industrie musteriane in Italia: problemi di derivazione di interpretazione culturale. *Rivista di Antropologia* 61:162–202.
  1982 The Mesolithic cultures in Italy: new activities in connection with Upper Paleolithic cultural traditions. *Veröffen.des Mus. für Ur-und Frühgeschichte Potsdam* 14/15:33–50.
  1989 Considerazioni sul significato e sull'utilizzazione delle liste tipologiche delle industrie Paleolitiche. *Atti della XXVII Riun. Scient. dell'Ist. Ital. di Preist. e Protostoria:* 147–163.

Bietti, A., M. Brucchietti, and D. Mantero
  1988b Ricognizione sistematica di superficie nella piana di Fondi (Latina). Primi risultati. *Quaderni del Centro di Studi per l'Arch. Etrusco-Italica* 16:389–396.

Bietti, A., and A. Burani
  1985 The late Upper Paleolithic in continental Italy: old classifications, new data and new perspectives. In *Papers in Italian Archaeology IV* (C. Malone and S. Stoddart, eds.), pp. 7–27. Oxford: BAR International Series S-244.

Bietti, A., S. Kuhn, S. Grimaldi, P. Rossetti, and J. Zanzi
  n.d. Technological, Functional and Experimental Perspectives on the Industry of the Lower Strata at Grotta Breuil. Proceedings of the symposium "The Fossil Man of Monte Circeo: Fifty Years of Studies of the Neandertals in Latium." (in prep)

Bietti, A., and A. M. Bietti-Sestieri
  1985 Problemi di teoria e di metodo in Archaeologia Preistorica. In *Studi di Paletnologia in Onore di Salvatore M. Puglisi* (M. Liverani, A. Palmieri and R. Peroni, eds.), pp. 13–29. Rome: Universitá di Roma.

Bietti, A., and A. Burani, and L. Zanello
  1983b An application of ISPAHAN to the typological classification of some Italian Upper Paleolithic endscrapers. *Pattern Recognition Letters* 1181–1186.

Bietti, A., S. Kuhn, and M. C. Stiner
  1988 Subsistence and settlement patterns for the Italian Epigravettian: the case of Riparo Salvini (Latium). Paper presented at the Colloque International sur le Peuplement Magdalenien. Chancelade, France.

Bietti, A., G. Manzi, P. Passarello, A. Segre, and M. Stiner
  1988a The 1986 excavation campaign at Grotta Breuil (Monte Circeo,

Latina). *Quaderni del Centro di Studi per l'Archeologia Etrusco-Italica* 16:372–388.

Bietti, A., F. Martini, and C. Tozzi
   1983a L'Epigravettien évolué et final de la zone moyenne et basse tyrrhénienne. *Rivista Scienze Preistoriche* 38:319–349.

Bietti-Sestieri, A. M., and R. Sebastiani, eds.
   1986   Preistoria e Protostoria nel territoria di Roma. Modelli di insediamento e vie di communicazione. *Quaderni del Centro di Studi per l'Arch. Etrusco-Italica* 12:30–70.

Binford, L. R.
   1962   Archaeology as anthropology. *American Antiquity* 28:217–225.
   1964   A consideration of archaeological research design. *American Antiquity* 29:425–441.
   1965   Archaeological systematics and the study of culture process. *American Antiquity* 31:203–210.
   1968   Post-Pleistocene adaptations. In *New Perspectives in Archeology* (S. and L. Binford, eds.), pp. 313–341. Chicago: Aldine.
   1971   Mortuary practices: their study and their potential. In *Mortuary Practices, Memoirs of the Society for American Archaeology No. 25* (J. A. Brown, ed.), pp. 6–29. Washington, D.C.: Society for American Archaeology.
   1972   Models and paradigms in paleolithic archaeology. In *Models in Archaeology* (D. L. Clarke, ed.), pp. 109–166. London: Methuen.
   1973   Interassemblages variability—the Mousterian and the "functional" argument. In *The Explanation of Culture Change: Models in Prehistory* (C. Renfrew, ed.), pp. 227–254. London: Duckworth.
   1977a General Introduction. In *For Theory Building in Archaeology* (L. Binford, ed.), pp. 1–10. New York: Academic Press.
   1977b Forty-seven trips: a case study in the character of archaeological formation processes. In *Stone Tools as Cultural Markers* (R. Wright, ed.), pp. 24–36. Canberra: Australian Institute of Aboriginal Studies.
   1978   *Nunamiut Ethnoarchaeology.* New York: Academic Press.
   1979   Organization and formation processes: looking at curated technologies. *Journal of Anthropological Research* 35:255–273.
   1980   Willow smoke and dogs' tails: hunter-gatherer settlement systems and archaeological site formation. *American Antiquity* 45:4–20.
   1981a Behavioral archaeology and the "Pompeii Premise." *Journal of Anthropological Research* 37:195–208.
   1981b *Bones: Ancient Men and Modern Myths.* New York: Academic Press.
   1982a Comment on White's "Rethinking the Middle/Upper Paleolithic Transition." *Current Anthropology* 23:177–181.
   1982b The archaeology of place. *Journal of Anthropological Archaeology* 1:5–31.
   1983a *In Pursuit of the Past.* London: Thames and Hudson.
   1983b *Working at Archaeology.* New York: Academic Press.
   1984   *Faunal Remains from Klasies River Mouth.* New York: Academic Press.
   1985   Human ancestors: changing views of their behavior. *Journal of Anthropological Archaeology* 4:292–265.
   1987a Data, relativism and archaeological science. *Man* 22:391–404.
   1987b Searching for camps and missing the evidence? Another look at the

Lower Paleolithic. In *The Pleistocene Old World: Regional Perspectives* (O. Soffer, ed.), pp. 17–31. New York: Plenum Press.

1989a   Response to Turner. *Journal of Archaeological Science* 16:13–16.

1989b   Styles of style. *Journal of Anthropological Archaeology* 8:51–67.

1989c   *Debating Archaeology.* New York: Academic Press.

1989d   Isolating the transition to cultural adaptations: an organizational approach. In *The Emergence of Modern Humans: Biocultural Adaptations in the Later Pleistocene* (E. Trinkaus, ed.), pp. 18–41. Cambridge: Cambridge University Press.

Binford, L. R., and S. R. Binford

1966   A preliminary analysis of functional variability in the Mousterian of Levallois facies. *American Anthropologist* 68:238–295.

Binford, L., and J. Sabloff

1982   Paradigms, systematics and archaeology. *Journal of Anthropological Research* 38:137–153.

Binford, S. R.

1968   Early Upper Pleistocene adaptations in the Levant. *American Anthropologist* 70:707–717.

1970   Late Middle Paleolithic adaptations and their possible consequences. *Bioscience* 20:280–83.

1972   The significance of variability: a minority report. In *The Origin of Homo sapiens* (F. Bordes, ed.), pp. 207–210. Paris: UNESCO.

Binford, S. R., and L. R. Binford

1969   Stone tools and human behavior. *Scientific American* 220:70–84.

Bischoff, J., R. Juliá and A. Mora

1988   Uranium series dating of the Mousterian occupation at Abric Romani, Spain. *Nature* 332:68–70.

Bischoff, J., N. Soler, J. Maroto, and R. Juliá

1989   Abrupt Mousterian/Aurignacian boundary at 40 ka bp: accelerator radiocarbon dates from l'Arbreda Cave. *Journal of Archaeological Science* 10:553–576.

Bisi, F., A. Broglio, A. Guerreschi, and A. M. Radmilli

1983   L'Epigravettien évolué et final dans la zone haute et moyenne adriatique. *Rivista Scienze Preistoriche* 38:229–265.

Blalock, H.

1972   *Social Statistics* (2nd Edition). New York: McGraw-Hill.

Blanc, A. C.

1937   Nuovi giacimenti paleolitici del Lazio e della Toscana. *Studi Etruschi* 11:273–304.

Blanc, A. C., and A. G. Segre

1953   *Excursion au Monti Circé.* Rome: INQUA IVᵉ Congrès International.

Bleed, P.

1986   The optimal design of hunting weapons: maintainability or reliability? *American Antiquity* 51:737–747.

Blumenschine, R. J.

1986a   *Early Hominid Scavenging Opportunities: Implications of Carcass Availability in the Serengeti and Ngorongoro Ecosystems.* Oxford: BAR International Series S-283.

1986b   Carcass consumption sequences and the archaeological distinction of scavenging and hunting. *Journal of Human Evolution* 15:639–660.

1987   Characteristics of an early hominid scavenging niche. *Current Anthropology* 28:383–407.

Boëda, E.
1988   Le concept laminaire: rupture et filiation avec le concept Lévallois. In *L'Homme de Néandertal, Vol. 4: La Technique* (M. Otte, ed.), pp. 41–59. Liège: ERAUL No. 31.

Boekschoten, G., and P. Sondaar
1972   On the fossil mammalia of Cyprus. *Proceedings of the Koninklijke Nederlandse Akademie van Wetenschappen* Series B, 75:306–338.

Bofinger, E., and I. Davidson
1977   Radiocarbon age and depth: a statistical treatment of two sequences of dates from Spain. *Journal of Archaeological Science* 4:231–243.

Bonifay, E.
1983   Circonscription de la Corse. *Gallia Préhistoire* 26:511–524.

Bonimovitz, S.
1986   Is the "Philistine Culture" really Philistine: problems in the methodology of the study of the Philistine Culture. *Bulletin of the Israel Association of Archaeologists* 1:11–21 (in Hebrew).

Bordes, F.
1950   Principes d'une méthode d'étude des techniques de débitage et de la typologie du paléolithique ancien et moyen. *L'Anthropologie* 54:19–34.

1953   Essai de classification des industries "moustériennes." *Bulletin de la Société Préhistorique Française* 50:457–466.

1958   Le passage du Paléolithique moyen au Paléolithique supérieur. In *Hundert Jahre Neanderthaler* (G. H. R. von Koenigswald, ed.), pp. 175–181. Utrecht: Kremink und Zoon.

1960   Le Pre-Aurignacien de Yabroud (Syrie), et son incidence sur la chronologie du Quaternaire en Moyen Orient. *Bulletin of the Research Council of Israel, Section G* 9G(2–3):91–103.

1961a   *Typologie du Paléolithique ancien et moyen.* Institut de la Préhistoire de l'Université de Bordeaux, Memoire No. 1.

1961b   Mousterian cultures in France. *Science* 134:803–810.

1967   Considérations sur les typologies et les techniques dans le paléolithique. *Quärtar* 18:25–55.

1968a   *The Old Stone Age.* New York: McGraw-Hill.

1968b   La question périgordienne. In *La Préhistoire: problèmes et tendances* (F. Bordes and D. de Sonneville-Bordes, eds.), pp. 59–70. Paris: Éditions du CNRS.

1969   Reflections on typology and techniques in the paleolithic. *Arctic Anthropology* 6:1–29.

1972   Du Paléolithique moyen au Paléolithique supérieur, continuité ou discontinuité? In *The Origin of Homo sapiens* (F. Bordes, ed.), pp. 211–218. Paris: UNESCO.

1972   *A Tale of Two Caves.* New York: Harper and Row.

1973   On the chronology and contemporaneity of different paleolithic cultures in France. In *The Explanation of Culture Change: Models in Prehistory* (C. Renfrew, ed.), pp. 217–226. London: Duckworth.

1975   Sur la notion de sol d'habitat en préhistoire. *Bulletin de la Société Préhistorique Française* 72:1–21.

1980   Le débitage Lévallois et ses variantes. *Bulletin de la Société Préhistorique Française* 77:45–49.

1981a   Vingt-cinq ans après: le complèxe Moustérien revisté. *Bulletin de la Société Préhistorique Française* 78:77–87.

1981b   Comment. *La Recherche* 12:644–45.

1984   *Leçons sur le Paléolithique. Tôme II: Le Paléolithique en Europe.* 3 volumes. Cahiers du Quaternaire, No. 7. Paris. Editions du CNRS.

Bordes, F., and D. Crabtree

1969   The Corbiac blade technique and other experiments. *Tebiwa* 12:1–21.

Bordes, F., and D. de Sonneville-Bordes

1970   The significance of variability in paleolithic assemblages. *World Archaeology* 2:61–73.

Bordes, F., J.-P. Rigaud, and Sonneville-Bordes, D. de

1972   Des buts, problèmes, et limites de l'archéologie paléolithique. *Quaternaria* 15:15–34.

Bosinski, G.

1988   Upper and Final Paleolithic settlement patterns in the Rhineland, West Germany. In *Upper Pleistocene Prehistory in Western Eurasia* (H. Dibble and A. Montet-White, eds.), pp. 375–386. Philadelphia: University of Pennsylvania Museum Monographs No. 54.

Bottema, S., and W. van Zeist

1981   Palynological evidence for the climatic history of the Near East 50,000–6,000 years ago. In *Préhistoire du Levant* (J. Cauvin and P. Sanlaville, eds.), pp. 112–132. Paris: Editions du CNRS.

Boule, M.

1910   Untitled review of *Le Préhistorique: origine et antiquité de l'homme* (third edition, 1909), by G. and A. de Mortillet. *L'Anthropologie* 12:427–431.

1911   L'homme fossile de La Chapelle-aux-Saints. *Annales de Paléontologie*
–13   6:111–172, 7:21–192, 8:1–70.

Bourlon, M., and J. and A. Bouyssonie

1912   Grattoirs carénés, rabots et grattoirs nucléiformes. Essai de classification des grattoirs. *Revue Anthropologique* 22:473–486.

Brace, C. L.

1964   The fate of the "classic" neanderthals: a consideration of hominid catastrophism. *Current Anthropology* 5:3–43.

1966   Comment. *Current Anthropology* 7:37–38.

1967   *The Stages of Human Evolution: Human and Cultural Origins.* Englewood Cliffs, NJ: Prentice-Hall.

1981   Tales of the phylogenetic woods: the evolution and significance of phylogenetic trees. *American Journal of Physical Anthropology* 54:411–429.

1988a   Punctuationism, cladistics and the legacy of Medieval Neoplatonism. *Human Evolution* 3:121–138.

1988b   *The Stages of Human Evolution: Human and Cultural Origins* (3rd ed.). Englewood Cliffs, NJ: Prentice-Hall.

1989   Medieval thinking and the paradigms of paleoanthropology. *American Anthropologist* 91:442–446.

Brace, C., F. Bookstein, S. Smith, K. Hunt, and P. Holck

n.d.   Neanderthal to modern cranial continuity: a rear end view. Manuscript in possession of authors. Museum of Anthropology, University of Michigan.

Bradley, B. A.
1975   Lithic reduction sequences: a glossary and discussion. In *Lithic Technology: Making and Using Stone Tools* (E. Swanson, ed.), pp. 5–14. The Hague: Mouton.

Braidwood, L. S., R. J. Braidwood, B. Howe, C. A. Reed, and P. J. Watson (eds.)
1983   *Prehistoric Archaeology Along the Zagros Flanks.* Chicago: University of Chicago, Oriental Institute Publications, Vol. 105.

Braidwood, R. J.
1958   Near Eastern prehistory. *Science* 127:1419–1430.
1975   *Prehistoric Men* (8th Ed.) Chicago: Scott Foresman.

Braidwood, R. J. and B. Howe
1960   *Prehistoric Investigations in Iraqi Kurdistan.* Chicago: Oriental Institute Studies in Ancient Oriental Civilizations No. 31.

Brain, C. K.
1981   *The Hunters or the Hunted?* Chicago: University of Chicago Press.

Braun, D., and S. Plog
1982   Evolution of "tribal" social networks: theory and prehistoric North American evidence. *American Antiquity* 47:504–525.

Breuil, H.
1906   Essai stratigraphique des dépôts de l'Âge du Renne. *Actes du Congrès Préhistorique de France,* Première session (1905):74–83.
1907a   Les gisements Présolutréens du type d'Aurignac. Coup d'oeil sur le plus ancien Âge du Renne. *Comptes Rendus de la XIIIᵉ Congrès Internationale d'Anthropologie et d'Archéologie Préhistorique,* Monaco (1906), tôme 1:323–346.
1907b   La question Aurignacienne. Étude critique de stratigraphie comparée. *Revue Préhistorique* 2:171–219.
1909a   La transition du Mousterien vers l'Aurignacien à l'abri Audi (Dordogne) et au Moustier. *Revue de l'Ecole d'Anthropologie* 19:320–340.
1909b   L'Aurignacien Présolutréen. Epilogue d'une controverse. *La Revue Préhistorique* 4:229–248, 265–286.
1913   Les subdivisions du Paléolithique supérieur et leur signification. *Congrès International d'Anthropologie et d'Archéologie Préhistorique* (Geneva, 1912):165–238.
1935   Untitled review of Peyrony (1933). *L'Anthropologie* 45:114–116.
1954   Le Magdalénien. *Bulletin de la Société Préhistorique Française* 51:59–64.

Breuil, H., and H. Obermaier
1914   Travaux de l'année 1913 de l'Institut de Paléontologie Humaine. II Travaux en Espagne. *L'Anthropologie* 25:313–328.

Brézillon, M. N.
1968   *La Dénomination des objêts de Pierre Taillée.* Paris: Editions du CNRS.

Bricker, H. M.
1976   Upper Paleolithic archeology. *Annual Review of Anthropology* 5:133–148.

Broglio, A.
1975   Le passage du Paléolithique supérieur au Néolithique dans la région Vénétie-Trentin-Frioul. *L'Epipaléolithique Méditerranéen,* pp. 5–21. Paris: Editions du CNRS.

1980   Culture e ambienti della fine del Paleolitico e del Mesolitico nell'Italia nord-orientale. *Preistoria Alpina* 16:7–29.

1984   Il Paleolitico Superiore (Aurignaziano, Gravettiano, Epigravettiano Antico). In *Il Veneto nell'Antichità. Preistoria e Prostostoria* (A. Aspes, ed.), pp. 233–243. Verona: Banca Popolare.

Brose, D. S., and M. H. Wolpoff
1971   Early Upper Paleolithic man and late Middle Paleolithic tools. *American Anthropologist* 73:1156–1194.

Brown, J. A.
1981   The search for rank in prehistoric burials. In *The Archaeology of Death* (R. Chapman, I. Kinnes, and K. Randsborg, eds.), pp. 25–37. Cambridge: Cambridge University Press.

1982   On the structure of artifact typologies. In *Essays on Archaeological Typology* (R. Whallon and J. Brown, eds.), pp. 176–190. Evanston, IL: Center for American Archaeology Press.

1987   The case for the regional perspective: a New World view. In *The Pleistocene Old World: Regional Perspectives* (O. Soffer, ed.), pp. 365–376. New York: Plenum.

Brush, S.
1989   Prediction and theory evaluation: the case of light bending. *Science* 246:1124–1129.

Bunn, H. T.
1981   Archaeological evidence for meat-eating by Plio-Pleistocene hominids from Koobi Fora and Olduvai Gorge. *Nature* 291:574–577.

Bunn, H. T., and R. J. Blumenschine
1987   On "theoretical framework and tests" of early hominid meat and marrow acquisition: a reply to Shipman. *American Anthropologist* 89:444–448.

Bunn, H. T., and E. M. Kroll
1986   Systematic butchery of Plio-Pleistocene hominids at Olduvai Gorge. *Current Anthropology* 27:431–452.

Burian, F., and E. Friedman
1973   Prehistoric hunters in the Halutza Dunes. *Mitekufat Haeven* 11:27–34. (Hebrew)

1975   Prehistoric sites in the Nahal Sekher area. *Mitekufat Haeven* 13:69–74. (Hebrew)

Burleigh, R., and J. Clutton-Brock
1980   The survival of *Myotragus balearicus* Bate, 1909, into the Neolithic on Mallorca. *Journal of Archaeological Science* 7:385–388.

Burney, D., R. MacPhee, J. Rafamantanantsoa, T. Rakotondrazafy, and G. King
1988   The roles of natural factors and human activities in the environmental changes and faunal extinction of late Holocene Madagascar. Paper presented at the International Conference: Early Man in Island Environments, September 25–October 2, 1988, Oliena, Sardinia.

Burton, J.
1980   Making sense of waste flakes: new methods for investigating the technology and economics behind chipped stone assemblages. *Journal of Archaeological Science* 7:131–148.

Busk, G.
1877   On the ancient or Quaternary faunas of Gibraltar. *Transactions of the Zoological Society of London* 10.

Butzer, K. W.
1971 *Environment and Archaeology.* 2nd edition. Chicago: Aldine.
1975 Patterns of environmental change in the Near East during Late Pleistocene and Early Holocene times. In *Problems in Prehistory: North Africa and the Levant* (F. Wendorf and A. E. Marks, eds.), pp. 389–410. Dallas, TX: Southern Methodist University Press.
1976 *Early Hydraulic Civilization in Egypt.* Chicago: University of Chicago Press.
1981 Cave sediments: Upper Pleistocene stratigraphy and Mousterian facies in Cantabrian Spain. *Journal of Archaeological Science* 8:133–183.
1982 *Archaeology as Human Ecology.* Cambridge: Cambridge University Press.
1986 Paleolithic adaptations and settlement in Cantabrian Spain. *In Advances in World Archaeology No. 5* (F. Wendorf and A. E. Close, eds.), pp. 201–252. Orlando, FL: Academic Press.
Butzer, K. W., and C. Hansen
1968 *Desert and River in Nubia: Geomorphology and Prehistoric Environments at the Aswan Reservoir.* Madison: University of Wisconsin Press.
Buzy, D.
1928 Une industrie mésolithique de Palestine. *Revue Biblique* 37:558–578.
1929 Une station magdalenienne dans le Negev (Ain el Qudeirat). *Revue Biblique* 38:1–18.
Byrd, B.
1987 *Beidha and the Natufian: Variability in Levantine Settlement and Subsistence.* Ph.D. dissertation. Department of Anthropology, University of Arizona. Ann Arbor: University Microfilms.
1988 Late Pleistocene settlement diversity in the Azraq Basin. *Paléorient* 14:257–264.
1989 The Natufian: settlement variability and economic adaptation in the Levant at the end of the Pleistocene. *Journal of World Prehistory* 3:159–198.
Cabrera, V., and J. Bischoff
1989 Accelerator 14C ages for basal Aurignacian at El Castillo Cave. *Journal of Archaeological Science* 16:577–584.
Cahen, D.
1984 Interprétations nouvelles pour le site paléolithique final de Meer II, Belgique. In *Upper Paleolithic Settlement Patterns in Europe* (H. Berke, J. Hahn, and C-J. Kind, eds.), pp. 241–250. Oxford: BAR International S-196.
Cahen, D., L. H. Keeley, and F. Van Noten
1979 Stone tools, toolkits and human behavior in prehistory. *Current Anthropology* 20:661–683.
Caldwell, J. R.
1964 Interaction spheres in prehistory. In *Hopewellian Studies* (J. R. Caldwell and R. C. Hall, eds.), pp. 135–143. Springfield: Illinois State Museum Scientific Papers No. 12.
Callen, E. O.
1967 Analysis of the Tehuacán coprolites. In *The Prehistory of the Tehuacán Valley (Vol. 1): Environment and Subsistence* (D. S. Byers, ed.), pp. 261–289. Austin: University of Texas Press.

Calley, S.
  1984   Le débitage Natoufien de Mureybet: étude préliminaire. *Paléorient*
          10:35–48.
  1986   *Technologie du débitage à Mureybet, Syrie, 9e–8e millénaire.* Oxford:
          BAR International Series S-312.
Campana, D. V.
  1989   *Natufian and Proto Neolithic Bone Tools.* Oxford: BAR International
          Series S-494.
Cann, R., M. Stoneking, and A. Wilson
  1987   Mitochondrial DNA and human evolution. *Nature* 325:31–36.
Carr, C.
  1985a   Perspective and basic definitions. In *For Concordance in Archaeological
          Analysis* (C. Carr, ed.), pp. 1–17. Kansas City, MO: Westport Pub-
          lishers.
  1985b   Getting into data: philosophy and tactics for the analysis of complex
          data structures. In *For Concordance in Archaeological Analysis* (C. Carr,
          ed.), pp. 18–41. Kansas City, MO: Westport Publishers.
Carrington, R.
  1962   *Elephants.* Penguin Books: Harmondsworth.
Carvalho, E., L. Straus, B. Vierra, J. Zilhão, A. Araújo
  1989   More data for an archaeological map of the county of Torres Vedras.
          Arqueología 19:16–33.
Casiano de Prado, L.
  1864   *Descripción Física y Geológica de la Provincia de Madrid.* Madrid: Aca-
          demia Real.
Cassoli, P. F.
  1980   L'avifauna del Pleistocene superiore delle Arene Candide (Liguria).
          Memoire dell'Ist. Ital. di Paleontologia Umana 3:155–234.
Cassoli, P. F., and F. Guadagnoli
  1987   Le faune del Riparo Salvini: analisi preliminare. In *Riparo Salvini a
          Terracina. Una Stazione di Cacciatori-Raccoglitori del Paleolitico Superi-
          ore*, pp. 43–48. Rome: Quasar.
Cassoli, P. F., A. G. Segre, and E. Segre
  1979   Evolution morphologique et écologique de la côte de Castro (Pou-
          illes) dans le Pleistocène final. In *La Fin des Temps Glaciaires en Eu-
          rope* (D. de Sonneville-Bordes, ed.), pp. 325–332. Paris: Editions du
          CNRS.
Casti, J.
  1989   *Paradigms Lost.* New York: William Morrow.
Cauvin, J.
  1978   *Les premiers villages de Syrie-Palestine du IXème–au VIIème millénaire
          avant J. C.* Lyon: Maison de l'Orient Mediterranéen.
  1985   La question du "matriarcat préhistorique" et la rôle de la femme
          dans la préhistoire. In *La Femme dans le monde méditerranéen* (J. Cau-
          vin, ed.), pp. 7–18. Lyon: Travaux de la Maison de l'Orient No. 10.
Cauvin, J., and M-C. Cauvin
  1983   Origines de l'agriculture au Levant: facteurs biologiques et socio-
          culturels. In *The Hilly Flanks and Beyond* (T. C. Young Jr., P. Smith,
          and P. Mortenson, eds.). Chicago: Oriental Institute Studies in An-
          cient Oriental Civilization No. 36.

Cauvin, J., and P. Sanlaville, eds.
1981   *Préhistoire du Levant.* Paris: Editions du CNRS.
Cauvin, M-C.
1966   L'industrie natoufienne de Mallaha (Eynan). *L'Anthropologie* 70:485–494.
1981a   L'Epipaléolithique de Syrie d'après les premières recherches dans la cuvette d'el Kowm (1978–1979). In *Préhistoire du Levant* (J. Cauvin and P. Sanlaville, eds.), pp. 375–389. Paris: Editions du CNRS.
1981b   L'Epipaléolithique du Levant. In *Préhistoire du Levant* (J. Cauvin and P. Sanlaville, eds.), pp. 439–441. Paris: Editions du CNRS.
1987   Chronologies relatives et chronologie absolue dans l'epipaléolithique du Levant Nord. In *Chronologies du Prôche Orient* (O. Aurenche, J. Evin, and F. Hours, eds.). Oxford: BAR International Series S-379(i).
Cauvin, M-C. and D. Stordeur
1978   *Les outillages lithiques et osseux de Mureybet, Syrie (Fouilles Van Loon).* Cahiers de l'Euphrate No. 1. Paris: Editions du CNRS.
Cavallo, J. A., and R. J. Blumenschine
1988   Larders in the limbs: expanding the early hominid scavenging niche. Paper presented at the 53rd Annual Meeting of the Society for American Archaeology, Phoenix.
Cervantes Saávedra, M. de
[1970] *Don Quixote de La Mancha.* Harmondsworth: Penguin (orig. published 1605).
Chamberlin, T. C.
[1965] The method of multiple working hypotheses. *Science* 148:754–759 (originally published in *Science* 15:92–96, 1890).
Chang, K. C.
1989   Ancient China and its anthropological significance. In *Archaeological Thought in America* (C. C. Lamberg-Karlovsky, ed.), pp. 155–166. Cambridge: Cambridge University Press.
Chapman, R., and K. Randsborg
1981   Approaches to the archaeology of death. In *The Archaeology of Death* (R. Chapman, I. Kinnes, and K. Randsborg, eds.), pp. 1–24. Cambridge: Cambridge University Press.
Chase, P.
1986a   Relationships between Mousterian lithic and faunal assemblages at Combe Grenal. *Current Anthropology* 27:69–71.
1986b   *The Hunters of Combe Grenal: Approaches to Middle Paleolithic Subsistence in Europe.* Oxford: BAR International Series S-286.
1987   Specialisation de la chasse et transition vers le Paléolithique supérieur. *L'Anthropologie* 91:175–188.
1988   Scavenging and hunting in the Middle Paleolithic: the evidence from Europe. In *The Pleistocene Prehistory of Western Eurasia* (H. L. Dibble and A. Montet-White, eds.), pp. 225–232. Philadelphia: University of Pennsylvania Museum.
1989   How different was Middle Paleolithic subsistence? A zooarchaeological perspective on the Middle to Upper Paleolithic transition. In *The Human Revolution: Biological and Behavioral Perspectives on the Origins of Modern Humans* (P. Mellars and C. Stringer, eds.), pp. 321–337. Edinburgh: University of Edinburgh Press.

Chase, P., and H. Dibble
 1987 Middle Paleolithic symbolism: a review of current evidence and interpretations. *Journal of Anthropological Archaeology* 6:263–296.
Cherry, J.
 1979 Four problems in Cycladic prehistory. In *Papers in Cycladic Prehistory* (J. Davis and J. Cherry, eds.), pp. 22–47. Los Angeles: UCLA Institute of Archaeology, Monograph No. 14.
 1981 Pattern and process in the earliest colonization of the Mediterranean islands. *Proceedings of the Prehistoric Society* 47:41–68.
 1984 The initial colonization of the west Mediterranean islands in the light of island biology and paleogeography. In *The Deya Conference of Prehistory: Early Settlement in the Western Mediterranean Islands and their Peripheral Areas* (W. Waldren, R. Chapman, J. Lewthwaite, and R. Kennard, eds.), pp. 7–27. Oxford: BAR International Series S-229.
 1985 Islands out of the stream: isolation and interaction in early east Mediterranean insular prehistory. In *Prehistoric Production and Exchange in the Aegean and East Mediterranean* (B. Knapp and T. Stech, eds.), pp. 12–29. Los Angeles: UCLA Institute of Archaeology, Monograph No. 25.
Childe, V. G.
 1942 *What Happened in History.* Harmondsworth: Penguin Books.
 1951 *Social Evolution.* New York: Henry Schuman.
 1952 *New Light on the Most Ancient East.* London: Routledge and Kegan Paul.
Christenson, A.
 1980 Change in the human niche in response to population growth. In *Modeling Change in Prehistoric Subsistence Economies* (T. Earle and A. Christenson, eds.), pp. 31–72. New York: Academic Press.
Clark, A. J.
 1986 Evolutionary epistemology and the scientific method. *Philosophica* 37:151–162.
Clark, G. A.
 1967 *A Preliminary Distribution Study of Burials at the Grasshopper Site. East-Central Arizona.* Master's thesis. Department of Anthropology, University of Arizona.
 1969 A preliminary analysis of burial customs at the Grasshopper Site, east-central Arizona. *Kiva* 35:57–86.
 1971a *The Asturian of Cantabria: A Re-evaluation.* Ph.D. dissertation. Department of Anthropology, University of Chicago.
 1971b The Asturian of Cantabria: subsistence base and the evidence for post-Pleistocene climatic shifts. *American Anthropologist* 73:1244–1257.
 1972 El Asturiense de Cantabria: bases sustentadoras y evidencias de los cambios Post-Pleistocenos. *Trabajos de Prehistoria* 29:17–30.
 1975a *Liencres: una Estación al Aire Libre de Estilo Asturiense cerca de Santander.* Bilbao: Seminario de Arqueología de la Universidad de Deusto, Cuadernos de Arqueología de Deusto No. 2.
 1975b El hombre y su ambiente a comienzos del Holoceno en la región Cantábrica. *Boletín del Instituto de Estudios Asturianos* 85:363–387.
 1976a *El Asturiense Cantábrico.* Madrid: Consejo Superior de Investigaciones Científicas.

1976b   Review: *Mathematics and Computers in Archaeology* (Doran and Hodson). *Computers and the Humanities* 10:369–372.

1978a   Review of *Spatial Analysis in Archaeology* (Hodder and Orton). *American Antiquity* 43:132–135.

1978b   A perspective on archaeological research in Spain. *Old World Archaeology Newsletter* 2:12–17.

1979   Spatial association at Liencres, an early Holocene open site on the Santander coast, north-central Spain. In *Computer Graphics in Archaeology* (S. Upham, ed.), pp. 121–144. Tempe: Arizona State University Anthropological Research Papers No. 15.

1981   On preagricultural coastal adaptations. *Current Anthropology* 22:444–446.

1982   Quantifying archaeological research. In *Advances in Archaeological Method and Theory, Vol. 5* (M. Schiffer, ed.), pp. 217–273. New York: Academic Press.

1983a   *The Asturian of Cantabria: Early Holocene Hunter-Gatherers in Northern Spain.* Tucson: University of Arizona Press.

1983b   Una perspectiva funcionalista en la prehistoria de la región Cantábrica. In *Homenaje al Profesor Martín Almagro Basch, Vol. 1* (A. Balil et al., eds.), pp. 155–170. Madrid: Ministerio de Cultura.

1983c   Boreal phase settlement-subsistence models for Cantabrian Spain. In *Hunter-Gatherer Economy in Prehistory* (G. Bailey, ed.), pp. 96–110. Cambridge: Cambridge University Press.

1984a   The Negev model for paleoclimatic change in human adaptation in the Levant and its relevance for the paleolithic of Wadi el Hasa (west-central Jordan). *Annual of the Department of Antiquities of Jordan* 28:225–248.

1984b   Review of *Early European Agriculture: Its Foundation and Development* (Jarman, Bailey and Jarman). *American Anthropologist* 86:190–191.

1987a   Paradigms and paradoxes in contemporary archaeology. In *Quantitative Research in Archaeology: Progress and Prospects* (M. Aldenderfer, ed.), pp. 30–60. Beverly Hills: Sage Publications.

1987b   From the Mousterian to the Metal Ages: long-term change in the human diet of Cantabrian Spain. In *The Pleistocene Old World: Regional Perspectives* (O. Soffer, ed.), pp. 293–316. New York: Plenum.

1988   Some thoughts on the Black Skull: an archaeologist's assessment of WT-17000 (*A. boisei*) and systematics in human paleontology. *American Anthropologist* 90:357–371.

1989a   Paradigms and paradoxes in paleoanthropology: a response to C. Loring Brace. *American Anthropolgist* 91:446–450.

1989b   Alternative models of Pleistocene biocultural evolution: a response to Foley. *Antiquity* 63:153–161.

1989c   Romancing the stones: biases, style, and lithics at La Riera. In *Alternative Approaches to Lithic Analysis* (D. Henry and G. Odell, eds.), pp. 27–50. Washington, DC: Archeological Papers of the American Anthropological Association No. 1.

1989d   Site functional complementarity in the Mesolithic of northern Spain. In *The Mesolithic in Europe* (C. Bonsall, ed.), pp. 596–603. Edinburgh: John Donald Publishers.

Clark, G. A., ed.

1979   *The North Burgos Archaeological Survey: Bronze and Iron Age Archaeology on the Meseta del Norte (Province of Burgos, Spain).* Tempe: Arizona State University Anthropological Research Paper No. 19.

Clark, G., and V. Clark
  1975   La cueva de Balmori (Asturias, España): nuevas aportaciones. *Trabajos de Prehistoria* 32:35–77.

Clark, G., N. Coinman, M. Donaldson, S. Fish, A. Garrard, J. Lindly, and D. Olszewski
  1988   Excavations at Middle, Upper, and Epipaleolithic sites in the Wadi Hasa, west-central Jordan. In *The Prehistory of Jordan* (A. Garrard and H. Gebel, eds.), pp. 209–285. Oxford: BAR International Series S-396(i).

Clark, G., N. Coinman, and J. Lindly
  1986   Paleolithic site placement in the Wadi Hasa, west-central Jordan. *Annual of the Department of Antiquities of Jordan* 30:23–40.

Clark, G. A., N. Coinman, J. Lindly, and M. Donaldson
  1987a   A diachronic study of paleolithic and aceramic neolithic settlement patterns in the Wadi Hasa, west-central Jordan. In *Studies in the History and Archaeology of Jordan III* (A. Hadidi, ed.), pp. 215–223. London: Routledge and Kegan Paul.

Clark, G. A., and S. Lerner
  1980   Prehistoric resource utilization in early Holocene Cantabrian Spain. *Anthropology UCLA* 10:53–96.
  1983   Catchment analysis of Asturian sites. In *The Asturian of Cantabria: Early Holocene Hunter-Gatherers in Northern Spain*, pp. 120–139. Tucson: University of Arizona Press.

Clark, G. A., and J. Lindly
  1988   The biocultural transition and modern human origins in the Levant and western Asia. *Paléorient* 14:159–167.
  1989a   The case for continuity: observations on the biocultural transition in Europe and western Asia. In *The Human Revolution: Behavioral and Biological Perspectives on the Origins of Modern Humans* (P. Mellars and C. Stringer, eds.), pp. 626–676. Edinburgh: University of Edinburgh Press.
  1989b   Modern human origins in the Levant and western Asia. *American Anthropologist* 91:962–965.

Clark, G. A., and M. Neeley
  1987   Social differentiation in European Mesolithic burial data. In *Mesolithic Northwest Europe: Recent Trends* (P. Rowley-Conwy, M. Zvelebil, and H. P. Blankholm, eds.), pp. 121–127. Sheffield: John R. Collis.

Clark, G., and L. Richards
  1978   Late and Post-Pleistocene industries and fauna from the cave site of La Riera (Province of Asturias, Spain). In *Views of the Past: Essays in Old World Prehistory and Paleoanthropology* (L. Freeman, ed.), pp. 117–152. The Hague: Mouton.

Clark, G., and L. Straus
  1975   Paleoecology at La Riera: Late Pleistocene Hunter-Gatherer Adaptations in Cantabrian Spain. Proposal submitted to the National Science Foundation, Washington, DC.
  1977   Cueva de La Riera: objetivo del "Proyecto Paleoecológico" e informe préliminar de la campaña de 1976. *Boletín del Instituto de Estudios Asturianos* 91:489–505.

1979   The North Burgos Archaeological Survey in perspective. In *The North Burgos Archaeological Survey* (G. Clark, ed.), pp. 247–260. Tempe: Arizona State University Anthropological Research Papers 19.

1983   Late Pleistocene hunter-gatherer adaptations in Cantabrian Spain. In *Hunter-Gatherer Economy in Prehistory: A European Perspective* (G. Bailey, ed.), pp. 131–148. Cambridge: Cambridge University Press.

1986   Synthesis and conclusions, part I: Upper Paleolithic and Mesolithic hunter-gatherer subsistence in northern Spain. In *La Riera Cave: Stone Age Hunter-Gatherer Adaptations in Northern Spain* (L. Straus and G. Clark, eds.), pp. 351–366. Tempe: Arizona State University Anthropological Research Paper No. 36.

Clark, G., and S. Yi

1983   Niche width variation in Cantabrian archaeofaunas: a diachronic study. In *Animals and Archaeology I: Hunters and their Prey* (J. Clutton-Brock and C. Grigson, eds.), pp. 183–208. Oxford: BAR International Series S-163.

Clark, G., D. Young, L. Straus, and R. Jewett

1986   Multivariate analysis of La Riera industries and fauna. In *La Riera Cave: Stone Age Hunter-Gatherer Adaptations in Northern Spain* (L. Straus and G. Clark, eds.), pp. 325–350. Tempe: Arizona State University Anthropological Research Papers No. 36.

Clark, G. A., et al.

1987b   Paleolithic archaeology in the southern Levant. *Annual of the Department of Antiquities of Jordan* 31:19–78.

Clark, J. G. D.

1971   *Star Carr: A Case Study in Bioarchaeology*. Reading, MA: Addison-Wesley.

1975   *The Earlier Stone Age Settlement of Scandinavia*. Cambridge: Cambridge University Press.

1980   *Mesolithic Prelude: The Paleolithic-Neolithic Transition in Old World Prehistory*. Edinburgh: Edinburgh University Press.

Clark, J. D., and J. W. K. Harris

1987   Fire and its roles in early hominid lifeways. *African Archaeological Review* 3:3–27.

Clarke, D. L.

1968   *Analytical Archaeology*. London: Methuen.

1972   Models and paradigms in contemporary archaeology. In *Models in Archaeology* (D. L. Clarke, ed.), pp. 1–60. London: Methuen.

1973   Archaeology: the loss of innocence. *Antiquity* 47:6–18.

1978   *The Mesolithic in Europe*. London: Gerald Duckworth.

Cleland, C. E.

1976   The focal-diffuse model: an evolutionary perspective on the prehistoric cultural adaptations of the eastern United States. *Mid-Continental Journal of Archaeology* 1:59–76.

CLIMAP

1976   The surface of the ice age earth. *Science* 191:1131–1137.

Close, A.

1989   Identifying style in stone artifacts: a case study from the Nile Valley. In *Alternative Approaches to Lithic Analysis* (D. Henry and G. Odell, eds.), pp. 3–26. Washington, DC: Archeological Papers of the American Anthropological Association No. 1.

Cohen, D.
1987   Refitting stone artifacts: why bother? In *The Human Uses of Flint and Chert* (G. de G. Sieveking and M. Newcomer, eds.), pp. 1–11. New York: Cambridge University Press.

Cohen, M.
1975   Archaeological evidence of population pressure in pre-agricultural societies. *American Antiquity* 40:471–475.
1977   *The Food Crisis in Prehistory.* New Haven, CT: Yale University Press.

Cohen, M., and G. J. Armelagos
1984   *Paleopathology at the Origins of Agriculture.* Orlando, FL: Academic Press.

Coinman, N.
1990   *Rethinking the Levantine Upper Paleolithic.* Ph.D. dissertation. Arizona State University. Ann Arbor, MI: University Microfilms.

Coinman, N., G. A. Clark, and M. Donaldson
1989   Aspects of structure in an Epipaleolithic occupation site in west-central Jordan. In *Alternative Approaches to Lithic Analysis* (D. Henry and G. Odell, eds.), pp. 213–235. Washington, DC: Archeological Papers of the American Anthropological Association No. 1.

Collins, D.
1970   Stone artifact analysis and the recognition of cultural traditions. *World Archaeology* 2:17–27.

Collins, M. B.
1975   Lithic technology as a means of processual inference. In *Lithic Technology. Making and Using Stone Tools* (E. Swanson, ed.), pp. 15–34. The Hague: Mouton.

Commins, S., and R. Linscott
1947   *Man and the Universe: The Philosophers of Science.* New York: Random House.

Conkey, M. W.
1978   Style and information in cultural evolution: toward a cultural model for the paleolithic. In *Social Archeology: Beyond Subsistence and Dating* (C. Redman et al., eds.), pp. 61–85. New York: Academic Press.
1980   The identification of prehistoric hunter-gatherer aggregation sites: the case of Altamira. *Current Anthropology* 21:609–630.
1985   Ritual communication, social elaboration, and the variable trajectories of paleolithic material culture. In *Prehistoric Hunter-Gatherers: The Emergence of Cultural Complexity* (T. D. Price and J. A. Brown, eds.), pp. 299–324. New York: Academic Press.
1987   New approaches in the search for meaning? A review of research in "paleolithic art." *Journal of Field Archaeology* 14:413–430.

Conklin, H.
1969   An ethnoecological approach to shifting agriculture. In *Environment and Cultural Behavior* (A. Vayda, ed.), pp. 36–49. New York: Natural History Press.

Connell, J. H.
1980   Diversity and coevolution of competitors, or the ghost of competition past. *Oikos* 35:131–138.

Cook, S. F., and R. F. Heizer
  1968   Relationship among houses, settlement area and population in ab-
            original California. In *Settlement Archaeology* (K. C. Chang, ed.). Palo
            Alto: National Press.
Cooper, M.
  1954   Progressive modification of a stone artifact. *Records of the South Aus-
            tralian Museum* 11:91–103.
Copeland, L.
  1975   The Middle and Upper Paleolithic of Lebanon and Syria in light of
            recent research. In *Problems in Prehistory: North Africa and the Levant*
            (F. Wendorf and A. E. Marks, eds.), pp. 317–358. Dallas, TX: South-
            ern Methodist University Press.
Copeland, L., and F. Hours
  1971   The late Upper Paleolithic material from Antelias Cave, Lebanon:
            Levels IV–I. *Berytus* 20:57–138.
Corchon, M. S.
  1971   *El Solutrense en Santander*. Santander: Institución Cultural de Can-
            tabria.
Cordell, L.
  1984   *Prehistory of the Southwest*. Orlando, FL: Academic Press.
Courty, M. A., P. Goldberg, and R. McPhail
  1989   *Soils and Micromorphology in Archaeology*. Cambridge: Cambridge Uni-
            versity Press.
Coverini, L., A. Giommi, F. Martini, and L. Sarti
  1982   Applicazione della "Cluster Analysis" alle strutture delle industrie
            litiche: contributo alla conoscenza dell'Epigravettiano Italiano. *Pre-
            istoria Alpina* 18:21–32.
Cowgill, G.
  1975   On causes and consequences of ancient and modern population
            growth. *American Anthropologist* 77:505–525.
Cremaschi, M., C. Peretto, and B. Sala
  1984   La Pineta, Molise. *I Primi Abitanti d'Europa*, pp. 129–131. Rome: De
            Luca.
Crew, H.
  1976   The Mousterian site of Rosh Ein Mor. In *Prehistory and Paleoenviron-
            ment in the Central Negev, Israel: Vol. 1., the Avdat/Aqev Area, Part 1* (A.
            Marks, ed.), pp. 75–112. Dallas, TX: Southern Methodist University
            Press.
Crusafont, M.
  1963   ¿Es la industria asturiense una evolucionada "pebble culture"? *Spé-
            leon* 14:77–89.
Daniel, G. E.
  1975   *A Hundred and Fifty Years of Archaeology* (second edition). London:
            Duckworth.
Dart, A.
  1986   *Archaeological Investigations at La Paloma: Archaic and Hohokam Oc-
            cupations in the Northeastern Tucson Basin*. Tucson, AZ: Institute for
            American Research Anthropological Paper No. 4.
Dart, R. A.
  1953   The predatory transition from ape to man. *International Anthropologi-
            cal Linguistics Review* 11:201–219.

Davidson, I.
1974　Radiocarbon dates for the Spanish Solutrean. *Antiquity* 48:63–65.
1976　Les Mallaetes and Monduvér: the economy of a human group in prehistoric Spain. In *Problems in Economic and Social Archaeology* (G. de G. Sieveking, I. K. Longworth, and K. E. Wilson, eds.), pp. 483–499. London: Duckworth.
1980　*Late Paleolithic Economy in Eastern Spain.* Unpublished Ph.D. dissertation, University of Cambridge.
1981　Can we study prehistoric economy for fisher-gatherer-hunters? In *Economic Archaeology* (A. Sheridan and G. N. Bailey, eds.), pp. 17–33. Oxford: BAR International Series S-96.
1983　Site variability and prehistoric economy in Levante. In *Hunter-Gatherer Economy in Prehistory: A European Perspective* (G. N. Bailey, ed.), pp. 79–95. Cambridge: Cambridge University Press.
1986　The geographical study of late paleolithic stages in eastern Spain. In *Stone Age Prehistory. Studies in Memory of Charles McBurney* (G. N. Bailey and P. Callow, eds.), pp. 95–118. Cambridge: Cambridge University Press.
1988　The naming of parts: ethnography and the interpretation of Australian prehistory. In *Archaeology with Ethnography: An Australian Perspective* (B. Meehan and R. Jones, eds.), pp. 17–32. Canberra: Australian National University.
1989　*La Economía del Final del Paleolítico en la España Oriental.* Valencia: Diputación Provincial.
n.d.　Freedom of information. In *Animals into Art* (H. Morphy, ed.). London: George Allen and Unwin. (In press)
Davidson, I., and J. Estévez
1985　Problemas de arqueotafonomía. Formación de yacimientos con fauna. *Quadernos* 1:67–84.
Davidson, I., and W. Noble
1989　The archaeology of perception: traces of depiction and language. *Current Anthropology* 30:125–137.
Davis, R. S.
1983　Theoretical issues in contemporary Soviet paleolithic archaeology. *Annual Review of Anthropology* 12:403–428.
Davis, S.
1983　The age profiles of gazelles predated by ancient man in Israel: possible evidence for the shift from seasonality to sedentism in the Natufian. *Paléorient* 8:5–15.
1984　Khirokitia and its mammal remains: a Neolithic Noah's Ark. In *Fouilles recentes à Khirokitia (Chypre), 1977–1981,* by A. LeBrun, pp. 147–162. Paris: Editions de la Recherche sur les Civilisations, A.D.P.F., Memoire No. 41.
1987　*The Archaeology of Animals.* New Haven, CT: Yale University Press.
Dawkins, R.
1983　Universal Darwinism. In *Evolution from Molecules to Men* (D. Bendall, ed.), pp. 26–41. Cambridge: Cambridge University Press.
Dayan, T., E. Tchernov, O. Bar-Yosef, and Y. Yom-Tov
1986　Animal exploitation in Ujrat el-Meked, a neolithic site in southern Sinai. *Paléorient* 12:105–116.

Debénath, A.
1987 Quelques préhistoriens de Poitou-Charentes: réflexions sur l'épistémologie d'une science. In *Préhistoire de Poitou-Charentes: Problèmes Actuels*, pp. 17–26. Paris: C.T.H.S.

Demars, P.-Y.
1982 *L'utilisation du silex au Paléolithique supérieur: choix, approvisionnement, circulation. L'exemple du Bassin de Brive.* Cahiers du Quaternaire No. 5. Paris: CNRS.

Denbow, J. R.
1984 Prehistoric herders and foragers of the Kalahari: the evidence for 1500 years of interaction. In *Past and Present in Hunter-Gatherer Studies* (C. Schrire, ed.), pp. 175–193. New York: Academic Press.

Dennell, R.
1980 The use, abuse and potential of site catchment analysis. In *Catchment Analysis: Essays on Prehistoric Resource Space* (F. Findlow and J. Ericson, eds.), pp. 1–20. Los Angeles: Anthropology UCLA No. 10.
1983 *European Economic Prehistory: A New Approach.* London: Academic Press.

Dever, W. G.
1973 Two approaches to archaeological method—the architectural and the stratigraphic. *Eretz Israel* 11:1–8.

Diamond, J. M.
1975 The assembly of species communities. In *Ecology and Evolution of Communities* (M. L. Cody and J. M. Diamond, eds.), pp. 342–344. New York: Belknap Press.
1978 Niche shifts and the rediscovery of interspecific competition. *American Scientist* 66:322–331.

Dibble, H. L.
1981 *Technological Strategies of Stone Tool Production at Tabūn Cave (Israel).* Ph.D dissertation. University of Arizona. Ann Arbor: University Microfilms.
1983 Variability and change in the Middle Paleolithic of Western Europe and the Near East. In *The Mousterian Legacy: Human Biocultural Change in the Upper Pleistocene* (Erik Trinkaus, ed.), pp. 53–72. Oxford: BAR International Series S-164.
1984 Interpreting typological variation of Middle Paleolithic scrapers: function, style or sequence of reduction? *Journal of Field Archaeology* 11:431–436.
1987a The interpretation of Middle Paleolithic scraper morphology. *American Antiquity* 52:109–117.
1987b Comparisons des séquences de réduction des outils Moustériens de la France et du Prôche-Orient. *L'Anthropologie* 91:189–196.
1987c Reduction sequences in the manufacture of Mousterian implements in France. In *The Pleistocene Old World: Regional Perspectives* (O. Soffer, ed.), pp. 33–45. New York: Plenum Press.
1987d Measurement of artifact proveniences with an electronic theodolite. *Journal of Field Archaeology* 14:249–254.
1988 Typological aspects of reduction and intensity of utilization of lithic resources in the French Mousterian. In *The Upper Pleistocene Prehistory of Western Eurasia* (H. Dibble and A. Montet-White, eds.), pp. 181–197. Philadelphia: University of Pennsylvania Museum.

1989   Implications of stone tool types for the presence of language during the Lower and Middle Pleistocene. In *The Human Revolution* (P. Mellars and C. Stringer, eds.), pp. 415–432. Edinburgh: Edinburgh University Press.

Dibble, H., and N. Rolland
n.d.   Beyond the Bordes-Binford debate: a new synthesis of factors underlying assemblage variability in the Middle Paleolithic of western Europe. In *The Middle Paleolithic: Adaptation, Behavior, and Variability* (H. Dibble and P. Mellars, eds.). Philadelphia: University of Pennsylvania Museum. (in press)

Dibble, H., and S. McPherron
1988   On the computerization of archaeological projects. *Journal of Field Archaeology* 15:431–440.

Dickson, D.
1990   *The Dawn of Belief: Religion in the Upper Paleolithic of Southwestern Europe.* Tucson: University of Arizona Press.

Dikaios, P.
1953   *Khirokitia.* Monographs of the Department of Antiquities of the Government of Cyprus, No. 1. London: Oxford University Press.
1960   A conspectus of architecture in ancient Cyprus. *Kypriakai Spoudia* 24:1–30.
1962   The stone age. In *Swedish Cyprus Expedition,* Vol. 1, part Ia, pp. 1–204. Lund: Swedish Cyprus Expedition.

Divale, W. T., and M. Harris
1976   Population, warfare, and the male supremacist complex. *American Anthropologist* 78:521–538.

Dobzhansky, T.
1972   On the evolutionary uniqueness of man. *Evolutionary Biology* 6:415–430.

Donahue, R. E.
1986   *Technomorphology: Tool Use and Site Function in the Italian Upper Paleolithic.* Ph.D. dissertation. Michigan State University. Ann Arbor: University Microfilms.

Doran, J., and F. Hodson
1975   *Mathematics and Computers in Archaeology.* Cambridge, MA: Harvard University Press.

Dormon, F.
1987   Analyses polliniques de trois sites Natoufiens (ancient, recent, final) dans la région de Salibiya-Fazael. *Paléorient* 13:121–129.

Dothan, T.
1982.   *The Phillistines and Their Material Culture.* New Haven, CT: Yale University Press.

Douglass, A.
1987   *Prehistoric Exchange and Sociopolitical Development: The Little Colorado White Ware Production-Distribution System.* Ph.D. dissertation. Arizona State University. Ann Arbor: University Microfilms.

Dray, W.
1957   *Laws and Explanation in History.* Oxford: Oxford University Press.

Dunnell, R.
1980   Evolutionary theory and archaeology. In *Advances in Archaeological*

Method and Theory, Vol. 3 (M. Schiffer, ed.), pp. 38–100. New York: Academic Press.
1982   Science, social science and common sense: the agonizing dilemma of modern archaeology. *Journal of Anthropological Research* 38:1–25.
Durham, William H.
1981   Overview: optimal foraging analysis in human ecology. *Hunter-Gatherer Foraging Strategies* (B. Winterhalder and E. A. Smith, eds.), pp. 218–231. Chicago: University of Chicago Press.
Earle, T.
1980   A model of subsistence change. In *Modeling Change in Prehistoric Subsistence Economies* (T. Earle and A. Christenson, eds.), pp. 1–30. New York: Academic Press.
1989   The evolution of chiefdoms. *Current Anthropology* 30:84–87.
Earle, T., and R. Preucel
1987   Processual archaeology and the radical critique. *Current Anthropology* 28:501–527.
Ebert, J., S. Larralde, and L. Wansnider
1986   Distributional archaeology: survey, mapping and analysis of surface archaeological materials in the Green River Basin, Wyoming. In *Perspectives on Archaeological Resource Management*. Omaha: I. & O. Publishing.
Eder, J.
1984   The impact of subsistence change on mobility and settlement pattern in a tropical forest foraging economy: some implications for archaeology. *American Anthropologist* 86:837–853.
1987   *On the Road to Tribal Extinction: Depopulation, Deculturation and Adaptive Well-Being Among the Batak of the Phillippines*. Berkeley: University of California Press.
Edwards, P. C.
1986   Tabaqat Fahl. The Wadi Hammeh. *Sonderabdruck aus Archiv für Orientforschung* 33:222–226.
1989   Revising the broad spectrum revolution: its role in the origins of southwest Asian food production. *Antiquity* 63:225–246.
Edwards, P., S. Bourke, S. Colledge, J. Head, and P. Macumber
1988   Late Pleistocene prehistory in the Wadi al-Hammeh, Jordan Valley. In *The Prehistory of Jordan* (A. Garrard and H. G. Gebel, eds.), pp. 525–565. Oxford: BAR International Series S-396(ii).
Eisenberg, J. F.
1981   *The Mammalian Radiations: An Analysis of Trends in Evolution, Adaptation and Behavior*. Chicago: University of Chicago Press.
Evans, J.
1973   Islands as laboratories of culture change. In *The Explanation of Culture Change: Models in Prehistory* (C. Renfrew, ed.), pp. 517–520. Pittsburgh: University of Pittsburgh Press.
1977   Island archaeology in the Mediterranean: problems and opportunities. *World Archaeology* 9:12–27.
Ewing, J. F.
1947   Preliminary note on the excavations at the paleolithic site of Ksar Akil, Republic of Lebanon. *Antiquity* 84:186–195.
Facchini, G., and G. Giusberti
1988   Sur la présence de l'homme dans l'île de Crète au cours du Würm

moyen. Paper presented at the International Conference: Early Man in Island Environments. September 25–October 2, 1988, Oliena, Sardinia.

Farizy, C.
  1990 La transition Paléolithique moyen/Paléolithique supérieur à Arcy-sur-Cure: aspects technologiques, économiques, et sociaux. In *The Human Revolution: Behavioral and Biological Perspectives on the Origins of Modern Humans* (P. Mellars and C. Stringer, eds.). Edinburgh: University of Edinburgh Press.

Farrand, W.
  1971 Later Quaternary paleoclimates of the eastern Mediterranean area. In *The Late Cenozoic Glacial Ages* (K. Turekian, ed.), pp. 529–564. New Haven, CT: Yale University Press.

Faure, M., C. Guerin, and P. Sondaar
  1983 *Hippopotamus minutus* Cuvier mise au point. *Actes du Symposium Paléontologique Georges Cuvier, Montbeliard* (E. Buffetaut, J. Mazin, and E. Salmon, eds.), pp. 157–183. Montbeliard, France.

Fernández Tresguerres, J.
  1980 *El Aziliense en las provincias de Asturias y Santander.* Santander: CIMA Monografías No. 2.

Ferring, C. R.
  1975 The Aterian in North African prehistory. In *Problems in Prehistory: North Africa and the Levant* (F. Wendorf and A. E. Marks, eds.), pp. 113–126. Dallas, TX: Southern Methodist University Press.

Feynman, R.
  1985 *QED (Quantum Electrodynamics): The Strange Theory of Light and Matter.* Princeton, NJ: Princeton University Press.

Fish, P. R.
  1979 *The Interpretive Potential of Mousterian Debitage.* Tempe: Arizona State University Anthropological Research Papers No. 16.
  1980 Beyond tools: Middle Paleolithic debitage analysis and cultural analysis. *Journal of Anthropological Research* 37:374–386.

Fish, P., S. Fish, A. Long, and C. Miksicek
  1986 Early corn remains from Tumamoc Hill, southern Arizona. *American Antiquity* 51:563–572.

Fish, S., P. Fish, and J. Madsen
  1989 Classic Period Hohokam community integration in the Tucson Basin. In *The Sociopolitical Structure of Prehistoric Southwestern Societies* (K. Lightfoot, S. Upham, and R. Jewett, eds.). Boulder, CO: Westview Press.
  1990 Sedentism and settlement mobility in the Tucson Basin prior to A.D. 1000. In *Perspectives on Southwest Prehistory* (D. Minnis and C. Redman, eds.), pp. 76–91. Boulder, CO: Westview Press.

Flannery, K. V.
  1967 Culture history vs. culture process: a debate in American archaeology. *Scientific American* 217:119–122.
  1969 Origins and ecological effects of early domestication in Iran and the Near East. In *The Domestication and Exploitation of Plants and Animals* (P. J. Ucko and G. W. Dimbleby, eds.) pp. 73–100. Chicago: Aldine Publishing.

1972   The cultural evolution of civilizations. *Annual Review of Ecology and Systematics* 3:399–426.

1973   Archaeology with a capital S. In *Research and Theory in Current Archeology* (C. Redman, ed.), pp. 47–53. New York: Wiley Interscience.

1976   The trouble with regional sampling. In *The Early Mesoamerican Village* (K. V. Flannery, ed.), pp. 159–160. New York: Academic Press.

1986   The research problem. In *Guila Naquitz, Archaic Foraging and Early Agriculture in Oaxaca, Mexico* (K. Flannery, ed.), pp. 7–10. Orlando, FL: Academic Press.

Flenniken, J. J., and A. W. Raymond

1986   Morphological projectile typology: replication, experimentation and technological analysis. *American Antiquity* 51:603–614.

Flenniken, J. J., and P. J. Wilke

1989   Typology, technology, and chronology of Great Basin dart points. *American Anthropologist* 91:149–158.

Folcy, R.

1984a   Putting people into perspective: an introduction to community evolution and ecology. In *Hominid Evolution and Community Ecology* (R. Foley, ed.), pp. 1–24. London: Academic Press.

1984b   Early man and the red queen: tropical African community evolution and hominid adaptation. In *Hominid Evolution and Community Ecology* (R. Foley, ed.), pp. 85–110. London: Academic Press.

1987   Hominid species and stone tool assemblages: how are they related? *Antiquity* 61:380–392.

1989   The search for early man. *Archaeology* 42:26–32.

Fontana, B., W. Robinson, C. Cormack, and E. Leavitt

1962   *Papago Indian Pottery.* Seattle: University of Washington Press.

Ford, J.

1952   Measurements of some prehistoric design developments in the southeastern states. *Anthropological Papers of the American Museum of Natural History No. 44.* New York: American Museum of Natural History.

1954   On the concept of types. *American Anthropologist* 56:42–54.

Ford, R. I.

1981   Gardening and farming before A.D. 1000: patterns of prehistoric cultivation north of Mexico. *Journal of Ethnobiology* 1:6–27.

Fortea, J., J. M. Fullola, V. Villaverde, I. Davidson, M. Dupré, and M. P. Fumanal

1983   Schéma paléoclimatique, faunique et chronostratigraphique des industries à bord abattu de la région méditerranéenne espagnole. *Rivista di Scienze Preistoriche* 38:21–67.

Fortea Pérez, J., and F. Jordá Cerdá

1976   La Cueva de Les Mallaetes y los problemas del Paleolítico superior del Mediterráneo Español. *Zephyrus* 26–27:129–166.

Fowler, D.

1987   Uses of the past: archaeology in the service of the state. *American Antiquity* 52:228–248.

Fox, W.

1987   The neolithic occupation of western Cyprus. In *Western Cyprus: Connections* (D. Rupp, ed.), pp. 19–29. Goteborg: SIMA, Vol. 77.

Freeman, L. G.
  1964   *Mousterian Developments in Cantabrian Spain.* Ph.D. dissertation. Department of Anthropology, University of Chicago.
  1968   A theoretical framework for interpreting archaeological materials. In *Man the Hunter* (R. Lee and I. DeVore, eds.), pp. 262–267. Chicago: Aldine.
  1973   The significance of mammalian faunas from paleolithic occupations in Cantabrian Spain. *American Antiquity* 38:3–44.
  1981   The fat of the land: notes on paleolithic diet in Iberia. In *Omnivorous Primates* (R. S. O. Harding and G. Teleki, eds.), pp. 104–165. New York: Columbia University Press.
Frison, G. C.
  1968   A functional analysis of certain chipped stone tools. *American Antiquity* 33:149–150.
Fritz, J., and F. Plog
  1970   The nature of archaeological explanation. *American Antiquity* 35: 405–412.
Fullola Pericot, J. M.
  1979   *Las Industrias líticas del Paleolítico superior Iberico.* Trabajos Varios del Servicio de Investigación Prehistorica No. 60. Valencia: Diputación Provincial.
Gallager, J. P.
  1977   Contemporary stone tools in Ethiopia: implications for archaeology. *Journal of Field Archaeology* 4:407–414.
Gallay, A.
  1989   Logicism: a French view of archaeological theory founded in computational perspective. *Antiquity* 63:27–39.
Gambassini, P.
  1970   Risultati della campagna di scavi 1964 nel Riparo C delle Cipolliane (Lecce). *Rivista Scienze Preistoriche* 25:127–181.
Gamble, C.
  1979   Hunting strategies in the central European Paleolithic. *Proceedings of the Prehistoric Society* 45:35–52.
  1982   Interaction and alliance in paleolithic society. *Man* 17:92–107.
  1983   Caves and faunas from Last Glacial Europe. In *Animals and Archaeology: I. Hunters and Their Prey* (J. Clutton-Brock and C. Grigson, eds.), pp. 163–172. Oxford: BAR International Series S-163.
  1984   Regional variation in hunter-gatherer strategy in the Upper Pleistocene of Europe. In *Hominid Evolution and Community Ecology* (R. Foley, ed.), pp. 237–260. London: Academic Press.
  1986   *The Paleolithic Settlement of Europe.* Cambridge: Cambridge University Press.
Gamble, C., and O. Soffer
  1990   Introduction. In *The World at 18,000 BP* (O. Soffer and C. Gamble, eds.), pp. 1–23. London: Unwin and Hyman.
García, L.
  1972   *The Balearic Islands.* London: Thames and Hundson.
Gardin, J.-C.
  1987   *Systèmes experts et publications savantes.* London: British Library Board.
Garrard, A., A. Betts, B. Byrd, S. Colledge, and C. Hunt
  1988   Summary of paleoenvironmental and prehistoric investigations

in the Azraq Basin. In *The Prehistory of Jordan* (A. Garrard and H. G. Gebel, eds.), pp. 311–337. Oxford: BAR International Series S-396(i).

Garrard, A., A. Betts, B. Byrd, and C. Hunt
1987   Prehistoric environment and settlement in the Azraq Basin: an interim report on the 1985 excavation season. *Levant* 19:5–25.

Garrard, A., B. Byrd, P. Harvey, and F. Hivernel
1985   Prehistoric environment and settlement in the Azraq Basin: a report on the 1982 survey season. *Levant* 17:1–28.

Garrard, A., and H. G. Gebel, eds.
1988   *The Prehistory of Jordan: The State of Research in 1986.* Oxford: BAR International Series S-396.

Garrard, A., and N. Price
1973   A survey of prehistoric sites in the Azraq Basin, eastern Jordan. *Paléorient* 3:109–126.

Garrod, D. A. E.
1928   Excavation of a Mousterian rockshelter at Devil's Tower (Gibraltar). *Journal of the Royal Anthropological Institute* 58:33–113.
1932a   Excavations in the Wadi el-Mughara, 1931. *Quarterly Statement of the Palestine Exploration Fund:* 44–51.
1932b   A new Mesolithic industry: the Natufian of Palestine. *Journal of the Royal Anthropological Institute* 62:257–269.
1942   Excavations at the Cave of Shukbah, Palestine, 1928. *Proceedings of the Prehistoric Society* 8:1–19.
1957   The Natufian culture: life and economy of a Mesolithic people in the Near East. *Proceedings of the British Academy* 43:211–227.

Garrod, D. A. E., and D. M. A. Bate
1937   *The Stone Age of Mount Carmel. Excavations at the Wady el-Mughara, Vol. 1.* Oxford: Clarendon Press.

Gebel, H. G., and M. Muheisen
1985   Note on 'Ain Rahub, a new Late Natufian site near Irbid, Jordan. *Paléorient* 11:107–110.

G.E.E.M.
1969   Epipaléolithique-mésolithique. Les microlithiques géometriques. *Bulletin de la Société Préhistorique Française* 66:355–366.
1972   Epipaléolithique-mésolithique. Les armatures non géometriques. *Bulletin de la Société Préhistorique Française* 69:364–375.
1975   Epipaléolithique-mésolithique. L'Outillage du fond commun. 1. Grattoirs, éclats retouchés, burins, perçoirs. *Bulletin de la Société Préhistorique Française* 72:319–332.

Geneste, J.-M.
1985   *Analyse lithique des industries Moustériennes du Périgord: une approche technologique du comportement des groupes humains au Paléolithique moyen.* Thèse du doctorat. Bordeaux: l'Université de Bordeaux I.
1988   Systèmes d'approvisionnement en matières premières au Paléolithique moyen et au Paléolithique supérieur en Aquitaine. In *L'Homme de Neandertal 8: La Mutation* (J. Kozlowski, ed.), pp. 61–70. Liège: ERAUL No. 35.

Gifford, D. P.
1981   Taphonomy and paleoecology: a critical review of archaeology's sis-

ter disciplines. In *Advances in Archaeological Method and Theory, Vol. 4* (M. Schiffer, ed.), pp. 365–438. New York: Academic Press.

Gilead, I.
1981   *The Upper Paleolithic in the Sinai and Negev.* Ph.D. dissertation. Hebrew University.
1984   Is the term Epipaleolithic relevant to Levantine prehistory? *Current Anthropology* 25:227–229.
1988   Le site de Fara II (Neguev septentrional, Israël) et le remontage de son industrie. *L'Anthropologie* 92:797–808.
n.d.   The Upper Paleolithic in southern Israel and Sinai and its relevance for the Levant. *Paléorient* 14(2). (in press)

Gilman, Antonio
1983   Explaining the Upper Paleolithic revolution. In *Marxist Perspectives in Anthropology* (M. Spriggs, ed.), pp. 115–126. Cambridge: Cambridge University Press.

Gingerich, P.
1984   Punctuated equilibria—where is the evidence? *Systematic Zoology* 33:335–338.
1985   Species in the fossil record: concepts, trends and transitions. *Paleobiology* 22:27–41.

Gjerstad, E.
1926   The stone age in Cyprus. *Antiquaries Journal* 6:54–58.

Gjerstad, E., J. Lindros, E. Sjoqvist, and A. Westholm
1934   *The Swedish Cyprus Expedition: Finds and Results of the Excavations in Cyprus* 1927–1931, Vols. 1 and 2. Stockholm: Swedish Cyprus Expedition.

Glock, A. E.
1985   Tradition and change in two archaeologies. *American Antiquity* 50:464–477.

Glover, I.
1973   Island southeast Asia and the settlement of Australia. In *Archaeological Theory and Practice* (D. Strong, ed.), pp. 105–129. London: Duckworth.

Godelier, M.
1974   *Economía, fetichismo y religión en las sociedades primitivas.* Madrid: Siglo XXI.
1977   *Teoría Marxista de las sociedades precapitalistas* (3rd ed.). Barcelona: Editorial Laia.

Goldstein, L.
1981   One-dimensional archaeology and multi-dimensional people: spatial organization and mortuary analysis. In *The Archaeology of Death* (R. Chapman, I. Kinnes, and K. Randsborg, eds.), pp. 53–69. Cambridge: Cambridge University Press.

González Echegaray, J., and L. G. Freeman
1971   *Cueva Morín: Excavaciones 1966–1968.* Santander: Patronato de Cuevas Prehistoricas.
1973   *Cueva Morín: Excavaciones 1969.* Santander: Patronato de Cuevas Prehistoricas.

González Morales, M. R.
1986   La Riera bone and antler artifact assemblages. In *La Riera Cave: Stone Age Hunter-Gatherer Adaptations in Northern Spain* (L. G. Straus and G.

Clark, eds.), pp. 209–218. Tempe: Arizona State University Anthropological Research Papers No. 36.

González Morales, M., and González Sainz, C.
1986   Las sociedades productoras. In *La Prehistoria en Cantabria*, pp. 295–310. Santander: Ediciones Tantín.

González Sainz, C.
1989a   Algunas reflexiones sobre el hecho artístico al final del Paleolítico Superior. In *Cien años después de Sautuola* (M. R. Gonzáles Morales, ed.), pp. 229–261. Santander: Diputación Regional de Cantabria.
1989b   *El Magdaleniense superior-final en la región Cantábrica.* Santander: Ediciones Tantin y la Universidad de Cantabria.

González Sainz, C., and M. R. González Morales
1986   *La Prehistoria en Cantabria.* Santander: Ediciones Tantín.

Goodman, D., L. Martin, G. J. Armelagos, and G. Clark
1984   Indications of stress from bone and teeth. In *Paleopathology at the Origins of Agriculture* (M. N. Cohen and G. J. Armelagos, eds.), pp. 13–49. New York: Academic Press.

Goody, J.
1976   *Production and Reproduction.* Cambridge: Cambridge University Press.

Goodyear, A.
1982   Tool kit entropy and bipolar reduction: a study of Paleoindian interassemblage lithic variability in the southeastern United States. Unpublished manuscript, Institute of Archaeology and Anthropology, University of South Carolina.
1989   An hypothesis for the use of cryptocrystalline raw materials among Paleoindian groups of North America. In *Eastern Paleoindian Lithic Resource Use* (C. Ellis and J. Lothrop, eds.), pp. 1–10. Boulder, CO: Westview Press.

Gopher, A.
1985   *Flint Tool Industries of the Neolithic Period in Israel.* Ph.D. dissertation. Jerusalem: Hebrew University.
1989   Diffusion processes in Pre-pottery Neolithic Levant: The case of the Helwan Point. In *People and Culture in Change* (I. Hershkovitz, ed.), pp. 91–106. Oxford: BAR International Series S-508.

Goring-Morris, A. N.
1980   *Late Quaternary Sites in Wadi Fazael, Lower Jordan Valley.* M.A. thesis. Jerusalem: Hebrew University.
1987   *At the Edge. Terminal Pleistocene Hunter-Gatherers in the Negev and Sinai.* Oxford: BAR International Series S-361.
1989   Developments in Terminal Pleistocene hunter-gatherer sociocultural systems: a perspective from the Negev and Sinai Deserts. In *People and Culture in Change* (I. Hershkovitz, ed.), pp. 7–28. Oxford: BAR International Series S-508.

Goring-Morris, A. N., and S. A. Rosen
1986   Final report to the Israeli Hydrological Planning Commission (TAHAL) on the results of prehistoric survey conducted by the Archaeological Survey of Israel and other projects conducted within 25 km of the site. Israeli Hydrological Commission (TAHAL), the Israel Electric Corporation, and the Archaeological Survey of Israel.

Gould, R. A.
  1979 Exotic stones and battered bones: ethnoarchaeology in the Australian desert. *Archaeology* 32:28–37.
  1980 *Living Archaeology.* Cambridge: Cambridge University Press.
  1982 To have and have not: the ecology of sharing among hunter-gatherers. In *Resource Managers: North American and Australian Hunter-Gatherers* (N. M. Williams and E. S. Hienn, eds.), pp. 69–92. AAAS Symposium No. 67. Boulder, CO: Westview Press.
  1985 "Now let's invent agriculture . . .": a critical review of complexity among hunter-gatherers. In *Prehistoric Hunter-Gatherers: the Emergence of Cultural Complexity* (T. D. Price and J. A. Brown, eds.), pp. 427–434. New York: Academic Press.
Gould, R., D. Koster, and A. Sontz
  1971 The lithic assemblage of the Western Desert aborigines of Australia. *American Antiquity* 36:149–168.
Gowlett, J. A.
  1987 The coming of modern man. *Antiquity* 66:210–219.
Graves, M., W. Longacre, and S. Holbrook
  1982 Aggregation and abandonment at Grasshopper Pueblo, Arizona. *Journal of Field Archaeology* 9:193–206.
Grayson, D. K.
  1983 *The Establishment of Human Antiquity.* New York: Academic Press.
  1985 Review of *Faunal Remains from the Klasies River Mouth* (Binford). *Science* 228:869–870.
Greenacre, M.
  1984 *Theory and Applications of Correspondence Analysis.* New York: Academic Press.
Grinnell, G. B.
  1962 *The Cheyenne Indians: Their History and Ways of Life.* New York: Cooper Square Publishers.
Gunneweg, J., I. Perlman, T. Dothan, and S. Gitin
  1986 On the origin of pottery from Tel Miqne-Ekron. *Bulletin of the American Schools of Oriental Research* 246:3–16.
Guerreschi, A., and P. Leonardi
  1984 La fine del Paleolitico superiore (Epigravettiano finale). In *Il Veneto nell'Antichità. Preistoria e protostoria* (A. Aspes, ed.), pp. 243–281. Verona: Banca Popolare.
Guthrie, D. R.
  1989 Woolly arguments against the mammoth steppe—a new look at the palynological data. *The Review of Archaeology* 10:16–34.
Hall, M.
  1984 The burden of tribalism: the social context of southern African Iron Age studies. *American Antiquity* 49:455–467.
Hahlweg, K.
  1989 A systems view of evolution and evolutionary epistemology. In *Issues in Evolutionary Epistemology* (K. Hahlweg and C. Hooker, eds.), pp. 45–78. Albany: SUNY Press.
Hahlweg, K., and C. Hooker
  1989 Evolutionary epistemology and philosophy of science. In *Issues in Evolutionary Epistemology* (K. Hahlweg and C. Hooker, eds.), pp. 21–44, 79–150. Albany: SUNY Press.

Hammel, E. A.
1964 Territorial patterning of marriage relationships in a coastal Peruvian village. *American Anthropologist* 66:67–74.

Hanson, R. N.
1961 *Patterns of Discovery: An Inquiry into the Conceptual Foundations of Science.* Cambridge: Cambridge University Press.

Hardesty, D.
1980 The use of general ecological principles in archaeology. In *Advances in Archaeological Method and Theory, Vol. 3* (M. Schiffer, ed.), pp. 158–187. New York: Academic Press.

Harlan, J. R.
1967 A wild wheat harvest in Turkey. *Archaeology* 20:197–201.

Harris, D. R.
1977 The origins of agriculture: alternative pathways toward agriculture. In *Origins of Agriculture* (C. A. Reed, ed.), pp. 173–249. The Hague: Mouton.
1978 Settling down: an evolutionary model for the transformation of mobile bands into sedentary communities. In *The Evolution of Social Systems* (J. Friedman and M. L. Rowlands, eds.), pp. 401–417. London: Duckworth.

Harris, M.
1977 *Cannibals and Kings: The Origins of Cultures.* New York: Random House.
1979 *Cultural Materialism: The Struggle for a Science of Culture.* New York: Random House.

Harrold, F. B.
1978 *A Study of the Châtelperronian.* Ph.D. dissertation. Department of Anthropology, University of Chicago.
1980 A comparative analysis of Eurasian paleolithic burials. *World Archaeology* 12:196–211.
1981 New perspectives on the Châtelperronian. *Ampurias* 43:35–85.
1983 The Châtelperronian and the Middle-Upper Paleolithic transition. In *The Mousterian Legacy: Human Biocultural Change in the Upper Pleistocene* (E. Trinkaus, ed.), pp. 123–140. Oxford: BAR International Series S-164.
1989 Mousterian, Châtelperronian, and early Aurignacian: continuity or discontinuity? In *The Human Revolution: Biological and Behavioral Perspectives on the Origins of Modern Humans* (P. Mellars and C. Stringer, eds.), pp. 677–713. Edinburgh: University of Edinburgh Press.

Hassan, F. A.
1977 The dynamics of agricultural origins in Palestine: a theoretical model. In *Origins of Agriculture* (C. A. Reed, ed.), pp. 589–609. The Hague: Mouton.

Haury, E.
1962 The greater American Southwest. In *Courses Toward Urban Life: Some Archaeological Considerations of Cultural Alternates* (R. J. Braidwood and G. R. Willey, eds.), pp. 106–131. New York: Viking Fund Publications in Anthropology No. 32.

Hawking, S. W.
1988 *A Brief History of Time: From the Big Bang to Black Holes.* London Bantam Press.

Hayden, B.
    1979   *Paleolithic Reflections.* Canberra: Australian Institute of Aboriginal Studies.
    1981   Subsistence and ecological adaptations of modern hunter-gatherers. In *Omnivorous Primates: Gathering and Hunting in Human Evolution* (R. S. O. Harding and G. Teleki, eds.), pp. 344–421. New York: Columbia University Press.
    1982   Research and development in the stone age: technological transitions among hunter-gatherers. *Current Anthropology* 22:519–548.
    1987   From chopper to celt: the evolution of resharpening techniques. *Lithic Technology* 16:33–43.
Haynes, G.
    1982   Prey bones and predators: potential ecologic information from analysis of bone sites. *Ossa* 7:75–97.
Headland, T. N., and L. A. Reid
    1989   Hunter-gatherers and their neighbors from prehistory to the present. *Current Anthropology* 30:43–66.
Held, S.
    1982   The earliest prehistory of Cyprus. In *An Archaeological Guide to the Ancient Kourion Area and the Akrotiri Peninsula* (S. Swiny, ed.), pp. 6–11. Nicosia: Zavallis Press.
    1989a   Colonization cycles on Cyprus 1: the biogeographic and paleontological foundation of early prehistoric settlement. *Reports of the Department of Antiquities, Cyprus, 1989,* pp. 8–28. Nicosia: Department of Antiquities.
    1989b   *Contributions to the Early Prehistoric Archaeology of Cyprus, Vol. 1: Environment and Chronological Background Studies.* Oxford: BAR International Series S-511.
Helms, S., and A. Betts
    1987   The desert "kites" of Badiyat Esh-Sham and North Arabia. *Paléorient* 13:41–68.
Hemingway, M. F.
    1980   *The Initial Magdalenian in France.* Oxford: BAR International Series S-90(i–ii).
Hempel, C.
    1965   *Aspects of Scientific Explanation, and Other Essays in the Philosophy of Science.* New York: Free Press.
    1966   *The Philosophy of Natural Science.* Englewood Cliffs, NJ: Prentice-Hall.
Henry, D. O.
    1973a   *The Natufian of Palestine: Its Material Culture and Ecology.* Ph.D. dissertation. Department of Anthropology, Southern Methodist University, Dallas.
    1973b   The Natufian site of Rosh Zin, Negev, Israel: a preliminary report. *Palestine Exploration Quarterly* 105:129–140.
    1976   Rosh Zin: a Natufian settlement near Ein Avdat. In *Prehistory and Paleoenvironments in the Central Negev, Israel, Vol. 1: The Avdat/Aqev Area, Part 1* (A. E. Marks, ed.), pp. 317–348. Dallas, TX: Southern Methodist University Press.
    1977   An examination of the artifact variability in the Natufian of Palestine. In *Eretz-Israel, Vol. 13* (B. Arensburg and O. Bar-Yosef, eds.), pp. 229–239. Jerusalem: Hebrew University.

1981 An analysis of settlement patterns and adaptive strategies of the Natufian. In *Préhistoire du Levant* (J. Cauvin and P. Sanlaville, eds.), pp. 421–432. Paris: Editions du CNRS.

1982 The prehistory of southern Jordan and relationships with the Levant. *Journal of Field Archaeology* 9:417–444.

1983 Adaptive evolution in the Epipaleolithic of the Near East. In *Advances in World Archaeology, Vol. 2* (F. Wendorf and A. E. Close, eds.), pp. 99–160. New York: Academic Press.

1985a Late Pleistocene environment and paleolithic adaptations in southern Jordan. In *Studies in the History and Archaeology of Jordan II* (A. Hadidi, ed.), pp. 67–77. London: Routledge and Kegan Paul.

1985b Preagricultural sedentism: the Natufian example. In *Prehistoric Hunter-Gatherers: The Emergence of Cultural Complexity* (T. D. Price and J. A. Brown, eds.), pp. 365–384. New York: Academic Press.

1987 The prehistory and paleoenvironments of Jordan: an overview. *Paléorient* 12:5–26.

1988 Summary of prehistoric and paleoenvironmental research in the Northern Hisma. In *The Prehistory of Jordan* (A. Garrard and H. G. Gebel, eds.), pp. 7–37. Oxford: BAR International Series S-396(i).

1989 *From Foraging to Agriculture. The Levant at the End of the Ice Age.* Philadelphia: University of Pennsylvania Press.

Henry, D. O., and A. Leroi-Gourhan
1976 The excavation of Hayonim Terrace: an interim report. *Journal of Field Archaeology* 3:391–405.

Henry, D. O., A. Leroi-Gourhan, and S. Davis
1981 The excavation of Hayonim Terrace: an examination of Terminal Pleistocene climatic and adaptive changes. *Journal of Archaeological Science* 8:33–58.

Henry, D., and G. Odell, eds.
1989 *Alternative Approaches to Lithic Analysis.* Washington, D.C.: Archeological Papers of the American Anthropological Association No. 1.

Henry, D. O., and A. F. Servello
1974 Compendium of carbon-14 determinations derived from Near Eastern prehistoric deposits. *Paléorient* 1:19–44.

Henry, D. O., and P. F. Turnbull, with A. Emery-Barbier and A. Leroi-Gourhan
1985 Archaeological and faunal remains from Natufian and Timnian sites in southern Jordan with notes on pollen evidence. *Bulletin of the American Schools of Oriental Research* 257:45–64.

Hespenheide, H.
1980 Comment: Ecological models of resource selection. In *Modeling Change in Prehistoric Subsistence Economies* (T. Earle and A. Christenson, eds.), pp. 73–76. New York: Academic Press.

Heywood, H.
1982 The archaeological remains of the Akrotiri Peninsula. In *An Archaeological Guide to the Ancient Kourion Area and the Akrotiri Peninsula* (S. Swiny, ed.), pp. 162–175. Nicosia: Zavallis Press.

Hietala, H.
1983 Boker Tachtit: spatial distributions. In *Prehistory and Paleoenvironments in the Central Negev, Israel, Vol. III, the Avdat/Aqev Area, Part 3* (A. Marks, ed.), pp. 191–216. Dallas, TX: Southern Methodist University Press.

Higgs, E. S., ed.
1972   *Papers in Economic Prehistory.* Cambridge: Cambridge University Press.
1975   *Paleoeconomy.* Cambridge: Cambridge University Press.
1976   *L'Origine de l'élévage et de la domestication.* Colloque XX. Nice: UISPP.
Higgs, E., and M. Jarman, eds.
1972   *Papers in Economic Prehistory.* Cambridge: Cambridge University Press.
Hill, K.
1982   Hunting and human evolution. *Journal of Human Evolution* 11:521–544.
Hillman, G. C., S. Colledge, and D. Harris
1989   Plant food economy during the Epi-Paleolithic period at Tell Abu Hureyra, Syria: dietary diversity, seasonality, and modes of exploitation. In *Foraging and Farming: The Evolution of Plant Exploitation* (D. Harris and G. Hillman, eds.), pp. 240–268. London: Unwin and Hyman.
Hillman, G. C., and M. S. Davies
1990   Measured domestication rates in wild wheats and barley under primitive cultivation, and their archaeological implications. *Journal of World Prehistory* 4:157–222.
Hodder, I.
1982   *Symbols in Action: Ethnoarchaeological Studies of Material Culture.* Cambridge: Cambridge University Press.
1983   *The Present Past.* London: Batsford.
1984   History vs. science: no contest. Review of *In Pursuit of the Past* (Binford) and *The Identity of Man* (Clark). *Scottish Archaeological Review* 3:66–68.
1985   Post-processual archaeology. In *Advances in Archaeological Method and Theory, Vol. 8* (M. Schiffer, ed.), pp. 1–26. New York: Academic Press.
1986   *Reading the Past. Current Approaches to Interpretation in Archaeology.* Cambridge: Cambridge University Press.
1989   Post-Processual Archaeology: The Current Debate. Paper presented at the 6th Annual Visiting Scholar's Conference "New Directions in Archaeology," Center for Archaeological Investigations, Southern Illinois University, April 28–29, 1989. Carbondale, Illinois.
Hodder, I., ed.
1982   *Symbolic and Structural Archaeology.* Cambridge: Cambridge University Press.
Hodson, F.
1970   Cluster analysis and archaeology: some new developments and applications. *World Archaeology* 1:299–320.
Hoffman, C. M.
1985   Projectile point maintenance and typology: assessment with factor analysis and canonical correlation. In *For Concordance in Archaeological Analysis* (C. Carr, ed.), pp. 566–612. Kansas City, MO: Westport Publishers.
Holdoway, S.
1989   Were there hafted projectile points in the Mousterian? *Journal of Field Archaeology* 16:79–86.

Hole, F.
1984   A reassessment of the Neolithic Revolution. *Paléorient* 10:49–60.
Holloway, R.
1981   Culture, symbols, and human brain evolution. *Dialectical Anthropology* 5:287–299.
Honea, K.
1975   Prehistoric remains on the island of Kythnos. *American Journal of Archaeology* 79:277–279.
Horowitz, A.
1979   *The Quaternary of Israel.* New York: Academic Press.
Hopf, M.
1983   Jericho plant remains. In *Excavations at Jericho Vol. 5* (K. Kenyon and T. Holland, eds.), pp. 576–611. London: British School of Archaeology in Jerusalem.
Hopf, M., and O. Bar-Yosef
1987   Plant remains from Hayonim Cave, western Galilee. *Paléorient* 13:117–120.
Hours, F.
1973   Le Kebarien au Liban. Reflexions à partir des fouilles de Jiita en 1972. *Paléorient* 1:185–200.
1974   Remarques sur l'utilisation de liste-types pour l'étude du Paléolithique supérieur et de l'Epipaléolithique du Levant. *Paléorient* 2:3–18.
1976   *L'Epipaléolithique au Liban. Resultats acquis en 1975,* pp. 78–106. Colloque III. Nice: UISPP.
Hours, F., L. Copeland, and O. Aurenche
1973   Les industries paléolithiques du Prôche-Orient, essai de correlation. *L'Anthropologie* 77:229–280, 437–496.
Houtekamer, J., and P. Sondaar
1979   Osteology of the fore limb of the Pleistocene dwarf hippopotamus from Cyprus with special reference to phylogeny and function. *Koninklijke Nederlandse Akademie van Wetenschappen,* Series B, 82:411–448.
Hovers, E.
1989   Settlement and subsistence patterns in the Lower Jordan Valley from Epipaleolithic to Neolithic times. In *People and Culture in Change* (I. Hershkovitz, ed.), pp. 37–52. Oxford: BAR International Series S-508.
Hovers, E., and O. Bar-Yosef
1987   A prehistoric survey of eastern Samaria: preliminary report. *Israel Exploration Journal* 37:77–87.
Howell, F. C.
1984   Introduction. In *The Origins of Modern Humans: A World Survey of the Fossil Evidence* (F. Smith and F. Spencer, eds.), pp. xiii–xxii. New York: Alan R. Liss.
Howell, F. C., G. H. Cole, and M. R. Kleindienst
1962   Isimilia: an Acheulian occupation in the Iringa Highlands, Southern Highlands Province, Tanganyika. In *Actes du IVe Congrès Panafricain de Préhistoire et de l'Etude du Quaternaire, Section III* (G. Mortlemans and J. Nenquin, eds.), pp. 43–80. Tervuren, Belgium: Musée Royal de l'Afrique Centrale.

Huckell, B.
  1990   *Agriculture and Late Archaic Settlements in the River Valleys of South-eastern Arizona.* Ph.D. dissertation. Department of Arid Land Studies, University of Arizona. Ann Arbor: University Microfilms.
Iltis, H.
  1983   From teosinte to maize: the catastrophic sexual transmutation. *Science* 222:886–894.
Ingold, T.
  1980   *Hunters, Pastoralists and Ranchers.* Cambridge: Cambridge University Press.
  1987   *The Appropriation of Nature: Essays on Human Ecology and Social Relations.* Iowa City: University of Iowa Press.
Irwin-Williams, C.
  1973   The Oshara Tradition: origins of Anasazi culture. *Eastern New Mexico Contributions to Anthropology* 5:1–30.
Isaac, G. L.
  1976   The activities of early African hominids. In *Human Origins* (G. L. Isaac and E. R. McGowan, eds.), pp. 483–514. Menlo Park, CA: W. A. Benjamin.
  1977   *Olorgesailie: Archaeological Studies of a Middle Pleistocene Lake Basin in Kenya.* Chicago: University of Chicago Press.
  1978   Food sharing and human evolution: archaeological evidence from the Plio-Pleistocene of East Africa. *Journal of Anthropological Research* 34:311–325.
  1980   Casting the net wide: a critical review of early hominid land use and ecological relations. In *Current Argument on Early Man* (L.-K. Konigsson, ed.), pp. 226–253. Oxford: Pergamon Press.
  1984   The archaeology of human origins. *Advances in World Archaeology* 3:1–89.
Jacobsen, T.
  1976   Seventeen thousand years of Greek prehistory. *Scientific American* 234:76–87.
Jaksic, F. M.
  1981   Abuse and misuse of the term "guild" in ecological studies. *Oikos* 37:397–400.
James, S. R.
  1989   Hominid use of fire in the Lower and Middle Pleistocene: a review of the evidence. *Current Anthropology* 30:1–26.
Jarman, M., G. Bailey, and H. Jarman
  1982   *Early European Agriculture: Its Foundation and Development.* Cambridge: Cambridge University Press.
Jelinek, A. J.
  1976   Form, function, and style in lithic analysis. In *Cultural Change and Continuity* (C. E. Cleland, ed.), pp. 19–35. New York: Academic Press.
  1977   The Lower Paleolithic: current evidence and interpretations. *Annual Review of Anthropology* 6:11–32.
  1981   The Middle Paleolithic in the southern Levant from the perspective of the Tabūn Cave. In *Préhistoire du Levant* (J. Cauvin and P. Sanlaville, eds.), pp. 265–280. Paris: Editions du CNRS.

1982   The Tabūn Cave and paleolithic man in the Levant. *Science* 216: 1369–1375.
1985   La coöperation Americaine-Française en archéologie préhistorique.
–86   *Nouvelles d'Archéologie* 22:64–67.
Jochim, M.
1976   *Hunter-Gatherer Subsistence and Settlement: A Predictive Model.* New York: Academic Press.
1981   *Strategies for Survival: Cultural Behavior in an Ecological Context.* New York: Academic Press.
1983   Palcolithic cave art in ecological perspective. In *Hunter-Gatherer Economy in Prehistory* (G. Bailey, ed.), pp. 212–219. Cambridge: Cambridge University Press.
Johnson, D.
1980   Problems in the land vertebrate zoogeography of certain islands and the swimming powers of elephants. *Journal of Biogeography* 7:383–398.
Johnson, G. A.
1978   Information sources and the development of decision-making organizations. In *Social Archaeology: Beyond Subsistence and Dating* (C. Redman, M. Berman, E. Curtin, W. Langhorne, N. Versaggi, and J. Wanser, eds.), pp. 87–112. New York: Academic Press.
1982   Organizational structure and scalar stress. In *Theory and Explanation in Archaeology* (C. Renfrew, M. J. Rowlands, and B. A. Segraves, eds.), pp. 389–421. New York: Academic Press.
Johnson, J.
1986   Amorphous core technologies in the Midsouth. *Midcontinental Journal of Archaeology* 2:136–151.
Jolly, C. J.
1970   The seed-eaters: a new model of hominid differentiation based on a baboon analogy. *Man* 5:5–26.
Jones, P. R.
1979   The effects of raw materials on biface manufacture. *Science* 204:831–836.
1980   Experimental implement manufacture and use: a case study from Olduvai Gorge, Tanzania. In *The Emergence of Man* (J. Z. Young, E. M. Jope, and K. P. Oakley, eds.), pp. 189–196. London: Routledge.
Jordá, F.
1955   *El Solutrense en España y sus Problemas.* Oviedo: Diputación Provincial.
1957   *La Préhistoire de la région Cantabrique.* Oviedo: Diputación Provincial.
1958   *Avance al Estudio de la Cueva de La Lloseta (Ardines, Ribadesella, Asturias).* Oviedo: Diputación Provincial.
1959   Revisión de la cronología del Asturiense. *Actas de Vᵒ Congreso Nacional de Arqueología,* pp. 63–66. Zaragoza: Universidad de Zaragoza.
Julien, M.
1982   *Les Harpons Magdaleniens.* Paris: Editions du CNRS.
Kafafi, Z.
1987   The pottery Neolithic in Jordan in connection with other Near Eastern regions. In *Studies in the History and Archaeology of Jordan III* (A. Hadidi, ed.), pp. 33–39. London: Routledge and Kegan Paul.

Kamermans, H., S. H. Loving, and A. Voorrips
  1985   Changing patterns of the prehistoric land use in the Agro Pontino.
          In *Papers in Italian Archaeology IV* (C. Malone and S. Stoddart, eds.),
          pp. 53–68. Oxford: BAR International Series S-243.
Kaufman, D.
  1986   A reconsideration of adaptive change in the Levantine Epipaleo-
          lithic. In *The End of the Paleolithic in the Old World* (L. G. Straus, ed.),
          pp. 117–127. Oxford: BAR International Series S-284.
  1987   Excavations at the geometric Kebaran site of Neve David, Israel.
          Quärtar 37/38:189–199.
  1989   Observations on the geometric Kebaran: a view from Neve David. In
          Investigations in South Levantine Prehistory (O. Bar-Yosef and B. Van-
          dermeersch, eds.), pp. 275–286. Oxford: BAR International Series
          S-487.
  n.d.   The Geometric Kebaran site of Neve David. In *Contribution à l'étude
          de l'évolution de l'homme au Sud Levant: anthropologie, préhistoire, paléo-
          environnement* (B. Vandermersch and O. Bar-Yosef, eds.). Oxford:
          BAR International Series. (in press)
Keegan, W., and J. Diamond
  1987   Colonization of islands by humans: a biogeographical perspective.
          In *Advances in Archaeological Method and Theory, Vol. 10* (M. Schiffer,
          ed.), pp. 49–82. New York: Academic Press.
Keeley, L. H.
  1982   Hafting and retooling: effects on the archaeological record. *American
          Antiquity* 47:798–809.
Kelly, R.
  1983   Hunter-gatherer mobility strategies. *Journal of Anthropological Re-
          search* 39:277–306.
  1988   The three sides of a biface. *American Antiquity* 53:717–734.
Kelly, R., and L. Todd
  1988   Coming into the country: early paleoindian hunting and mobility.
          American Antiquity 53:231–244.
Kenyon, K.
  1957   *Digging Up Jericho.* London: Ernest Benn.
  1981   *Excavations at Jericho, Vol. 3* (T. A. Holland, ed.). London: British
          School of Archaeology in Jerusalem.
Kirch, P.
  1980   The archaeological study of adaptation: theoretical and method-
          ological issues. In *Advances in Archaeological Method and Theory, Vol. 3*
          (M. Schiffer, ed.), pp. 101–157. New York: Academic Press.
Kirkbride, D.
  1968   Beidha: early Neolithic village life south of the Dead Sea. *Antiquity*
          42:263–274.
Kitchener, R., ed.
  1988   *The World View of Contemporary Physics.* Albany: SUNY Press.
Klein, Richard G.
  1973   *Ice-Age Hunters of the Ukraine.* Chicago: University of Chicago Press.
  1977   The ecology of early man in southern Africa. *Science* 197:115–126.
  1979   Stone age exploitation of animals in southern Africa. *American Scien-
          tist* 67:151–160.

1981   Stone age predation on small African bovids. *South African Archae-ological Bulletin* 36:55–65.

1986   Review of *Faunal Remains from the Klasies River Mouth* (Binford). *American Anthropologist* 88:494–495.

1987   Reconstructing how early people exploited animals: problems and prospects. In *Evolution of Human Hunting* (M. H. Nitecki and D. V. Nitecki, eds.), pp. 11–45. New York: Plenum Press.

Kleindienst, M. R.

1962   Components of the East African Acheulian assemblage: an analytical approach. In *Actes du IVᵉ Congrès Panafricain de Préhistoire et de l'Etude du Quaternaire. Section III* (G. Mortlemans and J. Nenquin, eds.), pp. 81–112. Tervuren, Belgium: Musée Royal de l'Afrique Centrale.

Klima, B.

1962   The first ground-plan of an Upper Paleolithic loess settlement in middle Europe and its meaning. In *Courses Toward Urban Life: Archaeological Considerations of Some Cultural Alternates* (R. J. Braidwood and G. R. Willey, eds.), pp. 193–210. Chicago: Aldine Publishing Company.

Kohl, P.

1981   Materialist approaches in prehistory. *Annual Review of Anthropology* 10:89–118.

Kozlowski, J. K.

1988   Transition from Middle to Early Upper Paleolithic in central Europe and the Balkans. In *The Early Upper Paleolithic: Evidence from Europe and the Near East* (J. Hoffecker and C. Wolf, eds.), pp. 193–235. Oxford: BAR International Series S-437.

Kristiansen, K.

1988   The black and the red: Shanks and Tilley's programme for a radical archaeology. *Antiquity* 62:473–482.

Kroeber, A. L.

1934   Uto-Aztecan languages of Mexico. *Ibero-Americana* 8:23–37.

1939   *Cultural and Natural Areas of Native North America.* Berkeley: University of California Publications in American Archaeology and Ethnology No. 38.

Kuhn, S. L.

1987   Artifact use intensity and raw material transport in the Mousterian of west-central Italy. Paper presented at the 52nd Annual Meetings of the Society for American Archaeology. Toronto.

1989a   Projectile weapons and investment in food procurement technology in the Eurasian Middle Paleolithic. *American Journal of Physical Anthropology* 78:252. (abstract)

1989b   Hunter-gatherer foraging organization and strategies of artifact re-placement and discard. In *Experiments in Lithic Technology* (D. Amick and R. Mauldin, eds.), pp. 33–47. Oxford: BAR International Series.

1990   *Diversity Within Uniformity: Tool Manufacture and Use in the "Pontinian" Mousterian of Latium (Italy).* Ph.D. dissertation. University of New Mexico. Ann Arbor: University Microfilms.

Kuhn, S. L., and M. C. Stiner

n.d.   Bones and stones: foraging practices, land use and technology in the Italian Mousterian. In *The Organization of Land and Space Use, and*

Technology (L. Binford et al., eds.). Albuquerque: University of New Mexico Press. (in press)

Kuhn, T. S.
1962   *The Structure of Scientific Revolutions.* Chicago: University of Chicago Press.
1970a   *The Structure of Scientific Revolutions* (2nd ed.). Chicago: University of Chicago Press.
1970b   Reflections on my critics. In *Criticism and the Growth of Knowledge* (I. Lakatos and A. Musgrave, eds.), pp. 231–278. Cambridge: Cambridge University Press.
1970c   Logic of discovery or psychology of research? In *Criticism and the Growth of Knowledge* (I. Lakatos and A. Musgrave, eds.), pp. 1–22. Cambridge: Cambridge University Press.
1974   Second thoughts on paradigms. In *The Structure of Scientific Theories* (F. Suppé, ed.), pp. 459–482. Urbana: University of Illinois Press.
1977   *The Essential Tension.* Chicago: University of Chicago Press.

Kurtén, B.
1971   *The Age of Mammals.* London: Weidenfeld and Nicolson.
1976   *The Cave Bear Story.* New York: Columbia University Press.

Kuss, S.
1973   Die Pleistozanen Saugetierfaunen der Ostmediterranean Inseln. Ihr Alter und Ihre Herkunft. *Rer. Naturf. Ges., Freiburg i. Br.* 63:49–71.

Laj Pannocchia, F.
1950   L'Industria Pontiniana della Grotta di S. Agostino (Gaeta). *Rivista di Scienze Preistoriche* 5:67–86.

Lamberg-Karlovsky, C. C., ed.
1989   *Archaeological Thought in America.* Cambridge: Cambridge University Press.

Lanfranchi, F.
1967   La grotte sépulcrale de Curacchiaghiu (Levie, Corse). *Bulletin de la Société Préhistorique Française* 64:587–612.
1974   Le néolithique ancien Mediterranéen, facies Curracchiaghiu, à Levie. *Cahiers Corsica* 43:39–48.

Lanfranchi, F., and M.-C. Weiss
1973   *La Civilisation des Corses: les origines.* Ajaccio: Cyrnos et Mediterranée.
1977   Araguina-Sennola, dix années de fouilles préhistoriques à Bonifacio. *Archaeologie Corsa* No. 2. Ajaccio.

Lanzinger, M.
1984   Risultati preliminari delle ricerche nel sito aurignaziano del Campon di Monte Avena (Alpi Feltine). *Rivista Scienze Preistoriche* 39:287–299.
1985   Ricerche nei siti mesolitici della cresta di Siusi (auf der Schneide, siti XV e XVI dell'Alpe di Siusi) nelle Dolomiti. Considerazioni sul significato funzionale espresso dalle industrie mesolithiche della Regione. *Preistoria Alpina* 21:33–48.

Laplace, G.
1959   Le problème des Périgordiens I et II et l'hypothèse du Synthétotype. *Bulletin de la Société Préhistorique Française* 56:168–169.
1964   Essai de typologie systématique. *Annali Università di Ferrara* n.s. 15:1–86.

1966   Récherches sur l'origine et l'évolution des complexes leptothiques. *École Française de Rome. Mélanges d'Archéologie et d'Histoire No. 4.* Paris: De Boccard.

1968   Récherches de typologie analytique, 1968. *Origini* 2:7–64.

Larick, R.

1985   Spears, style and time among Maa-speaking pastoralists. *Journal of Anthropological Archaeology* 4:221–241.

Lartet, E.

1861   Nouvelles recherches sur la coexistence de l'homme et des grands mammifères fossiles. *Annales des Sciences Naturelles (Zoologie)* 15:177–253.

Lartet, E., and H. Christy

1865–   *Reliquiae Aquitanicae: Being Contributions to the Archaeology and Pa-*
75   *laeontology of Perigord and the Adjoining Provinces of Southern France.* London and Edinburgh: T. Rupert Jones.

Lavallé, D.

1987   Nous, les élevés de Leroi-Gourhan qui travaillons au loin. *Bulletin de la Société Préhistorique Française* 84:415–416.

Laville, H.

1975   Climatologie et chronologie du paléolithique en Périgord: études Quaternaires. *Editions du Laboratoire de Paléontologie Humaine et de Préhistoire, No. 4.* Provence: Université de Provence.

Laville, H., J.-P. Rigaud, and J. Sackett

1980   *Rock Shelters of the Perigord: Geological Stratigraphy and Archaeological Succession.* New York: Academic Press.

Leacock, E.

1982   Relations of production in band society. In *Politics and History in Band Society* (E. Leacock and R. Lee, eds.), pp. 159–170. Cambridge: Cambridge University Press.

Leakey, M.

1971   *Olduvai Gorge, Vol. 3: Excavations in Beds I and II, 1960–63.* Cambridge: Cambridge University Press.

1975   Cultural patterns in the Olduvai sequence. In *After the Australopithecines* (K. Butzer and G. Isaac, eds.), pp. 477–493. The Hague: Mouton.

LeBrun, A.

1974   Cap Andreas Kastros: rapport préliminaire. *Report of the Department of Antiquities, Cyprus* 1974:1–23.

1981   *Un site Néolithique Préceramique en Chypre: Cap Andreas-Kastros,* Paris: ADPF.

1984   *Fouilles récentes à Khirokitia (Chypre), 1977–1981.* Paris: Editions de la Recherche sur les Civilisations, ADPF, Mémoire No. 41.

LeBrun, A., S. Cluzan, S. Davis, J. Hansen, and J. Renault-Miskovsky

1987   Le neolithique préceramique de Chypre. *L'Anthropologie* 91:283–316.

Lechevallier, M.

1978   *Abou Gosh et Beisamoun, deux gisements du VII millénaire avant l'ère chrêtienne en Israël.* Mémoires et Travaux du Centre de Recherches Préhistoriques Françaises de Jerusalem No. 2. Paris: Association Paléorient.

Lee, R. B.
  1979   *The !Kung San: Men, Women and Work in a Foraging Society.* Cambridge: Cambridge University Press.
Lee, R. B., and I. DeVore, eds.
  1968a *Man the Hunter.* Chicago: Aldine.
Lee, R. B. and I. DeVore
  1968b Problems in the study of hunters and gatherers. In *Man the Hunter* (R. B. Lee and I. DeVore, eds.), pp. 3–12. Chicago: Aldine Publishing.
Legge, A. J.
  1972   Prehistoric exploitation of gazelle in Palestine. In *Papers in Economic Prehistory* (E. S. Higgs, ed.), pp. 119–124. Cambridge: Cambridge University Press.
Lehavey, Y.
  1974   Excavations at Neolithic Dhali-Agridhi, Part 1: excavation report. In *American Expedition to Idalion, Cyprus, First Preliminary Report: Seasons 1971 and 1972* (E. Stager, A. Walker, and G. Wright, eds.), pp. 95–102. Philadelphia: American Schools of Oriental Research.
Lemonnier, P.
  1983   L'étude des systèmes techniques, une urgence en technologie culturelle. *Techniques et Culture* 1:11–34.
Lenoir, M.
  1975   Style et technologies lithique. *Bulletin de la Société Préhistorique Française* 72:46–49.
  1988   Le Magdalénien ancien en Gironde: conditions de gisement, variabilité typologique et technique. In *Upper Pleistocene Prehistory of Western Eurasia* (H. L. Dibble and A. Montet-White, eds.), pp. 397–410. Philadelphia: University of Pennsylvania Museum Monograph No. 54.
Leonard, R., and G. Jones
  1987   Elements of an inclusive evolutionary model for archaeology. *Journal of Anthropological Archaeology* 6:199–219.
Leone, M.
  1982   Some opinions about recovering mind. *American Antiquity* 47:742–760.
Leone, M. P., P. B. Potter, Jr., and P. A. Schackel
  1987   Toward a critical archaeology. *Current Anthropology* 28:282–302.
Leroi-Gourhan, A.
  1950   *Fouilles préhistoriques, techniques et méthodes.* Paris: A. and J. Picard.
  1964a *Les Réligions de la préhistoire.* Paris: Presses Universitaires de France.
  1964b *Le Geste et la parole I: technique et langage.* Paris: Albin Michel.
  1965   *Treasures of Prehistoric Art.* New York: Abrams.
  1968   The evolution of paleolithic art. *Scientific American* 209:58–74.
Leroi-Gourhan, A., and Audouze, F.
  1981   France: a continental insularity. *World Archaeology* 13:170–189.
Leroi-Gourhan, A., and M. Brezillon
  1966   L'habitation magdalénienne no. 1 de Pincevent près Montereau (Seine et Marne). *Gallia Préhistoire* 9:1–385.
  1972   *Fouilles de Pincevent: essai d'analyse ethnographique d'un habitat magdalénien.* Paris: CNRS.

1983   *Fouilles de Pincevent: essai d'analyse ethnographique d'un habitat magdalé-nien.* VIIème Supplement à *Gallia Préhistoire.* Paris: CNRS.
Leroi-Gourhan, Arl.
1981   Le Levant à la fin du Pleistocène et à l'Holocène d'après la pal-ynologie. In *Préhistoire du Levant* (J. Cauvin and P. Sanlaville, eds.), pp. 107–110. Paris: Editions du CNRS.
1986   The palynology of La Riera Cave. In *La Riera Cave: Stone Age Hunter-Gatherer Adaptations in Northern Spain* (L. G. Straus and G. Clark, eds.), pp. 59–64. Tempe: Arizona State University Anthropological Research Papers No. 36.
Lévêque, F., and J.-C. Miskovsky
1983   Le Castelperronien dans son environnement géologique. Essai de synthèse à partir de l'étude lithostratigraphique du remplissage de la grotte de la Grande Roche de la Plématrie (Quinçay, Vienne) et d'autres depôts actuellement mis au jour. *L'Anthropologie* 87:369–391.
Lévêque, F., and B. Vandermeersch
1980   Découverte de restes humains dans un niveau castelperronien à Saint-Césaire (Charente-Maritime). *Comptes Rendus de l'Académie des Sciences de Paris, Series 2* 291:187–189.
1981   Le néandertalien de Saint-Césaire. *La Recherche* 12:242–44.
Levinson, D., and M. J. Malone
1980   *Toward Explaining Human Culture.* New Haven, CN: HRAF Press.
Lewin, R.
1987   *Bones of Contention: Controversies in the Search for Human Origins.* New York: Simon and Schuster.
1988a New views emerge on hunters and gatherers. *Science* 240: 1146–1148.
1988b Conflict over DNA clock results. *Science* 241:1598–1600.
1988c DNA clock conflict continues. *Science* 241:1756–1759.
Lewontin, R. C.
1974   *The Genetic Basis of Evolutionary Change.* New York: Columbia Univer-sity Press.
Lindly, J.
1988   Hominid versus carnivore activity at Middle and Upper Paleolithic cave sites in eastern Spain. *Munibe* 40:45–70.
Lindly, J., and G. A. Clark
1987   A preliminary lithic analysis of the Mousterian site of 'Ain Difla in the Wadi Ali, west-central Jordan. *Proceedings of the Prehistoric Society* 53:279–292.
1989   On the emergence of modern humans. *Current Anthropology* 31:59–66.
1990   Symbolism and modern human origins. *Current Anthropology* 31: 233–262.
Lovejoy, C. O.
1981   The origin of man. *Science* 211:341–350.
Lumley, H. de
1969   Le paléolithique inférieur et moyen du Midi méditerranéen dans son cadre géologique. *Gallia Préhistoire, V. suppl.* Paris: Editions du CNRS.

Lumley, H. de, ed.
  1976   *La Préhistoire française. Tômes I et II. Les Civilizations Paléolithiques et Mésolithiques de la France.* Paris: Editions du CNRS.
Lupo, K.
  1990   Cutmarks and Carcass Acquisition Strategies: a Case Study from the Hadza of Eastern Tanzania. Paper presented at the 6th International Conference on Archaeozoology, May 21–25, 1990. Washington, DC.
Lurie, R.
  1989   Lithic technology and mobility strategies: the Koster Middle Archaic. In *Time, Energy and Stone Tools* (R. Torrence, ed.), pp. 46–56. Cambridge: Cambridge University Press.
Lyman, R. L.
  1987   Archaeofaunas and butchery studies: a taphonomic perspective. In *Advances in Archaeological Method and Theory, Vol. 10* (M. Schiffer, ed.), pp. 249–337. New York Academic Press.
Lynch, T.
  1966   The "Lower Perigordian" in French archaeology. *Proceedings of the Prehistoric Society* 32:156–198.
MacArthur, R. H.
  1968   The theory of the niche. In *Niche Theory and Application (1975)* (R. H. Whittaker and S. A. Levin, eds.), pp. 400–417. Stroudsburg, PA: Dowden, Hutchinson and Ross.
  1972   *Geographical Ecology.* New York: Harper and Row.
MacArthur, R. H., and R. Levins
  1967   The limiting similarity, convergence, and divergence of coexisting species. *American Naturalist* 101:377–385.
MacArthur, R. H., and E. Wilson
  1967   *The Theory of Island Biogeography.* Princeton, NJ: Princeton University Press.
MacDonald, B., G. Rollefson, E. Banning, B. Byrd, and C. d'Annibale
  1983   The Wadi el-Hasa Survey 1982: a preliminary report. *Annual of the Department of Antiquities of Jordan* 27:311–323.
MacDonald, B., G. Rollefson, and D. Roller
  1982   The Wadi el-Hasa Survey 1981: a preliminary report. *Annual of the Department of Antiquities of Jordan* 26:117–132.
MacDonald, B., ed.
  1988   *The Wadi Hasa Archaeological Survey (1979–1983), West-Central Jordan.* Waterloo: Wilfrid Laurier University Press.
Madden, M.
  1983   Social network systems among hunter-gatherers considered within southern Norway. In *Hunter-Gatherer Economy in Prehistory* (G. Bailey, ed.), pp. 191–200. Cambridge: Cambridge University Press.
Mallegni, F., C. Pitti, and A. M. Radmilli
  1984   Castel di Guido, Lazio. *I Primi Abitanti d'Europa.* Guidebook to the exhibition, pp. 176–181. Rome: De Luca.
Mandel, R.
  1987   Preliminary report of geomorphologic investigations at Akrotiri-Aetokremnos, Cyprus, 1987. Manuscript on file, Quaternary Sciences Center, Desert Research Institute, University of Nevada System, Reno.

Manhire, A., J. Parkington, and T. Robey
  1984   Stone tools and sandveldt settlement. In *Frontiers: Southern Africa Archaeology Today* (M. Hall, G. Avery, D. Avery, M. Wilson, and A. Humphreys, eds.), pp. 11–126. Oxford: BAR International Series S-207.
Marks, A. E.
  1973   The Harif point: a new tool type from the Terminal Epipaleolithic of the Central Negev, Israel. *Paléorient* 1:99–102.
  1976a Introduction. In *Prehistory and Paleoenvironments in the Central Negev, Israel, Vol. I* (A. Marks, ed.), pp. iv–vii. Dallas, TX: Southern Methodist University Press.
  1977a The Epipaleolithic of the central Negev: current status. In *Eretz-Israel No. 13* (Moshe Stekelis Memorial Volume) (B. Arensburg and O. Bar-Yosef, eds.), pp. 229–239. Jerusalem.
  1981a The Middle Paleolithic of the Negev, Israel. In *Préhistoire du Levant* (J. Cauvin and P. Sanlaville, eds.), pp. 287–298. Paris: Editions du CNRS.
  1981b The Upper Paleolithic of the Negev. In *Préhistoire du Levant* (J. Cauvin and P. Sanlaville, eds.), pp. 343–352. Paris: Editions du CNRS.
  1983a The Middle to Upper Paleolithic transition in the Levant. In *Advances in World Archaeology No. 2* (F. Wendorf and A. Close, eds.), pp. 51–98. New York: Academic Press.
  1989   Early Mousterian settlement patterns in the central Negev, Israel: their social and economic implications. In *L'Homme de Néandertal 6: Subsistence* (M. Patou and L. Freeman, eds.), pp. 115–126. Liège: ERAUL No. 33.
Marks, A. E., ed.
  1976b *Prehistory and Paleoenvironments in the Central Negev, Israel Vol. I.* Dallas, TX: Southern Methodist University Press.
  1977b *Prehistory and Paleoenvironments in the Central Negev, Israel Vol. II.* Dallas, TX: Southern Methodist University Press.
  1983b *Prehistory and Paleoenvironments in the Central Negev, Israel Vol. III.* Dallas, TX: Southern Methodist University Press.
Marks, A. E., and C. R. Ferring
  1988   The early Upper Paleolithic in the Levant. In *The Early Upper Paleolithic: Evidence from Europe and the Near East* (J. Hoffecker and C. Wolf, eds.), pp. 43–72. Oxford: BAR International Series S-437.
Marks, A. E., and D. A. Freidel
  1977   Prehistoric settlement patterns in the Avdat/Aqev area. In *Prehistory and Paleoenvironments in the Central Negev, Israel, Vol. II* (A. E. Marks, ed.), pp. 131–158. Dallas, TX: Southern Methodist University Press.
Marks, A. E., and P. A. Larson, Jr.
  1977   Test excavations at the Natufian site of Rosh Horesha. In *Prehistory and Paleoenvironments in the Central Negev, Israel, Vol. II*, (A. E. Marks, ed.), pp. 191–232. Dallas, TX: Southern Methodist University Press.
Marks, A. E., and A. H. Simmons
  1977   The Negev Kebaran of the Har Harif. In *Prehistory and Paleoenvironments in the Central Negev, Israel, Vol. II* (A. E. Marks, ed.), pp. 233–269. Dallas, TX: Southern Methodist University Press.

Marks, A. E., and P. Volkman
1986　The Mousterian of Ksar Akil, levels XXVIA through XXVIIIB. *Paléorient* 12:5–20.

Marshack, A.
1988a　The neanderthals and their human capacity for symbolic thought: cognitive and problem-solving aspects of Mousterian symbol. In *L'Homme de Néandertal 5: La Pensée* (O. Bar-Yosef, ed.), pp. 57–92. Liège: ERAUL No. 32.
1988b　La pensée symbolique et l'art. *Dossiers d'Histoire et d'Archéologie* 124:80–90, 97, 98.
1989　Evolution of the human capacity: the symbolic evidence. *Yearbook of Physical Anthropology* 32:56–85.

Martin, G.
1978　Ein Gev III, 1978. *Israel Exploration Journal* 28:262–263.

Martin, J.
1983　Optimal foraging theory: a review of some models and their applications. *American Anthropologist* 85:612–629.

Martin, M. K.
1974　*The Foraging Adaptation: Uniformity or Diversity?* Boston: Addison-Wesley Module in Anthropology No. 56.

Martin, P. S.
1971　The revolution in archaeology. *American Antiquity* 36:1–8.
1984　Prehistoric overkill: the global model. In *Quaternary Extinctions: A Prehistoric Revolution* (P. Martin and R. Klein, ed.), pp. 354–403. Tucson: University of Arizona Press.

Martin, P., and R. Klein, eds.
1984　*Quaternary Extinctions: A Prehistoric Revolution.* Tucson: University of Arizona Press.

Martini, F.
1978　L'Epigravettiano di Grotta della Cala a Marina di Camerota (Salerno). I: l'industria litica ed ossea e la cronologia assoluta dell'Epigravettiano evoluto. *Rivista Scienze Preistoriche* 33:3–108.
1981　L'Epigravettiano di Grotta della Cala a Marina di Camerota (Salerno). II: l'industria litica e la cronologia assoluta dell'Epigravettiano finale. *Rivista Scienze Preistoriche* 36:57–125.

Martini, F., and G. Pitzalis
1981　Il paleolitico in Sardegna. In *Ichnussa. La Sardegna dalle Origini all'Eta Classica.* Milano.
1982　Il Paleolitico Inferiore in Sardegna. *Atti degli 23 Riunione Scienzi Istituto Italiano Preistorici Protostorici* pp. 249–258. Rome.

Masterman, H.
1970　The nature of the paradigm. In *Criticism and the Growth of Knowledge* (I. Lakatos and A. Musgrave, eds.), pp. 59–90. Cambridge: Cambridge University Press.

Matson, R. G.
1990　Dietary Change in the Upland Southwest: the Coming of Agriculture. Paper presented at the 55th Annual Meeting of the Society for American Archaeology, Las Vegas.

Mauss, M. (in collaboration with H. Beuchat)
1904–　Essai sur les variations saisonnières des sociétés Esquimaux. Étude
05　de morphologie sociale. *L'Année Sociologique* 9:39–132.

May, R. M., and R. H. MacArthur
  1972   Niche overlap as a function of environmental variability. *Proceedings of the National Academy of Science* 69:1109–1113.
Mayr, E.
  1961   Cause and effect in biology. *Science* 134: 1501–1506.
Mazar, A.
  1985   The emergence of the Philistine culture. *Israel Exploration Journal* 35:95–107.
  1986   No more "Philistine Culture"? Response to S. Bonimovitz. *Bulletin of the Israel Association of Archaeologists* 1:22–27 (in Hebrew).
McNicoll, A. et al.
  1984   Preliminary report on the University of Sydney's fifth season of excavation at Pella in Jordan, *Annual of the Department of Antiquities of Jordan* 28:55–86.
McPherron, S., and H. Dibble
  1988   Hardware and software complexity in computerizing archaeological projects. *Advances in Computer Archaeology* 4:25–40.
Meignen, L.
  1988   Le Paléolithique moyen du Levant: synthèse. *Paléorient* 14:168–176.
Meignen, L., and O. Bar-Yosef
  1988   Variabilité technologique au Prôche Orient: l'exemple de Kébara. In *L'Homme de Néandertal 4: La Technique* (M. Otte, ed.), pp. 81–95. Liège: ERAUL No. 31.
Meignen, L., O. Bar-Yosef, and P. Goldberg
  1989   Les structures de combustion moustériennes de la grotte de Kébara (Mont Carmel, Israël). In *Nature et fonction des foyers préhistoriques* (J. Olive and Y. Taborin, eds.), pp. 141–146. Neours: Mémoires du Musée de Préhistoire d'Ile de France No. 2.
Mellars, P.
  1969   The chronology of Mousterian industries in the Périgord region of south-west France. *Proceedings of the Prehistoric Society* 35:134–171.
  1973   The character of the Middle-Upper Paleolithic transition in south-western France. In *The Explanation of Culture Change* (C. Renfrew, ed.), pp. 225–276. Pittsburgh: University of Pittsburgh Press.
  1985   The ecological basis of social complexity in the Upper Paleolithic of southwestern France. In *Prehistoric Hunter-Gatherers: The Emergence of Cultural Complexity* (T. D. Price and J. A. Brown, eds.), pp. 271–298. New York: Academic Press.
  1986   A new chronology for the French Mousterian period. *Nature* 332: 410–411.
  1988   The chronology of the south-west French Mousterian: a review of the current debate. In *L'Homme de Néandertal 4: La Technique* (L. Binford and J.-Ph. Rigaud, eds.), pp. 97–120. Liège: ERAUL No. 31.
  1989   Major issues in the emergence of modern humans. *Current Anthropology* 30:349–385.
Mellars, P., H. M. Bricker, J. A. J. Gowlett, and R. E. M. Hedges
  1987   Radiocarbon accelerator dating of French Upper Paleolithic sites. *Current Anthropology* 28:128–133.
Mellars, P., and C. B. Stringer, eds.
  1989   *The Human Revolution: Biological and Behavioral Perspectives on the*

Origins of Modern Humans. Edinburgh: University of Edinburgh Press.

n.d.   *The Emergence of Modern Humans.* Edinburgh: University of Edinburgh Press.

Mellaart, J.
1975   *The Neolithic of the Near East.* London: Thames and Hudson.

Meltzer, D.
1979   Paradigms and the nature of change in American archaeology. *American Antiquity* 44:644–657.
1990   Review: *Social Theory and Archaeology* (Shanks and Tilley). *American Antiquity* 55:186, 187.

Mercier, P.
1966   *Histoire de l'Anthropologie.* Paris: Le Sociologue No. 5.

Meyers, A.
1987   All shot to pieces? Inter-assemblage variability, lithic analysis and Mesolithic assemblage types: some preliminary observations. In *Lithic Analysis in Later British Prehistory* (A. Brown and M. Edmonds, eds.), pp. 137–153. Oxford: BAR International Series S-162.
n.d.   Reliable and maintainable technological strategies in the Mesolithic of mainland Britain. In *Time, Energy and Stone Tools* (R. Torrence, ed.). Cambridge: Cambridge University Press. (in press)

Mezzena, F., and A. Palma di Cesnola
1967   L'Epigravettiano della Grotta Paglicci nel Gargano (Scavi F. Zorzi 1961–63). *Rivista Scienze Preistoriche* 22:23–156.
1972   Scoperta di una sepoltura gravettiana nella Grotta Paglicci (Rignano Garganico). *Rivista Scienze Preistoriche* 27:27–50.

Miller, W.
1982   Uto-Aztecan languages. In *Handbook of North American Indians, Vol. 10: Southwest* (A. Ortiz, ed.). Washington, DC: Smithsonian Institution Press.

Minnis, P.
1985   Domesticating plants and people in the Greater American Southwest. In *Prehistoric Food Production in North America* (R. I. Ford, ed.), pp. 309–340. Ann Arbor: Museum of Anthropology, University of Michigan, Anthropological Papers No. 75.
1989   Prehistoric diet in the northern Southwest: macroplant remains from Four Corners feces. *American Antiquity* 54:543–563.

Mithen, S.
1988   Looking and learning: Upper Paleolithic art and information gathering. *World Archaeology* 19:297–327.
1989   Evolutionary theory and post-processual archaeology. *Antiquity* 63:483–494.

Moore, A. M. T.
1982   Agricultural origins in the Near East—a model for the 1980s. *World Archaeology* 14:224–236.
1983   The first farmers in the Levant. In *The Hilly Flanks and Beyond* (T. Young, P. Smith, and P. Mortensen, eds.), pp. 91–112. Chicago: Oriental Institute Studies in Ancient Oriental Civilization No. 36.
1985   The development of Neolithic societies in the Near East. In *Advances in World Archeology, Vol. 6* (F. Wendorf and A. E. Close, eds.), pp. 1–70. New York: Academic Press.

Moore, A. M. T., G. C. Hillman, and A. J. Legge
  1975   The excavation of Tell Abu Hureyra in Syria: a preliminary report. *Proceedings of the Prehistoric Society* 41:50–73.
Morala, A.
  1984   *Périgordien et Aurignacien en Haut-Agenais: études des ensembles lithiques.* Archives d'Ecologie Préhistorique. Toulouse: Ecole des Hautes Etudes en Sciences Sociales.
Morgan, C.
  1973   Archaeology and explanation. *World Archaeology* 4:259–276.
  1974   Explanation and scientific archaeology. *World Archaeology* 6: 133–137.
Morrison, I., and T. Watkins
  1974   Kataliontas-Kourvellos: a survey of an aceramic neolithic site and its environs in Cyprus. *Palestine Exploration Quarterly* 109:67–75.
Mortillet, G. de
  1867   Promenades préhistoriques à l'Exposition Universelle. *Matériaux pour l'Histoire Positive et Philosophique de l'Homme* 3:181–368.
  1873   Classification des diverses périodes de l'Age de la Pierre. *Comptes Rendus de la VIe Congrès Internationale d'Anthropologie et d'Archéologie Préhistorique*, Brussels (1872), pp. 432–456.
  1883   *Le Préhistorique. Antiquité de l'homme.* Paris: Reinwald.
Mourer-Chauviré, C.
  1989   Preliminary report on the Akrotiri birds. Université Claude-Bernard, Lyon. Letter report on file, Quaternary Sciences Center, Desert Research Institute, Reno.
Movius, H. L., Jr.
  1953   Old world prehistory: paleolithic. In *Anthropology Today* (A. L. Kroeber, ed.), pp. 163–192. Chicago: University of Chicago Press.
  1968   Note on the history of the discovery and recognition of the function of burins as tools. In *La Préhistoire* (F. Bordes and D. de Sonneville-Bordes, eds.), pp. 311–318. Paris: Editions du CNRS.
Muheisen, M.
  1985   L'Epipaléolithique dans le gisement de Kharraneh IV. *Paléorient* 11:149–160.
Mulvaney, D.
  1975   *The Prehistory of Australia.* Melbourne: Pelican.
Muñoz Salvatierra, M.
  1976   *Microlitismo Geométrico en el País Vasco.* Bilbao: Universidad de Deusto, Cuadernos de Arqueología No. 4.
Murdock, G. P.
  1949   *Social Structure.* New York: Macmillan.
  1967   *Ethnographic Atlas.* Pittsburgh, PA: University of Pittsburgh Press.
Mussi, M.
  1976   The Natufian of Palestine: the beginnings of agriculture in paleoethnological perspective. *Origini* 10:89–107.
Naroll, R. S.
  1962   Floor area and settlement population. *American Antiquity* 27:587–588.
Nei, M.
  1985   Human evolution at the molecular level. In *Population Genetics and*

Molecular Evolution (K. Aoki and T. Ohta, eds.), pp. 41–64. Tokyo: Japan Science Society Press.

1987 *Molecular Evolutionary Genetics.* New York: Columbia University Press.

Neitzel, J.
1985 *Rethinking Hohokam: Issues of Temporal and Spatial Variability in the Desert Southwest.* Ph.D. Dissertation, Arizona State University. Ann Arbor: University Microfilms.

Nelson, E.
1899 The Eskimo about Bering Strait. *Eighteenth Annual Report of Bureau of American Ethnology, 1887–1897.* Washington: U.S. Government Printing Office.

Neuville, R.
1934 La préhistoire de Palestine. *Revue Biblique* 43:237–259.
1951 *Le Paléolithique et le Mésolithique du désert de Judée.* Archives de l'Institut de Paléontologie Humaine No. 24. Paris: Masson et Cie.

Newcomer, M.
1971 Some quantitative experiments in handaxe manufacture. *World Archaeology* 3:85–94.
1972 *Analysis of a Series of Burins from Ksar Akil (Lebanon).* Ph.D. Dissertation. Institute of Archaeology, University of London.

Nissen, H. J.
1988 *The Early History of the Ancient Near East 9000–2000* B.C. Chicago: University of Chicago Press.

Nitecki, M., and D. Nitecki, eds.
1987 *The Evolution of Human Hunting.* New York: Plenum.

Noy, T.
1970 Prehistoric sites in the Halutza Dunes. *Mitekufat Haeven* 10:1–10 (Hebrew).

Noy, T., A. J. Legge, and E. S. Higgs
1973 Recent excavations at Nahal Oren, Israel. *Proceedings of the Prehistoric Society* 39:75–99.

Noy, T., and T. Schick
1973 Kurnub, a desert Natufian site. *Mitekufat Haeven* 11:6–26. (Hebrew).

Noy, T., J. Schuldenrein, and E. Tchernov
1980 Gilgal: a pre-pottery Neolithic A site in the lower Jordan Valley. *Israel Exploration Journal* 30:63–82.

Oakeshott, M.
1933 *Experience and Its Modes.* London: Cambridge University Press.

Obermaier, H.
1916 *El Hombre Fósil.* Madrid: Comisión de Investigaciones Paleontológicas y Préhistoricas, Memoria No. 9.
1924 *Fossil Man in Spain.* New Haven, CT: Yale University Press.

Olami, Y.
1973 The epipaleolithic site Haifa 1. *Mitekufat Haeven* 11:8–15.
1984 *Prehistoric Carmel.* Jerusalem: Israel Exploration Society.

Olszewski, D. I.
1984 *The Early Occupation at Tell Abu Hureyra in the Context of the Late Epipaleolithic of the Levant.* Ph.D. Dissertation. University of Arizona. Ann Arbor: University Microfilms.

1986a A reassessment of average lunate length as a chronological marker. *Paléorient* 12:39–44.

1986b *The North Syrian Late Epipaleolithic.* Oxford: BAR International Series S-309.

Onoratini, G.
1983 Le Gravettien et sa ligne évolutive dans le sud-est de la France. *Rivista Scienze Preistoriche* 38:127–142.

Orquera, L.
1984 Specialization and the Middle/Upper Paleolithic transition. *Current Anthropology* 25:73–98.

Ortea, J.
1986 The malacology of La Riera cave. In *La Riera Cave: Stone Age Hunter Gatherer Adaptations in Northern Spain* (L. Straus and G. Clark, eds.), pp. 289–298. Tempe: Arizona State University Anthropological Research Papers No. 36.

Ortner, D., ed.
1983 *How Humans Adapt: A Biocultural Odyssey.* Washington, DC: Smithsonian Institution Press.

O'Shea, J.
1981 Social configurations and the archaeological study of mortuary practices: a case study. In *The Archaeology of Death* (R. Chapman, I. Kinnes, and K. Randsborg, eds.), pp. 39–52. Cambridge: Cambridge University Press.

O'Shea, J., and M. Zvelebil
1984 Oleneostrovski mogilnik: reconstructing the social and economic organization of prehistoric foragers in northern Russia. *Journal of Anthropological Archaeology* 3:1–40.

Oswalt, W.
1976 *An Anthropological Analysis of Food-Getting Technology.* New York: John Wiley.

Otte, M., ed.
1988 *l'Homme de Néandertal, Vols. 1–8.* Liège: ERAUL Nos. 28–35.
/89
1989 Relations du Prôche Orient à l'Europe au Paléolithique supérieur. In *People and Culture in Change* (I. Hershkovits, ed.), pp. 397–404. Oxford: BAR International Series S-508.

Palma di Cesnola, A.
1971 Il Gravettiano evoluto della Grotta della Cala a Mariana di Camerota (Salerno). *Rivista Scienze Preistoriche* 26:259–324.

1983 L'Epigravettien évolué et final de la région haute-tyrrhénienne. *Rivista Scienze Preistoriche* 38:301–318.

1987 Panorama del Musteriano italiano. In *I Neandertaliani*, pp. 139–174. Viareggio: Museo Preistorico e Archaeologico "Alberto Carlo Blanc."

Palma di Cesnola, A., and A. Bietti
1983 Le Gravettien et l'Epigravettien ancien en Italie. *Rivista Scienze Preistoriche* 38:181–228.

Palma di Cesnola, A., A. Bietti, and A. Galiberti
1983 L'Epigravettien évolué et final dans les Pouilles. *Rivista Scienze Preistoriche* 38:267–300.

Parry, W., and R. Kelly
1987 Expedient core technology and sedentism. In *The Organization of Core*

Technology (J. Johnson and C. Morrow, eds.), pp. 285–309. Boulder, CO: Westview Press.

Patterson, T.
1989   History and the post-processual archaeologies. *Man* 24:555–566.
1990   Some theoretical tensions within and between the processual and post-processual archaeologies. *Journal of Anthropological Archaeology* 9:189–200.

Peretto, C., and M. Piperno
1984   Introduzione alla problematica del Paleolitico inferiore italiano. *I Primi Abitanti d'Europa*, pp. 101–103. Guidebook to the exhibition. Rome: De Luca.

Pericot García, L.
1942   *La Cueva del Parpalló*. Madrid: Consejo Superior de Investigaciones Científicas.

Perkins, D., and P. Daly
1968   A hunters' village in neolithic Turkey. *Scientific American* 219:96–106.

Perlés, C.
1977   *Préhistoire du feu*. Paris: Masson et Cie.
1979   Des navigateurs méditerranéens il y a 10,000 ans. *La Recherche* 10:82–83.

Perrot, J.
1966   Le Gisement Natoufien de Mallaha (Eynan), Israël. *L'Anthropologie* 70:437–483.
1968   *La Préhistoire Palestinienne*. In *Supplement au Dictionnaire de la Bible* 8:286–446. Paris: Letouzey et Ane.
1974   Mallaha (Eynan), 1975. *Paléorient* 2:485–486.
1983   Terminologie et cadre de la préhistoire recente de Palestine. In *The Hilly Flanks and Beyond* (C. T. Young, P. E. L. Smith, and P. Mortenson, eds.), pp. 11–42. Chicago: Studies in Ancient Oriental Civilization No. 36.
1989   Les variations du mode de sépulture dans le gisement Natoufien de Mallaha (Eynan), Israel. In *Investigations in South Levantine Prehistory* (O. Bar-Yosef and B. Vandermeersch, eds.), pp. 287–296. Oxford: BAR International Series S-497.

Peyrony, D.
1922   Nouvelles observations sur le Moustérian final et l'Aurignacien inférieur. *Association Française pour l'Avancement de la Science* 46:511–514.
1923   *Eléments de préhistoire*. Ussel: Eyboulet. (Fifth edition 1948. Paris: Alfred Costes.)
1932   *Les Gisements préhistoriques de Bourdeilles (Dordogne)*. Paris: Imprimerie Marechal.
1933   Les industries "aurignaciennes" dans le bassin de la Vézère. *Bulletin de la Société Préhistorique Française* 30:543–559.
1935a   Le gisement Castanet, Vallon de Castelmerle, Commune de Sergeac (Dordogne). Aurignacien I et II. *Bulletin de la Société Préhistorique Française* 32:418–443.
1935b   A propos du Périgordien. *l'Anthropologie* 45:489–490.
1936   Le Périgordien et l'Aurignacien. Nouvelles observations. *Bulletin de la Société Préhistorique Française* 33:616–619.

1939   De l'importance de l'étude géologique des gisements. *Revue Anthropologique* 1-3:54–62.

1948   Le Périgordien, l'Aurignacien, et le Solutréen en Eurasie d'après les dernières fouilles. *Bulletin de la Société Préhistorique Française* 45:305–328.

Peyrony, D., and E. Peyrony
   1951   Le Mousterien final et le Périgordien (type Châtelperron) en Périgord. *Bulletin de la Société Historique et Archéologique du Périgord* 78:120–121.

Phillips, J.
   1972   North Africa, the Nile Valley, and the problem of the late paleolithic. *Current Anthropology* 13:587–598.

   1975   Iberomaurusian-related sites in the Nile Valley. In *Problems in Prehistory: North Africa and the Levant* (F. Wendorf and A. Marks, eds.), pp. 171–180. Dallas: SMU Press.

Phillips, J., and E. Mintz
   1977   The Mushabian. In *Prehistoric Investigations in Gebel Maghara. Northern Sinai* (O. Bar-Yosef and J. Phillips, eds.), Qedem 7: Monographs of the Institute of Archaeology. Jerusalem: Hebrew University.

Pianka, E. R.
   1978   *Evolutionary Ecology.* New York: Harper and Row.

Piperno, M.
   1982   Considerazioni e problemi sul Paleolitico Inferiore italiano. *Atti della XXIII Riunione Scientifica dell'Istituto Italiano di Preistoria e Protostoria:* 39–50.

   1984   L'Acheuleano e il Musteriano nel Lazio. *Atti della XXIV Riunione Scientifica dell'Istituto Italiano di Preistoria e Protostoria:* 67–74.

Piperno, M., F. Scali, and A. Tagliacozzo
   1980   Mesolitico e Neolitico alla Grotta dell'Uzzo (Regione Trapani). Primi dati per un'interpretazione paleoeconomica. *Quaternaria* 22:275–300.

Plog, S.
   1980   *Stylistic Variation in Prehistoric Ceramics.* Cambridge: Cambridge University Press.

Popper, K.
   1972   *Objective Knowledge.* New York: Oxford University Press.

   1983   *Realism and the Aim of Science.* Totowa, NJ: Rowman and Littlefield.

Potts, R.
   1982   *Lower Pleistocene Site Formation and Hominid Activities at Olduvai Gorge, Tanzania.* Ph.D. dissertation. Harvard University.

   1984   Hominid hunters? Problems of identifying the earliest hunter/gatherers. In *Hominid Evolution and Community Ecology* (R. Foley, ed.), pp. 129–166. London: Academic Press.

Price, B.
   1982   Cultural materialism: a theoretical review. *American Antiquity* 47: 709–741.

Price, T. D.
   1983   The European mesolithic. *American Antiquity* 48:761–778.

Price, T. D., and J. A. Brown, eds.
   1985   *Prehistoric Hunter-Gatherers: The Emergence of Cultural Complexity.* New York: Academic Press.

Radmilli, A. M.
  1954   Una nuova facies del paleolitico superiore italiano presente in Abruzzo. *Bulletino di Paletnologia Italiana* 64:73–106.
  1974   Gli scavi nella Grotta Polesini a Ponte Lucano di Tivoli e la più antica arte nel Lazio. *Origini*. Florence: Sansoni.
  1977   *Storia dell'Abruzzo dalle Origini all'Età del Bronzo.* Pisa: Giardini.
Rafferty, J. E.
  1985   The archaeological record on sedentariness: recognition, development, and implications. In *Advances in Archaeological Method and Theory, Vol. 8* (M. B. Schiffer, ed.), pp. 113–156. New York: Academic Press.
Rapoport, A.
  1960   *Fights, Games and Decisions.* Ann Arbor: University of Michigan Press.
Redding, R. W.
  1988   A general explanation of subsistence change: from hunting and gathering to food production. *Journal of Anthropological Archaeology* 7:56–97.
Redman, C. L.
  1978   *The Rise of Civilization.* San Francisco: W. H. Freeman.
  1982   Archaeological survey and the study of Mesopotamian urban societies. *Journal of Field Archaeology* 9:375–382.
Reese, D.
  1975a   Dwarfed hippos: past and present. *Earth Science* 28:63–69.
  1975b   Men, saints, or dragons? *Expedition* 17:26–30.
  1988   The dwarfed Cypriot elephant. Ms. on file, Cyprus American Archaeological Research Institute, Nicosia.
  1989   Tracking the extinct pygmy hippopotamus of Cyprus. *Field Museum of Natural History Bulletin* 60:22–29.
  n.d.   A study of the dwarfed hippopotami of the Mediterreanean, Madagascar, and Africa with special reference to the dwarfed hippopotamus of Cyprus, *Phanourios minutus.* Ms. on file, Cyprus American Archaeological Research Institute, Nicosia.
Reher, C., and G. Frison
  1980   The Vore Site, 48CK302, a stratified buffalo jump in the Wyoming Black Hills. *Plains Anthropologist Memoir No. 16.*
Reidhead, V.
  1979   Linear programming models. *Annual Review of Anthropology* 8:543–578.
Renfrew, C.
  1973   *Before Civilization: The Radiocarbon Revolution and Prehistoric Europe.* London: Jonathan Cape.
Richardson, A.
  1981   The control of productive resources on the Northwest Coast of North America. In *Resource Managers: North American and Australian Hunter-Gatherers* (N. Williams and E. Hienn, eds.). AAAS Symposium No. 67. Boulder: Westview.
Riches, D.
  1979   Ecological variation on the Northwest Coast: models for the generation of cognatic and matrilineal descent. In *Social and Ecological Systems* (P. C. Burnham and R. G. Ellen, eds.), pp. 145–166. New York: Academic Press.

Rigaud, J.-P.
1980 Données nouvelles sur l'Aurignacien et le Périgordien en Périgord. In *L'Aurignacien et le Gravettien (Périgordien) dans leur cadre écologique* (L. Banesz and J. Kozlowski, eds.), pp. 213–241. Nitra: Institut Archéologique de l'Academic Slovaque des Sciences.

1982 *Le Paléolithique en Périgord: les données du Sud-Ouest Sarladais et leur implications.* Thèse de Doctorat d'État des Sciences, l'Université de Bordeaux I.

1985 Reflexions sur la signification de la variabilité des industries lithiques paléolithiques. In *La Signification culturelle des industries lithiques* (M. Otte, ed.), pp. 374–380. Oxford: BAR International Series S-239.

1988 The Gravettian peopling of southwestern France: taxonomic problems. In *Upper Pleistocene Prehistory of Western Eurasia* (H. L. Dibble and A. Montet-White, eds.), pp. 387–396. Philadelphia: University of Pennsylvania Museum Monograph No. 54.

1989 From the Middle to the Upper Paleolithic: transition or convergence? In *The Emergence of Modern Humans: Biocultural Adaptations in the Later Pleistocene* (E. Trinkaus, ed.), pp. 142–153. Cambridge: Cambridge University Press.

Rigaud, J.-P., and J. Simek
1987 Arms too short to box with God: problems and prospects for paleolithic prehistory in Dordogne, France. In *The Pleistocene Old World: Regional Perspectives* (O. Soffer, ed.), pp. 47–61. New York: Plenum Press.

1990 The last Pleniglacial in the south of France (24,000–14,000 years ago). In *The World at 18,000 BP* (O. Soffer and C. Gamble, eds.). London: Unwin and Hyman.

Roe, D.
1964 The British Lower and Middle Paleolithic: some problems, methods of study and preliminary results. *Proceedings of the Prehistoric Society* 30:245–267.

Rolland, N.
1977 New aspects of Middle Paleolithic variability in western Europe. *Nature* 266:251–252.

1981 The interpretation of Middle Paleolithic variability. *Man* 16:15–42.

Rolland, N., and H. Dibble
1990 A new synthesis of Middle Paleolithic assemblage variability. *American Antiquity* 55:480–499.

Rollefson, G.
1983 Two seasons of excavations at 'Ain el-Assad, near Azraq, eastern Jordan. *Bulletin of the American Schools of Oriental Research* 252:25–34.

1985 Late Pleistocene environments and seasonal hunting strategies: a case study from Fjaje, near Shobak, southern Jordan. In *Studies in the History and Archaeology of Jordan, Vol. II* (A. Hadidi, ed.), pp. 103–107. London: Routledge and Kegan Paul.

1988 Local and external relations in the Levantine PPN Period: 'Ain Ghazal (Jordan) as a regional centre. In *Studies in the History and Archaeology of Jordan, Vol. III* (A. Hadidi, ed.), pp. 29–39. London: Routledge and Kegan Paul.

Rollefson, G., and I. Köhler-Rollefson
1989 The collapse of early neolithic settlements in the southern Levant. In

People and Culture in Change (I. Hershkovitz, ed.), pp. 783–789. Oxford: BAR International Series S-508.

Rollefson, G., and B. MacDonald
  1981   Settlement patterns in southern Jordan: evidence from the Wadi el-Hasa Survey, 1981. *MERA Forum* 5:19–21.
Rollefson, G., and A. Simmons
  1988   The neolithic settlement at 'Ain Ghazal. *The Prehistory of Jordan: The State of Research in 1986* (A. N. Garrard and H. G. Gebel, eds.), pp. 525–565. Oxford: BAR International Series S-396(ii).
Ronen, A., ed.
  1982   *The Transition from Lower to Middle Paleolithic and the Origin of Modern Man*. Oxford: BAR International Series S-151.
Root, R. B.
  1967   The niche exploitation pattern of the blue-gray gnatcatcher. *Ecological Monographs* 37:317–350.
Roper, D.
  1979   The method and theory of site catchment analysis: a review. In *Advances in Archaeological Method and Theory, Vol. 2* (M. Schiffer, ed.), pp. 119–140. New York: Academic Press.
Rosen, S. A.
  1983   *Lithics in the Bronze and Iron Ages in Israel*. Ph.D. dissertation. Department of Anthropology, University of Chicago.
  1987   Demographic trends in the Negev Highlands: preliminary results from the emergency survey. *Bulletin of the American Schools of Oriental Research* 266:45–58.
Roughgarden, J.
  1983   Competition and theory in community ecology. *American Naturalist* 122:583–601.
Rupp, D., L. Sorensen, R. King, and W. Fox
  1984   Canadian Palaipahos (Cyprus) Survey Project: second preliminary report, 1980–1982. *Journal of Field Archaeology* 11:133–154.
Ruse, M.
  1986   *Taking Darwin Seriously: A Naturalistic Approach to Philosophy*. Oxford: Blackwell.
  1989   The view from somewhere: a critical defense of evolutionary epistemology. In *Issues in Evolutionary Epistemology* (K. Hahlweg and C. Hooker, eds.), pp. 185–228. Albany: SUNY Press.
Russell, F.
  1975   *The Pima Indians*. Tucson: University of Arizona Press.
Rust, A.
  1950   *Die Höhlenfunde von Jabrud (Syrien)*. Neümunster: Karl Wachholtz.
Sackett, J. R.
  1975   Reflections on Bordian methodology. Unpublished paper presented to the Seminar on Typology, Les Eyzies, France.
  1977   The meaning of style in archaeology: a general model. *American Antiquity* 42:369–80.
  1981   From de Mortillet to Bordes: a century of French paleolithic research. In *Towards a History of Archaeology* (G. Daniel, ed.), pp. 85–99. London: Thames and Hudson.
  1982   Approaches to style in lithic archaeology. *Journal of Anthropological Archaeology* 1:59–112.

1985   Style, ethnicity and stone tools. *Proceedings of the 16th Annual Chacmool Conference,* pp. 277–282. Calgary: University of Calgary.

1986   Style, function and assemblage variability: a reply to Binford. *American Antiquity* 51:628–634.

1988a   The Mousterian and its aftermath: a view from the Upper Paleolithic. In *Upper Pleistocene Prehistory of Western Eurasia* (H. Dibble and A. Montet-White, eds.), pp. 413–426. Philadelphia: University of Pennsylvania Museum Monograph No. 54.

1988b   The Neuvic Group: Upper Paleolithic open-air sites in the Perigord. In *Upper Pleistocene Prehistory of Western Eurasia* (H. L. Dibble and A. Montet-White, eds.), pp. 61–84. Philadelphia: University of Pennsylvania Museum Monograph No. 54.

Sahlins, M.

1972   *Stone Age Economics.* Chicago: Aldine-Atherton.

1976   *Tribesmen.* Englewood Cliffs, NJ: Prentice-Hall.

Sala, B.

1983   Variations climatiques et séquences chronologiques sur la base des variations des associations fauniques à grands mammifères. *Rivista Scienze Preistoriche* 38:161–180.

Salmon, M.

1975   Confirmation and explanation in archaeology. *American Antiquity* 40:459–470.

1976   "Deductive" versus "inductive" archaeology. *American Antiquity* 41: 376–380.

1982   *Philosophy and Archaeology.* New York: Academic Press.

Salmon, M., and W. Salmon

1979   Alternative models of scientific explanation. *American Anthropologist* 81:61–74.

Salmon, W.

1967   *The Foundations of Scientific Inference.* Pittsburgh: University of Pittsburgh Press.

Sampson, C. G.

1988   *Stylistic Boundaries among Mobile Hunter-Foragers.* Washington, DC: Smithsonian Institution Press.

Santonja, M. and P. Villa

1990   The Lower Paleolithic of Spain and Portugal. *Journal of World Prehistory* 4:45–94.

Sauer, C.

1934   The distribution of aboriginal tribes and languages in northwestern Mexico. *Ibero-America* 5:13–21.

Saxon, E. C.

1974   The mobile herding economy of Kebarah Cave—an economic analysis of the faunal remains. *Journal of Archaeological Science* 1:27–45.

1975   *The Prehistoric Economies of the Israeli and Algerian Littorals, 18000–8000 BP.* Ph.D. Dissertation. Department of Archaeology, University of Cambridge.

Schiffer, M.

1978   Some issues in the philosophy of science and archaeology. Unpublished paper presented at the State University of New York. Binghamton, in November, 1978.

1987   *Formation Processes of the Archaeological Record.* Albuquerque: University of New Mexico Press.

Schiffer, M. B., M. A. Sullivan, and T. Klinger
1978   The design of archaeological surveys. *World Archaeology* 10:1–28.

Schoener, T. W.
1974   Resource partitioning in ecological communities. *Science* 185:27–39.
1984   Counters to the claims of Walter et al. on the evolutionary significance of competition. *Oikos* 43:248–251.

Schoeninger, M.
1981   The agricultural "revolution": its effect on human diet in prehistoric Iran and Israel. *Paléorient* 7:73–92.
1982   Diet and the evolution of modern human form in the Middle East. *American Journal of Physical Anthropology* 58:37–52.

Schrire, C.
1980   An inquiry into the evolutionary status and apparent identity of San hunter-gatherers. *Human Ecology* 8:9–32.
1984   Wild surmises on savage thoughts. In *Past and Present in Hunter-Gatherer Studies* (C. Schrire, ed.), pp. 1–25. New York: Academic Press.

Schrire, C., ed.
1984   *Past and Present in Hunter-Gatherer Studies.* New York: Academic Press.

Schuldenrein, J., and P. Goldberg
1981   Later Quaternary paleoenvironments and prehistoric site distributions in the Lower Jordan Valley: a preliminary report. *Paléorient* 7:57–71.

Schwarz, H. P., W. Buhay, R. Grün, M. Stiner, S. Kuhn, and G. H. Miller
n.d.   Absolute dating of sites in coastal Lazio. *Proceedings of the International Symposium of the Fossil Man of Monte Circeo: 50 Years of Studies on the Neandertals in Latium.* Manuscript in preparation.

Seeden, H.
1982   Ethnoarchaeological reconstruction of Halafian occupational units at Shams et-Din Tannira. *Berytus* 30:55–96.

Segre, A. G.
1976   Quaternary geology of the Palidoro country, Rome. *Quaternaria*
–77   19:157–161.
1984   Considerazioni sulla cronostratigrafia del Pleistocene Laziale. *Atti della XXIV Riunione Scientifica dell'Istituto Italiano di Preistoria e Protostoria nel Lazio:* 92–101.

Segre, A., and A. Ascenzi
1984   Fontana Ranuccio: Italy's earliest Middle Pleistocene hominid site. *Current Anthropology* 25:230–233.

Segre, A. G., and M. Piperno
1984   Venosa-Notarchirico, Basilicata. *I Primi abitanti d'Europa,* pp. 186–188. Guidebook to the exhibition. Rome: De Luca.

Semenov, S. A.
1964   *Prehistoric Technology.* London: MacKay.
1970   The forms and funktions (*sic*) of the oldest tools. *Quärtar* 21:1–20.

Sergi, S.
1939   Il cranio neandertaliano del Monte Circeo. *Rendiconti delle Sedute della Reale Accademia Nazionale dei Lincei* 6:627–685.

Service, E. R.
    1963   *Primitive Social Organization: An Evolutionary Perspective.* New York: Random House.
    1978   *The Hunters.* Chicago: Aldine-Atherton.
Shackleton, N. J., and N. D. Opdyke
    1973   Oxygen isotope and paleomagnetic stratigraphy of equatorial Pacific core, V28–238. *Quaternary Research* 3:39–55.
Shanks, M., and C. Tilley
    1987   *Re-Constructing Archaeology: Theory and Practice.* Cambridge: Cambridge University Press.
    1988   *Social Archaeology.* Albuquerque: University of New Mexico Press.
Shapere, D.
    1971   The paradigm concept. *Science* 172:706–709.
Shea, J.
    1988   Spear points from the Middle Paleolithic of the Levant. *Journal of Field Archaeology* 15:441–450.
    1989   A functional study of the lithic industries associated with hominid fossils in Kebara and Qafzeh, Israel. In *The Human Revolution: Behavioral and Biological Perspectives on the Origins of Modern Humans* (P. Mellars and C. Stringer, eds.), pp. 611–625. Edinburgh: Edinburgh University Press.
Shipman, P.
    1983   Early hominid lifestyle: hunting and gathering or foraging and scavenging? In *Animals and Archaeology, Vol. 1* (J. Clutton-Brock and C. Grigson, eds.), pp. 31–49. Oxford: BAR International Series S-163.
    1986   Scavenging or hunting in early hominids: theoretical framework and tests. *American Anthropologist* 88:27–43.
Shipman, P., and J. Rose
    1983   Early hominid hunting, butchering, and carcass-processing behaviors: approaches to the fossil record. *Journal of Anthropological Archaeology* 2:57–98.
Shott, M.
    1986   Technological organization and settlement mobility: an ethnographic examination. *Journal of Anthropological Research* 42:15–51.
    1989   On tool-class use lives and the formation of archaeological assemblages. *American Antiquity* 54:9–30.
Sieveking, A.
    1976   Settlement patterns in the later Magdalenian in the central Pyrenees. In *Problems in Economic and Social Archaeology* (G. de G. Sieveking, I. H. Longworth, and K. E. Wilson, eds.), pp. 583–603. London: Duckworth Press.
Silberbauer, G. B.
    1981   *Hunter and Habitat in the Central Kalahari Desert.* Cambridge: Cambridge University Press.
Silberman, N. A.
    1982   *Digging for God and Country: Exploration, Archaeology, and the Secret Struggle for the Holy Land, 1799–1917.* New York: Knopf.
Sillen, A.
    1981   Strontium and diet at Hayonim Cave. *American Journal of Physical Anthropology* 56:131–137.

1984   Dietary change in the Epipaleolithic and Neolithic of the Levant: the Sr/Ca evidence. *Paléorient* 10:149–155.

Simberloff, D.
1983   Competition theory, hypothesis-testing, and other community ecological buzzwords. *American Naturalist* 122:626–635.

Simek, J.
1984   *A K-Means Approach to the Analysis of Spatial Structure in Upper Paleolithic Habitation Sites: Le Flageolet I and Pincevent 36.* Oxford BAR International Series S-205.
1987   Spatial order and behavioral change in the French paleolithic. *Man* 61:25–40.

Simek, J., and H. Price
1990   Chronological change in Perigord lithic assemblage diversity. In *The Human Revolution: Biological and Behavioral Perspectives on the Origins of Modern Humans* (P. Mellars and C. Stringer, eds.). Edinburgh: University of Edinburgh Press.

Simek, J., and L. Snyder
1988   Changing assemblage diversity in Perigord archaeofaunas. In *The Upper Pleistocene Prehistory of Western Eurasia* (H. L. Dibble and A. Montet-White, eds.), pp. 321–332. Philadelphia: University of Pennsylvania Museum Monograph No. 54.

Simmons, A.
1982   *Prehistoric Adaptive Strategies in the Chaco Canyon Region, Northwestern New Mexico.* Window Rock: Navajo Nation Papers in Anthropology No. 9.
1986   New evidence for the early use of cultigens in the American Southwest. *American Antiquity* 51:73–88.
1988a   Extinct pygmy hippopotamus and early man in Cyprus. *Nature* 333:554–557.
1988b   Test excavations at Akrotiri-Aetokremnos (Site E), an early prehistoric occupation in southern Cyprus: preliminary report. *Reports of the Department of Antiquities of Cyprus, 1988,* pp. 15–23. Nicosia: Department of Antiquities.
1989   Preliminary report of the 1988 season at Akrotiri-Aetokremnos, Cyprus. *Report of the Department of Antiquities. Cyprus 1989,* pp. 1–5. Nicosia: Department of Antiquities.

Simmons, A., I. Köhler-Rollefson, G. Rollefson, R. Mandel, and Z. Kafafi
1987   'Ain Ghazal: a major neolithic settlement in central Jordan. *Science* 240:35–39.

Simmons, A., D. Reese, and S. Held
n.d.   Extinct pygmy hippopotamus, early man, and the initial human occupation of Cyprus. *Proceedings of the International Conference on Early Man in Island Environments.* Sassari: Industria Grafica Stampacolor.

Simpson, G.
1940   Mammals and land bridges. *Journal of the Washington Academy of Science* 30:137–163.
1965   *The Geography of Evolution.* New York: Chilton Books.

Smith, F. H.
1984   Fossil hominids from the Upper Pleistocene of Central Europe and

the origin of modern Europeans. In *The Origins of Modern Humans* (F. Smith and F. Spencer, eds.), pp. 137–210. New York: Alan R. Liss.

Smith, F. H., J. Simek, and M. Harrill
1989   Geographic variation in supraorbital torus reduction during the later Pleistocene. In *The Human Revolution: Biological and Behavioral Perspectives on the Origins of Modern Humans* (P. Mellars and C. Stringer, eds.), pp. 172–193. Edinburgh: Edinburgh University Press.

Smith, F., and E. Trinkaus
n.d.   Modern human origins in central Europe: a case of continuity. In *Aux origines de la diversité humaine* (J. Hublin and A.-M. Tillier, eds.). Paris: Presses Universitaires de France.

Smith, J. M.
1978   Optimization theory in evolution. *Annual Review of Ecology and Systematics* 9:31–56.

Smith, P. E. L.
1966   *Le Solutréen en France.* Mémoires de l'Institut Préhistorique de l'Université de Bordeaux No. 5.
1972   Diet and nutrition in the Natufians. *American Journal of Physical Anthropology* 37:233–238.
1973   Family burials at Hayonim. *Paléorient* 1:69–72.

Smith, P., O. Bar-Yosef, and A. Sillen
1984   Archaeological and skeletal evidence for dietary change during the late Pleistocene/early Holocene in the Levant. In *Paleopathology at the Origins of Agriculture* (M. N. Cohen and G. J. Armelagos, eds.), pp. 101–136. New York: Academic Press.

Smith, P., and J. Young
1983   The force of numbers: population pressure in the central Zagros. In *The Hilly Flanks and Beyond: Essays on the Prehistory of Southwestern Asia presented to R. J. Braidwood* (T. C. Young, Jr., P. Smith, and P. Mortensen, eds.), pp. 123–137. Chicago: Oriental Institute of the University of Chicago.

Soffer, O.
1985   *The Upper Paleolithic of the Central Russian Plain.* New York: Academic Press.
1987   The Middle to Upper Paleolithic transition on the Russian Plain. In *The Human Revolution: Behavioral and Biological Perspectives on the Origins of Modern Humans* (P. Mellars and C. Stringer, eds.), pp. 714–742. Edinburgh: Edinburgh University Press.

Soffer, O., and C. Gamble, eds.
1990   *The World at 18,000 BP: High Latitudes.* London: Unwin Hyman.

Solway, J., and R. Lee
1990   Foragers, genuine or spurious? Situating the Kalahari San in history. *Current Anthropology* 31:109–146.

Sondaar, P.
1977   Insularity and its effect on mammal evolution. In *Major Patterns in Vertebrate Evolution* (M. Hecht, P. Goody, and B. Hecht, eds.), pp. 671–707. New York: Plenum.
1986   The island sweepstakes. *Natural History* 95:50–57.
1987   Pleistocene man and extinctions of island endemics. *Mémoires de la Société Géologique de France* 150:159–165.

1988 Report of the Coordinator and President of the Scientific Committee, International Conference: Early Man in Island Environments. Conference held September 25–October 2, 1988, Oliena, Sardinia.

Sondaar, P., M. Sanges, T. Kotsakis, and P. de Boer
1986 The Pleistocene deer hunter of Sardinia. *Geobios* 19:17–25.

Sondaar, P., M. Sanges, T. Kotsakis, D. Esu, and P. de Boer
1984 First report on paleolithic culture in Sardinia. In *The Daya Conference of Prehistory: Early Settlement in the Western Mediterranean Islands and their Peripheral Areas.* (W. Waldren, R. Chapman, J. Lewthwaite, and R. Kennard, eds.), pp. 29–47. Oxford: BAR International Series S-229.

Sonneville-Bordes, D. de
1955 A propos du Périgordien. *Bulletin de la Société Préhistorique Française* 52:597–601.
1960 *Le Paléolithique supérieur en Périgord.* Bordeaux: Imprimeries Delmas.
1966 L'évolution du paléolithique supérieur en Europe occidental et sa signification. *Bulletin de la Société Préhistorique Française* 63:3–34.
1972 Environnement et culture du Périgordien ancien dans le sud-ouest de la France: données récentes. In *The Origin of Homo sapiens* (F. Bordes, ed.), pp. 141–146. Paris: UNESCO.
1980 Cultures et milieux d'*Homo sapiens* en Europe. In *Les Processus d'hominisation,* pp. 115–129. Paris: CNRS.
1989 Préface. *Bulletin de la Société Préhistorique de l'Ariège* 44:5–17.

Sonneville-Bordes, D. de, and J. Perrot
1954 Lexique typologique du Paléolithique supérieur. Outillage lithique.
–56 *Bulletin de la Société Préhistorique Française* 51:327–335; 52:76–79; 53:408–412, 547–559.

Spaulding, A.
1953 Statistical techniques for the discovery of artifact types. *American Antiquity* 18:305–313.
1960 The dimensions of archaeology. In *Essays in the Science of Culture* (G. Dole and R. Carneiro, eds.), pp. 437–456. New York: Columbia University Press.
1988 Distinguished lecture: archaeology and anthropology. *American Anthropologist* 90:263–271.

Spence, M. W.
1981 Obsidian productions and the state in Teotihuacán. *American Antiquity* 46:769–788.

Spencer, F.
1984 The neandertals and their evolutionary significance: a brief historical survey. In *The Origins of Modern Humans: A World Survey of the Fossil Evidence* (F. Smith and F. Spencer, eds.), pp. 1–50. New York: Alan Liss.

Speth, J. D.
1983 *Bison Kills and Bone Counts. Decision Making by Ancient Hunters.* Chicago: University of Chicago Press.

Speth, J. D., and K. A. Spielmann
1983 Energy source protein metabolism and hunter-gatherer subsistence strategies. *Journal of Anthropological Archaeology* 2:1–31.

Spielmann, K. A.
1986   Interdependences among egalitarian societies. *Journal of Anthropological Archaeology* 5:279–312.
Spoor, C., and P. Sondaar
1986   Human fossils from the endemic island fauna of Sardinia. *Journal of Human Evolution* 15:399–408.
Spuhler, J.
1988   Evolution of mitochondrial DNA in monkeys, apes and humans. *Yearbook of Physical Anthropology* 31:15–48.
Stafford, T., K. Brendel, and R. Duhamel
1988   Radiocarbon, ^{13}C and ^{15}N analysis of fossil bone: removal of humates with XAD 2 resin. *Geochimica et Cosmochimica Acta* 52:2257–2267.
Stager, L. E.
n.d.   The periodization of Palestine from Neolithic through Early Bronze Times. In *Chronologies in Old World Archaeology* (R. Ehrich, ed.). Chicago: University of Chicago Press. (in press)
Stanley-Price, N.
1977a   Colonizations and continuity in the early prehistory of Cyprus. *World Archaeology* 9:27–41.
1977b   Khirokitia and the initial settlement of Cyprus. *Levant* 9:66–68.
Stanley-Price, N., and D. Christou
1973   Excavations at Khirokitia, 1972. *Report of the Department of Antiquities, Cyprus*. 1–33.
Stekelis, M., and T. Yizraely
1963   Excavations at Nahal Oren, preliminary report. *Israel Exploration Journal* 13:1–12.
Stephens, D. W., and J. R. Krebs
1986   *Foraging Theory.* Princeton, NJ: Princeton University Press.
Sterud, G.
1973   A paradigmatic view of prehistory. In *The Explanation of Culture Change* (C. Renfrew, ed.), pp. 3–17. London: Duckworth.
Steward, J.
1938   *Basin-Plateau Aboriginal Socio-Political Groups.* Bureau of American Ethnology Bulletin No. 120. Washington, DC: U.S. Government Printing Office.
Stiner, M. C.
1990a   *The Ecology of Choice: Procurement and Transport of Animal Resources by Upper Pleistocene Hominids in West-Central Italy.* Ph.D. dissertation. University of New Mexico. Ann Arbor: University Microfilms.
1990b   The use of mortality patterns in archaeological studies of hominid predatory adaptations. *Journal of Anthropological Archaeology* 9:305–350.
1991   The faunal remains from Grotta Guattari: a taphonomic perspective. *Current Anthropology* 32:103–117.
Stockton, E.
1968   Pre-neolithic remains at Kyrenia, Cyprus. *Report of the Department of Antiquities, Cyprus:* 16–19.
Straus, L. G.
1968   Reactions of supporters of the Constitution to the adjournment of

the New Hampshire Ratification Convention 1788. *Historical New Hampshire* 22:37–50.

1975a A Study of the Solutrean in Vasco-Cantabrian Spain. Ph.D. dissertation, Department of Anthropology, University of Chicago.

1975b ¿Solutrense o Magdaleniense inferior cantábrico? Significado de las "diferencias." *Boletín del Instituto de Estudios Asturianos* 86:731–790.

1976 A new interpretation of the Cantabrian Solutrean. *Current Anthropology* 17:342–343.

1977 Of deerslayers and mountain men: paleolithic faunal exploitation in Cantabrian Spain. In *For Theory Building in Archaeology* (L. Binford, ed.), pp. 41–76. New York: Academic Press.

1979a Mesolithic adaptations along the northern coast of Spain. *Quaternaria* 21:305–327.

1979b Caves: a paleoanthropological resource. *World Archaeology* 10:331–339.

1980 The role of raw materials in lithic assemblage variability. *Lithic Technology* 9:68–72.

1981 On the habitat and diet of *Cervus elaphus*. *Munibe* 33:175–182.

1982 Carnivores and cave sites in Cantabrian Spain. *Journal of Anthropological Research* 38:75–96.

1983a *El Solutrense Vasco-Cantábrico: una nueva perspectiva.* Centro de Investigación y Museo de Altamira, Monografía No. 10. Madrid: Ministerio de Cultura.

1983b Paleolithic adaptations in Cantabria and Gascony: a preliminary comparison. In *Homenaje al Profesor Martín Almagro Basch, Vol. I* (A. Balil et al., eds.), pp. 187–201. Madrid: Ministerio de Cultura.

1983c Terminal Pleistocene faunal exploitation in Cantabria and Gascony. In *Animals and Archaeology: Hunters and Their Prey* (J. Clutton-Brock and C. Grigson, eds.), pp. 209–225. Oxford: BAR International Series S-163.

1983d From Mousterian to Magdalenian: cultural evolution viewed from Cantabrian Spain and Pyrenean France. In *The Mousterian Legacy* (E. Trinkaus, ed.), pp. 73–111. Oxford: BAR International Series S-164.

1985a La collection Magnant: un témoin de la préhistoire charentaise. *Bulletin de la Société Archéologique et Historique de la Charente* 1985:21–31.

1985b Stone Age prehistory of northern Spain. *Science* 230:501–507.

1985c Chronostratigraphy of the Pleistocene-Holocene transition: the Azilian problem in the Franco-Cantabrian region. *Palaeohistoria* 27:89–122.

1986d A comparison of La Riera assemblages with those from contemporary sites in Cantabrian Spain. In *La Riera Cave: Stone Age Hunter-Gatherer Adaptations in Northern Spain* (L. Straus and G. Clark, eds.), pp. 219–236. Tempe: Arizona State University Anthropological Research Papers No. 36.

1986a Late Würm adaptive systems in Cantabrian Spain: the case of eastern Asturias. *Journal of Anthropological Archaeology* 5:330–368.

1986c Once more into the breach: Solutrean chronology. *Munibe* 38:35–38.

1986b The end of the paleolithic in Cantabria and Gascony. In *The End of the Paleolithic in the Old World* (L. Straus, ed.), pp. 81–116. Oxford: BAR International Series S-284.

1987a Paradigm lost: a personal view of the current state of Upper Paleolithic research. *Helinium* 27:157–171.

1987b Upper Paleolithic ibex hunting in southwest Europe. *Journal of Archaeological Science* 14:163–178.

1987c The paleolithic cave art of Vasco-Cantabrian Spain. *Oxford Journal of Archaeology* 6:149–163.

1987d Hunting in late Upper Paleolithic western Europe. In *The Evolution of Human Hunting* (M. and D. Nitecki, eds.), pp. 147–176. New York: Plenum.

1987e Preliminary archaeological explorations in Portugal. *Old World Archaeology Newsletter* 11:16–19.

1988a The reconstruction of Upper Paleolithic adaptations: the Biscayan regions as seen by an archaeologist from North America. *Munibe*, Suplemento No. 6, pp. 35–44.

1988b Abri Dufaure: site formation processes, functions and culture-geographic contexts in the Würm Tardiglacial of Gascony. In *Upper Pleistocene Prehistory of Western Eurasia* (H. Dibble and A. Montet-White, eds.), pp. 41–60. Philadelphia: University of Pennsylvania Museum.

1988c Preliminary prehistoric research in Algarve, Alentejo and Estremadura, 1987. *Arqueologia* 17:190–194.

1989a Age of modern Europeans. *Nature* 342:476–477.

1989b New chronometric dates for the prehistory of Portugal. *Arqueologia* 20:73–76.

1989c On early hominid use of fire. *Current Anthropology* 30:488–490.

1990a Underground archaeology: perspectives on caves and rockshelters. In *Archaeological Method and Theory, Vol. 2* (M. Schiffer, ed.), pp. 255–304. Tucson: University of Arizona Press.

1990b The last glacial maximum in Cantabrian Spain: the Solutrean. In *The World at 18,000 BP, Vol. 2* (O. Soffer and C. Gamble, eds.), pp. 89–108. London: Unwin Hyman.

n.d.a The "savage": noble or ignoble? Two views of the North American Indian (Lahontan and Mather). Unpublished manuscript.

n.d.b Social stratification in pithouse villages and population stress. Unpublished manuscript.

n.d.c The Mesolithic-Neolithic transition in Portugal. Unpublished manuscript.

n.d.d The early Upper Paleolithic of southwest Europe: Cro-Magnon adaptations in the Iberian peninsula ca. 35,000–20,000 BP. In *The Emergence of Modern Humans* (P. Mellars and C. Stringer, eds.). Edinburgh: University of Edinburgh Press. (in press)

n.d.f The Epipaleolithic and Mesolithic of Cantabrian Spain and Pyrenean France. *Journal of World Prehistory* 5. (in press)

n.d.h The role of raw materials in Upper Paleolithic and Mesolithic stone artifact assemblage variability in SW Europe. In *Raw Material Economy Among Prehistoric Hunter-Gatherers* (A. Montet-White and S. Holen, eds.). Lawrence: University of Kansas Publications in Anthropology. (in press) n.d.e   *L'Abri Dufaure: un gisement tardiglaciaire en Gascogne.* Paris: Société Préhistorique Française. (in press)

n.d.g   L'Abri Dufaure et la falaise du Pastou dans le système adaptatif du Magdalénien pyrénéen. In *Le Peuplement Magdalénien* (H. Laville, J-P. Rigaud and B. Vandermeersch, eds.). Paris: Editions du Comité des Travaux Historiques et Scientifiques. (in press)

Straus, L. G., ed.
1986   *The End of the Paleolithic in the Old World.* Oxford: BAR International Series S-284.

Straus, L., K. Akoshima, M. Petraglia, and M. Séronie-Vivien
1988   Terminal Pleistocene adaptations in Pyrenean France: the nature and the role of Abri Dufaure site. *World Archaeology* 19:328–348.

Straus, L., J. Altuna, G. Clark, M. González Morales, H. Laville, A. Leroi-Gourhan, M. Menéndez de la Hoz, and J. Ortea
1981   Paleoecology at La Riera. *Current Anthropology* 22:655–682.

Straus, L., J. Altuna, M. Jackes, and M. Kunst
1988   New excavations in Casa da Moura and at Bocas. *Arqueología* 18:65–95.

Straus, L., J. Altuna, and B. Vierra
1990   The *concheiro* at Vidigal: a contribution to the late Mesolithic of southern Portugal. In *The Mesolithic in Europe* (P. Vermeersch & P. van Peer, eds.), pp. 463–474. Leuven: Katholieke Universiteit.

Straus, L. G., and G. A. Clark
1978   Prehistoric investigations in Cantabrian Spain. *Journal of Field Archaeology* 5:289–317.

1986a   Synthesis and conclusions, part II: the La Riera excavation, chronostratigraphy, paleoenvironments and cultural sequence in perspective. In *La Riera Cave: Stone Age Hunter-Gatherer Adaptations in Northern Spain* (L. Straus and G. Clark, eds.), pp. 367–383. Tempe: Arizona State University Anthropological Research Paper No. 36.

1986b   La Riera archaeological remains—level contents and characteristics. In *La Riera Cave: Stone Age Hunter-Gatherer Adaptations in Northern Spain* (L. Straus and G. Clark, eds.), pp. 75–187. Tempe: Arizona State University Anthropological Research Papers No. 36.

Straus, L., and G. Clark, eds.
1986c   *La Riera Cave: Stone Age Hunter-Gatherer Adaptations in Northern Spain.* Tempe: Arizona State University Anthropological Research Papers No. 36.

Straus, L., G. Clark, J. Altuna, and J. Ortea
1980   Ice Age subsistence in northern Spain. *Scientific American* 242:142–152.

Straus, L., and C. Heller
1988   Explorations in the twilight zone: the early Upper Paleolithic of Vasco-Cantabrian Spain and Gascony. In *The Early Upper Paleolithic: Evidence from Europe and the Near East* (J. Hoffecker and C. Wolf, eds.), pp. 97–133. Oxford: BAR International Series S-437.

Straus, L., and A. Spiess
1985   Le Magdalénien final de l'Abri Dufaure: un aperçu de la chronologie et de la saison d'habitation humaine. *Bulletin de la Société Préhistorique de l'Ariège* 40:169–184.

Straus, L., and P. Walker
  1978   A technique for studying microscopic wear on artifact surfaces. In
          Views of the Past (L. Freeman, ed.), pp. 53–56. The Hague: Mouton.
Straus, L. et al.
  n.d.   The Middle Neolithic of Goldra Cave. *Journal of Archaeological Science*
          17. (in press)
Stringer, C., and P. Andrews
  1988   Genetic and fossil evidence for the origins of modern humans. *Sci-
          ence* 239:1263–1268.
Stringer, C., J. Hublin, and B. Vandermeersch
  1984   The origin of anatomically modern humans in western Europe. In
          The Origins of Modern Humans: A World Survey of the Fossil Evidence (F.
          Smith and F. Spencer, eds.), pp. 51–137. New York: Alan Liss.
Strong, D.
  1983   Natural variability and the manifold mechanisms of ecological com-
          munities. *American Naturalist* 122:636–660.
Stuiver, M., G. Pearson, and T. Braziunas
  1986   Radiocarbon age calibration of marine samples back to 9000 cal yr
          BP. *Radiocarbon* 28:980–1021.
Swiny, S.
  1982   The environment. In *An Archaeological Guide to the Ancient Kourion
          Area and the Akrotiri Peninsula* (H. Swiny, ed.), pp. 1–5. Nicosia:
          Zavallis Press.
  1988   The Pleistocene fauna of Cyprus and recent discoveries on the Akro-
          tiri Peninsula. *Report of the Department of Antiquities. Cyprus:* 21–24.
Taborin, Y.
  1987   Une certain lecture des sols d'habitation. *Bulletin de la Société Pré-
          historique Française* 84:353–357.
Taschini, M.
  1970   La Grotta Breuil al Monte Circeo. Per un impostazione dello studio
          del Pontiniano. *Origini* 4:45–78.
  1972   Sur le paléolithique de la Plaine Pontine (Latium). *Quaternaria*
          16:203–223.
  1979   L'industrie lithique de Grotte Guattari sur Mont Circé (Latium).
          Quaternaria 21:179–247.
Tchernov, E.
  1981   The biostratigraphy of the Middle East. In *Préhistoire du Levant* (J.
          Cauvin and P. Sanlaville, eds.), pp. 67–98. Paris: Editions du CNRS.
Tchernov, E., and O. Bar-Yosef
  1982   Animal exploitation in the Pre-Pottery Neolithic B period at Wadi
          Tbeik, southern Sinai. *Paléorient* 8:187–192.
Terrell, J.
  1977   Geographic systems and human diversity in the North Solomons.
          World Archaeology 9:62–81.
Testart, A.
  1982   The significance of food storage among hunter-gatherers: residence
          patterns, population densities, and social inequalities. *Current An-
          thropology* 23:523–537.
Thomas, D.
  1983   The archaeology of Monitor Valley I: epistemology. *Anthropological
          Papers of the American Museum of Natural History* 58:1–194.

Tixier, J.
1963 *Typologie de l'Epipaléolithique du Maghreb.* Mémoires du Centre de Recherches Anthropologiques, Préhistoriques et Ethnographiques d'Alger No. 2. Paris: Arts et Métiers.
1970 L'Abris sous roche de Ksar 'Aqil. La Campagne de fouilles 1969. *Bulletin de la Musée de Beyrouth* 23:173–191.
1974 K'sar Akil, Liban. *Paléorient* 2:187–192.
Tixier, J., M. L. Inizan, et H. Roche
1980 *Préhistoire de la Pierre Taillé I: terminologie et technologie.* Antibes: Centre de Recherches et d'Etudes Préhistoriques.
Todd, I.
1978 Excavations at Kalavassos-Tenta, Cyprus. *Archaeology* 31:58–59.
1982 Vasilikos Valley Project: fourth preliminary report, 1979–1980. *Journal of Field Archaeology* 9:35–79.
Torrence, R.
1983 Time budgeting and hunter-gatherer technology. In *Hunter-Gatherer Economy in Prehistory: A European Perspective* (G. Bailey, ed.), pp. 11–22. Cambridge: Cambridge University Press.
1989 Retooling: towards a behavioral theory of stone tools. In *Time, Energy and Stone Tools* (R. Torrence, ed.), pp. 57–66. Cambridge: Cambridge University Press.
Toth, N.
1985 The Oldowan reassessed: a close look at early stone artifacts. *Journal of Archaeological Science* 12:101–120.
Toulmin, S.
1983 The natural past and the human future: an introductory essay. In *How Humans Adapt: A Biocultural Odyssey* (D. Ortner, ed.), pp. 11–32. Washington, DC: Smithsonian Institution Press.
Tozzi, C.
1970 La Grotta di San Agostino (Gaeta). *Rivista Scienze Preistoriche* 25:3–87.
Trigger, B. G.
1983 Review of *Symbolic and Structural Archaeology* (Hodder, ed.). *American Scientist* 71:543.
1984 Archaeology at the crossroads: what's new? *Annual Review of Anthropology* 13:275–300.
Trinkaus, E.
1986 The neanderthals and modern human origins. *Annual Review of Anthropology* 15:191–218.
Trinkaus, E., ed.
1983 *The Mousterian Legacy.* Oxford: BAR International Series S-164.
Turner, A.
1984 Hominids and fellow-travellers: human migration into high latitudes as part of a large mammal community. In *Hominid Evolution and Community Ecology* (R. Foley, ed.), pp. 193–217. London: Academic Press.
1986 Correlation and causation in some carnivore and hominid evolutionary events. *South African Journal of Science* 82:75–76.
Turville-Petre, F.
1932 Excavations in the Mugharet el-Kebara. *Journal of the Royal Anthropological Institute* 62:271–276.

Underhill, R.
  1939 *Social Organization of the Papago Indians.* New York: Columbia University Press.
Unger-Hamilton, R.
  1989 The Epi-Paleolithic southern Levant and the origins of cultivation. *Current Anthropology* 30:88–103.
Upham, S.
  1981 *Polities and Power: An Economic and Political History of the Western Pueblos.* New York: Academic Press.
Upham, S., R. MacNeish, W. Galinat, and C. Stevenson
  1987 Evidence concerning the origin of maiz de ocho. *American Anthropologist* 89:410–419.
Upham, S., and F. Plog
  1986 The interpretation of prehistoric political complexity in the central and northern Southwest: toward a mending of models. *Journal of Field Archaeology* 13:223–238.
Valla, F. R.
  1975 *Le Natoufien. Une culture préhistorique en Palestine.* Cahiers de la Revue Biblique No. 15. Paris: Gabalda.
  1981 Les établissements Natoufiens dans le nord d'Israël. In *Préhistoire du Levant* (J. Cauvin and P. Sanlaville, ed.), pp. 409–420. Paris: Editions du CNRS.
  1984 *Les industries de silex de Mallaha (Eynan) et du natoufien dans le Levant.* Mémoires et Travaux du Centre de Recherche Française en Jérusalem No. 3. Paris: Association Paléorient.
  1987 Chronologie relative et chronologie absolue dans le Natoufien. In *Chronologies in the Near East: Relative Chronologies and Absolute Chronology 16,000–4,000 B.P.* (O. Aurenche, J. Evin, and F. Hours, eds.), pp. 219–245. Oxford: BAR International Series S-379.
  1988a Commentary on A. N. Goring-Morris' *At the Edge: Terminal Pleistocene Hunter-Gatherers in the Negev and Sinai. Mitekufat Haeven* 21:50–52.
  1988b Aspects du sol de l'abri 131 de Mallaha (Eynan). *Paléorient* 14:283–297.
Valladas, H., et al.
  1987 Thermoluminescence dates for the neanderthal burial site at Kebara (Mount Carmel), Israel. *Nature* 330:159–160.
  1988 Thermoluminescence dating of Mousterian "Proto-Cromagnon" remains from Israel and the origins of modern humans. *Nature* 331:614–616.
Valoch, K.
  1967 Le Paléolithique moyen en Tchescoslovaquie. *L'Anthropologie* 71:135–144.
van Zeist, W., and S. Bottema
  1982 Vegetational history of the eastern Mediterranean and the Near East during the last 20,000 years. In *Paleoclimates: Paleoenvironments and Human Communities in the Eastern Mediterranean Region in Later Prehistory* (J. Bintliff and W. van Zeist, eds.), pp. 277–321. Oxford: BAR International Series S-133.
Vandermeersch, B.
  1984 A propos de la découverte du squelette néandertalien de Saint-

Césaire. *Bulletins et Mémoires de la Société d'Anthropologie de Paris I* (série XIV):191–96.

Vega del Sella, el Conde de la
1916 *Paleolítico de Cueto de la Mina (Asturias).* Madrid: Comisión de Investigaciones Paleontológicas y Prehistóricas, Memoria No. 13.
1923 *El Asturiense: nueva industria Preneolítica.* Madrid: Comisión de Investigaciones Paleontológicas y Prehistóricas, Memoria No. 32.
1925 La transición al Neolítico en la Costa Cantábrica. *Actas y Memorias de la Sociedad Española de Antropología, Etnografía y Prehistoria* 4(4), Sección 34:165–172.
1930 *La Cuevas de la Riera y Balmori.* Madrid: Comisión do Investigaciones Paleontológicas y Prehistóricas, Memoria 38.

Verneuil, E., and L. Lartet
1863 Note sur un silex taillé trouvé dans le diluvium des environs de Madrid. *Bulletin de la Société Géologique de France* (2ème série) 20:698–702.

Vierra, R.
1982 Typology, classification and theory building. In *Essays on Archaeological Typology* (R. Whallon and J. Brown, eds.), pp. 162–175. Evanston, IL: Center for American Archaeology.

Vigne, J.
1983 *Les Mammifères terrestres non-volants du post-glaciaire de Corse et leurs rapports avec l'homme:étude paleo-ethno-zoologique fondée sur les ossements.* Thèse 3e Cycle. Paris: P. et M. Curie Université.
1987 L'extinction holocène du fonds de peuplement mammalien indigène des îles de Mediterranée occidentale. *Mémoires de la Société Géologique de France* 150:167–177.

Vila Mitja, A.
1984 Análisis funcional de tres complejos industriales del postglacial en Catalunya. In *Early Settlement in the Western Mediterranean Islands and in the Peripheral Areas* (W. H. Waldren, R. Chapman, J. Lewthwaite, and R.-C. Kennard, eds.), pp. 315–320. Oxford: BAR International Series S-229.
1985 Los instrumentos de trabajo en el paleolítico. *Revista de Arqueología* 20:24–31.
1987 *Introduccio a l'estudi de les eines litiques préhistoriques.* Bellaterra: Universidad Autónoma de Barcelona.

Vilanova Piera, J.
1893 *Memoria geognóstico-agricola y protohistorico de Valencia.* Madrid: Castellana.

Villa, P.
1982 Conjoinable pieces and site formation processes. *American Antiquity* 47:276–290.
1983 *Terra Amata and the Middle Pleistocene Archaeological Record of Southern France.* Berkeley: University of California Press.

Villa, P., and J. Courtin
1983 Interpretation of stratified sites: a view from underground. *Journal of Archaeological Science* 10:267–281.

Villa, P., C. Bouville, J. Courtin, D. Helmer, E. Mahieu, P. Shipman, G. Belluomini, and M. Branca
1986 Cannibalism in the neolithic. *Science* 233:431–437.

Villaverde, V.
   1988   Consideraciones sobre la secuencia de la Cova del Parpalló y el arte
            paleolítico del Mediterraneo español. *Archivo de Prehistoria Levantina*
            18:11–37.
Vita-Finzi, C.
   1973   Paleolithic finds from Cyprus? *Proceedings of the Prehistoric Society*
            39:453–454.
Vita-Finzi, C., and E. S. Higgs
   1970   Prehistoric economy in the Mount Carmel area of Palestine: site
            catchment analysis. *Proceedings of the Prehistoric Society* 36:1–37.
Vitagliano, S.
   1984   Nota sul Pontiniano della Grotta dei Moscerini (Gaeta), Latina. *Atti
            della XXIV Riunione Scientifica dell'Istituto Italiano di Preistoria e Pro-
            tostoria*, pp. 29–32. Firenze: Università di Firenze.
Vogel, J., and E. Visser
   1981   Pretoria radiocarbon dates II. *Radiocarbon* 23:43–80.
Vollmer, G.
   1987   On supposed circularities in an empirically oriented epistemology.
            In *Evolutionary Epistemology, Theory of Rationality and the Sociology of
            Knowledge* (G. Radnitzky and W. Bartley, eds.), pp. 163–200. La Salle,
            IL: Open Court.
Voorrips, A., S. Loving, and H. Kamermans
   1983   An archaeological survey of the Agro Pontino (Province of Latina).
            In *Archaeological Survey in the Mediterranean Area* (D. Keller and D.
            Rupp, eds.). Oxford: BAR International Series S-283.
Walker, A.
   1984   Extinction in hominid evolution. In *Extinctions* (M. H. Nitecki, ed.),
            pp. 119–152. Chicago: University of Chicago Press.
Walter, G. H., P. E. Hulley, and A. J. F. K. Craig
   1984   Speciation, adaptations, and interspecific competition. *Oikos* 43:
            246–248.
Wasburn, S. L., and C. S. Lancaster
   1968   The evolution of hunting. In *Man the Hunter* (R. B. Lee and I.
            DeVore, eds.), pp. 293–303. Chicago: Aldine.
Waterbolk, T.
   1962   The lower Rhine basin. In *Courses Toward Urban Life* (R. J. Braidwood
            and G. Willey, eds.). Chicago: Aldine.
Watkins, T.
   1979   Kataliontas-Kourvellos: the analysis of the surface collected data. In
            Studies Presented in Memory of Porphyrios Dikaios, pp. 12–20. Nicosia:
            Lions Club.
   1981   The economic status of the aceramic neolithic culture of Cyprus.
            Journal of Mediterranean Anthropology and Archaeology 1:139–149.
Watson, P. J.
   1990   Review: *Re-Constructing Archaeology* and *Social Archaeology* (Shanks
            and Tilley, eds.). *Journal of Field Archaeology* 17:219–221.
Watson, P. J., S. A. LeBlanc, and C. L. Redman
   1971   *Explanations in Archaeology.* New York: Columbia University Press.
   1974   The covering law model in archaeology: practical uses and formal
            interpretations. *World Archaeology* 6:125–132.

1984   *Archaeological Explanation: The Scientific Method in Archaeology.* New York: Columbia University Press.
Wendorf, F., A. E. Close, and R. Schild
1987   Recent work on the Middle Paleolithic of the eastern Sahara. *African Archaeological Review* 5:49–64.
Wendorf, F., and A. E. Marks, eds.
1975   *Problems in Prehistory: North Africa and the Levant.* Dallas, TX: Southern Methodist University Press.
Weinstein-Evron, M.
1986   The paleoecology of the early Würm in the Hula Basin, Israel. *Paléorient* 9:5–20.
Whallon, R.
1982   Variables and dimensions: the critical step in quantitative typology. In *Essays on Archaeological Typology* (R. Whallon and J. Brown, eds.), pp. 127–161. Evanston, IL: Center for American Archaeology.
White, J., and J. O'Connell
1982   *A Prehistory of Australia. New Guinea and Sahul.* New York: Academic Press.
White, J., and D. H. Thomas
1972   What mean these stones? Ethno-taxonomic models and archaeological interpretations in the New Guinea highlands. In *Models in Archaeology* (D. L. Clarke, ed.), pp. 275–308. London: Methuen.
White, L.
1959   *The Evolution of Culture.* New York: McGraw-Hill.
White, R.
1982   Rethinking the Middle/Upper Paleolithic transition. *Current Anthropology* 23:169–192.
1985   *Upper Paleolithic Land Use in the Perigord.* Oxford: BAR International Series S-253.
1989   Production complexity and standardization in early Aurignacian bead and pendant manufacture: evolutionary implications. In *The Human Revolution: Biological and Behavioral Perspectives on the Origins of Modern Humans* (P. Mellars and C. Stringer, eds.), pp. 366–390. Edinburgh: University of Edinburgh Press.
Whyte, R. O.
1977   The botanical neolithic revolution. *Human Ecology* 5:209–222.
Wiens, J. A.
1977   On competition and variable environments. *American Scientist* 65: 590–597.
1983   Avian community ecology: an iconoclastic view. In *Perspectives on Ornithology* (A. H. Brugh and G. A. Clark, Jr., eds.), pp. 355–403. Cambridge: Cambridge University Press.
Wiessner, P.
1982   Beyond willow smoke and dogs' tails: a comment on Binford's analysis of hunter-gatherer settlement systems. *American Antiquity* 47: 171–178.
1983   Style and social information in Kalahari San projectile points. *American Antiquity* 48:253–276.
Wilde, J., and D. Newman
1989   Late Archaic corn in the eastern Great Basin. *American Anthropologist* 91:712–719.

Willey, G., and J. Sabloff
1974 *A History of American Archaeology.* San Francisco: Freeman.
1980 *A History of American Archaeology,* Second edition. San Francisco: Freeman.
Williams, L., D. H. Thomas and R. Bettinger
1973 Notions to numbers: Great Basin settlements as polythetic sets. In *Research and Theory in Current Archeology* (C. Redman, ed.), pp. 215–237. New York: Wiley Interscience.
Wills, W.
1988 *Early Prehistoric Agriculture in the American Southwest.* Santa Fe, NM: School of American Research.
Wilmsen, E.
1973 Interaction, spacing behavior, and the organization of hunting bands. *Journal of Anthropological Research* 29:1–31.
1983 The ecology of illusion: anthropological foraging in the Kalahari. *Reviews in Anthropology* 10:9–20.
1989 *Land Filled with Flies: A Political Economy of the Kalahari.* Chicago: University of Chicago Press.
Wilson, E. O.
1975 *Sociobiology: A New Synthesis.* Cambridge, MA: Harvard University Press.
Winter, J.
1976 The process of farming diffusion in the Southwest and Great Basin. *American Antiquity* 41:421–429.
Winterhalder, B.
1981 Optimal foraging strategies and hunter-gatherer research in anthropology: theories and models. In *Hunter-Gatherer Foraging Strategies* (B. Winterhalder and E. Smith, eds.), pp. 13–35. Chicago: University of Chicago Press.
Winterhalder, B. and E. A. Smith, eds.
1981 *Hunter-Gatherer Foraging Strategies.* Chicago: University of Chicago Press.
Wissler, C.
1917 *The American Indian: An Introduction to the Anthropology of the New World.* New York: D. C. McMurtie.
Witter, D.
1988 From butchering caribou to butchering stone. In *Archaeology with Ethnography: An Australian Perspective* (B. Meehan and R. Jones, eds.), pp. 33–41. Canberra: Australian National University.
Wobst, H. M.
1974 Boundary conditions for paleolithic social systems: a simulation approach. *American Antiquity* 39:147–178.
1976 Locational relationships in paleolithic society. *Journal of Human Evolution* 5:49–58.
1977 Stylistic behavior and information exchange. In *For the Director: Research Essays in Honor of James B. Griffin* (C. Cleland, ed.). Ann Arbor: University of Michigan, Museum of Anthropology, Anthropological Papers No. 61.
1978 The archaeo-ethnology of hunter-gatherers, or the tyranny of the ethnographic record in archaeology. *American Antiquity* 43:303–309.

Wolpoff, M.
1980   *Paleoanthropology.* New York: Alfred Knopf.
1989   Multiregional evolution: the fossil alternative to Eden. In *The Human Revolution: Biological and Behavioral Perspectives on the Origin of Modern Humans* (P. Mellars and C. Stringer, eds.), pp. 62–108. Edinburgh: University of Edinburgh Press.

Wolpoff, M., et al.
1988   Modern human origins. *Science* 241:772–774.

Wood, W. and Johnson, D.
1978   A survey of disturbance processes in archaeological site formation. *Advances in Archaeological Method and Theory* 1:315–381.

Woodburn, J.
1979   Minimal politics: the political organization of the Hadza of north Tanzania. In *Politics in Leadership: A Comparative Perspective* (W. A. Shack and P. A. Cohen, eds.). Oxford: Clarendon Press.
1980   Hunters and gatherers today and reconstruction of the past. In *Soviet and Western Anthropology* (E. Gellner, ed.), London: Duckworth.
1982   Egalitarian societies. *Man* 17:431–451.

Woodbury, R. B., and E. Zubrow
1979   Agricultural beginnings, 2000 BC–AD 500. In *Handbook of North American Indians Vol. 9: Southwest* (A. Ortiz, ed.), pp. 43–60. Washington: Smithsonian Institution Press.

Wright, G. A.
1978   Social differentiation in the Early Natufian. In *Social Archaeology: Beyond Subsistence and Dating* (C. L. Redman, M. J. Berman, E. V. Curtin, W. T. Langhorne, Jr., N. M. Versaggi, and J. C. Wanser, eds.), pp. 201–224. New York: Academic Press.

Wright, H. E., Jr.
1968   Natural environment of early food production north of Mesopotamia. *Science* 161:334–339.
1970   Environmental changes and the origin of agriculture in the Near East. *Bioscience* 20:210–217.
1977   Environmental change and the origins of agriculture in the Old and New Worlds. In *Origins of Agriculture* (C. A. Reed, ed.), pp. 281–318. The Hague: Mouton.

Wylie, A.
1981   *Positivism and the New Archaeology.* Ph.D. dissertation. State University of New York at Binghamton. Ann Arbor: University Microfilms.
1984   Putting Shakertown back together: critical theory in archaeology. *Journal of Anthropological Archaeology* 4:133–147.

Wynn, T.
1985   Piaget, stone tools and the evolution of human intelligence. *World Archaeology* 17:32–43.

Yellen, J. E.
1977a   Cultural patterning of faunal remains: evidence from the !Kung Bushmen. In *Experimental Archaeology* (D. Ingersoll, J. E. Yellen, and W. Macdonald, eds.), pp. 271–331. New York: Columbia University Press.
1977b   *Archaeological Approaches to the Present: Models for Reconstructing the Past.* New York: Academic Press.

Yengoyan, A.
  1985   Digging for symbols: the archaeology of everyday material life. *Proceedings of the Prehistoric Society* 51:329–335.
Yesner, D. R.
  1980   Maritime hunter-gatherers: ecology and prehistory. *Current Anthropology* 21:727–750.
Yizraeli, T.
  1967   Mesolithic hunters' industries at Ramat Matred (the Wilderness of Zin): first report. *Palestine Exploration Quarterly* 99:78–85.
Young, T. C.
  1988   Since Herodotus, has history been a valid concept? *American Antiquity* 53:7–12.
Zohary, D. and M. Hopf
  1988   *Domestication of Plants in the Old World.* Oxford: Oxford University Press.

Site Index

Subject Index

Author Index

Contributors

C. Michael Barton
Department of Anthropology
Arizona State University
Tempe, AZ 85287

Ofer Bar-Yosef
Department of Anthropology
Harvard University
Cambridge, MA 02138

Amilcare Bietti
Dipartimento de Biologia Animale e
    dell'Uomo
Università di Roma 'La Sapienza'
Citta Universitaria
Piazzale Aldo Moro, 5
00185 Roma, Italia

Philip G. Chase
University Museum
University of Pennsylvania
33rd & Spruce Sts.
Philadelphia, PA 19104

Geoffrey A. Clark
Department of Anthropology
Arizona State University
Tempe, AZ 85287

Iain Davidson
Department of Archaeology and
    Paleoanthropology
University of New England
Armidale NSW 2351
Australia

André Debénath
Institut du Quaternaire
L'Université de Bordeaux I
33405 Talence, France

Harold L. Dibble
Department of Anthropology
University of Pennsylvania
33rd & Spruce Sts.
Philadelphia, PA 19104

D. Bruce Dickson
Department of Anthropology
Texas A & M University
College Station, TX 77843

Marcia L. Donaldson
Department of Anthropology
Arizona State University
Tempe, AZ 85287

Paul R. Fish
Arizona State Museum
University of Arizona
Tucson, AZ 85721

Suzanne K. Fish
Department of Arid Lands Studies
University of Arizona
Tucson, AZ 85721

Manuel R. González Morales
Colegio Mayor "Juan de la Cosa"
Universidad de Cantabria
Avenida de los Castros, s/n
39005 Santander, Spain

Francis B. Harrold
Department of Sociology,
  Anthropology & Social Work
University of Texas at Arlington
Box 19599
Arlington, TX 76019

Donald O. Henry
Department of Anthropology
University of Tulsa
Tulsa, OK 74104

Steven L. Kuhn
Department of Anthropology
University of New Mexico
Albuquerque, NM 87131

Catherine S. Mueller-Wille
109 Briton Way
Greenville, SC 29615

Deborah I. Olszewski
Department of Anthropology &
  Linguistics
Baldwin Hall
University of Georgia
Athens, GA 30602

Steven A. Rosen
Archaeological Division
Ben 'Gurion University of the Negev
Beer Sheva 84 105
P.O. Box 653, Israel

James R. Sackett
Department of Anthropology
University of California at Los
  Angeles
Los Angeles, CA 90024

Alan H. Simmons
Quaternary Sciences Center
Desert Research Institute
University of Nevada System
Reno, NV 89506

Mary C. Stiner
Department of Anthropology
University of New Mexico
Albuquerque, NM 87131

Lawrence G. Straus
Department of Anthropology
University of New Mexico
Albuquerque, NM 87131